WITHDRAWN. FOR FREE USE IN CITY
CULTURAL AND WELFARE INSTITUTIONS
MAY BE SOLD FOR THE BENEFIT OF
THE NEW YORK PUBLIC LIBRARY ONLY.

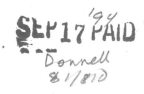

SEP 17 '94 PAID
Donnell
81/810

Sex and Sensibility

25-00
note
6|5

WITHDRAWN. FOR FREE USE IN CITY
CULTURAL AND WELFARE INSTITUTIONS
MAY BE SOLD FOR THE BENEFIT OF
THE NEW YORK PUBLIC LIBRARY ONLY.

SEP 17 1941

JEAN H. HAGSTRUM

Sex and Sensibility

Ideal and Erotic Love from Milton to Mozart

The University of Chicago Press

Chicago and London

The University of Chicago Press, Chicago 60637
The University of Chicago Press, Ltd., London

©1980 by The University of Chicago
All rights reserved. Published 1980
Printed in the United States of America
84 83 82 81 80   5 4 3 2 1

Library of Congress Cataloging in Publication Data

Hagstrum, Jean H
  Sex and sensibility.

  Includes index.
  1. English literature—History and criticism.
2. Love in literature.   3. European literature—
History and criticism.   4. Love in art.   5. Arts.
I. Title.
PR409.L67H3   809′.933′54   79-20657
ISBN 0-226-31289-5

Jean H. Hagstrum is John C. Shaffer Professor of
English and the Humanities at Northwestern University.
His many books include *Samuel Johnson's Literary
Criticism, The Sister Arts,* and *William Blake: Poet
and Painter,* all published by the
University of Chicago Press.

809.933
H

For Katherine Jeanne and Phyllis Ann

Contents

List of Illustrations   xi

Preface   xiii

1. Introduction   1

2. Milton and the Ideal of Heterosexual Friendship   24
    The "Rites Mysterious of Connubial Love"   26
    "True Manliness" and "Foul Effeminacy"   34
    The Narcissistic Sins   41
    Epilogue: Love and Death   46

3. John Dryden: Sensual, Heroic, and "Pathetic" Love   50
    Dryden's Sensuality   51
    Love and the Tears of Magnanimity   58
    The Heroic Hero in Love   62

4. Restoration Love and the Tears of Morbidity   72
    Aphra Behn and Restoration "Romanticism"   77
    Love, Madness, and Death: Lee and Congreve   82
    Otway's Tears of Morbidity and Dennis's "Vulgar Passions"   90

5. Woman in Love: The Abandoned and Passionate Mistress   100
    Dido   106
    The Portuguese Nun   112
    Calista, the Fair Penitent   117
    Eloisa: "Breathings of the Heart"   121

6. Friends and Lovers: The Witty and the Wise   133

    Witty and Spirited Lovers   135

    Pope's Women   137

    Swift's Vanessa and Stella   145

7. Sentimental Love and Marriage: "Esteem Enliven'd by Desire"   160

    Richard Steele   165

    Courtly and Bourgeois Love: *Jane Shore, The London Merchant,*
    and Hogarth's Sarah Young   173

    Henry Fielding and *Amelia*   178

8. Richardson   186

    Pamela I   191

    Clarissa   195

    Sir Charles Grandison: The Enlarged Family   214

9. Rousseau   219

    Emile: The Psychology of Postponed Sexuality   221

    La nouvelle Héloïse: Intense Friendship and Romantic Love   227

    The Confessions   241

10. The Aftermath of Sensibility: Sterne, Goethe, and Austen   247

    Sterne   247

    Young Werther   260

    Sense and Sensibility   268

    Epilogue: *Les liaisons dangereuses*   274

11. Love in Painting and Music: An Appended Survey   278

    Love in Painting: An Informal Overview   279

    Love in Music: A Brief Outline   285

    Watteau   297

    Handel   303

    Greuze   310

    Mozart   316

Appendix A.   Milton and the Visual Arts   333

Appendix B.   Chronology of Plays Referred To   333

Appendix C.   Watteau, *Le pèlerinage à l'Ile de Cythère*   335

Index   337

Illustrations

(Following page 178)

1a   James Barry, *Adam and Eve*

1b   Barry, *Adam and Eve*

2   Correggio (Antonio Allegri), *Ganymede*

3   Hugo van der Goes, *The Fall of Man*

4   Sir Peter Lely, *Lady Jane Needham, Mrs. Myddleton*

5   Sir Godfrey Kneller, *Francis Whitmore, Lady Middleton*

6   Peter Paul Rubens, *The Death of Dido*

7   Nicolas Poussin (?), *Dido and Aeneas*

8   William Hogarth, *A Rake's Progress,* pl. 4

9   Hogarth, *A Rake's Progress,* pl. 8

10   Sir Joshua Reynolds, *The Death of Dido*

11   Alexander Runciman, *The Origin of Painting*

12   George Romney, *Sensibility*

13   Thomas Rowlandson, *The Man of Feeling* (1788)

14   Rowlandson, *The Man of Feeling* (1785)

15   Jean-Antoine Watteau, *The Judgment of Paris*

16   Watteau, *Diana at Her Bath*

17   Watteau, *A Lady at Her Toilet*

18   Watteau, *Fête in a Park*

19   Watteau, *L'amour paisible*

20   Watteau, *Le pèlerinage à l'Ile de Cythère*

21   Louis Trinquesse, *Offrande à Vénus*

22   Watteau, *Reclining Nude*

23   Jean-Baptiste Greuze, *Seated Male Nude*

24   Greuze, *Seated Nude Woman*

25   Greuze, *Saint Mary of Egypt*

26   Greuze, *Aegina Visited by Jupiter*

27   Greuze, *La malédiction paternelle: le fils ingrat*

28   Greuze, *La malédiction paternelle: le fils puni*

29   Greuze, *Young Shepherd Holding a Flower*

30   Greuze, *The White Hat*

31   Greuze, *La prière du matin*

32   Greuze, *The Votive Offering to Cupid*

Preface

The following friends and colleagues at Northwestern University have read the manuscript and given valuable advice: Albert Cirillo of the English Department; Bernadette Fort of Romance Languages; Martin Mueller, director of Comparative Literature; and Judith Schwartz of the School of Music. Ronald Paulson of Yale has made learned and constructive suggestions about all aspects of the work. Paul Elmen, professor emeritus at Seabury-Western Theological Seminary, has rendered invaluable service by commenting on the entire manuscript. I am also indebted to Robert Mayo for good counsel, particularly on Richardson. Once again, my scholarly reputation is indebted to Scott Westrem of the Graduate School of Northwestern University, whose skillful and devoted labors have made this book much less imperfect than it otherwise would have been. I am also grateful to Marjorie Weiner, who typed a clear penultimate draft and so made contact possible with my learned colleagues. Flora Strohm, who typed the final draft, has once again won my gratitude; she transformed my difficult draft into a work of clarity and accuracy. Sean Shesgreen gave valuable advice on reproductions. Judith Colton of the Department of the History of Art at Yale made useful bibliographical and other suggestions. I am of course indebted to a large segment of the scholarly community, a debt inadequately acknowledged, even though my footnotes are many. One scholarly debt it gives me special pleasure to acknowledge. During the academic year 1976–77 a group of assistant and associate professors from all over the country pursued independent research at Northwestern University under Fellowships in Residence for College Teachers, awarded by the National Endowment for the Humanities. All eleven of them were helpful, in more ways than can be specified here, during a nine-month-long seminar devoted to the subject of this book. They will encounter in virtually every chapter familiar ideas, for some of which they might well assert proprietary rights. John Sekora, in addition to participating in the discussions, made bibliographical recommendations that have proved indispensable.

I wish to thank the following for generous support of my scholarship: the John Simon Guggenheim Foundation for the award of a fellowship during the academic year 1974–75 and the administration at Northwestern—particularly Dean Rudolph Weingartner, of the College of Arts and Sciences, and the Office of Research and Sponsored Projects—for released time and grants-in-aid.

The staffs of the following American libraries and museums have been unfailingly competent and courteous: the Northwestern University Library, in particular Russell Maylone, curator of special collections in the Deering Library, and Rolf H. Erickson, head of circulation; the Newberry Library; the Art Institute of Chicago, particularly the Prints and Drawings Department (I mention Harold Joachim and Anselmo Carini with special gratitude) and the Ryerson and Burnham Libraries; the Henry E. Huntington Library and Art Gallery, especially James Thorpe, director, and Robert Wark, curator of art collections; the Beinecke Rare Book and Manuscript Library of Yale University and the Yale Center for British Art; the Frick Art Reference Library; and the Pierpont Morgan Library. I am also indebted to magnificent collections abroad: the British Library; the British Museum, especially the Department of Prints and Drawings; and in Paris the Bibliothèque Nationale and the Louvre, particularly the Cabinet des Dessins.

Evanston, Illinois
January 1979

1. Introduction

ONALD BARTHELME ends "Rebecca" by telling why he wrote this story of the quarrel and reconciliation of two women lovers. "It was written for several reasons. Nine of them are secrets. The tenth is that one should never cease considering human love."[1] One wonders why the subject of so much human concern has so seldom received scholarly or critical attention. Several names do of course come to mind: C. S. Lewis, Denis de Rougemont, Irving Singer, Anders Nygren, Leslie Fiedler, Herbert Marcuse, Maurice Valency, John Bayley, J. B. Broadbent, A. O. J. Cockshut, Wallace Fowlie, Mark Rose, Frederick L. Beaty, and Edward Le Comte. However, considering the enormous amount of attention original writers have perennially paid to love, one can scarcely regard the critical commentary as being at flood tide. None of the scholars and critics named has concentrated on the Enlightenment; and, for whatever reason, no comprehensive study of love in the Restoration and in eighteenth-century English literary culture exists, even though that theme engaged its most creative and pioneering spirits.

A considerable space in this very large gap has been filled with Lawrence Stone's 800 learned pages on *The Family, Sex and Marriage in England, 1500–1800*,[2] a monumental example of the new social history. Its thesis is that in the late seventeenth century and all through the eighteenth there developed what Stone calls "affective individualism." This new *mentalité* can best be defined by its result: a different organization of the family, which the author calls "closed domesticated nuclear." The family was now based on the free choice of partner and on personal autonomy; it was bonded by strong ties of affection between the man and woman and between them and their immediate offspring. These all now lived together, separated often even from grandparents and other relatives—the new arrangement replacing older and more diffuse organizations established for convenience and gain. Along with the spread of the conjugal family came a growing desire for physical privacy and sexual pleasure, a condition that contrasted sharply with antecedent periods when families were founded on political, social, and financial interests; when affection was severely limited; and when sex was regarded as a "sinful necessity justified only by the need to propagate the race." This change from an

1. *Amateurs* (New York: Farrar, Straus & Giroux, 1976), p. 144.
2. New York: Harper & Row, 1977.

1

austere—even a bleak and relatively loveless—personal landscape to one of greatly increased psychological grace, comfort, and affectionate mutuality explains "the warmth and autonomy of the eighteenth century." One is not accustomed to have the age of reason, the period of prudence, described in such terms. But Stone's command of social fact is unrivaled, and after enormous labors he reaches this conclusion: what I have just summarized constitutes "perhaps the most important change in *mentalité* to have occurred in the Early Modern period, indeed possibly in the last thousand years of Western history." Literature, music, and art, as we now know better than our forefathers, are much more than mirrors of social reality; but the form and pressure of the times does leave its imprint on the imagination. And much in the culture of the late seventeenth and the eighteenth century reflects precisely the conditions Stone has so amply and ingeniously displayed (pp. 4, 5, 7, 119).

As a historian, Stone is more concerned with "concrete changes" in "historical reality" (p. 119) than with mental formulations, and he therefore leaves two large matters for the student of belles lettres to consider further. One is the change in language that reflects the rise of affective individualism. The other is the filiation—or the canon—of literary and artistic works that embodies the social changes. It would be surprising if in our period alterations of the magnitude that Stone investigates—a truly profound reorientation of human desires and habits—were not also accompanied by linguistic enrichment and a body of internally related literature and art—by works, that is, that possess the power to mythologize reality. Let us consider first the relevant words and their definitions.

The author of *The Family, Sex and Marriage* regards the family as the "only viable unit of study" (p. 19). The success of Stone's study demonstrates conclusively that for his purposes this focus was correct. However, in a study of parallel phenomena in art and literature, concentration must be on love. What interests the novelist, for example, is the emotion that leads to the creation of a family; when the wedding bells ring, the action is usually over—with the rare but important exceptions I shall subsequently examine. But concentration upon love brings its own special problems. The idea, in either its erotic or ideal aspect, is extremely difficult to define, so large and diverse are its cultural and philosophical meanings. These have been skillfully discriminated by Irving Singer in his indispensable *Nature of Love: Plato to Luther*.[3] It is tempting to apply to Restoration and eighteenth-century culture his fourfold analysis of love as *eros, philia, nomos,* and *agapē.* The period was not indifferent to *agapē,* or active divine love, as Milton and Richardson abundantly show; but in this aspect of their thought they were not typical, and the dynamic of Enlightened England did not lie in pursuing the soul to an "*O Altitudo!*" It may be true, as

3. New York: Random House, 1966. See esp. chaps. 10–13.

has been said, that "the only metaphor for *agapē* is *amor*,"[4] and no doubt a subtle student of human imagery, one of those whom the late Tucker Brooke called the "metaphor-phoroi," could find many analogues to divine love in the purely human pursuit of happiness. Certainly religion and love share and mingle essences in John Donne; and in the Romantic spousal of the soul with nature there lingered the idea of a rapturous union of man and God. But my concern is not with love as a metaphor—a subject almost infinitely extensible—it is with love as a reality. Singer rightly sees that in some thinkers and in some periods love can be seen as present in *nomos,* that is, submission to God's will and to religious law. Love, at important moments which I shall dwell on, does indeed enter the *nomos* of marriage and is then caught in the web of institutional law and obligation. But, as I have said, marriage is properly the focus of social history; love, that of literary study. John Bayley has said that "sexual love is for most people the most interesting and memorable aspect of life"—a debatable assertion. But he compels assent when he goes on to say that "it is this kind of love, *eros* rather than *agapē*, with which literature is most concerned."[5] We are left, then, with *philia* (love as fellowship) and *eros*. Each in its own way is crucially important during the period from Milton to Mozart. The ideal of religious brotherhood continues to exist, but as social benevolence rather than spiritual bonding; the Johannine lover of the brethren was secularized into the Man of Feeling. *Philia* as the friendship of individuals has a noteworthy eighteenth-century history. Its age-old rivalry with love, going back to the Greeks, reappears in *Clarissa* and *La nouvelle Héloïse* as dynamic, interacting juxtapositions (Clarissa and Anna vs. Clarissa and Lovelace; Julie and Claire vs. Julie and Saint-Preux); and these will require detailed analyses.

Even after these exclusions and distinctions, *eros* remains elusive. Swift's impatience is understandable:

> *Love,* why do we one Passion call?
> When 'tis a Compound of them all.
> [*Cadenus and Vanessa,* 772–73]

Once we have separated Eros from the other loves and declined to sentimentalize or exalt him, we still find that he is as elusive, as difficult to fetter, as Venus herself.[6] Plato, who refused to make him either god or man, concluded he must be a *daimon* and defined him as desire, lack, or appetency toward

4. J. B. Broadbent, *Poetic Love* (London: Chatto & Windus, 1964), p. 11.
5. *The Characters of Love* (London: Constable, 1960), p. 4.
6. C. S. Lewis in *The Four Loves* (New York: Harcourt, Brace & World, 1960), pp. 132, 136, revises Plato and makes Venus, not Eros, desire. She stands, generally, for the sexual element in love. It is her son, a later being—an offspring, a result, as it were—who directs us to the particular beloved. The distinction is interesting but not particularly relevant to eighteenth-century thought and practice.

something higher or better.[7] Thus, without ontological status in the world of ideas, he is nevertheless an important agent of upward intellectual mobility, though exactly how far up the dialectical ladder he has the power to lead or drive the mind it is very difficult to say. Paul Tillich, who considered Eros ontological, virtually an instrument of grace, sees him as "the moving power of life," which impels "everything that is towards everything else that is." Love becomes a drive toward "the unity of the separated" and so a repairer of the ravages of the Fall. It is not a "union of the strange" but "the reunion of the estranged."[8] These are rich and pregnant insights, but they tend to lead us away from our central concern. Spenser, who in his richly pictorial way displays Cupid as a powerful deity—quite unlike the cherubic rococo boy of later culture—never forgets the essential fact that his conquests are "all of loue, and all of lusty-hed." (FQ 3.11.29 ff.). Love in the title of this book means pretty much what plain common sense would understand it to mean. Descartes is quite unambiguous about the kind of love he places deep within man, since he makes it one of the six primitive passions of the human soul.[9]

A word needs to be said about the relations between the erotic and the ideal. These relations are profound and subtle, and the two cannot ultimately be separated, despite Anders Nygren's brilliant attempt to divide *agapē* and *eros*.[10] Our conception of ideal love is not essentially religious—or, more exactly, ascetic: it is, rather, the highest form of attraction, in which the physical, though it may be transcended, is never eliminated or left behind. The ideal that will concern us is not otherworldly or transcarnal; it is closely related to the modern psychoanalytical insight that in its highest condition love remembers its origins in sexual earth. The best minds of the eighteenth century understood clearly that crass motives could frequently cloak flattering idealism, and they often found the sexual lurking behind the most ethereal or pretentious affirmations. Then, too, men were becoming tired of the hoary

7. *Symposium* 202E (where Diotima calls Eros a *daimon*), 205D, 206C–207C.

8. *Love, Power, and Justice* (New York: Oxford University Press, 1954), p. 25.

9. *The Passions of the Soul* (1st ed. of English translation, London, 1650), article 69. It is extremely important to recognize the importance of the passions in a system so centrally rational as the Cartesian. Reason must control, but it loses its very genius and *raison d'être*—and the whole personality is impoverished—if there is nothing to control. See Louise K. Horowitz, *Love and Language: A Study of the Classical French Moralist Writers* (Columbus: Ohio State University Press, 1977), pp. 8–9.

10. *Agape and Eros,* trans. Philip S. Watson (Philadelphia: Westminster Press, 1953). Bishop Nygren makes, in fact, two sharp separations: (1) vulgar, earthly, sexual love (Plato's *pandemos* Eros) from *agapē.* (The two have absolutely nothing to do with each other.) (2) the heavenly (Plato's *ouranios* Eros) from Christian *agapē* (pp. 50–52). Neither of these is sensual; but the differences between a system in which the soul rises from the sensible to the supersensible and a system in which love descends to man from a God who chooses man without any precondition of worth and in so doing bestows value are radical indeed. Needless to say, these two ways of conceiving ideal love have often been rivals in human thought and culture. Although both these systems will impinge on my study, neither is peculiarly relevant to it.

admonitions to separate the physical from the spiritual; the whole course of post-Lockean sensationism was to unite them—to demonstrate that the pursuit of happiness need not lead to mortification of the flesh. Sterne, for example, was quite aware in his impish way that the expression "to *fall* in love" implied that "love is a thing *below* a man"—an implication that he imputed to Plato and rejected with amusing vigor.[11] Thus the titular presence of the two terms "erotic" and "ideal" is not in any way meant to imply a separation of the two in the belief that value resides simply and entirely with one and not the other. But having said all that, one must claim the privilege of dividing one from the other for purposes of analysis and of doing justice to those thinkers and artists who found the higher in strong ethical and religious opposition to the lower. Hierarchies in the moral and religious sphere tend to weaken immediately after Milton, but even late portrayals of the antithetical aspects of love which in no way deny a common physcial bond between them will nevertheless sharply insist on distinguished categories. In *The Magic Flute*, for example, Papageno (the bird-man) and Tamino (the noble, loving, and ultimately disciplined hero) march side by side for a while but in the end go off to separate, though related, destinies.

The most important definition of my subject comes, however, not from seeing Eros for what he truly is or from realizing that the bonds between lower and higher human love are indissoluble. It comes from perceiving the relationship between sex and sensibility; toward the furtherance of that perception this study is entirely devoted. It is possible, though the task would be formidable, to study love alone; and it is also possible to perceive a good deal about sensibility quite apart from love. My purpose is more limited: to study sex and sensibility at their intersection. Necessary groundwork must be laid here by surveying briefly the profound and revelatory changes that important historical words underwent—a discussion that will be continued all the way through the study as these essential words referring to the feelings are further defined and refined. Three sets or clusters of terms must be considered briefly: (1) those deriving from the Greek "pathē" (emotions), which, along with the "ēthē" (values) and the "praxeis" (deeds) of men, Aristotle enjoined the poets to portray; (2) the words "sentiment" and "sentimental," ultimately coming from the Latin verb "sentire" (to feel in body or mind); (3) words deriving from the Latin "sensus" (originally the past participle of "sentire"), notably my title word, "sensibility."

1. *"Pathetic."* Clinging to this word from its origins in antiquity are two etymological meanings that could have some relevance to eighteenth-century developments and usages. The Greek "path" is the root of "paschein," "to suffer"; and "pathos" signifies suffering. The word "pathic" was another term

---

11. *The Life and Opinions of Tristram Shandy, Gentleman*, vol. 6, chap. 37, ed. James A. Work (New York: Odyssey Press, 1940, 1960), p. 469.

for "catamite" ("a boy kept for unnatural purposes") and came from the Greek for "passive," that is, "pathikos."[12] These two ancient associations with passivity in pain and love could have had some underground influence on the eighteenth-century career of the term as it moved from associations of violence to delicacy. Two definitions from the *OED* give the terminus a quo and ad quem of that linguistic development. (*a*) The meaning listed as obsolete, for which the last example given comes from 1762, is "producing an effect upon the emotions; exciting the passions or affections; moving, stirring, affecting"; (*b*) the modern meaning is one to which the whole course of eighteenth-century thought and feeling moved: "affecting the tender emotions; exciting a feeling of pity, sympathy, or sadness; full of pathos." For the latter meaning illustrations are given from 1737 (Pope) to 1885. The very words in Johnson's *Dictionary* definition of "pathetick" in 1755 ("affecting the passions; passionate; moving") suggest why the term could have been associated earlier with violent, disruptive, and erotic passions. Joseph Warton associated it with strength, saying that "Rowe's genius was rather delicate and soft than strong and pathetic."[13] But it was toward implications of delicacy and softness that the term moved under profound social influence, in part mediated by Johnson himself, who in his criticism separated it from the sublime and regularly applied it to the domestic, gentle, quotidian emotions. The term did not thereby forfeit respect, for Johnson used it, so defined, to describe Shakespeare's most typical and successful literary effects, and some may even have regarded the newer meaning as revolutionary, since it was related to the democratization of life.[14] Not everybody rejoiced in the term or the changes it underwent. The repulsive, stereotypically masculine, mercenary James Harlowe, who hated the power of female goodness, denounced his sister Clarissa for her "whining pathetics."[15]

2. "*Sentiment*," "*sentimental*." These words derive from the Latin verb "sentire," which means both "to discern mentally" and "to feel physically." It is important to note that the etymological origin points to an ambiguity (or perhaps even an ambivalence) that remained with "sentiment" throughout the eighteenth century, when it was felt convenient to have a term that intellectualized emotions or emotionalized thought.[16] Even more important

12. See *OED* and E. Royston Pike, *Love in Ancient Rome* (London: Frederick Muller, 1965), p. 244.

13. *An Essay on the Genius and Writings of Pope* (1756, 1782), quoted in Scott Elledge, ed., *Eighteenth-Century Critical Essays*, 2 vols. (Ithaca, N.Y.: Cornell University Press, 1961, 1966), 2:745.

14. See "The Beautiful, the Pathetic, and the Sublime," chap. 7 of Jean H. Hagstrum, *Samuel Johnson's Literary Criticism* (1952; reprint ed., Chicago: University of Chicago Press, 1967), esp. pp. 137, 140–42.

15. Samuel Richardson, *Clarissa*, 4 vols. (Everyman's Library, 1932; reprinted, New York: E. P. Dutton, 1967), 1:262.

16. R. F. Brissenden has noticed that Nathan Bailey, in the 2d ed. of his *Dictionarium Britannicum* (1736), defines "sentiment" as "thoughts, mind, opinion, inclination," and "also passion,"

than this inherent duality is the change in meaning. "Sentiment" began as a word that expressed primarily a judgment of the mind and then became one that invoked a kaleidoscope of free-flowing, uncontrolled feeling. When Richardson denied that Lovelace was a "sentimental unbeliever" (*Clarissa*, 4:560), he meant that, whatever that rake's practice, he was not intellectually a skeptic, not an atheist in his mental conceptions. But when Sterne took his "sentimental journey," he spied out the nakedness of people's hearts, drenched his handkerchief in tears, and surrendered himself to the ecstasy of sensation. Erik Erämetsä has shown that five meanings of "sentimental" succeeded one another between Richardson and Sterne.[17] (*a*). It referred to opinions, thoughts, and judgments of the mind; that is, it was close to its parental noun, "sentiment." This was its meaning from *Clarissa* on; but, as Addison (who praised Milton for his sentiments, i. e., for his expression of thoughts) demonstrated, the noun bore this meaning even in the second decade of the century. (*b*) From 1749 on it referred more particularly to *moral* sentence, showing that progress toward an emotional meaning was perhaps encouraged by Richardsonian piety. (*c*) Between 1755 and 1765 it described a condition in which reason and feeling are both present, now one and now the other predominating. (*d*) During 1763–77 it referred to a state characterized by refined feeling and emotional elevation. (*e*) In the decade of the 1760s, thanks mostly to Sterne, it described refined, tender emotions that often involve amatory feelings. We can draw two conclusions from this brief discussion. One is that in learned discourse "sentimental" approached the meaning of "pathetic," as redefined. The second is that what "sentimental" came finally to mean—refined, tender emotions with an erotic coloration—described a literary reality that had existed considerably before Sterne popularized the word. Is there any reason why we cannot use the term whenever we meet combinations of sex and sensibility, provided that these phenomena seem to be more than fortuitous and belong to the currents that led to or flowed from the Sternean achievement?

3. *"Sense," "sensible,"* and *"sensibility."* These important eighteenth-century terms derive from "sensus" and so ultimately from "sentire," therefore bearing radical links with the words just discussed. When Tetty first met her future husband, Samuel Johnson, she remarked that he was "the most sensible man

the last perhaps being a low usage. Brissenden then goes on to discuss the meanings of "mental feeling" or "emotional thought." See "'Sentiment': Some Uses of the Word in the Writings of David Hume" in Brissenden, ed., *Studies in the Eighteenth Century* (Toronto: University of Toronto Press, 1968), pp. 89–107). Brissenden provides in *Virtue in Distress: Studies in the Novel of Sentiment from Richardson to Sade* (London: Macmillan, 1974), the most comprehensive and perceptive study as yet undertaken of "sentimental" and cognate words, in England, France, and Germany, and their relation to philosophical and literary trends. For a semantic analysis, see esp. pp. 11–22, 98–118.

17. *A Study of the Word "Sentimental" and of other Linguistic Characteristics of Eighteenth Century Sentimentalism in England* (Annales Academiae Scientiarum Fennicae, ser. B, vol. 74, no. 1 [Helsinki, 1951]). See esp. pp. 18–54.

that I ever saw in my life"; she may, as some have thought, have been grateful for his fire and passion rather than for his prudence.[18] And yet one must be cautious. Johnson himself in his *Dictionary* (1755) stigmatized "sensible," meaning judicious or prudent, as a term used only "in low conversation." Such vulgar meaning may have been present in many unrecorded usages for many generations and thus fully available to Tetty. Certainly during the early eighteenth century "sense" could mean what we today substantially intend when we use the terms "good sense" or "common sense." In 1783 John Murdoch, anticipating Jane Austen's antithesis and contrasting "sensibility" with "sense," defined the latter as judgment, a meaning he termed "popular or vulgar."[19] Both Swift and Pope were capable of using it in their poetry to mean natural understanding and practical intelligence—an interpretation that the *OED* (eleventh meaning) records as present in the language from 1684 on. Swift says that Stella entertains the men who crowd around her "with Breeding, Humor, Wit, and Sense" (*Stella's Birthday, Written A.D. 1720–21*, line 25), and Pope summarizes Apollo's gifts to his friend Martha Blount as "Sense, Good-humour, and a Poet" (*Epistle to a Lady*, line 292). These women will enter our story precisely because their great poet-friends regarded them as standing in opposition to the dominant meaning of "sense," which referred primarily to "the faculties of corporeal sensation considered as channels for gratifying the desire for pleasure and the lusts of the flesh" (*OED*). Anna Howe would not have referred to Lovelace as a "man of sense" if she had meant that he possessed cool judgment.[20] (He did not, and she was a clever and perceptive girl.) Her meaning (perhaps primarily that Lovelace was a man of feeling) is not totally unrelated to that of Congreve, who regularly used "sense" to signify erotic fire.[21] The unashamedly passionate Sigismonda of Boccaccio's *Decameron* says of herself in Dryden's couplet from the *Fables:*

18. Boswell, *Life of Johnson,* ed. Geroge B. Hill and L. F. Powell, 6 vols. (Oxford: Clarendon Press, 1934–64), 1:95. I was alerted to "sensible" in Tetty's comment as possibly meaning "fiery, poetic," by Gar.y Wills's "His Periwig Askew," a nationally syndicated column which appeared sometime during 1976.

19. See below, p. 271 and n.56.

20. *Clarissa,* 3:516. The possibility should be left open that Anna Howe is here using the word in its newer, popular meaning; if so, she is deliberately deceiving Clarissa in order to encourage her marriage. I consider this alternative unlikely. Cf. 2:28, where Anna earlier calls Lovelace a "man of sense," giving as evidence his willingness to "humble himself" and his ability to "keep a woman's passion alive."

21. See *The Way of the World,* ed. Kathleen M. Lynch, Regents Restoration Drama Series (Lincoln: University of Nebraska Press, 1965), p. 32 (2.4). See also ibid., p. 63 (3.280). In the first of these references, Mrs. Fainall says, "if [lovers] have fire and sense, their jealousies are insupportable." The passage is meaningless unless "sense" means "passion." Brissenden, who notes the complicated range of meaning that "sense" possesses (*Virtue in Distress,* p. 14), is fully aware of its association with sexuality (p. 78), an association that extends to "sentimental" (p. 107). But this subject Brissenden does not develop.

I please'd my self, I shunn'd Incontinence,
And, urg'd by strong Desires, indulg'd my Sense.[22]

"Sensibility" derives from "sensible" meaning acute pleasure or pain[23] and is related to "sense" meaning passion. The *OED* says that it was "rare until the middle of the 18th century." In that period it became a central term of complex and multiple signification covering such meanings as perceptibility by the senses, the readiness of an organ to respond to sensory stimuli, mental perception, the power of the emotions, heightened emotional consciousness, and quickness of feeling. C. S. Lewis makes an important point when he says that "sensibility," in its central popular meaning, "always means a more than ordinary degree of responsiveness or reaction."[24] The word is indeed related to fine excess or deplorable excess and in either meaning is a much stronger word than we now think of it as being. We need only remember what will in my penultimate chapter be the subject of close analysis—that in *Sense and Sensibility* Jane Austen applied the term to the deep ravage of Marianne Dashwood's emotions by love. And yet the most important fact about the eighteenth-century use of the word was not that its meaning of sexual passion was fully maintained but that it was concurrently civilized and "tenderized," if I may use the term, until it became almost indistinguishable from the latest eighteenth-century meaning of "sentimental." This development makes the sixth *OED* definition the central one for our purposes, provided we add to it the emotion of tender sexual love: "In the 18th and early 19th c. (afterwards somewhat *rarely*): Capacity for refined emotion; delicate sensitiveness of taste; also readiness to feel compassion for suffering, and to be moved by the pathetic in literature or art." The seeds of this development lay within the word "sense" itself. Dryden's Sigismonda, whose hot and raging blood we have already paused to consider, is also "of a softer Mould, with Sense endu'd" (424), where the term "sense" must refer to a more delicate type of emotion than her eager sexual desires, though that delicacy was still suffused with the erotic.

22. "Sigismonda and Guiscardo, from Boccace" (454–55) in *Fables*.

23. Toby, referring to the exquisitely painful location of his wound, says that "the groin is infinitely more sensible" than the knee (*Tristram Shandy* 8.19; p. 569).

24. *Studies in Words*, 2d ed. (Cambridge: Cambridge University Press, 1967), p. 159. Raymond Williams gives a broad spectrum of meaning in his discussion of sensibility, and he quotes (p. 237) Southey's description of "the sentimental classes" as "persons of ardent or morbid sensibility." Yet in general he ignores the presence of excess or of sensuality in the term. See *Keywords: A Vocabulary of Culture and Society* (New York: Oxford University Press, 1976), pp. 235–38. William Empson is similarly neglectful of these meanings, although he describes Austen's *Sense and Sensibility* as "a pretty full-blown piece of romanticism." (I take it that the last word must refer to excess in love and deep emotion generally.) Empson's analysis is intended to bring out the basic opposition in the reader's mental reception of and reaction to the two terms of Austen's title but also their underlying similarity. "Sense and Sensibility" in *The Structure of Complex Words* (London: Chatto & Windus, 1964), pp. 250–69, esp. p. 252n.

In summary, the three most characteristic eighteenth-century terms for the emotions ("pathetic," which began by referring to all the passions; "sentiment," which originally signified the product of intellection; and "sensibility," which at first included all feeling) came to refer specifically to the gentle, tender, loyal, courteous emotions, precisely those most amenable to domestic needs and desires. It is difficult not to believe that these and their cognate terms were being altered by the powerful tides of social and psychological change, an understandable drive toward civilizing gentleness in a culture tired of the aggressive emotions provoked by civil war and religious fanaticism. The linguistic developments which I have here introduced and which I shall continue to analyze in the course of this study all point to the steep rise in familial affection that took place in a period that some still regard as the age of cold reason and dry wit.

But can linguistic changes, *tout simplement,* be attributed to social forces alone? Not if we remember the effect of Sterne's writings on the fortunes of the word "sentimental"and not, surely, if we consider that sometimes, as in Milton's polemical writings and in *Paradise Lost,* important cultural developments seem to be not so much reflected as anticipated. Stone calls the reason for changes in real-life attitudes and relationships a "baffling phenomenon" and argues cogently against the much too simple view that the promulgation of an idea causes historical change. He gives two examples (p. 20). (1) In 1693 Locke in an influential book advocated abolition of regular beating for minor academic lapses; by the mid-eighteenth century some elite schools had abondoned the practice. "But between the idea and the action," writes Stone, "there yawns a vast gap. We do not know who read Locke, nor do we know how the readers responded to him. What seems to be involved is a far broader and prior shift in attitudes towards the child, which made the readership more responsive to Locke's message." (2) Since antiquity a stream of advice had been directed at mothers to breast-feed their babies. But a majority of English upper-class mothers heeded the advice only in the late eighteenth cnetury. "Here again, the key factor seems to be less the enunciation of the idea than a deep-seated change in the response of the readers, which at last made them more receptive to the advice." That kind of receptiveness is surely in part conditioned by literature and the arts, which are vastly more complex and also vastly more persuasive than didactic proclamation. The relation between social change and that many-layered form of expression we call a literary text (which can exaggerate, distort, complicate, or embody reality and also create a new world from the materials the outside world provides) will perhaps always remain elusive. But before I consider literature, perhaps a few commonplaces about art and history need to be uttered. Art does indeed spring from a social matrix, and the more we know of historical fact and circumstance, the less likely we are to fall under a "dangerous prevalence of imagination," a scholarly no less than a generally human mischief. But if we ignore the achievements of art (with all their power and complexity and also with their intellectual forms, which can organize life and thought), then there can arise in our perceptions an equally dangerous prevalence of flux. Art, alone and isolated, may be said to constitute a kind of innocence; the data of historical change, alone and isolated, a kind of experience; but when art is seen as a part of reality—cause as well as effect, its inspiration and organizing force as well as its result—then we have what for Blake was a higher, or Organized, Innocence, a condition of vision, not merely of sight.[25] Certainly literature and history are not discrete entities; as we learn from the structuralists, the same desires that create a novel can create a social institution. Marriage and *Tom Jones* have this in common: they have arisen from a human desire and fill a human need. Men's dreams and hopes press upon the imagination of the writer immediately from the individual psyche and mediately from society. They then press back upon society, which, now somewhat altered itself, presses once again upon the artist. "And all is done as I have told."[26] There is, then, an ecological chain in culture, a network of mutual dependency and influence between art and history that cannot be unraveled but that must nevertheless be respected.

Let us now turn to the literature that resulted from, accompanied, may have helped to create, and certainly helped to promote the revolution in manners which Stone has displayed; that is, to the canon of related works of art on the topic of love—to its beginning, middle, and end. It is difficult for the student of a topic or of a historical cycle to determine its end. We like to pursue the echoes we have raised down the corridors of continuing time. The student of a succeeding topic or later cycle will help to determine when the old dies by distinguishing as precisely as he can the birth of the new. Sex and sensibility are dead, long live Romantic love! Still, if we stay within a period even without considering very deeply what is to come, we get a strong sense of ending when we encounter satirical or humorous distancing with respect to a formerly serious topic. The witty playfulness of a Laurence Sterne or the moral censure of a Jane Austen do not appear in Richardson or Rousseau, in Fielding writing *Amelia* or in Pope writing *Eloisa to Abelard*. *Sense and Sensibility* and *A Sentimental Journey*—the very titles proclaim reflective thought and suggest the definition of terms. Sterne categorically, though playfully, lists the various kinds of journey it is possible to take.[27] Austen explores, with satirical intent, a pattern of behavior and analyzes its ingredients; she connects the boiling

25. The concept is implied in a note written by Blake on the pages of *The Four Zoas:* "Unorganiz'd Innocence: An Impossibility" (Geoffrey Keynes, ed., *Blake Complete Writings* [London: Oxford University Press, 1969], p. 380).

26. The last line of Blake, "The Mental Traveller" (Keynes, p. 427), a difficult poem that leads one deeply into an understanding of interacting historical cycles.

27. See "Preface: In the Desobligeant" in *Sentimental Journey.*

sensibility of her lovers to the picturesque movement in landscape gardening and painting, and she hisses her artfully modulated hiss at the deleterious effects of rearing children in the love-bonded nuclear family. In *Tristram Shandy* Sterne is a great consolidator and analyst, however whimsically his analysis proceeds. The more one reads that teasingly great novel, the more one senses in it the presence of the entire eighteenth century: there is scarcely an aesthetic posture that is not somehow represented. Thus relatively late works—by being ratiocinative and also by suggesting their sources, sometimes very slyly and indirectly—are extremely useful to the scholar when he analyzes his topic into its constituent elements and when he establishes his filiation. They also suggest the inescapable power of the movement at whose demise they hint. Eros and delicacy have impregnated the very pores of the jesting Sterne, his nerves and his blood cells; and he pulsates with their rhythms. It is impossible to disentangle the laughter from either the tears or the titillations in that delicate web that is at once fresh and fading. Its very oddity, about which Johnson exploded,[28] tells us that the hour is late for sex and sensibility and that this work will have no successors. And yet in that overflowing Sternean cup the wine that bubbles and winks at the brim is genuine, eighteenth-century-vintage erotic sentiment. Similarly, for all the wit and moral outrage with which Jane Austen accompanies her portrayal of sensibility, she respects it, however grudgingly, and yields to its attractiveness. Marianne, possessed by sensibility, is driven to the very brink of self-destruction by it, but we, like the author, never lose our love for her. It is as though the tormented girl through her very sensibility mysteriously reveals to us her own and its potential human worth. Sensibility is dangerous, no mistake about that. But it seems to grow in a soil of emotional richness, a richness that here produces nectareous fruit.

I need not say much about authors in the middle of our period, except to observe that they usually proclaim themselves unmistakably for what they are and that they breathe not a *fin de mouvement* air of ripeness, consolidation, or mortality but a spirit of continuing succession. No one mistakes Congreve's mourning bride, Rowe's Calista, Richardson's Harriet Byron and Clarissa, Fielding's Amelia, Rousseau's Julie for being anything other than heroines of sensibility and, whatever their own lives may have denied them, potentially fruitful literary mothers. No aesthetic distance, no satire, no laughter gives one the sense of being at the contemplative end of a movement. Middles tend to be relatively reticent about causes and origins, background and context. But they do embody hints that help us in a more difficult task, perhaps the most difficult task of all—the determination of beginnings.

Pope's *Eloisa to Abelard* was rightly regarded by critics of the eighteenth

---

28. "Nothing odd will do long. 'Tristram Shandy' did not last." Boswell, *Life of Johnson,* 2:449.

century as a masterpiece of pathos and sublimity and thus an integral part of the affective movement. What can one say, not about its formal generic and thematic sources but about the antecedent texts embedded in its texture? The lines, words, and phrases of what previous poets entered into Pope's magnetic field as he wrote and revised? A few from Crashaw, perhaps no more than four. Three or so from Milton. But from Dryden some thirty-five or thirty-six, making him the author to whom Pope owed the most in this, his most passionate poem. The bulk of these recollections come from the *Fables* and translations from the classics—perhaps not unexpectedly, since much of Dryden's own love poetry exists there. But a surprising number—ten, in fact (more than from Milton, Crashaw, and Cowley combined)—come from the heroic plays, specifically from *Tyrannick Love, Aureng-Zebe,* and *Don Sebastian.*[29] Similarly, in *Clarissa* and *Sir Charles Grandison,* two ample works of love and sensibility, Dryden and the heroic plays are frequently referred to, sometimes merely quoted but sometimes actually worked into the symbolic pattern of the novel. Thus Richardson and the Pope of the love poetry—and also other authors of the eighteenth century—point, not to the satire, wit, didacticism, or criticism of John Dryden but to his combination of eros and emotion.

The argument for this combination will appear in the chapter on Dryden. After the full display of evidence I hope it will not seem outrageous to say that David Hume's definition of love might have grown, in all its parts, out of a contemplation of the Restoration poet's achievements as a translator from the classics, as a versifier of fables, and mostly as a heroic dramatist. For the philosopher, love was a "compound" emotion in which three different passions are conjoined: (1) "the pleasing sensation arising from beauty," (2) "the bodily appetite for generation," and (3) "a generous kindness or good-will" (*A Treatise of Human Nature,* 2.2.11). Or, if we prefer a poetic statement and wish to observe the application to the private scene that Dryden did not make, we can turn to Thomson, who in *Spring* preached "sympathy of soul" in bodies aroused by nature and who praised "esteem enliven'd by desire," a combination of sentimental and physical love that he placed in the "well-ordered home." Thomson's hymn to marriage celebrates both sexual love and benevolence, as such words as "transport," "lavish hearts," "beauty," "rapture," and "bliss" abundantly attest.[30] Where shall we find a literary stimulus potent enough for this and indeed for the century-long fusion of sex and sensibility? Not in Dryden, for all his relevance. The answer must, after long reflection, be

29. These statistics are derived from counting the sources and parallels adduced in the notes by the editor of the definitive Twickenham edition (*The Poems of Alexander Pope,* vol. 2: *The Rape of the Lock and Other Poems,* ed. Geoffrey Tillotson, 3d ed. [London: Methuen, 1962; reprinted 1966], pp. 319–49).

30. From *The Seasons* (1746, or last ed. in Thomson's lifetime): *Spring* 1046, 1121, 1122, 1136, 1140, 1141; *Autumn,* 593, 603, 606.

in Eden—not the Eden of the Bible but that of Milton, Thomson's inspirer and mentor.

In making this choice we need not rely only on an unguided reading of *Paradise Lost*. There are insistent and recurring suggestions all through the Age of Sensibility that the Edenic Bower of Bliss had been "introjected"—as we say much too often these days—and that men and women, finding themselves in love or facing the frontier between innocence and experience or planning their futures with partners of the opposite sex, identified themselves with Milton's primal pair. Even as late as 1794, when writing to a man she loved, Mary Wollstonecraft said to Gilbert Imlay that she had always been half in love with Rousseau, one of the giants of the middle of our canon. But her invocation of Milton is more important, as it is less expected: "I like to see your eyes praise me; and Milton insinuates, that, during such recitals, there are interruptions, not ungrateful to the heart, when the honey that drops from the lips is not merely words."[31] Wollstonecraft's somewhat stilted language refers us to book 8 of *Paradise Lost*, where Eve leaves Adam and Raphael to their cosmological discussion, preferring to have such instruction from her husband and lover alone, for

> hee, she knew would intermix
> Grateful digressions, and solve high dispute
> With conjugal Caresses, from his Lip
> Not Words alone pleas'd her.
>
> [54–57]

In *Tatler* 149, Steele quotes the very same passage to shame a cold and ill-natured husband. Adam's temperance of his intellectual authority with gentleness and sexual play is regarded as exemplary. In fact the treatment of prelapsarian love in *Paradise Lost* ministered to one of the Spectator's aims, to increase domestic love and happiness; and Addison praised Milton for presenting a "noble Mixture of Rapture and Innocence" in poetry whose love sentiments were "chaste but not cold" (*Spectator* 345).

Addison was one of Richardson's culture heroes, and it is not surprising that the rich literary tradition on love inherited by the novelist should give prominence to the poet whom Addison praised. Many complex uses of Milton appear in all of Richardson's works, but in *Sir Charles Grandison* the poet seems virtually a part of the exemplary hero's excessively adoring but highly intelligent circle. More revealing than direct praise of Milton is the easy familiarity with which his Adam and Eve are treated, as though they had themselves been domesticated and were now members of the family. Sir Charles uses Eve's first response to Adam to make the point that ladies should not be

---

31. *The Love Letters of Mary Wollstonecraft to Gilbert Imlay,* Paris, Aug. 1793; Paris, 22 Sept. [1794] (London: Hutchinson, 1908), pp. 4, 46.

too easily won. Eve is sometimes treated with such levity as the hero is capable of: he calls her "the *old lady*" and uses her "*obsequious majesty*" toward her husband to chide his sister lightly for her rebelliousness.[32] Other examples will appear throughout this work—Fielding, for example, once identifies Amelia with Eve—but enough has been said here to suggest that our first parents as delineated by Milton had insinuated themselves into the erotic dreams and domestic concerns of some English young people. James Barry's *Adam and Eve,* painted in Italy and sent to England in 1770, is only indirectly related to the theme of love; but the painting does illustrate the leveling of the occupants of Eden to a common psychological condition (pl. 1a). However idealized the bodies, the expressions suggest quotidian reality: he looks confused and dependent, she reveals sensuality, guilt, and a nagging articulateness. The tragedy of the Fall, like other important tragedies, has been democratized and domesticated—a process even more apparent in the engraving than in the original oil (pl. 1b).

Unlike direct or overt literary influence, the kind of cultural insemination here being discussed does not proclaim itself; it must be investigated through suggestive hints and suppositions based upon them. But cumulatively these are sufficient to convince us that back of the eighteenth-century union of sex and sensibility lay Milton's Eden. Sometimes its ideal and unfallen qualities are realized—seldom in literature, seldom in painting, but luminously in Gluck's *Orfeo* and *Alceste,* in Mozart's *Magic Flute,* and in Beethoven's great work of uxorial love and heroism, *Fidelio.* More often the ideal glimmers in a fallen world, sometimes as a youthful dream, sometimes as a tormenting unrealized, even unrealizable goal. As the eighteenth century respected rhetorical and intellectual formulation, it must have discovered that the great power of love in *Paradise Lost* came in part from the clarity, force, and sophistication of the positions taken in the Divorce Tracts. These will be analyzed in chapter 2 in order to bring out the positive ideal which they contain and which reappears in the Edenic marriage of the great epic.

What the present book includes and excludes will surely seem anomalous to some, but these possible anomalies provide an opportunity to say more about the methods followed. At crucial points the sister arts are invoked for the enforcement or amplification of the themes discussed, and paintings or engravings are reproduced as illustrations or analogues of the literature. The long final chapter is devoted to visual and musical love. I do not claim in these pages the expertise of an art historian or a musicologist—only the experience of one who has explored the theme of love in many forms of expression and who, perhaps rashly, yielded to the temptation of commenting on parallel renditions outside literature. Anyone drawn to the allied arts could scarcely be expected to confine himself to a single literary genre. Important work has of

32. Ed., Jocelyn Harris (London: Oxford University Press, 1972), 3 vols., 2:97.

course been done on sentimentalism and sensibility by students of the drama or the novel. But the time has now come for the broader view which the theme in its sweep and amplitude requires. Had Joseph Wood Krutch not confined his attention to comedy alone, he would never have said that "in Restoration plays there is no hint that [love] possesses a 'seraphic part.'"[33] If one looks more broadly, one sees romance, ecstasy, even ethical and religious feeling.

Broadly though this book has been conceived, it has been subjected to rigorous limitation. The most important defining principle has been already mentioned: this is not a study of sensibility per se or love per se but of the two in interaction. Other exclusions have also limited the theme and kept it on the track of exploring sex and sensibility. The witty and rational friendships of Pope and Swift have been discussed not only because in profound and moving ways they are touched by—even as they touch—feelings characteristic of the age, but also because Richardson and Rousseau, the great masters of love-sensibility, show us that love is best explored in connection with friendship. The desire to see some form of contact between wit and sensibility proved irresistible. For the most part stage comedy and satire have been excluded, not because they are irrelevant to love but because they do not often illuminate sex and sensibility in combination. Similarly, some important authors have been excluded even though in important ways they touch upon aspects of the theme. Daniel Defoe, an admirable supporter of woman's advancement and a portrayer of such persistent and invincible lovers as Moll Flanders and Roxana, is not dealt with separately and at length because he is fundamentally less concerned with either erotic or ideal love than with essentially prudential relationships. His women lovers, for all their experience, do not often—perhaps ever—pledge either the heart or the body to deep or lasting emotion; they remain the female equivalents of the *homo economicus* Robinson Crusoe. Samuel Johnson appears frequently in these pages, since his wit and wisdom have not unexpectedly proved illuminating on several asepcts of my topic. He spoke with solemn and moving authority on friendship and marriage, and as a critic he appreciated and analyzed the literary theme of domestic love, making the "pathetic" one of his chief critical weapons. But these subjects have been dealt with elsewhere,[34] and as a public man, as a teacher of manners and morals, Johnson was not deeply interested in my central concern here, the passion of love. He in fact deplored its predominance in literature and culture.[35] Another great thinker and writer, Denis Diderot, has also with great

33. *Comedy and Conscience after the Restoration* (New York: Columbia University Press, 1924), p. 193.

34. See Hagstrum, *Johnson's Criticism,* chap. 7, and Sermon 1 in *The Yale Edition of the Works of Samuel Johnson,* vol. 14: *Sermons,* ed. Jean H. Hagstrum and James Gray (New Haven, Conn.: Yale University Press, 1978), pp. 3–15.

35. "Upon every other stage [than Shakespeare's] the universal agent is love, . . . For this, probability is violated, life is misrepresented, and language is depraved. But love is only one of many

reluctance been excluded from these pages. Diderot is not so much a master of *sensibilité* as its radical reviser into something a bit different. Under impulses from the Enlightenment and from post-Lockean French thinkers, he transformed sensibility into a kind of vitalistic materialism in *Le rêve de d'Alembert,* where he connects it with material, even insentient nature or matter, organizing its fibers and threads into formal, rationally controlled bundles of neural response. In this matter he seems to summarize one trend of the Enlightenment and look ahead to the Romantic materialism that influenced Shelley and even the young Coleridge. Similarly, with respect to love Diderot is a clear precursor of Shelley and other Romantic radicals. He attacks the institution of marriage and exposes the habits of courtship to the learned scorn of a world traveler and international anthropologist in his *Supplément au voyage de Bougainville,* where he also anticipates Blake in his attack on modesty, on embarrassed concealment, and on rituals of physical union that are compulsively nocturnal. Diderot would make an excellent introduction to the investigation of another phenomenon, the rise of Romantic love.

Three important associations peculiar to love which we shall encounter again and again in the ensuing pages require brief introductory comment here: love and imagination, love and death, and love and religion.

Sir Joshua Reynolds remarks early in his thirteenth discourse that one quality common to all the fine arts he is about to discuss is that they "address themselves only to two faculties of the mind, its imagination and its sensibility." Love in art both springs from the fancy and stimulates it—inevitably so; it therefore resembles everything else that has achieved belletristic status. My concern here, however, is not with this aesthetic commonplace but with the large human truth that love, by its very obsessive and monomaniacal nature, tends to seize on the imagination and dominate it. Unlike the animals, man is not subject to the periodicity of sexual impulse, and he can make love at virtually any time he chooses—a happy condition, said Diderot, which is owing to his peculiarly human endowment of thought and imagination, by which he can "suddenly recall to himself certain agreeable sensations."[36] It is nothing other than the imagination, which, by its ability to substitue a mental image for reality, feeds our night- and daydreams and even brings intense pleasure to the *vice solitaire.* It can substitute illicit for licit partners and pervert normality into unnatural forms. No wonder that the imagination was often regarded as

---

passions, and as it has no great influence upon the sum of life, it has little operation in the dramas of a poet, who caught his ideas from the living world." "Preface to Shakespeare," *Yale Edition,* 7:63.

36. Diderot goes on to refer to a woman who he says was more philosophical than she realized when she said that animals made love only at intervals because they were beasts (this is a pun, because *bêtes* means both "beasts" and "stupid"). This remark from the *Encyclopédie* is quoted by Arthur M. Wilson, *Diderot* (New York: Oxford University Press, 1972), p. 210.

possessing ardor and that Fanny Burney could refer to its "pulsations."[37] In one of his most disturbing but insistently human plays, Shakespeare explores the association of love and the imagination. The tragically alienated mind of Lear lays bare a raging libidinous fancy: "Let copulation thrive"; "To't, luxury, pell mell" (4.6). His great madness is by no means unique; on the contrary, its pathos is profound because it is typical, though greatly intensified. Perhaps one reason moralists have so unrelentingly inveighed against the imagination is that it seemed so hospitable to erotic images. One of the mischiefs of love is that, while turning us to another person, it can also paradoxically turn the gaze inward and lead to dangerous self-preoccupation. Freud saw that such preoccupation could produce what he called "the narcissistic overestimation of subjective mental processes."[38] The reverse is also true: preoccupation with mental processes can also lead to an overestimation of the self. In my analysis of Milton and in several subsequent pages I shall have much to say about the narcissistic sins and about a self-flattering love of similitude and consanguinity. Apparently a nexus exists between love in any form and the imagination, whose tendency is to lead away from life. The peculiar and fatal association of love and imagination may, then, lead us into some strange paths, but these must be explored if we are to do justice to the range and complexity of our topic.

The association of love and death goes back to the earliest expressions of human consciousness. In some periods, like the baroque and metaphysical seventeenth century, the intersection of love and death is at the very center of creativity. Three of the greatest medieval lovers were entangled in mortality: Abelard died a death in the sexual flesh before his general physical disintegration began and Eloisa lamented among the Gothic tombs; Isolde, deprived of Tristram through death, consecrated the *Liebestod;* and Francesca spoke for herself and Paolo when she said that "amor condusse noi ad una morte" (*Inferno,* 5.106). For Shakespeare black night was "death's second self that seals up all in rest" (sonnet 73), but the French refer to sexual climax as "la petite mort." The reasons for this immemorial association, though mysterious, do not entirely elude comprehension. Death is inexorable, and so too is love: "for love is strong as death," said the Preacher (*Song of Sol.* 8:6). What life denies death can be imagined as supplying, and many a lover has sought the grave. "Komm, süsser Tod!" In our highest joys we think of their end, and in our most ecstatic moments there is a sunset touch. From Shakespeare and

37. Burney is quoted by Patricia Meyer Spacks, who notes the quality of ardor that the imagination was believed to possess. See "'Ev'ry Woman is at Heart a Rake,'" in *Eighteenth-Century Studies* 8 (Fall 1974): 27–46, esp. p. 40.

38. "The 'Uncanny'" (1919), printed in *On Creativity and the Unconscious,* ed. Benjamin Nelson (New York: Harper & Row, 1958), p. 147. This essay contains a brilliant discussion of the "omnipotence of thought" and how that power affects both the imagination and reality.

Marvell to Wallace Stevens poets have known that the approach of death adds intensity and depth to affection:

> This thou perceiv'st, which makes thy love more strong,
> To love that well which thou must leave ere long.

Even in the love act itself—at its very climax or in its postcoital repose—there are intimations of mortality, as the ego is weakened, as consciousness fades. Church and state have perennially bound with their briars men's "joys and desires," and for centuries it was believed that seminal expenditure drained the body of vitality and the spirit of vivacity and that one paid for pleasure by suffering depleted energy. What art and imagination embroidered in metaphor and song social reality presented with stark immediacy. Stone, a careful student of mortality rates, has pointed out that in the 1640s, less than a generation before our period begins, life expectancy at birth in England was only thirty-two years. "The most striking feature which distinguished the Early Modern family from that of today . . . was the constant presence of death" (pp. 66, 68). Only in our own day is death the peculiar companion of age. The literature and art of the eighteenth century were born when death and youth, death and beauty, death and infancy were still intimately associated. From the plays of Nat. Lee and Otway to Goethe's *Werther* the grave, the charnel-house, self-destruction, and Gothic gloom are the dark companions of intersexual affection.

Even though my subject is, as I have said, *eros* rather than *agapē,* secular rather than religious sensibility, a few additional comments must be made on the most important implications of religion for eighteenth-century love. Religion enters our story even when we would least expect it to. As we shall see, Ovid continued to teach the learned classes of the eighteenth century, as he had taught those of the Renaissance, the *ars amatoria.* But perhaps the Bible was the truly effective instructor in love—even sensual love—of an expanded reading public, consisting of the middle classes, women, dissenters, and Latitudinarians. John Selden said in 1689 of Bible reading by the common people, "Lord, what Gear do they make of it!"[39] Apart from worry about turning the sacred into ridicule, as a man of the seventeenth century Selden was doubtless worried most about the political and religious dissension that private exegesis by untutored laymen might produce as

> The tender Page with horney Fists was gaul'd;
> And he was gifted most that loudest baul'd:
> The *Spirit* gave the *Doctoral Degree:*

39. *Table-Talk* (London, 1689), p. 3. The 2d ed. (1696) alters the spelling of "Gear" to "Jeer" (p. 7), showing how the word of the 1st ed. was pronounced and what meaning was primarily intended.

> And every member of a *Company*
> Was of *his Trade,* and of the *Bible free.*
> [Dryden, *Religio Laici,* 404–8]

But Selden might also have feared the incitements to amorous hope that Adam and Eve in their Edenic Bower of Bliss could provoke and the array of sexual perversion that the Old Testament could reveal. When Pamela, amazed by the alternation of love and hate in Mr. B, seeks a biblical example, she focuses on the love of Amnon and Tamar. The modest girl and her modest creator both knew, though they dropped no hint of their knowledge, that love changes to hate in that story because the lovers are brother and sister.[40]

The somewhat ambiguous instruction in love derived from the Bible points to the larger, central ambiguity of the entire Judeo-Christian heritage. On the side of positive encouragement, that great tradition made marriage a sacrament, proclaimed that God was love, required in its two greatest commandments (on which hang all the law and the prophets) both love of God and love of man, made love between man and woman the most important trope for the relations of God and Israel, Christ and the church, made marriage the metaphor for the consummation of all things, and sought to make the blessed and chosen community a fraternity of love and service. And yet the religious historical actuality is harsher and more hostile toward love than one would expect from doctrinal belief and ethical commandment. Christians met pagan love with a rigorous and fierce application of Mosaic law, if Gibbon's account may be trusted; and persecution and even torture, not loving persuasion, were sometimes used to stamp out irregular affection.[41] Paul's attitude toward marriage seems to be grudging at best, and many pages of patristic literature ring with shrill denunciations, repugnant to modern sensibility, of women and of sexual congress. More than one branch of the Christian church has created feelings of deep guilt even about legal and innocent love. One cannot say even of eighteenth-century Christianity that it was in the avant-garde in fostering eros and sensibility, though these did bear important relations to the religion of the West. Love in Rousseau is much more ambiguously indebted to the Christian tradition than is the love in the *Vita nuova* or the *Divine Comedy.*

Dante lived in a Christian civilization, Rousseau in one that was being secularized. The whole matter of how deeply religion affected social behavior

---

40. *Pamela,* letter 23 (Everyman's Library, 1914; reprint ed., New York: E. P. Dutton, 1933), 1:41–42. See 2 Sam. 13:1–22.

41. When Christianity was established, "the laws of Moses were received as the divine original of justice." Sexual frailty became as disgraceful as parricide, adultery was declared a capital offense, and unmanliness was met with cruel and implacable persecution: "A painful death was inflicted by the amputation of the sinful instrument, or the insertion of sharp reeds into the pores and tubes of most exquisite sensibility." *The History of the Decline & Fall of the Roman Empire,* ed. J. B. Bury, 3 vols. (New York: Heritage Press, 1946), 2:1475–76 (chap. 44).

and indeed the mind of the artist at the moment of creation is a vexed one. The problem is not made easier by the absence of a modern study of Christianity in eighteenth-century English culture. That its place was extremely important is attested by the fact that the greatest writers were Christians, that the Christian response to Deism surpassed the attack in intellectual as well as literary power, and that seminal and influential works of religious thought and exhortation continued to appear. England simply did not experience an Enlightenment—at least not one conveyed in the full sense of the French word "lumière." And yet a student of a topic like love is soon enough made aware that Christian values were being displaced, if not replaced; reinterpreted and transplanted, if not supplanted or eroded. Peter Gay's judicious statement is applicable to England: "To speak of the secularization of life in the eighteeenth century is not to speak of the collapse of clerical establishments or the decay of religious concerns. The age of the Enlightenment . . . was still a religious age. . . . Theological debates retained much of their old vigor and much of their popularity. To speak of secularization, therefore, is to speak of a subtle shift of attention: religious institutions and religious explanations of events were slowly being displaced from the center of life to its periphery."[42] That in England secularization affected love is abundantly evident if one compares Milton and Keats. For the earlier poet sensuality was a grievous sin whose "mortal tast / Brought Death into the World, and all our woe." But the Romantic poet, only a century and a generation later, called for "a Life of Sensations rather than of Thoughts."[43] Most in the eighteenth century would have been uncomfortable with Keats's longing, but that period did in subtle ways bridge the gulf between the two poets. It is a noteworthy fact that even some of the great idealizations of love and marriage which I shall later analyze are not presented in Hebrew or Christian dress. The book of Gluck's noble operas on love is based on pagan myth; Mozart relies on Masonic or some other form of Enlightened initiation; and Beethoven's opera mythologizes secular political protest and resistance. Enlightenment values can be credited with much good in the developing story of affective individualism. These mitigated the rigors of harsh Puritanical child rearing, made the pursuit of happiness a this-worldly, secular concern,[44]

42. *The Enlightenment: An Interpretation The Rise of Modern Paganism* (New York: Alfred A. Knopf, 1966), p. 338.

43. *Paradise Lost,* 1. 2–3; letter to Benjamin Bailey, 22 Nov. 1817, *The Letters of John Keats: 1814–1821,* ed. Hyder Edward Rollins, 2 vols. (Cambridge, Mass.: Harvard University Press, 1958), 1:185.

44. Milton justifies his place at the beginning of our story partly because, in his argument for divorce at least, he shifted from exclusive dependence on divine prescription to a reocgnition of the principle of human good, temporal as well as spiritual. He said, "Nothing can be recounted justly among the causes of our happiness unless in some way it takes into consideration both that eternal life and this temporal life." Milton's statement (*Prolusion,* 7.12.255) is quoted and commented on by Arthur Barker, *Milton and the Puritan Dilemma: 1641–1660* (Toronto: University of Toronto Press, 1942), p. 111.

exalted the position of woman, and created an atmosphere of greater freedom and joy in the relations of the sexes. Liberal thought produced other
results as well, some of them of highly dubious value. Growing secularization
undoubtedly had much to do with the melting away of Milton's indignant
disapprobation of the narcissistic sins: incest, sometimes overt, sometimes
prudently below the surface, was presented with surprising frequency as an
inevitable, if not acceptable, attraction. The whole relationship of belief and
practice is extremely complicated, but it is perhaps right to regard the Enlightenment heritage as being just as ambiguous with respect to love as was
Christianity. There could be something chilling to sex and sensibility in the
dry, rational, disillusioned wit of the eighteenth-century satirical and comic
spirit. And if the century's greatest Christian, Samuel Johnson, was not entirely happy about literary love, neither was the century's greatest skeptic,
Voltaire.

And yet the truth is that in its largest intellectual affiliations, sex-sensibility
drew upon both Christianity and Enlightened secularism. Johann Sebastian
Bach appears in the ensuing pages partly to show what the Christian "pathetic" could actually be at its greatest and purest. Dryden's Christian commitment doubtless favored the movement toward sensibility in his dramas; Steele
drew inspiration for sentimental love from his deep religious feeling; and
Richardson was an ardent and uncompromising Christian, admired by
Samuel Johnson for his firm spiritual control of the emotions. At the same
time, as I have said, love-sensibility at its highest moments could also be
pagan and secular, since love underwent the same process of transformation
and secular displacement that overtook other values and concerns. The
nineteenth century had some awareness of the complex coexistence in
eighteenth-century *amour-tendresse* of Christianity and secular modernity.
Leslie Stephen defined sentimentalism as "the effeminate element of Christianity," believing that sentimentalism took what was tender and pretty in that
religion and left out its sterner and more masculine ingredients. But he, like
so many other Victorians who commented on the century that preceded them,
is an untrustworthy guide because of his *furor criticus*. Sensibility he found to
be "a kind of mildew," and its masters he regarded with contempt. Richardson
he called "morbid." Sterne, "a literary prostitute," he believed to possess a
"corrupt heart and a prurient imagination," and he agreed with Byron that
greater moral danger lurks in *La nouvelle Héloïse* than in the open scoffing of
Don Juan.[45] We are now a century farther away from the Age of Sensibility
and ought to take a modern look, free of former inhibitions. If we need
earlier guidance, nineteenth-century France is perhaps more reliable than
Victorian England. Looking back, Jules Michelet said, "L'amour est grand au

45. *History of English Thought in the Eighteenth Century* (1876; reprint ed., 2 vols. [New York:
Harcourt, Brace & World, 1962]), 2:371, 374–76.

dix-huitième siècle. . . . Il est fort et réel, et il semble une religion, accrue des ruines de l'ancienne."[46] The eighteenth century is somewhat too early to illustrate Arnold's belief that poetry could supplant the Christian faith. But in purely human love the tendency toward secular displacement of values is, as I have said, clearly under way. Men have begun to see heaven in a domestic nest, eternity in a mutually felt romantic passion, the restoration of Eden in heterosexual friendship. The attempt to substitute a private—and somewhat chancy—human adventure for a religion ages old and putatively built on the rock of divine sanction may itself have caused the anxieties and neuroses that often attended affection in our period. However that may be, what I shall be concerned with in this book is not a creed but a pantheon, a gallery of imagined human characters, larger than life though related to it, more permanent than historical flux, with women and also some men who stand as permanent human forms and ideals to which our imaginations and even consciences advert. Eve, Adam, the Portuguese Nun, Almanzor, Belvidera, "Dear Prue," Eloisa, Stella, Clarissa, Julie, Rousseau the Confessor (for he too is partly fictional), My Uncle Toby, Marianne Dashwood, Werther, Alceste, Fiordiligi, the Countess Almaviva, Tamino, and Leonore were created in some kind of anticipation of or response to sex and sensibility. But they also helped to create us. Perhaps they are still creating us. It is owing to them and the likes of them that, in William Faulkner's language, "the past is never dead, it is not even past."

46. *Histoire de France* (Paris, 1893–97), 14:306. Quoted by R. S. Ridgway, *Voltaire and Sensibility* (Montreal: McGill-Queen's University Press, 1973), p. 35.

2. Milton and the Ideal of Heterosexual Friendship

*M*ILTON'S VISION of love and marriage encompasses two polarities. One is the ideal of heterosexual friendship, and the other is the sin of narcissism—or, more exactly, a cluster of sins involving sensuality, love of the self, and the attractions of similitude (the sins of spiritual and physical consanguinity). It is with these polarities that I shall be primarily concerned, although Milton's vision is so complex as to introduce several other elements, many of which will reappear in subsequent chapters. The vision itself is both conservative and forward-looking, at once a consolidation and a radical revision. Milton brings to fruition what had been present but often allowed to remain only latent in Judaism and Christianity—an exalted love between the sexes. That love, which Milton defined as mutual and as embracing both the spiritual and the physical, he made the very cornerstone of the institution of marriage, which was before and since able to exist and even thrive without it. At the same time, Milton recognized that an institution based upon human compatibility and mutuality in passion must be sensitive to personal change and also flexible enough in its arrangements to make accommodations when its chief ends were abrogated. He was therefore led to advocate one of the rarest and boldest positions in all of Christian history, the free and simple dissolution of the marriage bond when its essence, friendship between man and woman, had disappeared. Until very recently, the association of love and marriage has seemed to us as inevitable as the association of light and warmth. It was not so in Milton's day or in most antecedent Western cultures. His simple position was therefore extremely radical—that love creates marriage as the sun creates the day and that when love sets, it is night. More fundamental than the idea of marriage, then, is the idea of love, which, if properly understood, makes the position on divorce seem far less quirkish and perverse than it has sometimes been regarded.

Milton's views on love are embodied in a series of passionate prose tracts, especially *The Doctrine and Discipline of Divorce* (1643; revised and expanded 1644), which "glows with discovery" and was written with "almost fanatical courage."[1] They also appear in some of the most beautiful lyrical and pro-

---

1. William R. Parker, *Milton: A Biography* (Oxford: Clarendon Press, 1968), 1:240. The poetry of Milton is quoted from vols. 1 and 2 of *The Works of John Milton,* ed. Frank Allen Patterson, 18

foundly psychological passages of *Paradise Lost*. Before both the prose tracts
and the epic Milton had praised in *Comus* (1634) the "Sun-clad power of
Chastity" (781) to stay the "rash hand of bold Incontinence" (396). But this
delicate and lovely portrayal of "the unpolluted temple of the mind" (460) is
essentially fragile and cannot be said to be a mature vision of what man and
society need and desire. The Lady, the Brothers, and Comus lack the archetypal force of Adam and Eve or of Satan, Sin, and Death. The much later
Samson Agonistes (1671) also presents a partial vision of human affection. In
contrast to the soaring love of our first parents, the emotions of the fallen,
suffering hero of the Hebrews is, humanly considered, a compound of anger
and disillusion—a cry of devotion to God, certainly, but also a cry of despair
over man as a social creature, a shriek of hatred at the treachery of the female,
and a deep-fetched groan of shame at the "foul effeminacy" (410) of the male.
For all its Hebraic robustness and sublimity, *Samson* misses both the ideal
beauty of love in Eden and the symbolic force of the postlapsarian couple,
whose union typifies the achievement of Paradise within.[2]

---

vols. (New York: Columbia University Press, 1931–40); only titles of poems and line numbers are
given. For a scholarly and vividly written analysis of all the passages in Milton relating to sexuality
and love, see Edward Le Comte, *Milton and Sex* (New York: Columbia University Press, 1978).
Fully persuasive about how deeply sexual imagery had insinuated Milton's expression, Le Comte
also unflinchingly demonstrates the poet's reaction of disgust to the denials and trials of his first
marriage and his fear of female dominance, for a while hysterical and violent. But in the end Le
Comte does not find Milton to be a misogynist, and he says of the vision of ideal love: "But the
old-young dream of perfect bliss, which includes perfect sex, shines in the distance, beckoning,
'The happier *Eden*' (*Paradise Lost*, 4. 507)" (p. 120). For a perceptive analysis of love in *Paradise
Lost*, see Joseph H. Summers, "The Two Great Sexes," chap. 4 of *The Muse's Method: An Introduction to "Paradise Lost"* (Cambridge, Mass.: Harvard University Press, 1962). Summers says, "Milton
has consistently related the various motions within the poem to the 'two great Sexes which
animate the World.' Milton 'realized' his divine and all-embracing subject more often by sexual
than merely sensuous metaphor and allusion" (p. 88).

2. On Eve as a guide to repentance and as mother of the line that will produce the Redeemer,
see John Halkett, *Milton and the Idea of Matrimony* (New Haven, Conn.: Yale University Press,
1970), pp. 137–38. Halkett's view is substantially that of Tillyard, Stein, Fish, and Summers,
whose "romantic notion that it is Eve's love that leads Adam back to God" is challenged on mostly
theological grounds by Georgia B. Christopher, "The Verbal Gate to Paradise: Adam's 'Literary
Experience' in Book 10 of *Paradise Lost*" (*Publications of the Modern Language Association* 90 [Jan.
1975]: 69–77). For another view of *Samson Agonistes*, see Joyce Colony, "An Argument for Milton's
Dalila," *Yale Review* 66 (Summer 1977): 562–75. Colony argues that in altering his source in
Judges and transforming Dalila from a concubine to a wife, Milton gives her a place in the
redemption of the hero. Though hysterically angry at what she has done, he is still attracted to
her; his turning away from her is a true victory over his still powerfully sensual nature. She is thus
indirectly responsible for the recovery of his powers and his final redemptive exertion on behalf
of the Lord. I am myself attracted by this thesis that love is somehow present in this otherwise
harsh drama, but I am far from finding *Samson* to be a balanced statement of the Miltonic love
ideal.

The "Rites Mysterious of Connubial Love"

In *The Doctrine and Discipline of Divorce* (1.4) Milton hails wedded love as the "intelligible flame, not in Paradise to be resisted";[3] and in *Paradise Lost* (4.744 ff.) he separates himself from those "Hypocrites" who "austerely" preach abstinence, who talk of "puritie and place and innocence," but who in reality make impure what God has called pure and who ignore the divine command to increase and multiply.

> Our Maker bids increase, who bids abstain
> But our destroyer, foe to God and Man?
> [4.748–49]

For all his blame of sensuality, Milton, in prose and poetry, enforces with vigor and delight, the central importance of the sexual element in human love, unfallen and fallen. The "sensitive pleasing of the body" (*Divorce,* 1.2; 2:246) may not be the noblest or highest aim of marriage, but it is an essential one. It is so important that Milton uses biblical and liturgical language to describe its physical component. The term "one flesh" refers, quite without metaphor, to a union of bodies (though it can also be applied to fitness of mind and personality), and the biblical use of the word "flesh" is understood in *Tetrachordon* (1644) to "justify and make legitimat the *rites* of the Mariage bed" (2:606; emphasis added). Physical relations also constitute a "mystery," which was for the Protestant Milton a more solemn term even than "rite," since the Apostle Paul had used it of the resurrection of the body (1 Cor. 15:51). In *Colasterion* (1645) Milton vigorously attacked an opponent who objected that he had called marriage "the mystery of Joy" (2:749), and in *Paradise Lost* (4.750–51) he called "wedded Love," which is the "true sourse / Of human ofspring," a "mysterious Law." On at least one occasion he combined rite and mystery when he referred to sexual relations as "the Rites / Mysterious of connubial Love" (4.742–43).

Those who have questioned the presence in Eden of sexuality as we know it have seriously missed the point. Milton has made pleasure in the union between the primal pair as unmistakable as he could without being gross. Eve is a person of sweetness and grace, her golden hair curls in "wanton ringlets" (4.306). She displays without shame her "mysterious parts" (4.312; again the word "mystery" is associated with the sexual, even when openly displayed). And when she surrenders to Adam, "half her swelling Breast / Naked met

3. The divorce tracts and other prose works are quoted from *Complete Prose Works,* ed. Don M. Wolfe (New Haven: Yale University Press, 1953–). The quotation from *Divorce* 1.4 appears in *CPW,* 2:252. Similarly, later quotations will refer to the divisions of the work itself and also to the volume and page of the Yale ed., regularly abbreviated *CPW.* Vol. 2 (1959) of *CPW* is edited by Ernest Sirluck.

his" (4.495–96). Although the kiss that Adam presses on her lips is pure, it is sensual enough to provoke jealous desire in the arch-fiend from the place of envy and burning lust, who has been watching the "bliss on bliss" (4.508) of innocence. The bower consecrated to these blisses is flowery, lit at night by a moon that has arisen in "clouded Majestie" (4.607). The clothes of which Eve is totally free Milton calls "troublesom disguises" (4.740), and the delights of the new family are a "Perpetual Fountain of Domestic sweets" (4.760). That these include sexual dalliance and consummation is assured by the presence of Cupid, who "Reigns here and revels" and who "waves his purple wings" (4.764–65). Close to nature, though separated from the animals who are not allowed to enter the bower, the love of Adam and Eve is unmistakably physical and pleasurable, a love expressed in "conjugal Caresses" (8.56), a "Sweetness" in the heart, "the spirit of love and amorous delight" (8.475, 477). "Blushing like the Morn" (8.511), Eve enters—to the spousal descant of the birds—a bower from which offspring will issue forth.

Some have found Milton's portrayal of physical love extremely rare— "probably the last piece of imaginative literature before *Jude the Obscure* to treat sexuality in serious practical detail."[4] Some have deplored it—C. S. Lewis wondering if Milton was indeed wise to have painted such very "un-mysterious pictures" about paradisal sexuality, defying Augustine's warning not to describe an essentially unimaginable kind of love. Cardinal Newman also believed that Milton treated our first parents with intolerable freedom.[5] But whether pleased or offended, no one surely has mistaken—or indeed could mistake—Milton's meaning, least of all those writers and readers of the eighteenth century who looked to the bower in Eden as a sanction and source of their dreams of marital bliss. Raphael's smile "glow'd / Celestial rosie red" (8.618–19) when Adam asked him about the nature of angelic sexuality, and he gave an answer that some have regarded as evasive.[6] About human love in Eden, Milton is much less learnedly coy than his angel. He gives a direct answer, to which he applies sensuous embroidery and unmistakable nuance.

Sexuality in love, however important and basic, must be partial—for Milton as for any serious thinker. In his conception of heterosexual friendship the

4. J. B. Broadbent, *Some Graver Subject: An Essay on Paradise Lost* (London: Chatto & Windus, 1967), p. 245. For a discussion of sexuality in *Paradise Lost* and an appreciation of its centrality in Milton's conception of love, see Purvis E. Boyette, "Something More about the Erotic Motive in *Paradise Lost*," *Tulane Studies in English* 15 (1967): 19–30.

5. C. S. Lewis, *A Preface to Paradise Lost* (New York: Oxford University Press, 1961), pp. 122, 124.

6. Le Comte in *Milton and Sex* does not so regard it. "'We enjoy in eminence'—such is the blushing acknowledgment. It is superhuman, polymorphous, bisexual coitus that accomplishes mixing soul with soul in love supreme. It is every man's dream, and every woman's. Milton does not blush. He flaunts it, braving the reader's shocked reaction because of the depth of his own conviction that sex is not merely an animal activity, that 'marriage must not be called a defile-ment,' that flesh leads to spirit—therefore spirits scorn not flesh" (p. 93).

substantive is more important than the adjective, though the noun is colored by its modifier. Even "delight," to take one of the several words with romantic associations that the poet uses to describe the life together of the first couple, is by no means confined to moments of physical bliss. Men and women are refreshed by "apt and cheerfull conversation" (preface to *Divorce* 1; 2:235), "conversation" being a term that referred more broadly to total companionship than it does today. But "conversation" in our sense is also meant, for one of the noblest aims of union is a mutual discourse that is "meet and happy" (*Divorce* 1.2; 2:246) and that ministers to "the solace and love of each other" (2.16; 2:328). The last phrase is worth noting, since much has rightfully been made of Milton's egoistic demands in his own domestic life. In *Tetrachordon* Milton says that "there is a peculiar comfort in the maried state besides the genial bed, which no other society affords"—and that comfort arises more lastingly from "fitness of mind and disposition" than from sexual attraction.[7] Friendship in marriage thus assures a "free and lightsome conversation" (*Divorce* 1.11; 2:273) that "no mere amatorious novel" (1.6; 2:256) can provide.

The rich and complex ideal of the divorce tracts—a companionship that is amorous, relaxing, spirited, cheerful, comforting—is fully realized in the Edenic happiness of Adam and Eve. Its most endearing quality arises from its union of the contraries of total individuality and total mutuality. Eve, said Adam, is "Part of my Soul . . . / My other half" (4.487–88); and his rationality, his love of metaphysical and cosmological speculation, is balanced by her power of poetic, sensuous, descriptive, and narrative speech. When Adam, alone, longed for an equal, he longed for someone of his own species, not for someone to divide his authority and power. But, still, the mutuality that was established at once between him and Eve is so complete that it adumbrates if it does not fully satisfy the modern ideal.

> Among unequals what societie
> Can sort, what harmonie or true delight?
>   [8.383–84]

A total consonance of body, mind, and spirit nourished love in Eden. Such friendship, "unlibidinous" (5.449) but unashamedly physical, refined the manners, enlarged the heart, obeyed reason, and pointed upward to heavenly love. It recalled all that Agathon in the *Symposium* or Socrates in the *Phaedrus* said of love. It embodied the ascent to Oneness that Plotinus had envisioned. Eros has been immemorially thought of as pointing toward an ideal; and the Great Chain of Being is not only a connection of clearly defined and stable hierarchies but what Pope calls, in the third epistle of *An Essay on Man*, "the chain of Love / Combining all below and all above" (7–8).

---

7. *CPW*, 2:596, 605. See Halkett's fine discussion of "Fitness: The Conception of the Ideal Mate," in his chap. 2 (pp. 31–57).

From the general and insufficiently differentiated point of view I have been expressing so far, Milton can be seen as fulfilling in his vision of love a central Western tradition. But from a narrower, perhaps more discriminating and useful perspective, he can be seen to be a radical and seminal revisionist. Milton's thought shows in several places the imprint of "the divine volumes of *Plato*," from whom he learned early to cherish chastity and love and the "abstracted sublimities" of knowledge and virtue that love produces in the soul.[8] But the ideal of love that I have been describing inevitably represents a sharp break with the Platonic system. This divergence appears clearly if we compare *Paradise Lost* with the divorce tracts. In the poem Eve is brought to Adam

> in naked beauty more adorn'd,
> More lovely then *Pandora,* whom the Gods
> Endowd with all thir gifts . . . .
>
> [4.713–15]

Such a boon, Milton had said earlier, Plato and Chrysippus and their followers, the Academics and the Stoics, could not appreciate, for they "knew not what a consummat and most adorned *Pandora* was bestow'd upon *Adam*" (*Divorce* 2.3; 2:293). In commenting on God's creation of unmistakably distinguished sexes in Genesis 1:27, Milton flicks in *Tetrachordon* at the Jewish Platonists and at Plato himself, whose "wit" would have it that "man at first had bin created *Hermaphrodite*."[9] Since Milton must have been a careful reader of the *Symposium,* he knew that Plato's view was not necessarily that of Aristophanes, who fabled that we were once one sex and that love is a longing for our divided half. And if Milton knew the whole corpus of Plato's thought, as he surely did, then he was consciously breaking with the entire Platonic system of transcending earthly love and certainly with the homosexual matrix from which it sprang and which provided it with the analogies and metaphors it everywhere employs. The creator of Adam and Eve cannot have been finally in full sympathy with the position on love of a philosopher of whom it has

8. *An Apology for Smectymnuus* (1642) in *CPW,* 1:891–92. See Irene Samuel, *Plato and Milton* (1947; reprint ed., Ithaca: Cornell University Press, 1965), esp. chap. 7, "The Doctrine of Love," for an analysis of the insemination of Milton's mind by Platonic values and their persistence in *Paradise Lost,* which is regarded as a fulfillment of the *Apology for Smectymnuus.* I do not deny that Milton early held to an ideal of chastity and that he continued to believe spiritual love superior to the purely physical. The thesis of this chapter, however, is that Milton was more basically Christian than Platonic with respect to love and that in his maturest vision he united the sexual and the spiritual in ways undreamt of by Plato.

9. *CPW,* 2:589. On the rise during the Renaissance and seventeenth century of the hermaphrodite as a symbol of spiritual union in love, see A. R. Cirillo, "The Fair Hermaphrodite: Love-Union in the Poetry of Donne and Spenser," *Studies in English Literature, 1500–1900* 9 (Winter 1969): 81-95. Cirillo shows that Plato had influenced such commentators as Philo Judaeus to see in Gen. 1:27 reference to a genus, Man, that contained both the sexes, later separated into male and female (p. 87).

been said, "Of any ennobling individual relationship between man and woman Plato has no conception any more than his contemporaries."[10] Nor could Milton have been ignorant of the point of view that Robert Burton stated so categorically—that "Socrates used to frequent the Gymnasium because of the beauty of the youngsters, feeding his hungry eyes on that spectacle," and that Plato himself "delighted in Agathon."[11]

Even clearer is Milton's divergence from Augustine, whose position he calls "crabbed" and judges in *Tetrachordon* as being much too austere: "*Austin* contests [i.e., argues] that manly friendship . . . had bin a more becomming solace for *Adam,* then to spend so many secret years in an empty world with one woman" (2:596). Augustine's description of the consummation of a pagan wedding, with its invocation of many deities and its ugly use of the large and repulsive member of Priapus upon which the bride sat before her husband enjoyed her, reeks with disgust.[12] Predictably, his Eden is austere and largely sexless: loyal partnership, honest love, *concors mentis corporisque vigilia,* perfect peace of mind, no *turbidus calor,* sex acts totally and solely responsive to the free will and *sine libidinis morbo.*[13] In the end he wonders why we try to conceive of the inconceivable, particularly since in a fallen world we can associate sexuality only with turbulent lust. Milton, however, did try to conceive of the inconceivable and imaged it in some of his most memorable verse.

Augustine's shrinking reluctance to contemplate a joyful union of opposite sexes in Eden is itself a manifestation and an enforcement of the venerable and powerful tradition of Christian asceticism. That tradition tended to subordinate, even to denigrate, woman, who was considered sometimes a sink of loathsome sensuality, sometimes an incomplete man, often an intellectual nonentity.[14] Since marriage inevitably has much to do with woman, antifeminist loathing or indifference on the part of some Christian thinkers be-

---

10. G. M. A. Grube, *Plato's Thought* (London: Methuen, 1970), p. 89.

11. *The Anatomy of Melancholy,* 3.2.1,2. (1621; 3d ed., [Oxford, 1628], p. 652). The view that Plato introduced into Western culture a notion of love repressive to normal heterosexual relations has persisted to our day. See Herbert Marcuse, *Eros and Civilization* (New York: Vintage Books, 1962), p. 192. Marcuse believes, however, that the *Symposium* gives clear expression to the sexual origins of spiritual relations. "The road to 'higher culture' leads through the true love of boys" (p. 193). Observe that in *Areopagitica (CPW,* 2:523 and n.134) Milton wonders why Plato was not "a Law-giver to himself," and he calls his "epigrams and dialogues" "wanton," which they certainly are not, in language at least. It would appear that Milton is attacking them for their expression of homosexual love and attraction.

12. *De Civitate Dei* 6.9. See also 7.24. Augustine ill conceals his physical loathing, but these sections are also full of satirical and comical verve, particularly as he discusses the multiplication of pagan dieties.

13. Ibid. 14.26. Mark Rose comments, wittily: "Augustine, Paul's spiritual heir, was fated to struggle with a nature unusually passionate, and, having triumphed over his body, he bequeathed to Christianity a rather vicious portrait of his defeated enemy." See *Heroic Love: Studies in Sidney and Spenser* (Cambridge, Mass.: Harvard University Press, 1968), p. 7.

14. See "Mediaeval Sexual Ideal," chap. 3 of G. Rattray Taylor, *Sex in History* (New York: Vanguard Press, 1954, 1970).

came at best a grudging concession that this state was better than unlicensed lust. "It is better to marry than to burn" (1 Cor. 7:9)—but not all that much better; and even matrimony required unflagging vigilance against sensuality. As the *Parson's Tale* put it, "Man sholde loven hys wife by discrecioun, paciently and atemprely; and thanne is she as though it were his suster" (860). Just as Mary gloriously transcended Eve, so her condition of virginity was incomparably superior to that of our primal mother. Cardinal Bellarmine put the matter succinctly: "Mariage is a thing humane, virginitie is Angelical."[15] Even Luther confessed that celibacy had made marriage so disreputable that he could not think of that intimate union without a sense of sin.[16] So virginity was exalted, institutionalized, and made archetypical. Prophet and priest were separated from *l'homme moyen sensuel.* Against that tradition Milton's portrayal of marriage as a joyous heterosexual friendship constitutes one of the most eloquent protests in Christian history, allying him with the abandonment of ecclesiastical asceticism and the grant, to even the holiest of men and women, of Christian liberty to choose a mate and establish a small society bonded in sexual congress. It is little wonder that Milton's anger blazed against canon law and the canonists, "whose boistrous edicts tyrannizing the blessed ordinance of mariage into the quality of a most unnatural and unchristianly yoke, have giv'n the flesh this advantage to hate it, & turn aside, oft-times unwillingly, to all dissolute uncleannesse, even till punishment it self is weary and overcome by the incredible frequency of trading lust, and uncontroull'd adulteries" (*Divorce* 2.20; 2:341).

Milton was by no means the first to proclaim such powerfully antiascetic views, though he is perhaps the greatest English thinker and poet so to do; and of course it would be a grievous mistake to think that the entire Catholic world had been everywhere hostile to the flesh, capable only of an etherealized, otherworldly love. Saint Bernard had said that disembodied spirits long for their bodies and praised the body for its service to the soul: "And rightly doth the soul not will to be made perfect without that which it feeleth hath in every state served it in good things."[17] The Middle Ages

15. Quoted in James Turner Johnson, *A Society Ordained by God: English Puritan Marriage Doctrine in the First Half of the Seventeenth Century* (Nashville, Tenn.: Abingdon Press, 1970), p. 39. On later *angélisme,* see below, pp. 163–64. Rose in *Heroic Love* (p. 7) points out that Jovinian was excommunicated for suggesting that in God's eyes the married state was considered fully as desirable as virginity. Lawrence Stone, relying on John T. Noonan, *Contraception: A History of Its Treatment by the Catholic Theologians and Canonists* (Cambridge, Mass.: Harvard University Press, 1966), pp. 307–8, 320–21, 328–29, says that "it was not until the eighteenth century that Catholic theologians finally identified the purpose of intercourse with the spiritual purpose of marriage itself as a union of two human beings for mutual comfort and support." *Family, Sex and Marriage,* p. 625.

16. Quoted by Juliet Dusinberre, *Shakespeare and the Nature of Women* (London: Macmillan, 1975), p. 3.

17. Bernard is quoted in n. 4 to Dante, *Paradiso* 14, in the *Divine Comedy,* Carlyle-Wicksteed translation (New York: Modern Library, 1932), pp. 491, 493.

produced courtly love; and to the exaltation of heterosexual friendship, that amazing movement made at least one inestimable contribution. An authority on it has said that Aristotle, Virgil, and Paul would certainly have understood love to be an ennobling passion, but so patriarchal, so male-oriented were their views that these men would have been shocked to know that a woman could inspire such love.[18] What was new about the troubadors was neither the joy they found in love nor the refinement with which they adorned it but, rather, the object that aroused it. They loved women, and therein lay the seeds of revolutionary change. What many of the Fathers had made a vice the courtly lovers made a virtue. In this respect—and perhaps only in this—was Milton an inheritor of that great medieval tradition of poetic love: his society of affection was founded on love for a woman.

Spenser was indubitably one of Milton's forerunners, and even a brief comparison of their positions will bring out what is distinctive in the later poet. Like Milton, Spenser made the impulse toward sexual union part of the meaning and therefore the symbolism of Christian marriage. Consider the character of the female warrior Britomart, symbol of chastity. This symbol is complex, for it embraces church, state, and military might. But central significance lies in the fact that at Britomart's heart core is a love wound that cannot be healed until she is united with her lover, Artegall. Milton and Spenser share the view that chastity is not broken but is instead enriched when men and women love in sanctioned ways. There are also profound differences, for Spenser is drawn to what Milton sharply rejects, the Platonic imagery of androgyny. Venus herself is androgynous:

> She hath both kinds in one,
> Both male and female, both vnder one name:
> She syre and mother is her selfe alone,
> Begets and eke conceiues, ne needeth other none.
> [*FQ*, 4.10.41]

The first ending of the third book of *The Faerie Queene* portrays Scudamour and Amoret locked in a love embrace, so resembling the "fair *Hermaphrodite*, / Which that rich *Romane* of white marble wrought." Spenser may here be exalting a Neoplatonic love ideal.[19] To Milton such mythologizing is not congenial: he keeps his sexes sharply distinct and will have no traffic with the Platonic wit about the *ur*-sex or any kind of union that blurs the sharp contrasts necessary for productive sexual alchemy.

18. Maurice Jacques Valency, *In Praise of Love: An Introduction to the Love-Poetry of the Renaissance* (New York: Macmillan, 1958), p. 15. I am aware, by the way, that courtly love is no longer accepted unequivocally as a social movement. There is no doubt of its presence in poetry.

19. See Cirillo, "The Fair Hermaphrodite." By referring to the androgynous Venus and the hermaphrodite-like embrace, I do not wish to weaken either the force of post-Reformation marital ideals in Spenser or the revolutionary quality of his associating passionate physical love

Nowhere is the centrality of heterosexual friendship more evident than in Milton's bold redefinition of marriage and his radical view that divorcement must be the necessary and prime function of any Christian government. He was of course in complete accord with the Continental reformers in denying to marriage the status of a sacrament. But he came close to a sacramental view by asking *when* God does indeed join a pair. His answer is basic: "Only then, when the minds are fitly dispos'd, and enabl'd to maintain a cherfull conversation, to the solace and love of each other" (*Divorce*, 2.16; 2:328). When love, mutuality, and joy disappear, God disappears too; and the bonds are not only theoretically dissoluble, they must as a matter of religion and morality be dissolved, for marriage without love is a mockery and a hollow sham. Milton's rhetoric blazes at white heat when he asserts the Christian obligation to terminate a torture. The option of divorce follows inevitably from the definition of wedlock. And that definition, Milton stoutly insisted, rested on two important Christian virtues, liberty and charity—the liberty in which Christ set us free and the charity which is "the high governesse of our belief" (2.20; 2:340).

What a radical revision Milton's definition in fact is! The Book of Common Prayer (King Edward VI, 1552) stated that marriage had three aims: (1) procreation, (2) restraint and the remedy of sin, and (3) "mutual society, help, and comfort."[20] The third Anglican aim Milton moves up to the first and centrally defining place. Of the Roman Catholic aims (*proles, fides,* and *sacramentum*), Milton accepts the first two—he favored offspring and desired fidelity to the partner—but completely denies the third, calling it "that letter-bound servility of the Canon Doctors" (2.20; 2:342). Perhaps nowhere else is Milton so boldly antinomian, individualistic, and trustful of private human instinct guided by God. The theory espoused in the divorce tracts shows that he had severed relations with the Presbyterians, on whose side he had done polemical battle in 1641, and that he had gone far beyond the established thinking of both Anglican and Puritan.[21]

with the uxorial. Leslie Fiedler has rightly said of the Spenserian synthesis of which we are the heirs: "To identify the feeling which leads to and persists in marriage with the ennobling passion sung by the troubadours, this was a revolutionary step." *Love and Death in the American Novel* (1960; rev. ed., A Delta Book [New York: Dell Publishing Co., 1966]), p. 60. See also the highly discriminating article by Robert Ellrodt, "From Earthly Love to Heavenly Love" in *The Prince of Poets: Essays on Edmund Spenser,* ed. John R. Elliott, Jr. (New York: New York University Press, 1968), pp. 170–86. Ellrodt discusses Spenser's "frank acceptance of physical love" ("neither new nor surprising") and his identification of "l'amore honesto" with marriage (for which there is little or no precedence in the Neoplatonic literature of the Renaissance). See ibid., p. 175.

20. Johnson, *A Society Ordained by God,* p. 22, n.6 and p. 68, n.43. Luther believed that marriage was a civil matter, not a sacrament, though he regarded it as a blessed estate ordained by God; and English reformers were in general more conservative than their Continental brethren. See George E. Howard, *A History of Matrimonial Institutions* (Chicago: University of Chicago Press, 1904), 2:60, 71.

21. Halkett, *Milton and Matrimony,* p. 1. On the ends of marriage, about which Christian writers often disagreed, see ibid., p. 26. It should be noted that the aim of *fides* refers, not to saving faith, but to troth and fidelity.

Radical though Milton's demand for divorce may be, his conception of the intimate association in human love of the physical and the spiritual rests on traditional and orthodox foundations. In *Christian Doctrine* (bk. 1, chap. 7, "Of the Creation") he reveals the psychotheological roots of his position. He allies himself with the view of Augustine and virtually the whole Western church—Tertullian, Apollinarius, Jerome, and Gregory of Nyssa—in believing that the human soul was "not created daily by the immediate act of God" but propagated from father to son in a natural order (6:319). This belief led him to an acceptance of the doctrine of original sin, transmitted through the generations since Adam. But it also led him to two views congenial to his idea of heterosexual friendship. One is that body and soul are inseparable: "That the spirit of man is separate from his body, so that it may exist somewhere in isolation, complete and intelligent, is nowhere to be found in scripture, and is plainly at odds with nature and reason" (6:319). The other is that this union, in which soul is diffused through all parts of the entire being we call man, elevates the sexual. Milton asks, "How can the human seed, that intimate and most noble part of the body, be imagined destitute and devoid of the soul . . . ?" (6:321–22). From this position, in which even ideal love is placed squarely in nature, Milton draws an interesting corollary. God's ordination that man "shall cleave unto his wife: and they shall be one flesh" (Gen. 2:24) he regards as "neither a law nor a commandment, but an effect or natural consequence of that very intimate relationship which would have existed between Adam and Eve in man's unfallen state (*Christian Doctrine*, 1.10; 6:355). The words "unfallen," "natural," and "intimate" are all important. Milton is connecting the postlapsarian family with Eden, in a chain of natural causes; the "very intimate" relations of Adam and Eve become the prototype of man and woman in the married state. And consider what memorable poetic expression Milton gives to that state. When Adam reaches the climax of his first response to the sight of Eve, he says of himself and her, "And they shall be one Flesh, one Heart, one Soule" (*PL,* 8.499). The expansion of the original "Flesh" into a total fusion of being is as exceptional as it is beautiful, for Milton, who treated classical texts with the greatest freedom, usually leaves the biblical words intact.

"True Manliness" and "Foul Effeminacy"

What I have said of Milton so far clearly places him in the camp of the Moderns, not the Ancients, to use terms from a controversy that came to a head not long after Milton's death. He made the "endearment of friendships" (Jeremy Taylor's phrase: *Ductor dubitantium*, bk. 2, chap. 3, rule 9, sec.2) the sine qua non of marriage, and in *Colasterion* he sharply opposed the "amiable and attractive society of conjugal love" to the venerable pagan ideal of "grave freindship." He broke cleanly with the ascetic tradition. Though he of course conceded that the "deed of procreation . . . soon cloies," he was so far from wanting it abandoned that he urged that it be "cherisht and reincited with a pleasing conversation" (2:740). There were precedents for Milton's attack on ascetic rigor—writers like William Whately and Daniel Rogers invoked the ardors of marital affections, and many Puritan clerics "found in marriage a peculiarly absorbing field of personal experience for testing and enlarging upon the truth revealed in holy writ."[22] The tradition of Milton as the radical defender of liberty in thought and love, though it prejudiced his reputation in some eighteenth-century circles, kept it green for the Romantics. Shelley saw "the sacred Milton" as a son of the Renaissance, "the golden age of our literature," and adored him as "a republican, and a bold inquirer into morals and religion" (preface to *Prometheus Unbound*). The very qualities that endeared him to the Romantics also make him our contemporary. Unfortunately, modern sympathy may be offended by another side of Milton, his sense of hierarchy and order. Although much in Milton tempts us to turn to his biography and there discover with Byron "a harsh sire—odd spouse, / For the first Mrs. Milton left his house" (*Don Juan*, 3.91), we must resist the temptation to dwell on Milton the man and husband and confine ourselves to his writings. These alone provide ample evidence that their author believed profoundly that order must govern sexual relations, and they also reveal his indignant revulsion at lust, which he called foul and effeminate. The sense of hierarchy appears even in so forward-looking and humane a document as *The Doctrine and Discipline of Divorce*, where, as we have seen, charity and liberty play a large and impressive role. Even there Milton gives the impression that the solaces of marriage are primarily male-directed, that the "apt and cheerfull conversation of man with woman" exists to "refresh *him* against the evill of solitary life" (preface to *Divorce* 1; 2:235; emphasis added). But the definition of "true manlines" ("To the Parlament," *Divorce;* 2:227) may indeed be less personal than doctrinal. The superiority of the male rests on religious and metaphysical foundations, since the society of the family is a part of divine order and the paterfamilias is a surrogate on earth of the *Pater omnipotens*. God made only the male in his image, though he directly created two distinct sexes. Paul was Milton's teacher, and the Apostle to the Gentiles believed that "the head of the woman is the man" and that "she is the glory of the man" (1 Cor. 11:3, 7). Such theology leads to the inevitable conclusion that woman is

---

22. William and Malleville Haller, "The Puritan Art of Love," *Huntington Library Quarterly* 5 (Jan. 1942): 253. The Hallers also say that the Puritan divines endowed marriage with an "imaginative significance deeply felt" (p. 254). On the exaltation of marriage by Protestant divines, see also Lawrence Stone, *The Crisis of the Aristocracy 1558–1641* (Oxford: Clarendon Press, 1965), p. 669.

not directly or immediately in the image of God but only so in reference to man. Milton states the truth with chilling finality: "Hee for God only, shee for God in him" (*PL*, 4.299). Like Spenser before him, Milton was forced by history and experience to make exceptions. The great sixteenth-century poet had broken not only with the extreme Puritan view that woman was never fit to govern but also with the more liberal Anglican and Catholic view that woman was by her very nature fully qualified. Spenser believed that in general woman was not fit, but that in exceptional circumstances God might see fit to raise up a woman with the necessary qualifications, as he had when he provided Elizabeth I for the governance of England.[23] Milton transfers the national scene to the home. Man is of course the head, but "particular exceptions may have place, if she exceed her husband in prudence and dexterity, and he contentedly yeeld, for then a superior and more naturall law comes in, that the wiser should govern the lesse wise, whether male or female."[24] Milton has here forced a fairly broad opening without breaking order. Wisdom is not the prerogative of one sex, and natural law is allowed to prevail when common sense discerns exceptions to the divinely ordained norm.

Milton's conservative views animate *Samson Agonistes,* a work that includes an angry denunciation of dominating woman and an unrelenting dramatization of an enslaved sensual man. Samson had stooped to "foul effeminacy" (410) and, like the transvestite in Sidney's *New Arcadia,* had become a *haec-vir,* a womanish man.[25] Were that Latin phrase used today, it might refer to homoerotic feelings; during the pre-Romantic and Romantic period, it might

23. James E. Phillips, Jr., "The Woman Ruler in Spenser's *Faerie Queene,*" *Huntington Library Quarterly* 5 (Jan. 1942): 211–34.

24. *Tetrachordon* in *CPW,* 2:589. Le Comte in *Milton and Sex* also cites this passage and regards it as a "remarkable concession for a man of his time" (p. 59). But he prefaces this quotation with several from the *History of Britain* that reveal Milton's neurotic disgust with female rulers. But these outbursts Le Comte finds only in the first four books. "When Milton resumed work on it his spell of bitterness against presuming womankind was gone, all passion spent" (p. 57). Le Comte finds that the first part of the history—and presumably others like it—reflected the domestic difficulties that attended his first marriage (p. 58).

A modern commentator on Milton and love can scarcely ignore the fact that Milton—along with Paul and Freud—is regarded as a quintessentially patriarchial writer, whose enormous talents lie athwart the path of progress toward full equality for women. Such was Virginia Woolf's view, which is reflected in a stimulating article by Sandra M. Gilbert, who regards Milton as God the Father Almighty *redivivus*—"a male poet justifying the ways of a male deity to male readers," who makes woman secondary, derivative, emanational. See "Patriarchal Poetry and Women Readers: Reflections on Milton's Bogey," *PMLA* 93 (May 1978): 368–82, esp. p. 380. Even though I plead for a historical understanding of the idea of hierarchy and what it was intended to accomplish for mankind, I concede that Milton's conscious mind justifies much of the dismay that a modern, reforming sensibility inevitably feels. But can Gilbert be right in saying that Milton "excludes all females from the heaven of his poem"? Not, surely, if heaven is poetic achievement. (Eve, like Satan, is realized with the fullest poetic power.) Not, surely, if Eden and the New Jerusalem are taken into account, where Eve is not only a partaker but a cause of bliss and blessing.

25. Mark Rose, "Sidney's Womanish Man," *Review of English Studies* 15 (Nov. 1964): 353–63.

have referred to a taste for sensual similitude or closeness of relation. But in the Renaissance and seventeenth century it meant simply the prevalence of strong heterosexual passion, which allowed woman to work her own will, which was regarded as more libidinous than a man's, against his true interest and against reason and the will of God. Even in so radical a thinker as Blake, the Female Will, supported by Venereal power, is regarded as a great evil. *Samson* is one of the most powerful expressions of the idea. There slavery to the senses is regarded as "ignoble, / Unmanly, ignominious, infamous" (416–17). The wife, no longer a consolation and a cheerful companion, is a "Traytress," a "*Hyæna*," a "sorceress," and marriage has become a "snare" (725, 748, 819, 931). The Chorus, expressing the point of view of a *raisonneur* free of the personal suffering of the dramatic hero, finds that the "inward gifts" of woman are "unfinish't" (1026–27). Blind, old, lonely, disenchanted Milton, living on in Restoration England, now somewhat desperately interprets "Gods universal Law" as giving to the man "despotic power" over "his female" (1053–55).

A not dissimilar but more tempered and humane energy underlies the dynamics of the Fall in *Paradise Lost*. Hierarchy is present, but so, paradoxically, are freedom and mutual love. Obviously a system of thought other than the modern is operating. To us hierarchy and order suggest slavery and repression, not freedom and release. To Milton it was the hierarchy that guaranteed those values. To Adam, Eve was "Dearer thy self" than all the "joyes" of Eden, their "Sole partner and sole part" (4.411–12). Eve returns the love, aware that her husband is "Præeminent by so much odds" (4.447) and that both their love and their relative status is a sign of the benevolent power that created them. In fact, she finds her happiness even greater than Adam's, since her consort is superior to his. Adam is meant to exert gentle but unmistakable sway, and we confront very early a presage of the Fall when the transport he feels exalts his wife's loveliness to an absolute value and endows her with a self-completeness, an awe, an authority, and a reason that should belong to God alone. Well might Raphael contract his brow and administer a rebuke: cherish and honor Eve's beauty, but do not let passion create subjection (8.560 ff.). The angel even reminds Adam that the sensual touch is common to all creatures, as humbling a thought as it was for Donne when he realized that he shared an appetite for women with his manservant.

Milton's Eden is a more precarious state than Augustine's, precisely because it is imbued with greater joy. Its very ecstasy can threaten order and so bears within it the seeds of evil. Milton sensed what Blake in his revolutionary period knew and what Marcuse in our day has preached, that sexuality is a leveler, a potential enemy to established order. But what for Shelley was redemptive for Milton was in fact destructive, as the Fall abundantly demonstrates. Satan's machinations constitute a parody and perversion of the norms of Edenic sexuality that God had established. They are peculiarly insidious because the temptation that comes from below is not totally different in emotional appeal from the inspiration that comes from above. Satan inpregnates the serpent orally, entering the brute at the mouth to inspire it with intelligence. Man does not take the lead; woman does, for she "inspires" him to take and eat. He falls because, like Samson, he is "fondly overcome with Femal charm" (*PL,* 9.999). The doctrine that governs the poetry is inescapable—the Great Chain has been broken because man has become a sentimental slave, an effeminated man, a *haec-vir,* a moral transvestite. Where he should have led, he followed. But in the epic, unlike the later drama, male dominance is never called "despotic." It could not be in a land of free choice, where either is at liberty to choose evil. Eden trembles on the verge of error and destruction precisely because it is a place of freedom. Freedom coexists with hierarchy and tempers it. Woman is below man as a first mate is below a captain, as a prime minister is below a king; but she is not a slave or a victim. As a joyful partner, she is free to dream and in her dreams to embroider and sophisticate her pleasures. Even after the Fall she quickly regains dignity and place. It is through her that final deliverance will come, for it is the promise of the *protevangelium* that the seed of the woman "shall bruise / The Serpents head. . . ."[26]

I have so far presented Milton as a friend of both mutuality and hierarchy in love. There is little doubt that what influenced his eighteenth-century readers most was the mutuality. They must have felt that Milton, when seen steadily and whole, tended to pull back somewhat from his great and ennobling vision of heterosexual friendship, allowing the Hebraic and Pauline strain in his thought excessive influence. One wishes that he had instead absorbed the meaning and force of Spenser's memorable creation in the character of Britomart, which shows that the earlier writer could imaginatively, at least, break out of the confining hierarchical sexual position that he shared with Milton. Britomart is a woman who combines "amiable grace" and "manly terrour" (*FQ,* 3.1.46). Irrevocably in love, she remains feminine through all her exploits. She blushes vermillion at mention of her lover, she is subject to "feigning fancie" and grows pensive at amorous discourse (3.4.5); when unveiled, her blond hair falls in attractive waves. Yet she is a redoubtable warrior, able to unseat the stoutest knights, including her lover, and so manly in her full armor, with her beaver up, that the delicate Amoret, ignorant of Britomart's sex, fears her "will" (that is, her sexual passion). Spenser was revolted by a man dressed as a woman—a "lothly vncouth sight" (5.7.37). But he made a powerful symbol of a woman dressed as a male warrior—a chaste Diana *rediviva* but without that goddess's fear of men, a wise and armed

26. *Paradise Lost* 10.1031–32; Halkett, *Milton and Matrimony,* pp. 123, 130; Christopher, "Verbal Gate to Paradise," pp. 74–76. Milton is quoting Gen. 3:15.

Minerva but one desperately in love. Ultimately, after she releases her lover from the captivity imposed by the Amazon Radigund, she restores rule to him and reestablishes male authority. But during the time of her conquests, Britomart becomes a type of active femininity, of female masculinity, the reverse of stereotypical female delicacy. Although a tradition of warrior-virgins and of liberated brides seeking their husbands does exist, Britomart possesses a quality for which we really have no name but which, as we shall see, Beethoven embodied grandly in his Leonore. Unfortunately, Milton's Eve, for all her personal charms and redemptive powers, is never given the scope for active heroism.

No one who has been persuaded by my earlier discussion of Milton on heterosexual friendship can call him a joyless Puritan, condemning sexuality for its very delights. Yet Milton regarded foul, effeminating lust as one of the most dangerous challenges to true manliness and to a liberating and salubrious hierarchy. Upon it he mounted a lifelong attack. Why? Because the author of the *Areopagitica* felt that it enslaved first the senses and then the mind, thus toppling man from his free-born estate. *Comus* makes all this clear: the Lady, in a not unwarranted burst of confidence, says to the wizard, "Fool do not boast, / Thou canst not touch the freedom of my minde," and we are exhorted at the end to "Love vertue, she alone is free" (662–63, 1018). The freedom of the mind is precisely the quarry of lust, and not all virtue is so impregnable as that of the Lady in *Comus*. In *Samson*, as we have seen, lust leads to bondage and blindness.

It is fitting that *Paradise Lost,* which exalts love, should also provide the most unforgettable embodiments of its antithesis. In Eden delight is attended with danger, beauty is the peculiar prey of bestiality. From the unfallen Eve's person shoot "Darts of desire" (8.62); after the fatal eating, her "Eye darted contagious Fire" (9.1036). The noun and the verb "dart" show how closely linked are innocent love and sinful lust. Of the latter, Eve's dream is a dramatic foreshadowing, as it is also a psychologically suggestive revelation of a mind prepared by love to receive its congenial and attendant vice. Because Eve is beautiful, sensuous, poetic, open to imaginative stimulation, she is peculiarly susceptible to a corruption of her fancy.[27] Milton is here truly prophetic, for he has the Satanic toad squat at the ear of Eve and attack "The Organs of her Fancie" (4.802). As we have already seen, the period after Milton, both in praising and in censuring the imagination, associated it with solitary love fantasies. For it is precisely these that Satan plants in her aroused and receptive mind. The following morning she awakens with "Tresses discompos'd, and glowing Cheek" (5.10). Surely the dream is illicit, perhaps

27. These qualities are important but should not be overemphasized to the exclusion of others. Eve, a "complete" woman, is also rational, though less so than Adam. See Mary Ann Nevins Radzinowicz, "Eve and Dalila: Renovation and the Hardening of the Heart" in J. A. Mazzeo, ed., *Reason and the Imagination* (New York: Columbia University Press, 1962), pp. 155–81.

even sexually illicit, so powerful is the feigning fancy even in Eden. We know that the dream is a night-time contrast to the loving daylight joy to which Adam now invites her. Satan's temptation lies outside the bower and in the darkness, and we remember that Eve had wondered earlier about starry beauty and who enjoyed it. The prepared mind, again! Satan, a Romantic poet, tempts the woman to enjoy the nightingale, the moon, and then the forbidden fruit, fairer now in nocturnal illusion than in the uxorial actuality of sunlight. Satan himself eats. And Eve is clearly excited in the flesh as he holds to her very mouth the savory, appetite-quickening fruit he has plucked. And in the dream she too eats, after which in defiance of space she flies up to a cloud with Satan and sees the immense prospect of the earth below, only to sink down when left alone. The marvelous poetry is not meant to disguise the breathless sensuality; it in fact communicates libidinous excitement. Eve's dream is more sensual and physical than Faustian, the latter being the form that a dream by Adam might have taken. Eve is tempted not by illicit knowledge but by the delicious and the savory, by the expansion of the senses and the release of the body in flight. Adam's response, that his wife's dream is uncontrolled fancy, is true enough, but it is too intellectual and general by far. The dream has substituted for an idyllic love confined to one man a cloudy, aerial flight with another—a wandering on the earth in a luscious and distorting darkness which the moonlight does not dispel.

The presence of libido in the actual Fall is obvious and serves as a fulfillment of the delicious-dangerous imaginings of the dream. That fulfillment is of course in no way preordained or fatal. Eve is fully free not to act. But when she does act, she chooses to act out the dream. Under its unconscious influence, she takes the initiative in urging a division of labor. The very language is suggestive: she wishes to check a "wanton growth" that tends to become "wilde" (9.211–12), ironically blind as to what or who really needs the restraint. She will work alone among those Venereal plants and flowers, the rose and the myrtle, isolated work that interrupts the marital communion, which is a ritual of "Looks" and "smiles" and "Casual discourse" (9.222–23), an equivalent of the "apt and cheerfull conversation of man with woman" (preface to *Divorce;* 2:235) that Milton had made the very heart of the married state in his divorce tracts. Eve's departure from Adam actualizes the expansion of body and spirit she experienced in her dream. And the meeting with Satan is an encounter with someone who takes pleasure in her beauty and who is himself "pleasing" and "lovely" in shape (9.503–4). His very motion is wanton and seductive, and his speech lingers on the fair, ruddy, golden appearance of the fruit. The eating itself, described briefly in a few masterstrokes, wounds nature, but Eve experiences momentary delight. She eats death—and enjoys it and so forges an unbreakable link between love and mortality. Hers is no modest tentative nibbling but a giving of herself: "She ingorg'd without restraint" and is "jocond and boon" as though heightened with wine (9.791, 793). She is blithe and her cheeks glow as they had after her dream, and Adam, kindling, eats quickly as "Carnal desire" and the "lascivious Eye" are born (9.1013–14).

> As with new Wine intoxicated both
> They swim in mirth, and fansie that they feel
> Divinitie within them breeding wings
> Wherewith to scorne the Earth: but that false Fruit
> Farr other operation first displaid,
> Carnal desire enflaming, hee on *Eve*
> Began to cast lascivious Eyes, she him
> As wantonly repaid; in Lust they burne:
> Till *Adam* thus 'gan *Eve* to dalliance move.
>
> [9.1008–16]

Love has become lust.

Before we turn to the dreadful evil of the narcissistic sins, it is important to note that Miltonic love, unprotected as it is by ascetic prohibition, Stoic indifference, or Platonic denigration, is precisely the kind that might easily drive on toward lust. The fall is a predominance of that which made Eden alluring and lovely. More precisely and poignantly, the Fall occurred precisely because Eve was the loving, imaginative, poetic being that Adam—and Milton—loved. Feminine love can with fatal ease become effeminate lust. Whatever is to happen in later culture, we must remember that here Milton is not thinking of unnatural sexuality. Lust is called effeminate because woman leads man, as well as herself, into natural appetite and so subverts the divine hierarchy. Reason has given way to sense, and the Great Chain of Being has been broken.[28]

The Narcissistic Sins

In admonishing Adam about the danger of passion, Raphael is emphatic about the necessity of decent self-respect:

> Oft times nothing profits more
> Then self-esteem, grounded on just and right
> Well manag'd.
>
> [8.571–73]

And there is evidence that Milton himself, like his Romantic follower Blake, was powerfully motivated by an honest pride and an unblushing self-regard

---

28. There is abundant precedence for the view of "effeminacy" just presented. See Rose, "Sidney's Womanish Man," and also his *Heroic Love,* pp. 50–53.

that may have found much pious deprecation of the self intolerable. But such a feeling, not unlike the proper respect of oneself that underlies the Golden Rule, must be sharply distinguished from that complex of sins we call narcissistic. Why does Adam yield so quickly? It is not simply that he is overmastered by heterosexual passion, by the attraction of the flesh of the opposite sex. The primary attraction, the emotion that he feels more strongly than any other, is that of consubstantiality—not carnal contrast but carnal similitude. "I feel / The Link of Nature draw me: Flesh of Flesh," he says, remembering that Eve had been created from his side. The temptation to follow Eve to destruction is less the magnetism of sexual desire than the pull of the self by the self. It would appear to be a narcissistic circuit through which desire is here running.[29]

The joys of Eden were clearly heterosexual. Their termination results, on the physical level, from Eve's lust for illicit love and Adam's for similitude. How loathsome the sins of consanguinity are appears in the allegory of Satan, Sin, and Death, an anti-Trinity that presents a stark contrast to joyful heterosexual differentiation. The sins that this unholy family embody are those of self-enclosure and closeness of blood relation. Sin, a "Snakie Sorceress" (2.724) and the only woman in the family, is a Medusa or, if one wishes a modern analogue, Freud's phallic woman.[30] But for all her snakes, she is woman still, capable of the female role in sexual relations and another example of the traditional tendency to consider the woman as peculiarly libidinous. Like Athena, who sprang from the head of Zeus, she had sprung narcissistically from the head of her father Satan. Such self-engendered parturition suggests that Sin (she was so named in heaven) is the overweening fancy; if so, we have here another and of course almost archetypal example of an association between evil and the imagination, for Sin emerges from her father's head at the time he conceives of rebellion. She looks like him—she is in fact his "perfect image" (2.764: another grisly parody), and he immediately falls in love with her—in an incestuous passion that produces, once the war in heaven has been fought, her only son Death, so named in a parodistic christening at Hell Gate. A true son of his father, he immediately pursues his sister-mother

29. *Paradise Lost* 9.914. On perceptions of androgyny in the Genesis account of creation, see Cirillo, "The Fair Hermaphrodite." That temptation could run in latently or potentially narcissistic or homoerotic circuits seems to have been shown by Sidney in *The New Arcadia* when Musidorus comes upon his friend Pyrocles in womanish disguise but also tempting in his teasingly suggestive and alluring dress. Musidorus warns that the very habit will effeminate the mind and engender a "bastarde Love." *The Countesse of Pembrokes Arcadia,* ed. Albert Feuillerat (1912; reprint ed., Cambridge: Cambridge University Press, 1939), book 1, chap. 12 in *Complete Works* (Cambridge English Classics), 1:78.

30. Joseph H. Summers says, "The relations between Satan, Sin, and Death include narcissism, rape, sadism, and almost baffling complexities of incest" (*The Muse's Method,* pp. 88–89). For a brief discussion of Freud's curious but fascinating idea, see Jean H. Hagstrum, "Babylon Revisited, or the Story of Luvah and Vala" in *Blake's Sublime Allegory,* ed. Stuart Curran and Joseph A. Wittreich, Jr. (Madison: University of Wisconsin Press, 1973), pp. 108–9.

in hot lust, raping her and producing that breed of monsters who are hourly conceived and hourly born and who, in another in this complex nest of parodies, provide a kind of grotesque equivalent of consanguinity by gnawing at their mother's entrails. As a kind of climax to this "family romance," Sin projects it onto the future and dreams that she will reign at her father's right hand "voluptuous, as beseems / Thy daughter and thy darling, without end."[31]

The blasphemous trinity of Satan, Sin, and Death provides counterimages to many things, but most of all to love and the family. The peculiar sins of these creatures are narcissism and incest, and the allegory is useful in showing clearly central aspects of evil that might have escaped us from the rest of Milton's narrative, where Satan is the ambitious and rebellious angel or the voluptuous and attractive tempter of Eve. By stressing the family sins in his trinity of evil, Milton seems to provide another rejection of the fallen, pagan world whose myths of origin can be seen as embodying, with and without condemnation, the very narcissistic sins that he finds unfailingly horrible. The Titans were born of incest between Gaea (the Mother Earth) and Uranos, her own son; one of the twelve children was Chronos, who hated his father-brother and castrated him when he found him *in flagrante delicto* with Gaea.[32] From such ancient fabling the story of primal incest passed through the mind of Spenser, who associated the incestuous Argante and Ollyphant with the titans (*FQ*, 3.7.47–50), and was present in the eighteenth century, which obsessively illustrated Milton's allegory and which was not ignorant of its deep perversions:

> Then first, whilst Nature shudder'd with affright,
> Of Sin and Death was held th' incestuous rite.[33]

I have so far tended to stress the overt incestuousness in Milton's unholy family. But a deeper concern is with the more basic narcissism. The connection between the two kinds of evil was clear to the codifier of Hebrew law in Leviticus, who in prohibiting physical relations with all near kin (father,

---

31. 2.869–70. There are several parodies in the allegory of Satan, Sin, and Death, but can one view this family life as "essentially comic" (Joseph H. Summers, *The Muse's Method,* p. 46) or "hilarious" (Harry Blamires, *Milton's Creation: A Guide through Paradise Lost* [London: Methuen, 1971], p. 53)? The parodies seem, rather, to be grim; and if there is *humour,* it is *noir.*

32. On ancient incest myths, see Herbert Maisch, *Incest,* trans. Colin Bearne (New York: Stein & Day, 1972), p. 11 ff. The sources of Milton's allegory are more complex than this emphasis on the family sins would suggest. See J. F. Gilliam, "Scylla and Sin," *Philological Quarterly* 29 (July 1950): 345–47 and John Illo, "Animal Sources for Milton's Sin and Death," *Notes and Queries* 205 (Nov. 1960): 425–26. Both articles point to the ancient Scylla as a source, and she personified the libido.

33. From a poem by William Roscoe on the paintings by Fuseli inspired by Milton, quoted in John Knowles, *The Life and Writings of Henry Fuseli,* 3 vols. (London, 1831), 1: 429. Satan's confrontation of Sin and Death "became the most popular single scene [from Milton] with later artists." Marcia R. Pointon, *Milton & English Art* (Manchester: Manchester University Press, 1970), p. 14.

mother, father's wife, sister, half-sister, grandchildren) says, "Even their nakedness thou shalt not uncover: for their's is thine own nakedness" (18:10). The Hebraically oriented Milton seems to have absorbed Moses' point. Satan's primary sin is to beget a daughter upon himself, and the other fallen angels fall into the class of the irredeemable because of their narcissism, a condition from which man is exempt because he was tempted from the outside.

> The first sort [fallen angels] by *thir own* suggestion fell,
> *Self*-tempted, *self*-deprav'd: Man falls deceiv'd
> By the *other* first: Man therefore shall find grace,
> The other none. . . .
>
> [3.129–32; emphasis added]

Narcissus, as Bacon said, was "exceeding fayre and beautifull" but "so besotted and rauished . . . [that] hee pined away to nothing."[34] Into that condition Eve in Eden almost falls—even before she beholds Adam, her fleshly source, also her sexual antithesis and complement. In poetry of exquisite delicacy Milton describes Eve as seeing in the "Smooth Lake" a beautiful "Shape"; she is "pleas'd" (Milton uses the term twice) by what she beholds. She likes its "answering looks / Of sympathie and love." There she might have fixed her gaze and there she might have "pin'd with vain desire," but that she heard a voice warning her that she saw only herself—a voice that the Romantic poets seem not always to have heeded. That voice brings her to Adam, who is "no shadow" but her own very substantial and separate spouse, to whom she will "Inseparablie" belong and by whom she will become the mother of multitudes. That Eve is undergoing a real temptation, and not merely revealing a charmingly innocent unawareness and inexperience, is proved by the poet's language: she might have "*pin'd* with *vain* desire"; she might have loved the "smooth *watry image*" more than the manly and fertile husband, who at first seemed "Less winning *soft*, less amiablie *milde*" than her own reflection.[35] The creator of the allegory of Satan, Sin, and Death has exposed the poetically gifted Eve to a narcissistic temptation. Today we sometimes speak of healthy narcissism and even distinguish its several good varieties.[36] For Milton it was,

34. *The Wisedome of the Ancients*, tr. Sir Arthur Gorges (London, 1619), pp. 11–12. For an analysis of what the Narcissus myth stands for in Ovid and Spenser, and for a perception of the relations between Narcissus and the incestuous loves of Myrrha and Biblis, see Calvin R. Edwards, "The Narcissus Myth in Spenser's Poetry," *Studies in Philology* 74 (Jan. 1977): 63–88, esp. pp. 83–84.

35. *Paradise Lost* 4:449–91. The pejorative adjectives have been italicized. For the view that this episode (1) shows the fallibility of Eve and her need of an authoritative helpmeet and (2) satisfies the need to make of the union of the first pair a marriage based on consent after considering other possibilities (Adam follows Eve and claims her; Eve hears his plea and accepts him), see Dennis H. Burden, *The Logical Epic: A Study of the Argument of "Paradise Lost"* (Cambridge, Mass.: Harvard University Press, 1967), p. 85. For the view that Milton wishes us to distinguish Eve from Narcissus, see J. Max Patrick, "A Reconsideration of the Fall of Eve," *Etudes Anglaises* 28 (Jan.–March 1975): 15–21.

36. "I find no fault with a certain healthy narcissism." Anne Taylor Fleming, "The Fear of Being Alone" ("My Turn"), *Newsweek*, 13 December 1976, p. 17.

however beguilingly smooth, soft, and mild, totally unproductive—watery, unreal, vain, and self-reflective.

Did Satan ever take on the qualities of Eve's lovely reflection and so put the stamp of evil upon delicacy and alluring similitude? Satans other than Milton's did indeed possess the sweet, cherubic qualities of, say, Correggio's *Ganymede* in the Vienna Gallery (pl. 2). Raphael created a Satan who possessed breasts as well as a serpent's tail, young and sad-eyed as he (she?) looks longingly at Adam. Michelangelo in the Sistine Chapel painted a Satan with long hair and small breasts, who hands the apple to Eve but gazes at Adam. Nicolas de Brujn's Satan is a hermaphrodite who looks very evil indeed, with his breasts and forked tail, and in the *Très riches heures* Satan is a duplication of Eve herself, with blonde hair and very delicate features. Many other examples surely exist of the temptation conceived of as narcissistic and homoerotic. Milton, however, like Hugo van der Goes in *The Fall of Man* (also in Vienna) (pl. 3) presents an unmistakably male Satan, attractive to Eve precisely because he is assertively masculine, even though there may be hints of sexual ambiguity.[37]

But there is one point in the narrative at which Milton's archfiend does take on the qualities of an angelic androgyne, that lovely but sexually ambiguous creation of Florence, the girlish youth, the Ganymede-like being who may have been imagined as the kind of creature who would inhabit a sexless heaven, where there is neither marriage nor giving in marriage. Verrocchio set the type with his girlish youth: "a sad ephebe with a disturbing ambiguous beauty" that combines the charms of both sexes (see pl. 2).[38] Botticelli, Signorelli, many other Renaissance painters, and the Shakespeare of the romantic comedies and the sonnets in one way or another embody the type. Cesario-Viola and Rosalind-Ganymede suggest androgynous beings throughout much of the love-play. Men and women fall in love with they know not precisely what and in the final resolution make an easy transition from the disguised person who woos them to a person of a sex that cannot strictly be called "opposite."

> And so am I for Ganymede.
> And so am I for Rosalind.
> And so am I for no woman.
> [*As You Like It,* 5.2]

In the passage I am about to quote, Milton could possibly be reacting to Italian art or to Shakespeare's romantic comedies. But he is more likely to have been impressed with the unambiguous point that Josephus makes about

---

37. My examples come mostly from engravings after the artists I have mentioned which were inserted in that most amazing of extra-illustrated books, the Kitto Bible in the Huntington Library. See appendix A, below.

38. Jan Kott, *Shakespeare Our Contemporary,* trans. Boleslaw Taborski (1965; rev. ed., London: Methuen, 1967), p. 202.

the angels who visited Abraham and who also went to Sodom, where Lot (he had a dubious sexual record and was "much given to hospitalitie") invited them to lodge at his home. There the Sodomites, perceiving the "excellent beauty" of these angels, "began to offer outrage and villany to their persons" and continued to do so despite the exhortations of Lot and his offer to them of his daughters to use at their pleasure.[39]

Satan, having come on his journey as far as the orb of the sun, appears as "a stripling Cherube," a somewhat effeminated Hermes-figure, quite unlike the majestic and military Hermes-figure that is Michael, who appears "as Man / Clad to meet Man" (11:239–40).

> Not of the prime, yet such as in his face
> Youth smil'd Celestial, and to every Limb
> Sutable grace diffus'd, so well he feignd;
> Under a Coronet his flowing haire
> In curles on either cheek plaid, wings he wore
> Of many a colourd plume sprinkl'd with Gold.
> [3.636–42]

Satan's guise is related to the image of Eve in the smooth water. Both are delicate but disturbing manifestations of the inbred love that is more obviously evil when it appears in the cursed trinity that stands at the Gate of Hell.

Epilogue: Love and Death

The following schema is not an accurate summary of the foregoing pages, since it does not do justice to their distribution of emphasis. But it does provide the essential structure of Milton on love, against which subsequent adaptations and deviations can be perceived. The most important feature of the table is of course its absolute separation of good and evil.

LOVE

GOOD	EVIL
Order (God, man, woman) and reason	Lust (sensual predominance)
Heterosexual friendship	Narcissistic sins (incest, self-love)
Offspring, immortality	Death

39. *The Famous and Memorable Works of Josephus,* trans. Thomas Lodge (London, 1655), p. 15 (*Jewish Antiquities,* 1.11.3). There is little doubt that Milton gave considerable thought to the city of Sodom and the sins it represented. See Le Comte's discussion in *Milton and Sex* of the possible subjects for tragedy in the Cambridge or Trinity Manuscript (pp. 46–47); among these Sodom was prominent. See also Le Comte's discussion (pp. 83–84) of "the worse [that is, homosexual] rape" referred to in *Paradise Lost* 1.505.

Enough has been said in this chapter to show how the first two items in this schematic analysis of love become their sinful opposites—how hierarchy is challenged by a lust that effeminates man and dethrones him from rightful leadership, how the friendship of man and woman is parodied by love of self and the evil of similitude. But little has so far been said of what in the following pages will become a major theme, the association of love and death in bonds of sympathetic attraction. Milton associated them, of course, but in the repulsive and deeply tabooed embraces of Sin and Death at the mouth of hell. But these, though sexual, lead to physical agony and bestial procreation and stand as the antitype of that aim of marriage, *proles*, which Milton certainly accepted but did not, like the Catholic world, make primary. But though Death is capable of sex, he is not capable of love; and no one, not even Satan or Sin, is half in love with this monstrously "easeless" creature. Like Freud, Milton makes him the enemy of Eros, but unlike Freud, Milton does not allow life to move toward him in desire, to heed him gladly, to confuse him with rest or calm. If Denis de Rougemont is right, that in Western culture the true and dominant chord is "love *and* death,"[40] then Milton has been an exemplar only of what to shun. The Renaissance identified Eros with life after death but more especially with death itself.[41] Milton did not. His Cupid is placed in Eden, by the lovely and life-enhancing bower of innocence. Eros was a life principle. It was lust, in Milton the perversion of truly human love, that was embodied in Sin, the consort of Death.

If Milton diverged from one long tradition by separating love and death, he diverged from another one equally venerable by uniting what had been immemorially separated, love and friendship. Friendship without love, without woman, he found austere and exhausting, perhaps ultimately dehumanizing. In the union of friendship and love he found cheer, joy, relaxation, consummation—a union vastly superior to the mere marriage of true minds. So precious to him was this ideal that he called for the total and absolute dissolution of any marriage from which love and cheer had fled. The door that Milton opened rhetorically and imaginatively was not opened within the realm of Western social reality until fairly recent times. Of the many Restoration and early eighteenth-century plays devoted to the theme of marital discord, only one (Farquhar's pleasantly bracing *Beaux Stratagem*, 1707) presented divorce as a means of escaping from domestic misery—and even there

40. *Passion and Society*, trans. Montgomery Belgion (London: Faber & Faber, 1956), p. 15. Emphasis added.

41. See Edgar Wind, "Amor as a God of Death," *Pagan Mysteries in the Renaissance* (New York: Barnes & Noble, 1968), pp. 152–70. When love became associated with avant-garde thought, in the eighteenth century and the Romantic period, the link with death persisted. Perhaps Philippe Ariès has perceived the reason: "In the realm of the imagination it (death) became allied with eroticism in order to express the break with the established order." *Western Attitudes toward Death: From the Middle Ages to the Present*, trans. Patricia M. Ranum (Baltimore: Johns Hopkins University Press, 1974), p. 105.

it was only romantic vision.[42] Perhaps one reason for the failure of most subsequent literature to portray Milton's ideal and to erect instead a powerful friendship as a rival or parallel to the central love affair was that society provided no exit facilities for a loveless pair. If marital love should fail, as it usually did, then friendship with another of the same sex could provide solace to a spouse faced with a lifelong marital torment or deprivation.

The love embrace of unfettered joy occurs much more frequently in Milton than in his immediate successors.[43] One obvious reason is that his bower was located in Eden and the later ones in real experience. But the Miltonic ideal persisted, despite hostile realities, and was a seminal force in creating love-sensibility. However indirectly, the Edenic myth reached composers like Gluck, Handel, Mozart, and Beethoven, who imbued uxorial faith and joy with deep harmonies and ravishing melodies that Milton himself would have savored. At the end of the epic our "lingring Parents" look back on what was "so late thir happie seat" (12.638, 642). That backward glance may well stand for the frequently regressive and nostalgic tendencies that give poignancy to the love I shall examine. But the bower of Adam and Eve, through the force of art, could also beckon to the future. It challenged men to seek greater fulfillment than that provided by a passive acceptance of nature or of religious promise or by a timid acquiescence in existing reality. Milton believed in heaven, but his vision made his Restoration and eighteenth-century readers think of happiness on earth.[44] Perhaps no work of eighteenth-century art better illustrates the joyful naturalization of Eden than the attractive third part of Haydn's *Creation* (1798), whose libretto is directly derived from *Paradise Lost.* Adam and Eve praise and thank God for all the natural wonders

42. Robert D. Hume, "Marital Discord in English Comedy from Dryden to Fielding," *Modern Philology* 74 (Feb. 1977): 248–72.

43. Roland M. Frye in *Milton's Imagery* (see appendix A) says that Milton was "essentially innovative" in presenting Adam and Eve as a loving pair. If scholars like Mary Irma Corcoran and John R. Knott have found little anticipation of Milton's conception of Edenic sexual life in letters, neither has Frye in the visual arts (pp. 280–81). Fiedler has pointed out the paucity of work after Milton that successfully portrays conjugal love: "To make art of married bliss has proved impossible . . .; even in the novel it produces at best the mild, Biedermeier effects of, say, the domestic scenes in *David Copperfield*." *Love and Death in the American Novel,* p. 60.

44. Even the jaded Rochester, who found post-lapsarian sexuality a hell (a hell doubtless of his own making), could look back to the fresh physical delights of Eden:

> How blest was the created state
>   Of man and woman, ere they fell,
> Compared to our unhappy fate:
>   We need not fear another hell.
>
> Naked beneath cool shades they lay;
>   Enjoyment waited on desire;
> Each member did their wills obey,
>   Nor could a wish set pleasure higher.

"The Fall" (ca. Sept., 1680) in *The Complete Poems of John Wilmot, Earl of Rochester,* ed. David M. Vieth (New Haven, Conn.: Yale University Press, 1968), p. 86.

of creation. Then they turn to new joys within—to "unaussprechlich Glück," with its modest but obvious sexual overtones. Miltonic hierarchy is respected, since Adam is the leader, the more timid Eve a respondent. But in their magnificent duet each is given a power of rapture that is quite individual. Haydn has given us a monument to ordered joy and love that invokes at once nature and the benign intelligence behind it. The ideal of heterosexual friendship in marriage was of course not unknown before Milton. As Romeo descends from Juliet's balcony to leave for his Mantuan exile, she says, "Art thou gone so? Love, lord, ay, husband, friend!" (3.5). But nowhere is the ideal more powerfully and beautifully expressed than in the polemical prose and the great religious epic of Milton, who imprinted it on the consciousness of the eighteenth century.

3. John Dryden: Sensual, Heroic, and "Pathetic" Love

*C*OMING FROM Milton to Dryden, one has the sense of moving from an author for whom love was ontological to one for whom it was not. Had we proceeded to Dryden from Dante, or from Milton to one of Dryden's successors in the eighteenth century, that sense would have been overwhelming. But even so the feeling of change is striking enough, considering that Dryden and Milton were born and died within the same century and were both public defenders of the Christian religion. For Milton, a divinely ordained hierarchy governs the relations of God, man, and woman; and a gulf yawns between love and lust, between Edenic sexuality and sin. In Dryden love is hard to locate as a link in the Great Chain of Being. It is an energy within experience, a powerful drive available to the writer, an exploitable subject for comic, ironic, sensuous, heroic, even moral purposes. It does not, however, fit into a structural microcosm, as it does in *La vita nuova* or in the *Divine Comedy*. Dryden of course possessed a clear sense of right and wrong in love, as in other matters, but no Miltonic chasm separates the respective realms of good and evil. Dryden enjoys and transmits to his countrymen the sensuality of pagan classical verse. He is drawn to the physical heartiness of Chaucer and Boccaccio. And even the incestuous Sin, who in Milton stands with her paramours at the gate of hell, is somewhat more ambiguously placed in Dryden.

In expressing love and related emotions, Dryden was as much a pioneer, as much a creator of subsequent culture, as he was in writing satires or heroic couplets. Richardson inherited his heroic sensibility, as Pope inherited his wit and versification. My aim is to show how Dryden, under some contemporary impulses but nevertheless with great force and originality, created within a belligerent heroic world characters moved by delicate love, tender pity, and soft compassion. T. S. Eliot considered Dryden one of the creators of English culture and believed that "to him, as much as to any individual, we owe our civilization."[1] Eliot was talking chiefly about Dryden's triumph in modernizing the English language. It is also possible to see him as a creator of modern feeling, gentler than what has usually been known before, softer and more civilized. Dryden had found England raw, bleeding, and angry after the Civil

---

1. *John Dryden: The Poet, The Dramatist, The Critic* (1932; reprint ed., New York: Haskell House, 1966), p. 7.

War. He left it willing to subdue its raging passions and bend its neck to a yoke of mildness. Dryden does more than Milton can to justify the ways of man to man.

Dryden's Sensuality

If love in Dryden ends up as a civilizing and social affection, the reason for this does not lie in the elimination or even the weakening of physical passion. From his earliest plays to his very late translations and adaptations from foreign tongues, sexuality continues to burn with undiminished heat. No Restoration writer has been called Romantic more often than Dryden: "It would be hard to frame a definition of romanticism that should include *Marmion* and exclude *The Conquest of Granada*."[2] That "romanticism" embraces the treatment of love and its inescapable sexual ingredient, for Dryden in his own way was as sensual as Keats. He was of course writing for a newly liberated audience, for an age to which libertinism as a plausible philosophy and way of life was not unknown, during a century in whose middle years "pornography seems to have been born and grown to maturity."[3] But Dryden's sexuality seems to owe more to a source deep within him than to his age. His religious conversions did not extinguish it, and it survived his deeply felt poetic repentance for having added to the "fat Pollutions" of a "lubrique and adult'rate age"—more specifically to the "steaming Ordures" of the Restoration stage (*To . . . Mrs. Anne Killigrew* [1686], 63–65). Part of Dryden's zest in writing about sex must have been related to an age-old belief that it can cure low spirits and add spice to life—and also to language, spoken and written. Benedick says to Leonato in his own penultimate speech in *Much Ado about Nothing*, "Prince, thou art sad; get thee a wife, get thee a wife: there is no staff more reverend than one tipped with horn." That venerable wand Dryden waved over his readers throughout a long career. Looking to the future, we may note that by praising the hearty male and suggesting that the man with a past who has finally decided to direct his inclination to one woman only makes the best husband, Dryden provides a possible reason why Pamela, Sophia Western, and Marianne Dashwood were able to lead happy lives after all. In the comic subplot of a very early play, *Secret Love* (1667), a play seen three times by Charles II and at least eight times by Pepys, Florimell scorns foppish

2. George R. Noyes, "Biographical Sketch" in *The Poetical Works of Dryden* (Boston: Houghton Mifflin, 1950), p. xxv. See also Paul Spencer Wood, "The Opposition to Neo-Classicism in England between 1660 and 1700," *PMLA* 43 (March 1928): 182–97, esp. p. 191 and n.21.

3. David Foxon, *Libertine Literature in England, 1660–1745* (New Hyde Park, N.Y.: University Books, 1965), p. ix. This fact Foxon regards as the "most important and unexpected discovery" in his study, whose first three chapters originally appeared in *The Book Collector* (Spring, Summer, Autumn 1963), pp. 21–36, 159–77, 294–307.

solemnity and remains undisturbed when others tell of her wooer's previous flirtations:

> Give me a servant [that is, a *cavaliere servente*] that is an high Flier at all games, that is bounteous of himself to many women; and yet whenever I pleas'd to throw out the lure of Matrimony, should come down with a swing, and fly the better at his own quarry. [3.1.300–304][4]

If this book were concerned with sexuality in comedy, it would dwell on what can here be noted only in passing, that the play Dryden regarded as perhaps his best comedy, *Marriage A-la-mode* (written in the spring of 1671 and dedicated to the Earl of Rochester), contains a vigorous subplot full of high-spirited repartee and an earthy and refreshing wisdom about love, marriage, and sexuality.

One of Dryden's tasks, writing as he did after the Puritan dominance, was to reaffirm against the dourness of the "Saints" what the Renaissance had earlier affirmed against centuries of Christian asceticism, namely, the importance of the senses in life and art. Neither Dryden nor his Renaissance predecessors could do this with an absolutely easy conscience; and they turned to antiquity, especially to translating and enjoying Ovid, as an outlet for their own sensuality. If Dryden's sexualization of the decorous Virgil (see chap. 5 below) does not surprise, perhaps his intensification of Ovid's already assertive sexuality will. Just as the pagan love poet was more specifically erotic than his Latin predecessors, so Dryden surpassed in sexual meaning earlier English translators, reversing the tendency to tone down the ancient to please modern Christian taste. The time had come for boldness in language, and Dryden's heightenings of sexual *entendre* undoubtedly did nothing to impede the vogue that Ovid enjoyed as the seventeenth turned into the eighteenth century. Dryden's relations to his classical mentor are more complex than my discussion has so far implied. The ancient was a psychologist, concerned with the social implications of love; so was Dryden. Ovid was a master of pathos and delicacy, and Dryden praised him for these qualities, as for his naturalness, his shrewd and passionate pictures of psychological disorder, and his fidelity to the details and concerns of ordinary life. Ovid appears to have helped create

---

4. The act, scene, and line numbers given here come from *The Works of John Dryden* (Berkeley and Los Angeles: University of California Press, 1956–), vol. 9 (1966). No modern critical edition includes all the plays of Dryden. The dramas have been quoted from the best available editions as follows: *The Rival Ladies, The Indian Queen, The Indian Emperour, Secret Love, The Tempest, Tyrannick Love, The Conquest of Granada* I and II, and *Don Sebastian*—from the California edition of Dryden, vols. 8 (ed. John Harrington Smith and Dougald MacMillan), 9 (ed. John Loftis), 10 (ed. Maximillian E. Novak), 11 (ed. John Loftis, David Stuart Rodes, and Vinton A. Dearing), 15 (ed. Earl Miner); *All for Love* and *Aureng-Zebe*—from *John Dryden: Four Tragedies*, ed. L. A. Beaurline and Fredson Bowers (Chicago: University of Chicago Press, 1967); *Oedipus*—from *Dramatic Works*, ed. Montague Summers, 6 vols. (London: Nonesuch Press, 1932), vol. 4. Whenever possible, reference is made to act, scene, and line numbers. See Appendix B.

the Dryden we shall later be concerned with—the celebrant of pathetic love, the early Man of Feeling. At the very least, Dryden's translations from Ovid included many swift and buoyant lines of excited sexuality.[5]

Dryden also spiced the translation of the fourth book of Lucretius's *De rerum natura* (1685) with sexual heightenings, which coexist with a greater stress on familial love than the original contained. Sexuality is at once condemned as irrational and praised as necessary for the continuation of the human race. In one respect Dryden as critic, commentator, and translator is highly traditional. Like the great Renaissance painters, he christianizes what he can of his source and implies the destitution of pagan philosophy, while at the same time giving a high coloring to ancient sensuality. Quite apart from—and perhaps transcending—cultural and philosophical matters is Dryden's full enjoyment of Lucretius's love poetry, which he strives to turn into "luscious *English*." To Lucretius's "sublime and daring Genius," his "Masculine" thoughts, and his "fiery temper" the Englishman responds with an answering flame. Dryden concedes that, in the passages on coitus which he translated, the "Obscenity of the Subject" is "aggravated by the too lively, and alluring delicacy of the Verses." But "I own it pleas'd me." Dryden gladly supports Lucretius's defense of emotional expression over restraint and proudly displays the Lucretian Venus, who is not only the supplier of vital power to all that breathe but an earnest of universal peace. The goddess presages Enlightened sensibility.[6]

5. I have relied heavily on an excellent article by William Frost ("Dryden's Versions of Ovid," *Comparative Literature* 26 [Summer 1974]: 193–202), who discusses not only Dryden's erotic intensifications but also the appearance in the later novel of Ovidian influences. For important comments by Dryden on Ovid, see *John Dryden: Of Dramatic Poesy and Other Critical Essays,* ed. George Watson, Everyman's Library, 2 vols. (London: J. M. Dent & Sons, 1962), 1:98–99, 263, 265. The Ovidian translations, which Dryden contributed to the miscellany of 1693, called *Examen poeticum,* appear in California ed. of *Works of John Dryden,* vol. 4, *Poems 1693–1696,* ed. William Frost (1974), pp. 376–421. *Ovid's Amours* (Dryden's versions of Elegies 1 and 4) appear ibid., pp. 475–78, and his contributions to *Ovid's Art of Love* (book 1) ibid., pp. 480–506. An earlier work, Dryden's contributions to translations of *Ovid's Epistles* (1680), appear in *Poems 1649–1680),* vol. 1 of the California edition of *Works,* pp. 109–38. To the *Fables Ancient and Modern* (1700) Dryden contributed eight stories from Ovid, as many as from Boccaccio and Chaucer together.

6. In this discussion I am indebted to the definitive editorial work of Earl Miner, who comments on Dryden's alterations in translating Lucretius on the nature of love. See *Poems: 1685–1692* in California *Works* (1969), 3:57–65, 277–78, 285–86. The prose quotations come from Dryden's Preface to *Sylvae* (the title of the miscellany in which the translations of Lucretius appeared in 1685), ibid., pp. 10, 12. The Lucretian Venus is hymned in Dryden's translation of the beginning of Lucretius's first book (ibid., pp. 44–45). It is interesting to note that the invocation to Venus was freely translated by Rochester in one of the few poems to survive in his hand. For the implications of this invocation to Venus as the "delight of mankind" by whom "all things live" and its relevance to Rochester's sexual burlesques, see Reba Wilcoxon, "The Rhetoric of Sex in Rochester's Burlesque," *Papers on Language & Literature* 12 (Summer 1976): 273–84. I find indirect support for my view of the sensual Dryden in Thomas H. Fujimura's deduction from critical comments on Homer and Virgil that the poet's personality was vigorous, aggressive, passionate, though Fujimura is not discussing sexuality. See "The Temper of John Dryden," *Studies in Philology* 72 (July 1975): 348–66, esp. pp. 354, 356.

This section on translated sensuality ought not ignore the young, healthy, witty, and amorous Sigismonda of Boccaccio, who seeks out a husband of low degree and who, in Dryden but not in the Italian author, marries him in a union characterized by unabashed sexuality. The pair is discovered by the outraged father, who decrees the humble Guiscardo's death, which is followed by that of the heroine; her death, however, is preceded by her noble defiance of her father in all the dignity of heroic verse. Dryden has presented in English dress a heroine with "an amorous Mind," whose blood burns like a "raging Fire" and whose married love remains "ever eager, and . . . never cloy'd." The girl rises from rioting affection to love heroism at the end, when Dryden gives her a "Greatness of mind" that is also peculiarly feminine: "of a softer Mould, with Sense [that is, feeling or passion] endu'd." Sigismonda is a Woman of Feeling whose sensibility is exquisite and refined—and also prophetic of the age to come. Above all, she is unashamedly erotic:

> I pleas'd my self, I shunn'd Incontinence,
> And, urg'd by strong Desires, indulg'd my Sense.[7]

In praising Ovid for possessing the dramatist's ability to create "pleasing admiration and concernment," Dryden points to three characters from the *Metamorphoses*, Myrrha, Caunus, and Biblis (*Essay of Dramatic Poesy*, in Watson, 1:41). These are all guilty of incest, the first as a daughter, the second two as brother and sister. And other Ovidian stories that attracted Dryden are also concerned with what in discussing Milton I have called the circle of narcissistic sins. From Ovid's *Heroides* 11, Dryden translates in 1680 the story of the daughter and son of Aeolus who loved each other ("Canace to Macareus"), a story which Ovid and Dryden convey with gentle pathos, the sin, which leads to death, being viewed as entirely human and deeply pathetic.[8] In the *Examen*

7. The quotations in this paragraph come form "Sigismonda and Guiscardo" in *Fables*, 34, 58, 184, 395, 424, 454–55. Wordsworth seems to have been offended by Dryden's making Sigismonda's love "absolute sensuality and appetite": he "has no other notion of the passion." *The Early Letters of William and Dorothy Wordsworth (1787–1805)*, ed. Ernest de Selincourt (Oxford: Clarendon Press, 1935), p. 542. For a discussion of Dryden's poetical version and also its relation to subsequent criticism, drama, and painting, including Hogarth's *Sigismunda* in the Tate Gallery, London, see Charles H. Hinnant, "Dryden and Hogarth's *Sigismunda*," *Eighteenth-Century Studies* 6 (Summer 1973): 462–74. Dryden's use of "sense" (Sigismonda says, "I . . . indulg'd my sense") to mean passionate feeling or sexual appetite is also illustrated in I *The Conquest of Granada* 3.1.58–59: "Ah, why did Heav'n leave Man so weak defence / To trust frail reason with the rule of Sence?"

8. It is worth noting that this epistle has often been considered among Ovid's best because it arouses pathos without becoming mawkish. Altering his source (Euripides' *Aeolus*, in which the brother is a cruel aggressor), Ovid has tried to ennoble—or at least humanize—the act by making the passion reciprocal and giving his characters dignity. One can easily see why this story of profoundly illicit love would nevertheless appeal to the age of sensibility because of its gentle pathos, its treatment of the sin as fully human, its association of love and death, and its freedom from rant. See Howard Jacobson, *Ovid's "Heroides"* (Princeton, N.J.: Princeton University Press, 1974), chap. 9, pp. 159–75. The volume of Ovid's Epistles in which Dryden's translation appeared went through many editions after the first in 1680: 1681, 1701, 1705, 1712, 1716, 1720, for example.

poeticum (Third Miscellany, 1693) Dryden translates the "Fable of Iphis and Ianthe," from *Metamorphoses* 9, which portrays a lesbian love which is totally frustrated, the problem being solved only when Isis transforms one of the lovers to a boy.

In the adaptation of *The Tempest,* performed in November 1667, a hoydenish, comic view of incest is associated with Dryden's desire in that decade to humanize the devil and to shift the grotesque from the demonic realm to the sociopolitical, separating the supernatural from terror and tyranny. In adapting Shakespeare's play he gives Caliban an equally grotesque sister, Sycorax, and adds to their monstrous inhumanity the sin of incest. Trincalo comes upon the unlovely, loving pair in a *delicto* that is uncommonly *flagrante* but that is nonetheless treated in a burst of comic energy: "I found her . . . under an Elder-tree, upon a sweet Bed of Nettles, singing Tory, Rory, and Ranthum, Scantum, with her own natural Brother" (4.2.107–9).

After such roistering, the treatment of incest in two important plays seems complex indeed; it also reveals a degree of ambivalence perhaps not expected in the author of *Religio Laici* and *The Hind and the Panther.* In *Oedipus: A Tragedy* (performed 1678) Dryden collaborated with Nat. Lee in surrounding the parricide and incest with full-blooded Gothic imagery. The incest is regarded as an unnatural horror, an "offence to Kind," since nature abhors

> To be forc'd back again upon her self,
> And, like a whirle-pool swallow her own streams.
> [Act 1; Summers, 4:369]

But in a scene of the final act Oedipus and Jocasta are left alone. This scene, following the unspeakable agonies of mind that accompanied the revelation of their crimes, considerably mitigates the horror. At first Oedipus asks Jocasta to leave, but when she persists in staying, he, the unnatural criminal, feels the "pangs of Nature" and of "kindness" and melts with "a tenderness, / Too mighty for the anger of the Gods!" She proclaims her innocence and asks him to discover his: "You are still my Husband." He replies,

> Swear I am,
> And I'll believe thee; steal into thy Arms,
> Renew endearments, think 'em no pollutions,
> But chaste as Spirits joys: gently I'll come,
> Thus weeping blind, like dewy Night, upon thee,
> And fold thee softly in my Arms to slumber.[9]

9. Act 5 (4:419–20). Dryden says that he wrote the first scene of the play, all of act 4, and "the *first half,* or somewhat *more* of the *Fifth*" ("The Vindication of the Duke of Guise," quoted by Summers [ibid., p. 345], who believed Dryden also had a hand in act 3). Although this speech can, I believe, be used as evidence of an attitude of Dryden's since it appears in a collaborative effort which he helped plan in its entirety, I do not wish to claim that it is solely or even primarily his work. Robert Hume and Judith Milhous have suggested to me in private conversation that it may be too early for Dryden to be fully at ease in writing lovers' dialogue.

This tender speech is terminated when the ghost of Lajus rises and causes Jocasta to return to the world of condign and separate punishment. It is difficult to overstress the importance of a scene that brings Oedipus and his mother-spouse together in full knowledge of their relation but also in an access of tenderness and emotional affinity. The scene is part of a tendency that reached a climax in the Enlightenment and in Romanticism, to move incest from Milton's column of evil to a position in human sensibility where the *lachrymae rerum* could water it.[10]

The latest and best of Dryden's heroic, romantic plays, *Aureng-Zebe* (performed in 1675), concludes the series of wild lawless women (that scorner of weakness and virtue, Zempoalla in *The Indian Queen;* that unabashed libertine in love, Lyndaraxa of pt. 2 of *The Conquest of Granada*) with the character of the Empress Nourmahal, who is carried away—ultimately to foaming madness—by her love for the title character. As in the case of Phèdre's love for Hippolyte in Racine, this passion, conceived by a stepmother for her stepson, is called "incestuous" (3.352); for the attainment of it, "You must Divine and Humane Rights remove" (3.353). Nourmahal is perfectly willing to remove them all, for she is a Hobbesian "natural" woman, power mad as well as incestuous, a dedicated libertine who believes love is a sovereign power which either washes guilt away from any action she undertakes or, when it stains, stains beautifully. In her mad scene she is all fire, a burning lake, in full possession of hell even before her death, which takes place only eight lines before the curtain. The punishment meted out to her keeps Dryden safely within convention, but he does provide her, like his other Amazonian villainesses, with an uncommon amount of dramatic vigor.

In one of his best plays, *Don Sebastian* (December 1689), Dryden gives to unwitting incest a sympathetic and attractive delineation. The love between the king and queen (who are brother and sister, though the fact is unknown to either) is consummated in marriage, which is tragically dissolved immediately upon revelation of the truth. Don Sebastian is ready to take his own life until he realizes what the hereafter would then hold for him. He resolves instead to become an anchorite and remain in Africa, refusing to return to Portugal and pollute its throne by making incest seem to be "triumphant" (5.1.538). While he remains in a natural cave to live out his life as a lonely vegetarian, Almeyda

10. Robert Hume (see Appendix B) says that the Dryden-Lee *Oedipus* is "important historically as a step away from the popularity of 'admiration' and toward a pitying 'concernment' in tragedy" (*Development of English Drama*, p. 325). Roswell G. Ham finds the scene I have selected for emphasis a kind of climax of the perverse love of unnatural relations that had persisted from Elizabethan times: "Lee and Dryden were inclined to palliate the crime to the extent of a recall for one final scene of mad love" (*Otway and Lee: Biography from a Baroque Age*[New Haven: Yale University Press, 1931], p. 160). If one compares this play with the *Oedipus* of 1615, written by Thomas Evans and printed by Nicholas Okes, one finds the earlier play considerably less "horrific" and grotesque than the Dryden-Lee and considerably more normal and human.

goes to a convent, and the fact that brother and sister have married will be kept secret. Thus the action at the end obeys all the requisite proprieties. But in a climactic place the play includes lines about the sin that remove from it the stigma which the severe punishment has given it. The young king, kindling at the sight of his sister-bride and hearing her say that she must continue to love him, declares, "Nay, then there's Incest in our very Souls, / For we were form'd too like" (589–90). Love and guilt, in an almost proto-Byronic fashion, are intrinsically intertwined:

> Alas, I know not what name to call thee!
> Sister and Wife are the two dearest Names;
> And I wou'd call thee both; and both are Sin.
> Unhappy we! that still we must confound
> The dearest Names, into a common Curse.
>
> [608–12]

The king calls the night of his nuptials

> a glorious guilty night:
> So happy, that, forgive me Heav'n, I wish
> With all its guilt, it were to come again.
>
> [615–17]

How can sin reside in such bliss? If the two are allowed to be together one moment longer, then

> I shou'd break through Laws Divine, and Humane;
> And think 'em Cobwebs, spred for little man,
> Which all the bulky herd of nature breaks.
> The vigorous young world was ignorant
> Of these restrictions, 'tis decrepit now;
> Not more devout, but more decay'd, and cold.
>
> [629–34]

Dryden makes romantic love attractive even when it stands cursed by a powerful taboo. He both reflects the primitivism of the Restoration and anticipates defenses of the illicit by Enlightened thinkers and Romantic poets. But the incest has its dramatic antecedents. Ford, in *'Tis Pity She's a Whore*, portrays passionate love between Giovanni and his sister, who is pregnant with his child. The play has been condemned as morally monstrous by Gerard Langbaine, Vernon Lee, Stuart Pratt Sherman, and T. S. Eliot;[11] and Ford does indeed try to make the love seem sincere and appealing. But Dryden is

11. See Larry S. Champion, "Ford's *Tis Pity She's a Whore* and the Jacobean Tragic Perspective," *PMLA* 90 (Jan. 1975): 78–87, esp. p. 87, n.15.

much more tender and forgiving than his predominantly skeptical and hard-headed predecessor.[12] He allows the hero to express a sentiment of which the long and eloquent defense of incest by Mignon's father in Goethe's *Wilhelm Meister* is not much more than an expansion.

It is widely known that the *frisson* of much Gothic fiction and Romantic poetry arises from portrayals or suggestions of incest, but it has been thought that during the eighteenth century the theme remained out of sight.[13] This is not true. No less than five of Dryden's plays make it prominent, and Defoe and Fielding chose not to avoid it. But of course it did not become prominent and obsessive, nor did it receive powerful literary treatment, until that soaring—or searing—of the spirit that we call Romanticism or at least until respect for institutional control declined as the French and American revolutions became imminent.

Love and the Tears of Magnanimity

Every student of Restoration drama knows that "pathos" and "pity" are among the most important critical terms of the period. Chapter 1 discussed briefly the transformation of "the pathetic" from a term that refers to all the passions, including the most vehement, to one that refers largely to the tender and the soft, and I also referred to its paternity in the "pathē" of Aristotle's *Poetics.* Not nearly enough has been made of the relation of aesthetic pathos to Christ's *passio*—a relation that is obvious in music of the baroque when a composer like Bach creates special effects of awed tenderness for the incarnation and the crucifixion. Because love can soften the flinty heart and tears can avail to a repentance that saves the soul, aesthetic love and pity must surely, in a Christian culture, resonate with religious meanings. Chaucer's *Troilus* is con-

---

12. Earl Miner learnedly analyzes the theme of incest in this play in vol. 15 of California *Works* (1976), pp. 394–97. He finds Dryden's treatment "unique" because it combines these four differentiating conditions: the love is between brother and sister; their blood relationship is unknown to the participants; the love, unwittingly incestuous, is consummated; the blood relationship is subsequently revealed (p. 395). I have given the incest of this play special emphasis and have discussed it climactically in the section devoted to Dryden's sensuality. Reuben Brower, in contrast, has stressed the piety of the hero, whom he regards as a second Aeneas: in *Don Sebastian* Dryden reveals his deepest debt anywhere to Virgil. See "Dryden's Epic Manner and Virgil," *PMLA* 55 (Mar. 1940): 128–29. Can what I have stressed and what Brower sees be reconciled? If so, it is noteworthy that Dryden's softening and moralizing of heroic character by pathos and *pietas* is accompanied by sexuality, even of a perverse nature.

13. See Masao Miyoshi, for example, in *The Divided Self* (New York: New York University Press, 1969), p. 11. See also Montague Summers, *The Gothic Quest: A History of the Gothic Novel* (1938; reprint ed., New York: Russell & Russell, 1964), p. 397, where Summers accepts the categories for Gothic fiction of André Breton which, if they do not totally exclude incest, certainly do not make it prominent or definitive.

cerned with both love and pathos, and its portraits of love suffering are as heartrending as its portraits of dalliance are infectiously joyous. Spenser—the "inimitable Spenser" whom Dryden early and long admired[14]—steeps in tears those lines in *The Faery Queene* that introduce the loyal, fair, and forsaken Una (1.3.1–4). When Belphoebe comes upon the grievously wounded Timias, the author mollifies the asperities of his Diana by giving her *un coeur sensible*. The "soft passion and unwonted smart" that these lovers feel is underscored by comparing the woman with the mother of Jesus. Belphoebe was born of the morning dew, and no sin "ingenerate in fleshly slime" ever touched her (3.5.30, 3.6.3).

Dryden does not often follow Spenser in associating purity and pity. For him and his age it was more rhetorically effective and socially necessary to associate heroism and pity—a union that could best be made through the mediation of love. To explain and defend his infusion of tender, loving, forgiving feeling into heroic action, Dryden had a wide range of critical terms to draw upon—terms used to refer both to emotions he bestowed upon his characters and also to those he hoped to arouse in his audience. "Concernment" meant emotional involvement in tragedy: it could refer to fear alone but often could also invoke pity. "Compassion" was used frequently for Aristotelian pity; and "sense," which, as we have seen, did not yet mean practical, prudential reason, was "a feeling perceived in the mind, the heart." "Sensible" should be dissociated from its modern meaning and be allowed to refer to feeling, particularly (though not exclusively) of the refined, sensitive variety.[15] As early as 1668, in *An Essay of Dramatic Poesy*, Dryden used "compassion" and "concernment" to describe the effects of tragedy, and in the same work he associates the "soft passion" of love with the Christian dispensation in general and with Shakespeare and Fletcher in particular. In 1679, in "The Grounds of Criticism in Tragedy," prefixed to *Troilus and Cressida*, he reveals how much he admires pity, which works effectually to create charity, "the noblest and most god-like of moral virtues." Two years before, in the "Heads of an Answer to Rymer" (1677), he again specifically associated this eminently Christian quality with love: "We are not touched with the sufferings of any sort of men so much as of lovers; and this was almost unknown to the Ancients; . . . neither knew they the best commonplace of pity, which is love."[16]

Such, then, is Dryden's idea of love. It is modern, Christian, and peculiarly

14. See Charles E. Ward, *The Life of Dryden* (Chapel Hill: University of North Carolina Press, 1961), p. 8.

15. The words referred to are defined, with examples from Dryden, in H. James Jensen, *A Glossary of John Dryden's Critical Terms* (Minneapolis: University of Minnesota Press, 1969).

16. The quotations from Dryden's criticism may be found in Watson, 1:41, 46, 218, 245. Dryden's denial of tender love to the ancients is echoed as late as 1778 by Vicesimus Knox: "The character of Delicacy of Sentiment, so esteemed at present, seems to have been unknown to the antients." *Essays, Moral and Literary*, 1st ed. (London, 1778), p. 1.

relevant to the needs of his countrymen.[17] It is adumbrated in the early plays; it develops steadily, though complexly, in the heroic drama; and it reaches a climax in *All for Love,* which appeared in the very years in which Dryden made his full formulation of the idea in prose. In *The Indian Queen* (1663) four characters, including Montezuma himself, weep openly and in concert.

> Into my eyes sorrow begins to creep;
> When hands are ty'd it is no shame to weep,

says Montezuma (5.1.160–61). But here there is no particular association of love and sentiment. In *The Rival Ladies* (published 1664) love springs up like a straw fire, and, though it does not go out, it is forced to yield to "Obligement" (5.3.280) and the presence of anterior passion. In reworking *The Tempest* (1667), Dryden and Davenant had before them an example of a delicate and tender innocent in Miranda, who is first aroused to suffer ("with those that I saw suffer," 1.2.5–6) a tender distress which ends in romantic passion. But to Shakespeare's example the collaborators respond either with coarse jokes about male and female innocence awakening to experience or by the hoariest clichés that "Agéd Ignorance" ever dreamed up about heterosexual love.

By December 1677 Dryden was able worthily, though not with full success, to challenge Shakespeare and in *All for Love* to give noble embodiment to the new sensibility and idealism. To the magnificent excess of Shakespeare's lovers Dryden responds by portraying a love that is sensual and death defying but also refined, pitiful, courteous, and in its own way uxorial. The refinement of the new sensibility should not obscure Dryden's daring achievement in making sexual love attractive. He was at least bold enough to offend Johnson, who censured him severely for "admitting the romantick omnipotence of love."[18]

As if to anticipate one feature of the eighteenth-century landscape he helped to create, Dryden introduces Antony as a "Commoner of Nature"

---

17. On the idea of pity in Racine, Dryden, and others, see the important articles of Eugene M. Waith, to whom I am especially indebted: "Tears of Magnanimity in Otway and Racine" in *French and English Drama of the Seventeenth Century* (Los Angeles: Clark Memorial Library, 1972), pp. 3–22, and "Dryden and the Tradition of Serious Drama" in *Writers and Their Background: John Dryden,* ed. Earl Miner (London: G. Bell & Sons, 1972), pp. 58–89. So important do I regard the presence of benevolent, forgiving emotion in Dryden's thought that I am tempted to use an important eighteenth-century word ("sympathy") to describe it and to suggest that his example was operative in expanding "the nature and force of *sympathy.*" The last phrase is David Hume's, who goes on to describe how sympathy and passion operate—in words which, I believe, come close to describing the effect Dryden intended his magnanimous heroes to have upon the audience: "As in strings equally wound up, the motion of one communicates itself to the rest; so all the affections readily pass from one person to another, and beget correspondent movements in every human creature. When I see the *effects* of passion in the voice and gesture of any person, my mind immediately passes from these effects to their causes, and forms such a lively idea of the passion, as is converted into the passion itself." *A Treatise of Human Nature* 3.3.1.

18. Life of Dryden, *The Works of Samuel Johnson, LL.D.,* 9 vols. (Oxford, 1825), 7:268.

(1.132), a deeply melancholy man now "turn'd wild" (232) and inhabiting a Gothic setting. The "horrid Scene" (31) portrays a priest walking "a lone Isle o' th' Temple" (18) at midnight and also rising whirlwinds, opened graves, an armed ghost—and a ruin, the ruin being Antony, who paints himself in the red color of shame and the black of despair. His preeminent quality appears at once, his loyal love to the one who "deserves / More World's than I can lose" (368–69). Cleopatra is also temporarily without her lover, but not without her love, which she calls "a noble madness," a "transcendent passion" (2.17, 20). Giving the play a modern sentimental touch absent in Shakespeare, Dryden makes Cleopatra emphasize that, though Julius Caesar first possessed her person, Antony was her first true love. The lovers are mature and experienced, but their love is eager and untired, obsessive and exclusive. Consider the uninhibited, joyous, and poetic speech of Antony, "How I lov'd, / Witness ye Dayes and Nights" (2.281–82). Here no cynical Enobarbus mocks the passion; instead, Cleopatra, rejecting Augustus's offer of place and power and thinking only of death in Antony's absence, is all "that's excellent! / Faith, Honor, Virtue" (2.439–40). Dryden, reconceiving the values of the play, has made passionate love honorable without depriving it of sensuality: Antony is "a greater *Mars*" who "grow[s] rich by giving," and Cleopatra is a "brighter *Venus*" in a "perpetual Spring" (3.11, 12, 25, 28).

Shakespeare's lover is seen on the world stage, but Dryden's is not without heroic virtue, which coexists with a friendship for Dolabella that is almost Shelleyan and one for Ventidius that comes close in rivaling in intensity the love for Cleopatra. Of his love for the younger man, Antony says, "I was his Soul," "We were one mass," "For he was I, I he"—words that anticipate Heathcliff as well as Shelley (3.91, 96, 97). Both friendships of Antony, however, are transcended by romantic love; as is the uxorial, which is so far from being despised in this play that Antony bestows on his wife the heroic phrase "the greatness of your Soul" (3.314). The loyalty of Octavia is surpassed not only by the passion of Cleopatra but also by its union with those wifelike and gentle qualities that Shakespeare's generally greater heroine lacked. Antony too is a gentler being than history or myth would warrant, although Shakespeare's hero is also a generous man of tender feeling, over whom his comrades in arms shed tears and who insists that the defected Enobarbus receive the treasures that had been his own. In Dryden's apotheosis love also transcends war, and, in behavior that looks ahead to the antiheroism of the eighteenth century, Antony chooses a love death full of rich human emotion over an empty military conflict. For Cleopatra that love death is a spousal rite. The tableau at the end is carved in noble institutional marble, for Antony and Cleopatra sit in death as though they were the unacknowledged legislators of mankind. Dryden has indeed glorified tender and passionate love. To what it traditionally possessed he adds order, pity, kindliness, and a mitigated fury.

All for Love is the purest embodiment of Dryden's love pathos. It drove Shake-speare's greater play off the boards for over a century, for more reasons than can be accounted for in the somewhat bland term "classical." Neither respect for the dramatic unities and decorous discipline nor manageability as a piece of stage business alone can account for the eighteenth-century vogue of *All for Love*. Surely its expression in noble blank verse of a love ideal that was entirely human, at once passionate and tender, better explains its high place in the age of sensibility and humanism.[19]

The Heroic Hero in Love

However important the stage history of *All for Love,* it was the earlier heroic plays in rhymed couplets that touched the hearts of the broadened reading public who supported sensibility. If the tastes of Richardson's characters can be thought of as typical, it was Almanzor and other heroic lovers who caught the fancy of later generations and established models for conduct, not the civilized Antony, who "bates of his mettle; and scarce rants at all" (prologue, 11). Perhaps it was because the great Roman and Egyptian lovers indulged an illicit affection and were allowed to die that it became the lot of heroes who fought, forgave, and in the end married to provide examples of nobility to the sentimental eighteenth century.

In the *Cratylus* (398C–D) Socrates, in one possible etymology of the term, derived the word "hero" (ἥρως) from "eros" (ἔρως) and so established an as-sociation between the two that lasted for centuries. That link Dryden did not break in his heroic plays, where love is omnipresent and constitutes one of the basic themes. It will repay our effort to observe the nuances and trace the developments of this theme. In a collaboration with Robert Howard, *The Indian Queen* (performed 1663/4), "the first fully formed heroic play to be acted in London" (California *Works,* 8:283), Dryden develops a contrast be-tween the raging, passionate love of Montezuma and the virtuous, gentle love

---

19. The present reading should be compared with that of Bruce King, who says of the lovers: "Their deaths prove, and therefore symbolically legitimatize, their love." He also finds that the play displays many characteristics of the sentimental drama of the mid-1670s. See *Twentieth Century Interpretations of "All for Love,"* ed. Bruce King (A Spectrum Book; Englewood Cliffs, N.J.: Prentice-Hall, 1968), pp. 7, 9. Cf. also the article by Otto Reinert in the same collection ("Passion and Pity in *All for Love,*" pp. 83–98), which emphasizes Dryden's "rhetoric of sentiment and pity" (p. 85) but also says that the play "celebrates the passional life" (p. 97). Reinert demonstrates that in Dryden passion paradoxically triumphs over reason and that the ultimate victory is "romantic" as pity yields to passion and sentiment to grandeur (p. 98). Cf. also Clarence Tracy, "The Tragedy of *All for Love*" (*University of Toronto Quarterly* 45 [Spring, 1976]: 186–99), an article which sees the conclusion as an eternal triumph of love based on personal fulfillment (an amalgam of Egyptian and Christian ideas) over political love and duty, a Roman ideal that also possessed nobility.

of Acacis, both of whom court Orazia the daughter of the "Inca of Peru," for whom Montezuma now fights. The contrast influences the conduct of Montezuma himself, who, though he begins in passion and fury, ends as a well-tempered, magnanimous hero. His rival and ultimate model is a Mexican prince, son of the usurping Zempoalla, whose violent blood he has not inherited, and of a dead father, a mild and gracious ruler, from whom his heritage was nothing less than civilized virtue. This virtue appears in his release of captives and his display of chivalry toward his rival Montezuma. But it appears most strikingly in his noble love of the good Orazia, to whom he remains loyal unto death, a death administered by his own hand. The pagan Acacis is an *anima naturaliter Christiana* in an ambiguous world of loss and gain, violence and gentleness. He stands as an example of delicate and forgiving love to the once violent Montezuma, whose character he surely helps to form.

In the sequel, his own *Indian Emperour* (performed 1665), Dryden has continued the basic contrast between two noble characters in the pagan Montezuma and the Christian Cortez. Both are in love. Montezuma woos Almeria (the daughter of the now deceased savage Indian queen), who spurns him in haughty language that causes him to lament that his lion heart is caught in the toils of a passion for an unyielding woman. Cortez also falls in love with a pagan beauty, Cydaria, daughter of Montezuma, a girl who feels strangely and deeply stirred by the affection of a Christian conqueror. This love deepens on both sides, because the lovers are mature enough to discuss its nature and the social conditions that govern it. It is quite otherwise with Montezuma, who in his frustration over unsuccess with Almeria, seeks superstitious advice from a pagan high priest and even considers accomplishing the violent death of Cortez, of whom he is mistakenly jealous. It is the misfortune of the Indian emperor that he should love a woman in love with his rival, Cortez, who does not reciprocate her love, whom she had thought she hated, and to whom she does in fact administer a stab wound in the anger that follows the frustration of her love. In the end this violent woman dies by her own hand, still loving Cortez and receiving that good man's commendation, though not his love. Both Acacis the pagan of the earlier play and Cortez the Christian represent something more fundamental than doctrinal belief, and that is goodness of heart and civility in love. Cortez leads a band of greedy Christians, whose degeneracy of character the noble Montezuma exposes in a pitiless light. But in the end Cortez surpasses in moral dignity the pagan, whose death he survives. He is not a simple conqueror but a good and noble man who thanks the power above for the double blessing of "Conquest" and "Love" (5.2.379). In the end he wins his beloved because of his goodness as much as his passion. Once more Dryden rewards a love that consists of moderation and decency, of forgiveness and chivalry. Admirable though he is, the passionate Montezuma knows only frustration in love, partly, no doubt, because the object of it was a woman of impiety and violence.

Tyrannick Love (performed 1669) presents a contrast between baroque Christianity and paganism, the one as exalted as the other is base. On the Christian side, at its most ideal, "the least immodest thought" (2.1.218) is proscribed; when Saint Catharine goes to hideous torture, she goes "bare and naked," fearing most for her sacred modesty and praying, "Let not my body be the Tyrant's spoil" (5.1.307). Against so austere and unworldly an ideal (which was doubtless unrealistic even to Dryden), the romantic love present in the Roman court displays the frustrations of a real life torn between pagan and Christian values. That life is not without idealism, which the rantings of Maximin and the sapphire-studded glories of Catharine's apotheosis tend to obscure. The successful general Porphyrius is in love with the wife of Maximin, Berenice; but the emperor wishes to reward the general's valor with the gift of his daughter. Unfortunately, the young Valeria is more than willing and so supports her father's plan by offering herself to Porphyrius. He remains steadfast in his love of the empress, but Placidius, a trusted confidant of the emperor, adds to the complication by loving Valeria. The situation is at sixes and sevens, and the frustration that thwarts almost everyone is bound to end in violence. Catharine is delivered to her horrible-glorious death. Valeria stabs herself in the presence of her beloved Porphyrius; a love martyr, she "sighs her Soul into her Lovers eyes" (5.1.577). Placidius, deprived of Valeria by her death, stabs the tyrannical emperor, who retaliates in a series of counterstabs so fierce as to be ridiculous and decrees the death of his wife and her lover. But these two survive—the empress, who is revealed to be a Christian, and Porphyrius, who inclines toward Christianity. Dryden allows them to live because during the life of her husband, monstrous though he became at the end, Berenice would not hear of infidelity and looked to the hereafter for the fulfillment of her love. In the tangled world of tyrannic and sensual passion it is Christian mildness and civility in love that are rewarded. Catharine's love is of course too noble for this world and is appropriately rewarded with a martyr's crown. But the love of Berenice and Porphyrius survives violence and passion to be fulfilled on earth because it respects law and civil society and is moderate and mature, decent and forgiving.

These lovers indeed point the moral that Dryden constantly makes about love in the decade of the 1660s. It is approved when it is disciplined, orderly, civil; and it is opposed when it is passionate, wild, and excessively individualistic. In the comedies, love in real life can be racy and amusing. In the mythic world of heroism, love must obey the conventions of society and religion. Berenice passed the test triumphantly. While her husband lived, she was "Too ill a Mistress, and too good a Wife" (5.1.448); her love for Porphyrius while Maximin lived was pure, chaste, passionless, "As light transmitted through a

Crystal glass" (460). But with the creation of the greatest of the heroic plays, a more comprehensive ideal than that of social, civil love is developed. Love becomes intenser, more individual, more ennobling; by it the heroic hero is redeemed because it contains the saving ingredient of pity. Pity does not of course drive out terror, as the continuing presence of powerful and destructive villains demonstrates. Nor is pity swallowed by admiration, that new objective added to the purposes of serious drama by Minturno in the sixteenth century, an objective that became prominent in the Restoration and was specifically associated with love: Hobbes said that the "work of an heroic poem is to raise admiration, principally for three virtues, valour, beauty, and love."[20] For Dryden, as for most playwrights of the period, it is extremely difficult to define precise dramatic aims and to ascertain what emotions in the audience a particular play is intended to arouse. But if we concentrate on content and character within the plays rather than on putative responses, it is not far from the truth to say that the last and best of the heroic plays all embody pity, fear, and admiration—these three—and that the greatest of these is pity.[21] There is now no need for an Acacis or a Cortez separated from a Montezuma. The new hero has himself absorbed the values that Dryden had earlier found it necessary to distribute. If this analysis is right, we may have the clue to why the heroic play lived on in the newer sensibility of the eighteenth century. It united those qualities that later came to be regarded as the two chief nerves of poetry, pathos and sublimity (the latter concept including both terror and admiration).[22]

I shall now trace what Dryden himself approvingly termed the "pathetic vehemence" ("The Grounds of Criticism in Tragedy"; Watson, 1:259) that characterizes his portrayal of love in the major heroic plays. It has not been

20. Quoted by Bonamy Dobrée in *Restoration Tragedy: 1660–1720* (Oxford: Clarendon Press, 1929), p. 13.

21. See above, pp. 59–60, for expressions of Dryden's profound regard for pity in the drama. He of course also praised admiration: "above all, to move admiration . . . is the delight of serious plays" ("A Defence of an Essay of Dramatic Poesy" [1668] in Watson, *Critical Essays*, 1:114). But observe that Hobbes, quoted above by Dobrée, attaches admiration chiefly to "valour, beauty, and love." Two of these, beauty and love, are also intimately associated with pity. Observe, too, that Saint-Evremond (quoted by Robert Hume in *Development*, p. 178) explicitly makes the heroic the cause of tenderness in the spectator: "a greatness of Soul well expressed . . . excites in us a tender Admiration."

22. Joseph Warton said in 1756: "The sublime and the pathetic are the two chief nerves of all genuine poesy." Quoted in Scott Elledge, ed., *Eighteenth-Century Critical Essays*, 2:719. Jensen in *A Glossary of Dryden's Critical Terms* emphasizes in his definition of "admiration" qualities of transport, elevation, and even of being lost in pleasure. In one of his comments on admiration Dryden clearly anticipates Edmund Burke, who made silence an ingredient of the sublime (*A Philosophical Enquiry into the Origin of our Ideas of the Sublime and Beautiful* 2.6). Dryden says in dedicating *Amboyna* (1673) that "the greatest note of admiration is silence. . . . [Poets] have then gained over [their audience] the greatest victory, when they are ravished into a pleasure which is not to be expressed by words." *The Works of John Dryden,* ed. Walter Scott and George Saintsbury, 18 vols. (Edinburgh, 1883), 5:5.

sufficiently considered that the notorious exaggerations and bombastic violence of these plays may in fact be marks of struggle—a struggle within Dryden's own soul as he tried to forge an ideal for himself, for his age, and for the age to come. Certainly the canon of naturalism with which Dryden himself later judged his heroic achievement does not—perhaps cannot—do it justice.[23] What Dryden had tried to accomplish in his serious drama was to redefine greatness of soul in terms useful to a Christian society recovering from civil strife and turning toward unity, order, and civilization. His own contemporaries were aware that they were in the presence of a lofty ideal. Mrs. John Evelyn said of *The Conquest of Granada* that it is "so full of ideas that the most refined romance I ever read is not to compare with it; love is made so pure, and valour so nice, that one would imagine it designed for a Utopia rather than our stage." Mrs. Evelyn admired someone who could "feign such exact virtue" in an age of declining morality.[24] Dryden himself said of his hero Almanzor that he possessed "a frank and noble openness of nature, an easiness to forgive his conquered enemies, and to protect them in distress; and, above all, an inviolable faith in his affection."[25] He was a romantic Christian knight—forgiving, sensitive to suffering, and primarily a believer in the heart's affections.

In part 1 of this ten-act play (performed December 1670) Almanzor, a "noble Stranger" (1.1.235) of mysterious origins falls in love with the future queen Almahide, now a captive, who conquers him with one glance ("As I were stung with some *Tarantula*," 3.1.329), and he sinks immediately into a "Lethargy of Love" (3.1.337). We wonder if this man, whom Almahide finds "roughly noble" and even "Divine" in his "unfashion'd Nature" (3.1.305, 306) will go the way of Montezuma, forced to die frustrated, by his own hand. But another way is being prepared for the magnanimous but proudly and fiercely independent hero, who declares, "I alone am King of me" (1.1.206), for he now burns more for the beauteous captive's freedom than for her body. Almanzor is great, but that heroic quality is being redefined: "Great Souls by kindness onely can be ti'd" (4.1.54). Under a woman's influence, this "brave bold man" learns to damp his "inborn fire" (4.2.456, 469). He does not yet fully succeed: seizing his beloved's hand, he provokes the king to sentence him to death, a sentence changed to banishment through Almahide's entreaties. The fiery, eccentric, manly hero departs full of redemptive promise but not yet fully reclaimed, for he dreams of erecting empire on the "Conquer'd Necks" of the "best and bravest Souls" he can find (4.2.478, 479).

23. Dryden apparently regarded his heroic plays as an indulgence of the free imagination unrestricted by the limitations of mimesis. The essays of 1680–81 meant a return to nature and common sense as artistic norms. See Robert D. Hume, "Dryden on Creation: 'Imagination' in the Later Criticism." *Review of English Studies* 21 (Aug. 1970): 295–314.
24. Quoted by Waith in "Dryden and the Tradition of Serious Drama," p. 73.
25. Dedication to James, Duke of York, in *John Dryden (Three Plays)*, ed. Saintsbury, pp. 5–6.

Part 2 (performed January 1671) reveals that Almanzor achieves the ideal stated at the outset by Queen Isabella:

> Love's a Heroique Passion which can find
> No room in any base degenerate mind:
> It kindles all the Soul with Honours Fire,
> To make the Lover worthy his desire.
> Against such Heroes I success should fear,
> Had we not too an Hoast of Lovers here.
> An Army of bright Beauties come with me;
> Each Lady shall her Servants actions see:
> The Fair and Brave on each side shall contest;
> And they shall overcome who love the best.
>
> [1.1.145–54]

To the achievement of that ideal (which the popularity of this passage helped to propagate during the eighteenth century) there remain grave obstacles. Almahide is now married to Boabdelin and reigns with him as queen. Almanzor's own nature is as fiery as ever, a prey to a "quick imagination," a "boundless fancy" (2.3.73, 79) that believes the queen is still available. Of her continuing love there is no doubt: at one point death seems the only way out for one who loves another but is determined to remain loyal to her spouse. The obstacles to union are formidable, but they are all overcome. After Almanzor's banishment, his vows of poverty and separation from the world, and his sentence to death, the king and husband dies in battle, the discovery is made that Almanzor is of noble Christian birth, Granada is conquered by Ferdinand and Isabella, and the hero and heroine marry. Long before Dryden so rewards them, the values that justify the reward have been established. These constitute a pattern repeated again and again in the sensibility of the following century: a powerful imagination, irrepressible impulses for good, magnanimity, pity, and above all, passionate love.

The Conquest of Granada is a public play, displaying on a world canvas the conflict between Muslim and Christian. Its values are those of a Christian civilization, freshly imbued with a new, highly individualistic sense of love, realizing itself against fanatical and old-fashioned self-will. Love is thus given an international and interfaith setting. *Aureng-Zebe*, whose portrayal of incest I have already mentioned, is confined to the world of Muslim India, and the emotions are more narrowly focused on the primal and the domestic. Such wars and conquests as take place are almost entirely within the family, and Dryden says that "true greatness, if it be anywhere on earth, is in a private virtue; . . . confined to a contemplation of itself."[26] In this, his last and best heroic play, Dryden has clearly anticipated the domestication of heroism, which in

26. Dedication to John Sheffield, Earl of Mulgrave, ibid., p. 270.

Johnson's criticism, as throughout the eighteenth century, was transferred from the field of battle to the hearth and the heart. But in this intense familial setting there is no normative Christian character like Cortez or Isabella to establish sentimental, religious values. These—or at least a version of them— are learned anyhow: the lustful, power-hungry Morat, under the tutelage of a woman he loves illicitly, learns the truths of virtue, honor, mercy. The emperor, at first unnaturally lustful and as reckless as King Lear, is in the end softened by filial love. And Indamora, the heroine beloved of so many, is a plausible human being, not an automaton of ideal love and beauty. She contrasts strongly and favorably with the abject Melesinda, Morat's wife, a Muslim Griselda. Indamora loves but also wishes to live: she presents a contrast not only to Melesinda in this play but to Benzayda of the *Conquest* (pt. 1), a girl as faithful to her father as to her lover, her breast often and eagerly exposed to the avenging daggers of justice. Indamora, very humanly, fears death. Though completely innocent herself, she will dart a flirtatious glance at another man to gain a practical advantage, and she can pity the dying and formerly monstrous Morat while continuing loyal to her lover. This Kashmiri princess is a modern woman—beautiful, charming, decent, worldly, moderate, and virtuous. She is worth the winning.

And she is won by a hero, who is not so dramatically interesting as she but who, intellectually considered, is Dryden's completest union of the pathetic and the heroic. In a world of threatening parricide, fraternal rivalry, wounded minds, and unnatural affection, Aureng-Zebe establishes admirable human values. Unconquerable on the battlefield, he is also kindly and forgiving. A dutiful son and loving brother, he must win his prize against the rivalry of his father and brother. And he must also resist the amorous fury of his power-mad stepmother. His one fault (Dryden seems to make the point here and elsewhere that his heroes all do—indeed must—have blemishes) is that he is excessively and sexually emotional, a defect that he shares with others in the play, even the villainous Nourmahal.

> Love mounts, and rowls about my stormy mind,
> Like Fire, that's born by a tempestuous Wind.
> Oh, I could stifle you, with eager haste!
> Devour your kisses with my hungry taste!
> Rush on you! eat you! wander o'r each part,
> Raving with pleasure, snatch you to my heart!
> Then hold you off, and gaze! then, with new rage,
> Invade you, till my conscious[27] Limbs presage
> Torrents of joy, which all their banks o'rflow!
> So lost, so blest, as I but then could know!
> [4.533–42]

27. Observe this anticipation not only of Steele's famous title but also of the physical aspects of sensibility, emphasized particularly in France.

Is this fustian pure and simple? Or is it, rather, the dramatic expression of forgivable emotions in a man who loves with his body—humanly, physically, as Adam did in paradise? Dryden, who believed greatly in moderation and who had made civil conformity the dominant virtue in the earlier heroic plays, here, at the climax of his heroic inspiration, has chosen to deemphasize the value of moderation per se and to exalt what needs to be moderated, that is, energy and vitality. Aureng-Zebe is no plaster saint, no blue stocking sentimentalist, certainly no Saint Catharine, and not even a Christian hero like Cortez. But he is very much worth redeeming. His sexual energies make him susceptible to jealousy, and when this normally kind and forgiving man sees his beloved supporting the head of his dying brother, who kisses Indamora's hand, his anger blazes. The heroine leaves, too large spirited to abide a permanently jealous man, only to be brought back by a forgiven and forgiving father, who quickly restores Aureng-Zebe to his senses and his prize. This chapter began by considering Dryden's sensuality; it is tempting to see in this last of the heroic heroes (a passionate and sensual man whose excesses are fully forgiven) the lineaments of a self-portrait.

The approach taken in my reading of the heroic plays is somewhat different from that of those critics who have praised the ratiocinative in Dryden and found him weak in sentiment and passion.[28] It is diametrically opposite to the view of those who believe Dryden wishes to laugh at the absurd sentiments he allowed his characters to utter: Almanzor lives on ground dangerously enchanted by the self-indulging fancy, a victim of the notion that love is an enthusiastic fit.[29] It also differs from the view stated with such force by Samuel Johnson, who put emphasis on the "romantick heat" of these plays and on the "dramatic wonders," the "illustrious depravity, and majestick madness" of the characters and scenes. Johnson, though he grudgingly admires Dryden's bold treading on the brink of nonsense, denies to him a knowledge of gentle love, of "effusions purely natural," of "the simple and elemental passions, as they spring separate in the mind" (Life of Dryden, in *Works*, 7:259, 339–40, 341). Dryden's rhetoric does indeed tend toward rhodomontade, and even his most human ethical insights are expressed in hearty and overly rhythmic verse that tends to belie delicacy and gentleness. His characters are volatile and sometimes violent. Goodness is set off against an array of melodramatic sinners. But none of these qualities of characterization or versification should obscure

28. See Anne T. Barbeau, *The Intellectual Design of John Dryden's Heroic Plays* (New Haven: Yale University Press, 1970): each of Dryden's characters is a "rational construct, a walking set of attitudes" (p. 4). It is apparent from the foregoing pages that I take my place with those critics (Robert Hume, Eugene Waith, Arthur Kirsch in *Dryden's Heroic Drama* [Princeton, N.J.: Princeton University Press, 1965], and Eric Rothstein in *Restoration Tragedy: Form and the Process of Change* [Madison: University of Wisconsin Press, 1967]), who find, in the words of Hume, that Dryden is "basically *affective* in his outlook." *Development of English Drama*, p. 155 and n.3.

29. See Bruce King, *Dryden's Major Plays* (New York: Barnes & Noble, 1966), esp. pp. 61–67, 73, 75, 78, 81.

the fact that primitive passion is combined with "Mercy, Pity, Peace, and Love" to make Almanzor and Aureng-Zebe heroes of moral culture, forerunners of even Sir Charles Grandison. Through the mediation of Richardson, the villa at Clarens in Rousseau's best novel is organically connected with the benevolent aspects of Dryden's Agra and Granada.

It is possible to argue that Dryden's heroic plays are dramatically redeemable only by their vigorous, though monstrous, villains—Morat, Nourmahal, Lyndaraxa, and Maximin—and that their values of benevolence and love are kept alive only by their association with diabolical energy. Two considerations keep this approach from being fruitful. The first is that Dryden was no Milton, and his Satans, for all their raw power, lack the humanity or the negative moral coherence to make them fully plausible. The other is that, quite apart from intrinsic merit, Dryden's influence had waned by the time of Byron and Blake, who in *Manfred* and *The Marriage of Heaven and Hell* were eager to join the devil's party but were in no way tempted by Dryden's villains. It was different, however, at the beginning of the eighteenth century, when, though there was no identification with the diabolical energy in Dryden, there was a keen appreciation of the poet of both erotic and ideal love—of the translator of Ovid, the author of *The Conquest of Granada,* the creator of the adulterous but otherwise admirable Antony.

Apposite quotations from Dryden introduce works as diverse as the anonymous *Illegal Lovers; A True Secret History, Being an Amour Between A Person of Condition and his Sister* (London, 1728) and Jane Barker, *A Patch-Work Screen for the Ladies; or, Love and Virtue Recommended: In a Collection of Instructive Novels* (London, 1723). Charles Hopkins in *The Art of Love: . . . Dedicated to the Ladies* (2d ed., London, 1704) refers to the "great *Dryden,*" the "Sacred *Dryden*" (p. 3), urging his beloved to place him first in the list of writers to be read, ahead of Congreve, Wycherley, Cowley, Otway, and Lee. Thus Dryden was revered not only by Pope and the satirists, by witty users of the elegant and barbed heroic couplet; he was also remembered by Rowe, Richardson, and that "other" eighteenth century of tenderness and sentiment. Johnson called him "the father of English criticism." He may also be called the father of English sensibility.

From the perspective of this book, Dryden is of the highest importance because he embodied *both* sex and sensibility. The love he presents is *both* ideal and erotic—ideal in the sense that it is associated with a forgiving, humanizing pathos. For each of these, the full-bodied sensuality and the sensibility, there are abundant precedents. But for his combination of the two—a yoking of antithetical qualities that was at once powerful and prolific—Dryden must be credited with being something of a pioneer. Erich Auerbach has shown that the ancients, though they often treated love in literature, rarely made it the subject of elevated verse; he has also shown that the French, though they made love a tragically sublime and noble motif, presented it with barely a trace of overt sexual passion.[30] How different is Dryden, who owes much to both ancient and French drama! He endows the theme of love with the elevation, delicacy, and tenderness that antiquity lacked, and, in quite un-Gallic fashion, his *oeuvres* often throb with a bold and hearty physicality.

30. *Mimesis: The Representation of Reality in Western Literature* (Princeton, N.J.: Princeton University Press, 1953, 1968), p. 386.

4. Restoration Love and the
Tears of Morbidity

*B*ETWEEN DRYDEN AND RICHARDSON no writer on love is various or important enough to require a separate chapter. I face the necessity, therefore, of clustering authors around that aspect of my theme which they best illustrate and of thus imposing a topical coherence upon the flux of history—a coherence which, it is hoped, will not be excessively schematic and will do no harm to an attractive but sometimes bewildering variety. The aspect of the theme isolated for discussion in this chapter is highly emotional—love in association with death, violence, madness, primal instincts, and the passions, including the passions of tenderness and gentleness. There can be little doubt that such emotions as these were intimately related to the actual world of the Restoration writer—a fact that will surprise only those who still believe that the English literature of this period was only or even primarily neoclassical and was born in the stability that followed a royal restoration. Quite the contrary is true; the individual writer often suffered from the abuse of alcohol, from melancholy dreams, and from mental alienation, which was sometimes serious enough to require confinement. Collectively, the national experience was one of bitter controversy and tension between Puritanism and libertinism, between the demands of society and the desire for the primitive; and not infrequently distrust of the future—even dismay over political and religious developments—darkened the horizon. It has been suggested that the growth of sympathy, terror, and tender feeling in France from 1690 on was partly owing to the many famines and plagues that scourged the land and even to the ruinous taxation and inflation that precipitated many from comfort to distress.[1] England too had known fire and disease, which produced abundant opportunities to feel terror and tenderness, to say nothing of the tensions that came in the wake of the Civil War and must often have produced an intolerable psychological strain.

1. Geoffroy Atkinson, *The Sentimental Revolution: French Writers of 1690–1740*, ed. Abraham C. Keller (Seattle: University of Washington Press, 1965), pp. 169, 170. Since this is the first of several comparisons with France that will be made in this study, it is well to take note of Brissenden's important point: "Sexual freedom amongst the French aristocracy was not merely tolerated but encouraged to a degree unknown across the channel (except, perhaps briefly and rather self-consciously during the Restoration): and '*sentiment*', as defined and examined by countless French writers of the late seventeenth and early eighteenth centuries, came to stand for a highly civilized combination of erotic vivacity and delicacy together with an extremely sensitive moral awareness." *Virtue in Distress*, p. 87.

What historical words can legitimately be used to describe the morbidity, perversity, and violence that often accompanied Restoration love? Certainly the most accurate term is "the pathetic," whose general fortunes were outlined in chapter 1. This term, it will be recalled, could refer to all the passions, from the most violent to the most delicate, and it therefore places no excessive strain on "pathetic" to apply it to both Otway and Lee, to works that induce tears of morbidity as well as of magnanimity. It even bore the suggestion of eccentricity, since "pathic" (deriving from the same Greek root) referred to "catamite" (a boy kept for unnatural amorous purposes).[2] The great importance to subsequent English culture of the pathetic drama of the Restoration, with so influential a figure as Otway at its center, has been fully appreciated,[3] and I am therefore tempted to use, quite unhistorically, the term "sentimental" to describe the more delicate of the effects engendered in Restoration morbidity. This word did not of course come to mean full-blown literary emotionalism tinged with erotic feeling until the time of Sterne; but there is some value in invoking it now to call attention to the headwaters of the river that was to flow through the eighteenth-century landscape. One misses much in Restoration sensibility if one does not feel within it the seeds of sentimentalism. And because of the striking copresence of melancholy, madness, primal emotions, rural retirement, Gothic gloom, and picturesque settings, one is even tempted to bring out a term that literary scholars for more than a generation have been wary of using for anything much before 1798, the word "romantic."[4] The example of France, where "le mouvement rationaliste et le mouvement sentimental se développèrent en même temps,"[5] encourages us to see parallel developments in England. During the late years of Louis XIV, the regency, and the first years of Louis XV anticipations of Rousseau abound—of his peculiar association of delicate and trembling emotion with an external nature conceived to be so sensitive that it seemed to pulsate arterially and to flicker with illusion.

Whatever terms we use, we must never lose sight of the fact that the illicit in love was an object of central authorial concern. The desire to be sensational

2. See *OED*, s.v. "pathic" and above, pp. 5–6 and n.12.

3. See Eric Rothstein, *Restoration Tragedy*, esp. chap. 1.

4. On "romantic" broadly conceived, see Logan Pearsall Smith, "The History of Four Words," *Society for Pure English*, vol. 17 (Oxford: Clarendon Press, 1924). I am now somewhat more relaxed than I once was about using a term like "romantic" for particular artistic qualities and effects in combination that anticipate or recall the poetry and art of the very late eighteenth and early nineteenth centuries, whenever or wherever I find them, because we are not so period-bound as we once were, thanks largely to the brilliant polemics of Ronald S. Crane and Donald J. Greene—not so inclined, that is, to apply to an entire century or age a simplifying label. In fact, it is one purpose of this study to make the reader see how grotesquely inadequate such terms as "neoclassical" and "rationalistic" are to describe the cultural complexities of 1660–1800.

5. Geoffroy Atkinson, *Le sentiment de la nature et le retour à la vie simple (1690–1740)* (Geneva: Librairie E. Droz, 1960), p. 81.

and to exploit newly gained freedom of expression impelled writers to offer forbidden fruit. More complexly, the new tolerance, perhaps even the new sentimental softness of feeling, and certainly the impact—direct or indirect, positive or negative—of religion on all aspects of life tended to encourage an invincible curiosity about bowers of dark and prohibited bliss.[6] I have already noted that Dryden, a man of public political and religious commitment, was a nonetheless deeply sensual writer who more than once, with great dramatic emphasis, embodied the theme of incest, giving us a sense that the Miltonic boundaries between vice and virtue had been somewhat obscured. That tendency continues even as the moral sense quickens in the late seventeenth and early eighteenth centuries in reaction to excess. Growing modesty may have been accompanied by a growing knowledge of the Bible, a book which, as I have noted, can serve to heighten awareness of the many evils it so vividly exemplifies and condemns.[7] The attacks on art by Bishop Bossuet and the Reverend Jeremy Collier proceeded from minds that tended to find sexual evil lurking dangerously in the beauty that was portrayed by art or even in the love that was sanctioned by religious institutions. The French bishop and the English divine both felt that there was little distinction between the conjugal and the concupiscent. Bossuet believed that "all Marriage presupposes Concupiscence," and the mind of the English nonjuror turned "the tenderest language of love into language and imagery of foul concupiscence."[8] Well before the attack by Collier, the period of the Restoration, even when it thought itself the freest, was obsessed with religion. The uses of religious comparison in intensely erotic or wittily sensual expression did not die out with Donne; the wit of the glittering Dorimant, for example, is constantly laced with religious allusion. It was almost a commonplace observation, even among believers, that religion could and did arouse sensuality. Baxter found that the conversion of his wife aroused "*all* her passions," and Swift found that "*Zeal* is frequently kindled from the same Spark with other Fires, and from inflaming Brotherly Love, will proceed to raise That of a Gallant."[9]

6. For comparable developments in France, see Geoffroy Atkinson and Abraham C. Keller, *Prelude to the Enlightenment: French Literature, 1690–1740* (London: Allen & Unwin, 1971), pp. 25–26, 72.

7. See above, chap. 1, p. 20. One should not assume, however, a simple correlation between piety and decorum in culture and literature, on the one hand, and the reading of the Bible, on the other. See Lawrence Stone's graph 12 in *Family, Sex and Marriage*, p. 235. The production of editions of the Bible slumped from a peak in about 1630 to a low point in 1660; the number rose sharply to about 1680, then declined again in the next decade, rising slightly until about 1700. Despite increasing literacy the peak of 1630 was not approached until about 1760 and not surpassed (and then only slightly) in about 1780.

8. I here quote Aubrey Williams, whose vigorous defence of Congreve against Jeremy Collier and Bossuet is illuminating. See "No Cloistered Virtue: Or, Playwright versus Priest in 1698," *PMLA* 90 (March 1975): 234–46, esp. p. 242.

9. *A Breviate of the Life of Margaret, the Daughter of Francis Charlton, of Apply in Shropshire, Esq; and*

Intense religious experience and tender religious consciences can keep *agapē* and *eros* related, a relation which may of course be disapproved of by the conscious mind. In France there was a tendency for the erotic libertine to separate sharply from the sentimental romantic, partly for class reasons that are too subtle to be disentangled here. Certainly, as the *nouvelle* replaced the *roman,* as Honoré d'Urfé's *L'Astrée* (which was far from entirely Platonic and in which the senses were by no means despised) was succeeded by the chaste love of *précieux* fiction, two competing concepts of love developed;[10] and a subtle explorer of the passions, like Marivaux, found he had to use two terms even when the opposing tendencies were fused. These terms were "amour-désir" (the Ovidian, the realistic, the physical) and "amour-tendresse" (the Platonic, the ideal, the spiritual).[11] Since French romances, early and late, were translated into English and absorbed by English writers into their fictions, on and off the stage, the movement toward *pudeur,* toward concealment of feeling, was surely known. In certain areas of love, good *tendresse* was, for both ascetic and aesthetic reasons, kept away from bad *désir.* George Fox's journals, for example, show the founder of Quakerism shrinking from sexuality and procreation even in marriage, but at the same time referring to like-minded folk as the "tender" ones, the "very tender" ones; of other types of humanity he was often afraid.[12] Such separation of tenderness from sexual love must have been made often enough. But it is the thesis of this book that division of *tendresse* from *désir* was not ultimately successful. The power of Spenser, Milton, and Dryden was too great. The Protestant enshrinement of sexuality in marriage continued to be too potent an example. The determination to keep such discordant emotions and antithetical drives together in heterosexual friendship must often have caused strain. But desire and tenderness remained united, at whatever cost. It is a revealing fact that even the early English benevolist thinkers, often divines of the Church of England, could not avoid language suggesting sensuality when they recommended behavior that during the Restoration established the genealogy of the Man of Feeling. R. S. Crane's description of this as a "strain of egoistic hedonism" is accurate though too modest. In the divines he quotes and discusses, "tender sentimental feeling," "Self-approving Joy," or the "soft and tender Mind" soon becomes "the cherishing of our own Flesh," a "sensual Pleasure," "a natural

---

Wife of Richard Baxter (London, 1681), p. 44 (emphasis added); Swift, "A Discourse concerning the Mechanical Operation of the Spirit," in *A Tale of a Tub,* etc., ed. A. C. Guthkelch and D. Nichol Smith (Oxford: Clarendon Press, 1958), pp. 287–88.

10. Warren Roberts, *Morality and Social Class in Eighteenth-Century French Literature and Painting* (Toronto: University of Toronto Press, 1974), pp. xii–xiv, 9–12.

11. Valentini P. Brady, *Love in the Theatre of Marivaux* (Geneva: Librairie E. Droz, 1970), pp. 17–18, 27, 47–48.

12. *The Journal of George Fox,* rev. and ed. John L. Nickalls (Cambridge: Cambridge University Press, 1952), pp. 9, 17.

Deliciousness." Such feelings "some good Men have indulged and epi-curiz'd . . . till they have been tempted to call it downright *Sensuality*."[13]

If this be done in the dry tree, what shall be done in the green? That is, if divines recommending a spiritual, humanitarian virtue can be so suggestively physical, what should one expect of those who directly recommend love? Abraham Cowley provides an answer. In the "Elegie upon Anacreon," he praises one who indulged passion in old age and made love the very essence of his being.

> *Love* was with thy *Life* entwin'd
> Close as *Heat* with *Fire* is joyn'd.[14]

In "Platonick Love," from *The Mistress*, Cowley demands the presence of the body and of fully differentiated sexes as a means of avoiding the narcissistic sins and ultimately of achieving a full union of souls:

> For he, whose *soul* nought but a *soul* can move,
>   Does a new *Narcissus* prove,
>   And his own *Image* love.
>   That *souls* do beauty know,
>   'Tis to the *Bodies* help they owe. . . .
>
>   [P. 76]

It is not surprising, then, that in his "Answer to the Platonicks" he defends an affection that can beget offspring, an affection that, like the sun, warms the flesh and is "*Loves* noblest and divinest heat" (p. 81). Not all English writers—perhaps in the end very few—were able to achieve the relaxed boldness about the subject of love that characterizes Cowley. But it was in his anti-Platonic and pro-Miltonic direction that most subsequent writers wanted to steer their course.

William Walsh, in an interesting letter to Dryden dated 13 August 1691, discussed at length a treatise on the nature of love that he proposed to write but apparently never achieved. He planned to describe its benefits and its pitfalls.

> Wee will shew y^t Love is a tendency of ye Minde [to good] & y^t all ye Errony & Vices y^t proceed from Love, is loving ye lesser Good w^n it is accompanyd wth a greater Evil; not y^t it makes us love ye Evil, but ye Good does so blinde

---

13. Ronald S. Crane, "Suggestions toward a Genealogy of 'The Man of Feeling,'" *ELH: A Journal of English Literary History* 1 (Dec. 1934): 205–30; see esp. pp. 206, 218, 227, 228, 229. The piece has been reprinted in Crane, *The Idea of the Humanities,* 2 vols. (Chicago: University of Chicago Press, 1967), 1:188–213. For an important corrective of this influential essay, see Donald Greene, "Latitudinarianism and Sensibility: The Genealogy of the 'Man of Feeling' Reconsidered," *Modern Philology* 75 (Nov. 1977): 159–83.

14. *Abraham Cowley: Poems,* ed. A. R. Waller (Cambridge: Cambridge University Press, 1905), p. 60.

us, as to make us not take notice of yᵉ Evil. Wee will shew yᵗ Amorousness is so far from beeing a fault yᵗ it requires all yᵉ Wisdome & Vertue in yᵉ World to bee truly so.[15]

Walsh, almost as sensitive as Samuel Johnson or Reinhold Niebuhr to how the mind can deceive itself, makes the very goodness of love blind us to its evil, which creeps in unnoticed. If all the wisdom and virtue in the world be required to attain the greatest good in love and to protect us from its errors and vices, it would have to be said that the resources to obviate that unhappy end were not very often available, least of all, perhaps, in the Restoration. As we shall see in the remaining section of this chapter, the narcissistic evils that Milton feared and condemned and Cowley considered to be attendant upon Platonic love did insinuate themselves into literature in subtle and disturbingly morbid ways.

Aphra Behn and Restoration "Romanticism"

The term "romantic" is here used without rigor of definition to refer to a complex of qualities present in the best novel of "the admirable Astraea," *Oroonoko* (1688), sometimes considered the best English novel before Defoe. Its portrait, first in Africa and then in Surinam (which the author had visited as a girl), of a noble savage greatly superior to his white persecutors; its lively and detailed rendition of the picturesque beauty and primitive life of the New World; its social sympathy, expressed now in tears, now in blazing anger; its recollections of Eden and Milton; its exaltation of love—all these qualities anticipate aspects of Rousseau, Shelley, and Blake. The novel also possesses, in its earlier portions, a strain of delicate and suggestive morbidity and in its later a kind of Gothic sensationalism that look ahead to sensibility and the Romantic movement. Some of these qualities also suggest seventeenth-century roots. Rubens had painted noble and highly individualized heads of black men, and Dryden is a persisting presence in Behn. The noble, though flawed, Montezuma, whose nobility reveals his Spanish torturers as the vulgar sadists they really are, anticipates Oroonoko's superiority to the English villains who surround him. In fact Behn's black Apollo may be regarded as an Almanzor freed from the fetters of stage convention and the rhyming couplet to inhabit the freer world of prose fiction. *The Fair Jilt* (1688), a vividly sensational and episodic novel, also recalls Dryden in its portrayal of a woman of mad, raging, animal love, in whose veins runs the blood of a Lyndaraxa or a Nourmahal, even though she begins as an uncloistered nun who has not yet

15. *The Letters of John Dryden,* ed. Charles E. Ward (Durham, N.C.: Duke University Press, 1942), pp. 41, 159.

taken her final vows. But unlike Dryden, Behn rewards this sensual and wildly ambitious heroine, giving her "as perfect a State of Happiness, as this troublesome World, can afford"; a Defoe-like stroke of repentance is allowed to cancel the lurid past.[16] *The Dumb Virgin: or the Force of Imagination* (1700), a potboiler that certainly cannot be taken too seriously, is a domestic tragedy of passion which extends the world of *Aureng-Zebe* and *Don Sebastian* into the realm of sensational popular fiction and which, as its subtitle suggests, exemplifies what we shall observe recurringly, love and the fancy in close association. The plot eventuates in the unwitting incest of the heroine with her brother, her suicide, and parricide. The illicit sexual passions involved recall the tone and ambience of Otway's tragic world in *The Orphan*. At the climax, the "Dumb Virgin" loses both her maidenhead and her silence. Learning from her dying father that her own brother is his accidental murderer and her ravisher, she breaks the ligament that had tied up her tongue and cries out, "Oh! Incest, Incest." It is perhaps small wonder that one whose first speech should consist of only that word should immediately stab herself with her father's sword. Her language is somewhat enriched before she dies, as when, throwing herself into the arms of the newly revealed but now dying son of the family, she is allowed to exclaim, "O my Brother, O my Love." Since this is Restoration, not Romantic, incest, it must, like the parricide, be punished by death. But because the crimes were unwitting, they call for pity, not condemnation.[17]

In *Oroonoko* the black hero is more consistently noble than either Dryden's Montezuma (also a heathen worshiper of Nature's God) or Almanzor. But he is built of their soul-stuff and is of course larger even than the Nature which is the sole guide and nurse of his being. Like the heroic hero, he possesses "Humanity," "real Greatness of Soul," and above all "that absolute Generosity, and that Softness, that was capable of the highest Passions of Love and Gallantry." His attainment of this last was helped by his beauty, his finely shaped mouth, his "aweful" and "piercing" eyes, his Roman nose, and his skin, a "perfect Ebony, or polished Jet." Vile, oath-breaking Christians separate him from his family in Africa and take him to the New World as a slave, but only after his beloved wife had been sold at the order of his grandfather. He is reunited with Imoinda in Surinam, where his loyalty to his people and his own proud rebelliousness lead the hero, who has already achieved unbelievable exploits

---

16. *The Works of Aphra Behn*, ed. Montague Summers (London: Wm. Heinemann, 1915), 5:124. The polarities are evoked in the work itself. Behn says *The Fair Jilt* portrays a love that is like a "Fury from Hell" (p. 74), but she begins her story by calling love "the most noble and divine Passion of the Soul": "generous," full of "soft Impressions" and "tender Touches." The novel itself is sensational, but Behn's opening characterization of love shows the force in 1688 of the sentimental view.

17. *The Dumb Virgin* is quoted from 5:444. The subtitle, "The Force of Imagination," points to a century-long association of that faculty with morbid and illicit love.

in the hunt and in battles with American natives, to plan a new colony for blacks and to be condemned to death as an example to others. Nothing could be more violently sensational than that death, as Oroonoko suffers prolonged and brutally interrupted mutilation. He is ripped to pieces part by part as his captors throw his ears, nose, and limbs into the fire; and yet, though so cruelly diminished, he keeps smoking his pipe until it drops from his mouth in death. A tall tale from the New World, if there ever was one, *Oroonoko* is nevertheless a portrait of heroic nobility and gentle goodness of heart.

It is also a portrait of the heroic hero in love, a love that is fully sensual, totally un-Platonic, and as closely related as cause is to effect to the central and commanding goodness and heroism. That love begins and is put to its first test in Africa, where it takes on its peculiar qualities from an environment that seems to breed morbidity. Such morbidity might not have been present had the love of Oroonoko and Imoinda developed in unspoiled American nature rather than in a corrupt court where ancient custom sanctions such inhumanity as slavery and where the hero (who had a French tutor, knows Spanish, learned the ways of the world from an English trading gentleman, and studied English and Roman history) develops his virtues more by contrast than by imitation. Imoinda, a fair "Queen of Night," a "Black *Venus*," is introduced to him at court, and the attraction of the two for one another is that of similitude, not contrast: "She was Female to the noble Male." One gets a strong sense of brother-sister resemblance between this pair, and this suggestion of the Shelleyan ideal is not dissipated by what follows. The hero is softly passionate in his wooing, and he loves the "eternal *Idea*" of his beloved, an idea that will survive the ultimate decay of her flesh. Unfortunately, single-minded delicacy and passion, with a touch of Platonic idealism, are challenged soon after their marriage by the lusts of the ruler: "The old Monarch saw, and burn'd." He sends her the "Royal Veil," a summons to his bed which it is a mortal offense to disobey and which arrives before the consummation of her marriage. The passion of the king—if his feeble flame can be so denominated—is doubly improper: not only is he old, but he is Oroonoko's grandfather. Thus an unseemly filial conflict that recalls the situation in *Aureng-Zebe* is the chief obstacle to a love that has already struck the reader as existing between lovers who are excessively alike. The indignities Oroonoko suffers at observing the unnatural lusts of his own grandfather demand some kind of decisive resolution. This cannot be said to take place when the marriage is consummated by the young couple (Oroonoko "ravished in a Moment what his old Grandfather had been endeavouring for so many Months"), for the consummation does not put an end to the continuing interest of the aged ruler. Nor does Imoinda's reluctant falsehood—that she was raped by Oroonoko, who used force against her—do any more than gain a little time. The decisive action that breaks the hothouse dilemma of love in the court is the sale of the heroine into slavery in another country, at the order of the monarch. Why does he take so extreme a measure, which destroys his grandson's happiness and puts an end to his own titillations? An irresistible taboo demands it: "As it is the greatest Crime in Nature amongst them, to touch a Woman after having been possess'd by a Son, a Father, or a Brother, so now he [the old king] looked on *Imoinda* as a polluted thing wholly unfit for his Embrace; nor would he resign her to his Grandson, because she had received the *Royal Veil.*" The strict taboo that now separates the loving husband and wife bears some relation to English law and practice, and it is especially interesting to note that in Behn's Africa the fear of incest belongs, along with polygamy, to an old and now discredited way of life that Oroonoko has rejected by pledging loyalty to one woman alone. The hero, told that his beloved wife has died, assuages his grief with valiant military action until it is his turn to be sold into slavery in the New World, where he is reunited with Imoinda and finally suffers the sensational end I have already described.[18]

In Thomas Southerne's *Oroonoko* (November 1695), a fine adaptation of Behn's novel to the stage that remained popular through the eighteenth and into the nineteenth century, the mirror-like similitude of hero and heroine is completely shattered by making Imoinda white. Similarly, the mock-incestuous dalliance of the grandfather with his grandson's bride is changed to a love by Oroonoko's father for the bride, a love that is aborted short of incest but that leads nonetheless to the girl's banishment. All this, however, is in the past and is not shown on the stage; its effect, lingering on in the great grief of the hero, is quickly consoled when he meets and recognizes his wife. Oroonoko is nerved to take heroic action on behalf of his own people when he learns that the dissolute English governor may lay lustful hands on his wife. He now becomes a leader of the slaves. His action, heroic but never bloodthirsty, leads to his capture and death. The last does not come until there is no other way out, and then it comes to both him and his wife together, administered by their own hands, Imoinda dying first. The end is not crude and melodramatic, as in Behn, but a kind of *Liebestod* that is in keeping with the main action of the play. For Southerne has come close to making love the ruling principle of life, even above valor, which itself was valued highly since it transcended the meanness of "Christian" colonialism. The love that is exalted is truly heterosexual, totally free of the sins of narcissism. Oroonoko and Imoinda are transformed by Southerne into an Othello and a Desdemona who, however, never once suffer the slightest pangs of jealousy or undergo any misunderstanding whatever. In the main action of this play, then, Southerne takes his place with those in the Restoration who exalt "soft" love above "hard" military virtue and who define heroism as a thing of the heart and not of the mighty right arm.

18. *Works,* 5:135, 136, 137, 138, 140, 152, 154.

The dramatist removes the narcissistic sins from his main plot and embodies a version of them in his comic subplot, where they are laughed at and so purged from the world of the hero and heroine. Since this comic reduction constitutes a conscious revision of his source, it is tempting to think that Southerne may also be resisting what he senses as a trend in his culture toward morbidity. Well he might have, since his dramatic achievement came well after love irregularities in Lee and Otway. The prose intrigue of this play introduces two sisters now in Surinam, away from the fashionable life in London, where they have not been able to find mates. One, Charlotte Welldon, dresses herself as a man, and in that impenetrable disguise she arouses the love of a recently widowed heiress and mother, the widow Lackitt. Loving a woman disguised as a man could be taken as a straight comic convention except that it is here made real and truly operative in the action: the widow puts forward her booby son as a candidate for the love of Charlotte Welldon's sister Lucy, who must be married (it is thus that Charlotte stalls for time) before "he" can consider marriage. And that son turns out to be a hermaphrodite, a term the young man applies to himself: "I hardly know whether I'm a boy or a girl." Is the condition physical or spiritual? Apparently mostly spiritual: he is a mama's boy who prefers her apron to other forms of contact, but there is some hope of his being a capable enough male in time ("He that unties you makes a rod for his own tail"). Charlotte Welldon in disguise has married the widow Lackitt, but a man must stand in at night for the female husband. The comic plot is resolved when Welldon is revealed for what she is, the woman Charlotte, who now wins one Stanmore as husband. The widow takes her stand-in bed companion as her husband, and Lucy makes another attempt to "untie" the hermaphroditic son.[19]

I have already suggested what such ridiculous and tasteless farce means and why it is allowed a place in an excellent play whose main action portrays heroic love nobly and lyrically, a love which is, as we have seen, assertively heterosexual. Morbidity lurks even in Dryden, and Southerne seems determined to dissolve it amid peals of real and raucous laughter. Similitude in affection—love of woman for disguised woman, love of woman for effeminate male—is roisteringly exposed. It is as though the dramatist has said that morbidity is

19. The quotations come from 4.1 (p. 84 in the Regents Restoration Drama Series, ed. Maximillian E. Novak and David Stuart Rodes [Lincoln: University of Nebraska Press, 1976]). The editors take a somewhat different view of the subplot than the one expressed here; they believe that the desire of the Welldon sisters for a dignified marriage places them on the side of natural law and links them to the love of Oroonoko and Imoinda (p. xxv). I fully agree with them that the subplot is not traditional comic relief but is intimately associated with the serious plot in a new kind of texture (p. xxi). But I cannot concede that the grotesqueries of the subplot in any way constitute normative nature. My view could be seen as an elaboration of that of Robert D. Hume, who sees the subplot as an "example of Southerne's acute psychological perception and his ability to clarify by contrast" (*Development of English Drama*, p. 425). As the plays of this and subsequent chapters are discussed, the reader may wish to locate them in the chronological scheme provided in Appendix B.

disturbing when it remains intrinsic in love; placed extrinsically, it withers away. Can Southerne be credited with a healthy attempt to expunge a potential stain on the psyche and on society?

Love, Madness, and Death: Lee and Congreve

Death is insinuatingly and insistently present in Congreve's tragedy, *The Mourning Bride* (1697), and could not easily have been isolated and remanded to a subplot. It is embodied in the very setting, in the lovely verse, and in the character of the heroine. Similarly, the madness that tortured the mind of Nat. Lee the man is central in his plays and doubtless often accounts for their frequently very fine and powerful, as well as crudely sensational, effects. In this book I am concerned with madness only as it is related to love, and I also exclude the comically and satirically treated lovesick fool, who, as Steele wittily shows in the portrait in *Tatler* 1, possesses his own form of insanity. The love madness in Lee is made of sterner and more frightening stuff, but it is clearly related to our story even though it has even greater affinities with the Gothic and the Romantic imagination. But even within sensibility, as Dryden's heroic plays at the beginning and Goethe's *Werther* at the end clearly show, there persists an instinct for the brink and the abyss, for alienation and suicide.

The life of Lee provided his own age and posterity with another Restoration legend, comparable to the sins and skepticism of Rochester or to the tears and dissipation of Otway. Lee too may have been immoderate in his use of alcohol, his wastrel ways supposedly revealed by the boils and carbuncles of his countenance, the "Rubyes in 's Face," as Settle called them. He is said, after a week on a milk diet, to have drunk himself almost to death, indulging his craving so heavily that one night he fell down in the snow, where, some would say, he was run over by a coach. Lee was called "the mad poet" by his contemporaries, and portraits of him do indeed show a hairstyle that is strangely wild and eyes that stare menacingly to one side, as though he had seen something amazing or terrifying. He was in and out of Bedlam, where he was allegedly whipped and starved. His age regarded him as insane, and he fully reciprocated the compliment: in dedicating *The Rival Queens* (1677) to Mulgrave, he called his world a "wild, unthinking, dissolute Age; an Age whose Business is senseless Riot, Neronian Gambols, and ridiculous Debauchery."[20]

Lee's application of the adjective "Neronian" to his own environment alerts us to the possibility that the excesses portrayed in his first play, *The Tragedy of Nero Emperour of Rome* (1674), may be more than sensational escapism. The title character is a bloodthirsty and sexually unnatural sadist. Among the many enormities he commits are sodomy and incest, sins that spring from and

---

20. See Roswell G. Ham, *Otway and Lee,* pp. 50, 51, 154, 207, 211, 212, and 220.

are associated with madness, which does not here, as was traditional, *follow* the sin as a punishment. Quite the contrary. It accompanies and helps explain the deeds. Nero is unnatural because he believes himself above nature. He thinks himself a god who can pervert men's tastes out of their natural course. Of his sodomy he says,

> Virtue's a name; Religion is a thing
> Fitter to scare poor Priests, than daunt a KING.
> Swift, as quick thought, through every art I range:
> Who but a GOD, like me, could Sexes change?
> Sporus be witness of my Mighty art;
> Sporus, now Lady, once Lord of my heart.
> . . . .
> I ranksack Nature; all its treasures view;
> Beings annihilate, and make a new:
> All this can I, your God-like Nero do.[21]

Such megalomania will defy nature even further, as Agrippina says before she is executed by command of the son who had violated her person:

> This Monster, under Tyrian purple hid
> Did force a passage to his Mother's bed.
> . . . .
> Monster of men, who altered nature's course,
> The stream ran backwards, and found out the Source.
> [1.1.141–42, 147–48]

Nero exemplifies one kind of sexual madness—God defying, nature altering; the good Britannicus exemplifies another—a kind that may have been very close to what Lee himself suffered in real life. The evilly mad Nero drives the good man to another kind of insanity, the kind that dreams about ideal purity. Against the unspeakable Nero, Britannicus, "true Heire of the Empire," as he is called in the Dramatis Personae, brother of the emperor's wife Octavia, places the tender image of his beloved Cyara:

> Here's a soft calm, and there a blustring storm.
> My Painter so shall draw me day and night:
> Here horrid darkness stands; there, gaudy light:
> There, cruelty, like the red Sea appears;
> Here, melting mercy flows in pitying tears.
> Exquisite Emblems! perfect good and evil:
> A Heav'n, a Hell, an Angel, and a Devil.
> [4.1.50–56]

21. 1.2.31–36, 40–42. The plays of Lee are quoted from *The Works of Nathaniel Lee,* ed. Thomas B. Stroup and Arthur L. Cooke, 2 vols. (New Brunswick, N.J.: Scarecrow Press, 1954). This edition supplies the line numbers used.

This somewhat artificial juxtaposition, which may be Lee's version of the
important *topos,* Hercules at the crossroads, is less effective than earlier, truly
"mad" responses to the captive Parthian princess, the "Angel" whom Britannicus loves but who now wears the disguise of a boy. When she tells him, to
win his pity, that his beloved is dead, the news is too much for his tender mind,
since he has just before learned that Nero stabbed Britannicus's pure and
beloved sister. He falls into madness, and the disguised Cyara, knowing now
she has gone too far, reveals her true identity. But Britannicus continues to
call her "boy," thinking he is in Elysium, where he sees the airy shape of his
sister among the heavenly forms in a garden. Such a vision of purity and
beauty is not unlike the exquisite setting and music of the land of the blessed
in Gluck's *Orfeo,* but here the dazzling white soon changes again to melancholy
sable: "The whole cope is dark, black, dismal" (3.1.125). This mad chiaroscuro
vision of lost love and purity is piercingly authentic. In the Rome of Nero—
and by implication in the London of Lee—the black melancholy prevails, and
Britannicus ends by saying to his beloved, whom he still does not recognize,
continuing to think her dead,

> Ha! shough; yonder flyes a night-Raven
> In each black eye there rowls a pound of Jet.
> See how he fans, with his huge wicker wings
> The dusky Ayr. Come, boy, be gone
> I'le save thee, though I dye me self: go in:
> Run, run, I say, I'le fetch my Bow and shoot him.
> [3.1.127–32]

The play, for all its crudities, does portray with considerable power two
contrasting types of love mania, that of Nero and that of his victim Britannicus, the one a lustful maniac who thinks he can alter the course of nature,
the other an ineffectual good man, deprived of his public and personal heritage, whose alienated mind alternates between white illusions of purity in love
and a black vision of torment. Lee displays a tender sensibility in a cruel world,
so tender that madness is the only escape from pain. One of the genuinely
touching moments of the play comes when Britannicus refuses to believe his
beloved stands before him:

> She could not lye, for she was all perfection:
> All beauty sickned when she left the world.
> [3.1.113–14]

Sexual evil continued to haunt Lee, as is evident from that Websterian
portrait of degenerate "Christian" Italy in *Caesar Borgia* (late 1679?), a collection of hideous atrocities that even surpass in exquisite cruelty those perpe-
trated by Nero. Two characters deserve brief attention, Ascanio Sforza for his

revolting lusts, natural and unnatural, and Borgia himself for his madness. Ascanio, newly named cardinal, is

> A fine effeminate Villain, bred in Brothels,
> Senseless, illiterate, the Jear of Rome,
> A blot to the whole See! One fitter far
> For Hospitals, that paints and patches up
> A wretched Carkass worried in the Stews.
>
> [1.1.13–17]

He attempts to bribe Machiavelli, who proves to be a character of persuasive, though frightening, reality, by offering him "little American Boys with Boxes of Jewels in their hands" (1.1, s.d.). Ascanio—self-regarding, drunken, gaudy, illiterate, who kisses cardinals but also dreams of women and their "alluring flesh" (1.1.29)—is what Machiavelli calls him, a "walking lump of Lust" (1.1.203). He is also what Pope called Sporus, an "amphibious thing." It is hard not to believe that the contemporary audience saw in him a savage portrait of the Restoration fop. If so, his death by poisoning after grotesque suffering reveals the profound alienation of Lee's spirit from his age, on which he takes the revenge of a hideous *humour noir:*

> I burn, I burn, I toste, I roste, and my Guts fry,
> They blaze, they snap, they bounce like Squibs
> And Crackers: I am all fire—
>
> [5.3.232–34]

Toward the end of the play Lee brings into view the obsessive theme of madness caused by love and crime. Borgia, guided by Machiavelli, has accomplished the strangulation of his wife, Bellamira, whose infidelity he suspects, after she has been forced to witness the murder of her father and all the rest of her family. But his rage, which has been violent ("My Veins are all on Fire, / And I could wade up to the eyes in blood," 5.1.151–52), soon cools, only to be replaced by what he calls a "Melancholly, which will . . . destroy me" (5.1.240). When Machiavelli says that after Borgia is crowned emperor of Rome he will surely find a woman among his spoils, Borgia replies,

> Ha! no more, I charge thee.
> I swear I was at ease, and had forgot her:
> Why did'st thou wake me then, to turn me wild,
> And rouze the slumbering Orders of my Soul?
> To my charm'd Ears no more of Woman tell;
> Name not a Woman, and I shall be well.
> Like a poor Lunatick that makes his moan,
> And for a time beguiles the lookers on;
> He reasons well; his eyes their wildness lose,

> And vows the Keepers his wrong'd sense abuse:
> But if you hit the Cause that hurt his Brain,
> Then his teeth gnash, he foams, he shakes his Chain.
> His Eye-balls rowl, and he is mad again.
>
> [5.1.256–68]

The last part of this passage has been thought to be autobiographical, a description of Lee's own experience at Bedlam. More important is the sense it conveys of how precarious is the calm not only of a criminal but perhaps also of all fallen creatures, whose minds can be distracted by the mere use of a word, even a word that should invoke love, delicacy, and beauty. Borgia's is not a successful dramatic character and should not be analyzed too finely. But its very confusions and complications show the volatile nature of love, sometimes promising peace, sometimes opening the way to generous action, but more often than not torturing the mind to rage and madness.

Theodosius (Spring 1680?), a play profoundly ambiguous about the nature of Christianity and paganism and suggestive of Swift in its association of Christian enthusiasm and melancholy, continues to link love and madness. In its epistle dedicatory the playwright reveals himself as obsessed with the dangerous prevalence of his own wild imagination:

> It has been often observed against me, That I
> abound in ungovern'd Fancy; but I hope the World
> will pardon the Sallies of Youth: Age, Despondence,
> and Dulness come too fast of themselves.

The prologue presents the poet as inevitably cursed:

> On poets onely no kind Star e're smill'd;
> Curst Fate has damn'd 'em every Mothers Child.
> . . . .
> Tasso ran mad, and noble Spencer starv'd.
>
> [31–32, 36]

The play introduces a woman (Pulcheria) who is more of a ruler than her soft and kindly brother, and in Theodosius we see a Persian effeminacy that he is urged to cast aside. The play raises vexing questions about the power and place of woman, the feminizing of life that is sometimes seen as a Christian phenomenon, and the dangers to civilized life when sexual distinction is blurred. In the much misunderstood *Princess of Cleve* (1682?) the bisexual Nemours may be a direct attack on Rochester; if so, the portrayal may reveal a more profound revulsion at the Restoration rake than did the character of Ascanio Sforza.[22]

22. See Robert D. Hume, "The Satiric Design of Nat. Lee's *The Princess of Cleve*," *Journal of English and Germanic Philology* 75 (Jan.–April 1976): 117–38.

Lee's finest play, one that deserves much more attention than it has received, *Lucius Junius Brutus* (1680), can best be viewed not as a full-blown political allegory or a classical tragedy but as a pathetic or affective play and as a psychological family drama.[23] The title character, a powerful, noble, ascetic, and austere republican, is brought into the sharpest conflict with human sexuality and love. He demands that his son Titus renounce his bride Teraminta without touching her, even though she is "beautiful," "chastely good," and "most sweetly fram'd." He finds the thought of his son's marriage loathsome:

> Who would be there at such polluted Rites
> But Goats, Baboons, some chatt'ring old Silenus;
> Or Satyrs, grinning at your slimy joys?
> [1.1.214–16]

Small wonder the son proves to be impotent when attempting the consummation of his marriage! As a contrast to Teraminta's warmth and passion, Brutus admiringly points to the snowy chastity of Lucrece, and he everywhere resists the newer kind of sensibility that he associates with female predominance. If one takes the point of view of the tenderest victims, *Lucius Junius Brutus* arouses searing emotions of terror and pity. Can a father be admirable who also decrees the flogging and decapitation of one son, a fate from which the other son is spared only when a consul mercifully stabs him? And yet, despite his cruelties, it is very difficult to dethrone Brutus as a hero and transform him into a villain. It may be hard for modern flesh and blood to acquiesce in such harshness as Brutus exemplifies; but if the play is regarded as a psychological drama about the head of a family, then we are better prepared for it. For our age, of all ages, is surely the best prepared to understand the deep ambivalence that lies in fathers and fatherhood. Brutus is, above all else, a father, "aw-ful, God-like, and Commanding" (1.1.247):

> Thou would'st have thought, such was his Majesty,
> That the Gods Lightned from his awful eyes,
> And Thunder'd from his tongue.
> [2.1.490–92]

Toward such a father, as perhaps toward his own clergyman father, Lee must have had deeply ambiguous feelings, particularly because of Brutus's cruel offenses to normal human tenderness, sexual and familial. Nevertheless, an author who had been so much preoccupied with sexual and emotional excess and its attendant madness may also have felt that such stoical, indeed such

23. The exponents of this view are Rothstein in *Restoration Tragedy*, pp. 91–96, and David M. Vieth, "Psychological Myth as Tragedy: Nathaniel Lee's *Lucius Junius Brutus*," *Huntington Library Quarterly*, 39 (Nov. 1975): 57–76. I am deeply indebted to Vieth's highly persuasive psychological reading of this play, with its emphasis upon the father figure.

surgically cruel purity was sometimes necessary to purge society of rooted corruption. The power of the play may finally lie in its totally uncompromising portrayal of superegoistic austerity, at once loving and cruel, fearsome and indispensable. Brutus may indeed be the archetypal father of the Western world who has, off and on in history, extirpated from life sentimental and sexual excess. But to post-Romantic sensibility it may seem that Lee was never madder, though certainly never more dramatically effective, than when he suggested as the cure for the evils and dangers of physical love so single-minded a conscience as that possessed by Lucius Junius Brutus. Lee has given us the exact antithesis of the close association between sexual love and revolutionary energy that we find in Blake, Shelley, and Marcuse. For the Roman father of his country, lust and instability were linked evils; order and chastity, the heavenly twins. And he has also given us, well before its flowering, the antitype of sentimental tenderness and love.

It may at first seem totally illogical to include in a chapter on sexual abnormality and love morbidity a play like Congreve's so-called tragedy, *The Mourning Bride* (February 1697). It carefully and schematically distributes justice; it was written, according to its dedication, to "recommend and to encourage Vertue"; and it made nature, not art, its aim, "for only Nature can affect the Heart" (prologue). Because it was both virtuous and natural, moral and pathetic, the play won the approval of Samuel Johnson, who selected one of its most eloquent and orotund meditations on mortality as being "the most poetical paragraph" from the "whole mass of English poetry."[24] Almeria grieves over a supposedly dead husband, known for his "Worth, his Truth, and Tenderness of Love" (1.1.103), a husband she lost in a shipwreck on the same day she married him. He belonged to a rival city and was hated by her father the king. The "late" spouse was in general much kindlier than her own father, who now decrees her nuptials to one Garcia, and the prospect of marrying him casts her into a deep faint. Congreve seems to make more of this father-daughter misunderstanding than to regard it as either an isolated instance or a traditional *topos:* a genuinely intellectual and spiritual generation gap separates the paternal representative of the old, warlike order from the filial representative of the newer and more humane order of sentimental affection that can forget ancient feuds. In 1697 we are, then, in the presence of a sensibility very close to that of one of the reformers of English feeling, Richard Steele. Visiting the tomb of her husband, Almeria encounters some-

---

24. Life of Congreve, *Works* (1825) 8:31. The passage, beginning "It was a fancy'd Noise" and ending "affrights me with its Echo's" (2.1.52–69), is brought into a conversation between Johnson and Garrick, in which Johnson, much to Garrick's alarm for the reputation of Shakespeare, repeats and supports his superlatives. See Boswell, *Life of Johnson,* 2:85–87. *The Mourning Bride* is quoted from *The Complete Plays of William Congreve,* ed. Herbert Davis (Chicago: University of Chicago Press, 1967).

one who resembles him and who turns out to be none other than he himself. He is now in serious danger, because he is imprisoned by a hostile tyrant (Almeria's father) and loved by Zara, a determined and energetic rival to his wife. Zara's love turns to hatred when she discovers that someone else is preferred, whereupon she utters two famous lines that have become somewhat shopworn:

> Heav'n has no Rage, like Love to Hatred turn'd,
> Nor Hell a Fury, like a Woman scorn'd.
>
> [3.1.457–58]

Almeria's father sentences the husband to death by public execution, a decision enforced by his belated discovery that his prisoner is the Alphonso he had thought lost: so complicated do matters become that Almeria must kneel before her father and protest that she is innocent of planning parricide, revealing at the same time that the doomed prisoner is her husband, for whose life she pleads. Resolution comes because the obsessed Zara, despite her rage, continues to love Alphonso and desires to free him; because Gonsalez mistakenly kills the king, who has disguised himself as Alphonso; because Zara then mistakes the king for her beloved, whereupon she drinks poison. So evil recoils upon itself in wanton destruction, and in the end only the good live to rule Granada. The once mourning bride can wipe her tears and allow the marriage, which disaster interrupted on its first day, to be consummated.

But for all the decorous regularity and moral didacticism of the plot and the sentiments, *The Mourning Bride* is suffused with an attractive air of mortality. Its charnel house atmosphere does of course look back to the baroque preoccupation with skeletons, bones, graves, and ghosts. But it also looks ahead to the Graveyard Gothic and establishes a link between love and death. If death is here not so voluptuously presented as in earlier seventeenth-century painting and poetry, it is perhaps because the Restoration has added too much of the clear and commonsensical to its contemplations of mortality. But the gloom of this play is by no means dissipated by rational light; there is an almost erotic attachment to the funereal. At the opening Almeria kneels to pledge eternal faithfulness to her dead husband and dead father-in-law (another benevolent man). She visits the place of burial, which strikes her with "an Awe / And Terror" (2.1.63–64) that are far from unpleasing. She herself longs for death and labels as "Friendly" the "Yawn" of the open tomb (2.2.14). The imagery becomes unmistakably sensual:

> Death, grim Death, will fold
> Me in his leaden Arms, and press me close
> To his cold clayie Breast.
>
> [2.2.20–22]

Eternity—and here Almeria becomes as baroque as the Dryden of the sublime odes—she envisions as "liquid Light," and she imagines herself floating in "Seas of Bliss," in an "Exstacy of Thought," imagining herself reunited with her husband (2.2.27–30). The death wishes do not continue at quite so erotic a pitch (we must remember that the marriage was unconsummated at the time of the husband's "death"), but they do not disappear, either; and it is only the deus ex machina conclusion that releases us from the cold graves and clammy prisons, from headless corpses and icy bodies, all of which have been presented with a strange, attractive power. Although, as I have said, in structure and on the surface, all is scrupulously moral and healthy, throughout most of the play the bride continues to mourn and reveals herself as more than half in love with easeful death. Fidelity is not celebrated here as a happy sunlit state of matrimonial joy; its satisfactions derive from the grave. If Lee's morbidity ran to violence and madness, Congreve's in this play runs to a melancholy that creeps around his structures like Sandburg's and Eliot's fog. In this play he was, like Webster, "much possessed by death / And saw the skull beneath the skin."[25]

Otway's Tears of Morbidity and Dennis's "Vulgar Passions"

Thomas Otway fully deserves the reputation he possessed for over a century following his death—that of a tender, loving writer whose serious works, more than those of any other Restoration dramatist, aroused the pity that Aristotle required and who remained for generations the examplar *par excellence* of the pathetic. Since that quality was admired greatly as, along with the sublime, the very nerve of poetry, Otway's reputation as a tragedian was inflated until he occupied a position "next to Shakespeare" as a natural portrayer of human affections. It has not been sufficiently realized that the tears Otway shed and produced are as much the tears of morbidity as magnanimity, and it is not unreasonable to suppose that these qualities also may have colored the literary emotionalism of his many successors and raised on the cheek of eighteenth-century eroticism a blush of hectic red.

The legendary life of Otway prepares us for more than tears. Like Lee's, his "fiery face" was "painted with the juice of Vines,"[26] and he met, at the Christological age of thirty-three, an untimely end about which legends have clustered. Something of a vagabond, he is supposed to have been familiar with hunger, thirst, and cold. And, most romantically of all, he suffered from unrequited passion for the great Mrs. Barry, who immortalized the roles he

25. T. S. Eliot, "Whispers of Immortality," 1–2.
26. These phrases come from Shadwell's unpleasant verse picture of Otway. See Ham, *Otway and Lee,* p. 183.

created for her and who answered his ardors by loving the noble and licentious Rochester.[27] Otway's love was unfolded in those strange, undated *Familiar Letters,* perhaps written in 1682 and published in 1697, six missives without address, date, or superscription and with only an occasional signature, that seem to come from nowhere and may not be authentic.[28] But whether they are authentic or not, they constitute a good introduction to the man's response to love: if not written by Otway himself, they were doubtless produced by someone who knew the man and his plays and was attempting to create a believable extension of them. The letters contain professions of undying love in two complementary but fully distinguishable moods—one of tender purity of spirit that expresses itself in floods of unselfish devotion, the other of wild, frenzied, and violent passion and desire: "I *Love,* I *Doat,* I am *Mad,* and know no measure" (letter 2; 2:478).

Otway's slim collection of nondramatic literature also suggests that his "pathos" is more complicated than its later association with bourgeois domestic sentimentality would suggest. Like Dryden, he was attracted to Ovid and, again like Dryden, particularly to the incestuous stories, translating the heroic epistle "Phaedra to Hippolytus" and thus linking himself with the most famous play of Racine, whom he admired and whose tender and delicate sensibility he imitated. His poetry shows friendship to be a reinforcement of love. A *"much-lov'd Friend"* joins Otway in pastoral retreat, wasting the day in "shady, peacefull Bowers," and at its end each, taking his beloved to bed, fills every sense with "perfect pleasure": "With twining limbs, that still loves posture keep." Even political allegory and satire provide a romantic landscape and mood. The poet seeks the lonely heath. Like Gray in the next century, he is glued to a tree. He sheds tender and violent tears. He remembers his mother and his "much-lov'd fondled" boyhood. Above all, he thinks of the severe and "awfull" majesty of his beloved—as unavailable in rhyme as Mrs. Barry was in real life.[29]

The comedies, for which Otway was well known in his own day, are bitterly satirical, shockingly scabrous, full of sexual monsters, unfaithful friends, and cowardly cuckolds, with little optimism about the institution of marriage or indeed about the promise of any fulfillment in life or love.[30] The harsh realism of Otway's comic world is by no means an annihilating contradiction of the world of the tender tragedies or of his serious sensibilities. It complements

27. For a brief life of Elizabeth Barry, see John Harold Wilson, *All the King's Ladies: Actresses of the Restoration* (Chicago: University of Chicago Press, 1958), pp. 110–17.

28. These are printed in J. C. Ghosh, ed., *The Works of Thomas Otway,* 2 vols. (Oxford: Clarendon Press, 1932), 2:475–81 and discussed briefly, ibid., 1:13–14.

29. Ibid., 2:427–32 ("Phaedra to Hyppolytus"), 443–46 ("Epistle to *R. D.* from T. O.," 1, 30, 93, 95), 405–26 ("The Poet's Complaint of his Muse," 53, 107).

30. See Robert D. Hume, "Otway and the Comic Muse," *Studies in Philology* 73 (Jan. 1976): 87–116.

the elevated and mythical world which is our chief concern and shows that the morbidities I shall dwell on sprang from the frustrations of real life.

Our analysis of the amorous aspects of Otway's tragic muse can begin with his second play, *Don Carlos* (1676), since in this "Heroic Play" he tried to embody the pathos of Racine's *Bérénice* and believed he had succeeded in drawing "Tears from the Eyes of the Auditors, I mean those whose Souls were capable of so Noble a pleasure."[31] Certainly Otway's claim that his play was "pathetick" is vindicated by its conclusion, which—with sincere and mutual forgiveness all around before the death of the lovers and the madness of the greatly sinning king seal up all in silence—realizes with considerable success the Aristotelian aim of evoking pity. The central love in the story is illicit: the young prince, Don Carlos, continues to love the young queen, who had been intended for him before his father married her, and that affection is fully returned. The love is obsessively called incest by the madly jealous father, husband, and monarch, an epithet also used by the queen, though less frequently and in denial of any overt act. There are so many recollections of *Hamlet* in the whole first part of the play that Otway may be thought to have given Shakespeare's masterpiece a modern Oedipal reading. However that may be, the deep love between Don Carlos and the queen is viewed legalistically as a forbidden affection between stepson and stepmother, though it is actually a love between two young people protesting against the greater unnaturalness and illicitness of unions between youth and age. What is forgiven at the end by the father and what is repented of by the son (who concedes he should have been submissive to his father) is a quasi- or mock incestuous affection that is profound but never physically realized. Since the good and suffering queen never repents but exults in it as she dies on the bosom of her lover and contemplates an eternity of bliss with him, we must regard the love as good, however society or a jealous old monarch may classify it. And it receives the approval of the healthy and youthful Don Juan, a Restoration "naturalist" who attacks the "dull Law" that overrules nature and so destroys man's freedom to obey his "Godlike mind" (2.1.1, 6). One may be reluctant to call the love in this play morbid, but it is certainly unconventional and obsessive, and it attacks the very roots of social and political stability.

It was *The Orphan* (1680) and *Venice Preserved* (1682) that gave Otway the reputation, in Samuel Johnson's words, of being "one of the first names in the English drama" and, in Goldsmith's, of ranking "next to Shakespeare" as "the greatest genius England has produced in tragedy." His popularity was broadly based. Gay said in the early eighteenth century that "saunt'ring 'prentices o'er Otway weep," and the Romantics treated him as a legendary poet-lover whom society misunderstood and persecuted; they looked upon Jaffeir from *Venice Preserved* as a *schöne Seele* and Pierre as a Romantic rebel. Byron thought the

31. *Works of Otway*, 1:174. The line numbers used in quoting this play come from this edition.

last mentioned as immortal as the stones of his native Venice: "And Pierre cannot be swept or worn away."[32]

Because of its reputation for tender sensibility, we come to *The Orphan* expecting to shed tears of pity over the plight of its delicate heroine. Johnson said that "its whole power is upon the affections";[33] and Rowe, a disciple, had earlier praised it for touching the nerves of "good nature," of "tenderness or humanity."[34] The play does indeed satisfy the expectations aroused by such criticism. It is given a remote pastoral setting, far away from courts and cities, where a loyal but retired subject of the king lives with his two sons who love each other and also with a daughter and an adopted girl, the orphan of the title. Are we back in Eden? Are we in a land of romance and chivalry (the real boar hunt resembles a tapestry on castle walls)? Or are we in the land of late childhood or early adolescence (the young brothers dream of the future and their careers)? The heroine is gentle and dovelike, and it is not difficult to shed tears over her great sufferings, which never embitter her sweetness.

But one is not far into the play before discovering that the view of Otway as only, or even primarily, an artist of delicate pathos seems shallow and inadequate. We confront disturbingly morbid suggestions and gaze into psychological abysses. Rowe also had a sense of this, for in the midst of his praise of Otway's power to evoke pity he confessed to "an uneasiness"[35]—an extremely accurate word for the emotion that creeps over us as this isolated Eden turns into a place of primal fear. The two brothers, seemingly gracious and mutually devoted, soon quarrel over possession in love of the fair orphan Monimia, who has been raised with them as a sister. From this quarrel the whole tragedy proceeds. Monimia's brother, Chamont, who arrives home from the wars, has dreamed that she holds a wanton lover in each hand and that a witch has told him she is a pawn in a grim, fraternal game.[36] But the sensuality, which develops as the innocence of the house melts away, is more delicate than in Chamont's conventional dream—and more insinuating.[37] The

32. *Childe Harold's Pilgrimage,* 4.4. The other quotations in the paragraph are from: Johnson, Life of Otway, *Works* (1825), 7:173; Goldsmith and Gay, quoted in Aline M. Taylor, *Next to Shakespeare: Otway's "Venice Preserv'd" and "The Orphan" and Their History on the London Stage* (Durham, N.C.: Duke University Press, 1950), pp. 3, 245. See also ibid., pp. 4, 248–52.

33. Life of Otway, *Works* (1825), 7:175.

34. Quoted by Eugene Waith, "Tears of Magnanimity in Otway and Racine," in *French and English Drama of the Seventeenth Century* (Los Angeles: Clark Memorial Library, 1972), p. 19.

35. Quoted ibid.

36. Eric Rothstein, who believes the action of *The Orphan* "turns on the idea of Nature," shrewdly perceives that Chamont's is "a sort of perversely erotic dream that foreshadows the incest in the play." *Restoration Tragedy,* pp. 100, 102.

37. I find the evil in this play domestic, even "primal," to use a modern word; but Aline M. Taylor, in a sensitive reading, finds it to be "the atmosphere of court corruption," which somehow the old cavalier Acasto has brought with him to the country in his flight from the royal circle. She finds that convention therefore takes on the "external force of Fate." See her edition of the play in the Regents Restoration Drama Series (Lincoln: University of Nebraska Press, 1976), p. xxviii. My quotations and the act and line references derive from this edition of *The Orphan.*

older brother, Castalio, receives reports about Monimia's swelling breasts from the page, who is promised a pony if he brings further information—about the color of her stockings and her habit of gartering them above the knees. It is this brother whom Monimia loves and marries, who is at first assertive, then deceitful, about his intentions, and who ultimately becomes vengeful and fierce, his last hope being that confusion in nature and society will break the chain of causes and dissolve all forms and his last word being that he himself is nothing. The agent who produces the suffering and the tragedy is the younger brother, Polydore, who strikes out at Castalio in searing sexual rivalry for the love of a girl who is as close as a sister in this isolated familial society. The decisive act comes on the night the secret marriage is to be consummated. Monimia approaches the event with foreboding and "soft compassion" (3.1.276). The dangerously brooding Polydore, ignorant of the marriage, overhears the signal that will bring the bridal pair together in what seems to him like an illicit and faithless love tryst. Taking his brother's place that night, he reaps Castalio's fruit and commits what Laudian Anglo-Catholicism was firm in calling incest. The rightful husband is turned away from his nuptial door, and the bride is ravished in darkness by a brother whom she believes to be her husband. When the truth comes out the next day, she continues to love her lord, not her ravisher. She goes mad and drinks poison, but not before she is revealed as "the trembling, tender, kind, deceived Monimia" (5.1.453), who takes no comfort in her innocence but considers herself irremediably polluted. Here Otway reveals a striking contrast to Dryden, who in *Don Sebastian* kept even a blood incest emotionally guiltless since it was done in ignorance.

Polydore's reaction to the night of "rage and incest" (5.1.427), as he calls what he has caused, is also one of shock and disbelief—what he had thought was a more or less natural act of defloration he now learns was a betrayal of a brother which the law regarded as incestuous. Before he knows the full truth, he proposes the murder of the child that could result, and he envisions himself and Monimia going out into the world like the expelled Adam and Eve. In the accursed nature they would then encounter, adders sting and poisons "hang / Like gums against the walls" (4.1.454–55), a nature where "Desire shall languish like a withering flower, / And no distinction of the sex be thought of" (459–60). Natural humanity Polydore feels to be perverted even before the whole truth has been revealed to him.

The play is full of crude improbabilities, and these have been vividly pointed out from the time of Voltaire to the present. Of the wedding night, one critic has said, "O! What an infinite deal of Mischief would a farthing rush-light have prevented."[38] But a realistic standard of criticism is as egre-

---

38. David Erskine Baker, ed., *Biographia Dramatica*, new ed., 2 vols. (London, 1782), 2:266. Voltaire's views are discussed by Ghosh in *Works of Otway*, 1:51. Clifford Leach vividly summarizes

giously inappropriate as a purely logical one. In Otway's world of primal psychology, it can be said that his lack of Dryden-like coherence or the power of crisp, clear statement, his confusion of emphasis, his jarring and unresolved juxtapositions are in fact virtues, since they open doors upon the unplumbed depths of the soul. No Christian norms are invoked or even implied. The world is primitive, virtually a familial state of nature. Experience comes crashing in with a fatal accident that leads all the principals to suicide. They end loving and forgiving one another, to be sure—the pattern of *Don Carlos* being repeated—but they are kept destitute of the hope of immortality that the queen in the earlier play dreams of or that Shakespeare and Dryden gave to Antony and Cleopatra. Otway concentrates upon what became for the eighteenth century and the Romantics the most intense zone of psychological geography, the frontier between innocence and experience. The three leading characters all cross it, meeting pollution and anger, guilt and early sorrow. Love was briefer than a candle and was in its short career perverted before being blasted. Otway has discovered the fearful complications that lurk in familial love, in primal affections, and in unions of similitude.[39] The two brothers and their fair "sister" commit, with a kind of tragic and choiceless inevitability, the narcissistic sins against which Milton had warned. Anyone who follows in detail the career of eighteenth-century love will understand the steady popularity of a play that explores the intimate world of family love and exposes its potential morbidity.

Venice Preserved, a better but less typical play, is set in a public world of political plots and civil strife. It too is suffused with psychosexual energies and their frustration. Its most notorious sections, the Nicky-Nacky scenes, constitute a farcical *reductio* of a famous political leader to absurdity, but they also portray sexual perversion. "Nicky Nack" refers to the female pudenda, and old Antonio (Anthony Ashley Cooper, the first earl of Shaftesbury, Dryden's Achitophel)[40] is debased to wooing a prostitute, while crawling on his knees, bearing a bag of gold, talking baby talk, soliciting her kicks, barking like a dog, biting her, and howling with pleasure at her lashings. Taine has called all this "la grande buffonerie amère, le sentiment cru de la bassesse humaine."[41]

the improbabilities of the plot in "Restoration Tragedy: A Reconsideration," reprinted in *Restoration Drama: Modern Essays in Criticism,* ed. John Loftis (New York: Oxford University Press, 1966), p. 154.

39. In the early 1670s the propriety of marriage between first cousins was apparently much discussed. Opposing the papal prohibition, resisting the wave of opposition in England, and arguing that nothing in Scripture or Anglican polity forbids these marriages, Samuel Dugard(?) published in 1673 an interesting tract arguing that such marriage is "very innocent": *The Marriages of Cousin Germans, Vindicated from the Censures of Unlawfullnesse, and Inexpediency* (Oxford, 1673), p. 5.

40. On the political allusions in this play, see John Robert Moore, "Contemporary Satire in Otway's *Venice Preserved,*" *PMLA* 43 (March 1928): 166–81.

41. Quoted by Ghosh in *Works of Otway,* 1:59. Act, scene, and line references of *Venice Preserved* come from this edition (vol. 2).

Undoubtedly. But let us not confine the *bassesse* to Nicky-Nacky. The whole play is instinct with morbid or regressive sexuality; on one scholar's count, there are some thirty direct and indirect references to female breasts.[42]

Love and friendship do survive in the end, as they did in *The Orphan;* but they are here, as also in the earlier play, frustrated into tragic defeat and death and made complex and ambiguous. Always there is the suggestion of unexplained, unexplainable psychological depth. The love of Belvidera and Jaffeir, which began in a rescue of the lady during the venerable ceremony of the city's wedding with the sea, is confirmed in marriage and the birth of a handsome boy and then is suddenly and mischievously complicated when five years after the rescue and three years after the marriage, a jealous father feels his daughter has been stolen from him by a husband he now banishes from wealth and station. The young wife, in the crisis that ensues, proves soon to be an overmatch for her loving husband, whose weakness of character and infirmity of purpose appear in contrast. Belvidera is a bold as well as lovely woman, a civilizer as well as a leader of men, who is not ashamed to say to her husband,

> I joy more in thee,
> Than did thy Mother when she hugg'd thee first,
> And bless'd the Gods for all her Travel past.
>
> . . . .
>
> Oh lead me to some Desart wide and wild,
>
> . . . .
>
> Where I may throw my eager Arms about thee,
> Give loose to Love with kisses, kindling Joy,
> And let off all the Fire that's in my Heart.
> [1.332–34, 348, 353–55]

Quite a contrast to the trembling Monimia! But Belvidera's aggressiveness is no more availing against the forces of destruction than the orphan's gentle sweetness.

The rebels against the selfish authorities of the Venetian state may at first seem to be as good as the Romantics thought them. But Pierre's cry of hatred "Burn! . . . burn" (1.277–78) is not nobly but sexually and jealously motivated, since his basic complaint is that his beloved Greek prostitute Aquilina is being wooed by the old and lecherous Venetian senator. The rebellion as it develops and draws Jaffeir into its net also demands the sacrifice of healthy sexual love: the husband must apparently follow the revolutionary, who intends to banish "all tender humane Follies / Out of my bosom" (2.193–94), and then after his sacrifice must discover that his wife is being made the object of the illicit depredations of old Renault, an ally of Pierre and a man of

42. William H. McBurney, "Otway's Tragic Muse Debauched: Sensuality in *Venice Preserv'd,*" *Journal of English and Germanic Philology* 58 (July 1959): 393.

despicable sexual mores. The heroine may be extreme in her designation of the rebels as a pack of "Common stabbers, / Nose-slitters, Ally-lurking Villains" (3.2.162–63). But there is a spirit of moral ambiguity that hangs over their characters and action. As the plot moves to its climax, Jaffeir is torn between love of the now disillusioned Belvidera and loyalty to his word and to the leader of the conspiracy, whom he also truly loves. His love pulls him toward treacherous betrayal, his loyalty toward an ineffectual and doomed action. Jaffeir, being weak, is pulled in both directions—a fatality that leads to his wife's madness; his friend's death, preceded by his violent anger and then his forgiveness; and finally his own death, a divided soul wavering between conflicting duties. Are these duties and the hesitations they cause intellectually definable, like those of Dryden's Antony, torn between Egypt and Rome? Scarcely, for this is not so much a conflict of values as one of eroticisms. Jaffeir is nothing if not loving and emotional, and it is his loving *coeur sensible* that explains his fate.

> JAFF. No, *Belvidera;* by th' eternal truth,
> I doat with too much fondness.
> BELV.   Still so kind?
> Still then do you love me?
> JAFF.   Nature, in her workings,
> Inclines not with more ardour to Creation,
> Than I doe now towards thee; man ne'er was bless'd
> Since the first pair first met, as I have been.
> [5.266–71]

These expressions of love come after Pierre has been condemned, an act over which Jaffeir grieves and for which he feels agonizingly responsible. And when Pierre moves toward his death, the pull of friendship takes on almost the same erotic force as the heterosexual love.

> PIERRE.   Dost thou love me?
> JAFF. Rip up my heart, and satisfie thy doubtings.
> PIERRE. Curse on this weakness. (*He weeps.*)
> [5.438–40]

On the scaffold together, Jaffeir stabs Pierre and then himself, leaving the mad Belvidera to die alone in the final act.

As in *The Orphan,* the principals die without Christian hope (Pierre spurns the priest's attendance), and it is hard to find a normative character, intellectual or ethical, in the entire play, although Belvidera comes the closest. Dryden the critic did not even search for a choric center: he placed Otway's excellence in the portrayal of the passions, which are "truly touched" in *Venice Preserved* even "though perhaps there is somewhat to be desired, both in the grounds of them and in the height and elegance of expression." Otway's genius lay in expressing what Dryden in the same essay called the "passions and motions of the mind."[43] Those passions are, in both of Otway's best-known plays, at once tender and violent, arising alike from love and friendship and the conflict between them and with society—in the first the small society of the family, in the second the larger one of the state. The generation gap looms large in *Venice Preserved,* where youth and beauty, kindliness and love seem almost entirely the domain of the young, who are destroyed by their elders. In both plays, though more prominently in *The Orphan,* love is tinged with morbidity or ambiguity, and in the end lovers and friends are alike brought to destruction. Otway raises tender love and friendship and then destroys them in untimely death. Sensibility, no less than heroism, drives on toward the grave, which swallows up, in silence and with no hopes for futurity, all kinds of affection. The bold healthy love that Belvidera possesses is as surely destroyed as the quasi-incestuous love that tortured the queen in *Don Carlos* or the quasi-incestuous act that doomed the orphan Monimia.

Otway was at once a highly emotional and natural artist. But nature was less an ethical norm, a *frein vital,* than a stimulus to passion, a sanction of tears and sensibility. One demonstration that Otway was riding the tidal wave of the future is that he found almost at once a critic who appreciated his achievement and who embodied at the very heart of his critical system those natural emotional and psychological values implicit in his best plays. For John Dennis the sublime (the lofty, the fearful) was virtually the same as the pathetic (the emotional), nature was virtually equated with passion, and original genius expressed "Furious Joy, or Pride, or Astonishment." "Poetical Genius . . . is it self a Passion," and it is the task of the critic to inquire if the passion is "terrible and tender." Dennis provides a fitting conclusion not only to Otway but also to my discussion of the entire Restoration. An admirer of *The Orphan* as a play that moves compassion, Dennis was also deeply related to the movement whose beginning I have analyzed. He admired Milton as a Christian writer; and in fact for Dennis the coming of Christ altered nature so that reason and passion need no longer be at war, it being now possible to make the bliss of Eden a desideratum in real life. Dennis admired the fire and force of Nat. Lee, and he was close to Dryden during the last years of that poet's life and seems in fact to have inherited his whole concept of heroic love and pity and to have carried over into criticism the motion of his genius toward forgiveness and Christian

---

43. "A Parallel betwixt Painting and Poetry" (1695) in George Watson, ed., *Dryden: Critical Essays,* 2:201. H. James Jensen, quite properly, sees that this play "is not an imitation of an action in the Aristotelian sense but is rather an imitation of a series of motions. *Motion* in the seventeenth century is equivalent not only to the motion of action but also to emotion." *The Muses' Concord: Literature, Music, and the Visual Arts in the Baroque Age* (Bloomington: Indiana University Press, 1976), p. 92.

sensibility. Like Dryden, he found Virgil, especially in Book 4 of the *Aeneid,* productive of passion and compassion, and the love verses of Ovid, which Dryden had translated so skillfully and assiduously, he found "soft and . . . pathetick," "tender and yet . . . delicate." Such language summarizes the course I have followed so far and also looks ahead to the pages that remain.[44]

Dennis does not utter new truths so much as give critical support to impulses that were in fact transforming Western culture. Value was being shifted from an external and revealed standard to the arena of man's soul, and along with the subjectivizing and psychologizing of truth went its democratization. If it was revolutionary to discover that *all* men have souls, it was also revolutionary to discover that these souls could be trusted, emotionally and intuitively, to discover the truth. For Dennis poetry became an instrument of the new psychology. All poetry arouses passion, and this passion is of two large kinds: the "Enthusiastick" (that is, the contemplative, the meditative, which "belong[s] not to common Life") and the "Vulgar" (anger aroused by an affront, pity by sight of a mournful object). Of these two the more powerful is the vulgar. "Thus there are two sorts of Passion to be rais'd in Poetry, the Vulgar and the Enthusiastick; to which last, the Vulgar is preferable, because all Men are capable of being moved by the Vulgar, and a Poet writes to all" (1:338, 339; cf. 215). The statement is an important critical utterance, anticipating central positions of critics as diverse as Johnson, Wordsworth, and Shelley. Dennis is important in a study of love and sensibility because on the threshold of what has been too often called the age of reason he proclaims the primacy of the passions in art and justifies that primacy by their presence in all men everywhere. Growing inwardness and growing democratization may have characterized all the literature of the next hundred years; they are peculiarly associated with the literature of love. The profundity of that journey into the interior is revealed by the pain and embarrassment that it disclosed. It is therefore understandable that with deepening love-sensibility came morbidity. The price of achieving what Lawrence Stone has called "affective individualism"[45] was a *frisson* of terror as man tried to come to terms with a freer expression of his own erotic nature.

44. *The Critical Works of John Dennis,* ed. Edward Niles Hooker, 2 vols. (Baltimore: Johns Hopkins Press, 1939, 1943), 1:1, 47, 127, 133; 2:67, 121, 122, 196.
45. *Family, Sex and Marriage,* p. 4 and passim.

5. Woman in Love: The Abandoned and Passionate Mistress

*W*HAT DO THE FOLLOWING WOMEN have in common: an ancient Carthaginian queen brought strikingly to the attention of Restoration England in the vigorous couplets of Dryden, a young nun isolated in a convent in Portugal whose putative letters are published in literary French by a late seventeenth-century man of the world, a dramatic heroine who lives in Genoa and brings tears to the eyes of English audiences for the better part of a century, and a medieval French religious whose heart is revealed in the virtuoso couplets of eighteenth-century England's greatest poet? Generally considered, all belonged to the powerful current of eros and sensibility that was transforming English mentality and manners. More specifically, Dido, Marianna Alcoforado, Calista, and Eloisa had all been passionately in love and all exercised a large influence, through the medium of expressive and reflective language, upon subsequent literary and artistic culture. Three of them—for here we may have to exclude Calista, the heroine of Nicholas Rowe's play—stand in the pantheon of modern love as virtually mythic beings who transcend the heroines of Dryden, Lee, Otway, and Congreve and possess the literary immortality that belongs to the likes of Milton's Adam and Eve.

Bridging the historical period from the Restoration to Richardson, these and other women in love carry the passionate sensuality of the earlier period, when it was fully acknowledged, into the Augustan age, when it was not. The literature that embodies the dolors and delights of these heroines is unmistakably—sometimes powerfully—erotic and demonstrates that growing gentility in love did not quench, though it may have refined, physical ardor. Quite apart from any refining influence, but during exactly the same period, pornography was being domesticated. By the mid-seventeenth century, England was fully aware of the Continental outburst of illicit literature, being quick to import it. By 1748 England was ready to export Cleland's *Fanny Hill*, its first piece of original domestic pornography.[1]

Apparently thinkers of the age that succeeded the Restoration blamed the

---

1. David Foxon, "Libertine Literature in England, 1660–1745.III," *Book Collector* 12 (Autumn 1963): 301. See also Foxon's first two articles, ibid. (Spring 1963), pp. 21–36 and (Summer 1963), pp. 159–77. On definitions of "pornography" and "obscenity" in connection with a defense of Rochester's libertine poetry as literature, see Reba Wilcoxon, "Pornography, Obscenity, and Rochester's 'The Imperfect Enjoyment,'" *Studies in English Literature* 15 (Summer 1975): 375–90.

licentiousness of their immediate forebears[2] on the repressions of the Puritan ascendancy. Dennis, for example, explained Restoration behavior as the result of the iron control of natural instinct exercised by the "Saints" in power, whose harsh morality he described in salty language as "that beastly Reformation, which, in the Time of the late Civil Wars, was begun at the Tail, instead of the Head and the Heart; and which opprest and persecuted Mens Inclinations, instead of correcting and converting them, which afterwards broke out with the same Violence, that a raging Fire does upon its first getting Vent."[3] Puritanism, however, was seen not only as the cause of succeeding sensuality but also as being itself impregnated with the libidinous. I have earlier noticed the charge leveled against the dissenters by their most telling critic, Jonathan Swift, who also said of "Spiritual Intrigues" that "they may branch upwards toward Heaven, but the Root is in the Earth."[4] Erotic overtones can be heard in Roman Catholic mysticism, as the 1671 translation of *The Life of the Holy Mother S. Teresa* reveals, recalling in its own way Bernini's sensual-religious masterpiece portraying the saint's imminent impregnation by the flame-tipped spear of the angel. But the Puritans, though their religion may often

2. This characteristic of the age should not be too glibly assessed. Literary libertinism did certainly exist and was European in its scope, as Dale Underwood and others have shown. See Underwood's discussion of Rochester, Dorimant, the Don Juans of the seventeenth century and their worship of that permissive goddess Nature in *Etherege and the Seventeenth-Century Comedy of Manners* (New Haven: Yale University Press, 1957), chap. 2 ("The Fertile Ground"). It is also true that in the Puritan revolution, as in many revolutions, free love was prominent in theory and practice, and there was everywhere an attack on the celibate ideal, which was called "stinking chastity" by John Bale, Bishop of Ossory (1495–1563), sometimes known as "Bilious Bale." See Christopher Hill, *The World Turned Upside Down: Radical Ideas during the English Revolution* (London: Temple Smith, 1972), esp. pp. 247–56. On the other hand, modern social history tends to show that preindustrial England successfully controlled sexual conduct. The Restoration may have been no exception: during the reign of Charles II there was little perceptible increase in licentious behavior, insofar as that can be determined. See Peter Laslett, *The World We Have Lost,* 2d ed. (London: Methuen, 1971), esp. pp. 137, 138, 299. For the view that, in Elizabethan times at least, sexual offenses were common and lightly punished, see Stone, *Family, Sex and Marriage,* pp. 519–20.

3. *Critical Works,* 1:154. Dennis's and the opinions that follow can be related to Stone's comment that before the nineteenth century, "when medical opinion became more radically anti-sexual, doctors were as much concerned with the dangers of abstinence as with those of excess." He then cites opinions of Galen and Robert Burton, and Thomas Cogan's work of medical advice, *The Haven of Health* (1596)—all of which recommend sex as a means of releasing pent-up psychological energy (*Family, Sex and Marriage,* p. 497). Burton had "a keen perception . . . of the miseries and evils which arise from sexual suppressions and prohibitions." This may be an important reason why he quarrels with the warnings of the church fathers against love play; Burton finds it permissible for young people to "kiss coming and going . . . to talk merrily, sport, play, sing, and dance, so that it be modestly done, go to the Ale-house and Tavern together." See Lawrence Babb, *Sanity in Bedlam: A Study of Robert Burton's "Anatomy of Melancholy"* (East Lansing: Michigan State University Press, 1959), pp. 38, 41 (where Burton's comment is quoted from the ed. of A. R. Shilleto, 3:120).

4. "Mechanical Operation of the Human Spirit" in *A Tale,* ed. Guthkelch and Smith, p. 288.

have been accompanied by sensual as well as spiritual groanings, did not encourage the baroque fusion of body and spirit that we see in the poetry of Donne and Crashaw. In England there was alternation rather than fusion, either as one extreme followed another or, more subtly, as the coy and delicate reacted against, and sometimes even insinuated, the openly robust. During the eighteenth century, in fact, delicacy almost takes over sensibility.

Literary manifestations of sexuality cannot frequently be called, in Dennis's phrase, "a raging Fire"; nevertheless, a desire to express the naughty and the forbidden, particularly as it is experienced by women, remained an irresistible temptation to both male and female writers. Walter Charleton, who is thought to have written those crudely sensual early Restoration stories of *The Ephesian and Cimmerian Matrons,*[5] accompanied the narrative with theoretical defenses and definitions of heterosexual love as opposed to modern perversions. Restoration comedy and prose fiction—gamesome, frank, sometimes wittily indirect, sometimes offensively open—explored courtly intrigue, middle-class wives seeking adventure, and even the frontiers of that Erotopolis which was called "Betty-land" and which was said to adjoin "the Isle of *Man,*" a place described in unsubtle and indelicate language which, however, now and then recalled the Bible and anticipated Sterne.[6] Matrimony itself received abundant attention in popular tracts designed to give instruction and not infrequently to warn, as Defoe did in *Conjugal Lewdness* (1727), against physical excess by even lawfully yoked partners.

Women writers contributed to the growing literature of love, sometimes delicately, sometimes lustily. Mary de la Rivière Manley explored seduction with considerable psychological insight from perhaps as early as 1693, certainly from 1705 and on, in novels that exploited rape, incest, and both hetero- and homosexual orgies.[7] Mrs. Eliza Haywood, in seventy-odd volumes that appeared from 1720 on, expressed racy vigor and "palpitating passion." To this modern Sappho her contemporaries paid their tributes of aroused carnality, praising "the Force of Language, and the Sweets of Love" in her descriptions, which command the "throbbing Breast, and watry Eye":

> See! Love and Friendship, the fair Theme inspires
> We glow with Zeal, we melt in soft Desires![8]

Delicacy was the tone that Mrs. Elizabeth Singer Rowe strove to achieve from 1718 on, but the piety of this writer of the pastoral mode should not be

5. The title page continues: *Two Notable Examples of the Power of Love & Wit* (London, 1668).

6. ΕΡΩΤΟΠΟΛΙΣ: *The Present State of Betty-land* (London, 1684).

7. See the publication by Patricia Köster of four novels (1705 to 1714) in the series, Scholars' Facsimiles and Reprints (Gainesville, Fla., 1971), esp. pp. ix, xiv.

8. George F. Whicher, *The Life and Romances of Mrs. Eliza Haywood* (New York: Columbia University Press, 1915), pp. vii, 16, 17.

allowed to obscure the persistent eroticism or conceal in which sex it some-times arises:

> Lovely as Light, and soft as yielding Air.
> For Him each Virgin sighs.[9]

Pagan verse did for the eighteenth century what it had done for Renaissance literature and art: it provided an endlessly varied source of love themes and love images. The poems of Anacreon were translated and imitated all through the Restoration and the eighteenth century, appearing along with odes, epigrams, and fragments of Sappho, not frequently with the force and insight of a Cowley but often with his animus against spiritualized Platonic love and friendship. The "Soul" of Sappho is praised because it "seem'd form'd of Love and Poetry; she felt the Passion in all its Warmth, and de-scrib'd it in all its Symptoms."[10] Ovid, who was prominent in the Restoration because of the powerful sponsorship of Dryden as critic and translator and who continued to influence the eighteenth century under the same auspices, kept vividly alive myths and heroic stories of wild passion, incest, lesbian and homosexual love. Ovidian erotic stories were even applied to the political sphere, in a manner anticipating the later caricatures of Gillray and Row-landson.[11]

9. These lines come from "*Love* and *Friendship:* A Pastoral," which appears in Matthew Prior, *Poems on Several Occasions* (London, 1718), pp. 31–33.

10. Joseph Addison, ed. and trans., *The Works of Anacreon, Translated into English Verse; . . . To which are added the Odes, Fragments, and Epigrams of Sappho* (London, 1735), p. 255. It is important to note that pagan eroticism was dignified during the early eighteenth century with the enormously prestigious support of Addison, who says of this body of Anacreontic and Sapphic verse that it "has been look'd upon, in all Ages, as a little Assembly of the *Loves,* the *Smiles,* and the *Graces*" (ibid., sigs. A3v, A4r). The preface refers to "the inimitable Graces and Beauties of the Originals" (sig. A5r). It is clear that Addison has viewed the ancient love lyrists with a rococo eye. Anacreon and Sappho were imitated or translated by, among others, Thomas Stanley (1651), Cowley and John Oldmixon (1683), Ambrose Philips (1713), Francis Fawkes (1760, 1789), and, during the Romantic period, Thomas Moore, who even imagines "intercourse between Anacreon and Sappho," than which nothing was more delightful for the fancy to "wanton upon" (*Odes of Anacreon, translated into English Verse, with Notes* [Dublin, 1803]), p. 16. See also D. F. Foxon, *English Verse 1701–1750* (Cambridge: Cambridge University Press, 1975), vol. 2, s.v. "Sappho" in Subject Index.

11. The vogue of translating Ovid's amorous tales continued through the eighteenth century into the Romantic period. See, e.g., translations of Ovid's *Art of Love,* 1693–97, 1704 (published by Tonson in *Poetical Miscellanies*), 1709; the translation "by the Most Eminent Hands" of the *Epistles* (1725), of the *Metamorphoses* (1732), and of that special favorite *Sapho to Phaon,* which in one adaptation (1743) was apparently addressed to Lord Hervey by "a Lady of Quality" and entirely transformed from the erotic to the political. See also Foxon, *English Verse,* vol. 2, s.v. "Ovid" in Subject Index. Both Sappho (who, beside Phaon, had many lovers of her own sex) and Anacreon (who, though usually Venereal, also addressed love poems to the beauteous boy, Bathyllus) were bisexual—a fact that must surely have added piquancy to the vogue of these two poets. The story of Ganymede and Jupiter was well known; and a period that knew the visual arts well by virtue of travel and of engravings could have encountered versions of this homoerotic myth by

Modern eroticism, following perhaps unknowingly the lead of Milton's divorce tracts, separated itself from the fashionable aristocratic homosexuality that lay behind the Platonic dialogues. Although an aggressive heterosexuality could of course be crude, this at least must be said on its behalf, that it could not have existed without a profound concern—healthy or unhealthy, admirable or censurable—for women and even the status of women. The new woman, learned, literate, cultivated, sometimes rebellious, had emerged in English drama during the seventeenth century; she had, even earlier, alarmed a religious leader like John Knox and, much later, stimulated Daniel Defoe to an almost revolutionary reversal in 1697 of age-old stereotypes about the licentiousness and faithlessness of the sex: "All the World are mistaken in their practice about Women."[12] Eroticism also tended to produce antithetical responses: it sometimes exalted woman, as in the tradition of courtly love; it sometimes debased her to gross sensuality, as in both pagan and patristic satire and polemics. Ovid portrayed female aggressiveness in love both as an open, lustful lack of temperance and as a tendency to secret pleasure and dissimulation. I have noted in discussing Milton that a venerable tradition, which also included Sidney and Spenser, considered man's grossest sensualization to be his effeminization, his submission at whatever cost to the dominance of the female will. One memorable late seventeenth-century incident aroused considerable attention, the suicide for unrequited love of the classical scholar and poet, Dryden's admired friend, Thomas Creech (1659–1700) of All Souls', Oxford. Before this young clergyman hanged himself he had been madly in love, even leaving his mistress a generous legacy—behavior that after his death led to an outpouring of venom against the bestial appetite and the sex which aroused it and to a recommendation of that venerable clerical and academic escape, "the Vow of Virginity," the "most noble of all Vows."[13]

Michelangelo (a design at Windsor), Correggio (Vienna) (pl. 2), Annibale Carracci (at the Farnese, Rome), Rubens (the Prado), Rembrandt (Dresden), LeSueur (Louvre), C. Van Loo (Toulouse). John Dennis derided homosexuality and deplored its increase: "Let Fornication be ever so crying a Sin, yet Sodomy is a Crime of a thousand times a deeper Dye" (*Critical Works*, 2:314). He then goes on to say that since Collier's attack on the stage in 1698 the crime is on the increase: four persons were condemned for it at the last session (Dennis is writing in 1726) and several more were apprehended, "the like of which was never heard of in *Great Britain* before" (ibid.). See also Stone, *Family, Sex and Marriage*, pp. 492–93, 541–42. For a discussion of the views of philosophers, divines, and polemicists on incest, see A. Owen Aldridge, "The Meaning of Incest from Hutcheson to Gibbon," *Ethics* 61 (July 1951): 309–13.

12. Quoted by Jean Elisabeth Gagen, *The New Woman: Her Emergence in English Drama, 1600–1730* (New York: Twayne Publishers, 1954), p. 9; see also pp. 10–12.

13. See *A Step to Oxford: or, A Mad Essay on the Reverend Mr. Tho. Creech's Hanging himself, (as 'tis said) for Love. With the Character of his Mistress* . . . (London, 1700) and *Daphnis: or, a Pastoral Elegy upon the Unfortunate and Much-Lamented Death of Mr. Thomas Creech* (London, 1700). I owe knowledge of these pamphlets to private conversations with Earl Miner. On the relations of Dryden and Creech, see California *Works of Dryden*, vol. 3, *Poems, 1685–1692*, ed. Earl Miner (1969), p. 272. The quotation comes from *Daphnis*, p. 11.

"Courtly," Petrarchan, and *précieux* strains are increasingly heard in love literature. With greater emphasis than before and surely in part as a result of the growing admiration of the gentle virtues of pity and forgiveness, the "softer" sex was praised for its ability to refine manners into delicacy and civility. Milton said of Adam and Eve, "Som natural tears they drop'd, but wip'd them soon" (*PL,* 12.645). As we saw in the last chapter, not all the tears shed before 1700 were natural, and those of morbidity were not soon wiped away. But whether the tears are deleterious or wholesome, it is difficult to escape the feeling of Lucius Junius Brutus that the sweetening and softening of life was essentially feminine—that in fact there was everywhere a growing feminizing of the psyche. Although apparently the Parisian salon was not transplanted bodily to England during the Restoration, coteries sprang up around Mrs. Katherine Philips, the "matchless Orinda," and even Aphra Behn; and Hortense, the duchess of Mazarin and niece of the cardinal, established a genuine French salon in London, with the sometimes ludicrous Saint-Evremond as the hyperbolic celebrant of its virtues and charms.[14] These salons perhaps had little direct influence on English letters, but they must surely have ministered to the growing social spirit and the greater courtesy that now attended love. Combined with religious influence and the spreading bourgeois spirit, the presence of women on the aristocratic and the literary scene must have been felt as an influence. Certainly, *The Gentleman's Journal: or the Monthly Miscellany* of 1693, edited by P. A. Motteux, is impregnated with the feminine spirit. In the issue of October appears a prose address to the "Fair Sex," which says, "'Tis you that have been the Muses who have inspir'd Most of the Gentlemen whose Writings have grac'd this Journal: 'Tis you to whom . . . all our Sex owe, that Politeness, Easiness and Delicacy which a converse with you imparts more liberally than the most lavish Nature" (p. 324). The concern with art and music; the essays against hot pride and gaming; the short stories on love and courtship; the tunes by Blow, Purcell, and others; even the translations from Anacreon—all these breathe a civilizing feminine air as they invoke the theme of love in a manner that was soon to characterize Richard Steele.

But, as I shall say more than once, delicate love remains love still, and I must not here dwell on the sentimental, which I shall consider at length in a later chapter; erotic passion is my present concern. Lely's set of portraits known as "the Windsor Beauties" is related to the carnal concerns of the present chapter as Kneller's is to my discussion of sentimental love in chapter 7. The beauties by Lely were painted between 1662 and 1665 for Anne Hyde, the duchess of York, and were originally hung at Whitehall Palace (see pl. 4). To

14. Chauncey Brewster Tinker, *The Salon and English Letters* (New York: Macmillan, 1915), pp. 90–98.

portray the most beautiful women at court, as the duchess wanted him to do, Lely was challenged to exert all his considerable powers. His achievement is mostly erotic: his beauties possess glowingly white skin, partially exposed breasts, full and sensual lips pursed as though to invite a kiss, and languishing or flirtatious eyes. The actions in which they are engaged partially fulfill the amorous promise of their countenances, as they accept grapes from a kneeling Indian boy, hold their skirts up for a gift of fruit, or pluck a rose with delicate fingers, all the natural imagery being highly symbolic of erotic adventure. Hazlitt reacts with pre-Victorian priggishness when he calls them "a set of kept-mistresses, . . . without one spark of sentiment to touch the heart." Roy Strong has said, "These are no longer beauties of the sunset, they are bawds [surely this word is uncalled for] who welcome the oncoming night and its sports. They are voluptuous fleshy ladies. . . . For a moment beauty and sex are aligned in a triumph of unashamed sensuality."[15]

Such ladies may serve to conclude my brief and informal discussion of Restoration and early eighteenth-century carnality. They may also serve, though there are many differences, to introduce our four passionate heroines, Dido, the Portuguese Nun, Calista, and Eloisa, since, though only one is courtly (the Carthaginian queen herself), all are or have been sensual. One important difference should be noted right off: the women of this chapter do not invite passion in anticipatory relish; they recollect it in melancholy or suicidal tranquility, each with her own *Gestalt* of feeling, each in a profound or lyrical exploration of joy's aftermath. Though spiritually nobler—more loyal and steadfast—than the Windsor Beauties may have been, they possess the élan in love which their courtly counterparts seem to promise. The literary ladies had all been mistresses whom we remember not in their moments of allurement but in the agony of their lonely passion.

Dido

The position of Queen Dido in Western culture is much larger, of course, than the place that she occupied in the Restoration and eighteenth century, important though it was. After her death she was honored as a goddess and confused with Aphrodite or Astarte, so sublimely was she thought to have embodied the passion of love. Having almost stormed the pantheon, she easily won a mythic status in literature, music, and art, where she remained popular during three centuries, from the sixteenth to the nineteenth. She was, for

15. Hazlitt and Strong are quoted by J. Douglas Stewart in "Pin-ups or Virtues? The Concept of the 'Beauties' in Late Stuart Portraiture," *English Portraits of the Seventeenth and Eighteenth Centuries* (Los Angeles: Clark Memorial Library, 1974), pp. 4–5. The "Windsor Beauties" are represented, following the text of Stewart's lecture, on plates 1A, 2A, 5B, 7A, 8A and B.

example, painted by Rubens, Nicolas Poussin(?), Simon Vouet, Tiepolo, Reynolds, Fuseli, and Turner and caricatured by Gillray. Her position in art owes much though, as we shall see, not everything to Virgil, who immortalized her in the fourth book of the *Aeneid,* that "noble episode," as Dryden called it, "wherein the whole passion of love is more exactly describ'd than in any other poet."[16]

Dido has appealed to people of sensibility throughout the centuries because she embodies, along with love, the deepest passions, tender and terrible, beautiful and sublime. To the young Augustine she even became the rival of God in his heart, so moved was he by Dido dead, so relatively unmoved by the living "Deus, vita mea" (*Confessions* 1.13.20 [51]). She appears along with other great lovers in the second circle of *Inferno* 5, one of the carnal beings driven about in total darkness by a fierce wind in a howling darkness, which, as Dorothy Sayers says, is "simply the sin itself, experienced without illusion."[17] Dante stresses the wickedness of Dido's suicide and her breach of faith with the memory of her dead husband, Sichaeus. In other ancient Greek and Roman poets, love is usually a crisis brought on by the violation of a strict and fierce taboo. But the love of Dido and Aeneas violates no god-given or deeply felt law; it conflicts, instead, with civic obligation. It is a sexual union that originates in the profound carnal and psychic sympathy of two mature leaders, and no other ancient work binds lovers together with so rich and complex a chain of emotional, spiritual, and physical strands.[18] One reason this pagan love story appealed to even the religious seventeenth century, which translated the *Aeneid* so often and which singled out for special attention its fourth book, was surely that its author was an *anima naturaliter Christiana,* portraying love as well as foretelling the coming of the Messiah. The preoccupation of the baroque century with Virgil's Dido reached its climax in Dryden's great translation of 1697, a monument to the dying century and also an inspiration to the century about to be born.

Before I analyze Dryden's richly suggestive lines, it may be useful to consider two somewhat contrasting visual renditions of the story during the seventeenth century which provide a background for important developments during the eighteenth. Rubens's *Death of Dido* in the Louvre (pl. 6) shows the queen sitting on the bed that is soon to become a funeral pyre—a bed on which she has placed a bust of Aeneas. Since the expression on the queen's

16. "Dedication of the Aeneis" in *Poetical Works of Dryden,* ed. George R. Noyes, p. 501. This passage is omitted from George Watson's collection of Dryden's critical essays.

17. *The Comedy of Dante Alighieri: Hell,* trans. Dorothy L. Sayers (Harmondsworth, Eng.: Penguin Books, 1949), p. 102.

18. I am here indebted to Martin Mueller, "The Truest Daughter of Dido: Racine's Bérénice," *Canadian Review of Comparative Literature* 1 (Autumn 1974): 201–17. See also Irving Singer, "Erotic Transformations in the Legend of Dido and Aeneas," *Modern Language Notes* 90 (Dec. 1975): 767–83, a comparison of Virgil's, Ovid's, Chaucer's, and Marlowe's treatments.

face is not fully persuasive, it may be dangerous to try to interpret it. But it is difficult not to see in it a kind of ecstasy—the mouth is open; there is a touch of a smile on the lips; the eyes brim with tears, but they are raised expectantly as she is about to plunge the sword in her breast. Dido may be abandoned, but she is not a defeated woman. Still wearing a crown, she is a queen to the end and has achieved, even at the moment of death, a kind of transcendence of the earth that is usually the reward of religion but here is associated with love. Rubens's painting, though not one of his greatest, points to one of the most important psychological displacements in Western history, one crucially important for the story of love in the eighteenth century, when it began to assume the glories once associated with a triumphant religious faith. Another picture of the same century portraying Dido and Aeneas—for centuries attributed to Nicolas Poussin and now in Toledo, Ohio (pl. 7)—is of a radically different kind. Choosing to portray the love of the pair at its commencement rather than at its tragic *dénouement,* the painter presents an Aeneas whose kindling love is neither lust nor delirium but an intense and pleased interest in a virtually nude woman. It is Dido, full-breasted, seated, looking into the mirror which Aeneas holds, a look of pleasure on her profiled face, who embodies the erotic and psychological interest. She is at once delicate and sensual—a combination absolutely central to sensibility, as we shall see. And the contrasts between her profiled face and her full face in the mirror provide a subtle meaning. The profile is sweet and delicately eager; the reflected full face is kindly but potentially sad, even tragic, and so constitutes a haunting prophecy of doom after joy.[19]

Dryden's queen must be carefully distinguished from both the heroic Dido of Rubens and the loving but doomed human being of the last picture. Her character arises from the translator's exploitation of three qualities in the love story, each worthy of attention: (1) the sensual, (2) the pathetic, and (3) the ethical.

1. Apparently Dryden did not consider it inconsistent with the "grave, majestical, and sublime" tone that he felt ought to characterize a heroic poem ("undoubtedly the greatest work which the soul of man is capable to perform": "Dedication of the Aeneis," in Watson, 2:223–24) to intensify the sexuality of the original. That fact alone speaks volumes for Dryden's respect for

19. On Rubens's painting, see Emile Michel, *Rubens: His Life, His Work, and His Times,* trans. Elizabeth Lee, 2 vols. (London: William Heinemann, 1899), 2:178. Anthony Blunt denies the traditional attribution of the Toledo painting to Poussin. See "Poussin Studies XII: The Hovingham Master," *Burlington Magazine* 103 (Nov. 1961): 454–61, where Blunt argues that the paintings should be attributed to the "Hovingham Master," so called after Hovingham Hall, Yorkshire, where two paintings bearing characteristic features of this painter are housed, a totally unknown artist who imitated Poussin's early manner. See also Blunt, *The Paintings of Nicolas Poussin: A Critical Catalogue* (London: Phaidon Press, 1966), p. 174, item R 74, for references to the relevant scholarship. For Reynolds's strikingly different rendition of this theme, see pl. 10 and below, pp. 280–81.

physical love. The queen is beauteous as well as regal. Aeneas, ministered to by his mother Venus (who curls his locks, gives a gracious sparkle to his eyes, and makes his temples shine), is polished ivory touched with gold. And Cupid, not crudely by an arrow but by insinuation of the queen's whole personality, infuses the very being of Aeneas into her veins. Her dreams become troubled, and she becomes his temptress. When they unite in the cave, Hymen is present and Juno provides ritual sports, for the poet seems to make their love almost sacramental, giving it the status of marriage. Still, there is no doubt that what seized Dido was lustful pleasure, even though she does add maternal desires to the sexual and pleads with Aeneas to stay and father a child. The rage that ensues when she learns that Aeneas must depart is almost as sensual as the pleasure and may be even more brilliantly heightened by Dryden. The queen's suicidal melancholy is given Gothic trappings: owls appear, obscene songs are sung, the sacrifices are impious, the mad and the infernal feed her rage, and soon she takes her own life, a martyr to love.

The love wound never heals, and when the two lovers meet in Hades, she spurns the Trojan prince in what T. S. Eliot has called the "most telling snub in all poetry."[20] It is a snub administered by an abandoned sensual woman.

Perhaps one example will suffice to show how Dryden has sexualized the original. In Virgil Jupiter turns his eyes to the two "oblitos famae melioris amantis" (4.221). That is, he beholds the lovers forgetful of their better fame. Dryden expands this into something rather more and different:

> The lustful Pair, in lawless pleasure drown'd.
> Lost in their Loves, insensible of Shame;
> And both forgetful of their better Fame.
> [4.323–25]

A direct contrast to Dryden's heightening of the sexual in Virgil is Wordsworth's aversion to it. Even Venus herself the Romantic poet makes ornate and artificial, somewhat less sensual than the Roman poet's goddess and much less so than Dryden's. The insistent sexuality of Dryden's version, even though he does end the episode with moral disapprobation of the love, may in fact account for Wordsworth's impatience: Dryden, he believed, did not have a "tender heart nor a lofty sense of moral dignity."[21]

2. Wordsworth's comment is not without some justification, but it is excessively harsh. Although Dryden loves robust, hearty, and terse epigrams and distichs, the creator of the heroic hero who weeps, loves, forgives, and spares the lives of the innocent and sometimes even his enemies is by no means mute before Virgil's delicate *lachrymae rerum*. Dryden fully understands that the epic

20. *On Poetry and Poets* (London: Faber & Faber, 1957), p. 62.
21. Wordsworth's comment on Dryden is quoted by Willard Spiegelman in an article which finds much merit in the Romantic poet's translation: "Wordsworth's *Aeneid*," *Comparative Literature* 26 (Spring 1974): 97.

and tragedy share in the great aim of arousing "compassion" and that the "shining quality of an epic hero" is "his magnanimity," along with constancy, patience, piety (Watson, 227, 228). He concedes, following Segrais, that Aeneas might have shown a "little more sensibility" when he left Dido, "for that had been according to his character" (Noyes, p. 500). Dryden preserves the fear, the pity, the anxiety, the struggle within himself that the hero experiences when he hears the divine command to leave and when he delivers this news to the queen, although admittedly he does not emphasize these.

3. Predictably, Dryden is very much at home with the ethical-political dimensions of Aeneas's decision to obey Jupiter, who sees the love as lustful and dangerous. The decision to depart has been much discussed, and I need say only this of it here—that it is made by Dryden no more prominent than the sensuality I have stressed and that it is poetically less memorable than the description of Aeneas's beauty, Dido's response to it, her passion, and her madness. Dryden, in other words, is unmatched as the poet of the beautiful and the terrible in love, extremes to which the queen is driven, showing that he believed love to possess both the demonic and the divine. Still, the translator's great love of the erotic should not obscure his firm grasp of the religioethical. Once the god has spoken, Aeneas acts with unsentimental determination to do his duty and fulfill his destiny.

Dryden's failure to make of Virgil's famous episode a document of sensibility appears in the animus he shows toward Dido, whose character he weakens after he has so magnificently adorned her love and grief. The reason is obvious, though perhaps unforgivable—he is determined to preserve at all costs the dignity of his hero, his political and civic integrity; and he therefore presents not a faithless deserter of suffering goodness but a pious man who leaves an unworthy, licentious, and suicidal woman. Dryden's hostility becomes unrelenting. Virgil says of Dido's subjection to love and of her consequently grieving and grievous entreaties to Aeneas to remain,

> Improbe amor, quid non mortalia pectora cogis!
> Ire iterum in lacrimas, iterum temptare precando
> Cogitur et supplex animos summittere amori,
> Ne quid inexpertum frustra moritura relinquat.[22]

Dryden's translation reads,

> All-pow'rful Love, what Changes canst thou cause
> In Human Hearts, subjected to thy Laws!
> Once more her haughty Soul the Tyrant bends;
> To Pray'rs and mean Submissions she descends.

22. 4:412–15. These lines J. W. Mackail translates as follows in the Modern Library College ed.: "Injurious Love, to what dost thou not compel mortal hearts! Again she must needs break into tears, again essay entreaty, and bow her spirit down to love, not to leave aught untried and go to death in vain." *Virgil's Works* (New York: Random House, 1950), p. 73.

No female Arts or Aids she left untry'd,
Nor Counsels unexplor'd, before she dy'd.
[4.595–600]

The translator transforms unjust or injurious love to "all-pow'rful Love," and he transforms the weeping, suffering Dido (in painful subjection to love as she will try again to obviate, though vainly, a death which is bound to come) into a "haughty Soul," stooping to "mean Submissions" and "female Arts." For none of Dryden's pejorative epithets is there any justification in the original, and he almost obscures the fact that "tyrant" refers to "amor" by making it seem to refer to the queen. Thus Dryden takes his stand on Aeneas's side against a long tradition that considered him a cad and a coldly ambitious imperialist and that found in Dido a sympathetic human sufferer. That tradition Dryden knew well, for he translated the fountainhead of it, Dido's epistle in the *Heroides* of Ovid, where the queen is a much gentler being even than Virgil's, not extreme in anger or hatred but more rational, more thoughtful, less passionate. Ovid's Dido, though less grand and compelling than Virgil's, is more pleasing in her combination of the reasonable, the erotic, and the elegiac. And there is no question that Ovid's sympathy—and Dryden's while translating him—is squarely on the side of the suffering queen, to whom are given the following lines of lament over her lost chastity and faith to her dead husband, whose statue in the nearby chapel she now remembers:

Last night, methought, he call'd me from the dome,
And thrice with hollow voice, cry'd, *Dido,* come.
She comes: thy Wife thy lawful summons hears:
But comes more slowly, clogg'd with conscious fears.[23]

The passage is lovely and delicate. The word "conscious," which I shall examine later, anticipates sensibility, and the reiterated verb "come" must surely be a source of Pope's repeated use of the word, particularly when the haunting voice of the dead sister from the stone tomb invites Eloisa to "come . . . come" to cold oblivion.[24]

23. "Dido to Aeneas," 109–12. Translations from Ovid, *Epistles* (1680), in California *Works of Dryden*, vol. 1, *Poems 1649–1680*, ed. E. N. Hooker and H. T. Swedenberg, Jr. (1956), p. 135.

24. If Dryden's translation is indeed an anticipation of *Eloisa to Abelard* (257, 309–10, 317), then perhaps the suggestion of Murray Krieger (if I understand him correctly) that "come" possesses, among other resonances, a sexual implication is made less likely. See "'Eloisa to Abelard': The Escape from Body or the Embrace of Body," *Eighteenth-Century Studies* 3 (Fall 1969): 33. I have been assisted in my comments on Dido and Aeneas by the following, though my point of view and emphasis differ from theirs: L. Proudfoot, *Dryden's "Aeneid" and Its Seventeenth Century Predecessors* (Manchester: Manchester University Press, 1960); Mark O'Connor, "John Dryden, Gavin Douglas and Virgil" in *Restoration Literature: Critical Approaches*, ed. Harold Love (London: Methuen, 1972), pp. 247–75; and T. W. Harrison, "Dryden's *Aeneid*" in Bruce King, ed., *Dryden's Mind and Art* (Edinburgh: Oliver & Boyd, 1969), pp. 143–67.

The Ovidian Dido leads to the Tate-Purcell opera on the theme, a work first produced in 1689, some eight years before Dryden's translation of the *Aeneid* appeared. In this opera Aeneas is a poor thing who prefers convention to the human experience of love. The voice of Jupiter and the supernatural command to return are transmitted by cackling witches and a sinister sorceress, while Dido is raised to a heroine of tragic dignity and given the loveliest music of a generally inspired score. Her aria in act 1, "Mine with Stormes of Care opprest," expresses pity for the distressed as she confesses that her breast is "so soft, so sensible"; and the music, free flowing, relaxed, and tender, makes her a Woman of Feeling. Very little attention is given to her love of Aeneas, who is simply not worthy of her. When he so much as hints at departure, she moves into richly personal and tragic music and thinks at once of death. Her final aria (act 3), "When I am laid in earth," is a deeply moving *Liebestod,* with syncopations, melismata, and dissonances that express alternately disillusion, grief, and stabbing despair. The passion is intense and is only somewhat softened by the final chorus (especially at the words, "Soft and Gentle as her Heart"), which makes us remember the opening tenderness and achieves a kind of reconciling purgation through pity and love.[25]

In the plays of his maturity, Dryden was a pioneer in creating sensibility. But in his presentation of Virgil's Dido to his countrymen, though he achieved a powerful portrait of sensual love and sensual rage, his vision was limited by an uncompromising commitment to civic duty. Purcell's deeply subjective and moving music, besides providing a rich aesthetic experience valuable for its own sake, points more unmistakably to the future than does Dryden's *Aeneid,* book 4. The composer has undertaken a profoundly subjective plunge and so becomes himself a part of that revolutionary reorientation of the human spirit that went on in the psychologizing and internalizing of art that I have already noted in the criticism of John Dennis.

The Portuguese Nun

To the same movement toward inner human space belongs what has been called "perhaps the greatest single influence"[26] of the seventeenth century on subsequent literary culture, the *Lettres d'une religieuse portugaise,* which appeared some years before Dryden's translation of Virgil and Purcell's setting

25. For comments on both music and libretto, see Robert Etheridge Moore, *Henry Purcell and the Restoration Theatre* (London: Heinemann, 1961), chap. 2 (devoted to *Dido and Aeneas,* which Moore believes "maintains a sovereign superiority over any English opera to appear since" [p. 38]).

26. Charlotte E. Morgan, *The Rise of the Novel of Manners: A Study of English Prose Fiction between 1600 and 1740* (New York: Columbia University Press, 1911), p. 70.

of Tate—that is, in 1669, only nine years after the restoration of Charles II. Very soon it became the fashion in France to write "à la portugaise," and several of the writers discussed or mentioned in the preceding pages became aware of a powerful new influence. Aphra Behn was the first English imitator in her *Love Letters to a Gentleman* in 1676, and Mrs. Manley in 1696 produced direct imitations. Imitation was of course not confined to women, although it is noteworthy that they were among the first to respond. Sir Roger L'Estrange produced a translation in 1678, which was followed in 1680 by a second edition and in 1686 by a third. These translations, often accompanied by sequels consisting of the lover's response to the nun, are part of a European-wide vogue that has continued to our own day. The retired and love-abandoned sister of the letters has spoken directly to the hearts of important movers and shakers in Western culture, which the *Lettres* have penetrated more deeply than is indicated even by the long list of direct imitations, translations, sequels, answers, parodies, and even renditions into verse.[27]

We are here concerned with a masterpiece of *sensibilité*. Wherein does its power lie? In the "charme" of the letters, in "leur spontanéité, le naturel de leur désordre"?[28] Or in their sophisticated transformation of passionate feeling into the ordered development of a five-act Racinian tragedy?[29] Those who hold the first view believe that the *Lettres* are the authentic product of a retired *religieuse* living in a nunnery in Portugal, Marianna Alcoforado, who sprang from an old family in Béja, where she was born in 1640. They have constituted the dominant view: La Bruyère, Laclos (who believed that women are inevitably superior in love letters), Stendhal (who made this work the prototype of *l'amour-passion*), Sainte-Beuve (who found that writing to the moment produces the charm of disorder), and Rilke. But recent scholarship supports those who are uncomfortable with the notion that an untutored

27. Ibid., p. 73; James R. Foster, *History of the Pre-Romantic Novel in England* (New York: Modern Language Association of America, 1949), p. 21 and n.5; P. and J. Larat, "Les 'Lettres d'une religieuse portugaise' et la sensibilité française," *Revue de littérature comparée* 8 (Oct.–Dec. 1928): 619–39; *The Letters of a Portuguese Nun (Marianna Alcoforado)*, trans. Edgar Prestage (Portland, Me.: Thomas B. Mosher, 1900), pp. 47–54 (a list of translations, etc., 1678–1893). In 1975 there appeared a work produced in liberated Portugal by three Portuguese women, directly inspired by the nun's letters and entitled *The Three Marias: New Portuguese Letters*, trans. Helen R. Lane (New York: Doubleday & Doubleday). The three women, Maria Isabel Barreno, Maria Teresa Horta, Maria Velho da Costa, all mothers in their thirties, discuss many topics hitherto neglected in their culture, including female love.

28. Larat and Larat, "Les 'Lettres' et la sensibilité," p.626.

29. Leo Spitzer, "Les 'Lettres Portugaises,' " *Romanische Forschungen* 65 (1953): 94–135; *Lettres portugaises, Valentins et autres oeuvres de Guilleragues*, ed. F. Deloffre and J. Rougeot (Paris: Editions Garnier Frères, 1962). The latter work, which attributes the *Lettres* to Guilleragues and places them in a learned tradition, gives all the known facts of publication, establishes a modern text, summarizes the most important previous opinion and scholarship. Quotations from the *Lettres* are from this ed.

author could produce so universally acknowledged a masterpiece and attributes the work to Gabriel de Lavergne de Guilleragues, a French author and man of affairs. What he produced was a pastiche of recollections from Catullus and Ovid, from Molière, Racine, and La Rochefoucauld. The structure of the five-letter work has been thought to possess the progressive coherence of a classical tragedy in five acts, and its style has been analyzed as a sophisticated grouping into paragraphs of phrases that are tied each to each by carefully worked out thematic ligatures. The impressive edition of 1962, which attributes the work confidently to Guilleragues, has not, however, closed scholarly debate, which as recently as November 1976 produced the view that there are so many differences between Guilleragues's other works and the *Lettres* that at the very least a stimulus from real life must be postulated and that the French edition of 1669 may have to be regarded as some kind of translation, either from a real-life experience or from letters growing directly out of that experience.[30] Apparently the question of authorship is still wide open, and literary catalogers may well continue to hesitate between placing the letters under "Alcoforado" or "Guilleragues."

The analysis that follows is not intended to decide definitively between the schools of natural and artificial genius—to apply to this controversy the terms of a famous eighteenth-century debate. I shall not arbitrate between those who endorse the opinion, expressed even as early as 1701, that this work is "one of the most Artificial Pieces" of its kind "any where Extant" and those who, like Edmund Gosse, believe that the value of the letters lies in "their sincerity as a revelation of the heart" and that the nun taught "the secret of saying what was in the heart" with simple and untutored force.[31] If, however, a choice has to be made, one is more comfortable with the arguments for passionate, natural simplicity, which is accompanied by an almost uncanny ability to fix attention on psychological movement. That movement is less like that of a classical sonata than like the tentative statements, the sudden breakings off, the organically woven recapitulations of a symphony by Sibelius. The qualities in the nun's letters that must be honored are the emotional intensity that *seems* to be recorded during or just after the sensations are experienced; the presence of plausible contradiction, paradox, inconsistency; a sense that if at the end a balance has been achieved, it is a precarious one that can easily be upset. The oscillations of feeling may of course have come to an end; on the other hand, this pause could be temporary, and a cycle of similar emotions might easily resume.

30. See letters to the London *Times Literary Supplement* by Margaret C. Weitz (15 Oct. 1976, p. 1306) and Peter Dronke (5 Nov. 1976, p. 1397).

31. *Five Love-Letters from a Nun to a Cavalier. Done out of French into English by Sir Roger L'Estrange,* 2d ed. (London, 1701), sig. B3v; Edmund Gosse, "A Nun's Love Letters," *Fortnightly Review* 43 (1 Jan.–1 June 1888): 507, 513.

The nun begins her complaint to her ravager in the first letter, forcefully, even melodramatically. But the indignation over betrayal is not maintained, and she turns almost at once to the psychological—to the "mouvemens" (one of the key words of the text) of her spirit and to her fall from joy. We are made aware at the outset that this masterpiece focuses not on the moment of passion but on its aftermath in the soul. One of the subtlest combinations of emotion now experienced is pleasure in grief and loss: "Il me semble que j'ai quelque attachement pour des malheurs dont vous êtes la seule cause."[32] This paradoxical rejoicing in pain leads directly to the final injunction of the first letter: "Adieu, aimez-moi toujours; et faites-moi souffrir encore plus de maux."[33] Surely one reason for the pleasure-pain is that the love has produced "émotions violentes," "transports," "emportements"—words relating to the Longinian sublime in art that arose during the late seventeenth century and became prominent in the eighteenth.

The paradox of the first letter continues into the second, where it becomes even stronger. The lover is blameworthy, the nun is angry; he is incapable of a grand passion, she is extravagant, placing her love above religion and honor. *Sensibilité* was seldom more purely cherished than when the sufferer places her emotions above the "plaisirs languissants" of the *beau monde* and calls for the continuation of her passionate solitary grief: "Non, j'aime mieux souffrir davantage que vous oublier."[34] In letter 3 the "mouvemens de dévotion" appear, a new motif, but the writer is not yet willing or ready to resign her humanity, for she blazes up in fierce jealousy at her lover's French connections and recounts what she has sacrificed for him. But is she sorry she has loved? Not in the least! She detests the tranquility she knew before she met him and pities him for missing the richness of the emotions in which she exults. She is in love, if not with love, surely with having been loved, ravished, and aroused to violent suffering: "On sent quelque chose de bien plus touchant, quand on aime violemment, que lorsqu'on est aimé."[35] Love is a vital force, not something formed and molded; it is a *natura naturans,* not a *natura naturata,* and therein lies its splendor. Letter 4, in which there is much violent denunciation of the man, reveals that the burning core of her spirit is love-hate: "Que ferais-je, hélas! sans tant de haine et sans tant d'amour qui remplissent mon coeur?"[36] She now subsists on her passion, not even leaving her

---

32. P. 39: "It strikes me that I have a kind of attachment to the evils of which you are the sole cause." The page refs. are to the modern French ed. of Deloffre and Rougeot. The translations in the notes are my own. On *motion* as emotion, see above, p. 98, n.43.

33. P. 42: "Farewell, love me always; and make me suffer still more evils."

34. P. 44: "No. I would rather continue to suffer than to forget you."

35. P. 48: "We feel something much more touching when we love violently than when we are loved."

36. P. 54: "What shall I do, alas! without so much hate and so much love, which fill my heart?"

chamber except once to view the town nearby from that balcony on which she first felt her love. The rich array of her emotions passes in review: excess of grief, incertitude about her plans, changes in feeling, extravagance in her letters, confidences, hopes, jealousy. But now it is the love-hate within on which she feeds and from which she can get temporary relief only by writing. Nowhere has the venerable view that the writer *must* write when the heart is full been given more poignant expression. Give me the chance to write or give me death: the craving for expression is even stronger than Pamela's or Clarissa's. But ironically, the nun now begins to sense that, since all external matters are odious to her, she lives by recollected passion alone. Can she survive on such food? Will she—and her passion too—die of inanition? The last line is piercing in its pathos: "Je n'ose plus vous prier de m'aimer; voyes où mon destin m'a réduite! Adieu!"[37] She is reduced to a remembrance of things past, no more, no less, and now fears even a renewal of his addresses, since they would necessarily come, along with the lover, from the outside world, which she now loathes.

The last letter has been considered a resolution, a *dénouement,* or a sinking into a calm—or lethargy—of spirit. But is it? It is true that at the beginning the nun declares that this is the last time she will write, since she is sure he will never love her again. She returns all his gifts, including the portrait of himself, and says that she cannot continue to love and suffer when his actions have made him despicable to her. Above all, she realizes that she has been assiduously cultivating passionate suffering divorced from its cause, a love separated from its object, a rootless emotion that feeds on itself and looks to us like one of Milton's narcissistic sins: "J'ai éprouvé que vous m'étiez moins cher que ma passion."[38] She therefore commands him never to write again. She wishes him no evil; in fact, she hopes he will attain happiness. And she sees, as Pope's Eloisa will later see, that she has been idolatrous. But are all these signs that the passion has ended and that she has been healed? Or is this last another in a series of emotions awakened by her deep ravage? The ending does not permit us to say categorically that a catharsis has taken place. Compare the resolution with which this last letter begins and the one with which it closes. It begins, "Je vous écris pour la dernière fois." It ends, "Il faut vous quitter et ne penser plus à vous, *je crois même que je ne vous écrirai plus.*"[39] The last sentence is weak and wavers in spiritual doubt. Earlier in letter 5 the nun hinted that she might

37. P. 59: "I no longer dare beseech you to love me; behold, what my fate has reduced me to."
38. P. 62: "My experience was that you were less precious to me than my passion."
39. Pp. 61, 69: "I am writing you for the last time. . . . It is necessary to abandon you and to think of you no longer, I even believe I may not write to you any longer." Emphasis added. For another view of the conclusion of the *Lettres*—that the nun's passion is finally laid to rest, that she is released from the grip of obsessive passion—see Louise K. Horowitz, *Love and Language: A Study of the Classical French Moralist Writers* (Columbus: Ohio State University Press, 1977), pp. 125–43, esp. pp. 128, 140.

break her vow not to write just to demonstrate how tranquil she really was—an act that of course might, despite its bravado, reopen the wound and the whole cycle of anguish.

Dido ended her woes in suicide. For the Christian nun that route is not open. She tries to kill her passion, but the outcome of this duel is uncertain. But one thing is certain—this extended agony, in which internal emotion is substituted for the real person who caused it and which may never end though it is declared ended, is the lot of many, so many in fact that this set of simple letters has possessed continuing power from 1669 to our own day.

Calista, the Fair Penitent

The Portuguese Nun's letters have survived more than one revolution in manners, living on through many centuries and epochs. They thus meet Samuel Johnson's requirements of a classic. Rowe's *Fair Penitent* (1703), which was influential only in its own day and during the succeeding age, does not, and no one now claims that it does, even though it can certainly be regarded as a good play. It carried forward into Augustan England the pathos and perhaps also the morbidity of Otway's domestic drama, which influenced it; its Lothario is partly responsible for that magnificent creation, Richardson's Lovelace; and it possesses a few moments pregnant with anticipation of important things to come. Those moments spring from the fine rebelliousness of the title character and the poetically realized pagan mood and Gothic gloom that are made the objective correlative of the heroine's grief at the end.

We begin with the Gothic conclusion. *The Fair Penitent* uses as its epigraph a sentence from Dido's lonely night-time lament to herself, in which she decides on suicide: "Quin morere, ut merita es, ferroque averte dolorem."[40] In deciding to die by her own hand, Dido chooses a way open to a queen and a pagan but, as we have seen, not to a Catholic religious. Why does Rowe make suicide the fate of his Italian Calista, the heroine of an English drama whose chief aim was to excite pity in a "melancholy tale of private woes"?[41] Calista is unhappy partly because she has been unvirtuous but also because, no less than

---

40. *Aeneid* 4.547: "Why not die as you deserve and end your pain with a sword?"

41. Prologue, line 16. Reference is to the edition by Malcolm Goldstein in the Regents Restoration Drama Series (Lincoln: University of Nebraska Press, 1969). After writing this section on Rowe's play, I encountered J. Douglas Canfield's thoughtful study, *Nicholas Rowe and Christian Tragedy* (Gainesville: University Presses of Florida, 1977). Canfield persuades me that the overt values of the play center in Christian repentance and mercy and that Rowe stands in a definable tradition and context of Christian tragedy. (See esp. chap. 4, "Protagonist as Penitent [with Reluctance].") Nevertheless, the dynamics of the drama do not, I believe, support only a Christian reading. The powerful modern "affective" movement with some justice, seized upon the play as part of that tradition, and Samuel Johnson was right in sensing its moral ambiguity.

Dido or the nun, she is a woman abandoned, even though married and in the midst of society. In fact, marriage means for her primarily separation from the man who ravished her and whom she continues to love even after union with another and worthier man. Marriage, forced on her by her father, makes of her a lonely sufferer with only the recollection of passion and places her in the company of heroines high in state and church, like Dido and Eloisa. The fact that her situation is that not of a convent but of a household and that she appears in a literary form requiring a catastrophic end denies her the opportunity of dwelling on her passion, whose persistence makes of her a spiritual adulteress. She herself feels deeply stained with an "inbred, deep pollution" (5.158). The only solution is death, a death her father seems to suggest to her when he calls on her to repossess the ancient Roman spirit. When his mortal wound in a Genoese fray over the dead body of Lothario is reported to his daughter, she feels even more polluted than before, since she regards herself as the cause:

> For I am all contagion, death, and ruin,
> And nature sickens at me; rest, thou world,
> This parricide shall be thy plague no more.
> [5.232–34]

She then stabs herself, but not before her father comes in to forgive her and die.

The most noteworthy aspect of the suicide of the heroine is the ambiguity that attends the state of her soul, which does seem to be at peace as she gazes at her good though unexciting husband. But does she deserve to seem at peace either for the present or the future? Johnson complained that she "shows no evident signs of repentance" and that she "expresses more shame than sorrow, and more rage than shame."[42] Cibber said she should be called "the Fair Wanton," and Belford in *Clarissa* says that she is "a desiring luscious wench, and her penitence is nothing else but rage, insolence, and scorn."[43] Richardson's reformed rake exaggerates, and though he is right in observing a lack of repentance, we must remember that a truly Christian submission would have aborted suicide. The point I am making is that, though Christian values are present in the play, they are dramatically less powerful than other forces, and that what Calista feels very strongly is not the pull of heavenly bliss but the morbid attraction of death itself. We have noticed in *The Mourning Bride* a powerful connection between pious love and death. Here death is associated with an illicit passion that marriage does not terminate, a fact that makes its cold embrace doubly welcome. Even the good husband, Altamont,

---

42. Life of Rowe, *Works* (1825), 7:409.

43. Cibber is quoted by Malcolm Goldstein in the Introduction to his edition of the play, p. xviii; Belford's statement is made in *Clarissa,* 4:118 (Everyman's Library).

seeing that the heroine is bent on death, joins her in her wish for mortality. Such emotions in act 5 make the Gothic gloom of act 4 anything but gratuitous; these moments are more significant than the conventional and superficial gestures toward distributive justice that disposes of the illicit lovers. The compelling, substructural movement of the play is toward death, not toward justice. Sciolto tries to kill his daughter but is restrained by her husband, who himself longs for death and oblivion. Calista, in a charnel house with the corpse of her lover, Lothario, his deadly wounds displayed, throws aside the book of meditation and pious reform. She is dressed in black, and her hair hangs loose and disordered. The songs being sung are as Gothic as the ambience, with its damp horrors that freeze the blood; they tell stories of midnight phantoms and a fair maiden's imminent death. There is no priest, no confession; only a father who enters with a dagger, which he himself cannot use against her but which he leaves for her. It is all most melancholy—and musical, for Rowe, as has been widely recognized, is a master of sweetly harmonious verse and gentle poetical coloring. In these Gothic scenes he has given us an example of love turning toward death in a society that is beginning to lack the judging and classifying hierarchies of Milton and Dryden and beginning to luxuriate in the morbidities of the tender Otway without very many institutional restraints.

The Gothic ending comes after an even more effective episode in the play, the unrestrained and memorable rebelliousness of Calista. This transcends the somewhat conventional unconventionality of the gay Lothario, providing welcome relief from the cloying, though consciously approved, meekness and pity of Horatio and Lavinia. Horatio, a friend of the bridegroom Altamont, is married to Lavinia, and the married pair is regarded by the heroine's father as his own children. It is Horatio who declares the joys of virtue and who points to his loyal and passive wife as a contrast to the proud and sinful Calista:

> Then—to be good is to be happy. Angels
> Are happier than mankind, because they are better.
> Guilt is the source of sorrow; 'tis the fiend,
> The avenging fiend, that follows us behind
> With whips and stings; the blest know none of this,
> But rest in everlasting peace of mind,
> And find the height of all their heav'n is goodness.[44]

This is an example of *angélisme*, a concept I shall return to, since it is an influential ideal present in the eighteenth century and perhaps regnant in the Victorian ideal of love. Contrast such sentiments with those of Calista, who says,

44. 3.98–104. It is interesting to note that Richardson quoted this passage approvingly in a letter to Sophia Westcomb, 15 Sept. 1746, *Selected Letters of Samuel Richardson*, ed. John Carroll (Oxford: Clarendon Press, 1964), p. 69.

How hard is the condition of our sex,
Through ev'ry state of life the slaves of man!
In all the dear, delightful days of youth
A rigid father dictates to our wills,
And deals out pleasure with a scanty hand;
To his, the tyrant husband's reign succeeds;
Proud with opinion of superior reason,
He holds domestic business and devotion
All we are capable to know, and shuts us,
Like cloistered idiots, from the world's acquaintance
And all the joys of freedom; wherefore are we
Born with high souls but to assert ourselves,
Shake off this vile obedience they exact,
And claim an equal empire o'er the world?

[3.39–52]

Her use of the phrase "high souls" throws the mind back to the heroic drama
and reminds us of the newer tendencies to locate heroism in a domestic scene,
close to the business and bosoms of men. Calista's fine speech rings in our
ears, especially after Rowe bows his neck to the yoke of conventional rules and
rigors. One suspects that he distrusts them; at least he cannot make his bold
and attractive heroine bend to them too easily. He transforms frustrated will
into the death wish, which is better than meek submissiveness. It is difficult for
a modern to deny that Calista at her moment of fine, perceptive rebelliousness
breathes a more attractive spirit than Horatio, who preaches an angelic and
sexless kind of postmortem joy. Calista, for all her waywardness, seems somehow closer to the kind of fulfillment that Spenser and Milton sang than does
the bland Horatio.

It is difficult to say whether the playwright was aware of what I have called
the deep structure and the unconscious values of the play—the welling up of
personal rebellion in woman whom society forces into a movement toward
death. Almost to the very end the doomed heroine appears to blame her guilt
on the fact that she "loved, and was a woman" (5.73). The reader must surely
be chilled by her father's response: "Hadst thou been honest, thou hadst been
a cherubin" (5.74). The fact that many perceptive critics have noted the lack of
clear moral value in the play has encouraged us to discover in the strength of
the sinners and the weakness of the good some kind of symbolic value. The
absence of Christian order presages century-long developments that will substitute instinct for institutions, emotion for conscience and creed. The fear of
sexuality by the good and its embrace by the bad, who are given moments of
power and persuasiveness, seem to comment on the potential loss of morally
directed energy in modern man. It is noteworthy that the good husband
anticipates the Man of Feeling and at the same time is weak, timid, listless,
possessed of a death wish and called at the very end "a drooping flower"

(5.286). Can it be that the skillful Rowe, so often regarded as merely soothing, tender, and complacent, was more prophetic than he knew and penetrated more deeply into some of the effects of sensibility than we have realized? Did one whose melodious and traditional verse and whose historical plots recalled the golden age of English drama sense a reduction of sensual and imaginative power in modern man? He certainly had no full vision of the withering of the heroic spirit that was to overtake Western culture; but we, from our later vantage point, can see that Prufrock and Lambert Strether are not totally unrelated to Altamont and Horatio. Ibsen's Nora can scarcely be said to grow out of Calista's moment of proud identification with her oppressed sex. But Rowe has given us a glimpse of what a greater and freer spirit might have done with a female character determined to realize her identity in unconventional sexual behavior. We shall observe such another phenomenon as Calista in Lillo's prostitute Millwood, who, in one grand moment, is allowed to tower above the surrounding mediocrity.[45]

Eloisa: "Breathings of the Heart"

Pope's nun, unlike Calista, does achieve permanent dignity and identity as a rebellious and passionate woman. She has been regarded by distinguished authorities as a noble and sympathetic embodiment of the medieval spirit.[46] In the context of this book the poem represents at once a high point in the development of *sensibilité* and the best expression by Pope of his own "Romantick" spirit. His statement—that "the Epistle of Eloise grows warm, and begins to have some Breathings of the Heart in it, which may make posterity think I was in love"[47]—is at once personal and suggestive of the love tradition. Pope's poetic vocabulary has been seen as an example of "a new,

45. In addition to Johnson's Life of Rowe, these eighteenth-century perspectives on *The Fair Penitent* are useful: Joseph Warton's comments in *An Essay on the Genius and Writings of Pope* (1756, 1782), printed in Scott Elledge, ed., *Eighteenth-Century Critical Essays*, 2:745–46; *Biographia dramatica* (London, 1782), 2:113. On Lovelace and Lothario, see H. G. Ward, "Richardson's Character of Lovelace," *Modern Language Review* 7 (Oct. 1912): 494–98. On the enormous fame of *The Fair Penitent*, see the edition of Sophie C. Hart (Boston: D. C. Heath, 1907), pp. xvii–xviii. Allardyce Nicoll quotes Swift's fascinating comment that "the ladies frequent tragedies more than comedy. . . . In tragedy their sex is deified and adored, in comedy exposed and ridiculed." Nicoll, however, attributes the popularity of this tragedy among women to their delight in tears and pathetic situations. He sees the play as a link between Otway and Lillo. *A History of English Drama, 1660–1900*, 3d ed. (Cambridge: Cambridge University Press, 1965), 2:24, 59–60, 98–100. For a view of Rowe as mostly sentimental, with the concession that there is real drama, with turbulence and trouble, only in *The Fair Penitent*, see Dobrée, *Restoration Tragedy*, pp. 150, 151, 155, 156, 166.

46. See, e.g., Etienne Gilson, *Heloise and Abelard* (Ann Arbor: University of Michigan Press, 1963), p. ix.

47. Letter to Martha Blount (March 1716?), *The Correspondence of Alexander Pope*, ed. George Sherburn, 5 vols. (Oxford: Clarendon Press, 1956), 1:338.

tender, feverish way of experiencing passion—or, at least, a new way of wording the old passion." Ovid, Aphra Behn, the Portuguese Nun, Dryden's Virgil, and, perhaps more than any other (except of course the main source, John Hughes's translation in 1713 of the letters of Abelard and Eloisa), Dryden's heroic plays contributed to Pope's *locus classicus* of the "conscious abandon of mind and body to mood and moment."[48] One French scholar, who has counted the tears and sighs in various versions of Eloisa's story, finds that they steadily increase until in Pope they constitute "un déluge."[49]

Surely it can only be in relation to literary deserts that Pope's emotions can be called a flood. But emotion is powerfully present, and it is much more personal and poignant than has been realized. The poet handles, as directly and warmly as the decorum of his poem will allow, the physical facts of love, and his passion is much more than rhetoric, though it is surely that too. It will be helpful to discriminate the ingredient qualities of Pope's love-sensibility. It appears, full-blown, in the sister poem of *Eloisa,* the "Elegy to the Memory of an Unfortunate Lady," a lady who, like Dido and Calista, is surrounded with the trappings of horror and shudder—a ghost, the moonlight, the sword, the stab wounds. This poem was both severely censured and considerably praised by Johnson, and it apparently possessed enough authentic emotion to have stirred the logical and often disenchanted Hume, who read it aloud to Thomas Blacklock and witnessed how it threw the blind poet's whole body "into Agitation."[50] Pope's own "Romantick" feelings appear everywhere in his letters and are reflected in his garden and grotto as well as in these sister poems on love. Tenderness he calls "the very Emanation of Good Sense & virtue: The finest minds like the finest metals, dissolve the easiest." Melancholy is "pleasing" and gloom "agreeable." He loves to walk alone "by moonshine" and reflect on "the transitory nature of all human delights." He relates the sadness of women to their "natural softness," and he declares that a "Poetical Mind" will elevate the images of the beautiful autumn season to tenderness and sensibility. He loves romances, wild, exotic fairy tales and visions, the "Variety & luxuriancy of Description." And as if these were not

48. The quotations come from Geoffrey Tillotson's Introduction to the Twickenham edition, vol. 2, *The Rape of the Lock and Other Poems,* 3d ed. (London: Methuen, 1962, 1966), pp. 296, 297. For recollections of the works mentioned, see p. 295 and notes to the following lines of the poem: 24, 185, 323 (*Don Sebastian*), 31, 47, 73, 276, 313, 321, 322 (*Aureng-Zebe*), 104, 106, 189, 208, 217, 226, 229, 241, 273f, 353f (*Tyrannick Love*), 345 ff., 350.

49. Emile Audra, quoted by Henry Pettit in "Pope's *Eloisa to Abelard:* An Interpretation," reprinted in Maynard Mack, ed., *Essential Articles for the Study of Alexander Pope* (Hamden, Conn.: Shoestring Press, 1964), p. 299.

50. Twickenham ed., 2:358. Johnson (Life of Pope, *Works* [1825], 8:245) said of the "Elegy": "Poetry has not often been worse employed than in dignifying the amorous fury of a raving girl"—a comment often quoted. It is less frequently remembered that he also praised the poem for some parts written "with vigorous animation" and others "with gentle tenderness" (ibid., p. 327).

examples enough of Graveyard, Gothic, and Romantic sensibility, he reveals he has a strong conviction of the limited power of language: "It is however a most certain truth, that *one can never Express Any thing that one really feels.*"[51] And in a confessional mood he poetically contrasts his own feverish madness to the corrective and cool sanity of Bolingbroke:

> But when no Prelate's Lawn with Hair-shirt lin'd,
> Is half so incoherent as my Mind,
> When (each Opinion with the next at strife,
> One ebb and flow of follies all my Life)
> I plant, root up, I build, and then confound,
> Turn round to square, and square again to round;
> You never change one muscle of your face,
> You think this Madness but a common case,
> Nor once to Chanc'ry, nor to Hale apply;
> Yet hang your lip, to see a Seam awry!
> Careless how ill I with myself agree;
> Kind to my dress, my figure, not to Me.
> Is this my Guide, Philosopher, and Friend?
> This, He who loves me, and who ought to mend?[52]

It is not my purpose here to speculate on how or whether Pope's tender-melancholy and mad-sweet eroticism inspired the creation or suffused the enjoyment of his grotto, the "Shadowy Cave," that "lonely wondrous cave" which is both "palace and grave" and which one authority has described as "teasing to the modern imagination," a place where "reality and dream converge and blur."[53] Nor can we determine precisely how his grounds, gardens, cypress walks, and the obelisk to his mother at once reveal and relieve the same kind of "pronounced psychic overtones" and the same "subtle interplay between the human psyche and the landscape" that exist on an unrivaled scale in Hoare's garden at Stourhead.[54] Since I have placed madness within Pope's "Romantick" syndrome, a full account would have to relate love madness and hate madness and perhaps see the *Dunciad,* with its scatology, its ugly but powerful regressiveness, its images of obscenity and frenzy, as the obverse of the passion so nobly and sympathetically treated in *Eloisa to Abelard.*

In the *Dunciad* gross physical imagery is applied to the dunces to show that in this realm sex and fertility have become an obscene and ugly corruption

51. *Correspondence,* ed. Sherburn, 1:172, 330, 496; 2:202, 337. The letters quoted date from Feb. 1712/13 to Nov. 1725. Emphasis in last quotation is Pope's.

52. *Imitations of Horace,* Epistle 1.1.165–78 in Twickenham ed., vol. 4, *Imitations of Horace,* ed. John Butt (1939), pp. 291–93.

53. Maynard Mack, *The Garden and the City* (Toronto: University of Toronto Press, 1969), pp. 41, 47. The language describing the cave is Lady Winchilsea's, quoted by Mack, ibid., p. 41.

54. Ibid., p. 29, n.4; Kenneth Woodbridge, "Henry Hoare's Paradise," *Art Bulletin* 47 (March 1965): 116.

that can be best symbolized by whores, pimps, venereal disease, sick children, abortion, miscegenation, incest, lust.[55] But the vividness of this late vision of sexual perversion should not blind us to Pope's earlier conception of ideal love nor to his parallel but antithetical ability to embody love passion in noble and moving poetry and prose. That ability is nurtured by a philosophical belief ("The surest Virtues thus from Passions shoot," *Essay on Man,* 2.183) and by a dialectic, more Christian than Platonic, that progresses from the purely physical to the humanly tender:

> Lust, thro' some certain strainers well refin'd,
> Is gentle love, and charms all womankind.
>   [Ibid., 189–90]

Eloisa to Abelard was perhaps conceived and partially executed too early to make the whole poem the artistic counterpart to Pope's gallantry toward Lady Mary Wortley Montagu, although his emotions toward her surely explain some of the lines and personalize the basic situation of the poem. Since Pope is the brilliant but typically human artificer of letters that Johnson so shrewdly analyzes,[56] these letters are almost as aesthetically interesting as the poem, which is not to say that they are remote from actuality but quite the opposite—that they enter into it more deeply than merely casual effusions possibly can. Pope's prose is, then, a rich artistic analogue to the poem on the subject of love. He begins the correspondence with Lady Mary, for whom he has conceived an obsessive passion that makes him neglect everyone else when she is near, during a time of frequent meeting; but the letters achieve their fullest artistic intensity only after she has left with her husband for Constantinople—an intensity that diminishes remarkably upon her return some two years later and then disappears altogether. In describing his letters as "Shadows of me," as frank and "most impartial Representations of a free heart," Pope obscures somewhat the way his love is nourished, cherished, and expressed. His is a peculiarly literary and cultural kind of love, in which real life is given the shape and coloration of tradition. Thus he hopes on their sojourn abroad Lady Mary will look upon her husband "with the eyes of a first Lover, . . . with all the unreasonable happy Fondness of an inexperienced one,

---

55. On imagery of sexuality and madness in Pope's poetry, esp. *The Dunciad,* see Patricia Meyer Spacks, *An Argument of Images* (Cambridge, Mass.: Harvard University Press, 1971), pp. 20–21, 121–24. For a somewhat different view of madness in Pope, one that stresses its relation to imagination and to nothingness but that ignores its relation to sexual appetite, see David B. Morris, "The Kinship of Madness in Pope's *Dunciad*," *Philological Quarterly* 51 (Oct. 1972): 813–31. Martin Price sees clearly the reductive-regressive aspect of the dunces: "The psychological meaning of Dulness is . . . the surrender of thought to sensation." *To the Palace of Wisdom: Studies in Order and Energy from Dryden to Blake* (1964; reprint ed., Garden City, N.Y.: Doubleday & Co., 1964), p. 227.

56. Life of Pope, *Works,* 8:314–18. For interesting and relevant letters by Donald H. Reiman and Charles Rosen on the relations of life to art, see *New York Review of Books,* 26 June 1975, p. 38.

surrounded with all the Enchantments and Idæas of Romance and Poetry." Pope's prose song of innocence may appear somewhat less natural and more artful than Blake's, but it need not be regarded as less personally intense for all that, and Blake's verses and designs are also a tissue of literary and artistic allusions. As time and distance lengthen, Pope grows melancholy and even mad, but his imaginative wit still coruscates as classical and Christian allusions multiply and grow around his indulgence of sexual fantasies. "You have already . . . out-traveld the Sin of Fornication, and are happily arrived at the free Region of Adultery: . . . I shall hear how the very first Night you lay at Pera, you had a Vision of Mahomet's Paradise, and happily awaked without a Soul. From which blessed instant the beautiful Body was left at full liberty to perform all the agreeable functions it was made for." The "Idea" of the lady always lies "warm" and "close" in his heart, and news of her illness distracts him to mad "ravings"; but his "piece of madness" he is able to embroider with metaphor: it is like the "dreams of Spleenatic Enthusiasts and Solitaries, who fall in love with Saints, and fancy themselves in the favour of Angels, and Spirits, whom they can never see, or touch." Such is Pope's playful *angélisme*. Through it all Lady Mary remains cool, describes at length what she sees on her travels, teases him on now and then—though always without commitment on her part—and introduces romance and sensibility by quoting Turkish poetry—an interesting anticipation, by the way, of the later vogue for the "Oriental" verse prominent in Collins. Genuine and touching pathos arises when we realize that Lady Mary is unavailable in many more tragic ways than through her obvious geographical remoteness and that Pope's is the cry of a dwarfed and crippled man who must imagine pleasure and enjoy it only in the realm of romance. To that realm his fevered imagination floats, lost in "romantic thoughts," in "distant admiration" of her, as he lies dreaming of her "in Moonshiny Nights exactly in the posture of Endymion gaping for Cynthia in a Picture." The image is Keatsian in several layers, for it is sensual, mythological, and painterly, besides invoking the very story the later poet chose to convey his passion. The erotic raptures did not survive Lady Mary's presence in England, and Pope calms himself as she returns, though now and then the old passion flares before it sputters out in bitterness and is succeeded by satiric wit.[57]

57. *Correspondence*, 1: 352–53, 355, 363 ff., 368, 369, 383, 389, 390, 399 ff., 439. The letters that display Pope's passion date from about July 1716 to 1718. For an excellent discussion of this "affair" —one which sees beneath Pope's extravagance a deep desire to be taken seriously—see Robert Halsband, *The Life of Lady Mary Wortley Montagu* (New York: Oxford University Press, 1960), pp. 48, 58–64, 76, 97, 99. See also the perceptive discussion of this correspondence by James Anderson Winn, *A Window in the Bosom: The Letters of Alexander Pope* (Hamden, Conn.: Shoe String Press, 1977), pp. 111–14, 116–19. It is relevant to note the observation of Dustin H. Griffin that around the year 1720 the poet ceased thinking of himself as a lover. *Alexander Pope: The Poet in the Poems* (Princeton, N.J.: Princeton University Press, 1978), p. 42.

Both Pope and Lady Mary saw *Eloisa* in relation to themselves. In her copy of the poem she marked these lines,

> Still on that breast enamour'd let me lie,
> Still drink delicious poison from thy eye,
> [121–22]

putting a cross next to "eye" and at the bottom of the page writing "mine."[58] Pope wrote to Lady Mary in June of 1717, just after publication of the poem, that ·it contained one passage "that I can't tell whether to wish you should understand, or not" (*Correspondence,* 1:407). The likeliest candidate for the passage Pope had in mind cannot surely be direct expressions of love (that kind of fervent address he had made often, and Lady Mary would have understood nothing if not these), nor even those lines of the conclusion in which the poet refers to a "future Bard" who will join

> In sad similitude of griefs to mine,
> Condemn'd whole years in absence to deplore,
> And image charms he must behold no more,
> [359–62]

for he certainly could not have been embarrassed to have her think that as poetic creator he partook of Eloisa's feelings and related them to his love of the absent Lady Mary. Besides, he could scarcely have thought her so obtuse as not to see a general parallel. What really embarrasses him, I suggest, is that Lady Mary may perceive an identification between himself and the emasculated Abelard:

> Alas how chang'd! what sudden horrors rise!
> A naked Lover bound and bleeding lies!
> Where, where was *Eloise?* her voice, her hand,
> Her ponyard, had oppos'd the dire command.
> Barbarian stay! that bloody stroke restrain;
> The crime was common, common be the pain.
> I can no more; by shame, by rage supprest,
> Let tears, and burning blushes speak the rest.
> [99–106]

> Give all thou canst—and let me dream the rest.
> [124]

> For thee the fates, severely kind, ordain
> A cool suspense from pleasure and from pain;
> Thy life a long, dead calm of fix'd repose;
> No pulse that riots, and no blood that glows.
> [249–52]

58. See Halsband, *Life of Lady Mary,* p. 76.

> Cut from the root my perish'd joys I see,
> And love's warm tyde for ever stopt in thee.[59]

These several lines are among the most dramatic in the poem and give to it a modern cast and even modern symbolic value. The eighteenth century, however, was capable of regarding them as improper: the last two lines quoted were removed from the 1736 edition and Joseph Warton, who wished that lines 100–106 had been omitted, said that "the principal circumstance of distress is of so indelicate a nature, that it is with difficulty disguised by the exquisite art and address of the poet."[60] For Pope, then, to have assimilated his own tortured, dwarfed, and impotent body to that of the castrated Abelard would suggest a deeper personal intensity in the poem than most critics have dared to imagine. But it is of course not atypical of Pope to be a presence in his poetry, and if he in fact made Abelard's tragic inability a parallel to his own condition, we need go no further to account for his reluctance to have Lady Mary fully understand the meaning of the poem, which provides a dramatic analogue to the enormous distance that separated them. He must also have realized that if he can be regarded as Abelard, then Lady Mary becomes Eloisa, and the poet has imagined that all the rich and fiery passion is directed to him by a woman who in reality was noncommittal, proud, and distant.

Many of Pope's alterations of his source are designed to make the poem fit his own "Romantick" sensibility, which I have described earlier. After Abelard's emasculation, theological disgrace, and banishment from Saint-Denis, he chose as the site of his retreat a flat and deserted region; Pope made it rocky and mountainous. John Hughes only hints at the gloom of Eloisa's surrounding, Pope makes it a full-blown and amply developed "Gothic." The tradition of course included mystical rapture, but Pope reduces that while he heightens the erotic. Above all, Pope concentrates on Eloisa and makes of her a truly romantic heroine, passionate, suffering, but proud and unbowed. Both Romantic and modern critics have responded to her flame. "If you search for passion," said Byron, "where is it to be found stronger than [here]?" And the Twickenham editor of the poem has introduced it by saying, "Outside Shakespeare's plays and the novel, no woman in English literature expresses the degree of Eloisa's passion and despair."[61]

---

59. These two lines appeared after line 258 in 1717. Winn makes a just comment about Pope during the time he was creating the fantasies that appeared in his letters to Lady Mary: "Pope was reminded every day of the physical deformity that made him different from others." *A Window in the Bosom,* p. 113.

60. Joseph Warton's comment is quoted by William Lisle Bowles in his ten-volume edition of Pope's *Works* (London, 1806), 2:33.

61. On Pope's alterations of his sources, see James E. Wellington, ed., *Alexander Pope: Eloïsa to Abelard with the Letters of Heloise to Abelard in the Version by John Hughes* (1713) (Coral Gables, Fla.: University of Miami Press, 1965), pp. 11, 45, 53. Byron is quoted from his *Letters and Journals* by Tillotson in the Twickenham ed., p. 301, where the editor's comment is also to be found.

In an earlier chapter I considered the morbidity that overtook Restoration love-sensibility, and in this I have noted that the absence of the beloved object threw the Portuguese Nun back on her own depleted inner resources and led her to cultivate a love-hate that replaced a living lover. Suffering and passion became ends in themselves; the image in her soul made her idolatrous. Does such a fate overtake Eloisa? Is she self-obsessed to the point of neurosis and narcissism?[62] Has she committed the sin of the fallen devils in *Paradise Lost*? One draws back from the charge. The passion sears and, like the infernal flame, seems eternal: it is the worm that dieth not. But it always remains associated with the objective existence of the lover—his plight, his living image. Eloisa may be sinful, but she is not sick. And the libertinism she expresses is not presented as an ultimate evil, as in some of Dryden's superhuman villainesses, of whom Eloisa may in fact be a revisionary character; it is, instead, a protest of considerable dignity against institutions whose repressiveness can cause unbelievable suffering.

> How oft', when press'd to marriage, have I said,
> Curse on all laws but those which love has made!
> Love, free as air, at sight of human ties,
> Spreads his light wings, and in a moment flies.
> Let wealth, let honour, wait the wedded dame,
> August her deed, and sacred be her fame;
> Before true passion all those views remove,
> Fame, wealth, and honour! what are you to Love?
> The jealous God, when we profane his fires,
> Those restless passions in revenge inspires;
> And bids them make mistaken mortals groan,
> Who seek in love for ought but love alone.
> Should at my feet the world's great master fall,
> Himself, his throne, his world, I'd scorn 'em all:
> Not *Caesar*'s empress wou'd I deign to prove;
> No, make me mistress to the man I love;
> If there be yet another name more free,
> More fond than mistress, make me that to thee!
> Oh happy state! when souls each other draw,
> When love is liberty, and nature, law:
> All then is full, possessing, and possest,
> No craving Void left aking in the breast:
> Ev'n thought meets thought ere from the lips it part,

---

62. Patricia M. Spacks, in *An Argument of Images*, finds that Pope contemplated the inner struggle of Eloisa with "morbid enthusiasm" and that he locks us into her sensibility, giving us no alternative point of view (p. 234). Still, Spacks finds the psychological situation compelling in its way: "Only in *Eloisa to Abelard* does Pope present pathos as self-sufficiently interesting" (p. 253).

> And each warm wish springs mutual from the heart.
> This sure is bliss (if bliss on earth there be)
> And once the lot of *Abelard* and me.[63]

Can one admire Rowe's Calista or Lillo's Millwood and find Eloisa morbid, after so vigorous a desire for human freedom in love? Eloisa is passionate but not pathological, and Pope's imagination encompasses alternatives to the discontents of civilization and the repressions of religion.

Had the long passage just quoted appeared in Dryden, it would have led on to the relentless punishment of the speaker—to death, madness, suffering. Or the sentiment would have been repented. But Pope neither destroys Eloisa nor allows her to repent, and those err who believe that in her soul he allows grace to triumph over nature at the end, that her sufferings lead to the balm and equilibrium of salvation, that God finally replaces Abelard in her mind and heart. No, the aesthetic truth is quite different. So powerful is Abelard's sensual hold on Eloisa's imagination—and this is one of the most notable examples of the association of love and fancy in the whole eighteenth century—that she does not risk meeting him in heaven. Even the resurrected spiritual bodies of such lovers as these might renew carnal sin. And though for her lover Eloisa wishes the full baroque glory of a Rubens painting, for herself she comes in the end to desire only death. It alone—not heaven, not a prolongation of Christian consciousness, not salvation following repentance—can still her racing pulses. Her vision of her own future is not bliss in the beyond with a redeemed Abelard but a "kind" (343), shared, and quiet grave.

> Ah then, thy once-lov'd *Eloisa* see!
> It will be then no crime to gaze on me.
> See from my cheek the transient roses fly!
> See the last sparkle languish in my eye!
> Till ev'ry motion, pulse, and breath, be o'er;
> And ev'n my *Abelard* be lov'd no more.
>
> [329–34]

These climactic lines measure the intensity of a passion that requires so radical a cure as the final calm of death. Pope has not given his heroine the love of death that Congreve's mourning bride expresses or that Rowe (Pope's friend) gave to his fair penitent. Eloisa's is not a morbid love of death but an appreci-

---

63. Lines 73–98. Wellington, in his edition of the poem and Hughes's letters (pp. 126–27, n.29) shows that Pope follows his source in giving to his heroine the "long exposition of libertine naturalism" just quoted. He cites parallels from authors ranging in time from Cicero to Montaigne but curiously neglects the phenomenon in Restoration thought.

ation that, in her condition of intense and persisting passion, the only alternative is a fine and quiet grave where none embrace.[64]

Eloisa's most endearing quality is that she is a believable human being caught in the toils of a wholly probable and thoroughly understandable emotion. Religious hope and resignation give, as Johnson saw, "an elevation and dignity" to the poem, and the "gloom of a convent strikes the imagination with far greater force than the solitude of a grove."[65] Religion provided the terms of the conflict, even the conflict itself, what Pope called "the struggles of grace and nature, virtue and passion" ("The Argument"). But Pope gives no unambiguous resolution in favor of grace. Religion provided repression, not release. It also provided, to be sure, images of both gloom and glory; but it is the gloom that in reality predominates, since the glory remains only imagined. Religion constitutes an unattained and, for Eloisa, unattainable vision in this shatteringly human poem.

For all its universality, the poem is a child of its time and differs greatly from the sensibility of the Middle Ages that produced its characters. Intense and rhetorically powerful though it is, Eloisa's passion is more refined than that expressed in Abelard's own *Historia calamitatum mearum* (written as a letter to a friend about fifteen years after the drama), where the love story is frankly and even grossly sensual and violent. And, if we turn to an even greater story of love than Pope's, we find that Eloisa's passion is less impregnated with Christian sacramental pathos and final piety than Troilus's. That great medieval lover is marvelously sensual, and the radiant art of Chaucer that describes his joy does full justice to his sexual blisses. But in the end his soul rises, as Eloisa's does not, to the eighth sphere, where he can now laugh, as God laughs, at men's follies, including his own. But even before reaching this conclusion, so difficult for a modern spirit to enter into, hero, reader, and

64. It is apparent that my interpretation is consonant with those of Wellington, Tillotson (Twickenham ed.), and Frederick M. Keener, *An Essay on Pope* (New York: Columbia University Press, 1974), pp. 54–58, but perhaps not with those of Murray Krieger (*Eighteenth-Century Studies,* 3:28-47), who finds unresolved polarities; of Brendan O'Hehir ("Virtue and Passion: The Dialectic of *Eloisa to Abelard,*" *Texas Studies in Literature and Language,* vol. 2 [1960], reprinted in Mack, *Essential Articles,* pp. 310–26), who sees a theological resolution at the end, when nature and grace become reconciled in Christ, Eloisa's spiritual bridegroom; and also of Hoyt Trowbridge, who tentatively suggests that the calm that succeeds the tragic catharsis is religious—that a pious death swallows up love ("Pope's *Eloisa* and the *Heroides* of Ovid," *Studies in Eighteenth-Century Culture: Racism in the Eighteenth Century,* ed. Harold E. Pagliaro, vol. 3 [Cleveland, Ohio: Press of Case Western Reserve University, 1973], pp. 11–34). In an awkward but revealing picture entitled *Death of Héloise* (at Stourhead, Wiltshire), Robert Smirke appears to express the view of Eloisa that I have elaborated. Abelard, now an older, balding man, stands before her deathbed, an open book in one hand, the other pointing upward. She does hold the cross to her breast, but her mouth and her eyes deny she is repentant; and as he points up toward heaven, she points down to the earth. I have seen only the photograph in the library of the Frick Gallery, a negative of which is in the Courtauld Institute (B60/105).

65. Life of Pope, *Works*, 8:247.

poet shed tears of pity—pity of a sacramental and redemptive kind—for all who suffer in love. Illicit though the love of Troilus technically is, it is still one that borders on *agapē*. Christ is mysteriously in it, or we surely would not be invited by Chaucer to soften our hearts and make our spirits pliable before it. The passion, in short, partakes of the Passion. The poet is the *servus servorum* of love, and toward the lovers we are asked to "have . . . compassioun / As though I were their owne brother deare" (1.8). Pope makes no such direct appeal to our Christian brotherhood, and Eloisa, though she can surely be said to possess *gentillesse,* is not viewed *sub specie crucis.* Eloisa's is, as I have said, a fully human drama played out in a world that is still moral and religious enough to repress desire and demand discipline and where blasphemy and idolatry continue to mean something specific and serious. But the pathos does not redeem; it is a modern, post-Miltonic, unhierarchical emotion of fellow feeling for a purely human sufferer. What immortality exists is of the kind Shakespeare bestows in the sonnets or Gray in the *Elegy:* immortality through art, immortality that is achieved when future lovers drop a tear on the cold stone or a future bard grieves in song. Such immortality *Eloisa to Abelard* may itself be said to have won, although it has not received the suffrages of all modern critics. The eighteenth century found it "inimitable," and William Lisle Bowles exclaimed over "the singular beauties of this finished composition."[66] *Jane Eyre* echoes it at least twice (chaps. 24, 35), and Tess's deep love of Angel Clare seems to recall the idolatry of Eloisa: "She tried to pray to God, but it was her husband who really had her supplication" (chap. 33).

I began this chapter by asking what the Portuguese Nun, Dido, Calista, and Eloisa have in common and answered that it is surely sensual passion. In conclusion we ought now to ask what there was about that passion that related it particularly to Restoration and eighteenth-century England. Culture does what Samuel Johnson said Shakespeare—and all supreme art, for that matter—is capable of doing: it "approximates the remote, and familiarizes the wonderful."[67] We may be fairly certain that our period took the Carthaginian queen, the Italian heroine, the Portuguese religious, and the medieval French nun to its bosom not because it wanted to escape reality but because it wanted to understand and master it. From some points of view, the heroines' passion does seem remote and exotic enough, placed as it is within castle, convent, or palazzo walls. But what is its central quality? Intense devotion to a single man that is lifelong and irreversible and that lasts to the very edge of doom. Is not this in fact the very kind of obsessive devotion required of the Christian

---

66. Joseph Berington, *The History of the Lives of Abeillard and Heloisa,* 2d ed. (Birmingham, 1788), p. [v]; *Works of Pope,* ed. Bowles, 2:56.

67. "Preface to Shakespeare," *Yale Edition of Works of Johnson,* vol. 7, *Johnson on Shakespeare,* ed. Arthur Sherbo, p. 65.

marital commitment? The energy that burned in the hearts of these abandoned but loyal women was the flame that in some way would have to fuel the
domestic enterprise as it was being reconceived. I have pointed out, in discussing the heroic plays of Dryden—and I shall continue to emphasize the point
when I come to Richardson—that heroic behavior was being transferred from
the military field to the domestic scene. This chapter opens our eyes to the
possibility that passion which was frustrated within a religious vocation or by
royal responsibility might be realized in more familiar and familial places.

Pope undoubtedly chose the story of Eloisa because, with the publication of
Hughes's translation in 1713, it was becoming archetypal. Of what? Not,
surely, of religious conflict about love but of the sexual passion itself, which
was increasingly regarded as the foundation of individual love and marriage.
In "A Dialogue between Two Young Ladies, Lately Married, concerning the
Management of Husbands: Shewing how to make that Honourable State
more Easie and Comfortable" (its first edition appeared in 1696, and its third
edition was published in London in the same year as Hughes's translation),
Eloisa and Abelard figure in the consciousness of Amy and Lucy. Lucy, who is
getting on indifferently with her husband, is told the story of the lovers,
including the "unmanning" of Abelard, and at first she cannot understand
how a eunuch can cause so much fuss and feathers. But in the end Amy wins
her friend over to the newer romantic-sentimental view, that Eloisa is indeed
admirable because her love survives every conceivable obstacle and lasts as
long as her life. The sophisticated Pope is closer to these plain English wives
than to scholastic divines or philosophical critics. He celebrates not the
triumph of divine grace or of theological dialectic but the glorious persistence
of passion. He takes his place among the myth makers of modern love.

6. Friends and Lovers
The Witty and the Wise

Heav'n first taught letters for some wretch's aid,
Some banish'd lover, or some captive maid;
They live, they speak, they breathe what love inspires,
Warm from the soul, and faithful to its fires,
. . . .
Speed the soft intercourse from soul to soul,
And waft a sigh from *Indus* to the *Pole*.

[51–58]

$\mathcal{I}$N THESE LINES Pope's Eloisa, quite predictably, sees "letters" (the alphabet, all literature, epistolary art) as primarily the expression—and the relief—of the fiery breathings of love passion. By the early eighteenth century it had become a cliché that love and letters alike softened and civilized the soul; and this process of cultural mollification involved vastly more, of course, than providing an outlet for feelings "warm from the soul." It also tended to foster the elevation of woman to the intellectual and spiritual status of man; lovers of women and lovers of mere love might continue to satirize feminine foibles, to be sure, but the serious concern was to educate women in order to sophisticate the female mind and the heart. This meant above all, for a culture like that of the Restoration and of the England of Pope and Swift, making them capable of witty intercourse, of following the brisk lead of Shakespeare's Benedick and Beatrice, high-spirited lovers who do not abandon the mind either to or for love but sharpen their faculties in the very action of acquiring a lifetime partner. Such is surely one way of attaining the Miltonic ideal of heterosexual friendship—one different from the way of passion or of sentiment but a way highly congenial to Augustan *mentalité*, since it is frequently the way of the social world.

Early in the chapter on abandoned and passionate mistresses I described the court beauties painted by Lely in 1662 and stressed the sensual, passionate natures they seemed to embody. Toward the end of the century, in 1690–91, Sir Godfrey Kneller created a parallel and contrasting set of Hampton Court beauties. The differences between the courtly ladies of Charles II and those of William and Mary reflect some of the differences between love in the earlier and the later periods. Tom D'Urfey catches the spirit of the later beauties by calling them "Products of nicest Wit, and . . . of

Royal Huswifry."[1] They were wives, not mistresses; daylight, not night-time creatures; intellectual rather than sensual—qualities that are brought out in part by posture and facial expression but also by the statues, reliefs, and other emblems that accompany them. Where Lely's women possessed invitingly languorous and wanton grace, these stand erect, with their floor-length dresses of rich stuffs, wearing formal hair styles and presenting a manner much less free and cavalier than their predecessors. Some might find them a touch placid, stolid, and somber, with now and then an expression that could even be called unpleasant or stubborn (see pl. 5). They are beauties still, of course, and Fielding and Horace Walpole made them touchstones of feminine loveliness.[2] On the whole, they are much closer to the stuff of which wise, friendly, moral, sentimental, housewifely—and even witty—women are made than are the courtiers of Charles. Thus they fittingly introduce this chapter— and the next, too, on sentimental, virtuous love—chapters that discuss such women as Etherege's Harriet, Congreve's Millamant, Swift's Stella, Steele's "Dear Prue" and Indiana, and Fielding's Amelia.

Culture, influenced no doubt by the social currents of post–Civil War life and also by the Edenic ideal of Milton, was developing attitudes toward women that encouraged serious friendship between the sexes, the marriage of true minds. That prolific and typical publisher and editor, the Presbyterian Nonconformist John Dunton, produced in 1702 an anti-Jacobite work that he entitled *Petticoat Government: In a Letter to the Court Ladies,* urging his country-men to stick close to "Our Gracious Queen." The letter asserts that the world would be *"but a Desart"* without women, that the *"Gentle Sex . . . are the Moulds, in which all the Race of Adam are cast,"* that both men and women possess souls, and that there resides "an equal inbred Dignity to both." Dunton of course deplores the licentious and the libertine, but he goes out of his way to praise peculiarly feminine endowments like the female voice and female breasts. And yet, since he is almost modern in his desire for equality between men and women, he insists that *"There's no Sex in minds,"* a sentiment that Steele, a reformer but one anxious to preserve sexual distinction, was pointedly to deny.[3] Whether witty writers like Etherege, Congreve, Pope, and Swift lean toward Dunton or Steele in this matter, whether they in fact conceive of the relation between the sexes as entirely a masculine type of witty, Platonic friendship, it is partly the purpose of the chapter to determine. In any case, it is certainly to be expected that the Restoration and eighteenth century, which cherished wit and wisdom, should have created the spirited kind of inter-sexual rapport I shall now consider.

1. Quoted by J. Douglas Stewart in *English Portraits of the Seventeenth and Eighteenth Centuries* (Los Angeles: Clark Memorial Library, 1974), p. 16, where the Hampton Court beauties, as painted by Kneller, appear on pls. 1B, 2B, 3A and B, 6A and B.

2. Ibid., p. 4.

3. *Petticoat Government* (London, 1702), pp. A3r, 1, 2, 9, 10. For Steele's view, see below, p. 169.

Witty and Spirited Lovers

From the many "gay couples,"[4] as they were formerly called, of Restoration and early eighteenth-century drama, I select for brief discussion two who illustrate the kind of witty and articulate love one expects in a society that honors mental scintillation—Harriet and Dorimant from *The Man of Mode* (1676) and Millamant and Mirabell from *The Way of the World* (March 1700).[5] Many have denied that love of an admirable kind could possibly exist in the world of Etherege's play; and it is of course a love of neither the heroic nor sentimental kind that animates the breasts of the hero and heroine. Modern readers will have to forgive much in the handsome, well-dressed, brilliantly witty Dorimant, who glitters in mind as well as in dress and who possesses a deservedly sulfurous reputation. He is proud, he schemes and deceives, he spends a night with Bellinda while advancing his suit with the heroine, and he contemplates an affair with the good Emilia, but only after she has married Young Bellair: the candle, after it has been lit by a husband, will then be more easily relit by a lover. He also keeps an illiterate whore and denounces the lower classes. Still, he is by no means a moral monster but a typical Restoration gentleman who is set up not as an example to instruct but a human being to entertain us. It therefore in no way affronts probability to believe that he will be able to love steadily once he finds someone to match his verbal and mental acuity. That challenge he finds in Harriet, and there is no reason not to take him seriously when he says, "I love her and dare not let her know it" (4.1.139). In fact, all the asides of Harriet and Dorimant about the other are designed to tell us one thing chiefly, that the two are deeply and mutually attracted. What Young Bellair says of Harriet, that she is never well but when she is talking of Dorimant (4.2.164), can be applied to Dorimant's feelings about her. For the truth of the matter is that wit, intellectual affinity, and lively spirits, mental and animal, bring these two together, for reasons of intellectual pride if no other, for both are superior to their society, even to the good and certainly to the merely conventional members of it. They are young, full of sexual energy; and Harriet will gladly desert the dull country for the exciting town. One cannot guarantee that Dorimant will become a husband faithful and dutiful by later standards; but it surely promises something of value that two bright and amiable spirits are being drawn from a shoal of fools, cheap gallants, and conventional cits and are being united in the bonds of what the male lover calls love and passion.

4. See John H. Smith, *The Gay Couple in Restoration Comedy* (Cambridge, Mass.: Harvard University Press, 1948).

5. Etherege's play is quoted from the edition of W. B. Carnochan (Lincoln: University of Nebraska Press, 1966); Congreve's from the edition of Kathleen M. Lynch (Lincoln: University of Nebraska Press, 1965).

HARRIET. Whate'er you say, I know all beyond Hyde Park's a desert to you, and that no gallantry can draw you farther.

DORIMANT. That has been the utmost limit of my *love;* but now my *passion* knows no bounds, and there's no measure to be taken of what I'll do for you from anything I ever did before.

[5.2.142–46; emphasis added]

Even though we must tone down his words "love" and "passion" to an acceptable gentlemanly code, he should be believed. For love does indeed exist between these two, however unsentimental, intellectual, and amoral it may seem to be. Etherege has given us an example of Restoration minimalism, which will build a relationship on only the barest, stripped down mental and emotional essentials. These I have mentioned, and they stand in this world without religious, moral, or emotional sanctions. Yet they are real, and, however coolly, they do fulfill those Miltonic conditions for marriage, pleasing conversation and intellectual rapport. Harriet and Dorimant may in the etymological, though not the newer sentimental, sense be called "conscious" lovers. They *know* together, and among the elements of their shared knowledge is that they are superior in mind and body to the country primitives, town fops, and foolish and fearsome domestic tyrants of the older generation. They also know that they are united in a kind of intellectualized sexuality, or, if one prefers, of sexualized intellectuality. Their wit will play over such topics as religion, philosophy, society—and yes, over love itself, including the coupling of their own bodies.[6]

What prevents some of us from seeing the lovers' worth in *The Man of Mode*—the harsh lack of morality and sentiment in the world of the play—has to some degree disappeared from *The Way of the World,* thanks less (much less) to Jeremy Collier than to the whole development of tender, ethical sentiment that we have observed from Dryden on. Not that Congreve is softly sentimental: there is plenty of brittle glitter left, so much that the brief love expressions of the heroine chime out, by way of contrast, like crystal when it is struck. Millamant says, "I think I must have him . . . Well, if Mirabell should not make a good husband, I am a lost thing—for I find I love him violently" (4.258–59, 285–86). Harriet, who comes from the country, is more of an *ingénue* than Millamant; and Mirabell, though a man of the world guilty of its sins if not its crimes, puts much less strain on our sense of moral decency and feeling than does Dorimant. Otherwise, the situation does not differ greatly from that of

6. For another view of Dorimant and Harriet, see Hume, *Development of English Drama,* pp. 86–97. See also Brian Corman, "Interpreting and Misinterpreting *The Man of Mode," Papers on Language & Literature,* 13 (Winter 1977): 35–53. Corman says, "It is difficult not to take the relationship between Dorimant and Harriet as a serious one that is propelled almost irreversibly toward the marriage one expects at the end of a comedy. Dorimant and Harriet express their genuine feelings in a series of asides throughout the play" (p. 49).

the earlier play. Two high-spirited people, true wits in contrast to the wit-wouds and fools, the schemers and adulterers that surround them, are drawn together by the superiority of their minds, hearts, and palates. Congreve has made us rather more certain than Etherege that true and perhaps unshakable heterosexual friendship has developed between his lovers. There is warmth, if not heat, in this relationship, and spirits unite in mutual affection. Wit and energy bind the lovers, but there is also a marriage of true hearts. In the midst of a world that is neither lovely nor dignified, a world of metallic ambition and rusty boredom, Congreve establishes an ideal of equality in marriage, a friendship whose wit, raillery, and good humor lead to a permanent union in which each will give himself to the other "over and over again" (5.547).

Does Congreve emphasize the sexual in establishing this relationship? Never overtly so, for this is a modest play. Mirabell's refinement finds intolerable Petulant's "senseless ribaldry," which makes the ladies blush (1.472). When intimate physical matters are touched on, they are handled with witty indirection. Millamant says, "Ah! I'll never marry, unless I am first made sure of my will and pleasure"; and Mirabell replies, "Would you have 'em both before marriage? Or will you be contented with the first now, and stay for the other till after grace?" Millamant has the last word: "Ah! don't be impertinent—" (4.158–63). Such language is more delicate than the double entendre that plays around the speech and action of a Dorimant or a Horner, and indeed the love affair between Millamant and Mirabell breathes the air of eighteenth-century affective individualism.

Pope's Women

Writing to the Earl of Peterborough, perhaps in August of 1723, Pope refers to himself as being "abhominably Epicœne." He first mentions his "Merits as a Man"; and then when he turns to his qualities as a woman, he begins to write "pathetically," about love, in "the tender Strain" (*Correspondence*, 2:189). If we may adopt Pope's traditional and stereotypical metaphor for a moment, we could say that his poem about the passionate breathings of Eloisa's heart and the "Romantick" sensibility that lay behind it belong to the feminine side of his nature and the rational, witty, and moral satires to the masculine. The latter would of course not exclude women and friendship with women; Belinda in *The Rape of the Lock* and the ideal female portrait that concludes an *Epistle to a Lady* ("Of the Characters of Women") stand among the greatest achievements of the poet's social and ethical imagination. And these works embody at their heart what Pope's age would have called the manly qualities of good sense: "Charms strike the Sight, but Merit wins the Soul" (*Rape*, 5.34); the woman who is "Mistress of herself" is the recipient of Apollo's greatest gifts, "Sense,

Good-humour, and a Poet" (*Lady*, 268, 292). I have placed the moral satire on the "manly" side of Pope's nature, but it is necessary to point out that both the satire and the exaltation of woman are themselves "epicene," concerned with tender-amorous feeling as well as with moral judgment. It is now best to abandon these stereotypes of gender which, however historical, are crude at best; let us instead examine the essential ingredients of the poet's sensibility, which underlay both the exquisite poetic tribute to the tall and stately Martha ("Patty") Blount (1690–1763) and the letters the poet addressed to her and her sister. These ingredients are sexual, romantic, and ideal.

The friendship that produced both the epistolary and the poetic art was a long one, perhaps going back as far as 1705, and it was deepened by ties of mutual intellectual respect, high spirits on all sides, and a common religion (the Blounts belonged to an old Catholic family and the sisters were educated at Catholic schools in England and France).[7] The high spirits apparently tolerated the sexual jocosity which, without being excessive or offensive, appears now and then in the letters. Pope's energetic and witty bawdry, which appears prominently in his letters to Henry Cromwell, is frequently specifically phallic. He refers to the wide and well-worn passes of the "Nymphs of *Drury*" but more frequently to "my little Traveller," which he makes the subject of a naughty and fairly witty poetic *jeu:*

> Yet what more than all we prize
> Is a Thing of little Size,
> You know where.

This rondeau he asks Cromwell to show to "Sappho," perhaps Lady Mary Wortley Montagu. The same lack of reticence appears in the letters to Martha Blount and her slightly older and more attractive sister, Teresa. Addressing them both in one letter, as he so frequently did in the teens of the century, he calls them "blessed Saints," "Goddesses," "Most adorable Deities" but then lowers the tone abruptly in a burst of scatology: "But oh dear Angels! do not on any account Scratch your backsides: and oh heavnly Creatures! never leave the company to p——ss." In a strangely anonymous letter which pretends to be written by a brother to his sister but apparently was addressed to the Blount sisters, for fragments of its manuscript were found at Mapledurham, Pope says that he, a doctor, and a clergyman visited a home to see a hermaphroditic child. He reports, in language filled with bawdy meanings, that the doctor concludes his examination with a verdict that "upon the whole it was a woman; that whatever might give a handle to think otherwise, was a trifle, without being more common than for a child to be mark'd with that thing

7. See Pope, Twickenham ed., vol. 3.2, *Epistles to Several Persons*, ed. F. W. Bateson (London: Methuen, 1951), p. 46.

which the mother long'd for."[8] Such innuendos are offensive today, not because of their sexuality but because of the antifeminine tone that pervades them. But curiously, that tone survives to appear even in the verses that praise the ideal woman, verses in which, even more curiously, the laughable and monstrous hermaphrodite has been, as we shall see, transformed into the good androgyne.

The sexual is, then, present in the letters as an oxymoron—in a kind of elegant-robust, delicate-masculine way. Do we find any signs of the "Romantick," the kind of exotic sighing and elevated image making so prominent in the letters to Lady Mary which were studied in the last chapter? To some extent. Pope gives us several evocative descriptions of the romantic scenery at Stonor, Sherborne, and the Bath region when he writes letters to Patty about his travels.[9] He calls the sisters two of the "Youngest and Fairest" of their sex (that was perhaps in 1713, when Teresa was twenty-five and Martha twenty-three); he wonders that Teresa does not forbid all correspondence, "considering how often & how openly I have declared Love to you"; he wishes he were "the handsomest fellow in England for your sakes," so much does he love them and long to see them. And there is at least one moment of deep, though understated, pathos and affection. We all know what deep love tied Pope to both his parents. When his father died, he addressed to the Blount sisters one of the shortest—and most moving—letters in his voluminous correspondence: "My poor Father dyed last night. Believe, since I don't forget you this moment, I never shall." In this period of grief and ill health, perhaps in late 1717, one letter rises to the complexity and intensity of frustrated love:

> Let me open my whole heart to you: I have some times found myself inclined to be in love with you: and as I have reason to know from your Temper & Conduct how miserably I should be used in that circumstance, it is worth my while to avoid it: It is enough to be Disagreable, without adding Fool to it, by constant Slavery. I have heard indeed of Women that have had a kindness for Men of my Make; but it has been after Enjoyment, never before; and I know to my Cost that you have no Taste of that Talent in me, which most Ladies would not only Like better, but Understand better, than any other I have.
>
> I love you so well that I tell you the truth. . . .

In this amazing opening of the heart, poor Pope thinks of his twisted and tormented body, of possible sexual relations, and of the gallantry he has for years poured out to the girls. And he turns away from the grotesquerie of it all

---

8. *Correspondence,* 1:47, 42, 90, 516, 277–79. For an excellent comprehensive commentary on the correspondence of Pope and the Blount sisters, see James A. Winn, *A Window in the Bosom: The Letters of Alexander Pope,* pp. 101–10, 114–24.

9. This fact has been noted by Pat Rogers, "Pope and the Social Scene," in *Writers and Their Background: Alexander Pope,* ed. Peter Dixon (London: G. Bell & Sons, 1972), p. 140.

in wincing pain. Never after this point do the letters recapture their old verve and *joie*. Correspondence with Teresa apparently ceased altogether after a misunderstanding about investments and annuities. Letters to Martha continue, deepened and darkened by life's slow stain, as Pope remains a loyal, if somewhat melancholy, friend and as she shows some signs of petulance that must have ruffled the continuing friendship. After the outburst of 1717, and in the light of the tortured frustrations of feeling that it reveals, it is difficult to believe any of the rumors—that Pope and Martha intended to marry, that they did marry, that she was his mistress and visited his chambers. Even the gallantry before 1717 reveals something other than the singleness and obsession of romantic love, the love of an Eloisa or indeed of a Pope for Lady Mary. Indeed, Pope seems to distinguish it from what he called the romantic. Early on, perhaps in September of 1714, he calls himself "a truer Friend than ever any Romantic Lover, or any Imitator of their Style, could be." Some years later, in June 1717, he says, "I love you both, very sincerely and passionately, tho not . . . romantically (perhaps)." He compares his love of them with his love of himself ("I am in love with you both as I am with myself"), thus seeming to deny to this friendship the selflessness of a deeply passionate ravage. And if he divides his love of the girls with love of self, he also divides it, in the earlier letters, between the sisters and so misses the concentrated singleness of affection that romantic passion usually calls forth. The declarations of love are made to them both, not to Martha alone. On one occasion, perhaps in September 1714, writing from Bath to Teresa, he becomes frankly physical: at this watering place you can be "more modestly-half-naked than you appear any where else," and he refers to his "*violent* passion," but only to add immediately that this passion is directed to "your fair self and your sister" and that it has "been divided with the most wonderful regularity in the world. Even from my infancy I have been in love with one after the other of you." In writing to Martha on 24 November 1714 he says, "You have at last entirely gain'd the Conquest over your fair Sister," but then he almost at once pulls back from romanticizing rhetoric: "'tis true you are not handsome, for you are a Woman and think you are not."[10]

No, the correspondence with the Blount sisters (though it has moments of sexual passion and at least one moment of intense self-consciousness, though it has gallantry and some innuendo, and though it reveals the loyalty, the community of interest, and the respect that must characterize true friendship) cannot be called romantic. It must be sharply differentiated from the passion of the abandoned mistresses we have studied, and it does not fully fit the Miltonic ideal of heterosexual "conversation." But it is close—in its spirit and even in some of the details of the relationship (consider the doubling of the

10. *Correspondence*, 1:349, 379, 447, 456, 252, 409, 315, 257–58, 268.

gallantry and of the intimacies in addressing two women)—to the friendship between Swift and Stella.[11]

One can find evidence of rational friendship lit up with sober and loyal affection in the letters, but the clearest and certainly most concentrated embodiment of Pope's ideal is to be found in the portrait of the good woman that ends his *Epistle to a Lady,* "Of the Characters of Women." This brilliant poem Pope addressed to Martha Blount, and the concluding and climactic portrait arises from their long and steady friendship. One of the most striking and paradoxical features of this urbane, witty, and exquisitely Popean portrait is that at its highest the ideal is seen as illustrating this theme—*la donna é mobile; varium et mutabile est semper femina;* or, as Pope puts it, "Woman's at best a Contradiction still" (270). What is that contradiction? It is that at her ideal she is an alloy of male and female. Pope's panegyric recalls the good hermaphrodite of the Renaissance and anticipates the androgynous ideal of the late eighteenth century. Oddly, we remember in this moment of praise that he had bawdily described the hermaphroditic child in writing to the Blount sisters. Now, that bawdy merriment is strained through the filters of old thought and tradition, and Pope brilliantly emerges with an ideal becoming prominent in his day, that love and religion can civilize man by feminizing him:

> Heav'n, when it strives to polish all it can
> Its last best work, but forms a softer Man;
> Picks from each sex, to make the Fav'rite blest,
> Your love of Pleasure, our desire of Rest,
> Blends, in exception to all gen'ral rules,
> Your Taste of Follies, with our Scorn of Fools,
> Reserve with Frankness, Art with Truth ally'd,
> Courage with Softness, Modesty with Pride,
> Fix'd Principles, with Fancy ever new;
> Shakes all together, and produces—You.
> [271–80]

In the great Tory satirists the high and the low are never widely separated, and it is easy and natural to plunge from the sublime to the bathetic and vice versa.[12] The ideal woman, embodied in Martha Blount, is good-humored,

11. Whether Pope married Patty, promised marriage, or indulged in intimacies are questions that have persisted from Pope's to our own day, though the discussion has been much less frequent and intense than comparable speculations about Swift and Stella. See Pat Rogers, pp. 137–38; George Sherburn, *The Early Career of Alexander Pope* (Oxford: Clarendon Press, 1934), pp. 291–94; Bateson, ed., *Epistles,* pp. 45–46. Barring indisputable evidence to the contrary, it is best to regard both authors as incapable of marriage or physical intimacies—Pope for physical, Swift for psychological reasons.

12. On this topic, see Jean H. Hagstrum, "Verbal and Visual Caricature" in *England in the Restoration and Early Eighteenth Century,* ed. H. T. Swedenberg, Jr. (Berkeley and Los Angeles: University of California Press, 1972), p. 191.

commonsensical, able "To raise the Thought and touch the Heart" (250). But though she herself possesses an invincible and ever growing charm, she appears in a satirical portrait gallery of Cloes, Sapphos, Rufas, Narcissas, and Calypsos, who are "by turns all Womankind" (116) and who have "no Characters at all" (2). The paradox is even deeper than mere juxtaposition: the good woman, who builds her lasting élan and charm on humor and virtue, though a living woman of flesh and blood palpably present to the poetic speaker, is essentially a kind of unattainable exception to the frailties of most of her sex, a kind of ideal *lusus naturae*, less real than her ridiculous sisters or, if one wishes, real only to the extent that she participates in their inconsistencies.[13] For even in the "softer Man" a "Taste of Follies" and an unprincipled reign of "Fancy ever new" persist—perhaps as the very price of being human. Such a woman Pope can admire and love; a paragon he could not, for she might be only a Platonic version of the frigid "Decencies" of Cloe. Such, then, is the Popean ideal. It is admittedly not a dazzling sun but the mild moon's "more sober light" (254). Still, it is an ideal, however temperate. The sun is the realm of the vain and the transient, the moon of those who "raise the Thought and touch the Heart" (250). Pope seems to be saying that the masculine sun of the Ring and the Circus, of a flaunting, boastful, wagering society, is setting, while the moon of feminized sensibility is rising:

> Serene in Virgin Modesty she shines,
> And unobserv'd the glaring Orb declines.
> [255–56]

It is not, to be sure, Milton's Puritan-Protestant ideal of heterosexual friendship in marriage that the Catholic Pope praises. But the ideal of virginity and femininity, if we can believe the evidence of the many letters that lay behind the poetic lines, does not revive religious asceticism either. Pope and Martha Blount were both worldlings, deeply concerned with the affairs of contemporary life. It is difficult to believe that they remained untouched by the *nouvelle vague* of refined delicacy that arose when sensibility united with eros. Of that important cultural development Pope's serene moon may be one emblem.

In one of the earliest letters to Martha (25 May 1712) Pope encloses a copy of *The Rape of the Lock,* which he draws easily into the delicate, bantering, and flirtatious tone that so often characterizes this correspondence: "Our Virtue will be sooner overthrown by one Glance of yours, than by all the wicked Poets can write" (*Correspondence,* 1:143). In fact, the early letters to the sisters, those dating from 1712 to about 1718, reveal the matrix of high-spirited and affec-

13. On the relations of the portrait of "Patty" to the other portraits in this poem, see the discriminating analysis by Felicity A. Nussbaum, to which I am indebted: "Pope's 'To a Lady' and the Eighteenth-Century Woman," *Philological Quarterly* 54 (Spring 1975): 444–56, esp. pp. 451–54.

tionate raillery bearing serious implications out of which the witty mock epic must have sprung.

Pope at once loves and satirizes Belinda. She is a splendid and beautiful creature, an ornamental part of the glistening world of rustling silk and dazzling jewelry that Pope was fully prepared to admire. Could he otherwise have rendered it so alluringly in the resonating verses of *The Rape of the Lock?* The satire on the heroine and her world is that of an insider, a situation altered—even reversed—in *The Dunciad,* where the world portrayed is viewed with contempt and disgust by one who chooses to be an outsider. Belinda is a descendant of the heroines I have been discussing in this chapter, Harriet and Millamant, just as the poem in which she appears recalls *The Way of the World.* In the play members of a cabal "come together like the coroner's inquest, to sit upon the murdered reputations of the week" (1.48–49). In the *Rape,* "At ev'ry Word a Reputation dies" (3.16). In the play, Millamant pins up her hair with letters in verse, never with those in prose: "I fancy one's hair would not curl if it were pinned up with prose" (2.331–32). Belinda's curls are bound, less wittily, in "Paper-Durance" and are "wreath'd around" with "tort'ring Irons" (4.99–100). Both play and poem attack excesses in expressing love and present courtship as following the *précieux* code, in which women may be witty but must be modest and men may be aggressive but must be free of earlier entanglements. Above all, Belinda, like Millamant—and Harriet, too—possesses an animated mind in a responsive body: "Her lively Looks a sprightly Mind disclose" (2.9). And Mirabell dwells engagingly on Millamant's faults as of course Pope throughout the poem dwells on Arabella Fermor's.

If the two dramas do indeed provide an important context for the poem, one would expect—even though minimally—a love union that transcends and, in transcending, satirizes the immediate milieu. Instead, the *Rape,* unlike the plays, satirizes the lovers as well as the society that surrounds them and shows love in this world to be a truly diminished thing. The "dire Offence" arises from "am'rous Causes," but both cause and effect are relegated to the world of "trivial Things" (1.1–2). Attraction—in part sexual—there surely is. The morning dream of a glittering beau causes Belinda's "Cheek to glow," making her a part of a world where "Musick softens" and "Dancing fires" (1.24, 76). The Baron's heart is compromised, and so Belinda's lock cannot be saved—we sense "an Earthly Lover lurking at her Heart" (3.144). The loss of the lock is so filled with sexual innuendo that one must conclude that the curl stands for virginity and that in its rape there is at least a contemplation of lost physical virtue. But even with so serious an implication, it is not virtue that is lost but only reputation, miscalled honor.

> *Honour* forbid! at whose unrival'd Shrine
> Ease, Pleasure, Virtue, All, our Sex resign.
> [4.105–6]

Surely true honor could not require the loss of virtue; only reputation would demand that sacrifice.

In such a world love—even as understated and witty a love as that displayed by Harriet and Dorimant—is not allowed by Pope to exist except in exaggerated poses and parodies that recall the real thing only in distortion. The Baron burns his former love trophies to show he is free. He builds his altar of "twelve vast *French* Romances" (2.38). He blows on the fire with amorous sighs. In the melee that ensues, beaux and witlings die in metaphor and song, destroyed by killing eyes. And the fallen Baron addresses a kind of curse to any love victim who wishes to survive: "And burn in *Cupid*'s Flames,—but burn alive" (5.102). By comic exaggeration, Pope shows that real love in this glittering world has been trivialized and that the inheritance of Petrarchan and *précieux* traditions has been wasted.

The abundance of sexual reference indicates that genuinely physical love is buried beneath flounce and furbelow—and also beneath intellectual hypocrisy. For false honor, or reputation, has distorted out of all decent proportion the physical side of love and made a catastrophe out of what ought to be regarded from a rational perspective—even the very rape of the lock, the loss of physical honor. For among the important emotions that good sense must moderate are the outrage and fury with which society greets physical passion. Pope does not make this serious point with liberal or avant-garde pomposity or anything resembling libertine confidence. But it is inescapably present as an undertone in a symphony of brilliantly orchestrated effects. Do not, Pope seems to urge, exaggerate into evil the loss of what you are pleased to call honor; remember that there are many virtues superior to chastity. The emphasis is doubtless somewhat different here than in the lines to Martha Blount, where the Diana-like virtues of the sober moon are preferred to the sun's glittering social rays; but the dismay over distorting social convention is the same.

The enforcement of this liberal meaning regarding chastity explains the vigorous satire on prudery and repression that is conveyed by the machinery of the gnomes and by the symbolism of the Cave of Spleen. Gnomes are not irrevocably divided from sylphs, any more than coquettes are from prudes. Nymphs obsessed by gnomes are guilty of "Love deny'd" (1.82), and it is the gnomes who spread not gross evil but a gentle, fashionable, and life-denying mischief, since they "early taint the Female Soul, / Instruct the Eyes of young *Coquettes* to roll" (1.87–88). The Cave of Spleen is Pope's portrait of frustration and the illnesses that attend it. Libido explodes in these nether regions, as has been noted,[14] because it is dammed up—an idea familiar to the period, as we have seen in quoting Swift on dissenters and Dennis on Restoration ex-

14. By Martin Price in *To the Palace of Wisdom,* p. 153.

cesses. Those strange phantoms in the mists of the social underworld, "Dreadful, as Hermit's Dreams in haunted Shades" (4.41), obviously arose in part from religious causes, and Warburton invokes the temptations conjured up by female saints, visions which he says Pope regarded as "the effects of hypochondriac disorders."[15] Pope is openly sexual in some of his images:

> Men prove with Child, as pow'rful Fancy works,
> And Maids turn'd Bottels, call aloud for Corks.
>
> [4.53–54][16]

The eighteenth century was not ignorant of the fact that the gnomes of conventional repression and of hypocritical, canting respectability can cause "a sickly Mien" (4.31). It is relevant to note that *Tatler* 47 prescribed marriage as a cure for the spleen.

The "Romantick" Pope dreamed of love and created a masterpiece of passion in *Eloisa*. The rational and satirical Pope also sang of love, embodying it in the rational friendship with Martha Blount and, in reversed form, in the parody of true love that Belinda's world was guilty of. For that society possessed the form of love but, to its great cost in health and peace of mind, denied the power thereof. Belinda could well have used some of Eloisa's fire, since she and her kind had forgotten the truth that Pope later expressed in *An Essay on Man:*

> The surest Virtues thus from Passions shoot,
> Wild Nature's vigor working at the root.
>
> [2.183–84]

Swift's Vanessa and Stella

In one of the several brilliant allegories of *The Battle of the Books* Swift recalls in part the Satan, Sin, and Death of *Paradise Lost*. Momus bends his flight to the regions of a malignant deity called Criticism, who sits in a den atop a snowy mountain in Nova Zembla. On her right hand sits Ignorance, "her Father and Husband, blind with Age." The scene is of special interest because Criticism is made to embody the narcissistic sins that Milton decried. She subsists on a diet of her own overflowing gall, and "Her Eyes turned inward,

---

15. Note to 4:41 f in Twickenham ed., vol. 2, *Rape of the Lock and Other Poems,* ed. Geoffrey Tillotson, 3d ed. (London: Methuen, 1966), pp. 186–87.

16. It has been pointed out that the earthenware and the glassware of the Cave of Spleen "were commonplaces of scientific and semi-scientific literature" and that its crockery was "at least fifteen hundred years old when [Pope's] passage was composed." Lawrence Babb, "The Cave of Spleen," *Review of English Studies* 12 (April 1936): 165–76, esp. pp. 169, 170.

as if she lookt only upon herself." We are reminded of a Laputan's eyes, one of which turns inward as the other looks up at the zenith.[17]

The object of Swift's satire in these works is of course the learned, not lovers; but one can perhaps deduce from his attack here and also from other passages that he shares Milton's scorn and horror of incest, homoeroticism, self-love, and a morbidly excessive attraction to similars.[18] The point is worth bearing in mind because Milton's attitude was distinctly *not* shared by many pre-Romantics and Romantics, who, while they professed great love for the poet as literary examplar and even spiritual guide, nevertheless ignored his outrage at the autoerotic sins. In one extremely important matter, however, Swift demonstrates a striking divergence from Milton. Although a Christian divine, he shies away from praising marriage, or discussing it even in his sermons; and as a satirist he constantly reviles the institution for what it has become and reveals little or no sympathy for what it might have been. Such animus is strange for a minister of the Gospel and must surely have had personal psychological roots now buried too deep for our scrutiny. But one thing is abundantly clear: that Swift is not comfortable with the Miltonic ideal of heterosexual friendship as the sacramental essence of marriage. He may in fact have reverted to the old ascetic attitude of only grudging acceptance of that institution as suitable enough for the vulgar but as hardly a satisfactory physical or spiritual refuge for men of good sense and intellectual achievement. In fact, Swift mounted a lifelong and unrelenting attack on marriage that must have sprung from some kind of primal shudder. In "Phyllis, or, the Progress of Love" (1719) a prude, who forgets considerations of class distinction, elopes and ends in disgrace. The husband and the wife, once destined for better things, now keep a tavern, where as landlord and hostess they are

17. *A Tale,* etc., ed. Guthkelch and Smith, p. 240 and n.2. See *Gulliver's Travels,* voyage 3, chap. 2.

18. Because of Swift's own reticence and because of fierce social taboos, his attitude toward these matters is extremely difficult to deduce. When Burnet refers to "unnatural practices, not to be named" or to "much scandal of the worst sort," Swift comments marginally: "Only sodomy." See *Prose Works of Jonathan Swift,* ed. Herbert Davis (Oxford: Basil Blackwell, 1962), 5:278, 286. The reaction to these practices seems much milder than Swift's reactions to the excesses of Henry VIII (see below, p. 157) or to heterosexual sins in general. On the other hand, consider Swift's flick in *Gulliver's Travels* (voyage 3, chap. 8) at those who attribute chastity to sodomites—a habit in some academic and learned circles that he may well have observed and deplored. In talking to the Houyhnhnm master, Gulliver associates rape and sodomy in a list of heinous human evils (chap. 4), but he discovers that the loathsome Yahoos know nothing of the "politer pleasures" of "unnatural appetites in both sexes, so common among us" (chap. 7, last par.). In the *Battle of the Books* the unlovely Wooton and Bentley are made lovers, and morbid narcissism is rampant in the world Swift attacks in *A Tale of a Tub.* Phyllis Greenacre has found evidence of bisexuality in Swift and considers him capable of producing homosexual fellatio fantasies. But these deductions from the imagery and from biographical data are not compelling. See *Swift and Carroll: A Psychoanalytic Study of Two Lives* (New York: International Universities Press, 1955), pp. 98–99, 101, 109, 112–13.

"Cat and Dog, and Rogue and Whore" (100).[19] In "The Progress of Marriage" a young woman marries an old clergyman who dies—it is another inscrutable and imprudent match—but not before the old bridegroom has tried aphrodisiac waters to overcome his inability:

> The *horned* Floud, as Poets sing:
> . . . .
> For Husbands past their Youth to find.
> [110, 116]

Swift's comedy is hilarious and perhaps also personal, since the Dean of the poem may be in part a self-portrait. But the comic laughter is soon replaced by disgust: the husband dies and is succeeded by lovers in swarms; and finally a "broken Ensign," before he turns the widow out of doors, leaves her as a parting present "a rooted Pox to last for ever" (166).

One could accept the widely held view that these coldly reasoned but hotly felt attacks on bad marriages constitute an attack less on the institution than on the romantic love with which it was increasingly becoming associated—except that Swift's satire extends beyond romantic courtship to sexuality, parental love, and those parts of the body peculiarly and inevitably associated with the production and nurture of children, the genitalia and the breasts. In the now neglected constitution of Lilliput (chap. 6), which embodied a good many of Swift's ideals, parents and children are treated coldly and, by modern standards, even harshly. A child is under no obligation to the parents who begot him, and they are the last to be entrusted with his education. In the public nurseries an official is present during the twice-a-year parental visits to prevent fondling or any endearments. In the female nurseries the young girls are educated like males, dressed (without ornaments, of course) by servants of their own sex, and trained in habits of decency and cleanliness. In Brobdingnag (chap. 1) the female breast, through the device of enlargment which itself has been thought to be sexual, is nauseating, covered with spots, pimples, and freckles. It resembles indeed the male organ in a state of excitement, for Gulliver is placed astride it (chap. 5), like cupids in Pompeian charms and the children who ride the serpent in Blake's famous emblem. The breasts of the Yahoos (chap. 1) hang down between their knees when they walk, and the revolting Brobdingnagian monkey holds Gulliver as though she were about to suckle a child (chap. 5). The Reverend Doctor Swift would scarcely be placed in charge of diocesan marriage counseling by a forward-looking modern bishop.

19. Swift's poetry is quoted from *The Poems of Jonathan Swift,* ed. Harold Williams, 3 vols., 2d ed. (Oxford: Clarendon Press, 1958). When the title is given, only line numbers are referred to. Otherwise, volume and page refer to this edition.

Swift as a young clergyman made an offer of marriage; but more elabo-
rately qualified, reserved, self-regarding, tortuous proposals can scarcely be
conceived than those addressed to Jane Waring.[20] The key to Swift's discomfort with marriage must surely be his disgust with the physical, though the
union of the sexes provided many other affronts to good sense, prudence,
and selfish integrity as well, some of which (disparity in rank and age, for
example) I have already noted. Swift once said wryly that love and marriage
were under the rule of different goddesses: "*VENUS*, a beautiful good-
natured Lady, was the Goddess of Love; *Juno*, a terrible Shrew, the Goddess
of Marriage; and they were always mortal Enemies."[21] The author seems to
deplore this separation, but in actuality it was the union of Venus and Juno in
modern, post-Miltonic sex and sensibility that must in part have nerved Swift
to his savage attack on romantic folly.

That attack is considerably more nuanced than would at first appear, and it
is to the credit of modern scholarship that it has disclosed the range and
subtlety of Swift's satire, which is at once comic, moral, savage, tender, and
pathological. The folly of a wealthy suitor is measured brilliantly and devastatingly when he is emblemized as "a Gold Pencil tipt with Lead" (1:61). The
man whose flatulence rises with his passion is hilarious: "My Lord, on Fire
amidst the Dames, / F——s like a Laurel in the Flames" (1:66), as is Strephon
on his honeymoon, whose "Rouzer" affronts the nose of his blushing bride
(2:590). But Swift's many attempts to prove that the Queen of Love "rose
from stinking Ooze" (2:530) often merely turn the stomach. Then the author
looks less like a wit or an outraged priest than a dog returning to his vomit
or a Freudian patient repeating compulsively the particulars that produced
his trauma in the first place. Celia's dirty clothes, filled with her dandruff,
sweat, powders, lead, and hair—her handkerchief "all varnish'd o'er with
Snuff and Snot" (2:527)—represent her creator's pathological overkill and a
brutal trampling on the victim. But that indictment cannot be allowed to stand
as final, since in "A Beautiful Young Nymph Going to Bed" Corinna first
arouses amusement as "from her Gums / A Set of Teeth completely comes"
(19–20), then disgust as we see her "flabby Dugs," and finally genuine pity as
in great pain she "explores Her Shankers, Issues, running Sores" and bravely
unites her limbs and so "recollect[s]" her scattered parts. Swift even pauses to
ask how he can describe her arts "Or shew the Anguish, Toil, and Pain, / Of
gath'ring up herself again?" (69–70). It may be hard to believe that a strolling
battered toast has aroused the grand tragic emotion of pity. But she has, and
this fact reveals considerable benevolence on the part of her creator. And the

20. See the long letter to Varina, dated 4 May 1700 in *The Correspondence of Jonathan Swift*, ed.
Harold Williams (1963; reprint ed., Oxford: Clarendon Press, 1965), 1:32–36. See also ibid.,
1:18–23.
21. "Thoughts on Various Subjects" in *Prose Works*, 4:247.

polluters of female flesh, those men of whom poor Corinna is the victim, feel the lash of the indignant Christian moralist. No female sufferer from vice is so utterly destroyed as Baron Cutts, the salamander, whose "purulent and white" emissions spread corruption, leprosy, baldness on the skin they infect:

> SO have I seen a batter'd Beau
> By Age and Claps grown cold as Snow,
> Whose Breath or Touch, where e'er he came,
> Blew out Love's Torch, or chill'd the Flame:
> And should some Nymph, who n'er was cruel,
> Like *Carleton* cheap, or fam'd *Duruel*,
> Receive the Filth which he ejects,
> She soon would find, the same Effects,
> Her tainted Carcase to pursue,
> As from the *Salamander's* Spue;
> A dismal shedding of her Locks
> And, if no Leprosy, a Pox.
>
> [1:84–85]

Whether Swift's poetry of sexual disgust is in any way moral or optimistic it is not my purpose to discover. Suffice it to say here that it is poetry as vigorous as one finds in the annals of witty-satirical literature and that it possesses, besides, a richness, range, and complexity now increasingly appreciated.[22]

Poetic excellence can surely arise as well from hate and disgust as from attraction and fulfillment. And there can be little doubt that Swift's attack on romantic love quivers with psychosexual energy. But my use of the word "complexity" to describe Swift's poetic achievement was designed to suggest that mere revulsion is not enough to explain the range and variety we have encountered. Like Satan contemplating Adam and Eve in their bower, Swift may have envied what nature denied him. He did, as I have noted, make overtures

---

22. Swift's poetry has produced interesting recent criticism—didactic, Freudian, aesthetic, commonsensical, autobiographical. See Thomas B. Gilmore, Jr., "The Comedy of Swift's Scatological Poems," *PMLA* 91 (Jan. 1976): 33-43 and the discussion that followed in the next issue, 91 (May 1976): 464–67. See also Donald Greene, "On Swift's 'Scatological' Poems," *Sewanee Review* 75 (Autum 1967): 672–89; John M. Aden, "Those Gaudy Tulips: Swift's 'Unprintables' " in *Quick Springs of Sense: Studies in the Eighteenth Century,* ed. Larry S. Champion (Athens: University of Georgia Press, 1974), pp. 15–32; and Norman O. Brown, "The Excremental Vision," chap. 13 of *Life against Death: The Psychoanalytical Meaning of History* (Middletown, Conn.: Wesleyan University Press, 1959). Gilmore's shift in position (see *PMLA* article and discussion referred to above) is interesting and instructive. He does not move toward Greene's didactic position but instead modifies his own didactic views (that Swift was preaching good sense and good humor) to accommodate the disturbing presence of the poet in the poems. Swift's preoccupation with filth was indeed excessive, but he was finally victorious over himself and ends up a smiling conqueror. In the sex and love poetry, which must be distinguished from the scatological even though the two are related, Swift's own presence is unmistakable. The intellectual positions he takes indisputably reflect his own struggles with romantic love, heterosexual friendship, and marriage. I have in my commentary tried to be faithful both to general ideas and personal emotions.

regarding marriage while he was young, and one strange and teasing dream suggests the possibility that he may have identified himself with the rakish Bolingbroke. He was of course a friend and political ally of that spectacular mixture of weakness and strength. The strength he was quick to admire. He called Bolingbroke "the greatest young man I ever knew; wit, capacity, beauty, quickness of apprehension, good learning, and an excellent taste; the best orator in the house of commons, admirable conversation, good nature, and good manners; generous, and a despiser of money." The man's weaknesses Swift's rational and moral mind rebuked. He tries to "keep the toad from drinking," and he notes on a walk in the Mall that Bolingbroke steals away "to pick up some wench; and tomorrow he will be at the cabinet with the queen."[23] It is this noble and notorious man that Swift dreams about:

> Wednesday. Last night I dreamt that Ld Bolingbroke and Mr Pope were at my Cathedrall in the Gallery, and that my L^d was to preach. I could not find my Surplice, the Church Servants were all out of the way; the Doors were shut. I sent to my L^d to come into my Stall for more conveniency to get into the Pulpit. The Stall was all broken; the[y] s^d the Collegians had done it. I squeezed among the Rabble, saw my L^d in the Pulpit. I thought his prayer was good, but I forget it. In his Sermon, I did not like his quoting Mr. Wycherly by name, and his Plays. This is all, and so I waked.[24]

We cannot be absolutely sure, of course, that it was the licentious Bolingbroke who "preached" at Saint Patrick's in Swift's dream and not the gifted orator, the man of public affairs, the occasional Conformist, or even, ironically, the free-thinking Deist. But since the preaching Bolingbroke quotes Wycherley and his plays, it is likely that Swift has adorned his own pulpit with a charming, witty, and totally unreformed rake. There may have been some kind of subterranean identification in such a dream. If so—that is, if Freud is right that all dreams contain wish-fulfillment—it might explain the presence of some sympathy with sexuality even in the most scabrous verse and tell us why pity can accompany such searing anger or such devastating wit. Perhaps all we need to say is that Swift's poetry is as complex as his psyche and vice versa, letting it go at that. The psyche was, thanks in part to the cultural developments I have been concerned with, much more complex than, say, that of Posthumus in *Cymbeline,* who, feeling that he has a woman's side to him to which he attributes all mutability and corruptibility, determines to purge it by attacking the opposite sex: "I'll write against them."[25] Posthumus stands in

23. *Journal to Stella,* ed. Harold Williams (Oxford: Clarendon Press, 1948), 1:169, 339; 2:401.

24. *Prose Works,* 5:205–6. This passage comes from Swift's "Holyhead Journal, 1727," written in September of that year when he was delayed at Holyhead for a week because he had missed the packet boat (ibid., p. 203).

25. I owe the reference and the insight into Posthumus's motivation to Geoffrey Hartman. See "Literary Criticism and Its Discontents," *Critical Inquiry* 3 (Winter 1976): 218.

an old tradition that says that women, sensual themselves, are the cause of sensual mischief in men. Swift's attack, though it is sometimes conventional, is subtler and more modern than that.

Vanessa and Stella are relevant to my study because Swift mythologized them; he raised the real Esther Vanhomrigh and Esther Johnson into imaginative beings with a life of their own. We do not want to lose sight of history, and so the analysis of the poetry addressed to each will be preceded by an analysis of the letters to and from each. So much has been written about possible sexual relations with Vanessa and about a possible marriage with Stella that the air ought to be cleared at once of unnecessary speculation. The man who early in life made his offer of marriage virtually impossible for Jane Waring to accept and the mind that overflowed with disgust at all bodily functions could hardly have been eager for marriage with anyone at any time. And until decisive evidence appears, the best hypothesis is that Swift knew no copulation whatever, licit or illicit. He himself has put the matter virtually to rest, saying of himself poetically in *Cadenus and Vanessa:*

> He now cou'd praise, esteem, approve,
> But understood not what was Love.
> [546–47]

Swift's best biographer believes he told the truth when he said he lacked the "amative faculty."[26]

And yet there is no reason why what Swift felt about Stella and Vanessa and expressed in the poetry he addressed to them should not be called "love," even though he professed not to understand what that complex emotion consisted of. Like Arthur Lovejoy,[27] he distinguishes an idea with many ingredients from a simple or single idea, a "unit-idea."

> *Love,* why do we one Passion call?
> When 'tis a Compound of them all.
> [772–73]

It was hot and cold, sharp and sweet, with pleasure and pain, sorrow and joy, hope and fear paradoxically mixed. Surely somewhere in that compound is the emotion or combination of emotions that Swift expressed. In view of what I have said so far, it is obvious that what he felt was by no means what is usually thought of as love. The differences can be stated quickly and easily and do not need to be illustrated at length, because they appear obviously in the poems to Stella and in *Cadenus and Vanessa.* Swift's love is rational, sexless,

---

26. Irvin Ehrenpreis, *Swift: The Man, His Works, and the Age* (Cambridge, Mass.: Harvard University Press, 1967), 2:647. Ehrenpreis may, however, intend to confine the remark to the friendship with Vanessa.

27. *The Great Chain of Being* (Cambridge, Mass.: Harvard University Press, 1936), pp. 4, 20–21.

spiritual—based not on physical attraction, which disappears as we rot and rot, but on wit, virtue, and charity, which grow even as we ripe and ripe. I have suggested that even for so sober a satisfaction as this the word "love" is appropriate, but Swift himself would have it otherwise. He in fact chooses the traditional word "friendship," which, again traditionally, he opposes to love and eagerly prefers. For friendship is

> in its greatest Height,
> A constant, rational Delight,
> On Virtue's Basis fix'd to last,
> When Love's Allurements long are past;
> Which gently warms, but cannot burn.
> [780–84]

Such words describe exactly what I have called Swiftian love. Why then will not this, his own word "friendship," do? Partly because in the Western tradition since Plato the word has referred to admiration and association between people of the same sex and has often been directly opposed to heterosexual friendship. Some might argue that Swift virtually transformed his women into men and so earned the right to the traditional word "friendship." But mental transsexual change did not occur in any simple or understandable way in Swift's women, if it occurred at all, and we miss the essential elements of Swift's feelings for them if we fail to see that Stella and Vanessa were invincibly feminine—richly endowed and physically attractive members of the opposite sex. It is their feminine qualities that my analysis of the letters and poems will seek to disclose—and of course Swift's response to that femininity.

If Swift was attempting to escape the flesh and keep his love unspotted by physical stain, why not regard it as part of what the French call "angélisme," a European-wide phenomenon that we have already encountered and shall encounter again in connection with the sentimental movement and Richardson? The *Grand Larousse encyclopédique* (s.v. "angélisme") defines it as "désir de pureté extrême et d'évasion hors du domaine charnel" and illustrates it with a quotation from Gide that calls it "une sorte de frémissement tendre" that is to religious feeling what *joliesse* is to *beauté*. The concept was not unknown to the Swift circle. In Pope's *Eloisa* the heroine says that passion approached her "under Friendship's name" (60): in response, she Platonized love as her fancy "form'd [Abelard] of Angelick kind, / Some emanation of th' all-beauteous Mind" (61–62). But the nun's desperately defensive *angélisme* does not remain Platonic, and another of Eloisa's devices to evade love is to Christianize it: "Dim and remote the joys of saints I see" (71). This does not succeed either, and the heroine can imagine relief only in death. In *Stella's Birth-day* (1720–21) the sign of "the true old Angel-Inn" (14) tempts Swift to play with the term "angel" and try applying it to Stella:

> Now, this is Stella's Case in Fact;
> An Angel's Face, a little crack't;
> (Could Poets or could Painters fix
> How Angels look at thirty six)
> This drew us in at first to find
> In such a Form an Angel's Mind
> And ev'ry Virtue now supplyes
> The fainting Rays of Stella's Eyes.
>
> [15–22]

A witty tone does not, in Swift, obviate seriousness. And one could perhaps call a bright mind in a decaying body an "angel" and use the concept to mean a decent mind and decent manners: "Breeding, Humor, Wit, and Sense" (25). But still the word does not seem to do for Swift. It is too sentimental, too ethereal; and one of the crucial points to be made about Stella's body is that it exists, wrinkles and all, and these Swift does not want forgotten. Angels are simply too smooth and ageless, too Romantic or Victorian, for the robust Tory satirist.

And perhaps also too sexless because, as I implied earlier, for all his horror of physicality, Swift wanted his women to be women and not something else. Though earlier he had sought a wife, it was soon clear in his affair with Varina that he really desired a sister, a daughter, a pupil, and an entertaining companion. Stella and Vanessa amply fulfilled all these feminine roles. Esther Vanhomrigh was some twenty-one years younger than Swift when he at forty-one first met her, and Stella was a little girl of eight years when he became her tutor at Moor Park. The words used so far do not exhaust the possibilities in Swift's heterosexual friendships, which possessed qualities of play, tenderness, solicitude that invoke the sexual without arousing its ecstatic nature and that embody much that is domestic and uxorial. Swift's friendships fall far short of the Miltonic ideal—did not Adam interrupt his cosmological and theological instruction with kisses? (*PL*, 8.54–57). But they do recall what Milton wanted in cheerful conversation and companionship, something that was far more rewarding than the austerities of male friendship as he understood it. In his friendship with Vanessa, Swift wrote recurringly of their partaking of coffee, and Horace Walpole thought that a code word for sexual intercourse. The conjecture is not totally nonsensical, since "coffee" is indeed used in more than "its most literal and innocent meaning."[28] It refers to private meetings, slightly furtive, in which intimate and secret matters were discussed—episodes that Swift in his contemplated "Chronicle of 12 Years; from the Time of spilling the Coffee to drinking of Coffee" called "the

28. The phrase is J. H. Bernard's, who also quotes Walpole in his Introduction to *The Correspondence of Jonathan Swift, D.D.*, ed. F. Elrington Ball (London: G. Bell & Sons, 1910), 1:xxv.

Chaptr of hide, and whisper."[29] These meetings were suggestive enough to cause Vanessa to want them prolonged—and that under the protective cover of marriage. They also had enough emotional power in them to arouse an obsessive passion in the girl that ultimately required a separation and certainly induced the deepest kind of grief, if not death itself. Passion in no form could Swift accept, and "Mishessy," as he had affectionately called her, had to face the final tragedy alone. But he had shared grief and joy with her, professed to find in her all that nature ever gave a mortal: "l'honneur, la vertue, le bon sens, l'esprit, la douceur, l'agrement, et la firmitè [sic] d'ame" (ibid., 2:325). Some of these terms are sufficiently romantic, or at least feminine, to make Swift more comfortable in using a foreign tongue than his own. What we are analyzing is a kind of friendship plus, very rare in life and letters and therefore very hard to describe. Swift says, with jocular irony, that "Riches are nine parts in ten of all that is good in Life, and Health is the tenth, drinking Coffee comes long after, and yet it is the eleventh, but without the two former you cannot drink it right" (ibid., 2:427). Substitute "love" or "marriage" for "coffee," and the statement makes sense. To Swift, however, "coffee" is neither love nor marriage but, instead, a kind of substitute for both that partakes of many of their qualities.

It is the girl's determination to alter the relationship from "coffee" to love that causes the mischief described in *Cadenus and Vanessa*,[30] the poem which tells the story of Swift's relations with Esther Vanhomrigh. Cadenus (an anagram for the "decanus" of Saint Patrick's) imagines that "coffee" can continue indefinitely: he can even be coy about whether he really does allow love to enter. That secret "must never to Mankind be told, / Nor shall the conscious Muse unfold" (826–27). We can be sure that on his side Swift never allowed "coffee" to become amorous; he wanted it to go on forever in its titillating but, for him, satisfying way. Tragically, it could not. Society, at least in his day, did not make provision for it, nor could the girl allow this kind of intellectual-spiritual-emotional foreplay to continue indefinitely. Perhaps for most people—Swift in many more ways than the literary was a most exceptional being—nature itself does not permit the prolongation of "coffee." For most it almost inevitably invites Cupid to be a third guest, and in the poem that god does indeed arrive to shoot an arrow right through a book of Swift's poetry (this was to have been the girl's defense) and so pierce Vanessa's breast. Swift implies that the penetration came because his book was "feeble" (518): Had

29. *Correspondence*, ed. Williams, 2:356. For other references to "coffee," see ibid., 1:276, 308–9, 313; 2:355, 393, 427, 430.

30. Although in this commentary, I put emphasis on the relations between the poem and the reality protrayed in Swift's letters, it should be noted that he thought of literary antecedents for what he regarded as his own special brand of love poem and so he cites Ovid ("Book the Second"), Virgil ("*vide Dido*'s Case"), Tibullus, Cowley, and Waller (109–15).

not Plutarch's *Morals* blunted earlier darts? But, from a longer perspective than Swift himself can possibly provide us, we can interpret the episode to mean that something in Swift's own ideal of heterosexual friendship was peculiarly vulnerable to the aggressions of Eros he thought he was warding off. A powerful magnetism that we cannot at this distance explain was uniting sex and sensibility in Western culture, and it was a vain endeavor for Swift to try keeping them apart.

What failed with Vanessa succeeded with Stella. Perhaps because he never partook of "coffee" with Stella alone—she was always attended by her older friend Mrs. Rebecca Dingley; perhaps because he had helped form her character from very early childhood; perhaps because she was temperamentally cooler—for these or other reasons the friendship plus (this imitation of intimate love without the final intimacy) persisted through a lifetime. The relation must have been pleasing to both the man and the woman; for Swift it must have fulfilled primitive needs of his own being—a fact that gave it stability. He had depended on two women early in life, now two women depended on him. He could now be a kind of father, the titular head of a household, and so replace the father he himself had lost. These women with masculine traits joined in keeping heterosexual trauma from the relationship, but since they were women still and needed to be treated as such, they served to maintain the male identity he so desperately needed. This "fantasy family"[31] which he created thus ministered to his need for more than masculine friendship.

The brilliant *Journal to Stella* is the true literary monument to the real "love" that he felt. The poems define the ideal, but the letters embody the interplay of ideality and reality one finds in permanent art. The letters sparkle with high spirits and intimacy: Swift calls Stella and her companion "naughty girls," "rogues," "insolent sluts," "hussies," and the like. The letters have a "home" quality, a familial tone, and were usually written after Swift had gone to bed and was thinking deeply personal thoughts. Though for the most part they are chaste, they sometimes skirt the forbidden and even the obscene. Swift frequently chooses to omit a naughty word, but there is no secret about which one it is. The famous "little language" that is sprinkled through the correspondence and repeated with what looks like compulsive regularity in virtually each letter is the best evidence that, though the relationship with Stella is short of marital, sexual love, it is far beyond normal friendship. "So good night, myownlittledearsawcyinsolentrogues"—a passage that can be read without "translation." But "zoo must cly Lele and Hele, and Hele aden" is typical of a code that needs breaking: "You must cry There and Here, and

---

31. The phrase is Ehrenpreis's (*Swift*, p. 69), to whom I am everywhere indebted for far more than the language.

Here again."[32] Much speculation has been provoked by the baby talk of Swift in this *Journal.* Surely it is as wrong to find it totally innocent and playful as to find in every word a psychic substitution pregnant with meaning. Even if it is no more than nursery prattle, the very fact that it exists and is put on paper by a man at the height of his power as a writer and his position as a man of affairs is itself far from innocent. The most plausible view is that this language is full of psychosexual meaning that can never be completely unraveled. Freud asserts unequivocally that "children in dreams often stand for the genitals; and, indeed, both men and women are in the habit of referring to their genitals affectionately as their 'little ones.'"[33] Who could *prove* at this distance that Swift's "little" words have genital overtones? And yet such language certainly demonstrates all I seek to assert here—that Swift and Stella were bound together by more than the virtuous, rational, and adult rapport revealed in the poems he addressed to her.

The letters are generally more brilliant and interesting than the poems of praise, which, for all their cool charm, lack the energy and variety of the scabrous ones already discussed. Though the verses to Stella have moments of beauty, wit, and insight, they are in fact a bit dull, a quality that need not of course detract from their truth and nobility. In the letters Stella is an "Agreeable Bitch," in the poems she is "a noble generous Mind"—and the two phrases[34] pretty well measure the difference between the two art forms in which Swift chose to embody his "love." Stella in the verse embodies the uniform and universal virtues of the Houyhnhnms, but since she is not a horse she lacks their whimsical gravity. In the *Journal* at certain moments she is allowed to become a domestic kitten who frisks about in the domestic corners of her creator's brain.

Who, then, are Swift's women? They arise from life and enter his art, but even in life they are partly the creatures of his will and fancy. The reality from which the women spring is complex, molded by historical circumstances and shot through with Swift's own psychic needs. Today we encounter them not in their own or in Swift's world but in texts, where they exist as permanent art forms and take their place in the eighteenth-century mythology of love and friendship. These texts also have their contexts and subtexts, of course; and it is difficult not to believe that for Swift what I, for want of a better term, have called "love," or "friendship plus," is itself part of that current of eros and sensibility that I have been studying. A simple Platonic matrix for the friendship even with Stella will not do.

This last point needs further development. Both poems and letters combine

32. See *Journal to Stella,* ed. Williams, 1:22, 30, 67, 127, 170, 210 and n.34.
33. *The Interpretation of Dreams,* trans. James Strachey (New York: Avon Books, 1965), p. 392.
34. The first comes from *Journal,* 2:672; the second from "To Stella, Who Collected and Transcribed his Poems," 104.

to reveal that though Swift's women are not allowed sexuality, they are certainly not bodiless. Far from being ethereal essences or formal ideas, they are palpable flesh and blood. That flesh, wrinkled or unwrinkled, Swift insists—sometimes with compulsive anger—must be kept clean; but it is still earthy. His women weep, become angry, suffer from vanity, love gossip, act like children, and can envy rivals. They occupy physical space and produce in their creator puckish joy, embarrassment, and sometimes dismaying pain.

Of Stella, with whom he formed the greatest "love" of his life, he wrote deeply moving words that showed how much emotion this kind of relationship actually cost him and why I have felt it necessary to use not the word "friendship" but "friendship plus" of these strange and wonderful bonds: Stella and he "have been perfect Friends these 35 Years. . . . I am of Opinion that there is not a greater Folly than to contract too great and intimate a Friendship" (*Correspondence*, 3:141–42). Again, "I know not what I am saying; but believe me that violent friendship is much more lasting, and as much engaging, as violent love" (3:145). Swift's adjectives are revealing. He uses the noun "friendship," to be sure, since for him "love" will not do, possessing too many powerful and undesirable associations. But "friendship" he modifies by such potentially amorous terms as "violent," "engaging," "intimate," "great," and even "perfect."

I have said that Swift's women ministered to deep psychic needs which we cannot today fully perceive. One, not yet even hinted at, is now evoked by one of the adjectives I have just quoted, "violent." Can Swift's "love," like so much erotic love, be related to aggression? Epithets of hatred and scorn came quickly to his lips. He referred to Henry VIII as a "[H]ellish [D]og of a King" (*Prose Works*, 5:247), a "Dog, Villain, King, Viper, Devil Monster" (5:249)—an outpouring of vile epithets from an Anglican dean to the founder of his national church that may strike us as curious until we remember the immitigable sexuality of this monarch and Swift's loathing of carnal indulgence. Examples could be multiplied of angry, insulting language heaped on the living and the dead. Swift's hatred of dissenters seemed to know no bounds. He admired the old Cavalier fighter, Captain John Creichton (whose memoirs he may have helped to write) for breaking the pate of more than one Covenanter.[35] Swift may have admired even the decapitation of Roundheads, since, by the captain's own account, the violence was never unprovoked. Swift praised Stella for having once taken a pistol in hand and shot a thief dead in his tracks. Consider the cool approval that accompanies the recital of the circumstantial details: Stella, detecting danger, "stole softly to her dining-room window, put on a black hood, to prevent being seen, primed the pistol

---

35. See "Memoirs of Capt. John Creichton" (*Prose Works*, 5:120 ff.) and introduction by Herbert Davis (ibid., pp. xvii ff.).

fresh, gently lifted up the sash; and, taking aim with the utmost presence of mind, discharged the pistol loaden with bullets, into the body of one villain, who stood the fairest mark. The fellow, mortally wounded, . . . died the next morning."[36] The taste for violence—usually approved only if in a legal or a noble cause or as a personal necessity—enters Swift's literary art; and in *The Legion Club,* a late poem from 1736, it goes beyond what modern taste would regard as appropriate bounds. Swift wishes the following punishment on two Cromwellian brethren:

> Tye them Keeper in a Tether,
> Let them stare and stink together;
> Both are apt to be unruly,
> Lash them daily, lash they duly,
> Though 'tis hopeless to reclaim them,
> Scorpion Rods perhaps may tame them.
>   [153–58]

These lines were written when Swift was old and approaching his own end after much pain and madness. But the tendency toward violence had been in his personality from the beginning. He must have known—and perhaps even feared—that propensity. His own "love" for his women may have arisen in part to counteract the potential aggressions of his own powerful ego. It had been said immemorially—and was being said now more than ever with the rise of sensibility—that love softened and civilized life and manners. Swift's acerbities needed such mollifications. Unfortunately, perhaps, he could not bend his assertively masculine but warped nature to accept female love as it is usually pursued. The best he could do was to create a masculinized woman, who added Palladian virtue to Venereal endowments and so obviated the ravages of physical passion. Only in this way, as Swift saw it, could society "redeem the women's ruin'd cause, / Retrieve lost empire to [their] sex" ("To Dr. Swift on his birth-day, November 30, 1721," 50–51).

Swift contributed Vanessa and Stella to the gallery of witty and wise women that had been forming since the Restoration. It must have been the unconscious hope of post–Civil War and post–Puritan Englishmen that this gallery would help civilize the state and create a new man of peace and domestic virtue. Undoubtedly, as we saw in the previous chapter, the portraits of abandoned and passionate women contributed fuel to the domestic hearth, which required an access of personal affection if the new marriage of free choice and the new family growing therefrom were to survive. But though Swift was overtly hostile to romantic passion and also to marriage and sexuality, his portraits may have contributed in their own way to growing affection between

36. Ibid., p. 230 ("On the Death of Mrs. Johnson").

men and women. We have seen that the portraits of Vanessa and Stella, though they exalted rational benevolence and emotional control, were much more than coolly Platonic. In their own complex way they may have contributed to the bonding of men and women which increasingly sentimental mores required. If so, the dean, that great ironist, would have contributed an unexpected irony to the teasingly irregular flow of literary and cultural history. The enemy of romantic love would inadvertently have shown that marriages of affection depended as much on the warm esteem that glowed steadily in his extramarital affairs as on the more spectacular fires of the sexual passion that he may never have known.[37]

37. Perhaps this final perspective on Swift and marriage should be provided. Christian thought traditionally supported moderation in marriage. I have already referred to Defoe's cautionary book called *Conjugal Lewdness*. Jeremy Taylor said that marital chastity was a desirable condition that required being "restrained and temperate in the use of . . . lawful pleasure" (*The Rule and Exercises of Holy Living*, 2.3 in *The Whole Works*, 10 vols. [London, 1850], 3:64). The antiromantic Swift, a Christian divine, may well have stood consciously in that tradition—a fact that does not explain the complex psychological and aesthetic riches I have attempted to disclose.

7. Sentimental Love and Marriage
"Esteem Enliven'd by Desire"

*I*N CHAPTER 5, devoted to abandoned mistresses, I was primarily concerned with passion; in chapter 6, a study of the witty and wise friends of witty and wise poets, I was primarily concerned with esteem and friendship. In this chapter, of which the subject is "esteem enliven'd by desire," I am concerned with *both* love and friendship. These ancient rivals are at long last united—in marriage, of all places; and the radical nature of this conception of matrimony will impress especially those who are aware that Western man has more often than not found it inconceivable that the institution could possibly have anything whatever to do with either friendship or passion. Even in our own day, Denis de Rougemont has found passion and marriage totally "irreconcilable," so diverse in their origins and ends that they are of necessity mutually exclusive.[1] The union of the two, however, was precisely what the authors discussed in the present chapter recommended; and, indeed, I have suggested that the passion of deserted, grieving women in the Restoration and Augustan age was popular because it could be related to the uxorial need for erotic fire and that the witty friends, like Pope's "Patty" and Swift's Stella, were seen as embodying those rational and permanent qualities that marital friendship would require. With neither the mistress nor the friend, it seems, was marriage possible or perhaps even desirable. But writers like Steele, Addison, Thomson, and Fielding were obviously disciples of Milton, who regarded marriage as satisfying the demands of body, mind, and spirit in a union more total than any that had been hitherto conceived of as realistically possible.

For Steele the mission of true art was "to make the Mind and Body improve together." Another Spectatorial author, John Hughes, recommended a conjugal relationship that united friendship and love in such a refined degree that it was far above both the frivolous and the passionate but not without its own kind of intensity. For if the love of a wife cannot be called a "Feaver," a word perhaps more appropriate to a mistress, still marriage was successful only when it aroused "Vital Heat." For Addison, and perhaps also for the entire body of sentimental writers I shall now confront, the exemplar of this

---

1. *Love in the Western World,* 6.1, quoted by Robert G. Hazo, *The Idea of Love* (New York: Frederick A. Praeger, 1967), p. 360.

large union of body and soul is Milton's portrayal of unfallen love in Eden, which was a "noble Mixture of Rapture and Innocence."[2]

For a variety of complex historical reasons, the best adjective to describe this kind of marital union is "sentimental." In my introductory survey of that term we saw that its meaning was in the process of shifting from idea to feeling, from the rational and intellectual to the emotional and amatory. During that period of change, while the word was certainly undergoing pressure from the new against the old and while it still retained a good deal of ambivalence, it must have combined the meanings of both mental judgment and emotional intensity. Hume used it to refer to intellection but also to refer to taste as an intuitive alternative to reason. In fact the philosopher sought, in a central inquiry, to determine whether our moral attitudes are "derived from REASON or SENTIMENT; whether we attain the knowledge of them by a chain of argument and induction, or by an immediate feeling and finer internal sense."[3] Richardson, who himself exercised a profound influence upon the term "sentiment," tended to use it in its traditional sense, to refer to an opinion or judgment that was usually moral: "leading the life in the country every body should wish to lead," he rode and walked; but the hours from nine to eleven at night he "spent sentimentally" (that is, he devoted his evening to intellectual and edifying discourse). What is revolutionary in the novels is not Richardson's linguistic usage but the psychological and ethical elements that went into his treatment of the relations between men and women. He was under considerable strain as he tried to reconcile the physical-emotional and the ethical-religious, the two basic elements of sentimental love and friendship. In the following letter he is apparently defending himself for having become excessively chaste in his last novel:

> I want, methinks, to know what you delicate ladies think delicate, that I might form myself on your notions. Lord help me, I was foiled in the character I attempted of that kind [perhaps Sir Charles Grandison], to guess at delicacy, and have too often had the mortification to be censured even by ladies (of character too) as over-delicate.—Remember you not one instance in your own parlour, Abelard and Eloisa the subject? Give me therefore the Marlow notions [he is writing to Susanna Highmore, who was visiting at Marlow in Buckinghamshire] of delicacy, . . . I would fain reduce delicacy to a standard—Reduce, did I say? should not *exalt* be the word?[4]

2. *Spectator* 66 (16 May 1711), 525 (1 Nov. 1712), 345 (5 April 1712).

3. *An Enquiry concerning the Principles of Morals*, sec. 1, quoted by R. F. Brissenden, "'Sentiment': Some Uses of the Word in the Writings of David Hume," in Brissenden, ed., *Studies in the Eighteenth Century* (Toronto: University of Toronto Press, 1968), p. 92 and n.13. I am indebted to this excellent close analysis of Hume's usage.

4. The letter is dated July 1756 by internal evidence in *Selected Letters of Samuel Richardson,* ed. John Carroll (Oxford: Clarendon Press, 1964), pp. 326–27.

From this fascinating glimpse into a pioneering artist's mind we see that he was struggling with the union of the physical and spiritual and the problems that combining sexuality and morality entailed. This was the very union that the term "sentiment" was itself trying to accommodate.

For this reason "sentimental" is the word we are justified in using in order to describe adjectivally what was happening to those age-old nouns, "friendship," "love," and "marriage." My use of "sentimental" is at once broader and narrower than most other modern critical and scholarly conceptions of the term. I go far beyond its usual generic restriction to the drama, more specifically to comedy. I do not confine its application to middle-class life. Nor do I associate it inevitably with an optimistic morality that sees everything working together for good to those who love virtue and are charitable. And I resist its exclusive association with the lachrymose and the tender.[5] On the other hand, "sentiment" as a fusion of emotion and idea is not unrelated to the more restricted uses alluded to. The theater, close to popular taste, was doubtless an important force for change. Morality and more notably religion, as the example of Steele will show, are peculiarly close to love-sentimentalism. The example of Lillo is only one of the most striking adaptations of the once aristocratic emotions of tragedy, pity and fear, to the quotidian and bourgeois scene. And, as the reader of these pages will surely remember, one of my central concerns has been to observe the transfer of heroism from the military camp to the hearth, without forgetting that the heroic heritage included much of relevance to sentimental love. Remove from Ariosto's themes the knights and their bold and violent enterprises and you still have left "le donne, . . . gli amori, / Le cortesie."[6] It should be apparent, then, that my purpose is to resist excessive rigor of definition and to keep the term "sentimental" inclusive and evocative, associating it with a complex change in the mind and spirit of eighteenth-century man. Of its many associations, however, one in particular must never be ignored, for it is central to both intellectual and aesthetic meanings: the association with the emotions, primarily the emotion of love.

It is its emotional content that gives to "sentiment" the force and vivacity the term ought to possess, when it is seen in its proper historical context and delivered from an exclusive association with the second-rate and temporary in the drama. Pope (at least one strain in him), Richardson and Rousseau, the

5. For the various definitions of and approaches to sentimentalism referred to, see Arthur Sherbo, *English Sentimental Drama* (East Lansing: Michigan State University Press, 1957); Ernest Bernbaum, *The Drama of Sensibility* (1915; reprint ed., Gloucester, Mass.: Peter Smith, 1958); Paul E. Parnell, "The Sentimental Mask," in *Restoration Drama: Modern Essays in Criticism,* ed. John Loftis (New York: Oxford University Press, 1966), pp. 285–97; introduction to *Colley Cibber: Three Sentimental Comedies,* ed. Maureen Sullivan (New Haven: Yale University Press, 1973).

6. *Orlando Furioso,* 1.1.1–2. I have omitted from Ariosto's list "i cavallier, l'arme, . . . l'audaci imprese."

jesting Sterne, and the satirical Jane Austen are more profoundly sentimental than Colley Cibber or Henry Mackenzie ever dreamt of being. As one scholar has pointed out, "sentimental" may not even in our day have been adequately defined, but any one who has worked closely with its best artistic manifestations knows that it meant something "vivid and unmistakable."[7] If the term must be saved from the tepid and mawkish, it must also be preserved from the unctuously and blandly good. Blushing with the blood of feeling and passion, "sentiment" skirted the edge of the dangerous and even the immoral. Something self-delusive and egotistical lurks at its heart even when it professes virtue and joy. Its joy was in fact not a little self-approving and tended to approach a complacent ecstasy, if that oxymoron is not impossibly paradoxical. It is even arguable that sentimental love, for all its postures of self-abnegation, for all its religious and ethical avowals, did in fact come close to committing the narcissistic sins abhorred by Milton. The merely agreeable may indeed have been substituted for the truly moral as "sensationism" grew, and Milton's hierarchy of good and evil may have been watered down by teary self-approval. Thus the literature of sentiment, even when it is aesthetically or morally unsatisfying, can often be viewed as psychologically piquant and zestful.

One of the most interesting aspects of sentimentalism, hitherto insufficiently studied, is its impregnation by the feminine spirit. In introducing my discussion of passionate and abandoned mistresses, I cited Motteux's *Gentleman's Journal* and attempted to show that the issue for 1692/3 was replete with feminine attitudes. Such attitudes are even more prominent in John Dunton's *Ladies Dictionary*[8] of 1694, which fully treats the theme of love in its divine, heroic, and gentle aspects. It makes the now familiar point that love civilizes, that it can tame the savage breast, and that, by a "wonderful Sympathy," it can excite men to goodness. The love described is far from Platonic or prudish; indeed, women are urged to beautify their persons and to choose apparel carefully "for setting out the shape and proportion of the Body." But the *Dictionary* at the same time deplores carnal extremes and turns away in embarrassment and disgust from perversions of sexuality into lust and bestiality. And it praises virginity, not in order to prolong it, but in order, apparently, to make it too attractive to abandon heedlessly.

I have already introduced the concept of *angélisme,* to which I shall return in subsequent chapters and which Dunton invokes by describing virginity as a

7. Paul E. Parnell, "Sentimental Mask," p. 285. My entire paragraph is greatly indebted to this perceptive study.

8. The title continues in part: *...Being a General Entertainment for the Fair-Sex: a Work Never Attempted before in English* ...(London: 1694). See articles on "Apparel, or the Ladies Dressing-Room" (pp. 10–11), "Body the Beautifying thereof" (pp. 60–62), "Love" (pp. 263–305), "Virgins" (436–40), "Virgins, their state and behaviour" (pp. 440–41), "Virgins of the younger sort" (pp. 441–47). See also pp. 243, 267, 300, 440.

state "nearest to that of Angels." Surely this strongly Protestant Englishman does not intend to revive the Roman Catholic doctrine of a state holier than matrimony. He is apparently preaching discipline and virtue and urging that the mind and spirit prevail over the body, which, as I have said, he is far from scorning. Nevertheless, his use of the word "angel" reminds us that the notion of woman as too fragile for masculine handling was never totally absent from eighteenth-century sensibility. This tendency to make the angel in woman not only transcend but sometimes even deny her body was, as often in Western culture, associated with religious feeling and the hesitations in love induced by Christian asceticism. All this is lyrically expressed during the early eighteenth century by Elizabeth Rowe, whose music is, to quote one of her own lines about a "bright ethereal youth," of "a soft, beneficent, expressless grace."[9] We must not be taken in, however, by the professions of purity or the vague mystical lilt of the harmonies. As Richardson's Lovelace will show us, this odor of angelic sanctity possessed aphrodisiac properties, and the verse of "Philomela," as Mrs. Rowe called herself, does indeed breathe the erotic air of the Canticles.

> My Spouse! my Sister!—If beyond these names
> Of chaste affection, there are dearer ties,
> Still thou art more to me! My ravish'd heart
> Dwells on thy heav'nly beauties.[10]

Such *angélisme*, which was to persist through Shelley, Dickens, other Victorians, and a character like Hardy's Angel Clare right up to the frontiers of Modernism, where it appeared in other guises, gives us a perspective on the sexuality of sentimentalism, which indubitably exists but is sometimes so rarefied and etherealized that its physical roots are hidden from our sight.

As modern readers will be quick to recognize, one of the mischiefs of the sentimental exaltation of woman is that in the real world it does not exalt her at all. Trying hard to lift her to heaven, it succeeds only in leaving her gasping for vital breath on a sublunary shore. Sentimental love did of course require more than abject female slaves, and the masters of the movement succeeded in creating women of abiding dignity and power. But witty friendship also demanded more than modesty and obedience, and it is hard to defend the view that shared passion is per se a more liberating force than shared intellectuality. Defoe, who could never succeed fully in mythologizing the love

9. *The Miscellaneous Works in Prose and Verse,* ed. Theophilus Rowe, 2 vols. (London, 1739), 1:2. This is the first collected edition.

10. Ibid., p. 255. These lines come, in fact, from Mrs. Rowe's long and free paraphrase of *The Song of Solomon,* whose sexual implications she has by no means lost. The popularity of this languorous and delicate poet is attested by the number of editions her *Miscellaneous Works* went through: 2d ed., 1749; 3d, 1750; 4th, 1756; 5th, 1772. Earlier eds. of her work had appeared in 1731, 1734, and 1737.

relationship or in creating a woman authentically in love, was nevertheless one of the most enlightened polemicists on behalf of reform to improve woman's lot. Profession and practice were in this period, as in so many others, often at variance. And sentimentalism, which by virtue of its professions of esteem and affection ought always to have been in the vanguard, did nevertheless embody some reactionary forces. It was in this period that one ballad attained a kind of archetypal force, a centuries-old song that was modernized in John Old-mixon's *Nut-brown Maid* in 1707 and Prior's *Henry and Emma* in 1709. The old ballad was presented by Oldmixon to an early eighteenth-century audience as a "Compliment to the Fair Sex, who are often charg'd with Inconstancy" and by Prior as a portrait of "Unconquer'd Love."[11] But in fact these redactions present a woman who out-Griseldas Griselda, a grotesque of submissiveness who wins her lover's approval when she shows she is willing to be a hand-maiden to the woman she mistakenly thinks he loves. In order to be near him, she will become her rival's slave.

Richard Steele

Johnson said that Addison in his poetry "thinks justly; but he thinks faintly."[12] Can the same be said of Addison's literary twin, Richard Steele—that his emotions, though proper and decent, were lukewarm and callow? Only perhaps if one concentrates on *The Conscious Lovers,* formerly overrated because it was regarded as the *locus classicus* of sentimental feeling; but surely not if one considers those elegant and moving vignettes of common life in *The Tatler* or the exquisite and sincere letters of devotion to his wife.

Steele's literary career fulfills many of the tendencies that had been gathering force from the Restoration on: these he brings to a kind of synthesizing focus, adding the panache of his own lovable and whimsical personality. Though dashing and cavalier, Steele was a devout Christian, and he brought to the surface what many have felt in listening to the music of Bach and in contemplating the Passion and its implications for human behavior. In his *Christian Hero* (1701), his first prose work, written while he was on active duty as an ensign of the Guards and addressed to "Men of Wit and Gallantry," Steele does not scruple to rhapsodize about the crucifixion, suggesting to us who are students of the term "pathetic" that the sufferings of Christ perhaps constitute one of the fountainheads of that concept: "How his Wounds

11. See *The Literary Works of Matthew Prior*, ed. H. Bunker Wright and Monroe K. Spears, 2d ed. (Oxford: Clarendon Press, 1971), 2:909–10.

12. Life of Addison, *Works* (1825), 7:452.

blacken! His Body writhes, and Heart heaves with Pity, and with Agony!"[13] Turning from the religiously rhapsodic to the ethical, we see in *The Ladies Library* (1714) a Steele determined to fix the conduct of women. Out of the sentiments of the greatest English divines, he compiles a code of strict but not puritanical ethics. He attempts to establish a countertradition to the belles lettres of France and England that traduce and insult the female sex and that make it difficult to believe that the authors have ever had mothers, sisters, or wives.[14] In other literary forms he tried to redefine heroism in terms of benevolent action and became a leading—perhaps *the* leading—opponent of the duel. Although far from being the reformer of the status of woman that François Poulain de la Barre was in France or Defoe and Mary Astell in England, he did contribute greatly to the evolution of feminist thought in the large audience he commanded.[15]

The Letters to "Dear Prue"

It has been said that the *Pamela* sequel and *Amelia* are the first literary treatments of the good estate of marriage. But at least three decades before the novels of Richardson and Fielding began appearing, Steele had been exalting married love in his frank, guileless, and endearing letters to his second wife, Mary Scurlock, the "Dear Prue" of the correspondence. These were not, however, published until John Nichols brought them out in 1787—too late to influence the course of eighteenth-century sentiment but in time to impress at least one great Romantic poet, Coleridge, who adverted to them often. It is a pity they are not better known, for they belong to the great tradition of eighteenth-century letters—Pope's, Gray's, Walpole's, Cowper's—and their "frank and open demonstrations and assertions of love over a long period of years," in the words of Lawrence Stone, "are in striking contrast to the formal relations that were so carefully maintained in the sixteenth and early seventeenth centuries." Their charm lies in the fact that their author had no notion whatever of publication—which in no way distracts from their distinction in having been produced by a typical and complex sensibility, one that was at once the product and refiner of the tradition I have been elucidating.[16]

13. Quoted from *Tracts and Pamphlets by Richard Steele,* ed. Rae Blanchard (Baltimore, Md.: Johns Hopkins Press, 1944), p. 35. It is worthy of note that Shaftesbury's rhapsody to Nature was not the only rhapsody produced in the early eighteenth century. Steele's ecstatic responses to Christianity were widely read, this work going through some twenty editions in the course of the century. See ibid., p. 1.

14. See the 3d ed. (London, 1722), 1:1, 4, 17, 101, 102.

15. See Rae Blanchard, "Richard Steele and the Status of Women," *Studies in Philology* 26 (July 1929): 325–55.

16. See Calhoun Winton, *Captain Steele: The Early Career of Richard Steele* (Baltimore, Md.,: Johns Hopkins Press, 1964), pp. 86–90; George A. Aitken, *Life of Richard Steele* (Boston: Houghton Mifflin, 1889), 1:173 (ref. to Nichols), 177 (ref. to Coleridge); and Stone, *Family, Sex and Marriage,* pp. 361–62.

What the principals were like in real life need not concern us here, since my task is to regard them as lovers being mythologized in the art—even the artless art—of the personal letter. The letters take on some dramatic force by the contrast of lover and beloved. He is careless about money and likes to drink with boon companions. (In Michaelmas term, 1716, there were no less than eight actions for debt taken against Steele in the courts [Aitken, 2:109], and the shortest letter written to his wife was "Sober or not, I am / Ever Yours.")[17] Prue is penurious, excessively prudential (hence the nickname), quarrelsome ("Two or Three Quarrells will dispatch Me quite," 272) and she punishes him by denying him her favors ("You advise Me to take care of my soul, I do not [know] what you can think of Yours when you have, and do withhold from me your body," 510). But these contrasts merely add a fillip of reality to the devotion that reigns—to his love of her that continues to grow from 9 August 1707, when the letters commenced, to 23 June 1718, when they ended. Prue died on 26 December 1718, aged forty, the mother of one son and two daughters, and was buried 30 December in the south transept of Westminster Abbey opposite the monument to Dryden[18]—a far from meaningless juxtaposition if we remember not the poet's satires and comedies but his love poetry and heroic plays.

Tracing the professions of loyalty and affection for the woman whom Steele regarded as possessing "wit and Beauty" and also a "Good Understanding" (207), we note that their love is rich enough to have its paradoxes and that it is continually being refreshed by the living object—that it is guided by an unobtrusive religion, is fashionable in its forms of expression, and is both traditional and contemporary in its resonances. His is a "Generous passion" for her that is leveled with daily life and quotidian discourse: "I shall affect plainnesse and sincerity in my discourse to you, as much as other Lovers do perplexity and rapture. Instead of saying, I shall die for you, I professe I should be glad to Lead my life with you" (208). Steele loves his Prue, but he loves virtue as well, and he dislikes "low images of Love" as a "Blind Being" (211). Sometimes his passion takes on the vocabulary of the Longinian sublime, and he refers to "the pleasing Transport" that accompanies his thought of her "Youth Beauty and Innocence" (216). If he is sublime, he is also tender and "pathetic": his eyes are ready to "flow with Tendernesse," and he has a "gushing Heart" (217). After the marriage, love must coexist with suffering and the exasperations I have already noted. But nothing can quench the flame, which now burns brightly for her "Good sense" and

17. 16 Feb. 1717 (letter 512). See Howard Anderson, Philip B. Daghlian, and Irvin Ehrenpreis, *The Familiar Letter in the Eighteenth Century* (Lawrence: University of Kansas Press, 1966), p. 275. The letters of Steele are quoted from Rae Blanchard, ed., *The Correspondence of Richard Steele* (London: Oxford University Press, 1941) and referred to either by date or by the letter number assigned in this edition.

18. *Correspondence*, pp. 386–87, n.2 to letter 602.

her "True greatnesse of mind" (534), the latter surely a noteworthy phrase since in the application of the language of the heroic play to daily life Steele anticipates what Richardson was to do with obsessive frequency. During her long separation from him (November 1716 to December 1717, when Lady Steele was in South Wales attending to her properties), his affection remained "ardent" (542). He is a "Slave of Beauty," but he is intellectually more admiring than ever ("You are the Head of Us," 555); and he bows gladly to her rule in practical affairs. When he imagines her return, he thinks of agreeable clothes, cheerful conversation with a witty and handsome woman free of the worries of kitchen and nursery. Such are some of the emotions produced in Steele by his lady—"Poor Dear Angry Pleased Pretty Witty Silly Eve[ry]thing Prue" (566). The dominant emotion that suffuses the letters—"Love esteem and friendship and all that is soft" (575)—embodies many venerable traditions about love, perhaps the dearest and closest to Steele being that of love in Milton's Eden: he wrote to Prue less than a month before they married that "the Union of minds in pure affection is renewing the First State of Man" (210). Such sense of identification with both Milton and the sentimental movement places the correspondence fully in the central current of this book.

The Essays

In the love letters Steele addressed his wife only and expressed the private affections of his heart, revealing as he did so how much even these are guided by the *Zeitgeist* and by antecedent artistic formulations. In *The Tatler* papers Steele is a public man, who has joined with his "fellow-labourer[s], the Reformers of Manners," to civilize a nation.[19] England must be reformed from the nation of Wycherley, a society in which "love and wenching were the business of life" (no. 3), to a modern Christian state in which there prevails a gentle, civilized view of uxorial love and domestic happiness. The stage was of course one means of effecting reform, and Steele anticipated the view of Goethe's young Wilhelm Meister when he wrote in *Tatler* 8 that the theater can create "a polite and moral gentry." The periodical essay was perhaps an even more effective weapon than the drama;[20] and Steele's vignettes of family life, his short stories in prose with their tender portrayals of family joys and family woes, were designed, like the characters in Shakespeare's plays, to create "strong impressions of honour and humanity" (no. 8). Since newspapers in our own day will doubtless continue to portray sentimental scenes from domestic life as one of their staples, one could wish they possessed the style, wit,

19. No. 3, 16 April 1709. *The Tatler* essays are quoted from the edition by George A. Aitken, 4 vols. (London, 1898) and referred to by number and/or date.

20. Lawrence Stone comments on Steele's "influence in moulding eighteenth-century squirarchy attitudes to love and marriage through the pages of *The Tatler*" (*Family, Sex and Marriage*, p. 362).

and moral passion of Steele, which make forgivable his addiction to the tearful and cloying.

Steele's essays tell of the woes of lovers, parents, children; exploit the drama of the domestic scene; and emphasize the differences between the sexes in order to stimulate mutual love and respect. These several themes alternate in the columns of *The Tatler* from April 1709 to January 1710/11, the last number. In no. 45 (23 July 1709) he tells the story of the "unhappy Teraminta," a kept woman who passes life gorgeously dressed but immured, her only purpose in life being to satisfy the brutish appetites of her keeper. She pines away "in the solitude and severity of a nun, but the conscience and guilt of a harlot." No. 82 (18 October 1709) gives two tales of "exquisite distress," the first of a wife who died on the body of her husband which is washed ashore—Steele's version of Ovid's Alcyone and Ceyx, the subject at the end of the century of a drawing by Romney and a relief sculpture by Thomas Banks; and the other of a bridegroom discharging in jest a pistol he did not know was loaded and so slaying his bride just after the ceremony—a story that sounds like unadulterated melodrama in bare summary but that actually is unfolded with understated and piercing sentiment. ("Poor good old man!—" the grieving bridegroom writes to the father about his only daughter's death, "if it be possible, do not curse me.") Because Steele wants to portray real love and life known to his readers, he delicately satirizes, in no. 85, the vogue of extravagant love—romances set in Spain—and so prepares for the realistic fictions of Defoe, Richardson, and Fielding and for the approving criticism of Johnson. Now and then, as in no. 68 (15 September 1709), he calls attention to family pathos in Shakespeare, like the irresistible sorrow of Macduff in *Macbeth,* who cries out, "What, both children! Both, both my children gone!" In no. 149 he attacks the cruel and ill-natured private tyrant, the husband, and invokes *Paradise Lost* 8.39–58, the picture of Eve being lovingly instructed by Adam, which I have quoted in chapter 1. In no. 172 (16 May 1710) he asserts the extremely important idea that between the sexes there is difference but equality. "There is a sort of sex in souls," he says, in direct contradiction of what had been proclaimed by late seventeenth-century reformers.[21] But this unlikeness in the psyche (men inclining toward wisdom, women toward prudence) ought not to be regarded as a reason for inequality: "Our minds have different, not superior qualities to theirs" (172). Steele is far from being consistent, since wisdom *is* in fact superior to prudence; but his comment may reflect a high regard for a quality he lacked and his wife possessed in abundance. Sensibility is not always presented as an unmixed blessing, since it can lead to "an unmanly gentleness of mind," the

---

21. See above, p. 134, and cf. Erica Jong's comment, "The soul had no gender," in "Speaking of Love" ("My Turn"), *Newsweek,* 21 Feb. 1977, p. 11.

price one pays, apparently, for achieving "the softnesses of humanity" (181, 6 June 1710). Tears then give way to alcohol, and only the "generous and warming" wine can relieve the distress of contemplating the untimely death of beauty and innocence (181). In no. 198 (15 July 1710) Caelia, a lovely and virtuous girl, dismisses a husband who is faithless and who schemes to have her seduced. Infamy and innocence cannot dwell together, as Richardson will proclaim often in *Clarissa*. The modern woman whom Steele was delineating is too much a person of pride and integrity to remain in daily intercourse with a villain. Such a view constitutes a break with Jeremy Taylor, who believed that the wife had a mission to perform in reclaiming the wayward man and even with the Apostle Paul, who believed that the husband was sanctified in the wife. When he portrays men and women, Steele's sentimentality seldom offends modern taste: in fact he strikes us as being humane, witty, and sensible. But in enforcing filial piety, he can be intolerably mawkish and not a little silly. One cannot call *Spectator* 449 (5 August 1712) morbid, but it is scarcely healthy or vigorous: "Certain it is, that there is no Kind of Affection so pure and angelick as that of a Father to a Daughter. He beholds her both with, and without Regard to her Sex. In Love to our Wives there is Desire, to our Sons there is Ambition; but in that to our Daughters, there is something which there are no Words to express." To a father, therefore, the Fidelia of this essay gives up all, rejecting every one of her suitors to care for him. But even here Steele may have been saved by his whimsy, and one hopes that he actually rescues Fidelia from a monstrously bland devotion with a concluding stroke of irony: "What adds to the Entertainment of the good old Man is, that *Fidelia*, where Merit and Fortune cannot be overlook'd by Epistolary Lovers, reads over the Accounts of her Conquests, plays on her Spinet the gayest Airs, (and while she is doing so, you would think her formed only for Gallantry) to intimate to him the Pleasures she despises for his Sake."

"The Conscious Lovers"

Steele's inability to be persuasive in portraying parents and children in *The Tatler* carries over into *The Conscious Lovers*, his best-known but perhaps not his best play. It must be considered briefly, if only because of its great influence and popular success. The play went through some 48 editions in the course of the century, and between 1723 and 1773 it was performed some 316 times: 41 between 1723 and 1733, 85 in the next decade, 86 in the next (the decade of the triumph of the novel), 68 in the next, and 36 between 1763 and 1773 (its popularity seems to have declined with the success of Sterne).[22] The play was successful on the stage because it portrayed the sensibility that was gaining the

22. *The Plays of Richard Steele*, ed. Shirley Strum Kenny (Oxford: Clarendon Press, 1971), pp. 283, 288. References to the plays are to act, scene, and line numbers, which are taken from this edition.

day and because it addressed itself to a subject that concerned almost everyone, the possible conflict between duty to one's heart and to one's parents. As a work of art, Steele's play is less than satisfactory partly because successful reconciliation of that conflict was in Steele's day virtually impossible. How could one possibly be faithful at once to the desires of the heart and the desires of a father if these were in conflict?

The highly influential bishop William Fleetwood addressed himself to the problem in the second decade of the eighteenth century. About all he could do in untying the knotty problem was to urge charity and caution. God's commands superseded those of a parent, and so did the laws of the land. But disobedience to parents, coming into potential conflict, as it surely does, with the Fifth Commandment, must be considered only as a last resort, and then it must be undertaken with "great Modesty and Tenderness." If after neighbors and disinterested people are consulted and the parents are thought blameworthy in their resistance to marriage, then there can be a disobedience that is not sinful if the command is refused with decency and humility. But the worried bishop wanted to obviate that contingency if at all possible, and so he stressed the duty of parents to be alert to the presence of love, to respect it if it exists, and to reduce in importance considerations of fortune and estate.[23]

Let us consider how in the play Steele resolves a potential conflict and what lessons he enforces in the process. The complication is that Bevil Senior, considering the wealth involved, wants his son to marry Lucinda Sealand, whom the young man does not love but his friend Myrtle does. Bevil Junior is in love with Indiana, but his filial piety is such that he cannot disobey his father. That piety does not always look disinterested, since the son is a bit too anxious to preserve and augment his already considerable wealth. Steele, a friend of merchant wealth, of course wants the relations of father and son to seem exemplary, but perhaps the good old servant Humphrey is right in saying that "their fear of giving each other Pain, is attended with constant mutual Uneasiness" (1.1.117–18). The comment is revealing: strain must have developed when one tried to live out the new sentimental morality and reconcile it with the realities of bourgeois life. So loyal is Bevil Junior to his father's wishes that he never speaks to Indiana of the state of his heart but, instead, opens the sluices of charity to relieve her distress. An interesting and teasing association, this—between love and charity, an association that suggests that in the culture itself sex may often have lurked behind sensibility. When the two meet, they talk of esteem, a love-transcending quality which she calls "the Merit of the Soul" (2.3.36–37) and he says is something only "great Souls" (2.3.38) can possess. Steele is obviously doing what many of his successors did, attempting to transfer heroism from the military camp and the court

23. *The Relative Duties of Parents and Children, Husbands and Wives, Masters and Servants,* 2d ed. (London, 1716), pp. 25, 31, 34–35, 39, 44.

to middle-class life. But one wonders if such sentiments—along with Indiana's professed admiration of Griselda in the opera and Bevil Junior's praise of reflection as superior to sensation and his rhapsodies about charity—are not partly uttered *faute de mieux*. Had the young people been free of the restraints they were under, they might have been making love. Of course, this love even under restraint contrasts most favorably to the foolish modesty of Mrs. Sealand, Lucinda's mother, and the animality of the oafish pedant Cimberton, whom she wishes to foist on her daughter. When the recognition scene establishes Indiana as another daughter of the rich merchant Sealand, Bevil Senior is fully reconciled to the marriage; and the conflict of duties is ended by a kind of deus ex machina solution. Thus Steele really evades the issue and has, as Dennis saw,[24] created not comic laughter but only easily won joy—a mistaken aesthetic that obviates probability, instruction, and amusement. Parson Adams rightly called the play almost "solemn enough for a sermon" (*Joseph Andrews*, bk. 3, chap. 11), and the title word "conscious" refers partly to a kind of self-approving awareness that attends good behavior. But it refers primarily to love-sensibility, which suffuses the whole being with delicious, though potentially embarrassing, sensations.

In a fairly early letter, Richardson's Lovelace describes one of his victims as a "conscious girl." Of what did her "consciousness" consist and how was it manifested? She blushed, she was *"sensible all over,"* she was still innocent but at the same time encouraged the rake's amorous advances (*Clarissa* [Everyman's Library], 2:22). Richardson's full meaning of "conscious" is only potentially present in Steele, but the ingredients are there. Beneath the moralistic and highly proper social surface, physical love blushes and finally blooms. Bevil Junior and Indiana embody the gentle goodness and tempered affection based unmistakably on physical love that lay at the heart of Steele's sentimental formula and was expressed more attractively in the letters and essays I have earlier discussed. It is not impossible that the title adjective and all that it implies is the most enduring contribution to subsequent culture of Steele's once famous play.[25]

24. "Remarks on a Play, Call'd, The Conscious Lovers, A Comedy" (1723) in *The Critical Works of John Dennis*, ed. Hooker, 2:251–74.

25. In the play Indiana relates heroic greatness of mind to "Conscious Honour" and "Conscious Innocence" (2.3.204, 205), an important historical association that sees sensibility as a new version of old heroism. Bernbaum (*Drama of Sensibility*, p. 132) correctly defines "conscious" as possessing sensibility, that is, feeling—a meaning Gray used when he gave his "Favourite Cat" a "conscious tail" which "her joy declar'd" ("Ode on the Death of a Favourite Cat, Drowned in a Tub of Gold Fishes," 7). Thomson relates *conscious* to charity in the phrase "the conscious heart of Charity" ("Winter," 354). In his *Dictionary* (s.v. "conscious") Johnson records as the fourth meaning the moral one, which also must have been present in Steele's usage: "Bearing witness by conscience to any thing," and his first meaning of "conscience" is "The knowledge or faculty by which we judge of the goodness or wickedness of ourselves." These meanings—heightened feelings, blushing sexuality, charity, subjective moral approval—pretty well give the range for the entire eighteenth century.

Courtly and Bourgeois Love: "Jane Shore," "The London Merchant,"
and Hogarth's Sarah Young

The inadequacy of a social-class approach to the concept of sentimentalism is illustrated by juxtaposing Nicholas Rowe's *Jane Shore* and Lillo's *London Merchant*. Both are examples of the tenderest sensibility; both reek of the lachrymose and the "pathetic." Both clearly belong to the same movement of the human spirit toward the free expression of emotion. But the earlier play (1714) is concerned with a monarch and his former mistress; Lillo's play (1731) deals with a merchant, an apprentice, and a whore. It may indeed show a significant development that the setting of the later work is bourgeois and that of the earlier courtly. But the point that concerns us here is that tears of sensibility belong to no single level of society. Sentimentalism may have grown with the spread of bourgeois culture, but it is not the exclusive domain of the middle classes.

Nor do the tears of sentiment belong exclusively to a single genre, sentimental comedy or she-tragedies. It happens that these two plays are both based on traditional ballads and so have their roots in popular culture; both are inspired by the dramatic examples of two popular Restoration playwrights, Southerne and Otway; both are responsible for carrying sentiment to the very frontiers of the novel, a genre which both plays influenced—a literary condition, indeed, to which both plays aspire. Although what has just been said is truer of Lillo's realistic play (which, nunlike, frets at its genre's narrow walls) than of Rowe's stately and emblematic tragedy, the earlier play also cries out for a novelistic development of character contrast—between the former Jane of pleasure and the present suffering Jane, between the loving Jane and her jealous friend Alicia, and between the cruel Gloster and the good but impetuous Hastings.

In fact, so important is contrast to an understanding of *Jane Shore* that it is best analyzed by considering its opposition of good and evil or, more precisely, of the "pathetic" and the "Gothic," the latter being a clear anticipation of the Burkean sublime of terror. The term "Gothic," which was used of powerful scenes in Rowe's earlier play, is in this one appropriated by those characters who are set off against the pathos of the title character. The contrast between Jane (who deserves the title of Fair Penitent much more than Calista ever did) and the bluff and frank Alicia is indeed a moving one and may have been exemplary. The relationship of the two women could be said to anticipate that of Richardson's Clarissa and Anna Howe and Rousseau's Julie and Claire. But as the play proceeds Alicia ceases to be merely outspoken and frank; she first becomes jealous and then ends by railing against nature, mankind, and the order of the universe itself, like one of Dryden's wild and lawless women. At the close she is literally mad, denouncing her gentle and penitent friend as a beauteous witch and seeing apparitions in a bluish fire. Parallel to her ranting Gothicism is the evil of Gloster's perverted nature, who cynically stresses Jane's earlier wantonness and jollity in Edward's court, who calls her "this puling, whining harlot" (4.21),[26] who decrees for her a life of poverty and total deprivation that can be relieved only on pain of death, and who grows superstitious as his cruelty increases. And so he displays his withered arm and blames its condition on Jane, whom he now believes to be a witch as well as a whore.

Against the spectacle of a brutal man and a madwoman the goodness of the suffering heroine shines like a candle in the naughty world. She is charitable toward the poor, fond of children, severe on herself for her past sins ("sin and misery, / Like loathsome weeds, have overrun the soil" [2.193–94]), and mortified by the wooing of Hastings, who is sick with desire for the tender and repentant woman. Her sufferings deepen. She is now on the street, a burning taper in her hand, her tresses loose, a faint flush on her cheeks; and she leaves a trail of blood from her bare and wounded feet as she begs for bread, receiving some pity but more often scorn from those who throw filth on her. She longs for death, and, after she recognizes her good husband, who forgives her, she is in a position to attain her deepest wish:

> 'Tis very dark, and I have lost you now.
> Was there not something I would have bequeathed you?
> But I have nothing left me to bestow,
> Nothing but one sad sigh. O, Mercy, heav'n! *Dies.*
>
> [5.421–24]

Although pity and gentle love predominate in Jane's character, she has a colorful and sinful past; and the present is not without some expressions of spirit and rebellion. Jane decries the double standard by which a man can roam freely through the wilds of love, while if a woman ("sense[27] and nature's easy fool," 1.2.185) ever strays from convention, ruin and shame stalk her every step. What is true of Jane is true of her creator, for Rowe's vision is one not of untested purity and goodness but of virtue pitted against the external evil of foe and friend and also, more poignantly, against the comfortable evil of one's own sheltered past. Shore, recalling his past life with Jane, cries out when he hears of her present distress,

> When she was mine, no care came ever nigh her.
> I thought the gentlest breeze that wakes the spring

26. *The Tragedy of Jane Shore,* ed. Harry William Pedicord, Regents Restoration Drama Series (Lincoln: University of Nebraska Press, 1974), the edition which supplies the line numbers used. For an excellent discussion of this play, see J. Douglas Canfield, *Nicholas Rowe and Christian Tragedy,* pp. 146–78.

27. Observe this use of "sense" to mean passion, and see above, pp. 8–9, 54 and n.7.

Too rough to breathe upon her. Cheerfulness
Danced all the day before her, and at night
Soft slumbers waited on her downy pillow.
Now sad and shelterless, perhaps, she lies
Where piercing winds blow sharp, and the chill rain
Drops from some penthouse on her wretched head,
Drenches her locks, and kills her with the cold.
It is too much.—

[5.120–29]

The London Merchant, the best known of the eighteenth-century domestic tragedies and proclaimed by Diderot and Lessing[28] as marking a new epoch in culture, also submits to an analysis based on an antithesis of good and evil. For although this realistic problem play may be a distant ancestor of the work of Ibsen,[29] the ethics of a sentimentalized Puritanism shimmer through the entire action, making absolutely central a distinction between a tender love and a cruel illicit love. The good love is that which Maria, the merchant's daughter, conceives for the apprentice and which comes to full expression only at the door of death. It is characterized by melancholy on the girl's very first appearance, though we learn only gradually that George Barnwell is its object. Her love leads to charitable deeds and to at least one of slight moral dubiety when she agrees with the good employee Trueman to cover up an embezzlement by Barnwell and to make excuses for it. As George strides with giant steps into crime, Maria's malaise increases, a poignant accompaniment to the tragedy, since it is clear that he might have married the daughter of the merchant had he not deserted the path of virtue. The embrace of the lovers comes only in Gothic gloom at the end—by the light of a burning lamp in the dungeon where George is confined. Incidentally, Lillo's Maria, speaking the accents of love and death in the last scenes of the deepest pathos, is more moving than Sterne's poor, mad, loving Maria in *Tristram Shandy* and *A Sentimental Journey.* In the play the motionless form of her lover, who is about to die, is "so perfect that beauty and death, ever at enmity, now seem united there."[30] Her tongue is loosed at the brink of the grave; had it been articulate earlier—had the good woman been permitted by convention to take the initiative in love—life and sweetness might have crowned Maria's love. As it is, her embrace encircles the body of a condemned, though fully repentant, criminal. The association of

28. See Bernbaum, *Drama of Sensibility,* p. 151; Frederick S. Boas, *An Introduction to Eighteenth-Century Drama: 1700–1780* (Oxford: Clarendon Press, 1953), p. 244.

29. Allardyce Nicoll, *A History of English Drama: 1660–1900* (Cambridge: Cambridge University Press, 1965), 2:120. Nicoll calls this play a "landmark in the history . . . of European drama" (p. 121).

30. 1.9.8–9. *The London Merchant,* ed. William H. McBurney, Regents Restoration Drama Series (Lincoln: University of Nebraska Press, 1965), the edition which supplies the line numbers.

love and death has been noted before—in the morbid endings of Otway, even
in the finally optimistic *Mourning Bride* of Congreve, and in the concluding
scenes of *The Fair Penitent*. But seldom has the theme been more movingly
exploited than here, showing that memorable literature on *Liebe und Tod* was
not the exclusive province of the Jacobeans, the Romantics, or the nineteenth
century.

Millwood the prostitute presents a dramatically stark contrast to the melancholy and frustrated Maria. Like Rowe—and of course like Dryden and the
baroque seventeenth century—Lillo has learned to develop his meaning and
power through juxtaposed contrasts. Lillo said in his dedication that the aim
of tragedy is "the exciting of the passions in order to the correcting such of
them as are criminal, either in their nature or through their excess" (11–14).
George sins through excess, Millwood is evil in her nature. But what a deeply
etched portrait of evil it is, and how the dissenting Lillo surprises us by giving
his villainess a touch of greatness! She is presented as a hater of men who
desires for her present diet handsome and innocent youths. The eighteen-
year-old Barnwell meets all her qualifications, and the seduction proceeds
apace as Millwood reveals herself a Restoration naturalist of the kind we
have encountered in Dryden: moral goodness is a chimera; taste, eat, and
enjoy the fruit of life's tree. The further unmasking reveals Millwood to be a
lover of money as well as male flesh, willing to provoke her recently innocent
victim to hideous murder in a setting of Gothic gloom, the murder of an uncle
that has the look of parricide about it. Lillo brings his luckless hero into
melodramatic and primal disaster, his murderous act recalling those of Cain,
Nero, and Oedipus. After the deed, when the murderer returns bloody but
without money, repentant but poor, Millwood sinks to her lowest depths: she
laughs at conscience as a shadow and decides to turn her lover in as a murderer. But even at this her nadir, her quondam charms are praised by none
other than the merchant paragon, Thorowgood, who pays tribute to "the
powerful magic of her wit and form," which can "fire the blood that age had
froze long since" (4.16.80–82). Millwood ends, as we must surely expect, a
complete victim of distributive justice and a totally hardened contrast to the soft
and repentant apprentice. She is a superhuman figure of evil, suffering in this
life the earnest of her inheritance—the pangs of hell, chains, darkness,
wheels, racks, stinging scorpions, molten lead, seas of sulfur. She does not—
cannot—repent, and there is about her the large fatalism of a Byronic hero.
She is more than a stage villain, because before her hideous end on the
gallows, Lillo gives her a moment of dramatic power and human persuasiveness, revealing that Thorowgood is right in calling her mind "comprehensive,
daring, and inquisitive" (4.18.46–47). She blames the "barbarous sex" (11)—

men of all professions and classes—for despoiling and enslaving her. She merely followed her inclinations as the best and richest do every day. Her indictment of society and its laws is Swiftian in its savage vigor and brings this tribute from the good merchant: "Truth is truth, though from an enemy and spoke in malice" (57). Thorowgood goes on to fling this question at established society and the church: "You bloody, blind, and superstitious bigots, how will you answer this?" (58–59). Lillo's prostitute is a woman of uncommon beauty and intellectual penetration, and her indictment of society is not unlike that of the great Enlightened thinkers.

The plays of Rowe and Lillo have a primal power that Steele's *Conscious Lovers* lacks. It concentrates on unrelieved sentimental goodness, while they develop sensibility against forces of darkness and power and, at times, even perceptive and attractive evil. In Lillo one can even say that the seeds of *The Marriage of Heaven and Hell* are present. But the surprising stature of Millwood should not blind us to the superior force of sentimental goodness. Hogarth reminds us of Lillo's main point—that the wages of sin is death, that persevering goodness is its own reward. His emblematic series of 1747, *Industry and Idleness,* a work influenced by *The London Merchant,* portrays unrelentingly the decline into crime and death of Tom Idle, a far less complex character—in part owing to the nature of the medium—than George Barnwell. It is Sarah Young, however, Hogarth's richest and most interesting female character, who continues the tradition of the sentimental heroine. She appears on the first plate of *A Rake's Progress,* weeping, pregnant, holding a ring on her finger, obviously the victim of Tom Rakewell's seducing charms while he was at the university. As he sinks into folly and crime, her loyal goodness persists. On Hogarth's plate 4 (see pl. 8 herein), she appears, plainly dressed, to offer her earnings as a thrifty milliner to save Tom from imprisonment and debt. After his marriage to an older woman (who turns out to be a shrew) fails to divert him from his downward course, he is thrown into the Fleet for debt. Sarah, now a mother, visits him and faints in compassion at what she sees (Hogarth, pl. 7). Her most moving appearance is on the last plate (8) of the series, where, weeping, she attempts to succor her seducer, now mad and languishing in Bedlam, a shaven-headed, lice-infested, staring, and grinning shell of his former self (see pl. 9 herein). Of all Hogarth's women—the harlot Moll Hackabout, the middle-class bride of *Marriage à la Mode,* the wife of the industrious apprentice—only Sarah Young shows invincible goodness of heart and sweetness of temper under intolerable pressure. She is the daughter of a vengeful and unattractive mother, is herself the mother of an illegitimate child, and becomes the lover of a totally unworthy man. But because of the power of sentimental love and bourgeois virtue, she maintains a clean and wholesome dignity of person amidst corruption. It would seem that none of the bruising conditions of eighteenth-century London can harden a *coeur sensible* made tender by an early passion.[31]

Henry Fielding and "Amelia"

In the third book of *The Faerie Queene* (canto 10), the beautiful wife of the miser Malbecco deserts him to live outdoors with "the iolly *Satyres* full of fresh delight" (st. 44). When Malbecco discovers her, his all-night pleadings do not succeed in wooing her back to avaricious "virtue" away from the embraces and "busses" (st. 46) of the "rough and rude" goat-men (st. 48). Henry Fielding, who loved virtue as much as Spenser did, would have approved Hellenore's decision, given her choices. Sensuality could be forgiven, but a mean, materialistic spirit was truly the sin against the Holy Ghost.

The novelist's buoyant sexuality appears everywhere in *Joseph Andrews,* where it invigorates the conventions of courtship and of marriage itself with genuine human warmth. It everywhere creates human sympathy for *l'homme moyen sensuel* and his female equivalent (as embodied, for example, in Betty, the Tow-wouses' maid, whose "constitution" was "composed of those warm ingredients, which, though the purity of courts or nunneries might have happily controlled them, were by no means able to endure the ticklish situation of a chambermaid at an inn" (bk. 1, chap. 18). Parson Adams relentlessly exposes the lustful hypocrisy of Lady Booby by wondering that she could barbarously wish to deny young people "the common privileges, and innocent enjoyments, which nature indulges to the animal creation" (bk. 4, chap. 2). Fielding's tolerance of sexuality made him dislike coyness, hypocrisy, socially generated hatred of the male sex as monsters, and all manner of similar sexual fears and hesitations (see 4.7). The physical exuberance of the creator has been infused into his creations, and surely the full-bodied ecstasies which his good characters are capable of feeling have something of robust sexual energy and adventuresome animality about them. But Fielding's mixture is not accurately analyzed if we neglect a refining and softening sensibility that puts him squarely in the tradition I am exploring. To the "wanton Ringlets" of

31. Ronald Paulson enriches our appreciation of Sarah Young by suggesting that her *caritas* is a possible sublimation of *eros* and by adducing parallels between her and traditional *topoi* in Hogarth and elsewhere. See "Models and Paradigms: *Joseph Andrews,* Hogarth's *Good Samaritan,* and Fenelon's *Telemaque," Modern Language Notes* 91 (1976): 1186–1207, esp. pp. 1195–96, 1198. I am also indebted to the commentary of Paulson in *Hogarth's Graphic Works* (New Haven: Yale University Press, 1965), 1:165–66, 169–70, and of Sean Shesgreen, *Engravings by Hogarth* (New York: Dover Publications, 1973), pls. 28–35. I have reproduced the third state of Hogarth's plates 4 and 8 not only because it represents his final intention and gives us added dramatic elements (the stormy sky, the lightning bolt, and the ensemble of gambling children on 4 and the seal of Britannia on 8), but because on the latter Sarah Young's head has been retouched in order to close her eyes, define her chin more sharply, and mold her lips more carefully.

Illustrations

1a. JAMES BARRY, *Adam and Eve* (see p. 15).
Courtesy of the National Gallery of Ireland.

1b. JAMES BARRY, *Adam and Eve* (see
p. 15). Etching. By permission of the
Trustees of the British Museum.

2. CORREGGIO, *Ganymede* (see pp. 45, 284). Gemäldegalerie, Vienna; Bruckmann: Art Reference Bureau.

3. HUGO VAN DER GOES, *The Fall of Man* (see pp. 45,
333). Gemäldegalerie, Vienna; Bruckmann: Art Reference
Bureau.

4. SIR PETER LELY, *Lady Jane Needham, Mrs. Myddleton* (see pp. 105–6). Collection of Her Majesty the Queen. Copyright Reserved to H. M. the Queen.

5. SIR GODFREY KNELLER, *Francis Whitmore, Lady Middleton* (see pp. 133–34). Collection of Her Majesty the Queen. Copyright Reserved to H. M. the Queen.

6. PETER PAUL RUBENS, *The Death of Dido* (see pp. 107, 280). Musée du Louvre, Paris; Documentation photographique de la Réunion des Musées Nationaux.

7. NICOLAS POUSSIN (?), *Dido and Aeneas* (see p. 108).
The Toledo Museum of Art.

8. WILLIAM HOGARTH, *A Rake's Progress,* plate 4 (see p. 177). By permission of the Trustees of the British Museum.

9. HOGARTH, *A Rake's Progress,* plate 8 (see p. 177). By permission of the Trustees of the British Museum.

10. SIR JOSHUA REYNOLDS, *The Death of Dido* (see
pp. 280–81). Collection of Her Majesty the Queen.
Copyright Reserved to H. M. the Queen.

11. ALEXANDER RUNCIMAN, *The Origin of Painting*
(see p. 281). National Gallery of Scotland; Tom Scott,
Edinburgh.

12. GEORGE ROMNEY, *Sensibility* (see p. 282). Engraved
by Caroline Watson. Reproduced from William Hayley,
The Life of George Romney (1809).

13. THOMAS ROWLANDSON, *The Man of Feeling*
(1788) (see p. 282). Wilmarth Sheldon Lewis, Farmington,
Connecticut.

14. ROWLANDSON, *The Man of Feeling* (1785) (see p.
282). Wilmarth Sheldon Lewis, Farmington, Connecticut.

15. JEAN-ANTOINE WATTEAU, *The Judgment of Paris*
(see p. 284). Musée du Louvre, Paris; Alinari—Art Reference Bureau.

16. W A T T E A U, *Diana at Her Bath* (see p. 288, n.18).
Musée du Louvre, Paris; Jean H. Hagstrum.

17. WATTEAU, *A Lady at Her Toilet* (see pp. 298, 302, 303). Reproduced by permission of the Trustees, The Wallace Collection, London.

18. WATTEAU, *Fête in a Park* (see p. 298 and n.42). Reproduced by permission of the Trustees, The Wallace Collection, London.

19. WATTEAU, *L'amour paisible* (see p. 300). Charlottenburg, Berlin; Marburg—Art Reference Bureau.

20. W A T T E A U, *Le Pèlerinage à l'Ile de Cythère* (see pp. 301–2, 335). Musée du Louvre, Paris; Alinari—Art Reference Bureau.

21. LOUIS TRINQUESSE, *Offrande à Vénus* (see pp.
302–3). Musée de Dijon, Palais des Etats de Bourgogne;
Jean H. Hagstrum.

22. W A T T E A U, *Reclining Nude* (see pp. 302, 303). The Norton Simon Foundation, Los Angeles.

23. J E A N - B A P T I S T E G R E U Z E, *Seated Male Nude* (see p. 311). Bibliothèque Nationale, Cabinet des Estampes, Paris.

24. G R E U Z E, *Seated Nude Woman* (see p.
311). Courtesy of the Fogg Art Museum,
Harvard University. Bequest—Meta and
Paul J. Sachs.

25. G R E U Z E, *Saint Mary of Egypt* (see p.
312). Chrysler Museum at Norfolk, Virginia.

26. G R E U Z E, *Aegina Visited by Jupiter* (see p. 312). The
Metropolitan Museum of Art, Gift of Harry N. Abrams,
1970.

27. G R E U Z E, *La malédiction paternelle: Le fils ingrat* (see p.
313). Musée du Louvre, Paris; Alinari—Art Reference
Bureau.

28. G R E U Z E, *La malédiction paternelle: Le fils puni* (see p.
313). Musée du Louvre, Paris; Alinari—Art Reference
Bureau.

29. GREUZE, *Young Shepherd Holding a Flower* (see p. 313). Petit Palais, Paris; Bulloz—Art Reference Bureau.

30. GREUZE, *The White Hat* (see pp. 282, 313–14). Courtesy, Museum of Fine Arts, Boston.

31. G R E U Z E, *La prière du matin* (see pp. 282, 315).
Montpellier; Bulloz—Art Reference Bureau.

32. G R E U Z E, *The Votive Offering to Cupid* (see p. 315). Reproduced by permission of the Trustees, The Wallace Collection, London.

Joseph, Fielding's formal portrait[32] adds "a tenderness joined with a sensibility inexpressible" (1.8). The parallel portrait of Fanny endows her with a countenance "in which, though she was extremely bashful, a sensibility appeared almost incredible; and a sweetness, whenever she smiled, beyond either imitation or description" (2.12). Tom Jones—and by now we suspect the presence of a formula—possesses "a delicacy . . . almost inexpressible," and his eyes manifest "spirit and sensibility" (9.5). But once again, as if to avoid the implication of effeminacy that sensibility could obviously carry with it, Fielding insists that Tom also possesses a "most masculine person and mien." The whole of *Tom Jones* illustrates abundantly both the vigorously masculine and the delicately feminine qualities of the hero, a combination achieved, surely, by the pressure of tradition upon the highly yielding and receptive personality of the author.

The word "healthy" springs quickly to the tongue in speaking of Fielding on love. But since I have been concerned—and will be increasingly so as the century becomes "Romantic"—with signs of morbidity, I must raise the question of incest in *Joseph Andrews* and *Tom Jones.* When Parson Adams learns that Joseph and Fanny may be brother and sister, he falls on his knees and thanks God that "the dreadful sin of incest" (4.12) has not been committed; and until the truth of their respective origins is fully revealed, the hero and heroine take vows of celibacy and of a lifelong Platonic friendship, while Fielding refers to the fate of "Oedipus himself" (4.15). Unlike the brother and sister in Dryden's *Don Sebastian,* the lovers here escape crime, even though it is a close call. In *Tom Jones* the imputation of a worse form of incest is made against a relationship of full-blown sensuality, the love of Tom and Mrs. Waters, which led to the justly famous and unmistakably sensual eating scene of the movie version directed by Tony Richardson.

Why does Fielding give us these teasing brushes with morbid sin in developing the story of two loving heroes, one almost outrageously pure, the other almost outrageously imprudent, both men of combined vigor and gentleness? Apart from deep personal reasons, about which nothing is now known, one can suggest the following. Perhaps the author was being sensational about sex, like Mrs. Manley in her many scandalous tales and Defoe in *Moll Flanders,* where brother-sister incest is introduced. Perhaps he was, like Dryden and even Lillo in the portrayal of Millwood, anticipating the Enlightenment and Shelley, who believed that the sins of the spirit and of a repressive society were much more deeply staining than the sexual sins, even those prohibited by the severest taboo. If so, this was done by an adventurous, probing side of the

---

32. For a discussion of these portraits, see Sean Shesgreen, *Literary Portraits in the Novels of Henry Fielding* (DeKalb: Northern Illinois University Press, 1972), pp. 75–79, 126–31. Shesgreen says, rightly, that the description of Joseph is intended to make him sexually attractive (pp. 75–76); if so, we must note that sensibility has a place in that sensuality.

author's mind, but so tentatively and cautiously that the structures of religion and society remain fully intact, as they do not in Diderot, for example. But Enlightened argument does not seem to be what Fielding's indirect, even somewhat skittish, treatment of the issue suggests. Perhaps the best explanation, but one difficult to defend since it involves excessive speculation about psychological depths, is that love-sensibility contained within itself the embryo of that important cultural and psychological development later in the century which touched Rousseau and Goethe, Walpole and Beckford, and above all Byron and Shelley. Shelley declared incest to be a most poetical subject because it was related to his own love of similars, because he appreciated consanguinity and the attraction of closeness.[33] As the ingredient of delicacy became more prominent in love, the drive toward forms of unisexuality also became more prominent. It may be worth considering that in the spirit of so robustly a heterosexual man as Fielding delicate sensibility loomed larger than we have hitherto realized. With it may have come a deep and doubtless unconscious interest in incest, which emerges in the somewhat coy and devious ways I have described.

Fielding's commitment to Christianity had become more prominent when he wrote *Amelia*[34] (published in 1751), and no suggestion of morbid or irregular sexual sin is allowed to darken that already dark canvas. The novel, though flawed, may be regarded as a masterpiece of English sensibility, a climax of the tendency observed in Rowe and Lillo, to develop goodness against antithetical evil—love against powerful social and fatal forces. Fielding contrasts healthy domestic love with cancerous social evil, more deeply hated and feared than ever before in his pages. The love is also developed against the philosophical weakness of Booth, the husband, who until his conversion at the end (through reading the sermons of Barrow) has been wrong about the universe and about the forces that impinge on the destiny of man. Booth believes that man can achieve goodness by relying on the feelings alone and following their dictates, which cannot in any case be gainsaid. He is misled by this false philosophy (a kind of extreme sentimentalism without supernatural sanction, or perhaps it is a *reductio* of Pope's doctrine of the ruling passion) into trusting Colonel James, who scorns religion and virtue and who will in the end do him much harm. But weak though Booth's ideas are and necessary though it is to convert him from them to belief in Providence and a recognition of the need for prudential ethics, they are far better than those of the cynical Miss Matthews, who adheres to the ideas of Mandeville, a philosopher who deforms human nature by leaving out of it the best passion (love) that it is

33. On Shelley and on this subject generally, see Jean H. Hagstrum, "Eros and Psyche: Some Versions of Romantic Love and Delicacy," *Critical Inquiry* 3 (Spring 1977): 521–42, esp. pp. 527–38.

34. See Aurélien Digeon, *The Novels of Fielding* (1925; reprint, New York: Russell & Russell, 1962), p. 213.

capable of. To *that* Booth never stoops, since he is not one ever to believe that human nature is activated by pride and fear only. Booth's intellectual development, though treated with more sophistication than Tom Jones's, is not unlike it, for both heroes must acquire a respect for prudence, although both possess the promise of ultimate redemption because they love love and so are driven on by favorable winds.

The comments that follow are designed to bring out the theme of love and lust, with emphasis upon the qualities of the title character. It is to be borne in mind that the first part of the novel, concerning Booth's courtship and early married life, is told by Booth himself in prison just before he commits adultery with an old flame, his first love, Miss Matthews. Needless to say, in such a narrative situation we expect ironies. For the remainder of the novel—for the severest of Booth's and Amelia's trials and for their final happiness—we are in the good hands of the omniscient narrator. Fielding's narrational plan may account in part for the sense that, while the first three books seem now and then somewhat gauche, the remaining nine show so much authorial control and assurance that the reader feels securely and skillfully guided.

In the dedication Fielding alerts the reader to expect "the pleasure" of "tender sensation," and the very first sentence of the novel places the action in "the state of matrimony," a domestic setting that makes the author something of a pioneer, since marriage initiates the action instead of concluding it.[35] Since this is a novel of sensibility,[36] we are alerted at once to the sources of right feelings: they arise not from nature, which teaches only egocentricity, but from a beneficent Providence, the existence of which the Deist Robinson denies and about which his fellow prisoner, the learned Booth, is uncertain. Though he is not a metaphysical or cosmological fatalist, Booth does believe that man's emotions keep generating and hence controlling his actions. Behind the scenes Fielding is implicitly commenting on his hero's individualistic, emotional fatalism and simultaneously implying the desirability of making the emotions move at the command of virtue, a happy state of affairs that Johnson felt Richardson had realized.[37] If Booth had paused to think about

35. For a discussion of the pioneering quality of *Amelia*, the French and English reaction to it, and the novel as an embodiment of the conventional but enlightened opinion of the age about "idealized conjugal behavior," see A. R. Towers, *"Amelia and the State of Matrimony," Review of English Studies* 5 (April 1954): 144–57, esp. p. 156.

36. C. J. Rawson, who sees Fielding in *Amelia* as a novelist of sensibility, also finds the novel to present "a genuinely uneasy oscillation" between the indulgence of emotion and the silencing of it when painful or ineffable. See *Henry Fielding and the Augustan Ideal under Stress* (London: Routledge & Kegan Paul, 1972), p. 89.

37. For a discussion of the philosophical and ethical meanings of *Amelia* and their context in the age, see Martin C. Battestin, "The Problem of *Amelia*: Hume, Barrow, and the Conversion of Captain Booth," *ELH* 41 (Winter 1974): 613–48. Battestin does not find that the novel reaches an intellectual resolution, since the conflict within Fielding about the new psychology of emotion remains ambivalent.

what a fellow prisoner (Miss Matthews) revealed in her autobiography, he would have seen an example of the dangers implicit in passions that cause inner tumult and ultimately lead to crime. Ironically, Booth begins the account of his life in the room of Miss Matthews by referring to "that best and dearest of women" (2.1), his wife, to whom he is about to be unfaithful. And this theme of faithful love and loyal marriage, introduced so ironically, is the central theme of the novel, surpassing even the philosophical and ethical question of the emotions in human life, a question to which, however, it is closely related. The character of Amelia is exemplary precisely because it is suffused with the emotion of love made obedient to principles that transcend this very emotion, indeed all emotion.

One of the first of Amelia's merits to be dwelt on is her response to the crushing of her lovely nose in a chaise accident (ultimately she regained her beauty and retained only a scar): that response is sensible and even heroic, bringing out in her an attractiveness of mind that surpasses even the charms of her person (2.1).[38] Fielding is here as surely redefining the heroic as Steele and Addison had done before him. It is not too much to say that in Amelia's quiet triumph we have an example of the courage of one of Dryden's heroic heroes transferred to the quotidian sphere.

Booth's courtship of Amelia reveals him to be a man who has learned well the lessons of Steele: it is tender (tears and swoonings abound) and ethical (the mind is placed above the body), and it is accompanied by a deep family loyalty (all attention to the beloved is suspended when a sick sister, who finally dies in his arms, demands his ministrations: 2.4). In the courtship Amelia, who has chosen a man worthy though poor (she is supported in that choice by the good divine, Dr. Harrison, often, though not quite always, the author's *raisonneur*), is contrasted with her hot-tempered and materialistic mother and her selfish and mean-spirited sister. Dr. Harrison, by the way, fully honors the verbal proposal and the verbal acceptances made by Booth, Amelia, and Mrs. Harris, the *sponsalia per verba de futuro,* which no later suitor, however rich or well placed, can break (2.5). A solemn verbal betrothal, followed by consumma-

---

38. The accident to this part of her anatomy may bear the suggestion that Amelia is a woman fully capable of physical passion that in other circumstances could have gone wrong. Eric Rothstein comments, shrewdly, that "Fielding could hardly have chosen to give Amelia a damaged nose instead of a scarred chin or missing molar if he had not intended the semblance, belying the reality, of lewdness." See also the parallels from this novel which he adduces and the responses of critics to Amelia's condition which he cites. *Systems of Order and Inquiry in Later Eighteenth-Century Fiction* (Berkeley and Los Angeles: University of California Press, 1975), p. 174, n.11. A. O. J. Cockshut, in *Man and Woman: A Study of Love and the Novel, 1740–1940* (London: Collins, 1977), pp. 44–45, says, quite rightly, that Amelia, though chaste, loving, and loyal, is by no means a Victorian. She is worldly, realistic, unsurprised by the sordidness of life, vain of her beauty, tolerant of female frailty. She can lose her temper at her husband and call him, before her children, "a wicked man." And she reads the spicy Farquhar to cheer her during Booth's absence. This essential point should be borne in mind during the ensuing discussion of Amelia's character.

tion, is as sacramentally binding as a marriage.[39] Immediately on returning to England, Amelia and Booth spend three months in a rural happiness where love is at the center—a fully sensual love, as the bearing of several children clearly shows. But the idyll ends because their life is rooted in neither reality nor morality, though it is clear that the husband, a Man of Feeling, is vastly superior to his neighbors and indeed to almost every one else we have so far encountered except his beautiful wife and the good clergyman. It is as though Fielding is saying that sensibility, though it is not enough in and of itself, has the earnest of salvation in it when the proper ethical controls are applied—a combination of reason and emotion which we have found at the very heart of the word "sentiment."

When in prison Booth yields to the charms of Miss Matthews and lives for a week in what Fielding, who now tells the story directly, does not hesitate to judge severely as a "criminal conversation" (4.2), he falls from grace. That grace is embodied in and mediated by the deeply sacrificial love felt by Amelia, who earlier nursed him back to health when abroad and who shared poverty and indignity with him in her own country. From that marital Eden Booth now falls into the "sweet lethargy of pleasure" (4.2) with a siren—a fall that leads almost at once to melancholy on his part and to aggressive and selfish demands by Miss Matthews. Amelia appears on the scene just after the adultery and just after Miss Matthews has obtained Booth's release. Amelia, in contrast to the mistress and her hard egotism, is tender, soft, and good. She weeps often and faints not infrequently. Hugging her children to her, she is the central figure in a Victorian genre scene or, more historically, she constitutes the traditional emblem of Charity and her young. But in no sense is Amelia ever a prude, and she does not possess a self-righteous or vindictive bone in her body. Had Booth confessed his lapse at once, she would at once have forgiven the sin that Fielding does not excuse but finds fully pardonable.

Outside Newgate the marriage of the principals, however financially precarious their state, is contrasted with the cold, formal, loveless marriage of Colonel and Mrs. James and indeed with all the dark corruptions of the world. It is an oasis of goodness and love in a society where love, honor, wives, and families are prostituted for lust, financial gain, and political advancement. If Booth can scarcely be called an Adam, Amelia is compared fulsomely with the Eve of Milton (6.1), an Eve who is now approached by the tempter in the form of a "noble lord."[40] During this temptation the good Amelia is contrasted with

39. See Murial Brittain Williams, *Marriage: Fielding's Mirror of Morality* (University, Ala.: University of Alabama Press, 1973), pp. 124–29. Williams regards *Amelia* as "the first effort in English fiction to study realistically the problems of marriage" (p. 95).

40. Ronald Paulson has perceived the relevance of *Paradise Lost* to Fielding's fictions and the omnipresence of its central myth in the eighteenth century. See "The Pilgrimage and the Family: Structures in the Novels of Fielding and Smollett," in *Tobias Smollett: Bicentennial Essays Presented to Lewis M. Knapp*, ed. G. S. Rousseau and P.-G. Boucé (New York: Oxford University Press, 1971), pp. 67–69.

the slippery and bibulous Mrs. Ellison, one of the noble lord's confederates in the nefarious scheme, and particularly with a Mrs. Bennet, later Mrs. Atkinson (for she marries the faithful friend and military subordinate of Booth), a woman whose character is one of the most richly conceived in the entire novel. She earlier succumbed to the temptation that now awaits Amelia, whose superiority to the clever, classically learned Mrs. Bennet is the superiority of the guided heart to the undisciplined head. For the latter's intellectual gifts do not save her from a sexual fall, venereal disease, and what she herself regards as the virtual murder of her clerical husband. But it is a sign that this fascinating and much tormented woman has found grace when Amelia becomes fond of her and she becomes the wife of the good soldier Atkinson. Amelia, listening to her friend's story, one that might have been her own, demonstrates how Fielding must have wanted his stories responded to—by people who recognized them as close to life, which is the true source of the pathetic, and who reacted heartily with tears and even fainting spells. When Booth's former friend Colonel James begins a siege of Amelia's heart, we see being developed one of Fielding's fundamental antitheses—between innocence and guilt. On the side of innocence is love, on the side of guilt, lust; on the side of innocence, healthy sexuality, benevolence, tears of sensibility; on the side of guilt, monomaniacal passion, aggression, violence, calculation. Innocence needs to be fortified by prudence and sound doctrine, and these are achieved when Booth reads the great Dr. Barrow, who should not, however, be given all the credit. We must remember that Dr. Harrison for years by word and deed enforced upon Booth the example of Christian good works and supported sensibility with true charity. As the plot darkens and then brightens into a dawn of resolution, Amelia reveals that though she will never—*could* never—yield to evil seducers like the noble lord or Colonel James, there might conceivably be another way into her heart. When the good old friend, the loyal Atkinson (now married to Mrs. Bennet) seems to be dying, he gives to the heroine a picture of herself which he stole from her, had framed in gold and diamonds, and now hands over along with a virtual confession of passion. Amelia is flustered; but after taking waters and weeping, she becomes calm, and her chastity is in no way compromised. She did in truth feel "a momentary tenderness and complaisance" (11.6) that would have displeased her husband. Why? She was softened by Atkinson's "plain, honest, modest, involuntary, delicate, heroic passion" (11.6). Such is the way to a *coeur sensible.*

The last book of the novel (12) brings Booth to an acceptance of moral responsibility in his own ethics, now supported by Christian revelation, and Fielding rewards the faithfulness of the good wife by bringing to her the inheritance her wicked sister denied her. Now financially comfortable, the Booths, visited by the Atkinsons and continuing to love the good Dr. Harrison, raise a large family (two boys and four girls) in health and happiness away from London, that sink of corruption. And so ends an important novel of controlled sensibility, a story of Christian benevolence in a world that is largely evil. Amelia as a person lacks the moral grandeur and the psychological depth of Clarissa, and the novel of Fielding lacks the austere but harsh morality, the elevated philosophy, the fascinating and nuanced villainy of Richardson's masterpiece. But then *Amelia* is not Fielding's masterpiece. It is, however, far from being the failure it is sometimes regarded. One has difficulty finding its rival in English as a novel of domestic trials and triumphs, as an exploration of the pathetic mood, as a celebration of quotidian goodness, greatly tempted but ultimately triumphant. It creates an Eden in the wilderness and erects in English culture the Miltonic ideal of heterosexual friendship under an ethical and religious hierarchy, softened by the "pity" of the late Dryden, the tenderness of the she-tragedies, and the delicacy of Steele's vignettes of domestic life. It embodies the full range of meanings which it will take that great eighteenth-century word "sentimental" another decade to achieve. *Amelia,* like the very term "sentiment," is poised between the intellectual (it embodies thought and judgment about the central ethical problems of life and favors the sanctions of revelation) and the emotional (it makes refined, tender feelings, rooted in physical and sexual harmony, the motive power of existence).

Fielding's ideal is extremely close to Hume's definition of love between the sexes which I quoted in chapter 1.[41] It is equally close to the poetically expressed ideal of Thomson in *The Seasons,* also referred to earlier. It is in fact difficult to think of a more appropriate epigraph for Fielding's novel and indeed for the whole chapter on sentimental love than Thomson's phrase for domestic affection, "perfect esteem enliven'd by desire."[42] Milton did not have to wait too long for his ideal of heterosexual friendship to be realized, at least in the imaginations of men. The great poet created his bower of bliss in 1667. The two generations following applied his vision to daily life and attempted to transform his unfallen Eden into what we may call, following Blake, the condition of organized innocence. For Fielding and the sentimentalists did respect social organization and took comfort in the fact that so potentially lawless an emotion as love could come to rest in the sheltering arms of a divinely sanctioned institution like marriage.

41. See above, p. 13. In the *ELH* article cited above (n.37), Battestin makes the highly interesting and plausible suggestion that the thought of *Amelia* coincides with Hume's views on emotions in art and that an influence of the philosopher upon the novel is conceivable. See esp. pp. 641, 642–48. Fielding would doubtless have agreed with Hume about courtship ("the most agreeable scene in life") and about marriage ("The happiest marriages . . . are found where love, by long acquaintance, is consolidated into friendship"). He and the whole sentimental movement, however, might have boggled at Hume's immediately following sentence: "Whoever dreams of ecstasies beyond the honey-moon, is a fool." "Of Polygamy and Divorces" in *Essays,* The New Universal Library (London: George Routledge & Sons, n.d.), pp. 134, 138, n.1.

42. *Spring,* 1121. See above, p. 13.

8. Richardson

SAMUEL RICHARDSON, author of one of the century's greatest novels, was also one of its strongest Christians. But he was not, like Bunyan, a man of one book, nor should he be regarded as a Puritan. The context of his thought and feeling is large and complex; it cannot be subsumed under any category which he may seem at first to fit easily. As an Anglican, he was typically congenial to learning and to religious influence from both the Christian left and right, but apparently not to overtly Deistic propaganda.[1] There is of course a pietistic strain and a dissenter's idiom in him, but he can also reflect the baroque and Catholic Europe of the seventeenth century. In his novels literary allusion is impressive in range and significance, but it must be interpreted with care, for it is handled dramatically as part of his characterization. When Lovelace finds "blustering absurdity" in Dryden's "bouncing lines,"[2] he is revealing lineaments of his own fictional countenance and not necessarily displaying his creator's taste or approval. But patterns do emerge from a consideration of Richardson's intellectual milieu, and these assist us in handling what can justly be considered his central theme, the relations of women and men.[3] How does the treatment of this theme by the most important sentimental author of the century relate to the tradition of erotic mythmaking I have been exploring?

Richardson's roots lay deep in popular soil, and we do not yet understand fully his precise relations to books of piety, sermons of all denominations, manuals of self-help, didactic literature, tracts for the times, ephemeral drama, popular journalism and newspapers, and novels by and about women. Richarson must have absorbed impulses that range from the piety of Richard Allestree to the frank and scandalous sexuality of Eliza Haywood. But what needs to be noticed especially about a great mythmaker in the field of love and

1. See John A. Dussinger, "Richardson's 'Christian Vocation,'" *Papers on Language & Literature* 3 (Winter 1967): 3–19. See also Diana Spearman, *The Novel and Society* (London: Routledge & Kegan Paul, 1966), p. 191.

2. *Clarissa* (Everyman's Library), 4:511. This edition is hereafter cited by volume and page numbers.

3. Margaret Anne Doody says that "the love relationship is the focal point of Richardson's imagination": *A Natural Passion: A Study of the Novels of Samuel Richardson* (Oxford: Clarendon Press, 1974), p. 10. This is a learned study to which I am greatly indebted. Doody also says (p. 106) that "Richardson is the first major English novelist to present sexuality as a constant vital principle, . . . both conscious and subconscious."

sentiment like Richardson is that he was quickly swept into a European-wide movement and that he may have been influenced by its earlier manifestations even though his own reading was necessarily confined to books in English. Richardson of course absorbed the tradition of love-sensibility from Milton to Steele; but beyond that direct impingement upon him, he can be said to have been very close to the books and men who helped create and sustain that very tradition: the Bible, Anglican thinkers and popular interpreters of theology like Jeremy Taylor and Bishop Fleetwood, and of course Shakespeare, who from the Restoration on—as the criticism of Dryden clearly shows—was helping to create an English personality and an English position on most matters aesthetic and ethical. In attempting to revise Restoration mores, Steele appealed over the heads of writers like Etherege and Wycherley to Shakespeare and attempted to make him a source of pathetic and sentimental thought and expression. We should therefore not be totally surprised to find that behind Clarissa stands Ophelia; behind Lovelace—who, by the way, is fully at ease in referring to Shakespeare—Richard III and Iago. Indeed, one has the strong impression in reading Richardson that the Addisonian revolution in criticism ("revolution" may not be too strong a word if one thinks of his impact on Burke and therefore on the pre-Romantics) was a vital influence on his thought and led him freshly to the authors and works I have already alluded to. Richardson, who thought deeply about how to endow *Clarissa* with both tragic and sublime emotions, must have known that Addison called tragedy that "Noblest Production of Human Nature" (*Spectator* 39), that he finds the Bible rich in Oriental imagery and its language warmer than the cold European tongues (405), that the wild and solemn Shakespeare was a writer of natural genius (419), and that *Paradise Lost* achieved that rarest of literary qualities, sublimity (267, 279, 285), giving Milton the "first Place among our *English* Poets" as the creator of the noblest work of genius in our language (262). In *Sir Charles Grandison* Richardson has his hero say that to the works of Addison the female sex is "more obliged, than to those of any single man in the British world" (2:103).[4] Milton is also highly honored in the Grandison milieu, and the behavior of our first parents in love is referred to often enough to show that it had the force of living example.[5] Milton's achievement greatly surpassed that of Homer, whose *Iliad* was regarded as having done "infinite mischief" by inculcating a savage spirit. Charlotte Grandison, a wise and witty girl, asks if Alexander would have been "so *much* a madman, had it not been for Homer." The anti-Homeric bias of Richardson is much in evidence. The exaltation of Milton and the denigration of the classics perhaps had something to do with his tendency to swipe at Swift (Harriet deplores his

4. *The History of Sir Charles Grandison,* ed. Jocelyn Harris, 3 vols. (London: Oxford University Press, 1972), the edition quoted from in this chapter; references are to volume and page.

5. See above, p. 14. See also *Grandison*, 2:122–23.

frequent painting of "a dunghil" and his "abominable Yahoe story") and to downgrade Pope. Lovelace provides a revealing exception to his creator's anti-Augustan bias, for that dazzling rake does quote Swift and seems to reflect a central Popean idea when he refers to the one dominant passion that controls us all.[6]

Dryden is treated differently because, as we ought to know well, he possessed another side than that represented by "Jack" Dryden, as one of Lovelace's free and easy women always called the Restoration poet (3:276). The heroic plays—read, it would seem, as I have read them in this study—are among the most frequently cited literary works in all of Richardson. In *Sir Charles Grandison,* a novel whose basic image is music,[7] Handel joins Dryden as the object of special admiration, particularly for his setting of *Alexander's Feast,* which the hero calls the "noblest composition that ever was produced by man." That work of composite art, "as finely set, as written," was especially admired for the lines

> Happy, happy, happy pair! . . .
> None but the brave deserves the fair,

which were slightly altered and then directly applied to the relations of Charles and Harriet. At the danger of excessive reiteration, it must be said once again that one important reason why Richardson praised Dryden, Handel, and Milton and tended to undervalue the witty, mock-heroic English neoclassical writers was that he was deeply involved in the movement to redefine the hero. Far from being the violent, aggressive, bloody, ranting man of the central tradition, the hero ought instead to be a Christian, with a heart full of pity for the weak and the needy. In *Sir Charles Grandison* among the last words spoken by Harriet are that the "TRULY GOOD MAN" is superior to any hero. It is no disgrace for a man to be what men increasingly were calling women and what Harriet Byron calls her future husband, an "Angel," one who shames people into "amendment, by gentle expostulation, and *forgiveness.*" For this ideal Addison was a particular exemplar; he wrote in *The Campaign* that

> Great souls by instinct to each other turn,
> Demand alliance, and in friendship burn.

It is of considerable importance that Addison associates the obsessive phrase from the heroic drama, "great souls," with friendship and that this passage should be quoted by Sir Charles.[8]

6. *Clarissa,* 3:244, 486. The references to *Sir Charles Grandison* in this paragraph come from 3:197–98; 1:348. Charlotte's comment on Alexander and Homer I owe to Ian Watt, "Defoe and Richardson on Homer: A Study of the Relation of Novel and Epic in the Early Eighteenth Century," *Review of English Studies* 3 (Oct. 1952): 334.

7. Doody (*A Natural Passion,* p. 353) says that this imagery is not found in *Clarissa.*

8. The references to *Sir Charles Grandison* in this paragraph come from 1:239; 2:345; 3:88, 462; 2:375, 353; 2:103.

Others from the English tradition I have been studying do not perhaps have the crucial importance of Milton and Dryden in helping Richardson define love and friendship. But they too form a pattern in his intellectual context that make him a candidate for the terms "sentimental" and perhaps even "Romantic."[9] Thus he almost rapturously praises Spenser ("What an imagination! What an invention! What painting!") as an "Author of Fire, Fancy, Imagination; yet charmingly natural, and harmonious."[10] Otway's two famous plays—and also *Caius Marius*—are much in the minds of Richardson's characters, as are the *Oedipus, Borgia,* and *Theodosius* of Nat. Lee. Lothario of Rowe's *Fair Penitent* has been long seen as one of the sources of Lovelace; and Calista, as I earlier noted, is criticized by Belford, the repentant rake, as no more than "a desiring luscious wench." In that same play, however, Richardson saw an example of the angelic: "Rowe justly says,—To be *Good,* is to be *Happy:*—Angels are *happier* than Men, because they're *better.* If there were Sex in Heaven, good Women would be angels *there,* as they are *here.*"[11]

It is noteworthy that we must exclude from the context of Richardson the world of Daniel Defoe for the same reasons that this pioneering novelist is excluded from concentrated attention in the work as a whole. Though Richardson revised and printed some of Defoe's works[12] and though the two surely had much in common as students of female nature, Defoe is essentially antagonistic to love and sexuality, while Richardson celebrates the former and is always trying to come to terms with the latter. Defoe, in a work previously noted,[13] censures conjugal excesses and usually, even when he records passion, condemns it or presents it coldly. Richardson, on the other hand, presents it so warmly that he was much censured even in his own circle for his

9. For earlier uses of these terms, see above, pp. 73, 161–63. Ellen Moers sees clearly that Richardson was a novelist of sensibility, a precursor of Romanticism and of much in the Victorian age: "Women's Liberator," a review of Eaves's and Kimpel's biography of Richardson (see below, n.12) in *New York Review of Books,* 10 Feb. 1972, pp. 27–31, esp. p. 31.

10. Letters to Susanna Highmore, 22 June 1750, and to Lady Bradshaigh, 5 Oct. 1753, in *Selected Letters of Samuel Richardson,* ed. John Carroll (Oxford: Clarendon Press, 1964), pp. 161, 246.

11. Letter to Sophia Westcomb, 15 Sept. 1746, ibid., p. 69. Richardson refers to the passage in *The Fair Penitent* I have quoted and discussed earlier (above, p. 119). For the references to *Clarissa* in this paragraph and passages closely related to them, see 1:147; 2:339, 342, 372; 3:451; 4:118; and Doody, pp. 109–12.

12. T. C. Duncan Eaves and Ben D. Kimpel, *Samuel Richardson: A Biography* (Oxford: Clarendon Press, 1971), pp. 30, 37, 71–72.

13. See above, pp. 102, 159 n. The subtitle (*or, Matrimonial Whoredom*) to *Conjugal Lewdness* (1727) reveals the strength of Defoe's feeling on behalf of marital controls. The substituted title, *A Treatise concerning the Use and Abuse of the Marriage Bed,* and some sections of the work (pp. 26, 106) reveal that he does accept the ideal of marriage based on personal affection. But the emphasis (in the attacks on abortion, contraception, bastardy, and the physical enjoyed for its own sake) everywhere reveals that Defoe believes man's sexuality to be "a corrupt Principle" that dwells in him as a result of the Fall. Defoe's attack on sexuality extends of course to its unnatural expressions. Sodomy, "the highest and most unnatural of all Crimes," is growing in England—"to the shame of Society, and to the scandal even of the Protestant Profession" (p. 17); it should be punished by death (p. 12). The quotations come from the introduction by Maximillian E. Novak to the edition of this work in the series Scholars' Facsimiles & Reprints (Gainesville, Fla., 1967).

portrayals of "Fondling—and Gallantry." His purpose, as he said in his defense of his practice, was to "catch young and airy Minds . . . when Passions run high in them," and so he finds disapprovingly that Cheyne, his critic, was "very delicate in his Opinion of the Matrimonial Tenderness."[14] Richardson was certainly modest and, particularly when pressed and challenged, extremely defensive about his morality. But if the context I have set forth in this section is even partly correct, it must surely mean that Richardson took very seriously the examples of Steele, Addison, and Milton. He must have appreciated the fact that Milton had made marital sexuality and companionship a sign of indwelling divine grace—a condition, indeed, to which Richardson's own men and women aspired. Of that aspiration they often fell tragically short in the real world—a fact that explains our deep sense of loss in finishing *Clarissa,* a loss accompanied by the emotions of pity and fear which the Christian rewards and punishments do not entirely assuage. It is no exaggeration to say that Richardson is at his most intense when stubborn and unalterable circumstances thwart the psychosexual energies with which he endows his most memorable creations. On the human level—and it is on that level only that Richardson encounters the modern reader—he is a profound tragedian.

I have been so far occupied with Richardson's antecedents, but we must not overlook the stunning originality of his achievement in fulfilling the tradition that he inherited. Richardson has given us not ideas but a world; and in that world sexuality, love, and the desire for union in marriage serve as motives for action and as creators of the personal *Gestalt.* His world is vastly different from both the classical world of heroism and the romance world of courtly love, of the *dolce stil nuovo,* and of romantic comedy. Particularly in the romantic world, love, like valor, was a *donnée;* and in matters of the heart there was "the complete absence of practical motivation through a political and historical context. Love, being an essential and obligatory ingredient of knightly perfection, functions as a substitute for other possibilities of motivation which are here lacking."[15] Not so in Richardson's world. Women long for and move toward marriage, but they are fully capable of choosing virginity. Love is not a character trait mysteriously present in the personality. It is an achievement (hard won, when won at all) in the realm of the psychological, political, social, and religious life. Sentimental love is like Evangelical salvation—a gift freely offered but one that must be accepted and appropriated into the daily struggle and at last embodied in human institutions. Richardson could not therefore have been a novelist only of love; he must perforce have portrayed marriage too and indeed—since his canvas is society and the real world—the frustrations and sorrows of love defeated.

14. *Selected Letters,* p. 46 and n.14.
15. Erich Auerbach, *Mimesis,* p. 141.

"*Pamela*" *I*

This famous, much discussed, vulgar, but unforgettable and lively novel ends a long way from tragic defeat and social frustration; but it too needs to be approached from the perspective that my discussion of Richardson's context has provided. That approach does not permit us to see Pamela as a monster of chastity who reveals the twisted attitude toward sex of a repressed Puritanical author. She will appear, rather, as a somewhat normal Anglican girl of worldly aspiration who dances, sings, plays, and loves finery. The longing for a comfortable life is scarcely unnatural; to think otherwise might reveal a mind not entirely free of cant, a word that could perhaps be applied to those who have swallowed uncritically Fielding's caricature of the girl in *Shamela*. These readers do not seem to understand that Pamela's prudence and desire for worldly comfort do not necessarily make hypocritical her professions of strict morality or cries of sexual alarm. Pamela, a sensible girl realizing how much her society values premarital chastity in a bride, would have been mad to throw away a jewel of such great price. And if at times she seems fearful, crass, changeable, materialistic, and conventional, we must remember that she is only fifteen years old when the novel begins, that she is in real danger, and that her "foe" and tempter is ten years her senior, a man of wealth and position who embodies in some of his several roles the position of master, father, judge, and even God. The faulty Mr. B could by his very position evoke solemn and awesome resonances in Pamela—a fact evident in the quasi-religious language she uses in addressing him. She is his handmaiden, he is her lord; and she sometimes approaches him with the trembling reverence due a deity.

If we must reject the view that Pamela and her creator are Puritans, we must also modify the view that she is the embodiment of an almost otherworldly delicacy that anticipates the frailty and untouchable ethereality of Victorian womanhood.[16] Pamela blushes, faints, is linguistically proper, and is, like her parents, easily shocked by free expressions. (They regard even stockings as unmentionable.) Following Defoe, Richardson is thought to have decarnalized woman and transformed her from the dirty libidinous clay in which earlier cultures had cast her to rosy white china. But it does not take a reading of *Shamela* to alert one to the physicality of Pamela; sophomores penetrate quickly to the sexuality that palpitates beneath her modest exterior. There is

16. Ian Watt's brilliant and influential *The Rise of the Novel: Studies in Defoe, Richardson and Fielding* (1957; reprint, Berkeley and Los Angeles: University of California Press, 1971), pp. 154–73) believes that Richardson's religious tendencies were Puritan, that his creation of Pamela ministered to the ideal of delicacy, and that the novel was nevertheless a combination of modesty and prurience, providing a greedy public "with the combined attractions of a sermon and a strip-tease" (p. 173). My different emphasis does not detract from my admiration of Watt's psychological and sociological insights into Richardson's mind and method.

in *Pamela* a form of *angélisme*, to be sure; but, properly defined, it refers to fine and cultivated manners, to the appearance as well as the reality of goodness, and to physical attractiveness in this world—not to an otherworldly, disembodied superiority to the body. As Pamela approaches the consummation of her marriage, she feels awe and no little fear, but she is also a-tremble with the erotic desires that have characterized her all along. Pamela is not an innocent. She knows the Bible well, and, as we saw in chapter 1, that great anthology of human error and sin has informed her of passion—its concealments and even its perversions. She has read romances, and these instructed her as surely in the realities of love as in the ruses of escape and of furtiveness that she might have used. The kisses, the lap-sittings, the fondling, the several advances toward her bosom, her fainting, her cold perspiration—these last not entirely unlike sexual climaxes—are regarded as potentially dangerous and are called "foul"[17] by the conscious mind. But they permit no doubt at all of the fact that on both sides—Pamela's no less than Mr. B's—there is physical attraction, and that the ultimate marriage is firmly based on potent sexuality. What else can Pamela's attraction to Mr. B's person possibly mean? One need not remain in doubt. Pamela accurately describes her premarital emotions as constituting a love of which she was unconscious but which was indubitably present none the less. As for his "naughty" actions, "though I abhorred his attempts upon me [observe how the adjective and the concessive clause weaken the horror], yet I could not hate him, and always wish'd him well"—perhaps not quite so strong as the Italian "voglio bene," which can mean "I love." "But I did not know that it was love" (1:419). If the erotic attraction is granted, then many of the so-called inconsistencies and improbabilities disappear. Pamela does not choose escape, because, though terrorized, she is simultaneously attracted.[18] Once free and on her way home, she returns because her heart is with Mr. B, not with her parents. Ironically, the most famous scene in the novel—the near rape in which Pamela remains *virgo intacta*—is a kind of watershed for both parties. Pamela faints in terror but quickly recovers, relenting enough to allow Mr. B to kiss her. He moves toward a proposal, though he still has some pride to overcome. The whole motion of the novel is now toward marriage, despite some impediments raised by Mr. B's jealousy of Parson Williams. Most fascinating of all is the fact that the near rape leads to Mr. B's discovery in himself of a feeling much more respectable—and, as it turns out, even more obsessive—than lust, and he is henceforth determined to treat Pamela as a beloved. The physical attraction not only survives the forced intimacy but is deepened by it. And the physical basis of that deepening love Richardson keeps before us up to the end, when

17. *Pamela* (Everyman's Library), 1:28, the edition hereafter cited.
18. Pamela is herself, very early in the novel, aware of ambivalence in love: "Is it not strange that love borders so much upon hate?" (1:41).

Lady Davers, not yet knowing that her brother and Pamela are man and wife, comes upon them in bed. The marriage is intended to show a love that rises above the physical; but the physical is not abandoned, as in Platonic or Neoplatonic schemes of things; it is transcended. The ideal of heterosexual friendship portrayed by Milton is fully realized, even though the marriage itself and what follows is structurally anticlimactic.

Richardson makes his a love story by doing more than emphasizing early and repeatedly the presence of sexuality. The love that Pamela and Mr. B achieve melts the hearts of Mrs. Jewkes and Lady Davers, as true love was traditionally supposed to. It elevates a spirited and determined girl to high station and gives to the noble husband what his own class was prepared to deny him, a marriage of true minds, hearts, and bodies. For Richardson is careful to have his marriage stand as vastly superior to those entered into by most members of the British squirearchy. Such unions were passionate but loveless; or they were rapacious and violent; or cold and neurotic, with "the yawning husband, and the vapourish wife" mutually insupportable (see 1:412). Pamela provides a friendship and love far above such perversions of the Miltonic ideal, and for this kind of relationship the word "delicate," with all its Victorian connotations, simply will not do. The physical is too much present for that. "Civilized" would be a far better word; or, as I suggested in the last chapter, "sentimental," a word that combined the mind and the heart in this its period of great change, possesses its own kind of appropriateness. The love being developed and celebrated is far above the slaverings of Mrs. Jewkes as she urges Mr. B on and chides Pamela for her resistance. But the real contrast between Mrs. Jewkes and the heroine is not that the woman is carnal and the girl refined and spiritual but that the girl is truly feminine and the woman suspiciously masculine. The hints are unmistakable that the antithesis is not between sensuality and lack of passion but between two kinds of sensuality, the normal and the perverse, for Mrs. Jewkes obviously has lesbian tendencies. The love portrayed in this novel is not unlike the love in Dryden's heroic plays: in the end it leads to pity, trust, and forgiveness of even the unworthiest—of Mrs. Jewkes, Lady Davers,[19] and, not least, Mr. B himself. His willfulness, his aggressions, his previous affair with Sally Godfrey are all forgiven, and Pamela is willing to take in the daughter of sin, so removing the offspring of Mr. B and Sally from her orphan status. In his first fictional work

19. Unconsciously or intentionally, Richardson seems to have linked Lady Davers and Mrs. Jewkes, applying to the wealthy woman a phrase even more appropriate to the coarse servant: he calls the former one of those "termagant, hermaphrodite minds" (from "Introduction to the Second Edition of Pamela," 1741). I owe this quotation to Watt, *Rise of the Novel*, p. 163. C. J. Rawson finds that Pamela is made "hotly and pressingly aware" of Mrs. Jewkes's lesbianism (*Henry Fielding and the Augustan Ideal*, p. 60). Lesbianism, which was sometimes specifically included in attacks on "whoring and execrable Sodomy," was earlier and usually regarded as an Italian or a town vice. See John Dennis, "The Stage Defended" (1726) in *Critical Works*, 2:311, 314–15.

Richardson has produced a novel of tender benevolence as well as a novel of sensual loving, linking in an exemplary association both sex and sensibility.

The best perspective on *Pamela* comes from Richardson's own contemporaries. Like Thomas Salmon,[20] though without that writer's pre-Enlightenment spirit, Richardson made "an Attempt to reconcile the Male and Female World," preferring marriage to the single life and arguing that pleasure is not a crime, that sexuality is not synonymous with lust, and that "*Insensibility*" is not the "Result of a consummate Virtue." Impatient with those who advocate "a pretended angelick Purity," Salmon asks, "But would the most virtuous Lady really have her Lover believe she has no warm Desires?" To this question Richardson, though he is more modest and cautious than Salmon when writing outside the novel form, has answered a resounding no, as the many "warm" scenes of *Pamela* clearly reveal. A French admirer of the novel wrote Richardson praising the epistolary method for revealing the "fair Writer's most secret Thoughts": by means of it "the several Passions of the Mind must, of course, be more affectingly described."[21] Some of his contemporaries regarded Richardson as excessively passionate. His defense was that he took "Human Nature *as it is;* for it is to no purpose to suppose it Angelic, or to endeavour to make it so. There is a Time of Life, in which the Passions will predominate; and Ladies, any more than Men, will not be kept in Ignorance."[22] Richardson's first novel, which he wrote rapidly, as though in a kind of imaginative vision that swept him along,[23] has produced a story of love and sexuality that places its heroine on the border between innocence and experience, a zone that the eighteenth century and the Romantic period found particularly interesting. Richardson exploits its ambivalences and contradictions, and in its first part the novel fascinates us because love and fear, attraction and repulsion, alternately and continually seize the mind, which they fill with confusion and conflict. Even in a work that in its totality is considerably less than a masterpiece, the author has achieved a richness of psychological meaning not unworthy of the moral realist who won Johnson's famous praise. Pamela lives on because she vividly represents human nature in one of its most baffling crises, that induced by the coming of love.

And emphasis must be put on that last word. *Pamela* has been read as a moral tract, a hypocritical portrayal of lust, a work of Victorian delicacy, an embodiment of Puritanical fears of sexuality, a revelation of its author's sado-masochism. It has all too seldom been read for what it truly is, a love story with many resonances. Ellen Moers has said that in *Pamela* Richardson, "with a

20. If he is in fact the author of the anonymous *Critical Essay concerning Marriage* (London, 1724). The quotations come from pp. A4r, 17, 18.

21. I owe this quotation from Jean Baptiste de Fréval to Eaves's and Kimpel's publication of his letter to Richardson in the Riverside edition of *Pamela* (Boston: Houghton Mifflin, 1971), p. 4.

22. *Selected Letters*, p. 47 (to Dr. George Cheyne, 31 Aug. 1741).

23. Eaves and Kimpel, *Richardson: A Biography*, p. 90.

stroke of originality for which he has only recently been given credit, . . . made novel synonymous with love story, and made the classic English love story a tale of the love between a poor girl and a rich man. To the modern, marriage-oriented religion of sex . . . Richardson's novel supplies doctrine and ritual."[24]

"Clarissa"

Richardson's best novel, increasingly appreciated as one of the finest in English, contains a postscript, which concludes with a quotation from an un- named but eminent foreign author specifying the virtues that should charac- terize a long fictional "history" (see 4:562–63). These virtues Richardson's novel triumphantly achieves. Despite its gargantuan size, it possesses a spirit that breathes in all its members; its characters are natural and various, care- fully distinguished and maintained consistently throughout; and the variety of incident always keeps the reader awake, his attention riveted on the matter at hand. In addition to all this, Richardson has created two lovers of mythic dimensions who "mean" intensely on several different levels of human concern—the purely human, the socioeconomic, the psychological, the moral-religious. The more than one million words of text are anchored to a simple time scheme, for Richardson took pains about what he called the "fixing of dates." "The novel begins in January; it ends in December. Clarissa leaves home in the spring; the sordid climax occurs in June (actually on Midsummer night); she dies in September, shortly before the autumnal equi- nox; and Lovelace is killed in December, a few days before the winter sol- stice."[25]

The mass of insights about love that the novel embodies and implies can best be considered under the following heads: its sensibility, its sexuality, the char- acter and destiny of Clarissa, and the character and fate of Lovelace.

Sensibility

This complex word is being defined all through this study; predictably, a writer of Richardson's stature added meanings and nuances that require spe- cial attention. By "sensibility" I here refer to something broader than the feeling of heterosexual love, though sensibility often verges on love and may,

24. *New York Review of Books,* 10 Feb. 1972, p. 28. My reading is generally related to those who, like Walter Francis Wright, find Pamela to be "one of the first English heroines of sensibility" (*Sensibility in English Prose Fiction, 1760–1814: A Reinterpretation* [Illinois Studies in Language and Literature, vol. 22, nos. 3–4, University of Illinois at Urbana, 1937], p. 19). My serious dis- agreement with older interpretations, however, is that they tend to subordinate the love element and the sexuality to delicacy alone.

25. Frederick W. Hilles, "The Plan of *Clarissa*," *Philological Quarterly* 45 (Jan. 1966): 238.

in the spirit of Richardson, be a precondition of it. I also mean something narrower than a divine impulse, although, once more, religious love and goodness are not far away from the concept; Richardson's modern biographers are helpful and suggestive but somewhat too conservative and general when they say that his concept of *heart* is closer to Milton's idea of the Holy Ghost than to the promptings of passion.[26] In a fine phrase Anna Howe says of Clarissa, her dearest friend, that her mind is "vested in humanity" (4:17). But again a narrower focus is necessary, and "benevolence" may also be too broad and universal a term to be helpful. I refer, rather, to that cluster of historically generated qualities and emotions which we actually encounter in this novel, notably in the character of its heroine, and which we have already seen in the intellectual and spiritual milieu that pressed upon the novelist. One aspect of Richardson's sensibility, which he shares with his immediate precursor Steele, is his dislike of traditional male roles. Toward the end of his novel he opposes the practice of dueling; toward the beginning he combats the stereotypically masculine passions that Clarissa's odious, materialistic brother James embodies—coercion, revenge, envy. These are of course not exclusively masculine traits, as demonstrated by their presence in the character of the heroine's repulsive sister, Bella, who is said to lack "a *feeling heart*" (1:218), a phrase that looks directly ahead to Jean-Jacques Rousseau. Nevertheless, "the *heart* is what we women should judge by," as Clarissa says (1:198); and sensibility does have about it, all through the period, an unmistakable "odor di femina," to quote Mozart's Leporello. But Richardson is out to destroy all outworn sexual stereotypes, not create new ones; and it must be said that, in whichever sex sensibility had hitherto been the more prominent, the time was now come to extend it to the other. And one of the first questions Clarissa asks about the man with whom it is her fate to be eternally linked is this: whether he has a heart, for if he does not, "he wants everything" (1:202). This is the touchstone, then; and Clarissa rejects Solmes, the man her family intends for her, because *her* heart (here surely close to sexual feeling) recoils at the thought of him. When Anna Howe wonders and worries whether Clarissa's heart is committed to Lovelace, she associates sensibility and romantic emotion: "I would occasion no throb; nor half-throb; no flash of sensibility, like lightning darting in" (1:335). Long before Jane Austen's powerful use of the term, "sensibility" was already a strong word.

Two other sentimental[27] associations appear early in the novel, the associa-

---

26. Eaves and Kimpel (*Biography*, p. 608) are here stressing inner sentiment as ethical principle, not as Romantic feeling.

27. Compare Lady Bradshaigh's comment in 1749 on this term ("much in vogue among the polite") and her association of it with a walk out of doors: "Everything clever and agreeable is comprehended in that word . . . I am frequently astonished to hear such a one is a *sentimental* man; we were a *sentimental* party; I have been taking a *sentimental* walk." The lady would have apparently been surprised at my associating the term with death, but she should not have been. I owe the quotation to Wright, *Sensibility*, p. 24.

tion of love with death and with nature. As the rigors of the family persecution intensify, Clarissa thinks of death—and this early, flickering wish lights up during the long climax into a baroque religious blaze. And Clarissa shares with Shaftesbury, Thomson, and the Countess of Winchilsea the newer feeling for outdoor nature—for birds, for cascades, and for the open air: "Sometimes solitude is of all things my wish; and the awful silence of the night, the spangled element, and the rising and setting sun" (1:348)—a general enough description in truth but one that nonetheless reveals a deep feeling.

I tend to resist applying the word "delicate" to Pamela—at least in its later Victorian meanings—lest it obscure the sensuality of her character. But it must be used of Clarissa, even in a sense directly opposed to the sexual. Cousin Morden, the deliverer, whose Second Coming is awaited all through the novel and who does finally arrive for the apocalyptic conclusion, warns Clarissa of rakes and evil men, contrasting their sensibility with her delicacy, a distinction the heroine fully accepts. She requires this "feminine" quality of men too: for in one way delicacy is the very bond between the sexes, and the man must possess it in order *"to enter into those parts of the female character which are its glory and distinction"* (2:305). Of this quality Lovelace himself has had some notion, though he shows obvious signs of groping when he thinks of it. At first he laments that there is "no love, no sensibility" in Clarissa, and by these terms he means dalliance, love play, quickly responsive emotions (2:188); but he does not yet realize that by her standards sensibility must be related not so much to gratification as to human worth and virtue. (He came earlier, however, to the view that the *pathetic* consists not just of distress alone but of the sufferings of good and worthy persons: 2:69.) He tends to use hesitantly the very terms which Clarissa—or Richardson through Clarissa—is trying to define. A concept related to sensibility is generosity, which Clarissa elevates to a heroic ideal: "TRUE GENEROSITY is greatness of soul" (2:304). Dryden's phrase—and Dryden's example—is now being extended further into the female and benevolent realms of life. It will cost a traditional rake like Lovelace considerable anguish of spirit to accept this revolution. So Clarissa refuses Lovelace not out of "maidenly niceness" but out of "Principles" in the heart which were there planted "by the first gracious Planter" (2:306). (How profoundly inner and intuitve the Protestant Clarissa is!) Lovelace is soon enough made to perceive "evidence of a virtue and of a greatness of soul, that could not be . . . impeached" (2:389). The important differences between the sensibility Lovelace is capable of and that which Clarissa embodies comes out when he begins to put into execution one of his most elaborate designs upon his captive fair. Contemplating her plight, he experiences sensibility in the older meaning of mere feeling: aroused by beauty and tenderness in distress, he feels his nose tingle and his eyes glisten; and he sobs *"audibly"* (2:461). But his is not the true delicacy Clarissa embodies, for there is no reform of the will or transformation of the spirit in him. His sensibility is ephemeral, neural, fleshly; and it is significant that he turns from these tinglings to prosecute his shameful ruse (cf. 2:481). Lovelace's lachrymose response to Clarissa's exquisite tenderness must, then, be regarded as dangerous: it is a vicious parody of true feeling guided by virtue. On the other hand, Clarissa's weeping upon discovering that she has been kidnapped is truly noble; and as she renounces Lovelace forever (3:128), she bases sensibility upon principle. Her heart is against him, and that heart is not only *sensible* but fully tutored. She deserves the praise Samuel Johnson bestowed upon her creator: she had learned that the feelings must move at the command of virtue.

"Sensibility," which refers to all feeling, includes the lighter emotions and so can be congenial to delicacy. "Pathetic" tends by its origins to refer to the passions, especially the searing, overwhelming ones. Paradoxically, the pressure of the events in this novel made "sensibility" a heavier, darker word than by its nature it wanted to be; under parallel influences "pathos" became tenderer than etymologically it had been. Up to the point of Clarissa's rape under sedation, Richardson interprets the pathetic broadly to include fear, rage, even madness, as well as tears of gentle feeling. After the rape—even though he keeps insisting through Lovelace that the moral Clarissa has achieved heroic virtue or "greatness of soul" (3:237)—he now moves to what Rowe in *Jane Shore* had set as the exemplar of the pathetic, a beautiful, virtuous woman suffering. Persecuted, alone, cursed by her family, physically degraded, thrown into disgraceful confinement as Lovelace's orders are increasingly misunderstood, Clarissa becomes first a martyr and then a saint. Even here the example of Dryden is still potent: Clarissa becomes a Saint Catharine preparing herself for the spousals of the Lamb, as did the martyr in *Tyrannick Love.* In harmony with this great apotheosis there are answering repentances even in the Lovelace world, for Belford the rake repents and becomes a tender-hearted Christian. Tears, far from being unmanly, are in the process of replacing reason as the truest mark of "humane nature"—as indeed *"the prerogative of manhood"* (4:145), the latter phrase here attributed to Juvenal— evidence of why that Roman satirist was given special approval by Richardson's friend, Johnson. All the largest values of sensibility—the tender and the sublime—combine in Clarissa's preparations for death, which sometimes tend to recall the baroque rather than anticipate the Victorian. But when Cousin Morden finally arrives, Richardson does in fact paint a Victorian genre scene: the dying Clarissa, dressed in virgin white, lies asleep, with Mrs. Lovick's arm around her neck, one faded cheek resting on the good woman's bosom, one lily-white hand hanging lifelessly down. Richardson has even provided, as it were, a title for his canvas, "The Fair Sleeper" (4:332).[28] Mor-

28. Robert Palfrey Utter and Gwendolyn Bridges Needham (*Pamela's Daughters* [New York: Macmillan, 1936]) overstress the physical delicacy of Clarissa and then, somewhat surprisingly, find pictorial parallels to her in "the rococo fashion in heroines" (p. 176), citing Watteau, Lancret,

den, who witnesses this scene, must retire behind a screen to compose himself; and to the very end, though he disobeys Clarissa's request not to draw the sword and dispatches Lovelace in a duel, he continues to shed tears, which he calls "a repeated fit of humanity" (4:410).

Richardson is certainly one of the masters of sensibility, but from my analysis it is clear that the idea for him is not what Lovejoy called a unit-idea but a complex of emotions about emotion. It embraces death, romantic love, response to external nature, benevolence, forgiveness, Christian virtue, Protestant piety. But perhaps the most important feature of Richardsonian sensibility is that it is regarded as defining our humanity and measuring our dignity. It therefore is the sine qua non of love; since Lovelace does not evidently possess it—is capable throughout his lifetime only of a kind of parody of it—Clarissa cannot possibly give him her heart. Many modern readers—and some eighteenth-century ones, too—have felt that Clarissa is being finical in her continued resistance to Lovelace. Even Clarissa's best friend, the sensible and good Anna Howe, who better than any one else recognizes the "gentleness of your spirit," "the laudable pride of your heart," and "the just notion you have of the dignity of our sex in these delicate points," nevertheless urges the heroine to marry her kidnapper—"though we soil our fingers in lifting him up from his dirt" (2:294). But though a woman of Clarissa's independence of spirit would find this challenge appealing, she cannot possibly accept it. Lovelace has not passed the test of sensibility, and for Clarissa to give him her heart would be to forfeit her humanity. Only those whom a *coeur sensible* unites can join their bodies. Such, then, is Richardson's interpretation of Milton's ideal of heterosexual friendship, which he believes to require sentimental compatibility. That extension of meaning was made possible only because of the antecedent achievements of Dryden, Otway, Rowe, and Steele in portraying tender humanity and in laying the foundations of companionate marriage.

Sexuality

In the love scenes of *Paradise Lost* or the love poetry of Spenser, the ideal and the real seem to coalesce, and sexuality is strong and healthy. In Richardson, a much more modern writer, physical fulfillment is ideally a desideratum of the best characters but in reality a tortured nightmare of hopes disappointed and fears realized. Of such a nature is love in modern

---

Boucher, and Greuze. But the delicacy of the rococo, as we shall see in chap. 11, is vastly different. Although, as I have argued, the sexual is present in Richardson, it is not be be confused with French dalliance, and his delicacy is far from coquetry or Venereal flirtations in a park. D. H. Lawrence's memorable comment (cited by Watt, *Rise of the Novel,* p. 203), that Richardson united "calico purity and under-clothing excitements," seems to me more applicable to minor followers of Watteau than to the novelist. The parallel with Greuze has merit, however, and its implications will appear in my later discussion. See below, pp. 312–15.

society that rape replaces bridal union, and the heroine is forced to desert the flesh for sainthood. In this novel, unlike *Pamela,* Richardson gives full expression to his version of *angélisme,* or worship of purity; but this etherealization is forced on the heroine as a secondary good and is not sought as a primary ideal. Freud would have no difficulty in describing Clarissa's love of her bridegroom, Christ, as "love with an inhibited aim."[29] To understand the sexuality of *Clarissa,* we must attempt to answer two questions: Is the heroine in love with Lovelace? What is the nature of the friendship between Clarissa and Anna Howe?

Early in the novel it is clear that Clarissa has a "prepossession" in favor of her later ravisher—partly, no doubt, because a materialistic family is pressing the claims of a physically odious suitor (1:15). The fact that Clarissa agrees to a correspondence with Lovelace is itself, in the mores of the day, a sign of intimacy. Clarissa has knowingly entered a world of clandestine emotions and shared secrets—and the perceptive Anna, who uses such words as "glow" and "throb," recognizes that fact (1:45–46). Clarissa's analysis of her own heart is more reserved than her friend's: she prefers the person of the handsome, cavalier Lovelace to that of the bourgeois Solmes—a sure sign of sexual attraction—but she denies the heartthrobs and soon finds fear instead. The situation is clear enough even after Richardson's own revisions, made to reduce his heroine's culpability and enhance that of the seducer:[30] what Clarissa feels is not unlike what Pamela felt, though the girls are far apart in other respects—disapproval-attraction, fear-charm—that is, conflicting emotions ambiguously juxtaposed. However one wishes to describe Clarissa's feelings, they are strong enough to drive her into the seducer's arms, and one can scarcely fail to conclude that they are rooted in a deep and perhaps unconscious sexual appeal even though she protests against the imputation of *"throbs"* and *"glow"* (1:47, 57). The best that her rational mind is allowed to say is that Lovelace "might be liked well enough" (1:134) if he possessed a good character or if there were some hope of reclaiming him from his evil ways. To describe the condition of Clarissa's heart, "love" will not quite do, for it is too noble a word, invoking social and religious duty. But she could be driven into *"conditional liking"*—which in Richardson's brilliant substitutionary kind of style masks a strong desire to give herself to him sexually (1:203), an emotion in direct contrast to what she feels when she sees the ugly Solmes in his own grotesque physical rapture (1:404). Richardson is telling us that Clarissa is deeply a woman and not an angel; but she is a Woman of Feeling, as we have

29. *Civilization and Its Discontents,* trans. James Strachey (New York: W. W. Norton, 1961), p. 49.

30. Mark Kinkead-Weekes, *"Clarissa* Restored?" *Review of English Studies* 10 (May 1959): 156–71. Kinkead-Weekes finds that Richardson revised his first version in order (1) to defend Clarissa's purity and delicacy in love, (2) to emphasize the darker side of Lovelace, and (3) to underline the moral teaching. As the author points out, Richardson's heavy insistence on his heroine's perfection tends to deny his own earlier work, in which she shows some involuntary weaknesses.

seen, who requires delicacy and courtesy in love. The truth of the matter is that to be a woman of modern refined sensibility in Richardson's world was to *combine* the amorous and the angelical (just as the word "sentiment" combined judgment and emotion), both sides being equally beautiful and each side interacting with the other. Both mind and body had to be satisfied, and it is clear that at the outset Lovelace pleases the heroine's physical taste just as Solmes offends it: how can marriage relations, Clarissa wonders, which are "so *very* intimate" (2:167), be served with an odious hand? All this Clarissa calls "delicacy," fully acknowledging that "the finer sensibilities" do not make for easy happiness (2:167). It is true that as the novel progresses she comes to see that physical attraction must be distrusted ("Guard your eye," she says, 2:277), and from then on the heart replaces the eye as the guide of life (2:313). But the point needs to be stressed that Clarissa—and her emotion is fully shared by Anna Howe—dreamed of a man who would combine virtue with physical charm and that she hoped Lovelace would fulfill all the moral conditions as persuasively as he did the physical (see 2:103). If we deny or ignore this attraction, the novel loses much—perhaps all—of its tragic potential. When Clarissa praises marriage—and here Richardson anticipates the sermons of his friend Johnson—by saying that it is "the highest state of friendship" (2:192–93), we must never forget that at one time she had come close to marrying Lovelace, hoping apparently to build on the attraction she felt and redeem the libertine (2:197).[31] One of the most poignant of the letter fragments that survive the rape shows that Clarissa really wanted marriage—she longed to be courted and complimented and to make her parents rejoice (3:207). One of her last desires is that her dearest friend marry, and she prepares herself for death as though she were a bride going to meet her bridegroom: "As for me, never bride was so ready as I am. My wedding garments are bought. And though not fine and gaudy to the sight, though not adorned with jewels and set off with gold and silver . . . , yet will they be the easiest, the *happiest* suit, that ever bridal maiden wore" (4:303). Just as in *Pamela* the near rape, far from spoiling the sensuality, actually heightens it for both sexes, so here the attraction Clarissa feels for Lovelace persists until it is easily sublimated into a spousal love of God. One is led to remark that something irredeemably evil or ugly can scarcely be sublimated into the good or beautiful. In Clarissa's experience there has been no poisoning of the root of love. *Agapē* rises naturally and without hindrance from erotic denial. No unhealthy asceticism succeeds Clarissa's sufferings. Her dignity as a woman, as a human being, has been affronted, and she cannot possibly marry her persecutor. But

31. Although Clarissa repulses Lovelace, sometimes indignantly, sometimes gently, he apparently is nevertheless able to achieve a considerable degree of intimacy. By his own account, his cheek reclines on her shoulder, he embraces her, he kisses her lips. It was only at his invasion of the breast that she "flung from" him and made him lament, "But why makes she every inch of her person thus sacred?" (2:476).

she can and does forgive him, and she does not turn away retchingly from love and marriage. We are to feel the deepest pity that she is denied the love she desired, not relief that she has escaped it. And that tragic pity is simply not possible unless we perceive that Clarissa was indeed in love with the person of Lovelace and contemplated a deeply satisfying union of body and soul. Such love is only hinted at, but the hints are unmistakable. When Aaron Hill suggested that the lady be absolutely and avowedly in love, Richardson replied, "As to Clarissa's being in downright Love, I must acknowledge, that I rather chose to have it imputed to her, (his [Lovelace's] too well-known Character consider'd) by her penetrating Friend [Anna]; (and then a Reader will be ready enough to believe it, the *more* ready, for her not owning it, or being blind to it herself) than to think *her self* that she is."[32] Richardson opts for indirection, but he leaves no doubt that he wants Clarissa's heart compromised. Nor, if I may generalize about Clarissa's nature as a whole, is there any doubt that it bears an unmistakable appetency toward sexuality and pleasure. Her closest friend writes, in a posthumous summary of her character, "She acknowledged frankly, that were *person,* and *address,* and *alliance,* to be *allowably* the principal attractives in the choice of a lover, it would not have been difficult for her eye to mislead her heart" (4:494).

Our second question, concerning the nature of Clarissa's friendship with Anna Howe (whom, Richardson wrote, "I love next to Clarissa"),[33] is more difficult, but the answer that we must finally accept is fully consonant with the point that has just been made. The friendship is so profound—so early, so intimate, and even so erotic—that it is tempting to regard it as irreplaceable and to view the coming of Lovelace as a hideous intrusion on something pure and satisfying that should obviously have been prolonged. The word "erotic" used of the friendship may give pause, but Richardson's treatment is strong and suggestive. Consider Anna's behavior over Clarissa's corpse: "O my blessed friend! said she—my sweet companion!—my lovely monitress!— kissing her lips at every tender appellation. . . . And, kissing her again, Let my warm lips animate thy cold ones! . . . Again she kissed her lips, each cheek, her forehead . . . one more kiss, my angel, my friend, . . . why do I thus lament the HAPPY? And that thou art so, is my comfort. It is, it is, my dear creature! kissing her again" (4:402–3). The relationship was deep, to say the least; and at the loss Anna is, to use her own word, "frantic." The effect of Clarissa's death as well as the experiences of her life make Anna hate men as reptiles and make her renounce marriage, even with one so unlike Lovelace as her betrothed, Hickman (4:265), whom the dying Clarissa wanted her to marry. The two girls formed a friendship that is regarded both as innocence itself and also as "*fervent love*" (4:349), and one wonders why Richardson endowed it

32. Letter dated 29 Oct. 1746, *Selected Letters,* p. 72.
33. In a letter to Lady Bradshaigh dated 26 Oct. 1748, ibid., p. 97.

with the joy, morality, and even physical warmth that heterosexual relations lacked. A man and a woman together produce strain, danger, torture, lust—and finally death. The two women create a friendship that has become legendary and exemplary: it recalls that of Sidney's Pamela, the wise and proud, with Philoclea, the humble and playful, in the *Arcadia;* it anticipates that of Julie and Claire in Rousseau's *Nouvelle Héloïse.* Surely one of Richardson's greatest imaginative creations, this friendship unites the wit, shrewd intelligence, and pert realism of the friend with the nobility and humanity of the heroine. In the midst of her sufferings Clarissa writes to Anna, "How much more binding and tender are the ties of pure friendship, and the union of like minds, than the ties of nature! [Clarissa may refer both to familial and sexual ties, but primarily the latter.] Well might the sweet singer of Israel . . . say that the love of Jonathan to him was wonderful; that it surpassed the *love of women!* What an exalted idea does it give of the soul of Jonathan, . . . if we may suppose it but equal to that of my Anna Howe for her fallen Clarissa!"[34]

The language is, as I have said, strong and suggestive. But in the end we must conclude that the Anna-Clarissa love is neither morbid nor irregular. It is in fact entirely natural, a tried and tested love that provides psychological relief from the tortures of heterosexual lust. But it cannot be regarded, either, as the ultimate ideal that each sought—or that Richardson approved of. Both the long passages I have quoted are uttered in pain and grief. Even early in the novel, in the days of blooming heterosexual love, virginity looks attractive to the girls because it is known and familiar, while beckoning love is new and even at this time potentially menacing. At the time of her tragic bereavement Anna turns cynical and rejects both men and the erotic. But she is striking out at all experience, which has put an end not only to innocent friendship but to heterosexual love as well. Anna's fully understandable but hysterical emotions cannot be regarded as a norm, since they are regressive and express a nostalgia for what is irretrievably lost. She makes clear that she longs for a heaven that is only a repetition of innocence: "O may we meet, and rejoice together, where no villainous *Lovelaces,* no hard-hearted *relations,* will ever shock our innocence, or ruffle our felicity!" (4:403).

Richardson's ideal was that of Milton; but a fallen world presents to the good Clarissa, who longs for a virtuous physical union, only a cruel choice between an illiterate materialist, imposed on her by her family, and a Don Giovanni, imposed on her by post–Civil War society. Neither the safe commercial man nor the attractive libertine can fulfill the ideal, and the novel moves to suffering, death, and finally the substitution of heavenly love for the lost earthly love. The novel generates great power as it explores, like *The Book of Thel,* the crossing from innocence to experience. Anna, like Thel, runs

34. 3:517. See below, p. 305, for a discussion of David's lovely aria in Handel's *Saul,* one of whose themes is his love of Jonathan.

shrieking back to innocence when she beholds the ravages a world of sex and perversion can cause. Clarissa is driven forward to religion. One hopes that Richardson's vision is not typical, but the fact that his leading characters have taken on mythical status suggests that his vision embodies a modern truth about love and marriage.[35]

The Character and Destiny of Clarissa

So far I have considered Clarissa as a heroine of sensibility and as a woman to whom life denies the gratifications of heterosexual friendship. Of such friendship the coming of Lovelace into her life makes her mysteriously and disturbingly aware in the unconscious recesses of her being. I must now consider her as a rebellious daughter and then as a penitent daughter returning to her "Father's house." Apparently the motif of the prodigal son, upon which the art of the later eighteenth century rang so many fascinating changes, had earlier penetrated the consciousness of England and been transferred to the opposite sex. But before analyzing Clarissa as a daughter within the small but broadly symbolic society of the family, I ought to respond to the modern view that Clarissa is "the love goddess" of a life-denying middle-class culture. Does the presence of a commercial ethos in the novel tend to etherealize the erotic into a white and lifeless debility or pervert it into the death wish? Does the novel suggest as commendable familial qualities impotence and a desiccated instinctual life?[36] A counterquestion springs quickly to mind: How can one answer yes to these questions in view of Richardson's uncompromising condemnation of Clarissa's cruel, materialistic, and sexless family? Or, if I have been right in finding that Clarissa's initial response to Lovelace was sexually warm, how can we find the author loveless and bourgeois when he raises the

35. Mark Kinkead-Weekes in *Samuel Richardson Dramatic Novelist* (London: Methuen, 1973) provides a persuasive answer to excesses of modern and psychoanalytical readers who have seen Richardson as sex-obsessed, as a prurient peeping Tom. But in saying that the sexual scenes of *Pamela* are not about sex but about pride (p. 109), he denies the presence of a very important strain in that novel. Similarly, Eaves and Kimpel deemphasize Richardson's central theme when they say that *Clarissa* is no more about seduction and sex than *Antigone* is about burial rites and that rape is merely a conventional symbol, for both Lovelace and Clarissa (*Richardson: A Biography,* p. 269). Kinkead-Weekes is extremely perceptive about the sexuality in *Clarissa.* He understands Clarissa's image of the "pernicious Caterpiller" (which preys on "the fair leaf of virgin fame" and so poisons the leaves it cannot devour [3:207]) to refer not simply to the desecration of her virginity but to the destruction of her vitality and love. Rape is thus ultimately a "*desecration of true sex*" (p. 237). Those like Dorothy Van Ghent (see below, n.36) and Watt (*Rise of the Novel,* pp. 230–38), who have also deeply pondered the imagery, are similarly close to the truth. But their findings need to be guided by Richardson's consciously held ideals of love and marriage, against which psychopathological waves admittedly beat. It still remains an open question whether any image, except that of death and the grave, is obsessive enough to take on a double meaning, with indisputably sexual reference.

36. The language used in these questions is quoted from or suggested by Dorothy Van Ghent's stimulating but unhistorical analysis of *Clarissa* as a bourgeois myth in *The English Novel: Form and Function* (1953; reprint, New York: Holt, Rinehart & Winston, 1966), p. 50.

prospect—admittedly unrealized in life—for both Anna and Clarissa of uniting with men of spirit and sexual energy equal to them in intelligence and virtue? The picture drawn in the novel is scarcely that of "an expensive chattel"[37] being violated—a process of spiritiual and physical defloration that the reader is supposed to enjoy by proxy as he watches the spectacle unfolding before him. If anything is far from an appeal to voyeurism, it is that dimly lit rape scene, with the figures flitting in and out of the room. Nor does the story tell of a pure and debilitated woman incapable of sexuality and turning quickly and gladly to the comforts of religion and the consolations of death. Clarissa, though pure, is far from weak. She is solemnly majestic and powerful, shrinking those that come in contact with her to the schemers and villains they really are. She resists her persecutors not because she is unable to love but because she wants to be free to love on her own terms. Clarissa and Anna early on make as an absolute stipulation that they be pleased in love and marriage. The myth being produced by the story is that of a woman who demands respect, who had too much dignity and integrity to forgive her kidnapper and rapist, however rich, witty, attractive he may be. Clarissa is far from being *la femme moyenne sensuelle,* not because she is sexless but because she is never *moyenne.*

But though she is far from being exclusively or archetypally bourgeois, Clarissa is certainly a Protestant Christian, and it is to her role as a prodigal daughter, first rebellious, then forgiven, that I now turn. The importance of the topic and the unresolved dilemmas that it raises I have already confronted in my analysis of *The Conscious Lovers.* The historical reasons for the generational conflict have been made clear by Lawrence Stone:[38] even the growing importance of the conjugal family enforced the despotic authority of the husband and father. Patriarchy was strengthened by both church and state as the family became nuclear, and the authority that Clarissa—and later Rousseau's Julie—defy had acquired the solemnity of God and governor combined. Richardson, a far greater artist than Steele, probes the dilemma of conflicting wills to its depth and cannot rest satisfied with an easy evasion. If he does not succeed in the intellectual resolution of a conflict that could have torn the individual and society apart, his aesthetic response in exploiting the tragic form is moving and exemplary.

The old seventeenth-century view, expressed by the Marquis of Halifax in his famous letter of 1688 to his daughter, would no longer do. He told her she would have to accept a double standard, submit as a member of the weaker sex to having a husband chosen for her, yield to inevitable "Masculine Domination," and even be thankful for such husbandly faults as drunkenness and

37. Ibid.
38. *Family, Sex and Marriage,* pp. 150–59.

infidelity since they might make her man more complaisant in other respects.[39] And such marriage was called sacred! That Richardson was far from these conservative views he himself makes clear in a letter in which he says of those who do not consider the good of the child, "Let such Parents not only be disappointed, totally disappointed but besides be Anathema Maranatha."[40] He says he never believed that parents had a right to command children to marry against the current of their affections. And of course Clarissa's bold and radical defiance of the Harlowes—a blunt, high-spirited, and moral defiance fully supported by Anna, who lashes out even at the word "authority" (1:64)—is the best possible revelation of Richardson's liberalism on this issue, as is his degradation of the tyrannical family—brother, sister, father, even mother—to vile greed and envy. Though she kneels and pleads in their presence, Clarissa will employ ruses and finally have recourse to flight with Lovelace to outwit them, so outraged is she at the splay-footed cipher they wish to thrust upon her for life—and for gain. She rises to sublimity in her direct denunciations (1:395 ff.) in the presence of the intended and of his family, whom she clearly discomfits by the energy of her thought and language. Clarissa is a champion of the downtrodden woman of her day and all days, and with prophetic power she dominates the scene in behalf of a just cause.

No sooner has this liberated spirit eloped (and how powerfully that emotional and all but involuntary action is described!) than feelings of guilt arise at her defiance of her father's plain command. Eve has disobeyed an earthly god, and she now looks longingly back to her Eden, calling her action "my crime" (1:487). The countermovement has begun, and it would be well to understand what mighty forces now clash in the bosom of the heroine. Levitical law had made cursing a father or mother punishable by death (Lev. 20:9), and defiance of parental authority in choosing a mate was a form of cursing through action. Jeremy Taylor had said bluntly that children must obey their parents and that "it is unlawful for children to marry without and against the consent of their parents" (*Ductor dubitantium,* bk. 3, chap. 5, rule 8, sec. 7), even though, like Bishop Fleetwood after him, he had hoped the older gener-

39. See Robert D. Moynihan, "Clarissa and the Enlightened Woman as Literary Heroine," *Journal of the History of Ideas* 36 (Jan.–Mar. 1975): 159. Moynihan argues, correctly, that Clarissa and Anna belong to a liberal Protestant tradition and are both mature girls capable of freedom of choice (p. 163). On Lord Halifax, see also Stone, *Family,* p. 278.

40. Letter to Sarah Chapone, 2 Mar. 1752, *Selected Letters,* p. 205. Richardson's language is here angry in the manner of a Hebrew prophet. As Christopher Hill has clearly seen, there is indeed a prophetic, reforming side to Richardson, and one should not be surprised at the enthusiasm of Diderot and Rousseau. Richardson transmitted to Clarissa his radical vision of change: "She passed through and revolted against the feudal-patriarchal family and the tyranny of money; she looked forward to a society in which women shall have attained full equality of status." See Christopher Hill, "Clarissa Harlowe and Her Times" in *Essays on the Eighteenth-Century Novel,* ed. Robert D. Spector (Bloomington: Indiana University Press, 1965), pp. 62–63.

ation would exercise power with benevolence and wisdom and would never resort to force. Since it is now clear to Clarissa that she has gone off with a rake, for reasons that may have been partly sensual, she could well remember with horror Taylor's sentence: "Of all the dangers of a Christian none is more pressing and troublesome than the temptations to lust, no enemy more dangerous than that of the flesh, no accounts greater than what we have to reckon for at the audit of concupiscence" (*Holy Living*, chap. 2, sec. 3). Clarissa, like her creator—like so many, perhaps most, in the Christian tradition—greatly feared "Cupidity, or Paphian stimulus" (postscript, 4:559). And certainly a young girl so trained and now at the tender mercies of a sexual adventurer, living among whores and rogues, away from parental protection, and forced, as Anna says, to be "father, mother, uncle to yourself" (2:294), might well regard her escape and her defiance as the blackest of crimes. The self-judgment is harsh, but the heroine has fortitude even against herself. Clarissa's "perfect beauty" is described as possessing "something *so awful,* and yet *so sweet,*" something so "piercing, yet gentle" (2:243), that one thinks ahead to Burke's juxtaposition of beauty and sublimity. The awe and the authority surely arise in part from Clarissa's moral sense, which, while judging others, does not spare herself. Well might Lovelace ask, "Dear creature! Did she never romp?" (2:383).

But it is not only moral sublimity that drives Clarissa to seek parental forgiveness; her tender affections also have a hand in impelling her spirit homeward. Even Lovelace's pretended illness provokes her compassion before his hoax is revealed, and she says that hatred and anger are "but temporary passions with me" (2:437). As her deification proceeds, her spirit rises to heights of fiery anger and luminous judgment—she is sublime as she invokes the law as a freeborn Englishwoman (3:289)—but at the same time her heart softens into a kind of universal love and meekness that leads her to forgive her enemies, including Lovelace. Anna, typically perceptive, refers in writing to Clarissa to "your sweet meekness and superior greatness of soul" (3:378). Both the majesty and the humility (separately and together, godlike qualities) drive her back to her father. She is the *magna mater* to her tormentor-lover and his shabby set (see 3:391–92), but she herself also needs—badly needs—a father. She cannot die with his curse upon her. When it is lifted, she then actively seeks his favor and, on her knees, writes to her mother imploring the bestowing of both a maternal and a paternal blessing (4:52, 56–57, 63, 84). It is part of the pathos of the book that the daughter who even curtsies to the kind and fatherly doctor when she is dying (4:177) does not live long enough to learn that she has been restored to full paternal love. If Christ becomes her surrogate husband, God becomes her surrogate father, and it is very difficult to know which role her fervent religion best serves—replacing the erotic-uxorial through the Son or the forfeited paternal through the Father. It can be argued that the latter is more important. Clarissa seldom addresses Christ, though he is named in her last utterance, and it is curious that she seldom quotes the New Testament. Job and the Psalms constitute her meat and drink, and they of course present the cursing and finally forgiving Father. Richardson's amazingly perspicuous and intense portrayal of love includes, then, the familial. What makes the return of Cousin Morden so moving—a Messiah-like figure who is long awaited with passion—is that his ecstatic and tearful embrace of Clarissa, folding "the angel" in his arms as she sits (4:335), is the only purely enjoyed love embrace the poor girl receives from a man in the course of the novel. And that embrace is delivered within the closed circle of blood relationship.

The word "angel"[41] is used of Clarissa at the time of Morden's embrace. It should not be allowed to stand as her epitaph. "Woman" is in every way more satisfactory. Richardson uses it when he emphasizes that at the moment of her death she is "all that is woman" (4:348). It is a tribute to the liberalism of this author that "woman" included the rebel, the leader, the bold declarer of her own independence. It also, more conservatively, included *daughter,* and on the restoration of her filial position Clarissa's attainment of final integrity is adjudged to depend. A curious but interesting parallel comes from Blake, who could not end his career before he had restored to his myth the beneficent figure of God the Father, whom he had earlier stigmatized under the character of the oppressive, life-denying Urizen.

The Character and Fate of Lovelace

Lovelace, Richardson's most memorable creation, puts his creator squarely in the tradition of those writers—Milton, Rowe, Lillo, to remain within the filiation that this book traces—who develop good in contrast to evil and evil in contrast to good. That Satan, Calista, Millwood, and Lovelace are somewhat more interesting than their opposite numbers may be partly owing to the present condition of human nature, which now feels greater affinities with sin than sainthood, and partly to the greater opportunities for artistic variety and energy that evil produces. Certainly the fascination of Lovelace lies largely in his vivacious embodiment of complexity and conflict, and this entire chapter

41. For a discussion of this term in relation to Victorian sexuality, see Walter E. Houghton, *The Victorian Frame of Mind 1830–1870* (New Haven: Yale University Press, 1957), pp. 353–55. My own interpretation of Clarissa separates her from this tendency, though I acknowledge that one aspect of her is "angelic" and that that has exerted influence on subsequent culture. For an analysis of Clarissa that stresses her virtual abrogation of the body—even of the Christian notion of the idealized postmortem body, see Leo Braudy, "Penetration and Impenetrability in *Clarissa*" in *New Approaches to Eighteenth-Century Literature,* ed. Phillip Harth (New York: Columbia University Press, 1974), pp. 177–206. Braudy notes that Belford twice identifies Clarissa with Socrates and interprets this as evidence of her greater comfort with classical sublimation of the body than with the Christian resurrection of the body (ibid., p. 194, n.13).

might have been devoted to untangling the strands in his rich and complicated character. Our central questions must be these: Is Lovelace a man of
normal sexual energy? Does he possess sensibility and, if so, of what kind? Is
he the enemy of human love?

Since Lovelace's potency has come under suspicion, and he has even been
viewed as partially effeminate[42]—but especially since the appreciation of
Clarissa and what she lost depends in part on the character of her lover—it is
important to understand the nature of his sexuality. To begin bluntly and
assertively, it will have to be described as vigorous, normal in its nature, and
attractive to the opposite sex. Lovelace is not at first and not primarily a
sadistic monster, a tortuous villain denied common humanity, like Iago and
Richard III, although these help constitute a context for him. The man
Clarissa goes off with and trusts her destiny to is a brave, attractive, and
dashing rake, guilty of many sins of the flesh but a man of heterosexual
exuberance that accompanies—and helps to make zestful—a lively, witty mind
stocked with much learning, a disposition to do good, and an immitigable
charm of manner. If through him Richardson is castigating a Restoration type
of gallant who he thought was preying upon religion and culture (and there
are many signs that Lovelace is the avatar of an earlier, more gallant, but
tyrannical type of Englishman; see 4:130–33, 163–64), then a fortiori he must
be presented as a plausible sexual temptation to a girl of wit and spirit who, as
we have seen, is fully capable of falling in love with him. From his very first
appearance, Lovelace is a most appealing contrast to that mean-spirited creature James Harlowe. Lovelace is not a drinker or a gambler (1:17, 51), not an
intellectual unbeliever or a doubter or a jester about things sacred (2:161,
4:35); but a fluent writer, a discriminating reader, a man of quick memory
and wide-ranging imagination,[43] and a persistent and successful wooer of
women. A sensualist to the core, he appreciates Clarissa's beauty and shows in
his descriptions of her (1:148), descriptions that recall Milton's portrait of
Eve and are the only truly sensual passages in the novel, that his taste in
beauty can reach refinement and even exaltation while it remains essentially
carnal. He must be seen as a man of vital sexual power and charm. If we do
not grant him that basic quality, we will be at a loss to explain the responses of
Anna and Clarissa—and of sister Bella too, for that matter, since he woos her
first and wins a response.

His possession of a compassionate side is as requisite to his initial success
with Clarissa—and Anna too—as his physical charm (2:187). He can be extremely gentle and generous, is capable of good works (1:56; 2:56–59, 460),

---

42. See Judith Wilt, "He Could Go No Farther: A Modest Proposal about Lovelace and
Clarissa," *PMLA* 92 (Jan. 1977): 19–32.

43. "It is remarkable how intellectual Lovelace's world turned out to be." Kinkead-Weekes,
Richardson, p. 149.

possesses a sensitiveness to external nature (to birds, sunrises) not unlike Clarissa's, which he admires (3:147). He can also respond to Clarissa's exquisite tenderness, shedding tears of sympathy (2:481). But, as we have seen, his sensibility, unlike hers, does not move at the command of virtue and therefore is actually dangerous. Yet it is present and could have borne the seeds of salvation and a true friendship with Clarissa. And Lovelace can be said to come close to achieving that before he is seized by dark and perverted lusts. If one misses this trait in him, one fails to understand the conclusion of the novel, in which Richardson extends his powers of psychological analysis right up to the edge of the grave. Just before his death, Lovelace's ego is fully occupied defending his own actions in brilliant strokes of casuistry that show he is far from repentant (4:451). But in the duel, in which he dies at the hand of Cousin Morden, he acquits himself well. Though there is now and then a trace of the old swagger, his behavior reveals dignity and even sensibility. Above all, he demonstrates that he understands the central point of Richardson's book—that the good and gentle Clarissa is a "true heroine," a heroine of the new sensibility—and in achieving that insight Lovelace reveals considerable moral and spiritual sensitivity. As an "infidel only in practice" (4:559) and a potential Man of Feeling who, as far as beliefs go, can be called a Christian, he is spared the hideous death that overtakes an unrepentant rake like Belton or an unrepentant prostitute like Mrs. Sinclair. Instead, he dies cherishing the beauty of Clarissa's memory, his only joy being to think of her. As he falls, he breathes, "Oh, my beloved Clarissa!—Now art thou——" (4:529). And in the night of delirium that follows his fatal wound, he seems to have visions of Clarissa, whom he addresses as a "Blessed Spirit" (4:530). His last words are "LET THIS EXPIATE!" What can the profoundly contextual, as distinct from the literally grammatical, antecedent of "THIS" be? Surely not Christian repentance, for he has refused the last rites of the church. No more can it refer to his death in dueling, for that act had no seeds of salvation in it. It must refer to his love of Clarissa, that "Divine Creature," that "Fair Sufferer" (4:530). Such sentimental love cannot of course avail to salvation. But it does show that Lovelace does not end his days as an unrepentant persecutor and that we have not been mistaken in seeing in him the lineaments of a Man of Feeling. Unsaved, perhaps even irredeemable, he sees his beloved from across a great gulf like the one that separates Dives and Lazarus in the Gospels. Lovelace's dying moments are a sign he will be "condignly punished" (postscript, 4:557), for he is already in hell. Richardson would never have accepted more recent views that a *Liebestod* is inevitably redemptive. But, though lost, Lovelace is a figure of pathos who knows with torturing clarity that he has lost what he will never possess again. To deny him sensibility is to deny him his hell—to deprive his sufferings of their exquisitely painful essence. And that Richardson is unwilling to do. He is also unwilling to give

him what another unrepentant lover, Eloisa, longed for, the narcotic forget-
fulness of death. Richardson, with a kind of Dantesque appropriateness,
punishes Lovelace by making him love forever without reward. He is and will
be in hell, no mistake. But it is a hell worthy of a superior man who might have
been the instrument of realizing on earth the Miltonic Eden.

Ironically, during the course of his life Lovelace is fundamentally and compulsively the enemy of love—for all his charm, his occasional benevolence,
and his enormous potential as a husband and father of a family. He is, in fact,
the single most important destroyer of Clarissa's hopes in love. Of the many
crimes against love we witness in the novel, his is the greatest, for he destroys
the hopes that he himself has helped to arouse; and he is profoundly evil
precisely to the degree that he is potentially good. He is guilty of other crimes
too, some so monstrous that he becomes a rebellious Satan who has consciously chosen evil, others so deep in him that he could be regarded as an
abortion of nature. He is seldom in love without at the same time being in
hate: love of Clarissa early in the novel vies with hatred of her brother James
as his basic motivation. He wants to possess women, not respect and cherish
them, and his "arrogant and encroaching spirit" (2:10) with its desire for
power tortures animals, causes the deaths of young girls through unwanted
pregnancies (2:148), desires to "outwit and impel" Anna Howe to become his
prey (2:100), and is constantly piqued to conquest by the very purity and
virtue of Clarissa herself. Placing a low Calvinistic view on human nature, he
wishes to degrade human expectation to a depraved norm, and his imagination is gnawed by a hunger that preys incessantly upon goodness in order to
corrupt it to evil (2:102, 247, 498). Lovelace is Satanic precisely because his
attacks on love, purity, and beauty are not impelled by "gusts of violent passion," as in most men, but are a slow and nurtured growth of his perverse
nature (2:159). Often his dreams of life with Clarissa are dreams not of
mutual love and enjoyment but of realized power (2:251). Still this man,
hungry for power, suffers the indignity of being magnificently dwarfed by the
sublime object of his depredations—and he knows it as he cowers before her
(2:383). A man of an older, fiercer, presentimental order which was being
challenged by the growing appropriation of femininity into the individual and
his culture, Lovelace wonders how it would be to be dominated and deposed
by a woman of strength: "So *visible* a Superiority, to so proud a spirit as mine!
And *here* from below, from Below indeed! from these *women!* I am so goaded
on" (2:400).

Besides being an anti-Christ, an anti-Eros, an antibenevolist, and an antifeminist, Lovelace is made to embody the narcissistic sins that Milton condemned in *Paradise Lost.* The very essence of his being is love of self. He was
apparently indulged and spoiled by a mother who is not named but whose
presence seems to lurk behind his actions (2:10, 483), and he regresses to

childhood as Clarissa rises in moral majesty to become a kind of queen of heaven (3:290–92). I have already noted that he lusts for the witty and shrewd Anna, also an unavailable goddess who challenges his desire for conquest. That lust recurs (3:473) and is even dreamed about, for it has insinuated itself into the unconscious as well as the conscious mind. When the desire for Anna comes out as a dream, it has qualities of morbidity and perverseness. Lovelace dreams he has first produced a boy with Clarissa and then a girl with Anna who, when "they grow up, in order to consolidate their mammas' friendships (for neither have dreams regard to *consanguinity*), intermarry" (3:251). So what begins in the prostitution of Clarissa in a house of ill fame continues with a conquest of Anna, whom at this point he knows to be his enemy, and ends with an incestuous relation between the offspring of his concupiscence and his love of power. Shades of Satan, Sin, and Death! And so Lovelace is made to run the gamut of human evil. One is impelled to say that when the dying Clarissa forgives him, she forgives much. And yet Richardson, even in moments of savage condemnation, does not allow us to forget the good that might have been or even the love that has been banished by hate and persecution. At the time of the rape, when Lovelace's eyes are fierce and wild and his feelings violent, Clarissa sees in them even then the recollections of another and totally different mood; in a thrilling phrase she refers to the "*joy-suppressed* emotions" (3:370) of his gaze.

Is *Clarissa* a love story? It is, if a love story can be concerned with an earthly love denied to the heroine and perverted by the hero, with heavenly love substituted for the frustrated *eros,* and with a tormented love that exists eternally in that fiery infernal region of regret where the guilty sinner knows what he has missed. Is *Clarissa* a tragedy? Not if Christian hope and triumphant virtue completely exclude the memory of what might have been and completely reconcile the reader as well as the heroine to the loss and punishment of a brilliant and potentially satisfying lover. But the reader is not so reconciled: quite the contrary. He grieves deeply over the irretrievably lost opportunities and censures society for producing those very real and menacing creatures that can blight the promise of happiness. Richardson was clearly not one of those who found Christianity and tragedy irreconcilable. He found Christ relevant to art, but he also respected Aristotle—at least an Aristotle modernized and psychologized. And he hoped to achieve the great tragic emotions not through formally exact art but through evocative art produced in the context of the newer sensibility and its psychology. In this at least he was like Pope, for he desired to

> Encourage—compose—with more than magic art,
> With *pity* and with *terror* tear [the] heart.[44]

44. Richardson quotes Pope in the Postscript to *Clarissa* (4:555) and also the poet's classical source, Horace. The novelist is much concerned with tragic emotions and their realization in his fictions, although it must be said he does not reveal himself to be either sophisticated or consistent

Both a product of and a contributor to the eighteenth-century revolution that subjectified artistic aims and forms and transferred value from the finely shaped work—from the well-wrought urn—to the reader's emotional responses, Richardson obeyed the injunction of his friend Edward Young, himself a poet and critic in the vanguard, "to affect the human heart as deeply as you can." Young urged Richardson not to reward Clarissa cheaply, as many had advised, but to retain the tragic spirit and the tragic ending. Richardson's critics, Young said, would have "utterly ruined our three best plays" (*Venice Preserved, The Orphan,* and Lee's *Theodosius*) by making "the innocent and amiable" Belvidera, Monimia, and Athenais happy.[45] It was the genius of Richardson to rise to what his own age of important change demanded with respect to the emotions and to imbue an amazingly exact portrait of real life, close to the experience of the reader, with the venerable tragic emotions of "pathos and sublimity,"[46] in Young's modern terms for pity and fear. Primarily for this reason Richardson not only persuaded the Christian Samuel Johnson of his greatness but also French Deists, Romantics, and libertines—Didcrot, Rousseau, and Laclos, who approved of the fate of Clarissa. Even the Marquis de Sade appreciated Richardson's aesthetic integrity and his faithfulness to the mode of tragic sensibility he had chosen: "Que l'on réponde: si après douze ou quinze volumes, l'immortel Richardson eût *vertueusement* fini par convertir Lovelace, et par lui faire *paisiblement* épouser Clarisse, eût-on versé à la lecture de ce roman, pris dans le sens contraire, les larmes délicieuses, qu'il obtient de tous les êtres sensibles?"[47]

---

on the subject. On the subject in general, see John A. Dussinger, "Richardson's Tragic Muse," *Philological Quarterly* 46 (Jan. 1967): 18–33. For the view that *Clarissa* expresses seriousness and sorrow but not tragic emotion since the pious death of the heroine is emphasized, see Arthur Friedman, "Aspects of Sentimentalism in Eighteenth-Century Literature," in *The Augustan Milieu: Essays Presented to Louis A. Landa,* ed. Henry K. Miller, Eric Rothstein, and G. S. Rousseau (Oxford: Clarendon Press, 1970), pp. 247–61. See also Sheldon Sacks, "*Clarissa* and the Tragic Traditions," in *Studies in Eighteenth-Century Culture: Irrationalism in the Eighteenth Century,* ed. Harold E. Pagliaro (Cleveland, Ohio: Press of Case Western Reserve University, 1972), pp. 195–221. The last seems to me to be the definitive treatment of the problem. We must not forget the likely response of the Christian reader of the eighteenth century to the sufferings of Clarissa. George Jeffreys, who was "extremely pleased" with the novel, who professed himself a Christian, but who simply could not follow Richardson's injunction to "envy" the triumphant death of his heroine, writes: "What I mean by this is, that . . . the majority of readers (not excepting the clergy themselves,) can never be reconciled to the sufferings of Clarissa in this life, by the prospect of her happiness in another." It is well to remind ourselves that Christians are also human and can grieve over purely human loss, whatever the ultimate destiny. The letter from Jeffreys appears in [John Duncombe], *Letters by Several Eminent Persons Deceased* (London, 1772), pp. 149–53, where it is dated 21 Sept. 1749. I owe this reference to my colleague Robert D. Mayo, who will publish the letter in his collection of essays on Richardson in the Critical Heritage Series.

45. *Correspondence of Edward Young,* ed. Henry Pettit (Oxford: Clarendon Press, 1971), p. 180. Young's letter to Richardson is dated 20 June 1744.

46. Ibid., p. 342 (letter to Richardson, 7 Jan. 1749/50).

47. Quoted by Eaves and Kimpel (*Richardson: A Biography,* p. 603), who translate the remark: "Answer: if after twelve or fifteen volumes the immortal Richardson had *virtuously* ended by converting Lovelace and having him *peacefully* marry Clarissa, would you, in reading this novel taken in the opposite sense, have shed the delicious tears which it won from every feeling reader?"

"Sir Charles Grandison": The Enlarged Family

Richardson's last novel is considerably better than can be easily imagined by those who have only heard about it. But admittedly it represents a falling off after *Clarissa,* just as *Amelia* is a decline from the heights of *Tom Jones.* The portrait of the ideal husband in *Sir Charles Grandison* (1753) followed two years after Fielding's portrayal of the faithful and loving wife in *Amelia,* whose model of domestic loyalty is perhaps in the end more persuasive than Richardson's paragon. But if the palm for aesthetics must go to Fielding, Richardson comes off with greater intellectual honors, for Amelia does not sparkle with the many intellectual, spiritual, moral, and political facets of Richardson's diamond: Sir Charles is a modern Anglican knight of sensibility, more successful at disarming than destroying opponents, an early Broad Churchman hopeful of reconciling Englishmen and Italians, Anglicans and Catholics, Anglicans and Methodists. Despite broad, even international concerns, here as everywhere Richardson's canvas is chiefly the domestic life. The centrally important relationships of the novel are those of Sir Charles: with the ingénue Emily, who, though only fourteen, loves the hero with passion; with Olivia, the violent and volatile black-haired beauty from Florence whose fierce temper forever obviates a union with the hero; with the lively sister Charlotte, a parallel figure to Anna Howe; with the Lady Clementina, an Italian beauty whom the English gentleman would have married had religious differences been reconciled; and supremely with Harriet Byron—a delicate, beautiful heroine with a fresh country skin and a set of the highest principles, whom Sir Charles, when he is free of all debts of honor, makes his wife in an ideal union.

We are on familiar ground, since many—perhaps most—of the ideas and ideals we have seen developing since the Restoration here attain their climax. The term "hero" is obsessively applied to a new kind of man, the pacifist Sir Charles, who has disciplined his naturally violent passions into a religiously and rationally controlled order. Cliché terms from the heroic plays are also applied to Harriet, who possesses greatness of soul, and to Clementina, who reveals the same quality when she shows herself able to renounce passion for principle, that is, adherence to her Roman Catholic faith and Italian nationality. Richardson's novel thus represents a climax in the domestication of heroism, realizing nobility of action in the spheres of love, marriage, and quotidian duty. It is also a climax of sensibility in love and friendship; and tears are shed copiously and unashamedly not only by the heroine but also by the hero as their hearts unite and as they feel the warm presages of ultimate bodily copulation. Feeling, along with virtue, extends outward from the loving couple to their environment as they work toward uniting the good and redeeming the evil. Sir Charles's Christian heroism is forever active in obstructing the cruel, providing for the needy, encouraging the defeated, enforcing prudence in domestic arrangements, reconciling former enemies. Above all, *Sir Charles Grandison* is the portrait of how a good marriage should be created and sustained. Marriage is an "awful rite" (2:347), yet for all its majestic solemnity it is not stoical but rests on love and even sexuality at its base. Sir Charles, as Harriet says of him, may make no "ostentatious pretension to religion" (1:440) though he is unmistakably a Christian; but he does, somewhat ostentatiously, protest his susceptibility to physical love: "A susceptibility of the passion called *Love,* I condemn not as a fault; but the contrary. Your *brother,* Ladies (looking upon all three [the group includes Harriet, his adopted sister, who will become his wife]) is no Stoic" (1:414). Love must rise—need I say it?—far above the physical to the nobly spiritual; but in the calm of this novel, much more clearly than in the hectic world of *Clarissa,* Richardson makes crystal clear what I have assumed to be true everywhere in his thought and art, that the best love arises from physical attraction, grows with sympathy of mind, and achieves permanence only when two minds fully commit themselves to virtue and benevolence. Were not the excitements of sexuality placed well beneath the surface in this novel, it would be more widely read than it is now or has been in our century. But they exist and bubble underground like hidden springs. They make it clear that Richardson's model for love is the Miltonic, fusing the physical and the spiritual, not the Platonic, rising above and so transcending sexuality.

Two aspects of Richardson's treatment of love appear clearly in *Sir Charles Grandison* for the first time, the portrayal of love madness and the sense that true love is an extension of the familial. Clementina's wits are temporarily disordered by her great love for Sir Charles and its frustration by her family and life in Italy. Richardson's picture of love melancholy was greatly praised in the eighteenth century: Joseph Warton called it "deeply interesting," rating it above the madness of Lear and that of Orestes in Euripedes.[48] But to a modern it seems remote and enormously long in the portrayal, in part an abandonment of what Richardson does so brilliantly in "writing to the moment." It is unredeemed by the psychological depth one finds elsewhere; and even the political-religious contrasts, though of some interest, are not realized graphically. Transalpine, Catholic life was outside Richardson's ken—perhaps outside his sympathies, too (his index to the novel refers to "Men, Women, and Italians"); and though the laments of Lady Clementina have some lyrical beauty, they remain general and effusive, without redeeming particularity.

The presentation of the love of Harriet Byron and Sir Charles as an easy extension of the familial is successful and enormously suggestive to the student of English culture. Richardson continues his familiar polemic against

48. Warton's comment is quoted by Brian W. Downs, *Richardson* (1928; reprint, London: Frank Cass, 1969), p. 89.

parentally forced marriage and in favor of a child's freedom to choose a partner. He desires reform of the family into a community of love in which personality can freely flower. He is clearly a prophet of that great modern social movement toward Lawrence Stone's "affective individualism," which Richardson not only preaches but embodies in plastic literary forms. The environment of virtuous love which he creates attains its serenity—even its relaxation, I might say—because laughter and tears are both present. Charlotte Grandison possesses real wit and liveliness of mind, and these qualities are not overcome by tragedy as those of Anna Howe are in the greater novel. Even newer habits of love and "bonding" can be treated with relaxed lightness: when Charles kisses Harriet on the lips, Charlotte cries out, "O Lud! O Lud! how could you bear him afterwards in your sight?" (3:195). Tears are also a sign of personal rapport and goodness in action rather than tension, frustration, or fear. The lachrymose is called, with perhaps a slightly bemused touch, "kindly gush!" and it is regarded as divinely sanctioned: tears are "Dew drops of Heaven!" (3:144).

A potentially darker side to the familial in this novel must be analyzed perhaps less for its own sake than for what it seems to prophesy about the future direction of love-sensibility. Richardson's love fantasies in *Grandison* have been with some justice called polygamous.[49] His paragon is loved fervently by at least four women, and the question of whom he will choose for a life partner is left decidedly open until very late in the action. And once the decision is made, the former rivals, with some severe obstacles remaining, cease being that and accept their several positions in a relation of tearful love to one another. But in the end "polygamy" is not the appropriate word for the enlarged family[50] over which Sir Charles presides; his own perspective is fraternal: "Men and women are brothers and sisters." Richardson was religious enough to believe in the family of man and to give new meaning to that concept in exploring the love relationship. The hero's rescue of Harriet from the clutches of the rich, vain, hot-tempered, rakish Sir Hargrave Pollexfen brings her into the Grandison family,[51] where she becomes virtually a sister. That role is thrust upon her, but she accepts it gladly. She is obviously in it when she falls in love with her rescuer, and it is from the position of a kind of father-brother that he woos her. His endearments are mixed with instruction, exemplary deeds, practical leadership; lover and head of family are not alternating but fully blended functions as the two move through courtship to marriage. Thus the "company of angels" Harriet falls into is a "family of love,"

49. By Morris Golden, *Richardson's Characters* (Ann Arbor: University of Michigan Press, 1963), p. 21.

50. I follow the terminology of Lawrence Stone. The Grandison family is not "extended" vertically through generations but "enlarged" horizontally to include kin and others of the same generation (*Family, Sex and Marriage*, p. 23).

51. Freud says that rescue fantasies, particularly from water, are connected with giving birth. See *The Interpretation of Dreams*, p. 439 and n.2.

consisting of "true brothers and sisters" (1:133, 145), and she will surely look
upon the husbandly love that eventuates as simply an extension of "all the
tenderness of a brother" (1:167), which her rescuer has been manifesting
toward her ever since she joined the family. He also regards the relationship
in that fashion: he obsessively calls her his new sister (e.g., 1:144–45). Since
Harriet was orphaned at the age of eight (1:11), one thinks back to Otway's
famous and influential play, in which there is no blood relationship but the
orphan has taken a place as a sister before the amorous action begins.
Richardson knew Otways' work well; but it must be said that *Sir Charles Grandison* is entirely lacking in the morbidity of *The Orphan,* even though the novel
loosely repeats the play's situation, though not its action, and certainly implies
that close similarity, if not consanguinity, is a deep attraction. One reason that
Clementina, for all her loveliness and piety, will not do as the hero's wife is
that she comes from afar—she is dark, Catholic, Italian. Harriet is an English
"sister," and the ceremony of marriage is preceded by what can be regarded as
an antecedent ceremony—Sir Charles formally taking the orphan into his
family (1:44–45). Richardson made of the brother-sister relation in the Grandison family—both the actual blood tie and the symbolic one—something
noble, chivalric, and deeply sustaining, endowing it with all the respect and
idealism he was prepared to accord to true heterosexual love. The dynamics
of Richardsonian love must have been influential; perhaps unconsiously the
pre-Romantic, Romantic, and Victorian sensibilities were attracted to the
Grandison ménage precisely because it seemed to give so high a sanction to the
indigenous and the similar.

And yet it would be wrong to exaggerate this quality in Richardson's concept of love, which would be seriously distorted if morbidities were allowed to
intrude. The novelist was in fact an enemy of the narcissistic and the inbred.
He was careful to make the lesbianism of Mrs. Jewkes in *Pamela* completely
odious, and in this novel his heroine turns away from the irregular embraces
and kisses attempted by the violent and mannish Miss Barnevelt (1:43), who
apparently admires unbaptized ancient heroes and makes us wonder if
Richardson was anti-Greek partly because he saw sexual deviance in that
culture. Richardson, it can be said rather dogmatically, is not consciously
drawn to the abnormal. If anything, it is the forcefully heterosexual that
attracts him. In *Sir Charles Grandison* the paragon has a "keeping" rakish
father, who is nevertheless respected and obeyed, and a goatish and gouty
uncle (a brother of Sir Charles's saintly mother), for whom a wife is provided
in the course of the novel in one of the hero's redeeming actions. The hero is
himself sexually attractive, with a delicate complexion, curling auburn locks, a
manly stature and air, sparkling intelligence, and athletic prowess (1:359).
This paragon has an eye for feminine beauty, and one of his greatest satisfactions arises from his having wooed and won "one of the most perfect beauties
he had ever seen" (2:29). If one wishes to see clearly Richardson's ideal of

love, an ideal that perhaps did not change much in its essential features during his writing career, *Sir Charles Grandison* is an admirable source: as a novel of normality and daily life it is a corrective to the greater *Clarissa,* with the latter's hectic evil passions and almost equally hectic transcendence of even good passions. The later novel enables us to see clearly that "transcendence," not "denial," is the proper word to describe the sanctification of Clarissa. In the love between Charles and Harriet we have passionate-virtuous love realized in the social sphere, much to its edification. Indeed, that love becomes an example of what could in fact transform mankind into a family and so obviate the drive toward death and the afterlife that so powerfully motivates Clarissa when her earthly love falls in ruin.

All of Richardson's novels together enable us to see his achievement as one of the eighteenth-century climaxes in realizing the Miltonic ideal of friendship, love, and marriage and also the post-Edenic frustrations of that ideal. His range is as impressive as his penetration, and his entire treatment of love through all the novels is so encyclopedic that it is as much in need of an index as his last novel, which, like Pope's *Iliad,* was provided with one as a convenient guide to its sentiments. What an exploration of the recesses of the heart is stimulated by a full and careful contemplation of the following relations: Pamela and Mr. B; Pamela and the coarse, bisexual Mrs. Jewkes; Clarissa and Lovelace; Clarissa and the squat, toadlike Solmes; Clarissa and her sensible-fervent friend Anna;[52] Anna and her meek lover, Hickman; Clarissa and the reformed rake, Belford; Lovelace and Anna; Harriet and Charlotte; Sir Charles and each of his women; Sir Charles and Lady Clementina's brother Jeronymo; Harriet and her other "sisters." Even to give a partial list is to suggest the richness, the essential health, and the ambiguities: a richness that fulfills the adumbrations of Lee, Otway, Dryden, Pope in *Eloisa,* Rowe, Steele, Lillo; a health that impressed Samuel Johnson, Jane Austen, and the Victorians; and the ambiguities that have titillated Gothicists, Romantics, and Freudians. Richardson, as decades of adverse criticism and neglect have shown, is not hard to dismiss or ignore. But, as our age has come to realize, to dismiss him for his surface conventionality is to dismiss one of the most richly nuanced psychological artists English literature has produced. It is a pity that the length of his works and the frequent piety of his tone make him unavailable to many. In a study of eighteenth-century love he will have to be regarded as a watershed.

52. By concentrating on the theme of love I may not have done full justice to the intellectual range and to the high spirits that are especially to be found in the Anna-Clarissa correspondence. It is perhaps here that the greatest support can be found for Leslie Fiedler's comment that Richardson's morality had fully matured in *Clarissa,* where "his insight into the complexities of the female mind has become terrifyingly acute" (*Love and Death in the American Novel,* p. 64).

9. Rousseau

*R*ICHARDSON BEARS little responsibility for Rousseau the thinker, but Rousseau the novelist can be viewed as one of the Englishman's most considerable achievements. *La nouvelle Héloïse* is the finest embodiment of Richardsonian influence, which was Europe-wide in its scope and was accompanied by glowing critical acclaim, of which Diderot's enthusiastic *Eloge de Richardson* is only the best-known example. Rousseau's novel is worthy of the attention of modern English readers because it became virtually a classic of English letters in the generations following its publication[1] and also because, building on the foundations of *Clarissa,* it sophisticated, deepened, and aestheticized love-sensibility. That sensibility was already ambivalent and resonant in Richardson, but no one could deny that its moralistic rigidity was in need of artistic softening. Such mollification it received at the hands of one of the masters of the French language, and it is fascinating to observe how the psychological and moral vividness of the English author becomes lyrical music in French without losing its ability to penetrate the human depths. Rousseau was also a religious spirit—in his own way a believing Christian;[2] even so, he naturalizes Richardson's sublime baroque into a complex creation closer to the Romantic and the modern spirit. Clarissa becomes a saint, the bride of Christ, the daughter of God who sits on his right hand, forever divorced from Lovelace, who contemplates what he has lost across a great gulf. Julie becomes the bride of nature, mysteriously awaiting a reunion with her lover, Saint-Preux, and looking forward to a consummation in the beyond which is never explained but toward which the nerves and muscles of every loving character strain in anticipation. Richardson in the end rejects this world for the next; Rousseau also invokes the next, depriving love of its fulfillment here and now, while at the same time setting up enduring human structures that embody

1. See James H. Warner, "Eighteenth-Century English Reactions to the *Nouvelle Héloïse*," *PMLA* 52 (Sept. 1937): 803–19. "On peut même se demander si Rousseau n'est pas, aux environs de 1785, en passe de devenir outre-Manche un auteur classique" (Jacques Voisine, *J.-J. Rousseau en Angleterre à l'époque romantique* [Paris: Didier, 1956], p. 118). For eighteenth-century comparisons (mostly French) of Richardson and Rousseau, see Laurent Versini, *Laclos et la tradition: Essai sur les sources et la technique des "Liaisons Dangereuses"* (Paris: Librairie C. Klincksieck, 1968), pp. 281–84.

2. See his Fragments sur Dieu et sur la Révélation in *Oeuvres complètes,* 4 vols., Bibliothèque de la Pléiade (Paris: Editions Gallimard, 1959–69), 4:1031–55. All quotations from Rousseau come from this edition, which is hereinafter abbreviated *OC* and referred to by volume and page numbers.

Enlightened values but scarcely do justice to the romantic passion which must find its realization somewhere—and somehow—beyond. As my definition of "sentiment" has demonstrated, the age of Richardson felt it had to accommodate the claims of both reason and feeling in love, and when fusion did not succeed, it developed competing literatures of rationality and sensibility.

Rousseau, sensitive to these rival tendencies and surely deeply respectful of anyone who could have united them, sets his hand to a similar task. Julie and her husband, Wolmar, are notable embodiments, both taken together and considered separately, of the mind and the heart, although each gives primacy of one over the other. Richardson's dramatic light-dark conflict between his villain and his saint of sensibility is replaced by a complex field of force in which the emotions and the reason attract and repel, pull apart and cohere, and mysteriously but impressively confront each other, sometimes to achieve a kind of interpenetration that is quintessentially Rousseauist and Romantic and that perhaps deserves to be identified by Coleridge's crude but suggestive term, "interinanimation."

Rousseau's page is instinct with death, but it does not display either heavenly glory or the livid fires of Richardson's hell. These are replaced by Rousseauist nature, which, however, is full of nuance and complication. "Schiller affirme que Jean-Jacques 'a converti les chrétiens en êtres humains'";[3] but these human beings are not flat Enlightenment types. They continue to have something of the agony of fervent Christians seeking salvation, and they partake of the darker human passions despite Rousseau's denial or deliberate ignorance of the doctrine of original sin. Particularly in his private work, *The Confessions*, the first part of which is more a great novel of sensibility than a factual autobiography, Rousseau brings to the surface the morbidity that is latent in many English analyses of love, notably that of the "gentle" Otway. Love in Rousseau is tinged with obsession and deviance, and these we are able to see as the typical and influential configurations of a simultaneously pioneering and conservative spirit. What Rousseau does in his exploration of himself is both fulfillment and prophecy. He brings to a culmination the tendency toward the psychologizing of experience that I have noted from Dennis on; he also isolates those enduringly human elements in love that can destroy it, elements that have been present since man became man. He repeats in his own consciousness the story of the Fall, but like many people of neurotic sensibility, he is progressive as well as regressive. If he drives our thoughts back to primitive origins, to the childhood of the race and of individual man, he also predicts things to come, defining for pre-Romantics, Romantics, and moderns the terms of their own lovemaking, its

3. "Schiller affirms that Jean-Jacque 'transformed Christians into human beings'": Pierre Trahard, *Les maîtres de la sensibilité française au XVIIIᵉ siècle (1715–1789)*, 4 vols. (Paris: Boivin, 1931–33), 3:124.

occasional triumphs, its more frequent manifestations of mischief. In *The Confessions* Rousseau displays the kind of love that arises when age-old institutions begin to crumble and societies fall apart. In one sense his is an apocalypse of Protestant individualism, for the spirit of man must fall back upon itself without external guides and sanctions and cut its own path through the jungles of individual and social passion.

"Emile": The Psychology of Postponed Sexuality

The movement in England from the heroic to the pathetic has an answering or an antecedent development in the French concept of *vertu*. In earlier epochs that important term had meant force and military courage. In the seventeenth century it had come to stand for the obedience to duty. Now in the eighteenth century it meant "la conformité des actes aux émotions naturelles."[4] Thus some of the differences I have already noted between Richardson and Rousseau are explainable in part by differing national literary developments. Rousseau came at the height of sensibility in France and was responsible for producing its *période d'éclat;* but he sprang up by no means *ex nihilo*. He was preceded by writers who have no counterpart in English and who made their mark on his spirit and style. Prévost, for one, had already diluted the Christian morality of Bossuet and Pascal and, even while introducing the pathetic to the novel, had been guilty of excesses—*sensibilité* almost immediately becoming *sensiblerie*. Rousseau was also preceded and influenced by the subtle and refined Marivaux, who softened the brutality of nature by sensibility and who gave "à l'instinct cette dignité qui fait de l'amour, malgré tout, la plus belle partie de l'être humain."[5] No one of such radical and potentially subversive power in sensibility as Prévost or of such dedication to subtle exploration of love as Marivaux had preceded Richardson in England. Rousseau, writing in eighteenth-century France, was therefore the inheritor of much greater sophistication concerning love than was available to his English mentor.

In discussing the chief works of Rousseau on the subject of love, I shall begin with the most theoretical, *Emile,* and end with the most personal, *The Confessions,* allowing *La nouvelle Héloïse,* which partakes of both extremes, to stand in the middle and receive the major attention. It may surprise those who associate Rousseau only with Romantic release to discover in *Emile*—and almost everywhere, for that matter—a respect for reality and disciplined common sense worthy of Samuel Johnson, who nevertheless feared and

4. Ibid., 1:149.
5. Ibid., p. 72 ("to the instinct that dignity which makes love, despite everything, the most beautiful part of human existence").

loathed the French writer as a major social and moral menace. What concerns me is not, however, either the "Romantic" or the "classical" elements per se in Rousseau but his concept of love and ideas closely related to it. Like Coleridge after him and other Romantics, Rousseau appreciated the importance of early love and saw a happy home life as the best antidote to abuses of affection. The earliest education is the work of the mother, a fact that gives her a place of preeminence that all civilized men must respect. Lack of regard for the father can be excused, but lack of devotion to the mother breeds an unnatural monster (*OC,* 4:245 n.). And there is more than a hint in Rousseau of one modern view, that homosexuality is the product of extreme mother dependence. But *Emile* contains only the merest suggestion of possible aberration, and one must await *The Confessions* for a full exploration of the residues in life of an early and powerful mother influence—of attempts either to compensate for the lack of maternal affection or to escape the excesses of it. Nor is there any hint here that childhood, that great discovery of Rousseau, contains anything resembling the sexuality that Freud—or Blake, for that matter—saw in innocence. Quite the contrary. Rousseau's insight is that childhood must be loved for its own independent and unique sake and must be respected as an end in itself. Thus the child must be treated as a child and never as an adult; he must be respected as a child and not forced into adult roles—a basic insight often perverted in modern views of education in which the child is elevated into a repository of wise, rational powers of decision. For Rousseau the most obvious corollary of his respect for the autonomy of childhood is that it is completely free of sexual passion and so exists in a world quite apart from adulthood. His interesting discussion of the sense of touch—so different from Blake's and Gray's treatment of that important sense—gives to it only practical utility, as a sentinel that warns us of harm, the equivalent of eyesight by night, a means of self-preservation.[6] Although he recognizes the obvious fact that touch is a pan-corporal sense, present in almost every part of the body, he is far from seeing this as an invitation to heightened, though diffuse, pregenital pleasure. One would have to say that Rousseau's theory in *Emile* is surprisingly—and perhaps even suspiciously—far from his own practice as revealed in his autobiographical writing, which records his childhood delight in spankings, in strokings of the skin, and in a kind of preliminary, unfocused sort of dalliance.

The child of Rousseauist theory must be shielded from the passions as long as possible, and no little emotional intensity suffuses Rousseau's ominous warning of the sexuality that will one day invade the human fortress— "l'ennemi qui nous menace, et qui s'apprête à s'en emparer!"[7] When the

6. *OC,* 4:381, 388–91. For Blake on this sense, see S. Foster Damon, *A Blake Dictionary* (Providence: Brown University Press, 1965), p. 408 (s.v. "Touch"). For Gray, see Jean H. Hagstrum, "Gray's Sensibility" in *Fearful Joy,* ed. James Downey and Ben Jones (Montreal: McGill-Queen's University Press, 1974), p. 13.

7. *OC,* 4:466 ("the foe who threatens us and who is preparing to seize it").

passions come, they announce the tumultuous passage from autonomous, respected childhood to a complex, tormented adulthood. Even so, though potentially dangerous, the passions are few, natural, and God-given. Even the most basic of all, self-love—"passion primitive, innée, antérieure à toute autre"[8]—Rousseau does not regard as an evil. Here, however, I must pause to make a distinction, in order to bring out the complexity and the paradoxical nature of his thought. *Amour de soi* is one thing; *amour-propre*, though of course related, quite another. *Amour de soi*, coming from nature, is a good thing—a vital, self-preserving energy—and it is therefore closely related to the sensibility that springs from nature—"une exquise sensibilité qui donne à ceux qui en sont doués des jouissances immédiates." But if *l'amour de soi* is "un sentiment bon et absolu," it can become *amour-propre* (that is, "un sentiment rélatif"), into which enter all the mischiefs of society—comparison of self with others, demands for preference.[9] Joy it certainly can bring, but it is a negative kind of joy that lives not on the deep and true satisfactions of our nature but on the sufferings of others. Like Pope, who believed that the passions were a form of self-love and that this love was a good thing since it put wind in the sails of life, Rousseau accepts *love of self* as a natural good, attractive, gracious, beneficial to the personality. But, again like Pope, he sees that it can suffer a fall in society when it is diverted from its essential aim, and that *self-love* is a mischief that can deny us paradise and produce all our woes. The dangers of self-love Rousseau had early seen: in his first play, significantly entitled *Narcisse,* written when he was eighteen years old and staged in 1752, he attacks it as a capricious and bizarre passion and has his hero see the silliness of falling in love with his own picture, which has been "effeminated" in its retouchings and so only slightly disguised. The literary career of Rousseau went on to attack, with unforgettable vigor, the fop,[10] the transvestite, the unmanly urban dweller, and the unnatural effeminacies of an effete society. And yet one cannot

8. Ibid., p. 491 ("a passion primitive, innate, and anterior to every other").

9. *OC,* 1:668-69. The passage from which I quote comes from the first dialogue of *Rousseau Juge de Jean Jaques* and reads in part: "et voila comment l'amour de soi, qui est un sentiment bon et absolu, devient amour-propre; c'est-à-dire un sentiment rélatif par le quel on se compare, qui demande des préférences, dont la jouissance est purement négative, et qui ne cherche plus à se satisfaire par notre propre bien, mais seulement par le mal d'autrui" ("And here is how love of self, which is a good and absolute feeling, becomes self-love, that is, a relative feeling by which one makes comparison of oneself, which demands priorities, of which the joy is purely negative, and which no longer seeks self-satisfaction through one's own welfare but through harming others"). I am indebted to the Pléiade editors, who cite the parallels in *Emile* (ibid., pp. 1619–20) and to Juliet Flower MacCannell, "Nature and Self-Love: A Reinterpretation of Rousseau's 'Passion primitive,'" *PMLA* 92 (Oct. 1977): 890–902, esp. pp. 891–93.

10. The Pléiade editor Jacques Scherer points out that Valère in *Narcisse* is thrice called by Rousseau a "fat" or "petit-maitre" and that under these terms transvestitism and also homsexuality, which could not be directly named, were attacked (*OC,* 2:1862–63). Jean Starobinski perceives the subtlety in the presentation of Valère's character. For his narcissism to emerge, the portrait must be sufficiently feminized for him to *seem* to resemble someone of the opposite sex, someone else. But that is only a heterosexual disguise. The fundamental passion is narcissistic. "Sa passion . . . veut se porter sur *une* autre; mais c'est le moi qui se dupe et se fascine sous les traits de l'autre." *L'oeil vivant* (Paris: Gallimard, 1961), p. 177.

escape being somewhat haunted by the boldness and potential menace in Rousseau's radical and brilliantly aimed attack on traditional beliefs about the dangers implicit in the self and in his rehabilitation of the term "amour de soi" to mean something "bon et absolu." Has Rousseau forgotten the Miltonic shudder at the narcissistic sins, which all stem from the uncontrolled self and from an inward-oriented love of similitude? Has he sown the seeds of Romantic and modern egoism and helped turn man's adoring gaze from the author of his being to himself?

However one balances *amour de soi,* which is good, against *amour-propre,* which is evil, the truth is that in *Emile* the danger arising from aroused and undisciplined sexual passion is greater than that arising from the self, and sexual passion must be therefore delayed as long as possible. To prolong innocence is to gather strength for life; indulgence dissipates virility and threatens emotional and physical health. "Un des meilleurs préceptes de la bonne culture est, de tout retarder tant qu'il est possible. Rendez les progrès lents et sûrs; empêchez que l'adolescent ne devienne homme au moment où rien ne lui reste à faire pour le devenir."[11] The prolonging of innocence includes a strong prohibition against much feared self-indulgence, or onanism, the dangers of which haunted the mind of eighteenth-century man no less than the Victorians.[12] Rousseau apparently was one of those so haunted, fearing that the highly desirable deferral of the passions might be entirely thwarted if *le vice solitaire* were regarded with anything less than horror. Our own age has exposed the neuroticism that underlay such fear of masturbation. But Rousseau is striving for a more general and basic reform in his attempt to free childhood of passion. He wanted to eliminate, not anesthetize, early sexuality.

That desire for early purity underlies another important antithesis, this time between sensibility and imagination. Sensibility is good: it is the source of all our passions and closely related to nature. But imagination, which determines the bent or inclination (*pente*) of the passion, can by its errors (errors arising from being confined and limited and unnatural) transform the pas-

11. *OC,* 4:518–19 ("One of the best precepts of good cultivation is to hold back as much as possible. Make progress slowly and surely; keep the youth from becoming a man until nothing remains for him to do in order to become one").

12. Self-pollution, as the practice was called, was described by the most popular English manual on the subject as an "unnatural Practice" and was equated with sodomy and bestiality. It was indulged in by both men and women, but it was men who made it "so frequent, and so crying an Offence." *Onania: or, the Heinous Sin of Self-Pollution, and All Its Frightful Consequences (in Both Sexes) Considered: With Spiritual and Physical Advice to Those Who Have Already Injured Themselves by This Abominable Practice,* 18th ed. (9th of the Supplement) (London, 1756), pp. [iii], 1, 7. The work, which first appeared about 1710, ran through 19 editions, sold in some 38,000 copies, and was translated into French and German, popularizing the theory that masturbation causes mental and physical disease, an idea usually attributed to the nineteenth century. See Robert H. MacDonald, "The Frightful Consequences of Onanism: Notes on the History of a Delusion," *Journal of the History of Ideas* 28 (July–Sept. 1967): 423-31; and Stone, *Marriage,* pp. 514–16.

sions into vices. Even angels, when inhibited, can suffer this kind of fall.[13] Sensibility, when close to nature, can be sweet, healthy, and in due course of value to society. But imagination, particularly when cramped by physical and mental enclosure, can poison the passions; it can also poison them when it is dissociated from a beloved object and when narcissistic indulgence fills the mind with erotic titillations. Hard work, exhausting play, the learning of practical skills—all these accomplished away from the huddled urban masses—obviate such imaginings and cultivate a true sensibility which, when the time comes, can safely indulge the passions.

But the voice of the body must and will be heard, and that youth is singularly blessed if it is heard when he is strong and developed enough to make a socially useful response. Heard too soon, the voice will be a siren's song; heard at the right time, it will lead him into marriage, "la prémiére et la plus sainte institution de la nature."[14] Since, as the Savoyard vicar implies, this institution is primarily natural—not social or even creedally divine—the youth will find it a safe and pleasant harbor. But even though Rousseau uses here the sacred word "nature" and does give to passionate love a climactic place, it is quite surprising to those who do not know of his profound respect for discipline how carefully, even grudgingly, he treats the whole matter of sexuality. One gets more than a fleeting impression that the woman is the rival of the tutor, even his potential enemy, who could destroy in one premature attack the whole edifice of training he has reared. But Sophie does come— when Emile is ready for her—and part of that readiness is served by having her described to him in ideal verbal terms before she materializes in reality. One reason for this last caution is that, since she is as much a woman as Emile is a man, he must be allowed to focus on her mental and spiritual qualities away from the moment of physical attraction.

But though he postpones the advent of the physical, Rousseau never denies either its importance or its beauty. "Male and female created he them," as the Bible says, and Sophie is strong, very strong, precisely because she is different. Of women in general Rousseau says, "Plus elles voudront leur [les hommes] ressembler, moins elles les gouverneront, et c'est alors qu'ils seront vraiment les maitres."[15] When the time for love comes, we are to understand that by

13. *OC*, 4:501. For clear evidence that Rousseau is in part warning against masturbation and its debilitating effects on the body and its stimulating and hectic effects on the imagination, see ibid., pp. 496 and 1460, n.2.

14. P. 566 ("The first and holiest ordination of nature"). The comment is made by the good Savoyard vicar very early in his "Profession de foi," which is embodied in *Emile*.

15. P. 701 ("The more women wish to resemble men, the less they will control them, and it is then that the men will be truly the masters"). Later in *Emile* (p. 746) Rousseau deplores the confusion of the sexes: "Emile est homme et Sophie est femme, voila toute leur gloire. Dans la confusion des sexes qui règne entre nous, c'est presque un prodige d'être du sien" ("Emile is a man, Sophie is a woman, herein lies all their glory. In the midst of the confusion of sex that reigns among us, it is almost a miracle to be of one's own").

deferral of passion and passionate imaginings the woman has become as strong as the man in her own way and that the passions of both, by being postponed, have been strengthened rather than weakened. Since a rational and realistic foundation has been laid, illusion, enthusiasm, and imagination are now allowed scope. The delightful madness of passion can be indulged precisely because the whole character has been carefully disciplined by nature and nurture. Emile, with approbation, abandons himself to love; but love, that usually devouring passion, does not consume other good and amiable qualities and emotions because nature has already taught the essential law of conserving the best that it has itself implanted in the character. So in his love for Sophie, Emile is primarily attached to these traits in her: "la sensibilité, la vertu, l'amour des choses honnêtes." Similarly, Sophie loves in Emile those virtues that nature and natural education have already implanted in him: "la frugalité, la simplicité, le généreux desintéressement, le mépris du faste et des richesses." Has love changed him? Only in this, that he now has an additional reason for being truly himself.[16]

What has happened? Rousseau, by conceiving of nature not only as impulse but also as law, has made her worthy of crowning man's love with the abiding joys of regulated, institutional satisfactions. He transfers to nature the Miltonic ideal of heterosexual love, which the English poet believed must be governed by a religious hierarchy. Of the importance of heterosexual mutuality there can be no doubt. Rousseau insists upon mutual sexual enjoyment as essential to conjugal happiness, and he gives to the newly married couple a "recette contre la refroidissement de l'amour dans le mariage"—a recipe against the chilling of love in marriage: "Elle est simple et facile . . .; c'est de continüer d'être amans quand on est époux" (p. 862; "it is simple and easy . . .; it is to continue to be a lover when one is a spouse"). Of Rousseau's conception of the hierarchy of the sexes it is perhaps more difficult to be categorical. Rousseau frequently describes the role of woman and wife as inferior. But when the lovers are mature and nature has governed their physical and moral development, then even female dominance can sometimes be contemplated.

16. The entire passage in bk. 5 of *Emile* (p. 801) reads, "Emile aime Sophie; mais quels sont les prémiers charmes qui l'ont attaché? La sensibilité, la vertu, l'amour des choses honnêtes. En aimant cet amour dans sa maitresse l'auroit-il perdu pour lui-même? A quel prix à son tour Sophie s'est-elle mise? A celui de tous les sentiments qui sont naturels au coeur de son amant: l'estime des vrais biens, la frugalité, la simplicité, le généreux desintéressement, le mépris du faste et des richesses. Emile avoit ces vertus avant que l'amour les lui eut imposées. En quoi donc Emile est-il véritablement changé? Il a de nouvelles raisons d'être lui même; c'est le seul point où il soit différent de ce qu'il étoit." ("Emile loves Sophie, but what are the charms which first attracted him? Sensibility, virtue, love of things honorable. In loving such love as that in his beloved, will he himself lose it? As for Sophie, what did she require to be won? All the natural heart-feelings of her lover: esteem of the truly good, frugality, simplicity, generous unselfishness, scorn of pomp and riches. Emile possessed these virtues before love conquered him. Has he, then, really changed? He now has new reasons to be himself, only in this sense could he be said to be different from what he was.")

The conclusion of *Emile* points up the paradox. Having said to Sophie, "En devenant vôtre Epoux, Emile est devenu vôtre chef; c'est à vous d'obéir, ainsi l'a voulu la nature" ("In becoming your spouse, Emile has become your leader; you must obey him, such is the wish of nature"), the tutor immediately adds, "Quand la femme ressemble à Sophie, il est pourtant bon que l'homme soit conduit par elle; c'est encore une loi de la nature" (p. 865; "When the woman resembles Sophie, it is, however, good that the man be guided by her; that too is a law of nature").

I have said that with regard to the passions Rousseau was somewhat grudging; and so he was when he contemplated their premature arrival before the tutelage of nature had been completed. But when love, passion, and marriage come in the fullness of time, they come as a rewarding climax. And they come to man and woman mutually, man and woman regarded as essentially equal. Though the male seems generally to be the master, in love, tenderness, and related matters the woman rules. Just as Christ replaces the old dispensation, the Law, so now the wife replaces the natural tutor. She becomes the gentle guide of the heart and the tender affections, and she ensures that sensibility, which derives from nature, has been made a permanent feature of the human landscape. Thus nature seems ultimately to favor the woman, as apparently divine law never had—at least within our tradition. And natural love, far from being a childish, impulsive, immature thing, is the crown of human maturity. Like philosophy, ethics, and religion itself, it is an achievement of the fully matured mind. Such is the final lesson of *Emile*.

"La nouvelle Héloïse": Intense Friendship and Romantic Love

In 1758 Pope's *Eloisa to Abelard* was translated into French verse by Colardeau; it produced a delirium of enthusiasm that contrasted sharply with the relatively calm response the story had evoked before that date, even in previous verse and prose translations of the English poem. Toward the end of March 1759, while getting ready to write a preface to a new copy of his work, Rousseau wrote these three words, "la nouvelle Héloïse," after the earlier simple title *Julie* and before the subtitle, *Lettres de deux amans*. In this act he has been said to have placed his collection of letters under the patronage of the famous abbess who five centuries earlier had demonstrated that God and love were inseparable (2:lxviii, 1338). But matters are not quite so simple and categorical as that. If Rousseau really believed that the English poet had achieved a union of love and deity, he was out of step with the typical eighteenth-century readings of Pope's poem and indeed with the one given in this study. The point at issue is not, however, whether Rousseau read Pope accurately but whether he shared the poet's sense that a rich ambivalence inheres in the medieval story. From the three references and possible allusions that he makes in his novel, one judges that he did, since these add up to something rather more ambiguous than categorical. In the first of these references the lover, Saint-Preux, hopes his beloved Julie will soften her heart by reading the letters of Eloisa (her heart was made for love, while Abelard was a miserable creature, worthy of his fate since he was entirely dedicated to cold virtue). In the second reference Claire compares her beloved friend and cousin to Eloisa: Julie too once loved passionately and has now become pious—"plaise à Dieu que ce soit avec plus de succès!" Finally, in concluding his novel, Rousseau seems to recall the lovely lines of Pope's poem in which the dead nun, buried in the church, calls to Eloisa to "come, sister, come." So Claire hears the voice of the dead Julie: "J'entens murmurer une voix plaintive!...Claire, ô ma Claire, où es-tu? que fais tu loin de ton amie?...son cercueil ne la contient pas toute entiere....il attend le reste de sa proye....il ne l'attendra pas longtems."[17] These references and echoes seem to say three things. One is obvious: Julie, like Eloisa, has loved passionately. The other two are more ambiguous: Julie *may* not have been able to overcome that love even though she has turned to religion and an orderly, established arrangement like a good marriage. But the profoundest resonance comes from the echoing of the dead sister's voice: Claire says she and Julie belong together even in death and are not whole beings when one is separated from the other. In other words, Rousseau allows the antecedent love story, of which his may indeed be the most important revisionary text, to bring into competition the two loves that absorb the heroine's life—the love of Saint-Preux and the love of her female cousin-friend—even though for the opposition of the homoerotic and the heterosexual there is absolutely no authorization whatever in the source.

But if Pope and his medieval story are not relevant to the intense Julie-Claire friendship, Richardson indubitably is. To it the friendship between Clarissa and Anna Howe is so striking a parallel that it must be regarded as a direct and inescapable inspiration. The contrasting kinds of personality that unite in love and the very structure and dynamics of each friendship are all suggestively similar, and so is the intensity of feeling which is directly opposed to the heterosexual love. No study of love in *La nouvelle Héloïse* could possibly be complete without a thorough exploration of the friendship, but this must await analysis of another theme prominent in *Clarissa* and taken over by Rousseau, filial affection, or the relation of the heroine to her family, particularly to her father.

17. 2:85, 500, 745. In the last of these, the very last sentence of the novel, the elliptical periods are Rousseau's. ("I hear a sad voice murmur!...Claire, O my Claire, where are you? what are you doing far from your friend?...her coffin will not contain her entirely....he awaits the rest of his prey....he will not have long to wait.")

Filial and Marital Loyalty

We remember the impressive but, to a modern, almost incomprehensible anguish which Clarissa is made to suffer under the curse of a father who has committed an illiberal and un-Christian action against his own flesh and blood. Rousseau also treats the claims of a father with the greatest seriousness, as well he might since between 1639 and 1789 a noble French father possessed enormous powers, powers that were not greatly reduced even by the Revolution and the Napoleonic aftermath. Diderot was ordered to prison by his father, and other fathers used the *lettres de cachet* of the crown to imprison their children on vague grounds of disobedience, moral dissoluteness, or insults to family honor.[18] In a society so structured, the opposition of Julie's father to her low-born lover is almost irresistible. That Julie has, to an amazing extent, "internalized" filial duty is clear from her behavior. There can be no doubt of the depth of her love for Saint-Preux, her tutor; but even it stands below her love for her parents; and when it threatens to separate her from her family, she feels that she falls into an abyss. When the return of her father requires the departure of her lover, she does not hesitate to order him away with brisk dispatch. Because it does not fit his plans for his daughter (for whose happiness he seems really very little solicitous), the father rejects outright the offer of an enlightened young Englishman to provide an asylum for the lovers. All in all, he is presented as a cranky tyrant who is persecuting a Woman of Feeling in directly opposing her view (the modern, liberal one and surely Rousseau's own) that money and rank are less important than love. Curiously, although through the enlightened Milord Edouard the avant-garde Rousseau delivers a stinging rebuke to Julie's recalcitrant father (2:168–70), he is much less censorious of parental tyranny than is the pious Richardson, whose strong attack on Clarissa's family is equal in vigor to his attack upon the libertine persecutor. Rousseau is of course interested in doing more than make liberal or Enlightened points about domestic tyranny. He explores the emotional side of the filial attachment and so makes it a real competition for the heart of the maiden, really a conflict between rival loves that Clarissa does not feel at all, hers being an opposition purely of love and duty. How does Rousseau humanize, soften, and perhaps even eroticize a situation which in Richardson is legalistic and religious? The father in a rage strikes his daughter, draws blood, and then, after a period of silence at table, takes her on his lap, sighing as he embraces her, while she responds to physical violence by covering him with tears and kisses. The next morning he comes into her bedroom and presses her hands—but gives no hint of ever changing his views. Despite the "transports" of both father and daughter, Julie calls the

18. Arthur M. Wilson, *Diderot* (New York: Oxford University Press, 1972), pp. 103–4; Stone, *Family*, p. 478.

experience one of "douce et paisible innocence" and then moves toward a profound longing for death as friends arrange for her separation from Saint-Preux.[19]

When after three years Bomston ("Milord Edouard") intervenes again to offer an "azile à l'amour et à l'innocence" (p. 199) in York in Enlightened England, where the laws do not abridge nature, filial piety wins out once more: Julie simply cannot quit family and country for love. By this time the father's choice of a mate for her, the coldly rational Wolmar, has become apparent; and he now joins her father in supporting the claims of blood and nature and in enforcing the respect the girl already feels for the gift of life that her father has given. As if such violations of the romantic formula were not enough, Rousseau goes on to make the wedding that ensues—between a girl violated by romantic passion and an older man of rank and position but not of great wealth, another father, as it were—a union not only of duty but of deep religious feeling, Protestant piety, and a commitment deeply respected by the bride as sacramental, institutional, socially necessary, publicly rewarding. In the church the girl utters her first true prayer and dedicates herself to marital chastity and fidelity, which she regards as pertaining to the order of nature. Although in *Emile* the good Savoyard vicar expressed the highest possible respect for marriage, Rousseau, free to do what he wished in an imaginative creation like the novel, has surprised us: the wishes of the tyrannical but loving father who has violently opposed the currents of natural love have nevertheless established a relationship of trust and intellectual communion that is blessed with children and with a life of prosperity, order, and decency. The bride retains through the rest of her brief life the piety she gains at the marriage service, and in the end, on her deathbed, she wins her skeptical, Enlightened, Deistic husband to a personal faith. A kindly, fatherly man even when he is a Man of Reason with his "froideur naturelle" and his ability to judge with "une profonde sagesse" (p. 370), he becomes at the end not only a Christian but a Man of Feeling as well. This outcome, although striking, is not unanticipated. When Julie and Claire are reunited after a long separation and go into a delirium of emotion, Wolmar, instead of helping the fainting cousins, throws himself into an armchair "pour contempler avidement ce ravissant spectacle" ("to contemplate avidly this ravishing sight"). Here it is for the first time that "Wolmar lui-même, le froid Wolmar se sentit ému. O sentiment, sentiment! douce vie de l'ame! quel est le coeur de fer que tu n'as jamais touché?" (p. 599; "Wolmar himself, the cold Wolmar felt himself moved. O

19. 2:176–77. My word "eroticize" may of course be too strong (the mother is present), and Julie is careful to call this a "scene de la nature" (ibid.). There is a hint in the postscript of this letter (p. 178) that her father's blows and her fall may have caused a miscarriage. Other quotations from the novel in this paragraph come from pp. 39–40, 65, 72, 168.

feeling, feeling! sweet life of the soul! where is the heart of iron you have never touched?"). So the spirit of heart religion has touched the good, prudential husband, and at the end of the novel he is ready to shed literal tears of sensibility and so open the gates to sentimental grace. To passionate love Rousseau, the great reformer of feeling, has opposed not a cruel tyranny but a good, decent, rational way of life that at its most severe is always benevolent and that in the end wins supernatural sanction. Rousseau never allows the paternal relation to be broken, as Richardson does; he therefore does not have to restore it by the acts of faith and repentance that Clarissa undergoes before she can return to her "Father's house." Rousseau proceeds on a different path: he first softens the father by love, then has him replaced (even though he lives on in the retreat at Clarens) by a father-like husband, and finally allows the father-father and the father-husband, with the full cooperation of the obedient wife, to create a highly attractive and satisfying rural idyll, where temperance increases almost every kind of pleasure, including a keen pleasure in wine. Richardson's fathers alternate between being materialistic devils and forgiving gods. In Rousseau, though they may bark and rage a bit at the outset, they ultimately cooperate in helping to create—in certainly being the godlike instruments of—a "volupté tempérante" (p. 552), in whose kindly and relaxed ambience a woman can realize as daughter, wife, and teacher almost all the ideals of *Emile*. So congenial is the environment the husband-father provides that Julie, though she must die prematurely, can die the death of the joyful—not with the baroque sublimity of a Clarissa but naturally, eating and drinking to the last, confessing her faith without tension, and surrounded with the love and goodwill of all.

But for all its beauty, grace, and satisfaction, the marital idyll at Clarens lacks one thing, romantic passion.[20] It is therefore not ultimately ideal. Two other relationships also persist to the very end of the novel—and, by emotional extension, even beyond. These are the relationships of passion, and they are of the two kinds described earlier: the almost homoerotic friendship of the female cousins and the passionate love of the hero and heroine. (Julie, the title character, is of course the essential and most important partner in all three of the unions described in the novel; as wife, friend, and beloved she gives to each of them a feminine coloration.) The two relations of passion must now be discussed.

20. Julie, addressing Saint-Preux, reveals that she has persuaded herself that love is not really necessary for a happy marriage: "Ce qui m'a longtems abusée et qui peut-être vous abuse encore, c'est la pensée que l'amour est nécessaire pour former un heureux mariage. Mon ami, c'est une erreur; . . ." (p. 372; "What has misled me for a long time and has perhaps also misled you is that love is necessary in order to create a happy marriage. My friend, this is a mistake; . . ."). One side of Rousseau's mind may have approved what Julie says here; but a profounder side rejects it, as my ensuing discussion of romantic passion will show.

Intense Friendship

Rousseau's portrayal of intense friendship recalls Richardson's, as I have said, and is in itself so striking a feature of the novel and so intimately related to the theme of love that it requires separate analysis. In both novels, while the heroines are loving, devoted—one could say, sublimely serious—as they pursue their ideals, the friends, though also loving and intelligent, present an illuminating contrast by being earthier, saltier, wittier, more practical, more commonsensical. Neither friend rates love and marriage as highly as the heroines do, and both are capable of feelings for the heroines so intense that they resemble the erotic and hence seem to rival the heterosexual relationship that is the chief concern of the title characters' being.

Claire strikes us in her first letter as *sensible* as well as sensible; she possesses a tender heart and a clear head, and that heart is riven with love so deep that it must be called passionate. But though the heart may be compromised, the head is not: it remains, until the terrible bereavement at the end, sane and practical. Claire helps in emergencies, recognizes the danger Julie is in, supports the claims of the family, arranges for the departure of the lover, and comes to live at Clarens in order to be with Julie during the time of potential danger that arises when Saint-Preux returns to the society of his former mistress. It measures the distance between the moral Richardson and the more tolerant and sensuous Rousseau, who explores every aspect of love, that while enmity and hatred arise in Anna's heart toward Lovelace, no such emotions disturb the breast of Claire. Indeed, if there is a rivalry between the friendship and the love in Rousseau's novel, the lover does not seem to sense this, since he observes, applauds, and is even moved by the ravishing nature of Claire and Julie's embrace when they are reunited at Clarens. And the reunion is indeed wildly enthusiastic, the language used to describe it fully applicable to the consummation of a marriage. Both Julie and Claire faint, as though in ecstasy, and both the husband and the former lover are also deeply affected (see pp. 598–600). Although Claire will never follow Julie's advice to marry Saint-Preux, she loves him in her own way, a love which is that of a sister for a brother or a mother for a son.[21] Even before she marries her husband, who dies in the course of the novel, she confesses to him that friendship means more to her than love and that she will not marry him unless her beloved cousin is fully tranquil about the match (pp. 179–80). About herself and her relations to men, Claire is quite frank: she wonders if there is a sex in souls (Steele had said there was, John Dunton that there was not),[22]

21. Claire writes to Saint-Preux, "Toute la différence est que je vous aimois comme mon frere, et qu'à présent je vous aime comme mon enfant; . . ." (p. 319; "the whole difference is that I used to love you as a brother, and that now I love you like a child"). On the infantilism present in Rousseau's character and given to Saint-Preux, see the editor's comment, pp. 1524–25, n.3.

22. See pp. 204, 206 and above, pp. 134, 169.

since she herself has no sense of such a psychological division. She does indulge in some fantasies, but very few about love. She is perfectly willing to distinguish herself from Julie in these matters—Julie who radiates grace, beauty, delicacy, and above all love. Claire once tried to console Saint-Preux for his loss of Julie to her father's wishes by calmly assuring him that his beloved will remain forever youthful in his fantasy (p. 321); but of course she will also be forever unavailable, and the comment can scarcely be that of one who had herself known heterosexual passion. Claire is, to be sure, a Woman of Feeling, since she is endowed, if not with the "inépuisable sensibilité" (p. 322) she ascribed to Julie, at least with one more rational, more playful, and perhaps also more masculine. When her husband dies and she says that she will never marry again, gladly accepting Julie's invitation to come live at Clarens, she is far from expressing an unappeasable grief over the loss of her man and is accepting the dictates of her own independent nature, which was made more for friendship than for love.

And yet that friendship is amazingly deep and passionate, its depths not fully plumbed until the death of Julie. Before that tragic and searing event, Claire pulls back from Julie's wish that she marry Saint-Preux. That hesitation may be more surprising than it at first seems. Her feelings have in fact evolved from the maternal and sisterly to the sensual, a carnal feeling shared by Saint-Preux. In embracing him upon his return to the *ménage* Claire feels a trembling—an emotion compounded of the delicious and the fearful—that she has never before known (p. 641). Even so, during Julie's life she declines to take the step of marrying Saint-Preux, even though she confesses to desiring a nocturnal companion. After Julie's death she seems to recoil from the idea. Her outward explanation is that she cannot invade the domain of romantic passion that they have staked out for themselves and that will remain forever sacred to each of them. But the real reason must surely be that nothing on earth can replace the love she felt for her cousin. At the time of her loss she becomes mad and violent, and she is revealed as much more inconsolable than the husband or lover. In fact her haunting premonitions about Julie's death through the ominous dream of Saint-Preux and her behavior during and after the loss itself reveal that friendship can be said to go deeper than any love—at least for her. Friendships, as Richardson also saw, go back to the earliest years when tender, sensitive, and untroubled souls unite as they never can later. We need not imagine morbidity to be present; but we are certainly to understand that for some such friendship remains absolutely irreplaceable, a shrine that is guarded more passionately as life disappoints and destroys other hopes.

It must be significant that Rousseau gives to Claire the last letter of his epistolary novel—the letter in which she decisively rejects the idea of marrying Saint-Preux and resolves never again to talk to a man about love. She will keep the memory of Julie green against the time of their future reunion. Thus Rousseau gives to the friendship a pride of place, as if to suggest that, while both it and the love are passionate, the friendship is perhaps the more passionate of the two. It certainly possesses an intensity that the marriage lacks, and in this novel it is marriage that provides the rational contrast to passion that friendship traditionally did. There is no Stoicism in the Julie-Claire relationship, for Claire has been passion's slave as much as Saint-Preux. Like the Shakespeare of sonnet 144, Rousseau has two loves, not one; but unlike Shakespeare he cannot say that one brings comfort and the other despair, that one is fair and the other dark. Each one is a chiaroscuro, each unites the better and the worser spirit, for each is passionate. If we measure by emotional intensity alone, it is difficult to arrive at a priority between the intense friendship and the heterosexual love.

But can we measure by emotional intensity alone? Not if we remember the lessons of *Emile,* where marriage is the climax and the union of Sophie and the hero represents the coming of grace after the tutelage of law and discipline. Not if we remember that Julie, not Claire, is the *raisonneuse* of *La nouvelle Héloïse.* Not if we remember that in portraying the friendship Rousseau is, however intense, derivative, while in portraying romantic love he is a pioneer. And not, surely, if we remember what Claire herself says: that the woman of the future will and must have contact with men, that the sexes cannot live apart, and that sexual difference must be maintained for the happiness and welfare of the human race.[23] Since the friendship is as fiery and intense as the marriage is coldly rational, it is wise to keep them on the same level despite their contrasting qualities. Neither is ideal, for one lacks passion entirely, and the other lacks passion for the opposite sex. Rousseau gives subtler and more concentrated attention to the subject of passionate heterosexual love than to any other human relationship in this seminal novel. And it is this kind of love which he finally rewards with immortality and to which we must give climactic attention in discussing *La nouvelle Héloïse.*

Romantic Love

The love of Julie and Saint-Preux so triumphantly embodies the qualities of romantic love—it is intuitive, obsessive, passionate, lifelong, and extending to eternity—that we tend to forget that it was born in the age and in the spirit of

23. See p. 501. Claire goes on to defend chastity and delicacy in women, which is in one way fully consistent with what she has said: female modesty can even lend some coquetry to virtue and so minister to the sexual allure of differences in gender. On the other hand, one can see her defense of chastity as being a natural result of her desire to have Julie for herself—of her own deepest loyalty, that to the loving friendship. Of this friendship I do not scruple to use the word "homoerotic," not to mean consummated lesbianism (from which both girls would have recoiled) but to refer to the intensity of Claire's love, in which there was, I believe, a considerable admixture of the erotic.

sensibilité. Indeed, it fulfills the primary conditions that Clarissa laid down for passion—that it be based on mutual sensibility and a deep similarity of feeling, seeing, judging. The love of this novel begins as a marriage of true hearts, as what must have struck the eighteenth-century reader as a highly modern affection, in which a delicate and trembling sensitivity is more basic than either physical ardor or intellectual compatibility, although these are also present and important. The whole first part of the novel is devoted to a subtly nuanced development of that kind of love in a kaleidoscope of emotions at once intense and innocent. Julie's are streaked with guilt more because of paternal opposition and her strong sense of *bienséances* than because of contemplated sensuality, which she at first rules out. Saint-Preux's emotions are free to become rapturous almost at once, while Julie's remain at first more cautious, social, and prudential. The man's love spreads out from the sense of touch to his whole being, including the imagination, which attaches itself to external nature, specifically to the Alpine landscape in the vicinity. Love opens the heart to the newer Romantic taste in scenery—to such "sublime" objects as immense rocks, eternal torrents, and abysses with unsounded depths. These have their own kind of voluptuousness and are more tranquil than the passion, to which they become a special kind of objective correlative. Nature provides a beguiling accompaniment to love, since it is sentient and responsive but at the same time provides the comfort of a healing balm.

As the love seems destined to be blocked by parental opposition, sentient nature takes on the dark coloration of the lover's melancholy; but nature as a healer benefits only Saint-Preux, who alone is exposed to the Alpine solitudes during the first separation, while Julie is left to her own society in the parental home. There what has been a controlled kind of love, tinged with Calvinistic guilt, becomes "une passion plus terrible que la fièvre" (p. 94). The lover must be called back, at whatever danger, from natural solitude in the Valais to his former role as tutor. And he who seemed to be the greater sufferer in love because he was the more expressive becomes the stronger, the more open lover; while she who began as a leader is now the silent, mysterious sufferer, in need of his advice and consolation. If historical traditions can be seen to be operating here, it can perhaps be said that Saint-Preux is the newer type of lover: expansive, close to nature, unafraid of death as a solution—a lover, in brief, of pre-Romantic sensibility—while Julie is the traditional conservator of hearth and home, virtue and familial loyalty, who pays the price of her burden of restraint by being the first to break down completely.

Another feature of Julie's relative conservatism is that—perhaps in opposition to newer tendencies in sensibility, perhaps also to separate herself from what will be so brilliantly portrayed in the passionate friendship of Claire— she opts for sexual differences in mind and body between the man and the woman and thus strongly opposes the drive toward similitude. My emphasis upon her sense of guilt and her belief in restraint should not obscure the positive ideal of heterosexual love that animates her; it is a kind of divine fire, the lover is a hero, the heart has supplanted the reason but has taken over some of its functions in the control of animal passion. "Ni prude, ni précieuse" (p. 139), like Clarissa she demands respect, a respect which comes only to one who retains the traditionally feminine quality of modesty. For the man, who is less restrained, growing love becomes increasingly voluptuous without, however, losing delicacy. His imagination—that potentially dangerous faculty, as we saw in *Emile*—is more active than hers: it dwells on the beloved's chamber, her clothes and undergarments which inflame him almost to a sexual climax, her flowers, her blonde hair; and he tries, in the manner of Keats, to keep her image alive when he is afar, in a kind of languorous sensuality. That sensuality is tinged with sensibility and with the love of similarity. Saint-Preux, echoing the Song of Songs almost in the manner of Elizabeth Rowe earlier or of Shelley later, calls Julie "mon épouse, ma soeur, ma douce amie!" (p. 149). A delicate balance, this, of the carnal and the spiritual, the uxorial and the sisterly.

During the years of separation occasioned by the determination of her father that she marry another and by her obedience to his wishes, the love continues, though it of course alters when it alteration finds. The enlightened Englishman, Bomston, shames Saint-Preux out of suicide, but the hero still undergoes a kind of *anéantissement* and suffers through a purgatory as he circumnavigates the globe. On her side, Julie's spirit reveals in the period before her marriage to Wolmar the same habit of moving from rational coolness to rapturous palpitations of passion and sympathy, an alternation that never breaks down into total despair or suicidal melancholy but by its very existence makes clear to us that love in some form remains alive. Without love there would be nothing to restrain and nothing to feed the flames of desire. One role Julie, a potential leader, assumes with some ease is that of her lover's instructor, a reversal of their roles that persists almost to the end of the novel. In this role she can discuss love itself, defining it as a union of souls. But she can go further and discuss physical habits associated with love and sensuality. In what is surely one of the most unusual letters a delicate heroine ever addressed to her lover, she preaches a sermon against onanism. With powerful implications for one meaning of Johnson's haunting phrase "dangerous prevalence of imagination," she links that faculty with *le vice solitaire* and finds that "ces voluptés solitaires sont des voluptés mortes,"[24] thus enforcing the lesson we have encountered in *Emile*. Certainly one reason for her boldness in warning him about his solitary behavior is that in their relationship there is much to remember and to try to revive imaginatively. For their affair led to

---

24. P. 237. See also the editor's note on this amazing letter in *La nouvelle Héloïse*, in which he discusses Rousseau and "le plaisir solitaire" (pp. 1481–82, n.3).

the final intimacy and then to signs that Julie would become a mother (a hope that was disappointed, as it turned out). It is of some importance to note the fact of physical consummation.[25] Rousseau uses it partly to darken Julie's emotions and give additional reasons for her feelings of guilt besides disobedience to her parents. More important, he wishes to show that the love was a fully normal though deeply passionate one and that the eternity of affection which will be adumbrated as the novel comes to its climax is based on full physical realization on earth.

To take a more limited perspective for the moment, Rousseau does not neglect to show that love remains alive in Julie's heart right up to her marriage. She catches fire when she reads Saint-Preux's letter about his romantic agony on receiving her portrait, and she confides that her imagination is also active, full of sweet illusions, the "dernieres ressources des malheureux" (p. 289). She confides to Claire that she hoped to follow her mother in death; and when a serious case of smallpox almost leads to a fulfillment of that wish, her love is intensified by a visit of Saint-Preux during her feverish delirium, a visit she imagines for a while was a dream. When she learns of its reality, she makes a vow that undoubtedly governs her conduct at the time of her death—she declares to Saint-Preux in a letter that their love is a natural obligation of the heart that will last forever. At the same time she retains the rival obligations of friendship and filial obedience. Since these loves and obligations are profoundly irreconcilable, her reluctance to sacrifice any of them makes her own death inevitable. No earthly power can adjust such conflicting claims as these and still keep the spirit of each love sweet and whole. But long before her death comes her marriage, announced with stunning suddenness to Saint-Preux and the reader, who have just heard the ringing declaration of eternal faithfulness. This marriage, as we have seen, brings its calm joys and rational satisfactions, and so pleasant and rewarding are these that Julie assures Saint-Preux that if she had it to do all over again she would choose Wolmar and, open-eyed, accept a marriage without passion. Her person, mind, talents, morality—all belong to Wolmar and to the good estate of Clarens.

Despite all this, the very structure and dynamics of the novel demonstrate that the union of the two *coeurs sensibles* remains intact. This sentimental-romantic love survives all attempts at elimination or sublimation; it survives the stringent and therapeutic tests prescribed by the husband; it survives the

---

25. Letters 29–32 of pt. I are devoted to the physical "fall" of Julie (pp. 95–104), making the fact of full intimacy indisputable. For a discussion of the moral aspects and the psychological results, see the editor's note 2 (pp. 1398–1400). See also p. 111, and the letters that follow, especially the one (on pp. 113–15), in which Julie says: "Maintenant coupable et craintive, je tremble en pensant à eux [her parents], je rougis en pensant à moi" ("Now guilty and fearful, I tremble when I think of my parents, I blush when I think of myself"). The whole letter is filled with feelings of remorse over what took place but also guilt over her plans to deceive her parents again when they are gone.

lovers' determined and unrelenting search for *repos* and *oubli;* it even survives the distant proximity of the triangular arrangement at Clarens. Rousseau himself had difficulty resisting a *ménage à trois,* and for him to bring a disappointed lover into the home of his rival is not so bizarre as it would be in another author. It is quintessentially Rousseauist to have Saint-Preux return as a son in the family at Clarens—"l'enfant de la maison" (p. 527), as he is glad to say—a family over which Julie, now a mother, presides and where the elder Wolmar remains a somewhat remote, deistic father-god.[26] To the psychological substructure of that arrangement, *The Confessions* will force us to return. But here the primary consideration is not so much that Rousseau wishes to establish the kind of Oedipal triangle that brought him comfort as that he wishes to get all three kinds of love together for his climax—the uxorial, the homoerotic, the heterosexual.

Each of these is powerful in its own right, and for each strong claims are made. Which of them prevails at the time of Julie's demise? The very movement of the novel makes only one answer possible—the romantic and passionate. That prevalence has been prepared for by what I have already mentioned—the return and testing of the lovers in scenes of trembling devotion and spiritual union that are among the most beautiful in the whole literature of love-sensibility. Of these perhaps the loveliest is the ride on the lake when the storm arises and survival is assured only after a fierce struggle. The lovers have faced death alone. In the walk that follows their trial they come as far as those Alpine scenes, with the Jura in view, that Saint-Preux haunted years before when he was forced to leave Julie's home because of their love and where he wrote the passionate and fatal letter that made her yield. He shows her her name carved on the rocks. The emotions of the pair kindle: she seizes his hand, almost sighs, looks at him tenderly—and then breaks the spell. They are not to be united in the life of rational decency to which they return but ultimately in the death they have now so narrowly escaped. The earnest of that ultimate union is wordlessly pledged as they ride back, their hands clasped, across the moonlit lake. Perhaps only a Rousseau could be so lyrical about the earthly Almost—that is, about deferred zonal consummations and the substitute satisfactions of a chastened physical proximity. Tears of sensibility reconcile both to the oxymoronic state of intimate

26. See the editor's comment in the second note on pp. 1716–17 and Pierre Burgelin, *La philosophie de l'existence de J.-J. Rousseau,* 2d ed. (Paris: Librairie philosophique J. Vrin, 1973), pp. 382, 405. Burgelin takes a different view from the one propounded here: he is silent on the Oedipal implications but finds unity of being in the trinity of Wolmar, Julie, and Saint-Preux. He also believes that Rousseau's God sanctions, not love, but marriage, which creates a society because it purges men of the egotism of lovers. I prefer the view of Bernard Guyon, who writes this annotation on Julie's posthumous letter to Saint-Preux, pledging eternal love: "le roman s'achevait . . . par le triomphe de l'"amour-fou.'" This letter is "un grand cri d'adhésion au mythe romanesque de l'amour-vainqueur" (p. 1810, n.3; "the novel reaches its climax in the triumph of rapturous love . . . an exclamation of commitment to the romantic myth of conquering love").

separation (or of infinitely separated intimacy). Rousseau has resolved typically—in favor of lifelong unfulfillment. Julie remains truly a "still unravished bride of quietness."

The cup of sensibility is therefore both bitter and sweet, "amere et douce" (p. 733). But when its last drop is drained on Julie's deathbed, when the veil of the body is removed, and when Julie's spirit flies into immortality, a prospect is opened upon another sphere by her final letter, read posthumously. Addressed to Saint-Preux, absent in Rome at the time of her death, it declares that her love never died. The belief that the lovers were "cured" was only a blessed illusion—a phrase that has since been applied to religion; but illusion it was, however blessed, since the flames were never extinguished. Julie, who remains natural to the end, eating, drinking, talking, has not relinquished her deepest natural feeling. So another veil is being rent even before that of the body is removed, the veil of social convention: the heroine confesses without shame or remorse that, unmarried and married, her love for her ravisher continued unabated. And it will continue after death: "Non, je ne te quitte pas, je vais t'attendre" ("No, I do not leave you, I go to await you"). Virtue, which separated them on earth, will unite them in eternity. For herself, she is "trop heureuse d'acheter au prix de ma vie le droit de t'aimer toujours sans crime, et de te le dire encore une fois" (p. 743; "only too happy to purchase at the price of my life the right to love you forever without sin, and to tell you so one more time").

If we ask what Rousseau's love immortality can possibly mean, we are struck at once with its vagueness and suggestiveness compared with Richardson's vision of the future. The English author's orthodoxy permits us to imagine the lovers' future with some degree of clarity. Clarissa, already beatified in life, will possess a resurrected body (that is, an absolutely individual identity), but she will live on in a realm where there is neither marriage nor giving in marriage. Besides, she is eternally separated from her lover, who can now only cry out to her unheeding ears, if she hears him at all, across an eternally separating abyss. What can be said about the future of Rousseau's pair? Even though he possessed religious feeling and retained in its essence the faith of his fathers, it is not likely that the immortality conceived of in his novel is in any profound way religiously orthodox. Little evidence supports the hypothesis that in death a kind of individual salvation, mystical in its immediacy, takes the place of the Enlightened, collective *transparence* of Clarens, where men and women achieved a satisfying though fragile equilibrium.[27] Few signs from Rousseau's own vision suggest that the immortal life will be lived by the individual redeemed soul in a state of bodiless virtue and only spiritual ecstasy in

27. See Jean Starobinski, *J.-J. Rousseau: La transparence et l'obstacle* (Paris: Librairie Plon, 1957) pp. 149–50. See pp. 143–50 for a brilliant discussion of the notion of clarity and the imagery of the veil.

the presence of God. All we can say is that romantic passion will continue, and Keats perhaps best opens Rousseau's meaning—that immortality is a prolongation of the temporal, an extension of the earthly.[28] Such would seem to be the implication of Rousseau's doctrine of nature and of Julie's preparations for death. While Clarissa mortifies the flesh, subdues the spirit by Scripture reading and prayer, and diligently practices the Christian virtues with an intensity even she has not known before, Julie becomes more natural than ever. Her Protestant confession is free of agony, and she eats and drinks ordinary food and wine—but not sacramentally, unless we think of nature as providing a Holy Communion. Since love in Rousseau has not really transcended anything (it gives scope to what was already present in the heart and in nature), it will in eternity probably not be very much different from what it was in life. It is not explained how virtue will then reconcile the conflicting claims of love; but since hierarchy is hardly likely to reign, presumably love will express itself in any and all forms with equal freedom. Or will it be equal? One can speculate that for two reasons romantic love may be given priority. (1) The other loves had their own achievements on earth. Friends are allowed to be together, while an illicit lover must roam the seven seas and be forever deprived of his prize. And marriage achieves much in the here and now—children, a good estate, and *bonheur,* in the full meaning of that great Enlightenment word. None of these rewards attended passion, which is still in need of fulfillment and depends heavily on the compensatory adjustments of the afterlife. (2) If the artistic achievement of the novel and the language in which it is presented can be trusted, then romantic love has in and of itself a potential intensity that calls out for an eternity of realization. None of the other loves achieves the psychological subtlety of the Julie–Saint-Preux relation, the sublimity of its intercourse with nature, the delicacy of its feelings, the pathos that accompanies its denials and postponements, the profound melancholy that alternates with its joys. Of such stuff the eternity of an artist might well be made, and Rousseau was an artist. Saint-Preux in life is always a lover, never a husband; always a son, never a father; always a tutor, never a manager. He is desperately in need of fulfillment. And if ironically that fulfillment should be to continue as Rousseau always loved to be—a master of the preliminaries and not the ultimates in love—so be it. Jean-Jacques may have conceived of an eternity in which Saint-Preux was ever the suitor, never the husband: "Bold Lover, never, never canst thou kiss, / Though winning near the goal."[29] For perhaps the satisfactions of life were to be most fully

28. See Keats's sonnet "Bright star, would I were stedfast as thou art."

29. "Ode on a Grecian Urn," 17–18. In concluding my analysis I invoke Keats's poetry rather than dialectic because I believe that one enters into Rousseau's deepest meaning only through art. For an intelligent reading that considers the novel as an expression of Platonic structure in which Saint-Preux symbolizes "fol amour" and Julie "pur amour," see Jean-Louis Bellenot, "Les Formes de l'amour dans *La nouvelle Héloïse,*" *Annales de la Société Jean-Jacques Rousseau,* 33 (1953–55): 149–208.

realized by being "Pillow'd upon my fair love's ripening breast / . . . / Awake for ever in a sweet unrest" (Keats, "Bright star," lines 10, 12).

Back on earth society frustrates love, and nature strikes down lovers in death. *La nouvelle Héloïse* provides ample documentation of the obstacles, in both the individual and the community, to achieving the Miltonic ideal of heterosexual friendship. Contrary to one popular view, Rousseau does not put all the blame on corporate man. Love is sometimes guided by the realities of the natural individual psyche, but it can sometimes be distorted by them, too. These realities appear with amazing frankness in *The Confessions,* the psychological soil from which sprang the intellectual structures of *Emile* and the emotional configurations and lyrical effusions of *La nouvelle Héloïse.*

"The Confessions"

The first part (bks. 1–6) of *The Confessions* is more a novel than an autobiography. Its claims to accuracy and full frankness of revelation have rightly been challenged; but no one can challenge its breathtaking modernity, its unexpectedly penetrating gaze into the psychosexual depths. Perhaps never before and seldom since has there been so uninhibited and sophisticated an exploration of the sensuality of civilized man, the man of cultural discontents. Through the medium of this nostalgic book about childhood, adolescence, and young manhood (written from a temporal, physical, and psychological distance when Rousseau was fifty-four years old and living abroad in Staffordshire) we see into the recesses of the *coeur sensible.* No other document of belles lettres, philosophical discourse, or unadorned history throws so revealing a light upon the subject of love. Morally the book may be disgusting, intellectually it may lack coherence of vision or sharpness of verbal definition. But as an exploration of sensations felt in the blood and felt along the heart, it is unrivaled.

Part 1 in particular is a highly sensual book, one of the most sensual in our culture; but its sensuality is not of the gross bodily kind, although carnality is indubitably present. It is rather the sensuality of the Man of Feeling, and as such it is of much more interest to the student of civilization than the disrobings of Casanova or the shocks and titillations deriving from the Marquis de Sade. As Rousseau said in a later portion of the work, when he was about to set up relations with Thérèse, the most permanent of his needs was the need for heart intimacy, one he felt to be so singular that neither male friendship nor physical union sufficed to fill it. There are not many purely normal sexual relations in *The Confessions,* the only really satisfying one being the affair on the road with Mme de Larnage after he has left Les Charmettes. Rousseau's lifelong hatred of lust and prostitution is well known, and it is revealing that in one house of ill fame, despite all the unimpeachable physical inducements, his only achievement is to weep like a child. He is advised by his companion, in a cold and scornful voice, "*Zanetto, lascia le Donne, e studia la matematica.*"[30] Other forms of sensuality are equally unsatisfying. Two friendships, with Bâcle and Venture de Villeneuve, have moments of infatuation but remain abortive; and the attack on Rousseau by the Moor in the hospice at Turin is revolting, not least because of its retching climax (p. 67). Onanism we have already paused to notice as present in *Emile* and in a letter of Julie to her suitor; here it is presented in much the same way, as destructive of energy and peculiarly attractive to people of lively imagination. This method of cheating nature Rousseau himself indulged for some time, both to the depletion of his physical strength, as he thought, and the feverish stimulation of his fancy (pp. 108–9). One can also find some evidence of exhibitionistic display (pp. 88–89). But on the whole Rousseau kept himself unsullied long past most people's age of experience. He thus in his own life more or less fulfills the ideal expressed in *Emile,* even though sensuality burned in his blood, he says, almost from his birth (p. 16).

Perhaps the real reason for this relative "purity" is that the kind of sensuality Rousseau enjoyed most was not the full and final act but its foreplay. No one got more pleasure from touching or kissing a woman's hand—unless it was Sterne's Yorick taking the grisette's pulse—or kneeling before the beloved in postures of supplication. This intense enjoyment of the preliminary is conceivably related to the death of Rousseau's mother in the act of bearing him and the guilt he thereafter felt before women, whom he loved to supplicate. The origins of this peculiar kind of eroticism need not concern us so much as its manifestations, and of these one of the most striking occurs at Bossey, at the foot of Mount Salève, where the boy experiences a kind of Fall while staying at the parsonage of M le Pasteur Jean-Jacques Lambercier—an experience that teaches him the evil of being unjustly accused of something he had not done. At this time he also undergoes a Fall from sexual innocence when the pastor's thirty-year-old sister, Gabrielle (in actuality she was closer to forty) administers to the eight-year-old boy a series of spankings which they both find pleasurable. Mlle Lambercier is, according to Rousseau, acting as a loving mother in these chastisements, and he has all he can do not to provoke them, because with the pain and the shame comes sensuality: "Car j'avois trouvé dans la douleur, dans la honte même, un mélange de sensualité qui m'avoit laissé plus de desir que de crainte de l'éprouver derechef par la même main."[31] Pleasure and abjectness were ever thereafter associated in Rousseau's

---

30. *Confessions,* in *OC,* 1:322. Subsequent references to this work are similarly made, by volume and page, to the *Oeuvres complétes.* The Italian may be translated: let women alone, study mathematics.

31. 1:15 ("for I had discovered in the pain, even in the shame, an admixture of sensuality which had left me with more desire than fear of once more experiencing it [the punishment] by the

psyche; and punishment and admonition, meted out by a figure of authority, always proved to be titillating if not openly provocative.

The posture of supplication before an elder seen as sexually stimulating leads us directly to Rousseau's relations with Mme de Warens,[32] the notorious convert to Catholicism, who took him in both before and after his own submission, such as it was, to the church of Rome. She was twenty-nine years of age when Rousseau met her, he not yet sixteen. That famous and complex relationship, which to many seems to have about it an archetypal or at least essential quality, can best be understood in its chronological stages. When Rousseau first comes to stay at Annecy for an extended period with the woman he is to call "Maman" (she calls him "Mon Petit"), he recognizes that he is experiencing sensations and emotions quite new to him and perhaps quite different from any the human race has very frequently written about. This relationship is not like friendship with someone of the same sex, for the fact that Maman is a woman is of crucial importance. On the other hand, this is not ordinary passion either, for it is free of lust and even of impetuosity and is by no means always associated with love. But its delights are unsurpassable, and for these one becomes aware with Rousseau that a new vocabulary is necessary—a vocabulary of sensibility. For what we here confront is truly a "sensibilité du coeur," consisting of "sentimens affectueux"; it is an "autre sentiment" ("tendre," "doux," "exquis") than what is conventionally associated with giving oneself to another. For this is "plus délicieux" than friendship, certainly "plus voluptueux"; and it is "moins impétueux" than love (p. 104).

That Rousseau has, rather later in life than would be customary, entered an Oedipal state becomes even clearer as the story of this love proceeds. During the stay at Chambéry, Rousseau shares Maman with Claude Anet, a simple but skillful gardener and a man of many practical skills, who becomes the father in the *ménage à trois* and toward whom Rousseau curiously feels no emotions of jealousy whatever, even though he knows of the intimacies. Maman takes the

---

same hand"). Both in this chapter and in the next on Sterne, a good deal is made of the love of foreplay. Both authors may be reflecting the preferences of their own psyches for this kind of love over consummation. But there also may lie some social reality behind their preference. Fear of pregnancy and disease, the lack, until the nineteenth century, of brassieres and underpants (making the flesh more easily accessible to casual contact), and the lack of contraceptives—all these tended to discourage final penetration and to encourage fondling. Pepys, a man of many consummated adventures, nevertheless spent an incredible amount of time caressing the erogenous zones of surprisingly receptive women. See Stone, *Family,* pp. 554, 559. Rousseau and Sterne may, therefore, be reflecting a good deal of social reality. Nevertheless, I continue to find them both rather special, though not at all untypical of mid- and late-century sensibility.

32. For an interesting discussion of this fascinating woman, see Lester G. Crocker, *Jean-Jacques Rousseau,* vol. 1, *The Quest, 1712–1758* (New York: Macmillan, 1968), pp. 41–46, 65–70. Crocker, who believes Rousseau remained sexually on the oral-anal and the masturbatory levels, says little about possible Oedipal implications (pp. 67–68). Since, as Crocker points out (pp. 66–67), the term "Maman" was often used for the mistress of the house, interpretation should not rest solely or heavily on that usage.

initiative in establishing the sexual relations with the youth; and she always remains something of a cold partner, an instructress, one might say, rather than a tempting siren. But for the lad these "caresses maternelles," which are "ni transports ni desirs," produce "un calme ravissant, jouissant sans savoir de quoi." They are more like a dream of pleasure than present pleasure: "ravissemens inexprimables, sans songer même à la volupté des sens" (pp. 106–8). In fact Rousseau can achieve the height of pleasure only by substituting in his fancy another for Maman,[33] and it is significant that when he returns to her after his one truly ravishing experience (with Mme de Larnage) he can no longer enjoy "les caresses maternelles" without feelings of real guilt.

The climax of the idyll comes at Les Charmettes. (There some of the Oedipal quality is lost after the death of Claude Anet.) It is an enclosed garden and can be taken as a symbol of the womb to which Rousseau has so willingly retreated; and it brings its own rich joys. Years later Rousseau claimed to have total recall of all the features of this nest, which was itself regressive even at the time of the experiences. Les Charmettes continues to be a place of sexuality but also of gardening and study, of solitary walks and imaginative flights. Though delicious, the retreat is not fully satisfying—it is perhaps too much like the Vales of Har in Blake, that blood-chilling place of arrested innocence (*Tiriel*, 2.1–40). Claude Anet is missed and regretted; things fall apart at the center, Jean-Jacques is not well, Maman is bewildered. Above all, the idyll is darkened with guilt and impending doom and so of course must cease to be idyllic. Like Julie, Rousseau suffers from feelings of Calvinistic guilt: he throws stones at a tree trunk to learn if he is damned. Well might a relationship with so many incestuous overtones produce a feeling of isolation and damnation, particularly since the heart remains *sensible* and the spirit tender!

The whole arrangement collapses after Rousseau's return from his trip. Maman has been unfaithful; the youthful, callow, sensual Wintzenried has entered the nest, now a place of coarse sensuality, precisely the kind of love Rousseau cannot abide. So he leaves Les Charmettes for the world of struggle and eventual fame, and Maman retreats into the shadows, remembered today only because of her famous "son" and lover.

---

33. "Si j'avois cru tenir maman dans mes bras quand je l'y tenois, mes étreintes n'auroient pas été moins vives, mais tous mes desirs se seroient éteints; j'aurois sanglotté de tendresse, mais je n'aurois pas joui" (1:219; "If I had believed I was holding mama in my arms when I held her there, my embraces would have been less lively, but all my desires would have been quenched; I would have wept my heart out in tenderness, but I would not have had pleasure"). What happens here becomes a basic psychological mechanism in the erotic life of Rousseau. "Pour que Jean-Jacques soit heureux et sans anxiété dans l'acte du regard échangé, il faut que le désir se masque ou s'ajourne, qu'il se transmue en sympathie asexuée, en tendresse désintéressé, en amour filial." ("For Jean-Jacques to be happy and free of anxiety in the act of exchanging glances, it was necessary that desire be masked or that it cease, that it transform itself into asexual sympathy, into disinterested tenderness, into filial love.") Starobinski, *L'oeil vivant*, p. 118.

The idylls of Annecy, Chambéry, and Les Charmettes constitute together the basic configuration of Rousseau's love imagination. More than its bare lineaments appear in *La nouvelle Héloïse,* a fact that reveals how deeply it was part of the constitution of the author's personality. It is not by chance that when he wrote *The Confessions* (and that was fairly late in life), he compared (p. 104) his own arrival at Maman's house with Saint-Preux's arrival at Julie's estate at Clarens. For, as we have seen, that ideal community is in part a *ménage à trois,* though it is vastly more too, with the older husband as father, Julie as mother and now mistress of the establishment, and the former tutor and lover of the wife now her submissive disciple and the instructor of her children. The sensuality of *The Confessions,* with the male as supplicant and the woman as a figure of authority, has thus appeared earlier and in partial disguise, as a feature of love in the novel. Whether the maternal chord that Rousseau struck sounds for the many who still visit the thatch-covered cottage outside Chambéry, where the spirits of Rousseau and Mme de Warens communed more often than their bodies united, cannot of course be easily known. But it is certainly true that the literature, art, and sensibility that followed Jean-Jacques Rousseau reveal an intense, perhaps obsessive preoccupation with the maternal. Above all, of course, Rousseau, a kind of psychological prophet, has seen that the roots of human sexuality lie deep in childhood and has annexed for literature a whole new empire, the domain of the child, that "best Philosopher."[34]

The courtly love of the Middle Ages, as we know, exalted the woman but discovered passionate, romantic love only outside marriage in adultery. It created a new aristocracy, that of gentle hearts and courteous spirits; and it very often placed the lover on his knees before the woman, seeming to make the beloved a mother and the lover a trembling son asking for pity. If Rousseau had merely repeated what had been done earlier, he would still be a phenomenal figure, possessing the insight and the foresight to sound the courtly carillon at just the right moment of cultural time. But he is surely more a discoverer than a recoverer, and his exaltation of the child and childhood, his association of sensibility and sexuality, his perception of the maternal omnipresence, his profound awareness of how love, marriage, and friendship are in actuality related and how ideally they ought to be related—these are the achievements of a spiritual conqueror. With them comes much that is neurotic, regressive, partial—the desire, for example, to return to a primitive state, to what at the end of *The Confessions,* when he dreams of his retreat on the Ile Saint-Pierre in the Lake of Bienne (Neuchâtel), he calls "L'oisiveté . . . d'un enfant qui est sans cesse en mouvement pour ne rien faire, et

34. Wordsworth, "Intimations of Immortality from Recollections of Early Childhood," 111. On childhood and sensibility, see Jean H. Hagstrum " 'Such, Such were the Joys': The Boyhood of the Man of Feeling" in *Changing Taste in Eighteenth-Century Art and Literature,* intro. by Earl Miner (Los Angeles: Clark Memorial Library, 1972), pp. 43–61.

celle d'un radoteur qui bat la campagne tandis que ses bras sont en repos."[35] That last retreat is not pleasant or wholesome, even though he invokes the magic name of nature: "ô nature, ô ma mére, me voici sous ta seule garde; il n'y a point ici d'homme adroit et fourbe qui s'interpose entre toi et moi."[36] This is a kind of farewell to mankind, and it is the last lyrical note of Rousseau's fascinating autobiography.

No student of the Rousseauist aftermath can have failed to notice that he evoked a mixed response, even among those French writers who wept over *La nouvelle Héloïse,* who admired him, or who absorbed a part of his spirit— Choderlos de Laclos, Bernardin de Saint-Pierre, Restif de la Bretonne. The English who read and wept, who created their Rousseauist retreats, or who educated their children on the plan of *Emile* may not all have known the perverse implications of the revolution they were responding to. But the great Romantics did—Blake, Wordsworth, Shelley, and Byron, who hailed Rousseau as "the self-torturing sophist, wild Rousseau,"

> The Apostle of Affliction, he who threw
> Enchantment over Passion, . . .
>   yet he knew
> How to make madness beautiful, . . .
> His love was Passion's essence— . . .
> But his was not the love of living dame, . . .
> But of ideal Beauty, which became
> In him existence, and o'erflowing teems
> Along his burning page, distempered though it seems.[37]

35. P. 641 ("The idleness of a child who is ceaselessly active to no end, and that of a rambling talker who scours the fields without using his arms").

36. P. 644 ("O Nature, O my mother! Here I am under your sole protection; here no cunning rascal comes between thee and me").

37. *Childe Harold's Pilgrimage,* 3.77, 78. On Rousseau and the English Romantics, see Voisine, *J.-J. Rousseau en Angleterre.* Rousseau owed much to Richardson, who was, however, not flattered by the French debt: he professed himself "disgusted" by *La nouvelle Héloïse* (John Nichols, *Literary Anecdotes of the Eighteenth Century* [London, 1812–15], 4:598). Nevertheless, the influence of the novel on literature and *mores* was incalculable. Michelet, quoting Walpole, writes that "le mot d'*amour,* dit Walpole, avait été . . . rayé par le ridicule, biffé du dictionnaire. On n'osait se dire amoureux. Chacun, après l'*Héloïse,* s'en vante, et tout homme est Saint-Preux" ("the word *love,* said Walpole, had been streaked with ridicule, stricken from the dictionary. One dared not say he was in love. Everyone, after *Eloise,* boasted of it, and every man is now Saint-Preux"). Michelet is quoted from *Histoire de France,* 5:427, by Oscar A. Haac, "Faith in the Enlightenment: Voltaire and Rousseau Seen by Michelet" in *Studies in Eighteenth-Century Culture,* vol. 7, ed. Roseann Runte (Madison: University of Wisconsin Press, 1978), p. 483.

10. The Aftermath of Sensibility
Sterne, Goethe, and Austen

ONE OF THE THREE WRITERS now to be considered was the pioneer in treating love that Richardson and Rousseau were. Those mid-century masters of sensibility had their own antecedents and followers in combining sex and sensibility, to be sure, but no earlier or later writer produced such massive and central achievements in love-sensibility as *Clarissa* or *La nouvelle Héloïse*. My Uncle Toby, Werther, and the Dashwood sisters are likely to remain known, to the cognoscenti at least, as long as Western culture survives; but in terms of the movement I have been tracing they breathe a *fin d'époque* air. Sterne's best novel is, for all its absorption of eighteenth-century values and ideas, so special and eccentric that it could have no immediate successors and is therefore sui generis. *Werther* grows out of *sensibilité* but contributes less to the development of that movement than to the spirit of Romantic alienation that followed. And *Sense and Sensibility* is at once a consolidation of the love tradition and a criticism of it. Jane Austen, particularly through the mediation of her beloved Cowper, drank deeply at the fountains of emotional delicacy; but she also looked back to Samuel Johnson, who taught her to use the categories of ethical-rational wit in judging acts of love and passion. In other words, about the works discussed in this chapter there is a quality of aftermath even though the treatment of love is richly nuanced or emotionally powerful. Each draws the title terms of this book, eros and sensibility, into a suggestive and energetic union that looks more like a climax than a prophecy.

Sterne

Thomas Gray found that Shakespeare was able to produce three diverse emotions: he could "unlock the gates of Joy," release the flow of "thrilling Fears," and open the "sacred source of sympathetic Tears" (*The Progress of Poesy*, 3.1). Clearly Gray's critical categories were developed under impulses derived from his own age. On the last of the three Sterne bestowed the term "sentimental," subsuming under it "sensible" and "pathetic" and removing from it the meaning of intellectual or didactic sentence. For he consolidated and intensified the emotional tradition that began with Dryden's turning from heroic rant to heroic pity. "Sentiment," which once meant moral judgment and then in its period of transition came to stand for the combination of the head and the heart, now refers primarily to feeling, sometimes passionate but more often delicate, refined, civilizing, and always copious and irrepressible. Not everyone accepted easily the linguistic change, and even Sterne was himself capable of using "sentiment" in its oldest meaning.[1] John Wesley contemptuously dismissed "sentimental" as "not English" and "not sense," finding it a fashionable term notable only for its "oddity, uncouthness, and unlikeness to all the world beside."[2] But "Courtney Melmoth" in "The Tears of Genius" represents the *nouvelle vague* when he apostrophizes the "gentle Yorick": there was a "milky and humane temperature about thy pulses." "Gracious God, what a throb was there!" "SENSIBILITY took thee by the hand."[3] Ralph Griffiths, praising that portion of *Tristram Shandy* to which I shall pay particular attention, perceived at once a connection with the creator of Pamela, Clarissa, and Harriet Byron: "*Richardson*—the delicate, the circumstantial RICHARDSON himself, never produced any thing equal to the amours of Uncle Toby and the Widow Wadman!"[4]

"Sensibility" in Sterne is a term of large meaning that embraces joy and sorrow, martyrdom and religious reward, even God himself, who is a vibrating "Sensorium" of sympathy, the eternal fountain of our feeling.[5] Like Rousseau before him, who in theory at least separated impulses arising from the loins from those arising from the heart (*The Confessions,* in *OC,* 1:106–7), Sterne is careful to elevate the sentimental above the sensual. At least this is true in his *Journal to Eliza* and *A Sentimental Journey:* the pleasures of the heart Sterne certainly believed to be far above those that "the grossest Sensualist" feels.[6] And yet as these works, the letters, and especially the Sternean masterpiece *Tristram Shandy* show, affection and benevolence cannot be kept on separate levels, isolated from one another. Sexual love and tender feeling are like the body and soul, which Sterne compares to a jerkin and its lining: "rumple the one," says My Father in a strikingly modern insight, and "you

1. Writing to Garrick in April 1762, Sterne says of an English translation of Diderot's *Fils naturel:* "It has too much sentiment in it,...the speeches too long, and savour too much of *preaching." Letters of Laurence Sterne,* ed. Lewis P. Curtis (Oxford: Clarendon Press, 1935), p. 162.

2. Quoted from Wesley's *Journal* in *Sterne: The Critical Heritage,* ed. Alan B. Howes (London: Routledge & Kegan Paul, 1974), p. 229.

3. Samuel Jackson Pratt, who used the pseudonym "Courtney Melmoth," is quoted ibid., pp. 224, 225. The apostrophe to "Dear sensibility! source inexhausted of all that's precious in our joys, or costly in our sorrows!" occurs in *Sentimental Journey,* "The Bourbonnois," pp. 277–79. I quote here and elsewhere from the edition of Gardner D. Stout, Jr. (Berkeley and Los Angeles: University of California Press, 1967).

4. *Sterne: The Critical Heritage,* pp. 166–67.

5. On "sensorium" see *Sentimental Journey,* pp. 277–78 and the notes by Stout. See esp. Appendix E, pp. 353–54.

6. The phrase comes from *The Journal to Eliza* (1767), 24 April, in *Letters of Sterne,* p. 330.

rumple the other."[7] So Sterne remembers his beloved and the "quiet, sentimental Repasts" he had with her; and he weeps like a child. A "turn of Sentiment" he seems to define as "Truth, fidelity, honour & Love mix'd up with Delicacy" (*Journal to Eliza,* pp. 324, 365). In *A Sentimental Journey* Yorick calls love a "passion" which leads to generous action:

> L'amour n'est *rien* sans sentiment.
> Et le sentiment est encore *moins* sans amour.
>
> [P. 153]

A sentimental journey is "a quiet journey of the heart in pursuit of NATURE" (p. 219), on which the traveler finds that the moment he is kindled by love, he is also "all generosity": "If ever I do a mean action, it must be in some interval betwixt one passion and another" (pp. 128–29). If one is seeking an emblem typical of Sterne, one could do worse than the mimosa, the sensitive plant which "feels, alive through all her tender form,"[8] a plant which is surely tended by "Cupid! prince of God and men" (p. 131).

There can be no doubt that sex and sensibility unite in Sterne, that love vibrates in tune with the "great—great Sensorium of the world!" (p. 278). But what is the nature of Sterne's eroticism? Is the sentimental traveler who protests he comes to spy out the nakedness of the ladies' heart really a voyeur who has come to spy out the nakedness of their bodies? Despite his protests of innocence and guilelessness, Yorick's manner offended sensitive and squeamish readers, and the uncompromisingly moral Johnson understandably roared out his disapproval. Yorick drives off in the night with the Marquesina da F*** after the ballet of bumping bodies at the concert in Milan (p. 172), and he seems to have tumbled the *fille de chambre* on the bed after sentimental discourse: "Nature has so wove her web of kindness, that some threads of love and desire are entangled with the piece" (p. 237). But in reading this work at least, one keeps wondering if the mutual blushes are not those of forepleasure rather than those of consummation and if Sterne is not emotionally akin to Rousseau, in whose *Confessions* we noted eroticism of the early adolescent, pregenital, pan-corporal kind in which touch is all in all and the intensest pleasures come from kissing and fondling the hand. What are we to make of Sterne's own allegations about himself? Suffering apparently from a venereal disease whose cause he was at a loss to determine, outraged that he of all people, with "all his sensibilities," must suffer "the chastisement of the

---

7. *Tristram Shandy,* ed. James A. Work, 3.4; p. 160. The first two numbers refer to volume and chapter, the third to the page in Work's edition (New York: Odyssey Press, 1940). On the sympathetic bonds between body and soul, see *A Sentimental Journey,* pp. 162–63 n.

8. Erasmus Darwin, "The Loves of the Plants" in *The Botanic Garden,* pt. 2, canto 1, line 251. Darwin, who makes the mimosa the symbol at once of love and sensibility, devotes sixteen lines to the "sensitive plant."

grossest sensualist," he protests that he has had no commerce with the sex, not even his wife, for fifteen years and that he has "not an ounce & a half of carnality" about him, that there was "an act he *could* not do, or think of."[9] "Do": perhaps Sterne is to be believed here, though there is little evidence for an opinion one way or the other; "think of": hardly, for though incapacity is conceivable, the purity of his thought is belied by every other page of his *oeuvres*. Whatever the biographical truth, there is little doubt that Sterne himself chose to wear a public mask of impotence. On the Sunday following his own marriage, he preached on Luke 5:5, giving it a sexual *entendre:* "We have toiled all the night, and have taken nothing."[10] And there is no doubt either that he endows his fictional creations with the same reputation he gave himself. One scholar has said, referring to "the strange passionlessness of the Shandys," that there is an air of impotence about all the Shandy males, including the bull.[11] Another scholar has said that in Sterne and his context, "women are randy, men impotent."[12]

Sterne's adequacy as husband and lover need not concern us as much as what has been described as "the crazy veering between 'delicacy' and 'concupiscence'" in the fictions.[13] Each of these polarities has, as we know well, an important contemporary history. Delicacy was of course the bond that united Rousseau and Sterne, as it connected both to Richardson and him in turn to Rowe, Otway, and Dryden. Ovid, whom mention of Dryden brings to mind and who can be allowed to stand for another, though related, tradition of love, does not separate delicacy from consummated sexuality; he makes, in fact, a strong association between love and refinement: "Love first disarm'd the Fierceness of their Mind, / And in one Bed the Men and Women join'd." Indeed Ovid's 1764 editor applies what the Latin poet says of wanton love to "the Art of loving the Sciences" and so creates for education an "*Emblem* . . . not disagreeable."[14]

Some mid- and late eighteenth-century men of feeling, however, were far from accepting Ovid's fusion of sex and sensibility or even from Sterne's juxtaposition of the two. Goldsmith, who loved and cultivated feeling, criticized the free physical expression of love in Italy: "But small the bliss that sense alone bestows, / And sensual bliss is all the nation knows" (*The Traveller,*

9. *Sentimental Journey,* p. 243. Preceding references come from a facetious letter to a "Mrs. F——" in *Letters of Sterne,* p. 241, and from the *Journal to Eliza,* pp. 329, 343.

10. See Work's introduction to *Tristram Shandy,* p. xviii.

11. Ibid., pp. 1x–1xi.

12. Patricia Meyer Spacks, *Imagining a Self: Autobiography and Novel in Eighteenth-Century England* (Cambridge, Mass.: Harvard Universtiy Press, 1976), p. 133. These opinions about male impotency I shall later qualify somewhat in discussing My Uncle Toby's wooing.

13. Martin Price, *To the Palace of Wisdom,* p. 325.

14. *Ovid's Art of Love, in Three Books. Together with his Remedy of Love* (London, 1764), p. A3r. The quotation from Ovid comes from *The Art of Love,* bk. 2 (p. 66 of this ed.). Translations are by Dryden, Congreve, and others.

123–24). Some literary sentimentalists could be downright silly in their loyalty to the quiverings of refinement, like Robert Potter when he said of Samuel Johnson in 1789 that "his vigorous mind being perhaps vitiated or degraded by the grossness of his body, vibrated not to the delicate touches of a Shenstone and a Hammond."[15] We can be grateful today for the absence of such vibration in Johnson, but historically it is interesting to note how serious a deficiency it was held to be. Cowper, who shared Potter's opinion of Johnson, censures him as an inadequate judge of "writers upon the subject of love, a passion which I suppose he never felt in his life."[16] The word "passion" is hardly the one that springs to mind in remembering Cowper on heterosexual love; it is singularly appropriate, however, to his fear of being a spiritual castaway and to his convulsing emotions on receiving his mother's portrait long after her death. And his biography provides exquisite examples of the kind of love that sensibility without passion might produce. The two- or three-year friendship between the poet and his cousin Theadora is modest, delicate, shy, familial, tender—but no more. It ended abruptly and was treated by the poet with complete silence. But the evidence on which to build a judgment of Cowper's early life is slight; and the poet's later delicate, fastidious, and sexless friendships with women may not have been totally unaffected by his easily alienated and guilt-ridden mind. Without trying to determine what is owing to nature and what to nurture, we may note intriguing similarities between Cowper's sensibilities and those that appear in the love affair Mackenzie describes in *The Man of Feeling* and the manifestations of delicacy by men and women portrayed by Romney, Blake, Flaxman, Canova, Shelley, and many others.[17]

The combination of avant-garde psychology and sexual delicacy appears also in the work of the associationist Hartley, the influential thinker after whom Coleridge named a son. Hartley was a "vibrationist" who anticipated Sterne in using the term "sensorium," which he derived from Newton's reference to the human receptor that could observe a glowing coal in circular motion and of that impression make an entirely subjective circle of fire. Hartley also made "sensorium" synonymous with the mind and fancy as the seat of the sensitive soul. Thus sensibility was for him basically the "Power of receiving Vibrations." Such thought obviously has affinities with Sterne's, particularly in *Tristram Shandy*. But there the parallel ceases, for Hartley, afraid of art, poetry, and novels, shows himself to be very squeamish as well about sexuality, urging in such matters the development of "Steadiness and

15. See James T. Boulton, ed., *Johnson: The Critical Heritage* (London: Routledge & Kegan Paul, 1971), p. 309.
16. Ibid., p. 274.
17. On Cowper and Theadora, see Charles Ryskamp, *William Cowper of the Inner Temple, Esq.* (Cambridge: Cambridge University Press, 1959), pp. 119–34. See also pp. 135–44.

Sobriety of Mind" and of a spirit watchful against "Intercourses with the World in general, and with the other Sex in particular." Not all those who could be called delicate were as afraid of corporality as Hartley seemed to be, but it is perhaps more than fortuitous that an influential psychologist should also favor the kind of antisensual sensibility that we have seen to be a growing trend.[18]

The permeation of Sterne's works by sexuality—to turn now to the other polarity present in his treatment of love—is itself a phenomenon worthy of analysis; but in the context of an age increasingly filled with fastidious sensibility, his carnal allusiveness stands out strikingly. It certainly separates Sterne from virtually all the Men of Feeling who preceded and from most who followed him. But though his combination of sexual nuance and tender sensibility is as rare and volatile as his combination of tears and laughter, there is abundant context for his sexually suggestive double entendres (considered by themselves) in mid-century England. For salacious writing, sometimes artful, sometimes merely provocative, did survive the decades-long post-Restoration attempts to cleanse the mind and tongue—an assault mounted mostly by the sentimentalists. Some examples come easily to mind: one is perhaps related to sensibility, another is its witty enemy, and still another is a legendary commender of prudential caution. John Cleland has been called a "romantic sentimentalist,"[19] and in *Fanny Hill,* which James Boswell called "that most licentious and inflaming book,"[20] there is considerable success at indirection: periphrases for the vagina abound, and there are some fifty variants or so for the penis. Cleland is in his way as delicate as Henry Mackenzie.[21] John Wilkes's *Essay on Woman* (1763) is a work at once so naughtily and religiously allusive that many of its strokes of wit will have to be called either blasphemous or tasteless. Wilkes outdoes Wycherley and Etherege, both of whom liked

18. See David Hartley, *Observations on Man: His Frame, His Duty, and His Expectations,* 2 vols. in one (Gainesville, Fla.: Scholars' Facsimiles & Reprints, 1966), pt. 1, pp. 9, 10, 44, 242, 403. This is a facsimile of the 1749 ed. and has an introduction by Theodore L. Huguelet. It is possible to relate the moral scrupulosities of writers like Goldsmith, Cowper, and Hartley, who do indeed reflect sensibility, to an important trend in late-eighteenth-century *mentalité* which we can call, in the phrase of Maurice Quinlan, "Victorian Prelude" (see his book under this title [New York: Columbia University Prtess, 1941]). Lawrence Stone discusses the signs from the 1770s and on of Victorian-Evangelical-Methodist censorship of sexual freedom: authoritarian tendencies in the family, iron self-control, preoccupation with moral control (*Family,* p. 673).

19. The characterization is that of Peter Quennell, quoted by Michael Shinagel, "*Memoirs of a Woman of Pleasure*: Pornography and the Mid-Eighteenth-Century English Novel" in *Studies in Change and Revolution,* ed. Paul J. Korshin (Menston, Eng.: Scolar Press, 1972), p. 223.

20. *Boswell for the Defence,* ed. William K. Wimsatt and Frederick A. Pottle (London: William Heinemann, 1960), p. 84. Boswell called Cleland a "curious figure." *Boswell in Search of a Wife, 1766–1769,* ed. Frank Brady and Frederick A. Pottle (New York: McGraw-Hill, 1956), p. 316.

21. See Shinagel, p. 225. *Fanny Hill* was published on 21 Nov. 1748. By 1750 three editions were available to the English reader. William H. Epstein, *John Cleland: Images of a Life* (New York: Columbia University Press, 1974), pp. 3–4.

to use religious metaphors in a salacious context, as he sexualizes or feminizes such terms as the Fall, the Resurrection of the Flesh, the Red Sea, the entry into the Temple. Perhaps the direct parody of Pope is more acceptable: "Thy lust the Virgin dooms to bleed to-day, / Had she thy reason would she skip and play?"[22] The sober and cautious Benjamin Franklin, who recommended marriage as the proper remedy for violent natural inclinations, did urge those who refused to marry but did not renounce sexual congress to choose older versus younger women, one of the reasons being that the lower parts age least, so that below the girdle the old are indistinguishable from the young.[23] Thus in addition to the scabrous and sexually suggestive literature in many tongues and from many epochs that have been so amply displayed as a background for Sterne's bawdry, one can adduce examples from his contemporary milieu.

My main interest is not in sources or context but in meaning. Perhaps a few miscellaneous examples may bring to mind the whole surprising range of impolite allusions in *Tristram Shandy,* which must form a background to any discussion of the relations of sensibility to sex in Sterne.[24] Dr. Kunastrokius delighted in combing asses' tails and plucking the dead hairs out with his teeth, allowing the tweezers he always carried to remain in his pocket—both the doctor's name and his habit making obvious allusions to an oral-anal perversion (1.7; p. 13). The learned Kysarcius discourses casuistically on whether a mother is kin to her child and raises the question of incest (4.29; p. 328). A man, it is alleged, can be lit at both ends if a sufficient wick appears (8.15; p. 553). And there is more than one suggestion—a decisive one being My Father's long whistle—that Obadiah's new child, as hairy as his father, who had not shaved for three weeks, is a product of bestiality, the male culprit being the Shandy bull, who has hitherto been much maligned for his inadequacy (9.33; p. 646). If this animal receives the major attention at the end, the other half of this Cock and Bull story has certainly not been neglected earlier: perhaps the most obsessive of all the double meanings in the novel are phallic.

Are these verbal allusions (and the copresence of situational bawdry) merely gratuitous and sensational, or can they be regarded expressions of vitality by

22. *An Essay on Woman and Other Pieces Printed at the Private Press in Great-George Street, Westminster, in 1763, and now Reproduced in Fac-Simile from a Copy Believed to be Unique . . . London Privately Printed, September MDCCCLXXI,* lines 81–82 (p. 19).

23. Benjamin Franklin, *A Letter of Advice to a Young Man Considering Marriage,* Airedale Series, no. 2, 1926 (n.p.: Privately published). The headnote says that this "letter" was written on 25 June 1745.

24. See Frank Brady, "*Tristram Shandy:* Sexuality, Morality, and Sensibility," *Eighteenth-Century Studies* 4 (Fall 1970): 41–56. Jean-Jacques Mayoux, "Laurence Sterne" in John Traugott, ed., *Laurence Sterne: A Collection of Critical Essays* (Englewood Cliffs, N.J.: Prentice-Hall, 1968), pp. 108–25; and Michael O. Houlahan, "Sexual Comedy in *Tristram Shandy,*" Ph.D. diss., Northwestern University, 1970.

one who loved life but was not destined to live long? The answers to these questions may arise from an analysis of Sterne's sexual humor as it culminates in the courtship of the Widow Wadman by My Uncle Toby, a deliciously amusing and warmly human episode that is prepared for by the entire course of the novel. In fact the theme of masculine impotence, which jostles for attention with bawdy references to virility all through *Tristram Shandy,* is a pertinent background for the abortion of Toby's amours at the end.

The novel, almost at the very beginning, refers to the animal spirits, those subtle, almost noncorporeal particles that pass through the nerves. These, which must allude, among other things, to sexual force and adequacy, are precisely what the Shandy family lacks (1.1; p. 4 and n.2). The homunculus, or spermatazoon, that will become Tristram is not properly conducted to his destined place because these vital spirits are dissipated, and the "little gentleman" comes to the end of this, his journey from My Father to My Mother, miserably spent, his own élan "ruffled beyond description" (1.2; pp. 5–6). So the newest Shandy comes into the world somewhat depleted and inadequate, possessing a trait, as I have said, that he shares with most male members of his family. The domestic situation is not typical of the whole world, however, as Slawkenbergius's tale about the stranger with the enormous nose riotously demonstrates. That "nose" arouses all the libidinal energies of Strasburg which, when combined with the fancy, produce an overmastering obsession. "Noses have ever so run in their heads, that the *Strasburgers* could not follow their business." Slawkenbergius's moral is, "I fear [the city] will not be the last fortress that has been either won—or lost by NOSES" (vol. 4; p. 271). This comic vision anticipates Blake's darker vision of a sex-crazed society created by the phallic Orc, and it also anticipates Sterne's own kingdom of Navarre, where whiskers bear the same association as noses—and "pump-handles—and spigots and faucets" (5.1; p. 348). But it is directly antithetical to the sexual calm that ususlly prevails in the Shandy family, where "unhappy *Tristram!* child of wrath! child of decrepitude! interruption! mistake! and discontent!" (4.19; p. 296) suffers further indignities to his manhood. When for want of lead weights (which Trim removed for Toby's mock battles) the sash comes down on the boy's foreskin, he may have suffered no damage at all, as he himself protests, but the reputation of vital loss hangs over Tristram's as over Sterne's own head. That reputation Toby suggests removing by having the boy fully displayed to the public at the market cross. But "'twill have no effect, said my father" (6.14; p. 433), a melancholy comment by the head of a household much maligned on this score, a household that has reason to know how persistently such a reputation could cling.

When the Widow Wadman enters the story, toward its end, she enters a kind of desolate void, for it is now time for the demolition of Dunkirk to be carried out in imitation of the melancholy military events on the Continent.

On the darkening Shandy green there is no longer the laughing, whistling, and singing that accompanied the progress of British and allied arms. Now that Sterne has replaced mock military battles with My Uncle Toby's siege of a lady's heart, the time has come for one of those playful but significant Sternean contexts. Through Burton, Plato is invoked (6.36; p. 467 and n.3), and we are especially urged to remember Milton and Eden. The "heroine" of the love story is presented as "a daughter of *Eve*" who, though modest, is the aggressor in temptation , guided as she is by "Love-militancy" (8.8; p. 546; 8.14; p. 552).

My Uncle Toby brings his long past to bear on his present adventures. He suffered unspeakable miseries when he was wounded in the groin years before in real military action across the Channel, when his four-year confinement was caused by a most dismal crushing of his hip bone and ilium. Such ancient disabilities present less of a handicap now than the fact that he "know[s] nothing at all" about women, not even, as Walter says, "so much as the right end . . . from the wrong" (2.7; p. 101). Such, then, is our somewhat battered and aging ingénu, who must now undergo the widow's siege. It begins skillfully and appropriately in the sentry box, where the lovable old captain's heart and senses are attacked to the accompaniment of Sterne's most lyrical language about the various kinds of human eye. *We* hear Sterne's richly modulated voice; Toby sees only the darting eye, which, however, succeeds almost at once in penetrating the good man's heart. " 'I am in love, corporal!' quoth my uncle *Toby*" (8.27; p. 580). Certainty has overtaken this modest and otherwise reluctant bachelor because in riding his horse he experienced discomfort in the lower regions, apparently owing to a blister raised by chafing; but the persistence of the discomfort even after the disappearance of the blister suggests an unmistakably Venereal origin. My Uncle Toby has—there can be no doubt of it—experienced physical desire, for upon Walter's pressing him as to when he knew he was in love, he replies simply, "When the blister broke" (8.32; p. 585). Not possessing his brother's intellectual baggage about love—or about anything else, for that matter—My Uncle Toby reveals himself to be a thorough traditionalist: desire is simply that which will "make a man marry, and love his wife, and get a few children" (8.33; p. 586). Walter may have his Platonic categories about love, and women may have their fifty-odd reasons for marriage. Toby has only the most obvious and least disputable ones of the Book of Common Prayer: procreation and the establishment of a family.[25]

The comic verve becomes irresistible when the Widow Wadman is concerned with the "whereabouts" of her suitor's wound. A full range of verbal

25. Vol. 9, "The Eighteenth Chapter," pp. 634–35. On the aims of marriage, see above, pp. 13, 33, 160–62, 185.

misunderstandings arising from Toby's habitual and thoroughly innocent military metaphors, the earthiness of the widow's desires in contrast to his idealization of her, the traditionally religious antifeminism of Walter (rich in learning and deeply suspicious of the sex act)—all these delectable meanderings are woven together in Sterne's best manner and made to seem relevant to the suit. But then suddenly the wooing stops, and the affair is aborted. Toby has been frightened into a retreat. Apparently he learns of the widow's strong physical desires—"which shock you know I should not have received, but from my total ignorance of the sex" (2.7; p. 101). This is a rich irony, since Toby fully accepted his own aroused sexuality as a sign of love and hoped for the usual fruits of holy matrimony. How these could have come about without his partner's full physical cooperation he does not bother to ask. He only knows that when he finds passion more prominent than compassion in the daughter of Eve he has chosen for a wife, he returns precipitately to his status quo ante and becomes once more a denizen of the male world only. The whole novel is now close to breaking off, but we must surely believe that My Uncle Toby returns to being the lovable combination of goodness and innocence that is quite unrivaled in the annals of sensibility and that might have withered in the hotter regions of procreative desire.

Can more be said about Sterne's intentions, which are mercurially elusive at this climactic stage of the novel? Perhaps three possible explanations of Toby's aborted suit can be suggested. (1) Sterne remands Toby to the state of innocence, never allowing him to cross the frontier of experience, because his whole existence would have been threatened by the new, untried world. "Women in the novel," as Patricia Spacks has rightly said, "have considerably more sexual gusto than the men—another cause, perhaps, for male fear."[26] And, as I have pointed out in discussing Milton, a venerable tradition, classical and Christian, regarded woman as more libidinous than man, and on discovering carnality in the object of his suit Toby withdraws, as Adam should have done, from the tempting fruit. Sterne could be said to be taking the side of friendship against love, a point of view brilliantly articulated by Richardson's Anna Howe and Rousseau's Claire—an opinion frequently present in the literature of sensibility and here, for once, allowed to prevail. There are, however, several reasons for thinking that this view is not close to Sterne's desires as a man or a novelist. Although he cannot be said to have carefully or penetratingly portrayed any woman in his fictions—and therefore we must guard against interpreting their desires and motivations too closely or sympathetically—it would seem that the widow's concern about the location of the wound and about My Uncle's capacity were fully justified: did not her first husband have a sciatica that kept him from performing his duties, and

26. *Imagining a Self,* p. 132.

should she be asked to accept, sight unseen, as it were, another liaison that promises a similar state of inaction? My Uncle Toby is by no means impotent himself, as his kindled desires and as his wish for a family indicate; his is a case of long preserved virginity, not inherent lack of ability.[27] And surely someone who has spent so many pages devoted to phallic nuances—to filling the mind of the reader with sensual thoughts, if not desires—can scarcely have regarded a state of permanent innocence as in any way desirable. (2) Perhaps Sterne, at the climax of one of the great novels of sensibility, is recommending the doctrine of Clarissa or of Julie—that though the physical may properly be present in love, it must be transcended by the truly sentimental and moral. If looked at from this perspective, the courtship of the Widow Wadman is aborted because between her and her suitor there is no true compatibility. My Uncle Toby wants procreation; but the pleasures of sex he regards as only utilitarian and perhaps compensatory (they overcome the boredom of the quotidian), while she has no view of anything other than immediate pleasure. During the lonely nights of her widowhood her servants each night pinned together the bottom of her nightgown; but now, when her hopes of marriage are aroused, she kicks away the pins and prepares for nocturnal action. It is all too obvious: the sentimental Toby and the carnal Widow Wadman must part, for they are not compatible, she being unable even to conceive of the Miltonic ideal. This interpretation fits the tradition of sensibility that lay behind Sterne; but does it fit him? It would seem too solemn, too categorical for so sensual, so subtle, so noncommital an author. (3) The final possibility is that Sterne may have continued loving My Uncle Toby but found him lacking in the vitality that the scabrous portions of the novel, in their strange, involuted, and perhaps sometimes offensive way, keep recommending. *Tristram Shandy* is undoubtedly about impotence, but Sterne, though portraying it as present in a family that he loves, regards it as a limitation and not the inevitable or invincible condition of man. Death, as has been finely said, "makes all men impotent";[28] but Sterne does not submit meekly to it. He defies it, laughs at it, flees from it, mocks it, and ultimately transcends it through art. It is not impossible that, beneath the complex surface of this nondescript novel, he is actually satirizing the sentimental movement for divorcing itself, in its latter days, from the fructifying forces of human physicality.

27. Sterne says nothing was "ever better" than Toby's "fitness for the marriage state." He then lists his qualifications: sweetness of temper, humanity, trust, and "the other causes for which matrimony was ordained—." That these are sexual is indicated by Sterne's long list of mock-modest asterisks and by his concluding comment: "The DONATION was not defeated [not "defended," as James A. Work's text mistakenly has it] by my uncle *Toby*'s wound" (9:22; p. 626). For this textual correction and a welcome defense of Toby's physical endowments, see Mark Sinfield, "Uncle Toby's Potency: Some Critical and Authorial Confusions in 'Tristram Shandy,'" *Notes and Queries* 25 (Feb. 1978): 54–55.

28. Spacks, *Imagining a Self*, p. 134.

The family bull is only one of three Shandean animals whose emblematic meanings it is instructive to establish. The ass Walter Shandy uses to symbolize the lower parts of the body, an ungentle creature, which must be mounted and mastered, for " 'tis a beast concupiscent" (8.31; p. 584). It must of course be distinguished from that "sporting little filly-folly" (ibid.), the hobby-horse—a useful beast that can carry one away in a canter from life's cares. My Father's bull is neither gentle, frisky, nor kicking; its most important characteristic is that it has the unshakable reputation of being impotent. Walter rejects that imputation and defends his animal: if the cow does not calve, it could be the cow's fault, and besides, since the parish is large and well supplied with other cows, the bull's failures are at least understandable.

Can these animal fables be interpreted further and applied to human love? The hobby-horse is of course the Shandean animal par excellence; but it is also a peculiarly human animal, a part of our very being, as it were—"as tender a part as [a man] has about him" (2.12; p. 115). But it can, for all that, pull against a truly humane sensibility and therefore partakes of the nature of original sin. The beast can be comfortable to ride, as Walter suggests, but only because it carries a man into the solipsistic recesses of his own being: self-indulgence is always flattering, easy, and pleasant. Because the hobby-horse is so essentially human it can be lovable and even kindly, as indeed the Shandys are. Sterne says that one can apparently be "generous (tho' hobby-horsical)" (3.22; p. 206). Nevertheless, this beast is inward-driving and cannot therefore be the true instrument of love and charity. When Toby retreats from the widow, he is riding his hobby-horse back into himself; he is being human, to be sure, but not largely or redemptively human.

That symbol of libidinous energy, the ass, kicks and paws up dirt all through the novel, and it is difficult not to see him as a countersymbol to the lack of vital spirits that enervates most of the Shandy men. Stretching the symbol a bit, we can perhaps assume that it is this defiant creature which the dying but laughing Sterne rides through southern France and Italy, escaping that whoremonger death. Speaking of death, we must certainly say that Sterne does not invest it either with the baroque, Christian immortality that Clarissa achieves or with the kind of continuing passion after death that Shakespeare and Dryden seem to reserve for the postmortem Antony and Cleopatra or that Rousseau vaguely promises Julie and Saint-Preux. The art of Sterne provides no hint at all of futurity. There is only the ass. And on him the coughing, consumptive Sterne, with his spindly legs, rides with merry and defiant pleasure. His vital spirits never desert him; and the celebration of life and energy—even of sexual energy which through the insistent presence of bawdry impregnates almost every page—persists to the very edge of doom. It is thus that he flings an impudent challenge at death—in a peal of impish laughter. The homunculus from which *he* grew was not a diminished or spent thing, and Sterne in his affirmation of life and energy is neither a Tristram nor a Yorick.

Like the Shandy men and Sterne himself, the bull has the reputation of impotence. But is it deserved? If the long suggestive whistle of My Father on hearing the description of Obadiah's hairy son means what it seems to, the bull does not deserve his reputation; and Walter must be trusted when he says that he is as good as any that ever "p-ss'd"; he "might have done for *Europa* herself in purer times."[29] Sterne for once may be speaking through the learned head of the Shandean household when he says that in town circles the loss of reputation for virility is regarded as loss of character itself. What the facts are about Stern's own sexual abilities, as I said earlier, need not concern us. The important matter is that he makes of impotence (surely one of the oldest themes of the comic spirit, and also the most recent) not only a delectable drama about the dilemma of debility but also an assertion of vitality— partly the vitality of the libidinous and kicking ass but more centrally that of the humorous artist, celebrating human warmth against the encroaching cold.

Sterne was preoccupied, then, with both physical love and sentimental delicacy, both being the kinds of love that bind humanity together. Such sensibility possesses its own kind of power. Even the vigorous Smollett softened his late, delightful creation, Matt Bramble, into a Man of Feeling and gave him a tender heart beneath his barking manner. But *Tristram Shandy*, particularly in its concluding books, shows us Sterne drawing from deeper wells and artistically tapping sources of energy that may have been denied him in life. In one sense he can be said to have brought a great eighteenth-century movement, the cult of feeling, to its climax. In another, perhaps more comprehensive view he can be said to have revived an older and more basic conception of Eros, the one expressed by Bacon. For the earlier writer, Cupid is the cause of all union, including that of sentimental fraternity: for on him "euery exquisit simpathy doth depend." At the same time the son of Venus, the youngest of the gods, is also the one who attaches desire to each "indiuiduall nature," "a desire of coniunction and procreation."[30] Sterne worshiped both these incarnations of the god of love.[31]

29. 9.33; pp. 646–47. The behavior of the Shandy bull, if I have interpreted Sterne correctly, raises the whole question of bestiality, about which I have done no particular research except to note warnings against it. French eroticism was capable of introducing a small dog for lascivious purposes—a fact which may explain the presence of the spaniel in Watteau's *A Lady at Her Toilet* (see pl. 17). See Donald Posner, *Watteau: A Lady at Her Toilet* (New York: Viking Press, 1973), p. 83. Posner says the dog as a real sexual partner was a frequent theme in carnal literature (pp. 80–81).

30. *The Wisedome of the Ancients*, trans. Arthur Gorges (London, 1619), s.v. "Cupid, or an Atome," pp. 76–84.

31. In this discussion of Sterne I have turned aside from the biographical, but the evidence should be reviewed. His latest biographer pulls away from concluding that "Sterne was actually impotent; but he may have suffered anxieties about his adequacy—altogether a different matter."

Young Werther

One of the literary subjects which preoccupied Goethe, that universal man, was love; and it is difficult to think of any author, work, or movement touched on in this study which does not in some way enter the background of his art. The love that Wilhelm Meister comes to feel—at the climax of the *Lehrjahre*—for his "Amazon," Natalie, has in it elements of the baroque-religious we have observed in *Clarissa.* The lovely idyll of Mignon and the Harper in the same novel, concerned as it is with incestuous love and its fruit, is related to an important Enlightenment theme and to an essential ingredient of pre-Romantic sensibility. The Gretchen tragedy of *Faust,* with its final exaltation of *das Ewig-Weibliche,* is in form traditionally religious, recalling the Christian pathetic; but it is concurrently an expression of the avant-garde feeling that was at once feminizing and civilizing life and manners. And the love affair in *Elective Affinities (Die Wahlverwandtschaften)* between an older married man and a very young girl exalts the delicate and precocious Ottilie to the Eternal Child, partly by removing her from life and making of her in death a change-less work of marmoreal art. In these and other expressions of love Goethe has fully realized the meaning of "sentiment" at the moment of its greatest rich-ness and ambiguity: he has united carnal delight and spiritual transcendence. But at the same time he has entered deeply into the implications of "sensibil-ity" in its postmeridian developments, imbuing ideal forms with the inescap-able features of morbidity and even perversion. The last are insistently, though by no means grossly or obviously, present in that amazing work which was written hastily in 1774 and thoroughly revised in 1787, *Die Leiden des Jungen Werthers,* a product of *Sturm und Drang,* the German equivalent of sensibility and a potent influence on subsequent life and letters.[32] This work merits our attention not simply because it falls within my period and because it is a fascinating *Schlüsselroman* based on its author's own youthful experiences of life, but also because it shines in the Rousseauist afterglow and powerfully explores and extends the nature of love-sensibility. These backward- and

---

Arthur H. Cash, *Laurence Sterne: The Early & Middle Years* (London: Methuen, 1975), p. 84. See the discussions of Sterne's relations with Miss C——, Elizabeth Lumley, his wife, and Eliza Draper (pp. 78–85).

32. Quotations in German come from *Goethes Werke,* Hamburger Ausgabe, 14 vols. (Hamburg: Christian Wegner Verlag, 1949–), vol 6 (1st ed., 1951; 6th printing, 1965), ed. Erich Trunz. References are to volume and page. The English text is quoted from *The Sufferings of Young Werther,* trans. Bayard Quincy Morgan (New York: Frederick Ungar, 1957). For an excellent summary of the *Werther* vogue, see Harry Steinhauer, "Goethe's *Werther* after Two Centuries," *University of Toronto Quarterly* 43 (Fall 1974): 1–13, and the definitive work by Stuart Pratt Atkins, *The Testament of Werther in Poetry and Drama* (Cambridge, Mass.: Harvard University Press, 1949). For Goethe's relations to cultural movements in Germany, see Roy Pascal, *The German Sturm und Drang* (Manchester: Manchester University Press, 1959).

forward-looking qualities will emerge if we consider the love of Werther for Lotte in four connections: with (1) *nature,* (2) *death,* (3) *regression to childhood* and the childish, and (4) the shadowy but hauntingly real presence of an *Oedipal triangle.* This fourfold approach is intended to modify, if not reject outright, the traditional view that Werther's suicide represents an intense but understandable response to the frustration of a normally passionate, though deeply poetic, love for a woman—a frustration made unavoidable by her obligations to the state of matrimony. Such a view is implicit in Rowlandson's parody in 1786 of the by then famous novel. (Parodies, as we know, have a way of disclosing the essentials of a popular and influential interpretation.) Lotte is bare breasted and looks lascivious, her husband on the wall as a picture is ridiculously got up in an enormous military hat and apparently stands for foolish convention among other things, and Werther is a mad romantic, distraught by love as he tears his hair. The picture hanging between the lovers, of Tantalus in the water reaching for tempting but eternally unavailable fruit, epitomizes their plight.[33]

1. *Nature* does seem to proffer a Rousseauist nest at Wahlheim, an hour's walk from town, a sequestered, homelike place. But Werther cannot derive from it the intense, if somewhat troubled, delights which the Confessor drew from Les Charmettes because of his taste for what Burke called the sublime of terror and Freud the "oceanic" feeling, both real menaces to adulthood, however exploitable they may be by the creative artist. Werther wants to lose himself in the distant hills and valleys, which are vast and dim: he longs for the rapture of one great emotion. But his feeling is as unspecific and undifferentiated as the details of reality (developed in the course of the novel) are concrete and sensuous. Early one morning Werther experiences in the presence of nature a piercing sense of Coleridge's "vain endeavour": he is winning nothing but despair from the outward forms he contemplates.[34] Very soon the soft, sexual, maternal feelings mediated by nature (these predominate at first) are drowned in a growing din of torment as nature becomes a devouring monster: the grave gapes, streams dash themselves to pieces on

33. The etching, *The Sorrows of Werter—the Last Interview,* is in the collection of Wilmarth Sheldon Lewis of Farmington, Conn. Although her reaction was more refined, Jane Austen's probably did not differ in kind from Rowlandson's. One of the characters in her burlesque, "Love and Freindship" (1790), is doomed to marry a "Sensible, well-informed man" who "had never read the sorrows of Werter" and therefore had "no soul." See the edition by G. K. Chesterton (London: Chatto & Windus, 1922), p. 24.

34. *Dejection: An Ode,* 42–46:

> It were a vain endeavour,
> Though I should gaze forever,
> On that green light that lingers in the west:
> I may not hope from outward forms to win
> The passion and the life, whose fountains are within.

the rocks, storms flood the valley and ruin the summer arbor; and Cowper's frightening vision in *The Castaway* is repeated. Not quite at once: there are a few remissions, which, however, only accentuate the dryness and emptiness that contact with nature now produces.

2. The theme of nature—and its ultimate disappointments—is fatally accompanied by whispers of *death*. These adumbrations of mortality are so carefully, consistently, and increasingly suggested by the natural scene and also by the developing human relationships that the careful reader does not regard Werther's suicide as gratuitous or melodramatic. One senses danger early on when the "oceanic" in nature blurs Werther's perceptions as a painter and weakens his sense of form, as everything external swims and sways before his inner being. This loss of shape is a sure sign of *Dumpfheit* (dullness of soul) and makes us appreciate more Blake's insistence on the "bounding line," the "hard and wirey line of rectitude and certainty."[35] Feeling lethargy within, Werther finally sees a dark abyss in the outside world and only one welcoming presence, that of an all-encompassing death. And this is precisely the union that Werther seeks when the mutually rapturous love embrace with the now married Lotte is perceived to be tragically ultimate. The suicide is grimly presented: Werther shoots himself above the eye and spills his brains, achieving death only after lingering from midnight to noon of the next day.

Werther's example was enormously influential, but it had antecedents and parallels. Donne, Hume, Voltaire, and Rousseau—each in his way an advanced thinker—had defended suicide; and the English, so much admired by the best minds of Goethe's youth, were also thought to be peculiarly inclined to self-destruction. Goldsmith, a writer with European fame, had associated suicide with gloom, ruins, sensibility, and the night—providing it with the orchestration of the most avant-garde sensibility.[36] James Boswell, both progressive and conservative in his tastes, was depressed by the links between love and murder, causing him to issue a "solemn . . . Warning of the dreadful Effects that the *Passion of Love* may produce."[37] Herbert Croft (who contributed to Johnson's *Lives of the Poets* the biography of Young, rightly considered a critical liberal) wrote a kind of English *Werther* in *Love and Madness* (1780), a

---

35. "A Descriptive Catalogue," no. XV, in Geoffrey Keynes, ed., *Blake: Complete Writings* (London: Oxford University Press, 1969), p. 585.

36. "A City Night-Piece" in *The Bee* (*Collected Works*, ed. Arthur Friedman [Oxford: Clarendon Press, 1966], 1:430–33). Goldsmith has the solitary suicide lift his arm against himself at 2 A.M. in the deserted city. On the greatly exaggerated reputation of the English for suicidal tendencies, see Roland Bartel, "Suicide in Eighteenth-Century England: The Myth of a Reputation," *Huntington Library Quarterly* 23 (Feb. 1960): 145–58.

37. Letter to *The St. James's Chronicle*, 15–17 April 1779. Boswell is commenting on the murder committed by the Rev. James Hackman, who was executed and whose trial and sentencing Boswell attended. The letter is reprinted in *Boswell Laird of Auchinleck, 1778–1782*, ed. Joseph W. Reed and Frederick A. Pottle (New York: McGraw-Hill, 1977), pp. 86–89.

story which includes a sympathetic account of the death of Chatterton, recounts the actual story of the Reverend James Hackman's murder of Miss Martha Ray in what Boswell called "a fit of frantick jealous love," and demonstrates the ease with which love, when frustrated (as it was here by the victim's love of another), can become madness.[38] The tendency to associate love and death and to portray both in settings of Gothic gloom was, as we have seen, present in the Restoration. But the tendency was now growing, and the young aesthetician Edmund Burke advanced it mightily when he defined the sublime of fear as consisting of "great and confused" images of nature, of the privative qualities of darkness and obscurity, and of the presence of the "king of terrors" himself.[39] All these qualities are present in the imagination of young Werther.

Burke went even further and associated the sublime with evil: Milton's Satan stands as an unrivaled example of grandeur. Is Goethe Burkean in this sense also? Does the sublime that Werther feels include the Satanic? It does, though in complex ways. The Satan present is not the grand rebel cherished by the Romantic imagination, nor is he the power-maddened overreacher of the orthodox tradition. He appears to be the Evil One of that unholy trinity, Milton's Satan, Sin, and Death, a familial triangle which became one of the obsessive images of the period. For the psychological and moral condition that produces the suicide is essentially narcissistic, and Werther is driven, deep within, by love of self and love of similitude. But so inevitable and even endearing had the culture that Goethe inherited made the narcissistic sins that he himself could look back on his own embodiment of these sins and regard his hero's sufferings as no more than "ungratified desires," "thwarted happiness," and a part of "the life-process of every individual."[40] The analysis that follows may seem to fly in the face of this criticism, written in Goethe's old age. But scholarship has fortunately never felt bound by an author's paternal, and sometimes conventional and sentimental, views of his own intellectual offspring.

3. If, then, as moderns using critical tools now available to us, we examine closely the nature of Werther's desire, his frustration, and his life process, we find that it bears close resemblances to *the regressive* and the primal. When Werther became a man, he simply did not heed the Apostle Paul's advice and

38. This work recounts the murder in entirely fictional letters between Hackman and Miss Ray. In one of Hackman's supposed letters Croft introduces genuine letters of Chatterton and his sister. See Boswell, *Life of Johnson*, 3:383.

39. *A Philosophical Enquiry into the Origin of our Ideas of the Sublime and the Beautiful*, ed. James T. Boulton (London: Routledge & Kegan Paul, 1958), pp. 59, 61, 62.

40. Goethe's comments are quoted by Georg Lukacs, *Goethe and His Age*, trans. Robert Anchor (New York: Grosset & Dunlap, 1969), p. 47. For my disagreement with Lukacs's view that Werther is the pioneering spirit of a new age, see "'Such, Such Were the Joys,'" *Changing Taste*, pp. 52–53.

put away childish things. Quite the contrary. He seems to have tightened his hold upon the childish and become one of the longish list of pre-Romantic and Romantic children. It is of course no sign of regression that he should love the child or even that children he met should, of all living and inanimate beings, be the closest to his heart. He felt that we are all children under God—and that idea certainly has a venerable history and should not give us pause; but when he conceived of God as one who allows his children to live in pleasant illusions, we perhaps have a right to be disturbed and to think ahead to how brilliantly the first part of *Wilhelm Meisters Lehrjahre* disposes of that notion as the hero grows up to become a man. During the first summer in the time scheme of the novel Werther continues to indulge this fantasy—that we are all children and that he too is a child, even as suicidal fancies are being born. And when the novel nears its shattering climax, during the Christmas festivities when the whole environment reverts to worshiping the Child and reaffirming the beauty and value of childhood, Werther becomes less an earthly than an everlasting boy (*das Ewig-Kindliche*), begging for forgiveness of his Heavenly Father and promising, while awaiting Lotte in the next world, to seek out her mother, now a redeemed facsimile of the one he has loved on earth as an angel and thus consolatory as nothing terrestrial can possibly be.

4. If Werther has become a child, who is the father? Not the natural father he lost in death. Who is his mother? Not the one he visits briefly—without noteworthy emotion—after he has lost his position at court. No, the "parents" of the "child" Werther are Albert, the husband, and Lotte, his wife, whom Werther adores. Goethe thus adapts to his purposes the *Oedipal triangles* of Rousseau, Claude Anet, and Mme de Warens in *The Confessions* and of Saint-Preux, Wolmar, and Julie in *La nouvelle Héloïse*.[41] Each of these "arrangements" is broken—by the departure of Rousseau the "son," by the death of Julie the "mother," and by the suicide of Werther the "child"—for the same reason: the situation in each instance approximates the Oedipal and so falls under a deep and ineradicable taboo that may indeed operate below the level of consciousness in the participants.

Like Saint-Preux vis-à-vis Wolmar and the Confessor vis-à-vis Claude, Werther's relations with Albert are so free of normal sexual jealousy that one is invited to treat the two as "father" and "son" rather than rival lovers. At least in the central sections, Albert's role as husband and father, as mentor and guide, supersedes his position as Lotte's suitor and lover. He is a force for law and order, particularly familial order. Like a stereotypical father, he is undiscriminatingly on the side of established value and insensitive to the individual suffering that custom and tradition entail. Toward him Werther feels

41. For the influence of *La nouvelle Héloïse* upon *Werther,* see Georg Brandes, *Wolfgang Goethe,* trans. Allen W. Porterfield, 2 vols. (New York: Frank-Maurice, 1925), 1:214.

only the jealousy of the child, mixed with admiring love. The lover, almost like Rousseau, who helped establish the pattern, looks to the husband as to the embodiment of stern duty from whom he half expects the ministrations of the rod.

The Werther-Albert relationship does not, however, exhaust the father-son implications that this rich novel possesses. Additional ones arise from the persistent religious metaphor which underlies much of the thought and action. About to take his life, Werther writes, "O Lotte! I shall go before you! go to my Father, to your Father. To him I will make my complaint, and he will comfort me, until you come."[42] At the moment of his climactic action the hero is more a child than ever—now a kind of cosmic child ready to act sub specie aeternitatis. One might well ask, Why does he have a sense that he goes directly to the Father without the mediation of the Son? The reason is surely not that Goethe is making a point so often raised in Catholic-Protestant polemics about the intermediary nature of Jesus but, rather, because Werther *is* Christ in his fevered and distorted fancy. The young man has, as it were, replaced him and therefore no longer needs him. When he says he will "go to my Father, to your Father," he is not only quoting the words of Christ but assuming the Messianic role, as he does when he utters the cry from the cross: "My God! My God! why hast thou forsaken me?"[43] He can in fact regard the sacrifice of his life not as an act of despair but as a sacrifice for another, resulting from "the certainty that my sufferings are complete." Like Christ, he is about to make a perfect sacrifice that will avail to the salvation of their loving hearts. What does this large identification mean? Not, one would guess, that Werther is a Romantic maniac, swollen with overweening pride, about to fall into the abyss like the original Son of the Morning. He is, rather, the eternal, archetypal son, even usurping the place of the Son, so demanding is the role which he assumes—or which his nature and circumstances have thrust upon him—in his human relationships.

Lotte, both before and after her marriage, is more a mother than a fluttering girl or a trembling bride. She is at the very outset surrounded, like a Victorian child-mother in nineteenth-century novels and paintings, by eight brothers and sisters. Kindly, intelligent (she reads Goldsmith), avant-garde in her taste (she sighs the name of the *Sturm und Drang* writer Klopstock during a tempest), controlled and calm when others whimper in fright, she is a leader as well in the festivities, the establisher of arrangement at the dance. Fresh,

---

42. P. 151. "O Lotte! Ich gehe voran! gehe zu meinem Vater, zu deinem Vater. Dem will ich's klagen, und er wird mich trösten, bis du kommst" (6:117). Werther is here quoting Christ's post-Resurrection words to Mary Magdalen regarding his Ascension: "I ascend unto my Father, and your Father" (John 20:17). The original of course contains the same echo of the German Bible, which reads: "Ich fahre auf zu meinem Vater, und zu eurem Vater."

43. P. 113. "Mein Gott! mein Gott! warum hast du mich verlassen?" (6:86).

young, healthy, she nevertheless likes older people and is liked by them. In her relations with Werther she is more often like an older woman than a beloved. She gives him sweets as though he were her little boy, and Werther kneels before her, like another Rousseau; toward her white form he stretches out his arms, like the Blakean child toward a lamb. Until the climax she remains sacred, untouchable, an "angel," as she is obsessively called by him and others.[44]

The climax of this relationship—a passionate embrace, the only one in the novel—is followed by a gory suicide, which would perhaps be considered sensational and insufficiently motivated had Werther loved conventionally. But as a member of an Oedipal triangle, he has violated a dark taboo big with vengeance, and he must reject himself with finality. And Lotte too must reject him—with as much finality. She brushes the dust from the pistols owned by Albert and hands them to Werther's servant. Instruments of death belonging to the "father" are transmitted by the "mother" to an Oedipally infatuated boy, who uses them to remove himself from the "family" in the most decisive way imaginable. On the eve of his act Werther cries out: "Sin? . . . I am punishing myself for it. . . . I shall go before you! . . . And see your mother! I shall see her, shall find her, ah, and pour out my whole heart to her! Your mother, your image."[45] In love-sensibility from Shakespeare to Rousseau and Keats, immortality is regarded as a prolongation of the present—but without pain, frustration, and death. And so Werther projects onto a future beyond the grave the same image he has adored here and gives to it and indeed to the whole configuration in which it grew up and flowered the ultimate sanction of the Heavenly Father.

Exaltation of the maternal, the sisterly, the childlike lies at the heart of pre-Romantic delicacy, and Goethe continues to exploit the theme—with modifications—in some of his greatest poetry and fiction. Such delicacy is also present in English fictions that immediately preceded *Werther,* notably in Mackenzie's *Man of Feeling* (1771), in which the bland and bashful lovemaking, if so it can be called, seems somehow smothered by an unseen maternal presence, and also in the same author's *Man of the World* (1773), in which the unwitting incest almost committed is by no means regarded with horror or even disapproval. In Diderot's first play, *Le fils naturel* (published 1757; produced 1771) the benevolent, melancholy, dutiful, sentimental hero Dorval

44. For passages in which Lotte is called an angel or appears strikingly angelic, see the English translation, pp. 28, 53, and the German original, 6:19, 39. It is interesting to note that while Albert addresses Lotte with the formal *Sie,* she uses *Du,* in return, the pronoun that she and Werther employ reciprocally. See p. 77 of the translation; 6:58 of the original.

45. P. 151. "Sünde? . . . ich strafe mich dafür; . . . Ich gehe voran! . . . Deine Mutter sehen! ich werde sie sehen, werde sie finden, ach, und vor ihr mein ganzes Herz ausschütten! Deine Mutter, dein Ebenbild" (6:117).

loves and is loved by an orphan, who is revealed to be his half-sister just in time to prevent the consummation of an incestuous love. Thus incest, which was the *haut goût* of picaresque stories and tales of travel, is also prominent, though sometimes slightly disguised, in sentimental drama and fiction.[46] It would therefore, as previous discussion has also shown, be a serious mistake to regard the exploitation of this theme as a peculiarly Romantic preoccupation, although it is true that writers of the early nineteenth century made it more obvious, lurid, and appealing. In discussing Fielding I suggested that this theme might have been introduced for reasons of sensationalism, a consideration that could of course be relevant here too. But evidence mounts that late eighteenth-century sensibility found incest and proto-incest congenial and seems often to have been stimulated by the idea of consanguinity. Of all stages of human society—the family, the tribe, the aggregation to protect property, the state—the earliest and most primitive (that is, the family) is the most productive of sentiment. Such at least were the views of James Macpherson in introducing the Ossianic poem *Temora* (1763): "As the [family] is formed on nature, so...it is the most disinterested and noble" (p. xii). We recall that before the passionate embrace of Werther and Lotte, their spirits are melted by reading the wailing cadences of Ossian that describe dead young heroes mourned by mothers and sisters in a misty landscape. It was not always so; at one time Werther admired the clear, bright, worldly, sunny Homer. Not only Ossian replaces Homer; *Hamlet* too, with its famous triangle and its heartrending frustration of the life and loves of a delicate, poetic, melancholy hero, constantly lurks behind the images and scenes of Goethe's novel.[47] There is much, then, in the sensibility of Goethe's age and in the literature that influenced it to account for the stress on the familial that I have made the central feature of my interpretation.

Final emphasis should fall not on this, however, but on the larger and more fundamental sensibility that includes it. What Werther prizes in himself more

46. J. M. S. Tompkins, *The Popular Novel in England, 1770–1800* (1932; reprint, Lincoln: University of Nebraska Press, 1961), pp. 62–65. Even philosophers and theologians discussed incest. In 1785 the influential and respected William Paley reveals that his abhorrence of adultery and fornication is greater than his aborrence of incest. Fear of incest should be inculcated early, not apparently because of any evil in a close degree of kinship, but in order to "preserve chastity in families and betwixt persons of different sexes." He closes his discussion by citing the permissive laws of Egypt, Athens, and Chaldea. *The Principles of Moral and Political Philosophy* (London, 1785), pp. 260–61.

47. *Werther* echoes *Hamlet* in at least the following passages: p. 115 ff. (original, 6:88 ff.), where the crazed man gathering flowers in winter recalls Ophelia; Albert's contemplated banishment of Werther, which recalls Claudius's removal of Hamlet from England (p. 127; original, 6:97); and the parallels in melancholy, sensitiveness, and maternal orientation between the two heroes. If it can be proved that Goethe's was an Oedipal reading of *Hamlet*—as seems likely from our interpretation of the novel—then Freud and Ernest Jones have been strikingly anticipated.

than intelligence, artistic ability, or imagination, is his *coeur sensible:* he complains that the Prince, a candid and simple person whom the hero by no means dislikes, "prizes my intelligence and my talents more than he does this heart, which is after all my sole pride, which is the only source of everything I have, of all my force, all my bliss, and all my misery. Oh, anyone can know what I know—only I possess my heart."[48] No further evidence is needed to show that the largest affiliation of *Werther* is not nascent Romanticism or German *Sturm und Drang* but the whole development of Western sentiment, with its profound emphasis upon the human affections.

"Sense and Sensibility"

Two anomalies arise from using Jane Austen's *Sense and Sensibility* as the last literary work to be discussed at length in a study of Restoration and eighteenth-century love. The first concerns the date: commenced in late 1797, the novel was not published until 1811, a year that could be said, very approximately, to divide the first from the second generation of Romantics. Still, if the time is not right, the content is; and it must be remembered that Austen's sensibility was actually formed by writers of the eighteenth century— Richardson (including the Richardson of *Sir Charles Grandison*),[49] William Cowper, and Samuel Johnson. The second anomaly arises from the fact that the spirit of Jane Austen is, in one dimension, comic, and I have hitherto largely excluded from consideration the witty comedies and satires that constitute one of the glories of our period. But exceptions have been made, for some comic works—by Etherege, Congreve, Swift, and Pope—have been discussed; and now a large one must be made for *Sense and Sensibility*. The very title words will suggest why. It is also useful, after what Frederick Pottle has called a "shift of sensibility"[50] has taken place, to see how a rational and categorizing mind responds to the earlier clichés and stereotypes.

Had I been concerned with the inheritors of the spirit of Shakespeare's Benedick and Beatrice—with the witty couples of Restoration comedy and the plays of Sheridan and Goldsmith—then *Pride and Prejudice* would have been a fitting choice, with its sophisticated and highly verbal lovers whose initial

48. P. 97. "Auch schätzt er meinen Verstand und meine Talente mehr als dies Herz, das doch mein einziger Stolz ist, das ganz allein die Quelle von allem ist, aller Kraft, aller Seligkeit und alles Elendes. Ach, was ich weiss, kann jeder wissen—mein Herz habe ich allein" (6:74).

49. The draft of a play by Jane Austen has recently come to light, perhaps written about 1800. It is entitled "Sir Charles Grandison or The Happy Man, a Comedy," and is a free adaptation of Richardson's last novel. *New York Times,* 14 Dec. 1977, p. C21.

50. Frederick A. Pottle, *The Idiom of Poetry* (1941; reprint, Bloomington: Indiana University Press, 1963), chap. 1.

faults and preconceptions are deepened and then overcome before Elizabeth and Darcy unite in marriage. Had I concentrated on the theme of
marriage—on the ideal of a prudent and wise union—then my final analysis
might well have been devoted to *Emma,* a novel in which the dangers and
errors of a meddling and obsessive fancy are exposed and marriage to a good
and seasoned man brings rational satisfaction. Had the Gothic element or
Burke's sublime of fear been a central concern instead of a recurring sub-
theme, then *Northanger Abbey,* with its deflation of fearful rapture, would have
been the appropriate text. Or if I had the space to explore the love myth of
Jane Austen herself—that is, the psychological pattern her imagination
formed of mothers, fathers, brothers, sisters—then all the novels, along with
her letters, her juvenilia, and other scraps of writing, would have been grist
for my mill.[51] But for a study of love, passion, and sensibility, only one choice
seems right: the imperfectly plotted, somewhat atypical, but deeply moving
Sense and Sensibility. The most important point that will emerge from our consideration of the characters of Marianne Dashwood (Sensibility) and her sister
Elinor (Sense) is not the antithesis that is developed between them but their
dynamic interaction and its contribution to the final equilibrium.

Coming to this novel from the violence and suggestive morbidity of *Werther*
and the bawdry of *Tristram Shandy,* we might easily allow the considerable
modesty of Jane Austen to obscure the real passion that seethes beneath the
controlled and witty surfaces. To speak generally of the author herself for a
moment, anyone so seemingly cool and rational has of course invited speculation about what is being kept out of sight. The jokes she put into an adolescent
book have been thought to suggest an awareness of homosexuality, and Mary
Crawford's pun in *Mansfield Park* about *"Rears* and *Vices"* has been considered
"anatomically intended." Impropriety has been thought occasionally to break
through the surface and now and then to evade the tendency to repress the
indelicate. In *Sense and Sensibility,* when Willoughby "rapes" a long lock of
Marianne's hair that was "all tumbled down her back," the author perhaps
intends to reveal sexual play, for the couple talk and whisper excitedly as the
ravisher kisses and then secretes the hair. It is not impossible that when
Edward Ferrars, beloved of Elinor, in a moment of suppressed excitement
ruins both a pair of scissors and its sheath by cutting the container to pieces,
he may be guilty of a sexually symbolic gesture. But though such interpretation seems likely, the kind of imagery that invites it occurs most in-

---

51. See Geoffrey Gorer, "The Myth in Jane Austen" in *Art and Psychoanalysis,* ed. William
Phillips (New York: Criterion Books, 1957), pp. 218–25. Gorer's article, which appeared first in
American Imago (1941), attempts to prove that the psychological myth that underlies her novels
(except for the last, *Persuasion,* which rejects it) is a crying out against her love-starved life and
against the father and sisters who starved it.

frequently.[52] More important than suggestive metaphor or trope are the very movement of the plot and the juxtaposition of characters in certain intellectual and physical attitudes by which the author succeeds in creating an intensity that suggests love and desire. Whoever regards her as cold and unfeeling has not responded to the structural and colloquial excitements of Jane Austen. But modest she surely is—a fact that cannot be wondered at in view of the powerful censorship of sex provided by the central Western tradition and in view of the specific inhibitions that Austen's intellectual milieu enforced upon her. I have commented on the trembling modesty of her mentor Cowper; the admired Samuel Johnson excluded from his dictionary many of the basic, necessary, and widely used terms for love and sexuality, particularly if they had a hint of irregularity about them.[53]

   The passion that Marianne conceives for Willoughby and that leads only to frustration and suffering is a deep ravage. It is introduced as "violence of affliction" (p. 72), it threatens institutional life, it becomes a screaming "agony" (p. 158), it settles into gloomy dejection, it develops into what is called a putrid fever but is really a psychosomatic state; and if the girl had not survived, her death could have been regarded as suicide. "Had I died," says Marianne, as she returns to health and sanity, "it would have been self-destruction" (p. 303). Why does Austen call this "potent" drive toward love and death "sensibility" (p. 71)? Surely in part because she perceives that although the revolution in feeling could be accompanied by the silly and harmless manifestations she satirizes (love of ruins, Gothic settings, dead leaves, smoking chimneys, and brawling brats), it was also potentially cruel, unsocial, selfish, dogmatic, and harsh. It could lead to distortion of observation, and Marianne Dashwood (like Emma Woodhouse) sees life and nature through the skewing spectacles of fancy. The wish has become master, and sense observation ceases to be trustworthy. More important is the dethronement of reason and its replacement by that "hunger of imagination which preys incessantly upon life" (Johnson, *Rasselas,* chap. 32). Fanny Burney describes the heroine of *Camilla* in a situation not unlike that of Marianne, in

52. For a discussion of the passages that I have mentioned and some others, see Brigid Brophy, "Jane Austen and the Stuarts," in *Critical Essays on Jane Austen,* ed. B. C. Southam (London: Routledge & Kegan Paul, 1968), esp. p. 25; Tony Tanner's introduction to the Penguin English Library edition of *Sense and Sensibility* (Baltimore, 1969), p. 18; and Alice Chandler, "'A Pair of Fine Eyes': Jane Austen's Treatment of Sex" in *Studies in the Novel* 7 (Spring 1975): 88–103. For the passages in *Sense and Sensibility* referred to, see the Oxford University Press edition of the novel (London, 1970), ed. Claire Lamont and James Kinsley, pp. 51, 315. See also p. 84. Subsequent references to the novel come from this edition.

53. Johnson, for example, omits these words entirely: "buggery, " "clitoris," "mastupration," "masturbation," "penis," "onanism," "paederasty," "sodomy"; he gives no hint of sexual meanings in "emission," "orgasm," "pollution," or "sense," though these were present in eighteenth-century usage.

which "the ardour of her imagination . . . shook her Judgment from its . . . unsteady seat, and left her at the mercy of wayward Sensibility—that delicate, but irregular power."[54] And not only writers in the school of Johnson (in *Rambler* 28 he juxtaposes sensibility and "perturbation") found it a destructive emotion. In *The Mysteries of Udolpho* Mrs. Radcliffe has the father warn the heroine of the real dangers of heightened sensibility.[55] William Cowper provided, in his own life and in poems like *The Castaway* and *On the Receipt of My Mother's Picture Out of Norfolk,* a picture of bleeding if not burning sensibility, his heart still freshly wounded over the death of his mother some fifty-three years before.

Over against sensibility, which Austen here as elsewhere associates with the "luxury of a raised, restless, and frightened imagination" (*Northanger Abbey,* chap. 7), the author sets up the character of the heroine, Elinor, who embodies sense. "Sense" must, on the obvious level, refer to the judgment; it was so used in 1783, when that usage was called "popular" by John Murdoch, who also anticipated Austen's title antithesis: he addressed himself to "the sensibility, rather than to the judgment, or what is popularly called the Sense, of the reader."[56] In Austen sense is an attractive quality—dry, witty, given to understatement, clearheaded and clear-eyed, virtuous; it leads to love of cleanliness and comfort and above all to moral responsibility and an unselfishness alive to familial and civic duty. But paradoxically its finest quality is that it possesses feeling—even deep feeling. One of the most endearing qualities of Elinor's character is that she suffers with and for her sister, that she subordinates her own grief at what she thought was the permanent loss of *her* lover, and that the needs of others are regularly placed before her own. It is a rare and touching moment when she learns that her lover has *not* married another—and much inferior—woman but is in fact truly her own:

> But Elinor—How are *her* feelings to be described?—From the moment of learning that Lucy was married to another, that Edward was free, to the moment of his justifying the hopes which had so instantly followed, she was

54. *Camilla* 4: 399. I owe this reference to Patricia Meyer Spacks, "'Ev'ry Woman is at Heart a Rake,'" *Eighteenth-Century Studies* 8 (Fall 1974): 40.

55. 1st ed., 4 vols. (London, 1794), 1:13–14. The enormous fear of heightened sensibilities and warm imagination is attested to in *A Father's Legacy to His Daughters* (Boston, 1794), annexed to Lord Chesterfield's *Principles of Politeness and of Knowing the World,* in which Dr. John Gregory of Edinburgh warns his daughter to "shun, as you would do the most fatal poison, all that species of reading and conversation which warms the imagination, which engages and softens the heart" (p. 128). Even the Marquis de Sade tried to expose the weakness of sensibility and of a "Gothic" imagination in *Justine.* See R. F. Brissenden, "*La Philosophie dans le boudoir*; or, A Young Lady's Entrance into the World" in *Studies in Eighteenth-Century Culture: Irrationalism in the Eighteenth Century,* ed. Harold E. Pagliaro (Cleveland, Ohio: Press of Case Western Reserve University, 1972), p. 119. Brissenden sees parallels between *Justine* and *Sense and Sensibility.*

56. *Pictures of the Heart, Sentimentally Delineated in the Danger of the Passions, an Allegorical Tale,* 2 vols. (London, 1783), preface.

everything by turns but tranquil. But when the second moment had passed, when she found every doubt, every solicitude removed, compared her situation with what so lately it had been,—saw him honourably released from his former engagement, saw him instantly profiting by the release, to address herself and declare an affection as tender, as constant as she had ever supposed it to be,—she was oppressed, she was overcome by her own felicity;—and happily disposed as is the human mind to be easily familiarized with any change for the better, it required several hours to give sedateness to her spirits, or any degree of tranquillity to her heart. [Pp. 318–19]

The language is warm with emotion, even passion; and we are to understand from so important an ingredient in her character that the sister who possesses *sense* does not thereby become cold, dry, unemotional. Indeed, the title antithesis breaks down under the pressure of life and experience. Sense becomes sensibility, and sensibility becomes sense. Like all of Austen's admirable characters, Elinor—the first to be in love, the first to be rewarded in marriage—indisputably possesses sensibility too. It is no exaggeration to call her a Woman of Feeling in love who ought to be placed squarely in the tradition I have been tracing. Austen is of course not opposed to feeling, only to the excess of it, only to lack of control, only to the abandonment of the whole being to its dominance.[57]

While showing that sense, to be human and attractive, must possess sensibility, Austen shows, conversely, that people with sensibility are very much worth caring about and worth redeeming from their excesses. She is no moral absolutist, pitting black against white, but a subtle explorer of the nuances of feelings and their interpenetration. Marianne's faults spring from an excess of virtues: she is open, frank, fresh, beautiful, alert, clever. And her lover, even after he has committed not only follies but a crime, is conceded to be handsome and talented, possessing "a disposition naturally open and honest, and a feeling, affectionate temper" (p. 290). Perhaps the greatest tribute sense pays to sensibility is that Elinor feels keenly the powerful attractions of Willoughby—even after he has almost destroyed her sister, even after his

57. See Stuart M. Tave, "Sensibility," in *Some Words of Jane Austen* (Chicago: University of Chicago Press, 1973), pp. 74–115, and Ruth apRoberts, "*Sense and Sensibility*, or Growing Up Dichotomous," *Nineteenth-Century Fiction* 30 (Dec. 1975): 351–65, to which I am indebted for the interesting and relevant information that the words of the title were translated into the French words *raison et sensibilité*, both being related to love by the subtitle, *où les deux manières d'aimer* (p. 354). The present chapter places Jane Austen in what its title calls "The Aftermath of Sensibility." It was a Rousseauist aftermath. Lionel Trilling does not argue in *Sincerity and Authenticity* for an influence from Rousseau upon Austen (the only work of his that we know her to have read was *La nouvelle Héloïse*), but he does argue for "an affinity, a common concern for the defence of the 'honest soul', with its definitive quality of single-mindedness and sincerity" (Cambridge Mass.: Harvard University Press, 1972), p. 72.

villainy with a young girl has been made known, even while he is expressing a still ardent love for Marianne which for a married man "it was not even innocent to indulge" (p. 292). For if that marvelous scene, when Willoughby bursts in upon Elinor to find out how Marianne is and to explain his action, means anything at all, it must mean that she is physically drawn to him:

> Willoughby, he, whom only half an hour ago she had abhorred as the most worthless of men, Willoughby, in spite of all his faults, excited a degree of commiseration for the sufferings produced by them, which made her think of him as now separated for ever from her family with a tenderness, a regret, rather in proportion, as she soon acknowledged within herself—to his wishes than to his merits. She felt that his influence over her mind was heightened by circumstances which ought not in reason to have weight; by that person of uncommon attraction, that open, affectionate, and lively manner which it was no merit to possess; and by that still ardent love for Marianne, which it was not even innocent to indulge. But she felt that it was so, long, long before she could feel his influence less. [P. 292]

This man she cannot get out of her mind. She "for a moment wished Willoughby a widower" (p. 294); and though no selfish thought of possessing him for herself is allowed to arise from the unconscious, Elinor does desire momentarily that he might be a member of the family, a husband to her sister whom he has wronged so grievously. But then she returns to what becomes the final solution and the concluding equilibrium of the novel, in which the dashing Willoughby is neither condignly punished nor transformed into a guilty Byronic hero. "He lived to exert, and frequently to enjoy himself" (p. 334).

Sense and Sensibility, then, is no simple antithesis of light and dark, good and evil, honor and love, reason and emotion, the spirit and the flesh. It is perhaps in part owing to the forces that developed out of Dryden and grew in power throughout the eighteenth century that so witty, so prudential an author as Austen felt, like her mentor Samuel Johnson, the influences of domestic pathos, the tears of sensibility, and the civilizing passions of love. She remained unsentimentally loyal to right reason, which is never allowed to extinguish the fires of feeling. And the struggle of these contraries, in which qualities on the one side mix with and energize qualities on the other, is perhaps closer to Blake and Coleridge than we have sometimes realized. I have reserved to the last the best piece of evidence that Austen transcended the antithesis of her own title or any simple moralistic attitude deriving from it. This evidence is that she enters so deeply—mostly through the sympathetic responses of her heroine and *raisonneuse*—into the passionate and suffering heart of Marianne and therefore into the violent emotion of love itself. George Moore appreciated the power of that identification and of that "supreme scene" when Willoughby rejects Marianne and makes that rejection known to the stupefied girl: "Miss Austen gives us all the agony of passion the human heart can feel; she was the first; and none has written the scene that we all desire to write as truthfully as she has; . . .it is here that we find the burning human heart in English prose narrative for the first, and, alas, for the last time."[58] It is a tribute to Austen that her ability to portray the passions should betray another novelist into so striking an exaggeration of her power and uniqueness.

Marianne does not, to be sure, marry the handsome lover but the much older, the very decent Colonel Brandon, "who still sought the constitutional safe guards of a flannel waistcoat" (p. 333). Even so, marriage is in the end more than equilibrium and stable repose: "Marianne could never love by halves; and her whole heart became, in time, as much devoted to her husband, as it had once been to Willoughby" (p. 334). So Venus, if we remember the myth of Cupid and Psyche, does after all come to bless with her own presence the wedding of her son and is fully reconciled to her daughter-in-law.

Epilogue: "Les liaisons dangereuses"

But it had not always been so. Though Milton's Adam and Eve established a pattern of friendship based on sexuality that became the sacramental center of marriage, that pristine bliss was seldom achieved again. We do see approximations of it in some of Dryden's plays; in Congreve's *Mourning Bride;* in Steele's essays, letters, and plays; in *Sir Charles Grandison* and *Amelia;* in the precarious happiness of Rousseau's Clarens; and now, at the very end, in Austen. Most such marital fulfillments come at or close to or even after the endings of the works in which they are portrayed. I have been chiefly concerned, however, with the time of Venus's persecutions of Psyche—with the obstacles to her marriage and even with disordered, perverted, thwarted, unrealized love. Such tragic or pathetic abortions of realized love we encounter in Otway, Rowe, Lillo, Sterne, Goethe. But all through these shine glimpses of the Miltonic ideal, sometimes for no other purpose than to make the tragic loss of Eden more poignant and to show how pitifully short of the ideal human substitutions fall. Boswell, whose life, one is tempted to say, embodied almost as many lapses from the ideal as the entire tradition we have been studying, nevertheless lifted the banner high: "The primary intention of Marriage is that most perfect gratification of love and friendship between the sexes." He also said that "there has perhaps been no period when Marriage

58. *Avowals* (New York: Boni & Liveright, 1926), pp. 50–51. I owe this reference to Claire Lamont in the introduction to the Oxford edition of *Sense and Sensibility*, p. xxi.

was more the general topick of conversation than at present."[59] Why should this be so? Certainly in part because the institution was about to be shaken by powerful and hostile forces that Boswell had the wit to discern in their early rising. His comment was made on the eve of the French Revolution and less than a generation before the powerful attack on the institution mounted by some of the Romantics.

But these future revolutionary shocks do not explain the preoccupation with marriage, nor does the soberer skepticism of some of the *philosophes* about marital value. The mid-century debate about marriage and the new restrictions contained in Lord Hardwicke's Marriage Act of 1753—restrictions designed to stabilize unions and to further the propertied interests of the propertied classes—did turn the attention of journalists, polemicists, and other writers to important social changes.[60] But the really fundamental reason for the profound concern with marriage was profound concern with love itself, with the possibilities for human happiness in this life, with the enlargement of human potential, with its tragic frustration. Surely one tribute to the power of the movement we have been studying is that, with some modifications, love-sensibility was adopted by the Romantic movement in England and on the Continent. For example, when Shelley's Prometheus arises to bring redemption, he does so in a pitying, loving, and forgiving act of free will that Dryden's Almanzor would have understood fully.

It would be a mistake, therefore, to conclude this literary investigation with exclusive emphasis upon marriage—upon the domestic and the purely sentimental. For Etherege, Congreve, Pope, Swift—and, I might add, Richardson's witty Lovelace and the jesting Sterne—have also been prominent in the story. They have been so not only because they themselves were touched by sensibility but also because they either reached formulations important to an understanding of love or their work bore powerful implications for the expansion of its semantic significance or its development in human culture. The names mentioned in this paragraph introduce laughter and humor and lead us to consider the relations of the judging wit to the concerns of the heart. Can one discover deep relations within the eighteenth century between wit and sensibility, and dare one suggest a priority between them? If so, which should be considered the more fundamental: the tears or the laughter, the emotional revolution that accompanied the opening of the *coeur sensible* or the consolidating ethical insights that sprang from the witty, rational mind? Richardson's Lovelace, that larger-than-life character who embodied both wit

---

59. *The Hypochondriack*, ed. Margery Bailey, 2 vols. (Stanford, Cal.: Stanford University Press, 1928), 2:71 (no. 43, April 1781), 54–55 (no. 41, Feb. 1781).
    60. Stone, *Family*, pp. 35–37.

and sensibility, may provide guidance. In a penetrating and revelatory letter, he says that his levity is owing to a deep concern: "I struggle and struggle, and try to buffet down my cruel reflections as they rise: and when I cannot, I am forced, as I have often said, to try to make myself laugh, that I may not cry; for one or other I must do."

He then goes on to show how different his conquests of his psychic tumults are from the "apathy nonsense" of Seneca, Epictetus, and the Stoics. The modern character "in the very heart of the storm" is able "to quaver out a horse-laugh. . . . This high point of philosophy, to laugh and be merry in the midst of the most soul-harrowing woes, when the heartstrings are just bursting asunder, was reserved for thy Lovelace" (4:262–63). The passage is a haunting anticipation of Laurence Sterne, who frisked as death pursued him and who said in a letter to Garrick, "I laugh 'till I cry, and in the same tender moments *cry 'till I laugh*" (*Letters,* p. 163). Can there be any doubt that in both these transcendences of Stoical control the suffering is basic and the laughter is compensatory and secondary? It may not be far wrong to say that sensibility—not the cliché term of much superficial thought but the ravaging passion that Austen explored in the sufferings of Marianne—is the deep current in Restoration-to-Romantic culture, and not the more structured formulations of wit and prudence.

A perspective on this elusive but fascinating problem may come if we consider briefly and finally the copresence of sentiment and wit in Choderlos de Laclos's *Liaisons dangereuses* (1782), a great novel which brings to a culminating death both aspects of the century and leaves us with a strong hint as to which of these is the more elemental and basic. The first part of the novel develops the witty graces of the Vicomte de Valmont and the Marquise de Merteuil, who represent an apotheosis of the *ancien régime* values of reason, social polish, prudence, brilliance of verbal style; so great is their charm that we almost wish them well. But their great aim is vengeful seduction, and their first victim is a simple, sentimental, convent-raised *ingénue*, Cécile, who is easily degraded from the embraces of her true lover to the experienced, calculating, and clever sensuality of Valmont, abetted by his equally brilliant colleague in seduction, the hypocritical Marquise. At first confederated worldliness seems to win the day. But in the second part of the novel Valmont, acting alone and like Lovelace determined to debauch a saint, turns his attention to Mme de Tourvel, the Présidente, pious, beautiful, loyal in marriage. Here, in a true confrontation of old sex and new sensibility, sex seems at first to win. But in the fall of the good Présidente, three powerful ends are achieved. First, the alliance of the two witty sinners is completely shattered, and each goes to an ignominious fate, he to death and she to a kind of life-in-death. Second, the Présidente has suceeded, though this fact is quite unknown to her, in opening Valmont's heart to true, sentimental love, thus making inevitable a split with his quondam witty confederate in crime. Valmont does seem, before he dies, to have been touched by a kind of secular grace, mediated to him by Mme de Tourvel. Third, the broken and seemingly defeated Présidente rises to true humanity, achieves disinterested love—an almost Christlike kind of love for someone unworthy of her, her debaucher—and in the end, by her mystery, her uniqueness, her inexplicable power, dominates the landscape. The spiritual dignity the Présidente ultimately achieves should not obscure the harrowing completeness of her fall— her feelings go first, then her body; and then her mind is given over to complete illusion. It is a fall worthy of a Clarissa or Julie, so deep that it makes one see what their corruption might have been like had Richardson or Rousseau allowed it to happen. But if one wishes to determine priorities between wit and sentiment in this *fin de mouvement* masterpiece, one need not hesitate. Both sides fall; but wit, for all its brilliance, retires in hatred and recrimination, at civil war within itself, while sentiment goes to its grave in spiritual triumph. The conclusion that arose from considering the combination of reason and emotion in both Lovelace and Sterne is borne out by their clashing opposition in Laclos's novel. Feeling, guided by value and capable of achieving love, is both more basic and more permanent. Perhaps we can now say with some confidence that the deepest if not the most attractive legacy of the Age of Reason is the *coeur sensible*.

11. Love in Painting and Music
An Appended Survey

A STUDENT OF UNIVERSAL THEMES in the literature of England during the eighteenth century feels impelled to consider the sister arts of painting and music. That country witnessed the establishment of a pioneering school of painters; many of them worked under the direct inspiration of literary masters, who were themselves often either painters or very closely associated with practicing visual artists. The aesthetics of *ut pictura poesis* was uninterruptedly influential, and Alexander Pope, himself a painter, said that images were reflected from art to art.[1] Among such images are those related to the theme of love. If we consider the culture of the Continent as well, we are struck with the fact that during the eighteenth century music reached one of its apogees. No greater composers than Bach, Mozart, and Haydn have existed in any period; and if we add Handel and Gluck to the list, it becomes apparent that love is one of the central themes of operatic and vocal music as it is of literature and painting. The greatest masters of sensibility were extremely close to music. Rousseau was himself a performer, composer, and theoretician, keenly interested in the history and present state of the art; and Richardson, through his characters (particularly that of his paragon, Sir Charles Grandison), expresses deeply spiritual approval of Handel and his settings of sacred and secular texts. It was in fact the peculiar genius of that distinguished composer to marry great English texts to a music fully worthy of them, sometimes indeed surpassing them. Pope hailed him as a "Giant," come to England "to stir, to rouze, to shake the Soul," and he called the music Handel wrote or superintended "ravishing."[2] Handel set important

1.   The verse and sculpture bore an equal part,
          And Art reflected images to Art.
                ["To Mr. Addison, Occasioned by his Dialogues on Medals," 51–52]
          Smit with the love of Sister-arts we came,
          And met congenial, mingling flame with flame; . . .
          How oft' our slowly-growing works impart,
          While images reflect from art to art?
                                    ["Epistle to Mr. Jervas," 13–14, 19–20]
The Twickenham Edition of the Poems of Alexander Pope, vol. 1, *Minor Poems,* ed. Norman Ault and John Butt (London: Methuen, 1954), pp. 156, 204.

2. *The Dunciad* (B), 4:65–67; *Correspondence,* ed. Sherburn, 1:338 and n.4 (letter to Martha Blount, March 1716?). In the letter Pope does not mention Handel by name but praises the music at Lord Burlington's estate, which was in the charge of the composer.

texts by two authors most prominent in this study of love, Milton and Dryden, thus providing interpretative glosses, as it were, on literary passages and episodes that stand at the fountainhead of sensibility.

The visual and musical arts are capable of making precisely the same contribution to the important movement of "affective individualism" as literature: they at once reflect reality and mythologize it. A common social reality of revolutionary force can help to explain the consonance at the deepest level that characterizes all the arts of the period when expressing love. Artists of every kind were responding to a dynamic and popular theme—a fact that had important implications for the state of the arts. The growth and prestige during the eighteenth century of such forms as the novel, the *conversation galante,* the domestic genre painting, and the continuing and even greater triumphs of the lyric opera are doubtless in part explainable because each of these was peculiarly congenial to eros and sensibility.

Love in Painting: An Informal Overview

It is the genius of painting to be vivid, and that vividness can be relied on to bring to light many of the obscurer corners of the human response to love. Viewed from the perspective of my topic in its profounder, even unconscious aspects, the painting of the eighteenth century can be seen to be a more subtle and complex phenomenon than it is sometimes taken to be. There is a sentimental, or romantic, side to Sir Joshua Reynolds—a strain in him of "pathetic" softness, perhaps even of morbidity.[3] Most of his portrayals of children belong to his attractive and sunny side and are healthy, humorous, good-natured—and very English. But his renditions of childhood can also have suggestions of eccentricity, psychological depth, or even perversion, particularly when myth or history is invoked in those works Reynolds called his "fancy pictures." Consider, for example, his *Saint John in the Wilderness* (1776), a painting in the Wallace Collection. Saint John is very special indeed; he is not a mature, angry prophet but an almost nude, smooth-skinned boy who sits by a lamb. His "sweet round mouth" seems formed rather to sing "Ha, Ha, He!" than to proclaim "Repent ye, for the kingdom of heaven is at hand."[4]

---

3. See Chauncey B. Tinker's Charles Eliot Norton lecture, "Reynolds: Romantic Tendencies" in *Painter and Poet: Studies in the Literary Relations of English Painting* (Cambridge, Mass.: Harvard University Press, 1938), pp. 46–69. Elie Faure refers to the *"songes niais"* of Reynolds and calls this side of him perverse. See R. H. Wilenski, *English Painting,* 4th ed. (London: Faber & Faber, 1964), pp. 146, 152.

4. Matt. 3:2. See Blake's "Laughing Song" in *Songs of Innocence.* The composition, with the delicate face and the raised arm pointing upward, recalls Leonardo's and Guido Reni's Baptists even as it anticipates Blake's, though in none of these cases is the preaching forerunner of Christ

Saint John the boy may be no more than sentimental, but Reynolds's *Robin Goodfellow, or Puck* (Earl Fitzwilliam, 1789) seems to produce overtones of perversion. In a densely wooded landscape, a baby sits on a toadstool with a napkin under him that almost covers his loins. His stomach is fat, his head is almost macrocephalic, he has ass's ears; and his small eyes, which look almost drunken, are apparently intended, with the somewhat crinkly mouth, to express the mirth that Shakespeare gives him. It is not impossible that Reynolds has created a monstrous joke—that the boy Puck recalls the baby Bacchus or is a parody of the famous Silenus by Valerio da Settignano in the Boboli Gardens, where a chubby-legged, drunken old man rides a turtle, his enormous belly and his *membrum virile* thrust out toward the spectator along with his gesturing left hand. If so, it is clear that Shakespearean joy has been here compromised by an aged demon possessing the body of a somewhat animalized child, and the effect is chilling.[5] When Reynolds turned to the myth of Cupid and Psyche in 1789, he did not go to the sentimental heart of the story, like Raphael, or to its sensual core, like Giulio Romano; instead, choosing that most popular episode when Psyche, against Cupid's precise and stern orders, holds up a light to reveal her husband asleep, he portrays not a mature man capable of performing husbandly duties but a mere boy in slumber. Can this child, we ask, have possibly given Psyche the sexual delights she had been enjoying night after night? There is some iconographic precedence for this, but once again Reynolds disturbs us by a reduction to childhood that is even more unusual than the "puerilizing" of the prophetic Baptist. When Reynolds treats the venerable baroque theme of the death of Dido (pl. 10), he is also surprising. Gone is the heroic act performed by Rubens's queen (pl. 6). Dido, already dead, lies stretched out. One nude foot appears sexually tensed. The eyes are not yet closed. The mouth, round like that of the Greak tragic mask (an emblem of sexual passion as well as of the theater and

the mere child that Reynolds portrays. Another version of this painting is now in Minneapolis. See Ellis Waterhouse, "A *Child Baptist* by Sir Joshua Reynolds" in *Minneapolis Institute of Arts Bulletin* 57 (1968): 51–53. Ronald Paulson's striking idea that the Reynolds child is the seed of the ideal man, "the general truth from which the man will . . . particularize himself," can be fruitfully applied to many of his children but not, I believe, to Saint John or Puck, where the mature person will, or ought to, reverse what we see in the child. See *Emblem and Expression* (Cambridge, Mass.: Harvard University Press, 1975), p. 90. For a learned discussion of the Child Baptist, see Marilyn Aronberg Lavin, "Giovannino Battista: A Study in Renaissance Symbolism," *Art Bulletin* 37 (June 1955): 85–101; "Giovannino Battista: A Supplement," ibid. 43 (Dec. 1961): 319–26. I have no evidence that Reynolds knew this tradition, and nothing that Lavin reproduces or discusses looks like a direct source.

5. Reynold's oil on panel, painted for Alderman Boydell's gallery, is now owned by T. W. Fitzwilliam of Milton Park. It is reproduced as pl. 294A in Ellis K. Waterhouse, *Reynolds* (London: Kegan Paul, Trench Trubner & Co., 1941) and as pl. 24 in Raymond Lister, *British Romantic Art* (London: G. Bell & Sons, 1973). Lister calls this painting "undeniably Romantic" and finds it to have "overtones of perversion" (p. 49).

the muses), looks like frozen ecstasy. Above all, because the head tends to hang back, the breast is thrust out almost assertively. But anatomical reasons do not explain the insistent and pervasive rhythms of arrested sexuality, as though this were not a postmortem but a postcoital rigor. Reynolds has sexualized the model Romano gave him of a chastely clad sleeping Psyche, and in what Edgar Wind has called his "greatest attempt at the truly 'grand' style" he shows that he was not untouched by sex and sensibility. Since Fuseli was influenced by Reynolds's figure of Dido in creating his *Nightmare,* we should not be surprised that the Romantic painter greatly admired the older work. He called it "supreme beauty in the jaws of death" and said that he himself had observed "the throes which it cost the author before it emerged into beauty, assumed the shape, or was divided into the powerful masses of chiar'oscuro which strikes us now."[6]

If even Reynolds occasionally reflects both romantic passion and perversion, we can expect to find it often enough in eighteenth-century art. Toward the close of the century, one theme frequently repeated was the origin of painting, as it was adapted from a story by Pliny to endow the art itself with erotic beginnings. David Allan (1773; National Gallery of Scotland), Wright of Derby (National Gallery, Washington); and Alexander Runciman among many others exploited the theme. Runciman's rendition (pl. 11) in particular brings out the love implications: a youth with long hair and effeminate features lies asleep; his profile is reflected on a wall by the shadows that the moonlight causes; those shadows are being traced by a girl in white, whose hand is being guided by Cupid.[7] John Opie also painted ladies in white, and his canvases suggest that we must remove implications of Victorian purity from some eighteenth-century whiteness and that Clarissa even at her most

6. Fuseli is quoted by Nicolas Powell in *Fuseli: The Nightmare* (New York: Viking Press, 1972), p. 68. For Wind's comment and the reproduction and discussion of the source in Romano, see "Borrowed Attitudes in Reynolds and Hogarth," *Journal of the Warburg Institute* 2 (1938): 182–85. For the Cupid and Psyche, see Waterhouse, p. 81 (1789 [179]). For other works by Reynolds that may be touched by the kind of feeling we have noted or that in other ways may be related to the theme of this book, see Waterhouse, *Reynolds,* pls. 124, 137, 141B, 228A, 229, 242B. A peculiarly egregious instance of Reynold's sexualized sensibility appears in *Snake in the Grass, or Love Unbinding the Zone of Beauty* (Tate Gallery), in which Cupid, looking up at his mother, begins to undress her. Venus, covering one half of her face with an upraised arm and a dangling hand—a gesture of extremely unpalatable coyness—looks, not at us, but at Cupid, who, however, is close to the larger of the bare breasts, which have more than a hint of lactation about them. The rhythms of the painting are languorous and seductive. I have spared the reader a reproduction here; but see Wilenski, *English Painting,* pl. 57.

7. Robert Rosenblum has investigated this popular subject, which came from an ancient Greek legend about a Corinthian maiden Dibutade, who, knowing that her lover must depart, traces his silhouette on the wall as a memento of her love. See "The Origin of Painting: A Problem in the Iconography of Romantic Classicism," *Art Bulletin* 39 (Dec. 1957): 279–90. Rosenblum calls the mode of this and other related paintings the "Neoclassic Erotic" in *Transformations in Late Eighteenth Century Art* (Princeton, N.J.: Princeton University Press, 1967), p. 20.

intensely achromatic moments may not be untouched by love-sensibility. Choosing to portray an amorous scene from Thomson's *Seasons* (Damon peeping on his beloved Musidora, who is about to bathe), Opie clothes her in a billowing white dress, as she exposes one breast to view. A similar combination of modesty and display appears in the filmy garment and the partial exposure of *Ariadne* or of *Hobnelia, or the Spell*.[8] So sex and sensibility coexist in a union observable on many an eighteenth-century canvas. The full- and moist-lipped Lady Hamilton, whose mouth so often recalls that of Greuze's girls (see pls. 30, 31), Romney had portrayed as Circe, Calypso, a bacchante, and the Magdalen; but never were the words of my title more patly united than when he portrayed the buxom lady as Sensibility: she looks with mild and longing eyes at the mimosa plant, which the painter's friend William Hayley had suggested as an iconic sign[9] (pl. 12). Earlier I turned to caricature to bring out essential configurations in my theme. Rowlandson penetrated with unfailing instinct to the erotic core of sensibility and did so with vulgar but hilarious effect. On one occasion his Man of Feeling is a don who sits in front of his fire in his academic study, while another don peeps through the Gothic window and observes his friend stroking the bottom of the doxy on his lap.[10] Another scene (pl. 13), which is set out of doors, shows the Man of Feeling, fat, florid, and red-nosed, a copy of Wilkes's *Essay on Woman* emerging from his pocket, with thick sensual lips parted in a hungry leer, caressing the bosom of a pert and pretty country lass. In another indoor scene, this one very shabby, while the bumpkin husband is asleep on the bed, a similarly gross man even more suggestively seduces an overdressed country wife (pl. 14). In all these prints and drawings "feeling" is interpreted with gross physicality, and in the stocky sensualist who personifies it Rowlandson seeks to explode the whole myth of sentimental purity, refinement, and reserve.

Another extremely important association, between the imagination and

8. I have not seen originals of the paintings by Opie, only the photographs in the Henry E. Huntington Art Gallery. I have relied on the data there provided. *Hobnelia* and *Ariadne* remain untraced; *Damon and Musidora* is at Petworth House.

9. William Hayley, *The Life of George Romney, Esq.* (Chichester, 1809), pp. 120–21.

10. This hand-colored aquatint is at the Art Institute of Chicago. Rowlandson turns his devastatingly scabrous attention to another cant word of *sensibilité* in his "Sympathy I" and "Sympathy II," reproduced as pls. 46 and 47 in *The Amorous Illustrations of Thomas Rowlandson*, with an introduction by Gert Schiff (n.p.: Cythera Press, 1969). James Gillray responded with reductive humor to at least two of the topics that have been discussed earlier. In a vigorous ink drawing, at the Huntington, *Eloisa and Abelard,* Gillray creates a fat and grossly featured woman—one panel portrays the tumult in a Vestal's veins and in the other he places a veiled and starched nun to portray the morning delights of the groves. In *Dido in Despair* his insulting pencil portrays a very fat Lady Hamilton, caught in a swirl of bedclothes, looking out the window for Lord Nelson, who has "gone to fight the Frenchmen, to lose t'other arm and eye." T. S. R. Boase reproduces the essential detail of this color print at the British Museum as pl. 4b of *English Art: 1800–1870* (Oxford: Clarendon Press, 1959); see also p. 57 and n.3.

sexuality, appears with suggestive force in the visual arts. Many irate fathers of young girls in drama and fiction reveal that reading was considered particularly stimulating to the amorous fancy. Carle Van Loo, in his fine painting *La lecture espagnole* (Hermitage, Leningrad), uses the book to illustrate total absorption in the presence of an outside stimulus.[11] Two handsome girls listen, *en plein air,* as a man in Spanish dress reads from a book. As a younger girl releases her pet bird to fly while attached to a string, kite fashion, a young nurse or maid drops her sewing, either to listen herself to what must be a story of romantic love or to watch its potentially dangerous effect on the imagination of two girls, whose expression and attitude show the deepest interest and concern. Rowlandson also broaches this theme in *The Force of Imagination* (see the two pen and watercolor drawings in the Huntington). As two people look through a door in amazement at what they see, a soldier kneels on one knee and clasps his hands as if in prayer before a teatable, which is not, however, the object of his perverse adoration. That is a hall tree on which the infatuated youth has hung a nightgown, a nightcap, and a plume which he has rummaged from a nearby trunk.

Painting, as an important and accurate analogue of what was happening in literature and society, records the obverse side of Edenic love. Milton's allegory of Satan, Sin, and Death (severely criticized by Samuel Johnson—perhaps on the unconscious level because it portrayed the narcissistic and incestuous sins which the lexicographer preferred to ignore) was the most widely illustrated episode from *Paradise Lost.*[12] It cannot be said that designs by Hayman, Burney (who makes Satan and Sin look like brother and sister), Barry (who creates a scene of great power), Romney (who did only sketches of the allegory), Blake (whose renditions are classics), and Fuseli (who humanizes Death and makes Sin an erotic link with both him and Satan) penetrate very deeply into Milton's suggestions of perversion, though such morbidity is present in later Romantic art. The most important response of the eighteenth century to Milton's allegory was to forget Milton's horror at the sins of consanguinity and similarity. In Hogarth's *Satan, Sin, and Death,* while Satan is a stereotype of evil (though a fairly human one) and Death a well-drawn skeleton with flamelike hair, Sin is sweet faced, white skinned, lovely in breast and neck, and even gentle, as she looks longingly at her father-consort. She has become a Woman of Feeling; she might even represent Clarissa caught in a painful conflict between her father and her seducer. Could eighteenth-century painting have grasped Milton's central point, that narcissistic love and

11. This painting is reproduced as fig. 10 in Michael Fried's "Absorption: A Master Theme in Eighteenth-Century French Painting and Criticism," *Eighteenth-Century Studies* 9 (Winter 1975–76): 139–77.

12. See Johnson, Life of Milton, in *Works* (1825), 7:137; Marcia R. Pointon, *Milton & English Art,* pp. 20, 48, 57–59, 88, 90, 104, 117–18, 123, 126, 144, 146.

love of sameness were dangerously related? Hardly—since painting, even pornographic painting, was too vivid a medium to permit direct treatment of what was regarded as perversion. And yet on this subject painting—though it can never be so explicit as the work of a Casanova, who loved to expatiate on his strong erotic attachments to the bodies of men and women, boys and girls alike—can be suggestive and revelatory. Ganymede, the shepherd boy swept up into the heavens by Jupiter for his own delectation, was made popular by Michelangelo, Correggio (pl. 2), Peruzzi, Girolamo da Carpi, and others.[13] Ganymede united male and female beauty in one form, as did the hermaphrodite, best known in Bernini's statue, now in the Louvre. And Cupid and Psyche were so often portrayed with sexual differences suggestively smoothed over that androgyny or some form of unisexuality strikes one as the underlying message. Perhaps this motif was present during the early eighteenth century in pictorial renditions of the story of Hercules and Omphale, as in the painting by François Le Moyne (1688–1737) at the Louvre. Omphale, a delicate blonde nude to the waist, embraces Hercules with one arm, as he holds the distaff and spindle in his hands and looks meltingly at the woman. This bearded hero, who is also blond, may of course be a late version of a man effeminated by excessive love of the opposite sex, the *haec-vir* discussed in the chapter on Milton.[14] On the other hand, he may with equal plausibility represent a reduction of sexual difference and stand as a direct antithesis to the Mars and Vulcan who love Venus in manly ways. These are largely uncharted waters, and such post-Miltonic developments are reintroduced here mostly to suggest the need for further study.

These deviant tendencies may not be unrelated to the position of Venus in Watteau's magnificent *Judgment of Paris* (pl. 15), in which the goddess is partially unveiled to Paris, to the other goddesses, and to Cupid, who helps to undress her while we see only her totally nude back. Watteau has centered all the power of his art on this part of the goddess: line, color, light all focus the attention on the standing nude. The other figures, in partial shadow, serve only to give the curvaceous, modeled back, with dimpled shoulders and buttocks, and the thin, "modern," unbaroque legs even greater luminosity. Velázquez's *Rokeby Venus* (National Gallery, London) was perhaps the prototype

13. See Frederick Antal, *Classicism and Romanticism: With Other Studies in Art History* (London: Routledge & Kegan Paul, 1966), p. 134 and pl. 37a and b; John Bell, *New Pantheon,* 2 vols. (Huntington Library extra-illustrated ed., London, 1790), vol. 1, part 2, p. 349, and antecedent illustrations of representations of Ganymede on onyxes.

14. François Boucher has created a singularly erotic scene of Hercules kissing Omphale in a dazzling canvas in the Pushkin Museum, Moscow (pl. 5 in Raymond Charmet, *French Paintings in Russian Museums,* trans. Muriel Dubois-Ferrière [Geneva: Nagel Publishers, 1970]). See Hagstrum on Cupid and Psyche in *Critical Inquiry* 3 (Spring 1977): 521–42. It is noteworthy that Greuze, in a pen-and-ink drawing now at the Museum in Tournus, was attracted by the theme of Omphale (or love) triumphing over a bearded but now effeminated Hercules.

in our period for this kind of beauty in reverse, a painting in which the goddess's face is seen in a mirror but which presents her back directly to us. That back in its upper part can perhaps be regarded as somewhat thin and uninteresting, but at the bottom it is rounded and full, the anal cavity being the most prominent and the most energetically rendered of all its features. This painting is perhaps less strangely "dispassionate"[15] than it is strangely passionate, one reason for its considerable appeal being precisely the posture of its subject. The eighteenth century seems to have responded enthusiastically to Velázquez's—or possibly Bernini's—invitation to portray the woman *à l'arrière*. Boucher in *The Odalisque* (Louvre, 1743) paints shoulders, legs, feet, but emphasizes the bottom. Watteau, following the lead of Jan Steen, who vulgarly but amusingly presents a clyster as a cure for love, shows in *The Remedy* an attendant with a syringe approaching a lovelorn maiden from behind. (In such scenes Watteau is unusual in showing exclusively the front of his subjects.) However she is presented, the meaning is obvious in these erotic paintings: the woman is voluptuously expectant, and the "remedy" is a visual metaphor for the male member.[16] But still the preoccupation in many of these works is with the back, and in these one cannot help wondering whether love has chosen to pitch his tent in the usual place.

These last examples, including Watteau's *Judgment of Paris,* are admittedly more suggestive than completely persuasive in meaning. What do they suggest? Perhaps they keep alive the Miltonic theme of narcissism, but lacking the sense of sin with which the poet imbued it. One aspect of sensibility tended to make all love attractive, even love of self and love of the similar. Concurrently, as these irregular, enclosed circuits were being wired, male-female separation was becoming more difficult to bridge; and the raptures of Eden, though still regarded as ideal, were in reality becoming more remote. Eve, like Venus, was beginning to turn her back.

Love in Music: A Brief Outline

The informal survey of painting I have just completed seems to have drawn us into a consideration of the eccentric and even the morbid; and we saw that the most frequently illustrated Miltonic episode was the narcissistic and abnormal allegory of Satan, Sin, and Death. Music—at least the highly selective and distinguished music to be considered here—pulls us in the opposite di-

15. Kenneth Clark, *The Nude: A Study in Ideal Form* (1956; reprint, Garden City, N.Y.: Doubleday, 1959), p. 209. Lord Clark discusses, wittily and learnedly, the increasing display of the back in art (pp. 209–11, 496–97).

16. See Donald Posner, "Watteau's *Reclining Nude* and the 'Remedy' Theme," *Art Bulletin* 54 (Dec. 1972): 383–89.

rection: toward Eden, the natural and healthy Bower of Bliss, and the Miltonic ideal of heterosexual friendship. Of all the arts such music is the least sullied by the Fall; perhaps by its very nature it is congenial to an expression of the ideal and the sublime: certainly Gluck, more than the Goethe I have considered, renews the contact of the human spirit with elemental spirituality. All this is not to say that music—particularly in the operas and oratorios to be examined—did not cover a broad spectrum of love emotions, from vulgar, earthy comedy to exalted idealism. Musical drama can possess as much variety as verbal drama, and works of the lyrical stage during the Restoration and eighteenth century provide a rich analogue of love in many moods and in many essential thematic configurations. But the truth is that nothing in the literary or pictorial art I have considered equals the exaltation to be found in the musical masterpieces now to be confronted. In these the motion upward is extremely strong, and indeed the single most important reason for considering music is that it expresses, more nobly than any other art of the period, the ideal aspect of my theme.[17]

This probably means that no one can understand sensibility in its full richness and complexity without knowing—if not as a scholar reading scores, at least as an amateur listening to performances—the settings by Bach, Handel, Gluck, Mozart, and Beethoven of libretti that speak the language of love. Bach's *Saint Matthew Passion* produced a broad range of powerful responses: anger, wonder, exaltation, pity or tenderness, joy, hope, serenity. Of these perhaps the greatest are pity and exaltation—or, to use the language of literary criticism, the pathetic and the sublime. Behind the *literary* tradition I have considered stood the exemplary pathos of Racine, who helped lead Dryden and the whole school of emotional drama that followed the Restoration into the paths of pity and compassion. The *visual* culture of the eighteenth century was also indebted to a French master of the pathetic, the Racine of painting, Nicolas Poussin. His sense of tragic humanity, developed in part from contemplating antique nudes that expressed suffering, was never more moving

17. I comment in the musical sections of this book mostly on acknowledged masterpieces. Undoubtedly different views would appear if the theme of love were traced in seventeenth-century operas, in the librettos of Zeno, Metastasio, and Goldoni, and in the dramas of the French and Italian stage that influenced the musical stage. A brief, highly selective survey, like mine, must, however, concentrate on authentic art with the power to mythologize reality and to influence subsequent culture; and in these works an idealizing tendency is strong. Another cautionary word concerns the librettists, who were sometimes independent and influential: consider, for example, Calzabigi (librettist of *Orfeo ed Euridice* and *Alceste*), who could boast that he had taught Gluck how to write recitative. (See Alfred Einstein, *Gluck,* trans. Eric Bloom [1936; reprint, New York: McGraw-Hill, 1972], pp. 64–69.) I do not have the space nor the expertise to distinguish constantly between the contribution of the composer and that of the librettist; when I use the name of the composer I should be understood to refer to whatever combination of musician and librettist produced the quality or effect being described. In general, however, I believe in the primacy of the music. See n.34, below.

than when he exploited the great subjects of Christian pathos. Does eighteenth-century *music,* which was greater than the other arts in portraying ideal pathos and ideal love, have a similar forerunner? Perhaps the revolutionizing Claudio Monteverdi (1567–1643), particularly as the composer of the *Madrigali guerrieri ed amorosi,* published in 1638, can be regarded as the John the Baptist of musical eros and sensibility. One madrigal at least ("Hor che 'l ciel e la terra,"), for six voices and two violins, contains a spirited contrast of *guerra* and *pace* within love itself; and the marvelous *Combattimento di Tancredi e Clorinda* (1638), as it moves from anger and warlike emotions in the new *concitato* style to the pathos of death, where love, forgiveness, and tender religious resignation blend to produce a musical pathos of rare emotional power, presages Dryden's heroic drama and indeed the whole movement of Western culture from fierceness to gentleness, from love as a respite from war to love as a fulfillment in domestic tranquility. Two fighting knights prove to be a man and woman in love—a woman whom death overtakes, to the unspeakable anguish of her "victorious" lover.

The Restoration composer Henry Purcell (1659–95), a composer closely in touch with literary development, whose *Dido and Aeneas* is discussed above in connection with Dryden, was precisely such a master of love combined with religious pathos. This quintessentially baroque combination Purcell deepened and humanized with psychological insights and freely indulged subjective feelings—qualities that appear strongly in the lines "To Thee all Angels cry aloud" from the *Te Deum* in D major of 1695 (lines that call poignantly for mercy) and in the love pathos of Laura's plaint ("O Let me ever, ever weep / My Eyes no more shall welcome Sleep") in the epithalamium (act 5) of *The Fairy Queen* (1692). Purcell, a genius of many more successful modes of expression than the sentimental comedy that followed him, was also a master of delightful humor: consider the drunken poet versus the fairies in *The Fairy Queen* (act 1) and that charming country dialogue when Coridon tries to kiss the reluctant Mopsa (act 3). Purcell, a deeply religious artist, could nonetheless express Restoration libertinism and the desire for variety in love and even give such sentiments to a woman, as in the "Song by a Nymph," "When I have often heard young Maids complaining" (*Fairy Queen,* act 3)—sentiments that Steele and Richardson in subsequent generations were to resist. But in the very same work he could reaffirm the values of marriage (Hymen's bass aria, "See, see, I obey," act 5), and in a series of "Chinese" songs he could reflect the newer sensibility of natural kindness and generosity (ibid.). Though not directly related to love, the passion of Saul is deeply introspective: consider the solemn but psychologically penetrating lyricism of Saul's aria "Oh! I'm sore distressed" from *In Guilty Night* (1694?), a work which in its musical reflection of the visit to the witches is an example of the mystery and terror that I have called "Gothic" and that is often associated with the tragic aspects of love. The immemorial association of love and nature, which was to be so characteristic of sensibility, is present in Purcell's *Fairy Queen,* where the musical onomatopoeia that imitates the songs and movements of birds, the murmuring of streams, and the pleasures of sleep produces virtuoso pieces of incomparable freshness (act 2).

Parallels to the delicacy of eighteenth-century literary love and to rococo eroticism abound in music, but few examples from great musical art spring to mind that illustrate the narcissism I have found so prevalent in literature and art. Mozart, that universal genius, may reflect the tendency in the character of Cherubino, but the vigorous eroticism of Handel, Haydn, and Gluck, though often touched with tenderness, seems usually to have been free of morbidity— even of the disapproving portrayal of morbidity that Milton gives. Sometimes life-denying fear is associated in art and myth with the figure of Diana; and indeed the cantata, *Diane et Actéon* (published 1732) by Joseph Bodin de Bois-mortier (1689–1755) does contain a section that seems to illustrate and antic-ipate the strain of excessive delicacy that we associate with the rococo and with some pre-Romantic sensibility. The work does, to be sure, end with an "Air tendre" that states the moral: there is no need to eschew peeping or to avow chastity for all time; just choose "moments favorables," and you will avoid the doom of becoming a stag. The power of the work, however, lies in the "Air vif," in which Diane's anger blazes, and in the "Air gai," which dismisses lewd fauns and satyrs and shows that the goddess really fears savage (that is, erotic) love. So she summons sexless or homoerotic nymphs and naiads, who will provide her not with love, which she loathes, but admiration, which she demands. This sylvan retreat, devoted entirely to female delicacy, is given a very appropriate and skillful musical expression by Boismortier, who resembles both Rameau and Watteau.[18]

The towering genius of Johann Sebastian Bach (1685–1750) should perhaps not be used briefly to point a passing moral and adorn a historical tale; but for the student of eros and sensibility his work is vastly instructive and should be explored more fully. His moving but always dignified employ-

18. The work was in fact formerly attributed to Rameau. It is relatively unknown and may be heard in a recording produced by Nonsuch (H-71159). Watteau's *Diana at Her Bath* (Louvre) provides an interesting analogue to this opera (pl. 16). The blonde goddess is full-breasted and her pink skin is attractive. But the painter seems mostly to be saying negative things about this immortal virgin: the vegetation is skimpy and the tree is broken, twisted, and partly dead; the head is small and the expression suggests self-preoccupation and self-satisfaction; the eyes are lowered in modesty, perhaps because the misty distance (so unlike that in the truly erotic pieces) really is not much to look at. The painting shows chastity as a somewhat starved and diminished thing. But there is a further irony. A.-P. de Mirimonde suggests that Diana has the small head of a Parisian girl without her coiffure and that her posture suggests, as does the statue in the *Fête in a Park* in the Wallace collection, the emblem of *Occasio,* or Opportunity, here sexual opportunity. See "Statues et emblèmes dans l'oeuvre d'Antoine Watteau" in *La Revue du Louvre et des Musées de France* 12 (no. 1, 1962): 16 and n.17. See also below, p. 298 and n.42.

ment of sentimental pathos shows us how vastly different post-Miltonic culture might have been had the erotic and the emotional not been severed from their traditional moorings. But within the hierarchy of beliefs which commanded his loyalty he was fully free to be completely modern—deeply and delicately subjective and emotional. The currents of sensibility that were transforming literature and culture did not leave this profoundly formal and structured mind untouched. Consider a very few examples: the sixth English Suite (in D minor), with its transformations of a dance in *lento* triple time to a chromatic meditation (in the sarabande) full of subjective emotional expressiveness; his plea for secrecy and mystery in love in the *Notenbüchlein für Anna Magdalena Bach*, "Willst du dein Herz mir schenken";[19] or the thrilling alternation of the chorus of believers with the tenor, who sings, "Ich will bei meinem Jesu wachen" (*Saint Matthew Passion*), where the bittersweet of religious devotion recalls the traditional oxymoron of love and death:

> Drum muss uns sein verdienstlich
> Leiden recht bitter und doch süsse sein.
> [On that account we must be worthy:
> Sufferings can be bitter and also sweet.]

The last words bring to mind the "coupe amère et douce" that Rousseau's Julie drinks and that symbolizes one of the central paradoxes of the love tradition. In Bach, as in many masters of the seventeenth-century literary and artistic baroque, it is impossible to separate the religious from the secular, *agapē* from *eros*. The chorales are instinct with a pious sweetness which could be offensive without controlling musical form but which within that form breathe the attractive lyricism of erotic love. Many of Bach's cantatas proclaim the joy of birth, love, marriage, uxorial bliss, and maternal tenderness; and these festive celebrations produce emotions and declarations not entirely different from the religious affirmations that praise the *Patrem omnipotentem* in the B Minor Mass (1733?–38) or that invoke the future "vitam venturi saeculi" in the "Confiteor" of the Credo. Bach was an artist of powerful and redemptive contrasts, which did not, however, pit the sacred against the secular, the spirit against the flesh. Such traditional polarities were transcended by deeply and humanly emotional alternations of fear and hope, suffering and jubilation,

---

19. "Wilt thou give me thine heart?" The verse continues: "so fang' es heimlich an, dass unser Beider Denken Niemand errathen kann" [let us begin secretly, so that no one can divine our mutual thought]. See *Die Klavierbüchlein für Anna Magdalena Bach: 1722 und 1725*, ed. Georg von Dadelsen in *Neue Ausgabe Sämtlicher Werke*, ser. 5, vol. 4 (Basel: Bärenreiter Kassel, 1957), p. 126. It has been suggested that this famous love song, called the "Aria di Giovannini," may not in fact have been written by Bach. But its presence in the Notebook shows that it was liked and sung in his family and was part of the regnant sensibility. See Arnold Schering's preface (trans. Kurt Oppens) to *The Little Notebook* (New York: Edwin F. Kalmus, 1949), p. 112n.

the hushed pathos of the "sepultus est" followed by a burst of exaltation at the "Et resurrexit."

It is not surprising, then, that Bach can transfer, without much change, a melody or a musical theme from a pagan to a religious setting. Like many in the eighteenth century, Bach was attracted by the Socratic story of Hercules at the crossroads, where the hero must make a choice between pleasure and duty, between Venus and Minerva.[20] In Bach's secular cantata, as elsewhere, Hercules chooses virtue and dismisses pleasure. But Bach does not imbue the moment of decision with black-white contrasts as the hero turns away from the flesh and follows the spirit, as he rejects ease for military hardship. Bach's hero dismisses *Wollust* (Pleasure) with nobility, gentleness, and beauty of sound; and when he unites with *Tugend* (Virtue) in a lovely duet ("Ich bin deine, Du bist meine"),[21] the music follows the words in portraying sexual enjoyment and marital tenderness: the verb "küsse" is sensually embellished as two *concertante* violas add warmth and gentleness. The seventeenth century gave us the *madonna voluttuosa,* and the poetry of Donne and Crashaw expresses the religious-erotic. Without rejecting that, Bach produces something much rarer and "Enlightened": he blends the amorous and the virtuous in what could be called the ethical-erotic.[22] In the same work Pleasure sings a lovely aria in B-flat, "Schlafe, mein Liebster," an invitation to the beloved to sleep that ends with an injunction to recognize no restraints ("erkenne keine Schranken") and to indulge passion ("schmecke die Lust der lüsternen Brust").[23] This sensual invitation by Wollust is, in the *Christmas Oratorio* (1734),

20. "Die Wahl des Herkules" (or "Herkules auf dem Scheidewege") (1733). For a discussion of the "Choice of Hercules," an obsessive theme during the eighteenth century, see Jean H. Hagstrum, *The Sister Arts* (1958; reprint, Chicago: University of Chicago Press, 1974), pp. 190–94 and pls. VI–VII.

21. Compare movement 6 (Aria duetto) of cantata 140, *Wachet auf, Bach Cantata No. 140,* ed. Gerhard Herz (New York: W. W. Norton, 1972), pp. 95–99, 144–47. This dialogue between Jesus (basso) and the Soul (soprano) quotes the Song of Solomon 2:16, 4:5, 6:3; Psalm 16:11; and Isaiah 35:10, revealing how close religious expression could be to the erotic.

SOUL: Mein Freund ist mein!
JESUS: Und ich bin sein!
BOTH: Die Liebe soll nichts scheiden!
    Ich will mit dir ⎫
               ⎬ in Himmels Rosen weiden, Da Freude die Fülle,
    Du sollst mit mir ⎭
    da Wonne wird sein!

22. See above, pp. 75–76, for voluptuous vocabulary in ethical and philosophical discussions of benevolism.

23. ("Taste the sweets of the yearning breast.") For information on Bach's transfer of this aria, see Philipp Spitta, *Johann Sebastian Bach,* trans. Clara Bell and J. A. Fuller-Maitland, 3 vols. (New York: Dover, 1951), 2:576. The two arias may be compared in *Weinachts-Oratorium,* ed. Walter Blankenburg and Alfred Dürr in *Neue Ausgabe,* ser, 2, vol. 6 (Basel: Bärenreiter Kassel, 1960), pp. 75–85 and "Lasst uns sorgen lasst uns wachen" in *Festmusiken für das Kurfürstlich-Sächsische Haus,* ed. Werner Neumann, ibid., ser. 1, vol. 36 (1963), pp. 32–38.

changed to the key of G, imbued with more interior warmth, and then given almost intact as a lullaby to the Virgin Mary. In both versions Bach has created a song of unrivaled beauty, totally without sentimentality but full of both eros and sensibility. If this untransformed song is typical, we can say that Bach's spirit did not rise to the One on an ascetic Platonic ladder; it grew, in the Christian manner, from organic earth to a living flower:

> So from the root
> Springs lighter the green stalk, from thence the leaves
> More aerie, last the bright consummate floure.
> [*PL*, 5.479–81]

Such is Milton's metaphor to describe movement from matter to spirit. It will serve admirably for Bach's ascent from *eros* to *agapē*.

Christoph Willibald Gluck (1714–87), who, like so many in the later eighteenth century was inspired by Greek myth, who simplified melody and form, and who achieved an amazing coherence between his music and the text which he set, devoted his great powers of construction and concentration to the theme of love, both ideal and passionate. The union of these qualities, so often regarded as contradictory, seems to proclaim that without passion love could not soar and was not worthy of celebration. Gluck's penchant for pathos meant that he was perforce concerned with separation and loss, for only in suffering could he bring out nobility of soul and fervent dedication to the beloved. His happy conclusions, though they sometimes seem shallow, are earned through a noble mastery of affliction; both the joy and the sorrow arise from complex and suggestive depths, and the psychological panorama is varied and interesting. In his two great operas, Gluck is concerned with married love, a theme dear to the heart of sensibility. Although the mythic-musical art of Gluck necessarily differs from that of the sentimental realists writing prose fiction, and although he is of course related to the long and continuous treatment of his myths in baroque and classical music, he can be said, by his concentration on mature couples bound to each other by vows and commitments, to be a successor of Steele, Richardson, and even Rousseau.

The heroine of *Orfeo ed Euridice* (1762) is introduced at the very opening, when Orfeo utters her name in a beautiful musical sigh, breathed out against the chorus of nymphs and shepherds, who themselves penetrate to the inner meaning of such words as "pianti," "lamenti," and "sospiri" as they sing the stately music of grief before the funeral urn of the deceased wife. Orfeo is presented not primarily as a musician or hero but simply as a weeping husband here uttering exclamations of lyrical beauty and soul-shuddering sadness. Because he expresses such deep human love, even when defying those implacable tyrants, the gods, he wins the support of Amor, who here, in a role not always given him, defends and supports uxorial love. Other human qualities of Orfeo emerge as he begins his test and comes to the underworld, a place of terror, fear, and hatred, where he stands out as a Man of Feeling. For it is in that role, and not as a musician, that he stills the Furies, revealing that the inferno itself is a psychological condition that he bears within his grieving soul. His cry, "Ho con me l'inferno mio: / Me lo sento in mezzo al mio cor" (act 2), is a distant echo of Satan in *Paradise Lost,* "Which way I flie is Hell; my self am Hell."[24] The Elysian Fields, where Euridice is to be found, are a kind of purified, innocent Nature, which Gluck clothes in music of exquisite delicacy and harmony—music that pays tribute to the white chastity of the place and the "alma sicura, pura" that inhabits it. Nevertheless, even though there the "soul" is "safe and pure," it is a realm below that of love, and Euridice quickly deserts its elegant grace for a reunion with her husband once he has paid tribute to its inexpressible beauty. Gluck's Elysium was praised by Rousseau for its reflection of naturalistic philosophy; but Orfeo gladly turns to human life, which is superior to its "dolce lusinghiera armonia."[25] Thus the mythic musician has celebrated neither art nor nature but human love as the only cure of human suffering. The chorus, in the same spirit, redefines Elysium and locates it in human marriage: "Uno sposo sì fedel" constitutes "un altro Eliso."[26]

Gluck's psychological penetration continues as he makes subtle human drama of the pair's return to earth. The reunion, so ecstatic to begin with, moves quickly to misunderstanding because her husband's coldness is incomprehensible to Euridice. As a woman of sensibility and sensuality, she prefers death to loveless indifference. Her "qui sto" in act 3 (a Luther-like "Here I stand") is paralleled by Orfeo's bold and Enlightened rebelliousness against the "Numi barbari": the couple are naturally loving human beings subjected to antihuman laws imposed from on high.[27] The suffering, now in its later and more searing phase, comes to a heartrending climax as Euridice dies for a second time and Orfeo sings the famous aria "Che farò senza Euridice?" ("What shall I do without Euridice?"), the middle section of which expresses pure despair. The ending, made happy by the sudden intervention

24. *PL* 4.75. The cry of Orfeo may be literally translated: "I have my own hell with me: I feel it in the center of my heart."

25. Act 2. ("sweet, deluding harmony"). See Ernest Newman, *Gluck and the Opera* (London: Bertram Dobell, 1895), pp. 145–46, where Rousseau is quoted as praising the perfect congruity and equality of the blessed spirits in the Elysian scene.

26. Act 2 ("a spouse thus faithful [is] another Elysium.") For a learned and readable discussion of the Orpheus theme in opera, particularly of the theme in Monteverdi and Gluck, see Joseph Kerman, *Opera as Drama* (1956; reprint, New York: Vintage Books, 1959), pp. 25–49.

27. Einstein (*Gluck*, p. 74) refers to the fine copper engraving, perhaps approved by Gluck, that illustrates, in the 1764 Paris edition of the score, the couple's return to earth. Orfeo is shown as turning away in pain, but the imperious and haughty Euridice is at once passionate, jealous, and angry.

of Amor just as the stricken husband is about to take his own life, restores somewhat too patly the wife to the embrace of the husband and praises abstract love, not the loving couple—a touch of moralizing sentimentality not fully in keeping with the purely human joys and sorrows hitherto prominent. But if we overlook the superficiality of the resolution, we must surely be impressed with what Gluck has achieved: seldom has love-joy been given a more graceful and sublime, or love-grief a more poignant, musical expression.

Alceste (1767) is another masterpiece of eros and sensibility; its similarly simple mythic plot and appropriate music alternate between tenderness and majesty. In *Orfeo ed Euridice* purely human emotions prevail; *Alceste* is generally more ideal. That quality is suggested at the very outset when Alcestis decides to undertake the Christlike mission of offering her life so that her husband may be allowed to live and reign. As in the earlier opera, the divine decrees are regarded as barbarous (here they are called sinister), and the love of husband and wife is presented as a purely human affection suffering the persecutions of supernatural tyranny. The great aria of act 1, "Divinités du Styx," is the outpouring of a proud, loving, grieving woman who will die for the man she loves but will not abjectly supplicate the cruelly whimsical deities for pity. Defiant and free human courage, in the spirit of Byron or Shelley, is opposed to pious fatality, a mood also dear to the Enlightenment and to sensibility. The plot would end at once but for the fact that the husband's love matches his wife's in fervor: Admetus rejects life without Alcestis and sublimely opposes his human dignity to the supernatural cruelty. All doors opening upon life having been closed, the couple now face death and long for it in majestically beautiful solos and duets. The *Liebestod* of long tradition certainly reaches one of its apogees in act 3. As in the earlier opera, the resolution, in which Hercules appears as a friend and rescuer and Apollo as a celebrant of uxorial loyalty, comes too quickly and accounts for some loss of pathetic dignity at the very climax.[28] But the greatness of the opera survives its closing scene: it resides in the noble musical realization of ideal and human love combined, a love that remains untouched by supernatural menace and the seeming inexorability of death. In both Gluck's masterpieces a purely human Eden is reclaimed from the encroaching dark by a musical loveliness that is at once grave and soaring.

28. The appearance of Hercules was added to the French revision in 1776 (for the Paris performance) of the Italian version (1767); some scholars regard the earlier as the superior version. See Martin Cooper, *Gluck* (New York: Oxford University Press, 1935), pp. 134–35. Einstein (*Gluck*, p. 107), who believes that Gluck's great masterpiece is *Alceste*, thinks the ideal performance for our own day would be a compromise between the Italian and the French versions. See also Rudolf Gerber's Foreword to his edition of *Alceste* in *Sämtliche Werke*, ser. 1, vol. 7 (Basel: Bärenweiter Kassel, 1957). He traces the evolution of the plot from Euripides via Calzabigi to du Roullet's version, suggesting the likely reasons for changes in dramatic motivation.

Joseph Haydn's last opera, not performed during its composer's lifetime (*L'anima del filosofo ossia Orfeo ed Euridice,* 1791) seems by its title to promise a continuation of Gluck's great achievement on the theme of love and marriage. And Haydn does create, at the end of act 1, a duet ("Come il foco allo splendore") that expresses a deep union of souls:

> Il mio cor dal tuo bel core
> Mai diviso non sarà.
> [My heart from thy lovely heart
> Ne'er divided will be.]

In such music Haydn truly fuses love and sensibility. But he intended really to create an opera "entirely different from that of Gluck,"[29] and he in fact succeeded. His *Orfeo* is a grim and doom-ridden work from its beginning, and it ends in an almost universal tragedy which includes the hero's renunciation of sexual pleasure forever. This opera rises to magnificence, but it does not breathe the air of eighteenth-century love-sensibility. It is stark, violent, tragic.

Beethoven, however, presents in *Fidelio* a worthy successor to Gluck's celebrations of uxorial love. The music, the setting, the active heroism of the woman, all differ markedly from *Alceste,* but in its essentials Beethoven's opera represents a continuation of Gluck's theme in the combined ideality and humanity of the love. In Beethoven a world of human political oppression replaces the pantheon of cruel gods; and a cold, damp, suffocating prison, built by tyrannical men, supplants Hades and the Styx. Love defies and defeats these human tyrants with memorable art, and that victory of light over dark is a purely human and female act.

From the source (a libretto by Bouilly: *Léonore, ou l'amour conjugal,* 1798) through the final revised opera, *Fidelio oder: Die eheliche Liebe* (1814), the main theme remains the mature and mutual love of Leonore and Florestan. The opera has been called "a genuine rescue opera"[30] (*Sir Charles Grandison* in its opening action is another notable example of the type), and the plot is in fact a tense and exciting story of the penetration of an unspeakable Spanish prison

---

29. Quoted by H. C. Robbins Landon in "The Operas of Haydn," *The Age of Enlightenment: 1745–1790,* ed. Egon Wellesz and Frederic Sternfeld (London: Oxford University Press, 1973), p. 181. See also the edition by Helmut Werth (Munich: G. Henle Verlag, 1974) and the *Analytical Notes* (Boston: Haydn Society, 1951).

30. Paul Henry Lang, "French Opera and the Spirit of the Revolution" in *Studies in Eighteenth-Century Culture: Irrationalism in the Eighteenth Century,* ed. Harold E. Pagliaro (Cleveland, Ohio: Press of Case Western Reserve University, 1972), pp. 97–112. Lang provides a persuasive and precise musical context in the neo-Buonapartean rescue operas, which were often exciting to the common man, who was keenly interested in prison scenes. Lang draws attention to a larger context, which, if it did not influence the librettist Bouilly and Beethoven directly, certainly influenced the culture that produced them. For a description of the salient characteristics of the rescue opera, see R. Morgan Longyear, "Notes on the Rescue Opera," *Musical Quarterly* 45 (Jan. 1959): 49–66.

by a disguised wife to effect the escape of her husband. Freud interprets rescue fantasies in dreams as obsessively erotic,[31] and it would reveal a limited vision to deny that below Beethoven's stormy and heroic surfaces there is a substructure of physicality. But Beethoven as man and artist consciously seems to separate love from underground passion and liberates it into the light of piety, moral courage, political idealism, and social redemption. The panorama of virtues that the opera unfolds is a civic one. But this civic salvation arises, as so many in the Enlightenment thought it should, from uxorial love, which first created the society of the family; and Beethoven in fact elevates not young, passionate, premarital, consuming, or irregular love but mature, already established, married love to the pitch of high moral and political intensity that not only can coexist with the civic virtues mentioned but actually energizes and activates them. So, although he comes on the scene late, Beethoven has contributed a masterpiece to the process of ennobling domestic virtue that had been going on for over a century. The great achievement of *Fidelio* is not so much to contribute to the gallery two highly individualized lovers as to mythologize and idealize familial fidelity and courage.[32]

   That Beethoven belongs in a discussion of eighteenth-century love appears very early in the opera, since like Richardson and Rousseau he accompanies the heterosexual love of the hero and heroine with the homoerotic love which the jailer's daughter, Marzelline, conceives for the heroine (here of course the result of Leonore's disguise as a man). It may be an eloquent fact that the conclusion rewards the heroic wife and leaves the romantic girl speechless, without letting us know if she ever marries the man she should have loved all along, the loyal and persistent Jaquino. How far above infatuation is the love Beethoven celebrates appears in the great aria of act 1, "Komm Hoffnung," which is a hymn to hope and to the binding obligation of married love—to the "Pflicht / Der treuen Gattenliebe" ("the pledge of true marital love"). Similarly, in Florestan's magnificent "Lebens Frühlingstagen," surely one of the peaks of all operatic literature, the rapture rises to exaltation as the tempo quickens and the tenor goes into the upper registers.[33] Florestan, in the lines

   31. See *The Interpretation of Dreams*, p. 439 and n.2.
   32. I call attention to a fine insight in Irving Singer, *Mozart & Beethoven: The Concept of Love in Their Operas* (Baltimore, Md.: Johns Hopkins University Press, 1977): "That Beethoven should have written the greatest opera about conjugal love while never finding it for himself is . . . not a paradox. . . . For he writes about the striving and not the achievement, . . . And possibly Beethoven could not have written about conjugal love at all if he himself had undergone the confusing complexities of the real thing" (p. 128). See Alexander W. Thayer, *The Life of Ludwig van Beethoven*, ed. H. E. Krehbiel (New York: G. Schirmer for the Beethoven Association, 1921), 1:121 ff., 317 ff.; 2:166. See also chap. 7 ("Conflict with Women") of Edith Sterba and Richard Sterba, *Beethoven and His Nephew: A Psychoanalytic Study of Their Relationship*, trans. Willard R. Trask (New York: Pantheon, 1954), pp. 97–111.
   33. Act 2: recitative, beginning "Gott! Welch' Dunkel hier!" (O God, what gloom is here!"); aria,

beginning "Und spür' ich nicht linde, sanft säuselnde Luft?" ("Do I not feel a gentle, softly murmuring breeze?") is lyrical not about physical love but about the "Freiheit" of the "himmlische Reich" ("freedom of the heavenly kingdom") and about his wife, who is now "ein Engel im rosigen Duft" ("an angel with the scent of roses"). It is exciting to encounter in this context of familial heroism that obsessive word "angel"; but here, surely, we are not in the presence of the kind of escapist *angélisme* we have frequently encountered, which substitutes the ethereal for a feared sexuality. In this opera the vision is necessarily rarefied, since the prisoner has languished in solitary confinement, without sufficient food and without human companionship. The vision is inevitably pure and takes on dramatic force for that very reason. We are to feel deeply tragic emotions over the fact that Florestan, in the prime of his life, should be dreaming of heavenly release, not earthly consummation. At the end, in an inspired duet, Beethoven brings together not two political activists—not even, primarily, a man and woman—but a faithful married couple, who in the fierce intensity of the music pronounce their names, Florestan and Leonore, and so renew their vows. The nobility with which this opera invests married love is rare indeed in art and recalls that equally rare moment in fiction when Rousseau endows with religious sublimity the nuptials of Julie and Wolmar. The chorus fittingly concludes the entire work by praising the lovely wife who is also a courageous "Retterin des Gatten" ("savior of her spouse"). The value most intensely rendered in Beethoven's music[34] is not physical love, certainly not the passive womanly love so frequently exalted in Western culture, and not even the ethereal, almost unworldly love the hero sings about in his confinement. The highest value is embodied in the loving woman who undertakes a heroic deed in society and so frustrates the schemes of a cruel tyrant. The reunited husband and wife are blessed by the king's minister, Don Fernando, essentially a Man of Feeling, who also frees the political prisoners, deposes the tyrant, and praises human brotherhood.[35]

Beethoven is a long way from Milton, chronologically and culturally. Human individualism and freedom, the new spirit of equality, even between the sexes, the concept of the heroic woman, the doctrine of a purely human

---

beginning: "In des Lebens Frühlingstagen ist das Glück von mir geflohn!" ("In the very springtime of life, joy has fled me!")

34. All through this discussion of Beethoven I mean to imply that the music is both emotionally intense and intellectually conceptual, and of course primary. I therefore welcome Singer's comment: "The music dominates throughout, the orchestral design overwhelming the singers on occasion. Far from serving as the illustration of anything, the work becomes the tonal *embodiment* of the abstract concepts to which it is devoted" (*Mozart & Beethoven*, p. 120).

35. His aria, "Des besten Königs Wink und Wille" ("the wish and will of the best king"), ends thus: "Es sucht der Bruder seine Brüder, / Und kann er helfen, hilft er gern" ("the brother seeks out his brethren, and when he can help, he does so joyously").

benevolence—all these are post-baroque, though Milton anticipated some of them. But the placing of a triumphant marital friendship at the center of a redeemed human community may be viewed as one way of restoring Eden, and Beethoven has done more than Milton by making the loving, married pair the very agents of salvation. Paintings, like novels, are usually closer to mundane reality than musical sounds, and Watteau and Greuze may, more than Bach and Beethoven, keep the physical side of sex and sensibility before us. But the point of most of my analyses, even of the most ideal love, is that the body remains somehow present even when it is subordinated. The music that Beethoven gives to Florestan, even at its most ethereal, when he has a vision of his beloved as an angel in a rosy olfactory mist, is not without intense, though mostly implied, libidinous energy.

Watteau

Watteau was a contemporary of Pope, and like the author of *The Rape of the Lock* was capable of a shimmering, kaleidoscopic delicacy that can belie the essential earthiness of his vision and obscure his connections with the new freedom and even irrationality that characterized French culture in the early eighteenth century. That culture consciously sought after *charme, coeur, esprit,* and *sentiment;* and Watteau, along with Lancret, Pater, and De Troy, contributed to the dissolution of the academic and the slackening of formal rules.[36] Certainly, provocative displays of the female body, owing much to the pearly and ample eroticism of Rubens, were both a sign and a cause of the newer freedom.[37] Watteau's modeled flesh is the voluptuous elevated to the pictorially lyrical. How this assertion of heterosexual verve contrasts with the drive toward unisexuality already noted as characteristic of the later eighteenth century appears strikingly if we think of some of Canova's most famous sculptures. His men and women—adolescent boys and girls, rather—tend to be amazingly alike, divisions, as it were, of one unified being. Watteau is different. In his *Spring, or Flora crowned by a Zephyr*[38] the woman has large breasts and thighs, and the male, though hardly Michelangelesque, is assertively manly. In an oil painting *L'amour désarmé* (Musée Condé, Chantilly)[39] the mythical beings are humanized into an unconventional, though

36. Walter Friedlaender, *David to Delacroix* (Cambridge, Mass.: Harvard University Press, 1952), pp. 1–6.

37. Clark, *The Nude*, pp. 205–7.

38. Reproduced as illustration 6 in Donald Posner, *Watteau: A Lady at Her Toilet.* The oil painting is now, unfortunately, destroyed.

39. Reproduced in color in Jean Ferré (and others), *Watteau*, 4 vols. (Madrid: Editions Artistiques Athéna, 1972), 2:622. See also 3:834–37. Numbers following the title of Watteau's pic-

delicate, ensemble of two nude bodies. Cupid places a hand on his mother's heart, as his body casts a shadow across hers, in the manner of Veronese. The quietly beautiful Venus, her hair slightly disordered in the back, is no conventional recollection of an ancient goddess. She is seated facing us, her legs crossed, a gauzy veil over her pudenda, her body otherwise totally nude. The gentle aggressiveness of this almost chaste pose is suggested by Venus's possession of the arrows and bow, which Cupid is forced to reach for. *He* may be disarmed, but his mother is not—she is ready and willing to provoke love. The figure in the lovely and highly sensual *Lady at Her Toilet* (pl. 17) turns to face us, allowing us to gaze directly on her charms. It is only by careful attention to slight details that we realize that Venus and Cupid are indirectly present. They are not, however, beings in a mythological history but metaphorical invitations to love in a real-life setting. If we allow our minds to leap to another contemporary of Watteau, we realize that nothing could be further from the interiors in which Swift introduced the nymphs and Venuses of his poetry. Here there are no tawdry or sordid details—no rings, trinkets, baubles, or soliciting gestures. Nor is there the slightest hint of disapproval by the artist, who has portrayed a free and joyous offering of self in a "pose of wonderful receptivity."[40]

Watteau's group paintings have been said to constitute his "comédie sentimentale."[41] The phrase has much to recommend it, but we must not think of Steele and the English *comédie larmoyante*. Watteau's world is too brittle and amoral to invoke *The Conscious Lovers*—and too imaginative. For his women are bedecked in the rich costumes of the day, his men dressed as stock figures from the *commedia dell'arte* or as other well-known stage figures. And his nude, lifelike, almost breathing, sensual park statuary interacts with the human drama and sometimes makes it seem frivolous and artificial (pl. 18).[42] All this brings us into the realm of social and artistic *féerie*. but "sentimental" is still a

---

tures in my text or notes refer to this work. Vol. 2 contains the plates, which are given page numbers on the reverse side. Each plate refers to other parts of the work which discuss the painting in question.

40. Posner, *Watteau*, p. 74. This monograph provides an exhaustive and sensitive scholarly commentary.

41. The phrase is that of Saint-Paulien in Ferré, 1:77.

42. In this dazzling picture in the Wallace Collection (*Fête in a Park*), the most striking feature is perhaps the contrast between the erotic play (in various degrees) of the brilliantly clothed and skillfully disposed couples and the nude fleshly statue, which is so lifelike that one wonders if it is indeed made of stone. Its exact meaning has been disclosed by Mirimonde (see above, n.18). The one leg folded under the other, the long braid of hair, and the sensuality of the flesh identify the statue as the emblem of *Occasio,* or sexual opportunity (pp. 16–17). Mirimonde says that Watteau's park statues are not, except in one instance, identifiable as statues but can be analyzed precisely as emblems easily understood in Watteau's day. They enter the drama and meaning of the scene portrayed: "Les statues qu'il place dans ses parcs traduisent les sentiments et les pensées de ses personnages" (p. 12; see also pp. 11, 13).

good word, for behind the characters, attitudes, and ensembles we sense the animating presence of grace and love. In these outdoor scenes Watteau's vision is at once erotic and delicate, invoking both sex and sensibility. The sensual passion lies beneath the graceful poses and the fluttering, shimmering garments of social life and the stage; it is never suffocated by the superficies. The men and women, who sing, play musical instruments, read or hear stories, walk, sit, converse amid feathery trees that anticipate Gainsborough and by lakes and reflecting pools that recall Nicolas Poussin, are almost all engaged in the preliminaries of love play. They have all embarked, or will soon embark, on a journey to Venus's isle. Some remain indifferent, reluctant, fearful, but one feels that the titillating flutter will soon enough impel them on with the rest.

I have already mentioned the eighteenth-century love of the female back and considered one of Watteau's splendid and frankly sensual portrayals of it. In his many *fêtes champêtres* the lady with her back toward us bears rather more solemn and subtle meanings. In *Les deux cousines* (2:624; Paris, Hubert de Ganay) the seated girl is voluptuous, but it is the one who walks away from us who arouses the greatest interest. Mysterious as she moves toward the misty distance, she seems to be making her own lonely way to Cythera, walking past her cousin, who is with her lover and seems already to have arrived. Similarly, in *Assemblée dans un parc* (2:638; Louvre), a painting in which the magnificent park dwarfs the human figures, a preadolescent girl, her back to us, stands near a dog and seems to stare at the water. Separated by a subtle arrangement from both younger children and adults, she seems to be innocent but on the edge of experience. *Fête d'amour* (2:642; Dresden, Gemäldegalerie) is surely one of Watteau's most voluptuous works.[43] Its colors are the golden ones of autumn, not the usual dark green, though the distant mountains, suggesting Cythera, are blue and white. Much amorous play goes on in the foreground, including that of a couple committed to love who walk away from us but look back. Among those who remain one woman pushes away an over-eager lover, one touches her breasts; but, once again, the most interesting of all may be one of the women who present their backs—the one who seems ashamed or perturbed as she rests her weight on her hand while her lover looks complacent and a nearby dog barks angrily. Watteau's backs do not constitute a single or simple effect, nor do they, in these park scenes at least, point to perversion.

43. The Art Institute of Chicago possesses the preliminary study in sanguine, chalk, and pencil, for this painting. For all the amorous suggestiveness of the final work, the drawing is even more erotic. In the very center of the drawing a man kisses a woman and presses her breasts, while she turns her head up to him, extending and bending her nude legs. Dalliance remains in the final version, to be sure, but the overt erotic play has been somewhat muted. The drawing, unique of its kind, supports the feeling that Watteau's *fêtes* in oil are full of controlled, if not suppressed, sexuality.

What they do suggest is the complications that accompany pleasure—delay, reluctance, loneliness, perturbation, shame. The woman who turns her back is a mysterious and enriching presence in the world of love that Watteau has created.

At the very least the woman who faces the other way is one among several subtle variations of dalliance that Watteau's delicate pencil traces. He is not always subtle, of course; but in the aristocratic and theatrical world of the *conversations galantes* he is allusive rather than overt, delicate rather than direct. This mode of expression is exquisitely suited to the foreplay Watteau continually suggests—as important an aspect of rococo sensibility as it is of the lovemaking of Rousseau and Sterne. How endlessly diverse and subtly nuanced it can be on the canvases of Watteau! The enchanting *Amour paisible* (pl. 19) may be taken as typical. It is useless to ask where we should locate Venus's isle in this picture. Is it in the misty, blue-gold distance, where green-brown trees accompany and blue-green cliffs support solid architecture, giving substantial reality to love dreams? Is it in the stream that runs through the middle ground and beckons to unknown places? Or could it be—and this would be very subtle in a picture—in the past recollections of the three couples who are in the foreground? Perhaps the most enriching hint the picture conveys is that the human beings are even now on Venus's isle, which is a heaven of foreplay, the only kind of satisfaction Watteau really promises. But the placing of ultimate pleasure in the well-dressed couples does not fully satisfy either, for these are, as it were, sculpted like marble and are much less animated—and erotic—than Watteau's garden statuary can be; and here they are in fact separated from the surrounding landscape, which includes in its shadows a shepherd who watches them. From what are these chiseled beings separated? From reality, surely, but perhaps also from the consummations of Cythera, which would account for the melancholy that suffuses the broad expanses of this picture.

The qualities I have noted—variety in the dalliance, exquisite grace of posture, attitude, and dress, the indescribable sense of melancholy—are present in the paintings obviously alluding to the enchanted island, the symbol of love's *toute puissance*. The pilgrimage thereto—and also therefrom—had been the subject of the literary art of La Fontaine and the musical art of Couperin, but it is Watteau whose name will always be indissolubly linked to the enchanted, amorous isle. In *L'Ile de Cythère* (2:596; Paris, Collection Heugel) a gondola with five tiny winged Cupids is ready to embark. A *maréchal* of Cythera with two attendants, one of each sex, directs the human passengers, while two other Cupids descend from the sky to point the way, trailing the mantle of divinity, the blonde flourishing the bow, the brunet the torch. One on the ground gently pushes a reluctant and frightened girl toward the boat, showing that these divinities are more then rococo decoration and represent propelling erotic energy as well as the almost religious omnipresence of love in Watteau's world. Passengers begin to form couples, though there seem to be more women than men in the total of thirteen; these, like most of Watteau's lovers, are fully clothed, their dress gleaming with the golden light that attends some of the Cupids and suggesting that garments are not merely decorative either but are themselves a part of love's body. The old Titianesque antithesis of naked truth and clothed art has vanished. Clothed or unclothed, Watteau's couples are in full amorous play, of which the garment is insistently a part.

Watteau's masterpiece, *Le pèlerinage à l'Ile de Cythère* (pl. 20) is a rhythmically elegant movement of people in real time and space toward an embarkation for ecstasy; and its chromatic tonalities, human juxtapositions, play of emotions, and landscape effects have been brilliantly described by the Goncourts, Théophile Gautier, Rodin, and many art historians. My concern is to bring out its qualities as a vision of love. A rich park setting with feathery trees is animated by strong horizontal movement of line, for this painting, like most of Watteau's, has replaced with earthly parallels the upward diagonal thrust of the baroque. On the right, from which the human motion toward love proceeds, stands a statue of Venus on a pedestal, bare breasted but covered with flowers, garlands, and a quiver full of arrows, the offerings of lovers and of Love himself. Underneath this statue—in actuality a herm, which is far less animated than some of Watteau's other park sculptures and which here stands the farthest from the action of embarkation—a reluctant woman who gazes downward, perhaps in shame, is urged on by a partly clothed Cupid tugging at the hem of her gorgeous garment and also by the solicitations of her gallant. The couple that appears next as the eye moves leftward toward the water is already in movement, the man raising a willing blonde beauty from the grass by both her hands, while the next pair (the central and largest figures in the group) already walk toward the boat, having reached the top of the curve of ground that may symbolize the sphere of the earth itself, the lady looking back with a bemused expression at the couple just rising from the ground. A group of carefully differentiated couples descending to the water are motioned on by a nude Cupid, as two couples are about to embark, a lady delicately and suggestively lifting her skirt to mount the bark, which is decorated with Venus's golden shell, dark lavender hangings, and nude female statues. One cupid prepares the vessel for occupation, seven more form an ensemble in the sky that drives on toward Cythera, two others fly about the vessel as if to inspire the seminude oarsman. One supposes from all this that the voyage will be pleasurable; but the posture of one of the boatmen does recall that of Charon, suggesting that these waters are the antitype of the Styx and that the destination is not a place of shades and shadows but of flesh and fulfillment. Watteau's pictorial dynamics make of the embarkation a movement of real people in different states of real eagerness and real reluctance toward erotic experience. But though the sense of reality is strong and the dominant tone here may be optimistic, Watteau remains an artist of rich complexity. The reality is suffused with imagination, as the decorated bark clearly shows. And a most delicate sense of melancholy— perhaps no more than a future *post coitum tristitia*—plays over the scene in the softly gleaming water, the pink-rose mist, the rocks and the mountains in the distance that look more like ice or blue glass than solid rock as they blend easily with sky and water. The suggestion is quiet but inescapable that Cythera *could* be a mirage, separated from the hopeful couples by infinite space and an ever receding haven. Or pleasure can be thought of as real enough, with only its permanence in doubt. Particularly in his breathtakingly beautiful and delicate renditions of distant destinations and dreams, Watteau is too complex and ambiguous to allow us to say simply that *The Embarkation for Cythera* portrays "le bonheur en marche."[44]

Watteau is in fact more delicate and subtle than his *confrères* or followers in socially erotic art. For one thing, his range is larger and more varied. This man of Flemish background and spirit, even in his lifetime called *célèbre* as the *peintre du Roi* and often engraved and widely distributed, covered many subjects besides those I have discussed: country fêtes, rural love, blacks, peasants, some nudes (see pls. 17, 22), a few landscapes as such. His *oeuvres* were widely studied, and he was treated almost like Raphael as the source and standard for the portrayal of heads and attitudes. The attractive and competent Nicolas Lancret (1690–1743), who also painted Italian comedians and couples making music and love in park scenery with statuary and trees, lacked the subtlety of contrapuntal rhythm, the individuality of face and figure, and the suggestiveness of distance that Watteau possessed. Jean-Baptiste Pater (1695–1736), Watteau's only pupil, presents gorgeously dressed couples in dalliance, but his ensembles are without the sharp and suggestive differentiation that makes one "read" Watteau with endless fascination, nor is his landscape so ample and rich. That ravishing painter and lover of life, François Boucher (1703–70), who engraved after Watteau and was generally indebted to him, is often overtly mythological, while Watteau's reality only suggests myth; and when he portrays actual society, Boucher does so with greater artificiality— not only the clothes and attitudes but the very skin of his men and women suggest artifice and study. Watteau's portrayal of love is richer, then, than any of these—richer even than the masterpieces by Fragonard at the Frick Gallery that portray contemporary gallantry. What he possessed in such inimitable subtlety we regret keenly when we see his manner imitated but his spirit totally lost. In the Musée de Dijon, the *Offrande à Vénus* (1785?) shows that Louis

44. Saint-Paulien in Ferré, 1:178. See Appendix C, below.

Trinquesse has challenged comparison with the master (pl. 21). But the statue of Venus and Cupid lacks a plastic relation to the lovemaking of couples on the grass, which is characterized by obvious excitements and gross anticipation. The brunette is vulgarly confident; the blonde, more delicate but offensively coquettish. "Où sont les neiges d'antan?"

Watteau is important in our story not solely—or even primarily—because he was a great artist. He portrayed a theme central to English sex and sensibility. In a visual idiom akin to the rich verbal textures of his English contemporary Alexander Pope, he represents the erogenous zones of society, notably the border between innocence and experience. This fact is revealed by the frequent presence in his rich and gorgeous parks of reluctant and fearful women, withdrawn and withdrawing innocents. The frontier between innocence and experience is precisely the area that Richardson and Rousseau, Jane Austen and Blake set out to explore—a place where the eighteenth-century imagination liked to linger and from which it could not always escape. Watteau revealed the unabashed delight in the female body so evident in his *Lady at Her Toilet* (pl. 17), which, as we have seen, is open and hearty in its invitations, and his *Reclining Nude* (pl. 22), where the rhythmic whiteness of the bed sheets vies in allure with the richly endowed body and the woman's sense of its mystery. At the same time the fully clothed, socially elegant dalliance in the park breathes an air of preliminary or anticipated pleasure. Watteau in both dress and undress anticipates Sterne, whose imagination combined a fingertip type of promissory flirtatiousness with bawdy allusiveness. It is not surprising that an artist with so many cultural connections should also influence other artists, and Watteau's Europe-wide influence touched such diverse English painters as Hogarth, Reynolds, Gainsborough, Blake, Romney, Turner, and Constable. The influence extended beyond the profession of art. In 1805 Pilkington's *Dictionary* said that the works of Watteau "seem to advance daily in the esteem of the public."[45] But quite apart from influence, the French painter's achievement is monumental and deserves study for its own sake. He brought the expression of erotic love to one of its eighteenth-century summits.

Handel

Since it was one of the important accomplishments of this period to feminize sensibility, there are few Restoration and eighteenth-century por-

---

45. From an unsigned article in Matthew Pilkington, *A Dictionary of Painters, from the Revival of the Art to the Present Period* (London, 1805), p. 640. This work was first published, under a slightly different title, in 1770.

trayers of love to whom the word "delicacy" cannot be applied. Of these few George Frideric Handel was surely one. He expressed pity, approved forgiveness, depicted the tenderness of women and children, and found sympathy in heterosexual love; but his genius as a whole cannot be said to be soft and effeminate; and this German bachelor, deeply influenced by Italian and English culture, appears untouched by any kind of irregularity that may have been associated with the feminization of the spirit. In fact, in a fairly early composition of 1706–8, the cantata for soprano voice, *Tu fedel? tu costante?* (in which Handel anticipates the democratization of society and enforces the right of an aggrieved woman to be heard and to take action), he completely reverses the later cultural situation. He masculinizes the feminine and tries to extend male assertiveness to an area from which it had hitherto been excluded. The woman who sings of a faithless lover denounces him in simple forthright musical sentences that mount in intensity to hate and that in the end express her decision to turn to the "antica libertà" normally reserved for men.

Dryden, another creator whose genius could seldom be called *delicate* but who nevertheless contributed greatly to sensibility, was understandably an author for whom Handel felt the deepest affinity. The writer had anticipated the musician in the creation of protesting and vigorous women who cried for liberty and revenge. But it is more typical of the innermost being of both men that they should be attracted to the civilized Acis in Ovid's story from the *Metamorphoses* (bk. 13), in which the crude love of Polyphemus for the nymph Galatea is sharply opposed to the gentle shepherd's.[46] With the giant, Handel is less successful in his first theatrical piece in English, *Acis and Galatea* (performed 1721), than he is with Acis. The giant's offer of his hand and hearth in Ovid and Dryden has a kind of noble primitivism about it, but in the music, as "Polyphemus, great as Jove / Calls to empire and to love" (act 2), Handel simply refuses to be either imperial or amorous and decides instead to create a very human and sympathetic buffoon. This he does with energy and amusement; but what does he make of the tender and kindly love that ends tragically, as Polyphemus kills the shepherd with a boulder that he tears from the side of a mountain? He creates for it a pastoral setting in music that imitates birds in the flutes and piccolos and that expresses loveliness and desire in the soprano voice ("Hush, ye pretty warbling quire," act 1). Acis's air ("Love in her

46. The music was perhaps written in 1718, though certainty is apparently impossible. See Winton Dean, *Handel's Dramatic Oratorios and Masques* (London: Oxford University Press, 1959), p. 159. The poem on which Handel based his masque is by John Gay; and Pope, Dryden, and John Hughes contributed lines. For an excellent analysis and defense of Gay's pastoral opera and of how Handel's music interprets it, see Bertrand H. Bronson, "The True Proportions of Gay's *Acis and Galatea*" in *Facets of the Enlightenment* (Berkeley and Los Angeles: University of California Press, 1968), pp. 45–59.

eyes sits playing," act 1) is melodic but never sentimental, and its music responds not to the panting, fiery love of the text but to the foreboding tragedy. Elsewhere, the love music tends to be brisk rather than languishing, though now and then erotic hints arise. Handel's real achievement is to express the pathos of Acis's death ("Mourn, all ye Muses!" act 2) and, in the loveliest music of the whole work, to celebrate his union as a river god with nature's diurnal round (Galatea's recitative "'Tis done" and air "Heart, the seat of soft delight," act 2). It is typical of Handel's eighteenth-century genius that physical love should be transcended not by piety or renunciation but by harmony with nature. That union is rendered in an exquisite waving orchestral accompaniment that suggests softly rolling water as Handel responds to the "Crystal flood" and the "bubbling fountain" of his text. If the word "delicate," to which I have given many special meanings, is not appropriate here, "beautiful" certainly is. In fact *Acis and Galatea* shows us a Handel who consciously declines both the erotic and the sublime of terror and rises to musical heights in portraying natural consolations.

Some twenty years later, in *Saul* (1739), Handel once again, despite the feeling of sympathy his own mental distress must have given him for the alienation of the king's mind, achieves distinction not so much in expressing the sublime of fear that Endor and the king's agitated spirits might have evoked as in developing the love of David and Michal and the friendship of David and Jonathan. Gracious in Michal's "Ah! lovely youth" (1.2), more darkly beautiful in "Fell rage and black despair" (1.4, where the girl expresses her serenity of spirit as she turns from her father's madness to David's music, which is both spiritual and amorous in the love duets), the love music is progressively enriched as the oratorio proceeds until the magnificent chorus "Is there a man" (2.5) exalts the couple's love to the level of religion and virtue. Handel, like Richardson and Rousseau in their great novels, accompanies love with friendship, which in this work he makes transcendent. No doubt the death of Jonathan permitted him to add to manly love the still sad music of pathos, in which he was already a master—a pathos, by the way, which is full of plastic beauty but, like Beethoven's, without a shred of the meretricious or undignified. Like the writers mentioned when describing the homoerotic love of Clarissa-Anna and Julie-Claire, Handel in the last line of Jonathan's aria ("Of thee, thou darling of my soul," 2.2) lingers over and beautifully embellishes the erotic implications. At the very end, when political order is restored in the baroque beauties of David's and the chorus's lament over the dead king, even these are superseded by the heartrending loveliness of the new king's lament with the chorus ("Oh Jonathan! how nobly didst thou die," 3.5) over his personal loss and his moving tribute to friendship ("And more than woman's love thy wond'rous love to me!" 3.5).

No piece of music is more often praised in *Sir Charles Grandison* than

Handel's setting of *Alexander's Feast, or the Power of Music,* which appeared in 1736 (preceding the novel by some seventeen years) and which, after *Messiah,* became during the eighteenth century the most admired work of Handel.[47] Its greatest single quality is dignity, though there are also beguiling human touches, as in the softening into a long sigh of the tenor recitative at the words "The lovely Thais by his side" (pt. 1). Without ever falling into bathos, Handel exploits the pathetic and can be said to give it an erotic force which, however, never subverts the formal discipline. "He chose a mournful Muse" (pt. 1) is lovely and introspective, and Handel makes us feel the bodily implications of the line that follows, "Soft pity to infuse." The soprano air that laments Darius dead on the field of battle, with its fivefold "fall'n" and the phrase "With not a friend to close his eyes," verges on "tears" (pt. 1). These are in the text, and the music accompanies them by slow and caressing musical phrases that Dryden invites in "For pity melts the mind to love" (pt. 1). The more purely erotic sections Handel treats with equal skill and feeling, as the soprano and the cello interweave melodies that create fully sensual music and as the word "pleasures" is ornamented and enjoyed. Love can alternate between violins in unison briskly leaping up to echo words like "sigh'd" and "look'd" and instrumental sound reduced to faintness and somnolence, to accompany "sunk upon her breast" (pt. 1). Music is itself the main theme of *Alexander's Feast,* but next to it come love and pity, which the poet uses as emotions to calm and dispel military hate and the lust for destructive violence. Handel's music here obeys the libretto and explores a quintessentially eighteenth-century topos.

Handel's *Samson* (1743) is based on an adaptation of Milton's drama, but the music also invokes the heroic sublime and the pathetic of Dryden, with a strong admixture, when appropriate, of the Restoration playwright's sensuality. When Micah arrives with the Israelites, Handel moves with striking sureness into musical pathos in both the recitative and the beautiful aria "O mirror of our fickle state!" (act 1, sc. 1), addressed to the hero and his lamentable condition, its last word, "woe," being profoundly echoed in the music. The rich vein of subjective musicality that we have encountered in Purcell's *Dido and Aeneas* Handel even more deeply explores in Samson's lament "Oh loss of sight!" and in the aria, "Total eclipse!" (1.2), a haunting musical equivalent to Milton's several poetic responses to his blindness. The truly magnificent aria "Why does the God of Israel sleep?" (1.3) is a climax of the baroque sublime and shows that in his maturity Handel was not afraid of emotional exaltation, achieving it best in connection with religion. But sensuality does not appear

47. For an analysis of the musical expression both of the passions and of abstract ideas related to love, see Bronson, "Some Aspects of Music and Literature," in *Facets,* pp. 91–118. See also the discussion of Handel's setting of Dryden's "Ode for St. Cecilia's Day" in 1739 (ibid., pp. 99–107). For a learned survey of critical responses to the Dryden-Handel *Alexander's Feast,* see Robert Manson Myers, *Handel, Dryden, & Milton* (London: Bowes & Bowes, 1956), pp. 34–44.

until Dalila sings a gracious love song, "With plaintive notes," balanced by Samson's vigorous and antithetical lust song, rendered in accusatory anger and less successful than the virgin's aria that provoked it. The conception of Dalila's character, psychologically interesting and assertively sensual, is peculiar to the oratorio and is without direct or obvious sanction in *Samson Agonistes*.[48] "My faith and truth" (2.2) is a song of pure desire, whose languorous sensuality is introduced by the wife and echoed by the virgin. First and second sopranos voluptuously unite their voices in love pleas, with echoes; and the repetition of the air in unaccompanied voice is as alluring as it is nakedly simple. When Samson and Dalila unite in a duet, the effect is that of baroque antithesis. As she turns away, rejected, the hero becomes public, civic, traditional; and sensuality vanishes from the work. Other musical characterizations are skillfully done—for example, the dignity of Manoah and the triumphant heroic piety of Samson—but the opening pathos of Samson's condition and the physical allure of Dalila make a part of this oratorio a masterpiece of the erotic-pathetic worthy of a place in the story of sex and sensibility.

Semele (1744), a secular oratorio based on a text by Congreve, tells a pagan tale and can therefore concentrate on the theme of love more fully than *Samson* could possibly have done. This concentration is, as an eminent authority has said, energetic and ardent: "*Semele* is an opera of love, a radiant work celebrating, with a kind of ecstasy of the senses, the glory of woman's form and presence."[49] No other work discussed in this study—literary, pictorial, or musical—possesses its special combination of languorousness and sublimity, of physicality and the blazing destruction of a lovely body. Fire fights fire, as Semele's desires are burned out by desire itself. "Endless pleasure, endless love" (1.4) is a spirited baroque aria in which Semele describes the love play of the disarmed Jove, but it gives no hint of the profound truth that the king of the gods reveals, that he and love are one and it may be dangerous for a mortal to confront pure essence. Handel, even in his best work, was not always able to rise to the complexities suggested by his book. But he is a master of dramatic contrast, and even before the issues become clear in the text,

---

48. Paul Henry Lang comments that Handel has transformed Milton's Dalila from a "despicable harlot into a persuasive woman of beguiling feminity." *George Frideric Handel* (New York: W. W. Norton, 1966), p. 398. Winton Dean in *Handel's Dramatic Oratorios* says, "There is no evidence that Handel regarded sensuality with disgust or was enamoured of chastity; his works suggest that, if the balance tilted at all, it was in the other direction" (p. 331).

49. Lang, *Handel*, p. 410. Richardson demonstrates that the myth, thanks doubtless to Handel and Congreve, was not difficult to identify with if one possessed enough verve and arrogance. Lovelace, in saluting Clarissa with passion, says: "There was, I believe, a kind of frenzy in my manner which threw her into a panic like that of Semele perhaps, when the Thunderer, in all his majesty, surrounded with ten thousand celestial burning-glasses, was about to scorch her into a cinder." *Clarissa* (Everyman's Library), 2:98.

Handel with great subtlety and force contrasts the calm, long phrases of Jupiter in love with the short, breathless, ecstatic pants of the infatuated woman. The mortal now longs to put on immortality, but the lovemaking does not end therewith. It becomes richer: zephyrs sing a very lovely and highly rhythmic tribute to "soft delights" (2.3), and Jove himself tries to assuage ambition with Arcadian delights that conclude with a lovely verse from "Summer" in Pope's *Pastorals,* "Where'er you walk" (2.3). Handel's virtuosity extends to a breathtaking recitative that expresses levitation and an air that praises music (in "But hark! the heav'nly sphere turns round," 2.4) as an ecstasy of sound. In the delicious *scène de sommeil,* when Somnus sings his marvelous "Leave me, loathsome Light" (3.1), the languid, muted music is sensuous rather than sensual. And sensuality itself becomes hectic and fiery when Jupiter and Semele next meet, she now full of impious desires for immortality, he still alluring in "Come to my arms, / My lovely fair" (3.4). Semele calls for "all in full excess" (3.4), and Jove grants, though with moving reluctance, her desire to see him in all his glory. It is now too late for repentance; and crying out in language that anticipates Shelley and recalls Nat. Lee ("I burn, I burn, I faint," 3.7), she is destroyed by celestial fire—but not before she achieves final dignity in her F minor arioso. The opera is, up to its very last scene, a work of concentrated power that explores with memorable musical effect a wide spectrum of eroticism—the humanly sensual, the pastoral, the dangerous, and the blasphemous. It is not fire, however, that ends the opera but smoke. The priests sing in terror and astonishment, and the music hints, in smokelike, wispy phrases, at the postincendiary state of the heroine. The concluding D major chorus, which promises guiltless pleasure all around, is not fully persuasive in its optimism.

Solomon (1748) is more a splendid pageant than a dramatic exploration of character, but it is nonetheless perhaps Handel's finest expression of human sensuality and love. Its most beautiful sections contain the exquisite love music that Victorian England regarded as indecent blots on an otherwise chaste composer and expunged from his work—a censorship that measures the distance between the eighteenth century and the nineteenth with respect to my theme.[50] The opera includes pathos as well as love and belongs indubitably to the tradition of eros and sentiment. In the overture the allegro fugue and the music in triple measure must as surely anticipate the marital joy of Solomon as the maestoso, or grave, section prefigures his heroic piety. And in the powerful double chorus, in which the priests sing "With pious heart" (1.1), the leaping joy (always within a carefully designed baroque frame) that accompanies the words "distant nations catch the Song / And glow with holy flame"

50. Winton Dean has mounted a welcome attack on "the false and fatuous tradition that Handel's oratorios were intended as glorified anthems." *Handel's Dramatic Oratorios*, p. 284.

(1.1) must also anticipate, though here in a religious and not a natural context, the love of Solomon and his queen. Purely human love in the late Handel possesses both a sacred and a naturalistic dimension, each expressed in exquisite music. What we have seen him eschew early in his career, the sublime, he is fully comfortable with here. Zadok's recitative and aria ("Sacred raptures," 1.1) are full of Longinian transports as the music illustrates "descending flames," "rushing tides," "swelling heart," and "warm enthusiastic fires." Indeed we are tempted to think of ourselves on the Romantic frontier when we witness the flexible musical expression of "panting bosom," "hope of bliss," and "ravish'd soul" (1.1). The chorus that follows Zadok's emotional forthrightness enforces the impression that for Handel love is best in a Christian context—if that is not being anachronistic about the time of the action: forgiveness as well as power is being affirmed, and even nature flourishes best when the quality of mercy drops like the gentle rain from heaven. Solomon's aria ("What though I trace each herb and flow'r," 1.1) is that kind of naturalism, and the morning dew of the text evokes the tenderest and most exquisite response in the music. Handel reflects Dryden's heroic mercy, to which has been added the gentle naturalism of Pope's pastorals and Lady Winchilsea's lyrics.

When Solomon addresses his queen and, like Milton, hails "wedded love," she makes an alluring sensual response that begins, however, as a dancing tribute to wisdom. (Surely intellectual judiciousness cannot often have been celebrated in such an engaging triple measure!) As the queen ascends the nuptial bed, the erotic feeling grows ("But completely bless'd the day, / On my bosom as he lay," 1.2), and the music becomes less rhythmic and more lyrical. Nor does the magic disappear when triple measure returns and the word "bed" is fulsomely decorated. The duet of the king and queen ("Welcome as the dawn of day") is purely amatory, in no way directly religious, as the words of address, "my lovely king" and "my queen," are antiphonally sung. Solomon is urgent ("Haste, haste") as the richly erotic music impels the couple to the "pleasing gloom" and the "murm'ring rill" that the eighteenth century loved but seldom could animate with such life as breathes in this music. The splendid air "With thee th' unsheltered moor I'd tread," in long, sinuous, legato phrases, is deeply sensual music. Do we need to remind ourselves that such music from the lips of the queen does not in the least shadow her chastity, for after Spenser, Milton, and indeed the entire Reformation chastity was defined to include and even encourage the wife's glad honoring of her marital obligations? The climax of the erotic love of act 1 is the "Nightingale Chorus" ("May no rash intruder"), a ravishing anticipation of postcoital sleep, with its slow trills, heady repetitions, lullaby phrasing, and shimmering languor. Such language may seem to make of Handel an impressionist like Debussy, but it is impossible to exaggerate the amorous suggestiveness of the music.

The other important motif of *Solomon* relevant here is the pathos embodied in the character of the First Harlot, who cannot bear to have her child divided, in contrast to the cruel vengefulness of the Second Harlot, who can sadistically prefer the death of the child to surrendering it. The First Harlot represents maternal tenderness ("my soft darling"), sheds real tears, and pierces the air with her cry, "Spare my child" (2.3).[51] Handel cannot let this emotion go. Having forgiven her sins because of her sacrificial maternal love, he now in her final aria ("Beneath the vine, or fig-tree's shade") gives to the pathos an exquisite G major pastoralism in slow triple measure. The rest of the oratorio, with its praise, during the visit of the Queen of Sheba, of art, benevolent power, and religion, introduces nothing at variance with the themes of conjugal and parental love. Handel's several affinities with Dryden were noted earlier; here Handel rivals Milton's verse in portraying the Edenic love of *Paradise Lost*. It is difficult to think of music in the eighteenth century that might more appropriately have accompanied the innocent ardors of our first parents than the solos, duets, and orchestral accompaniments of Solomon and his queen.

Greuze

Jean-Baptiste Greuze more than any other painter illustrates the union of sex and sensibility. His work constitutes a kind of climax of the trends I have been developing out of Milton—a climax not in quality but certainly in typicality. We should not—indeed we *cannot* any longer—patronize his abilities;[52] but though his star is once more on the ascendant, he will perhaps never regain the enormous reputation he enjoyed in his own day. For all his triumphs he will always stand well below Watteau—a pity, really, for though Greuze embodies mid-century sentiment, he cannot be said to exalt it, as Watteau exalted the salon eroticism of his own day; and mid- and late eighteenth-century sensibility therefore lacks an absolutely compelling pictorial embodiment. Like Watteau—and other parallels can be found between the two masters[53]—Greuze, whose origins were outside the capital and the

51. Dean regards the air in F minor, "Can I see my infant gored?" in which the First Harlot offers her child ("Take him all") as "the supreme depiction in music of torn maternal love." Ibid., p. 522.

52. The appearance of the catalog of the exhibition of Greuze shown at Hartford, San Francisco, and Dijon from 1 Dec. 1976 to 31 July 1977 opened the eyes of many to the considerable power of this artist. See Edgar Munhall, *Jean-Baptiste Greuze: 1725–1805* (Wadsworth Atheneum, Hartford, Conn.). Item, figure, and page numbers following mention of Greuze's works in my text refer to this catalog (*Cat.*).

53. A beautiful black-and-white chalk drawing by Watteau at the Morgan Library, *Seated Woman*, one of some one hundred designs engraved by Boucher, seems to me to anticipate

fashionable world, did not allow Paris to refine away his original rustic tastes and instincts. He was frequently described by his contemporaries as "unique" (*Cat.*, p. 8). The epithet indicates that they were struck not so much by a powerful originality as by a forcefully presented familiarity that aroused an echo in every bosom. Greuze, like Hogarth, won enormous acclaim from the humble and sophisticated alike, and it is significant that the great *philosophe* who praised Richardson was equally lyrical about Greuze. Diderot, for all his pioneering genius, was very much a man of his time, and he sensed that both the novelist and the painter embodied the newer forces of democratic sensibility that were sweeping through culture.

The rising acclaim accorded Greuze in our own day has really nothing to do with sensibility; it is, rather, a tribute to his power as an artist, and on those grounds it is well deserved. But if we look closely at some of the drawings that reveal his essential powers, we find that they betray not only pure skill but also a specific ability to produce sentimental feeling. The black-and-red chalk drawing *Seated Male Nude with Left Leg Outstretched* (1758, pl. 23), is vastly more than the academic exercise it most surely is, showing admirable anatomical skill.[54] Nor is it notable chiefly for the energy instinct in every line, an energy not entirely unworthy of Michelangelo, who may indeed be its distant inspiration. The arresting quality is the pathos one feels in the curved back, the folded hands, the position of the head. As the muscles tighten in tension, the whole figure seems to give itself over to grief. Similarly, in *Seated Nude Woman* (1767, pl. 24) Greuze recalls tradition and expresses originality. He brings to mind Rubens's rendition of the famous *topos* Charity[55] and, in the hands and the breasts, the Venus Pudica in the Uffizi. But the powerfully drawn nude has the stamp of individual feeling: her intent gaze is related to the clasping of the breasts with nervous fingers and the pressing together of the legs. Even bolder is *Cimon and Pero* in the Louvre (*Cat.*, no. 60), a version of *La charité romaine,* in which a determined, even fierce, daughter breast-feeds her imprisoned father who had been doomed to die of starvation—a scene that has

---

Greuze. A girl, who could be a peasant though her face has some aristocratic qualities, looks up and reveals only a profile. She is obviously intent upon something and reveals the "absorption" of *sensibilité.* The famous Greuze in Warsaw, *The Fowler* (*Cat.*, no. 12)—and also the ink and wash drawing of the same subject at the Bibliothèque Nationale (*Cat.*, no. 11)—seems to recall Watteau in color and in treatment of the musical instrument and the clothes, although there are also profound differences.

54. That this drawing is academic, however good, will appear from examining *Eighteenth-Century French Life-Drawings*, ed. James Henry Rubin (Princeton, N.J.: Art Museum, 1977).

55. This theme is one of the most persistent in Western culture, prominent from the Middle Ages to Bouguereau. Charity is usually presented as a seated figure, with one or more children (usually more) clinging to her. Her breasts are ample and often one is bared, for Charity, who sometimes also gives bread to beggars, is usually *lactante.* See the folio Td 24, tome 1, at the Bibliothèque Nationale, s.v. "Charity."

haunted Western imagination even up to the concluding scene of Steinbeck's *Grapes of Wrath.* Greuze's dark, forboding black- and gray-ink wash over pencil, big with menace, unforgettably expresses aged gratitude and dependence on womanly kindness, anger, and fortitude combined. Two portrayals of Saint Mary of Egypt bring us, though indirectly, to the subject of sexual love, one of Greuze's most important themes. In one (Musée de Dijon; *Cat.,* no. 110), the nude, kneeling saint holds a skull as she looks up to the divine light, her expression one of religious wonder tinged with fear, while her body is charged with erotic excitement or the recollection of it. This drawing demonstrates that Greuze, like Richardson, had a strain of the baroque in him. In the oil painting (pl. 25) erotic power is still present as the dark-haired nude beauty kneels on penitential stairs. No religious light shines on this grief-stricken repentance over a debauched life. The body, still voluptuous, absorbs and reflects all the light, and its curve and posture, the shape of the lip and the sadness of the eye, reveal a master of sorrow and sensuality combined.

If Greuze eroticizes sacred story, he sentimentalizes classical myth and legend, which were already erotic, and so brings both great traditions into the stream of eighteenth-century feeling. One neoclassical drawing, *Anacreon in His Old Age Crowned by Love* (*Cat.,* no. 101), celebrates the ageless eroticism of a Greek poet well known in Greuze's epoch. But it is the graceful, slender Eros, standing on the poet's knee, who catches the contemporary *ésprit.* A kind of laughing antitype of tears, he smiles the smile and conveys the cheerfulness of *un coeur sensible. Aegina Visited by Jupiter* (pl. 26)—and attended by a fully clothed and concerned domestic—is a large and compelling picture to which uncolored reproduction is extremely unjust. Although Aegina's marmoreal body lacks the brilliant chromatic variety of the bed sheets, through her the essential psychological drama is fully conveyed. As her domestic attendant (very well portrayed) tries to soothe her tense fears, the girl strikes one as much more like Pamela on her wedding night (with its "awful" fears) than the eager and ambitious Semele of Handel's music. Taken as myth in the *gusto grande,* the expression on Aegina's face would be unpersuasive; taken as the portrayal of an ordinary mortal on the edge of unknown erotic experience, her look is just about as profound as it ought to be, a combination of fear and innocent curiosity. The same essential theme appears in a genre Greuze rarely used, an allegory, *Innocence Carried off by Cupid* (Louvre; *Cat.,* no. 100), a late painting, which though more ambitious is less successful. The story is brilliantly conceived and very much worth describing: a clothed maiden is caught between the concerned and restraining family and the voluptuous and smiling Cupid and his train, who propel her toward experience in a swirl of ribbons and gowns. This is a one-person embarkation for Cythera, and if it is less successful than its great forerunner or even than Greuze at his best, the reason is that Innocence is weak and simpering. It is sad that the expression, meant to convey simultaneous longing and reluctant fear, did not come off, since we might then have had a successful visual epitome of the central erotic concern of the century.

In the famous genre scenes that portray family life, Greuze reflects other great themes of eighteenth-century prose fiction. Some communicate only in general terms the new sense of family unity achieved when a pious and authoritative father reads from an open Bible to a family that shows varying degrees of attention but is essentially unified and respectful. In the oil painting entitled *The Well-Beloved Mother* (*Cat.*, fig. 4), the traditional *topos* of Charity is transferred to the hearth: a woman in white is fondled and pressed in on by her many children as an adoring husband and nurse look on. When a father dies, illness and death make it impossible to sentimentalize him, but he is mourned deeply by his many children (no. 51). Greuze is the poet of the family bonding that took place as "affective individualism" came to dominate English and French culture. But Greuze's sense of drama is too strong to allow him to remain content with easy pieties, and in fact his greatest genre paintings retell the story of the Prodigal Son, giving it a tragic twist at the end. The sister paintings in the Louvre, both entitled *La malédiction paternelle,* portray the force of feeling that went into paternal anger and the responses to it in the novels of Richardson and Rousseau. In the first of these, *Le fils ingrat* (pl. 27), a handsome son is stunned and fearful, the cursing father is unrestrained in his anger, and the entire family is shaken as the tense body of the father stretches out in malediction toward the object of his wrath and so ruptures the unity of the family. In the sequel, *Le fils puni* (pl. 28), the prodigal returns, not to eat the fatted calf and be restored to his inheritance but to behold the dead body of the father, whose departing soul (invisible to us) the grieving family behold leaving the body. One could dwell on the many compelling details of this domestic drama; the important point is that Greuze has created a tragedy and that he provides an illuminating gloss on the spirit of a Clarissa bent under a fatherly curse which, though undeserved, is nonetheless fearsome. In both the novel and the painting the pathos lies in the intervention of death before the curse can be lifted or the blessing bestowed.

A man of such familial sensibility, to say nothing of his own personal propensities toward gallantry, could hardly have been kept from a portrayal of love. And a very special and characteristic kind of portrayal it was. The *Young Shepherd Holding a Flower* (pl. 29) shows a boy in love, about to blow away the dandelion gone to seed in order to learn whether his love is reciprocated; it is an altogether graceful and haunting portrayal, particularly in the eyes and mouth, of very young male love, a subject not often undertaken. In *The White Hat* (pl. 30) a beautiful young woman, older than the shepherd, is irresistibly voluptuous—consider the exposed breast, the teasingly light garment, the slightly pursed lips, the lowered eyes—but at the same time tenderly, perhaps a bit suavely innocent.[56] It is the same theme we keep encountering, here with an emphasis upon delicacy and only a hint of experience to come. In 1765 Greuze painted a more obviously sensual and aggressive woman, *Une jeune fille qui envoie un baiser par la fenêtre, apuyée sur les fleurs, qu'elle brise,* which was hung in the Salon of 1769.[57] The girl is young and appears in a suggestive *déshabille.* Having just received a note from her lover, she blows him a kiss from her window. Diderot finds the girl sensual: "Il est impossible de vous peindre la volupté de cette figure. Ses yeux, ses paupières en sont chargés! . . . Elle est ivre."[58] Then he goes on to describe her abandonment to passion, and incidentally his own, in an interesting revelation of how a successful eighteenth-century love painting was reacted to: her left arm crushes a pot of flowers, the billet falls from her hands, her fingers and indeed her whole body breathe carnality. Perhaps Diderot sees too much if he in fact discovers a fully robust and uninhibited sexuality. There seems to be delicacy and coquettishness in the pleasure, as we can see from our longer perspective. Indeed the picture loses both its individual charm and its mid-century typicality if those qualities are overlooked. It is assertively erotic, but its spirit is also *sensible.*

Perhaps a morphology of Greuzian sensibility, based on many portraits of girls by Greuze that are often well below excellence and are sometimes even revolting, will be helpful in summarizing his impact. Anita Brookner has called these girls "Lolitas" and has described the artist's production as "decent pornography." David Kunzle has said that Greuze reflected "the sentimental and moral preoccupations of his age" in "that endless series of liquescent, yearning girls, strange fusions of protesting innocence and complacent depravity. With them Greuze unites in a single physiognomic statement the pleasures of sin and the pleasures of remorse."[59] The word "depravity" is too strong (it smashes "delicacy" to a thousand pieces); but the comment is sensi-

56. Garry Wills's comment on this painting, which is reproduced in color in *Cat.* (no. 91), is vividly phrased and fully just: *"The White Hat* . . . sifts light and color through or over feathers, lips, eyes, breasts, silk in a way that makes Renoir's *Madam Henriot* look like an amateur's first approach to the way light uses clothes to color skin, skin to color clothes." "Machines for Sentiment," a review of the Munhall catalog in *New York Review of Books,* 17 Feb. 1977, p. 42.

57. Reproduced by Fried (see above, n.11), fig. 22.

58. Quoted ibid., p. 172 ("It is impossible to describe for you the sensuality of that figure. Her eyes, her eyelids are full of it! . . . She is intoxicated").

59. David Kunzle, *The Early Comic Strip* (Berkeley and Los Angeles: University of California Press, 1973), p. 393 (vol. 1 in *History of the Comic Strip*). Anita Brookner is apparently quoted (p. 391) from her University of London dissertation on Greuze. In her book (*Greuze* [London: Paul Elek, 1972], pp. 83–84, 90, 128–29) Brookner shows that some of the most offensive heads of girls were produced by Greuze in his later years (their production reached a peak in the late 1780s) when his popularity was waning and his need for cash was clamant. For additional examples of the Greuzian girl, see Brookner, pls. 69, 75–78, 81–82. Munhall, for understandable reasons, includes almost nothing of this work in the catalog. For a brief but perceptive analysis of Greuze, see Robert Rosenblum, "The Greuze Exhibition at Hartford and Elsewhere," *Burlington Magazine* 119 (Feb. 1977): 145–49. This essay, which appeared after this chapter was written, tends to enforce

tive in seeing an uncomfortable hint of sin in the sensibility and scenting out the almost evangelical pleasure in remorse that helps to account for the enormous popularity of this work. One must insist that Greuze is capable of healthy joy and an infectious vivacity in some of his female studies, and some can be quintessentially Greuzian and yet attract and compel. But a composite of many of the *têtes d'expression,* consisting of the following, will show why Greuze has provoked outrage and dismay: moist, full, red lips that are present even in young children; elevated eyes that recall the Magdalenes and saints of Guido Reni, Domenichino, and even an artist as early as Perugino; the head tilted to one side; partially exposed breasts and a suggestion of self-embrace, particularly if they are large; a mouth slightly open but not in laughter; considerable white showing in the eye; the caressing of a pet animal or bird; a coy placement of one hand or even one finger; and melting languor in the face that seems to anticipate rather than remember pleasure. Sometimes even the youngest girls seem to squirm with desire; and the nostrils flare, the hair curls suggestively, the expression is intolerably sweet and humble, and the faces are round and soft. Two paintings by Greuze, both ambitious and skillful works well above the quality of most of the female heads just described, embody many of their qualities and at the same time make the religious metaphor overt. About *La prière du matin,* a faulty but revealing painting in Montpellier (pl. 31), one is led to ask what kind of morning prayer is being offered. The bare shoulder, the falling hair, the expectant mouth, the loosely clasped hands, the bare feet, and the eyes all persuade us that the girl is beseeching a visit from Jove, not from Jehovah, and that the ecstasy yearned for is scarcely a union with the Ancient of Days.

If the content of the maiden's *prière* should be in doubt, another painting, *The Votive Offering to Cupid* (pl. 32), ought to dispel it. Here the object of the prayer is portrayed as an animated statue whose flesh, posture, and expression suggest that the kneeling maiden has found a living god in Cupid. The allegory unlocks the Greuzian mystery, if there ever was one. The girls of this enormously admired and typical painter comprised, as no other artistic creations ever did, sex and sensibility, *Schmachten* inspired by *Liebe.*

It is one of the special merits of Greuze that he tells cultural time so accurately. We are well past rococo refinement, though in this last painting the statue and its base recall Watteau. We have not yet come to the passionate

---

my belief in Greuze's relevance to the basic themes of this book. Rosenblum believes the painting called *Jupiter and Aegina* in actuality describes Jupiter's descent to Semele. He also says that *Saint Mary of Egypt* is an "astonishing mixture of the voluptuous and the chaste"; if so, Greuze is here close to some of Richardson's and Rousseau's central effects. Rosenblum's analysis of *Lot and His Daughters* (a work of "unmitigated carnality," a "gross but powerful representation of geriatric nudity, incest, and drunkenness") is related to my discussions of sexual morbidity from Milton's allegory of Satan, Sin, and Death through Otway all the way up to Rousseau and Goethe.

Romantic abandonment, though there is much in Greuze that anticipates Gros, Girodet, or Prud'hon. We are at exactly the point, well after Milton, very shortly before Mozart, and precisely during the vogue of *A Sentimental Journey,* when sensibility was being eroticized and feeling, as in immediately pregenital adolescence, was spread pan-corporeally to all the nerves and receptors of the body.

Mozart

Mozart, whom it is not entirely absurd to consider the apogee of all music, is certainly that for the Age of Sensibility. Clarissa, we remember, made fellow feeling, tenderness of heart, an absolute precondition of heterosexual love, and her tragedy lay in being courted—and assaulted—by a sadist and not a Man of Feeling. Would Mozart have passed Clarissa's test? Triumphantly, for his ideal seems to be a union of sexual love with a *coeur sensible.* In *The Abduction from the Seraglio* (1782) the love of Belmonte and Constanza is in the end blessed by the ennobled Muslim, the Pasha Selim, who abjures cruelty (not in music, alas! for in this *Singspiel* he has a spoken part only) and then turns to benevolence, shaming the Christians by his forgiveness.[60] He recalls Montezuma, Almanzor, and Aureng-Zebe, and his movement from cruelty to forgiveness is in the pattern Dryden established during the late Restoration. Toward the end of his career, in *La clemenza di Tito* (1791), Mozart accompanies the love story with action in which the Roman emperor is revealed as a Man of Feeling, perhaps even a proto-Christian, who also possesses the cultural and ethical values of the Enlightenment. He has so much respect for mutuality that he renounces the woman he is wooing because she already loves another, and he delights in the courage and sincerity that impel her to reveal the commitment of her heart even if that revelation disappoints the one who has the power to destroy her.

Mozart's four greatest operas are also concerned with love—in both original and typical ways. The composer has produced musical equivalents of most of the tendencies and themes I have discussed. When he does not suffuse the emotions with love, he develops them in contrast to or in conflict with love. Subtly and complexly the Mozart of the operas is always concerned with eros and sensibility. Each of these qualities, as we now know well, is definable in history and philosophy; it is no exaggeration to say that in Mozart's most exalted music the two unite to become a single beauty

60. For an excellent discussion of this opera, which emphasizes the passion and the sensuousness of its protrayal of love and the final transcendence of both qualities, see Singer, *Mozart & Beethoven,* pp. 105–8. For the background, see Miriam K. Whaples, "Exoticism in Dramatic Music, 1600–1800," Ph.D. diss., Indiana University, 1958.

truly blent, whose red and white
Nature's own sweet and cunning hand laid on.
[*Twelfth Night,* 1.5]

"The Marriage of Figaro"

Love in *The Marriage of Figaro* (1786) is itself a skillful blend of four distinguishable kinds, each worthy of brief attention: (1) masculine love contrastingly portrayed in the conventional Count and the adventuresome Figaro, the new man; (2) the narcissistic, childlike love that flutters Cherubino's heart; (3) the unashamedly frank love that Susanna and the Countess express, with differences appropriate to their respective social stations; and (4) the pathetically disappointed and unrealized love felt by the Countess.

1. I have called the love experienced by both the Count and Figaro masculine, but what a contrast the two present! They are brought into conflict at the very opening. That the title character is deeply in love with his future wife, Susanna, is evident immediately in the lovely duet Mozart gives them as well as his jealousy of the Count, who has apparently threatened not only to invoke the *jus primae noctis* but also to make further depredations that the proximity of the bedroom will facilitate. Figaro's spirited and impudent *cavatina*, "Se vuol ballare" (act 1; p. 76),[61] is a challenge to a contest of wit and manliness and a declaration, if not of social and class independence, then certainly of powerful unwillingness to cower before such an affront as the ancient *droit du seigneur* or the power of social place to invade a humbler bedroom at any time. It is important to see this conflict not primarily as a general class or political challenge but as a confrontation of two lovers, one a healthy, witty servant who is alive to his amorous rights, the other an avatar of class-conscious sexual privilege and of old-fashioned mores in love. As the marvelous first act comes to a close and it becomes clear that by exchanging clothes Susanna and the Countess are going to spring a trap on the two proud men they love, the music becomes irresistibly, almost fatefully rhythmic. Mozart's is a world of comedy, and his beat is by no means Beethoven's cosmological and ominous pulse. The music makes us virtually certain that the trap will be sprung easily by the likes of Figaro. But the *dénouement* is vastly more than a quick comic resolution that conventionally tidies up the loose ends. The Count is brought to his knees and to a plea for forgiveness, the opera thus working to frustrate and humiliate the old double standard of Almaviva, and indeed of sporting love in general, for the Count has been flirtatious with all and sundry but neglectful of his

61. For the convenience of the literary student who wishes to study the words, a page reference is given after each important Mozart aria, to the libretto as printed in *The Great Operas of Mozart* (New York: W. W. Norton, 1964). On the facing page is an idiomatic English translation supplied, variously, by W. H. Auden, Chester Kallman, Ruth and Thomas Martin, and John Bloch. Nathan Broder supplies the general essay on Mozart and one on each opera. The act and scene numbers are supplied whenever possible.

wife. More than that: the word "perdono" (act 4; p. 154) produces a resolving richness of harmony that suggests a deep and satisfying equilibrium. Stendhal remarks that "Mozart concludes his *Folle Journée* with the most beautiful piece of church-music that can be heard anywhere."[62] The remark is sensitive and just and implies that something important and basic was present in the madcap pranks to warrant the choral blessing at the end. What could it have been? Undoubtedly the virility which Figaro and even the Count possessed, which Susanna and the Countess longed for, and which a growing eighteenth-century current was making the indispensable basis of enduring marital compatibility. Mozart is typical of his age in both celebrating libidinous energy and then finally directing it to the institution of marriage.

2. What is Mozart's response to the complex blending of the old and the new that Cherubino represents, whose delicacy is such a contrast to the manly passion of Figaro? It is in part to create brilliant music that does not dispel the erotic ambiguousness of the page, who in "Non più andrai" is called "Narcisetto, Andoncino d'amor." This little Narcissus, this small Adonis who is, as Susanna insists, "ancora fanciullo" (act 1, p. 90), looks back to the Cupids of Watteau, Boucher, and the rococo; but he is also highly typical of the pre-adolescent androgyny that *sensibilité* loved to portray, a sexual ambiguity emphasized by his being dressed as a girl. Cherubino, standing on the edge of experience, is all aflutter with love. He reveals in his first aria, "Non so più cosa son, cosa faccio" (p. 82), that he is not yet accustomed to his newly felt flames, not yet sure of his sexual identity. But this amorous butterfly is highly attractive to the ladies—one reason that Figaro consigns him so vigorously to martial dangers and exertions. Susanna's flirtatious, girlish "Venite, inginocchiatevi" (2; p. 96) shows the regressive pleasure she and the Countess feel as they dress this doll in women's clothes. There is more here than meets most people's eyes, and perhaps Beaumarchais penetrated deeply into an important cultural trend when he required that the role be entrusted to a pretty girl "pour en bien sentir les finesses."[63]

3. If Figaro and the Count represent a simple contrast of manly rivalry and Figaro and Cherubino represent a rich and complex opposition of mature manliness and a sexually dubious adolescence that appeals to women even at the moment they long for something more normal, then Susanna and the Countess represent a contrast arising out of a quality they have in common.

62. Quoted by Singer, *Mozart & Beethoven,* p. 85.
63. ("in order better to feel the refinements.") This comment is quoted by Singer (p. 81). I owe the comment about Cherubino as Narcissus to Leonard Barkan. It is important also to note that Cherubino invokes the old Petrarchan conceits when he asks in the enchanting "Voi che sapete" (pp. 94, 96) what love truly is. The translation (p. 83) somewhat obscures the meaning of "Non so più cosa son, cosa faccio": "I can't give you a good explanation / For this new and confusing sensation." Literally translated, what Cherubino says is: "I no longer know what I am, what I do; / Now I am of fire, now of ice."

Both are frank about their longings. The clever, sporting servant girl, who is willing to risk a compromising game with the Count up to a point, really loves and desires her man, the virile Figaro. Her aria "Deh! vieni, non tardar" (4; pp. 144, 146) shows that her play with the delicate Cherubino was part of a richer and more ambiguous sensibility than is sometimes conceded her, in which the normal and healthy wins out. If Susanna's longings are open and frank, the same can be said of the Countess's, though we must take some account of class decorum in the expression. In act 1 she acknowledges that her desires are sexual and need to be satisfied by human contact. Surely her playful response to Cherubino's special kind of youthful charm and her joining the plot with Susanna are motivated by that need.

4. But the Countess's longings are also deepened by tragic feeling, a fact that makes her unique in this opera and that lifts her to a higher level of love. In the great "Porgi amor" (2; p. 92) the word "morir" is a leitmotiv: a mature woman, wounded by a marriage that has flouted her desires and insulted her integrity, longs for death. Mozart has enriched the venerable *topos* of love and death with the profoundest melancholy: like Julie, the Countess knows that the cup of *sensibilité* is at once "douce et amère." The Countess's torment has a modern side to it: she is disillusioned with the aristocratic way of life; she protests its double standard and its insult to the dignity of woman. In "Dove sono i bei momenti?" (3; p. 130) this woman, still young and attractive, crystallizes her malaise into nostalgia for past ecstasy and hope for future restoration of joy. That restoration is achieved in the solution of the plot, and the Countess, proving herself resilient, forgives her husband to the accompaniment of festive music that asserts the dominance of the comic spirit but that at the same time, in its hymnlike, quiet solemnity and tenderness, reminds us that a human heart has almost been broken and that the old and irresponsible social behavior cannot satisfy the deep longings of body and soul.[64]

"Don Giovanni"

Watteau's Don Juan makes his advances in a situation that involves music. On one canvas he is about to embrace a gorgeously dressed actress, perhaps

---

64. Stendhal, who finds this opera to be a sublime *mélange* of witty *esprit* and melancholy, believes that the Countess, that loving, unloved figure, provides the melancholy, of which there is no hint in Beaumarchais. See Michael Levey, "Aspects of Mozart's Heroines," *Journal of the Warburg and Courtauld Institutes* 22 (Jan.–June 1959): 132–56, esp. pp. 144–45. Levey finds that the Countess, who can be said to gain control of herself in "Dove sono," achieves a kind of apotheosis of charity and harmony at the end. Although Levey makes the climax excessively religious (I find it, rather, a triumph of sensibility over convention), I prefer it to the view of Singer, who finds the Countess "self-pitying" in "Porgi amor," dreamily nostalgic in "Dove sono," and in general too gentle for any kind of sensuous or passionate emotion (*Mozart & Beethoven*, p. 83). Yet in the end, Singer believes, the Countess triumphs through her "extraordinary gentleness" (p. 85). The present work hopes to show that sex and sensibility are inseparable in the fullest visions of human happiness. Mozart's achievement in creating the Countess seems to rise to that level.

poised to sing. Her response, a complex one that combines pleasure and surprise, requires more than colored forms on canvas to bring out its meanings and calls for the expatiating skills of a novelist or the suggestive skills of a musical composer to develop the pictorial hints. On the same canvas the seduction is accompanied by four lovers who, a short distance away, are engaged in a music lesson.[65] The music that Watteau—and of course others too—associated with the archetypal lover was abundantly provided by Mozart, whose *Don Giovanni* (1787) is the richest, as it is the most complex, response to the legend in our culture. The paradoxes and ambiguities that arise from the *buffo* and *serio* sides of the hero's character can be understood only in relation to the three women of the opera, each highly individual, each different from the others: Zerlina, Donna Elvira, and Donna Anna.

Zerlina has been adjudged a flirt, a fool, a hypocrite, a scamp, a vivacious *ingénue,* a rural Venus, an embodiment of the life force. Since Mozart's music invites the comparison, she must be seen as the parallel in this opera to Susanna of *Figaro;* but she is even more gaily sensual, her sparkling, dancing charms being one of its enduring glories. The duet with the Don, however seductive he may be, however flirtatious she, is big with sensual promise that does not, however, move passionately to fulfillment: the love seems on her part to be what it is called, an "innocente amore" (1.3; p. 184). Those who believe that a premarital consummation with the Don takes place offstage are wide of the mark. Such melodrama would considerably dull the sparkle of what Mozart's music seems to suggest is a winsome and ambiguous foreplay by a girl of a bold spirit but an essentially good heart. Zerlina's consolation (in "Vedrai carino," 2.1; p. 220) of her awkward, innocent man, whom the Don has beaten, shows clearly who will be sexually aggressive in their union, despite her humble protests of submission in "Batti, batti" (1.4; p. 194). The "balsamo" she promises him for his wound does not come exclusively from the heart, and her other double entendres are not difficult to penetrate.[66] The girl is vivacious and indiscreet, but not seriously censurable and certainly far from tragic. The presence of this charming girl in the opera suggests that an encounter with "Donnish" charm is precisely what country cloddishness now and then needs.

Donna Elvira, a more complex being, is given greater musical attention. Her rage—with its violent and bloody thoughts of revenge ("Ah! Chi mi dice mai," 1.2; p. 172)—is accompanied by the Don's sensually caressing addresses, "Poverina! Poverina! . . . Signorina! Signorina!" (p. 174). This juxtaposition of seductive consolation and blazing love anger shows that the deserted woman is

---

65. Ferré, 2:670. See also ibid., 1:103–8.

66. Singer (p. 63) says illuminatingly that "in Ovid, Zerlinas populate the countryside," suggesting that her role is like that of the Ovidian Cupid who wounds with the arrow in one hand and with the other applies the sexual unguent. Zerlina cures the evil she inflicts.

still sexually hungry, and her cries should be seen not so much as evidence against her permanent character as signs of the possession of a formidable sexual nature. The musical exploration of Elvira's ambivalence must have greatly interested Mozart, for it continues in "Ah! fuggi il traditor!" where difficult, unconventionally accented music burns with a hatred that is almost at once cloaked in gentle concern as she warns Donna Anna of the Don's wiles (1.3; p. 184). Rage and love continue to tear this woman's breast until the very end. "Ah! taci, ingiusto core!" (2.1; p. 210) is lyrical because Donna Elvira continues to love; and Leporello, disguised as the Don, is able to lead her off because her desires are still strong. When the disguised servant leaves her, her rage bursts out like a Roman candle, in the theatrical but brilliant "Mi tradì," which is perfectly sincere in its expression of pure hatred, an aria made interesting by intermittent expressions of tenderness that show the lady could still love.[67] During the Don's last meal Donna Elvira arrives to kneel before him, showing that her cruel lover had indeed filled her whole being with an obsessive sensuality. In Milton or Dryden such sensuality expressed in a serious work of art was almost always accompanied by punishing moral disapproval. Mozart understands its essential selfishness as he relentlessly portrays its gripping hold on her spirit. But he does not seem to judge her or condemn it.

Musically, he rates Donna Elvira's sensuality slightly below the moral sublimity and pathetic tenderness of Donna Anna's emotions, which are those of an aggrieved beloved and of a bereaved daughter. Surely this character is conceived partly in mythical terms; the myth concerns neither the remotely cosmological nor the grandly institutional but the personal and the familial. The demonic lover has attempted to sully personal love, and his murderous hand has dispatched a father. And so the call for revenge in Donna Anna's "Or sai chi l'onore rapir a me volse" (1.3; p. 190) is, though not overtly religious, a cry for justice; and all through the opera this austerely conceived woman possesses Clarissa-like traits of an aroused conscience. In the duets with her lover she provides the fire and force of moral indignation; in the ensemble that Donna Elvira joins she contributes religious and moral solemnity. Her character requires the complementary sweetness of Don Ottavio's love, which has sometimes been harshly judged as lacking in dignity and depth. It should not, however, be viewed alone, any more than his beloved's anger should be; both are parts of a larger whole. Together, the two constitute an impressive portrayal of love, which possesses enough energy to overcome

---

67. Cf. the lines, "Ma se guardo il suo cimento, / Palpitando il cor mi va" ("But if I look on his face, my heart beats with excitement"). For the text of the recitative "In quali eccessi" and the aria "Mi tradì," see Mozart's *Werke,* ser. 5, no. 18, *Opern* (reprint of the Leipzig ed.; Ann Arbor, Mich.: J. W. Edwards, 1955), pp. 261–70. The aria does not, curiously, appear in the libretto in *The Great Operas.*

the limitations we feel in the individual characters when separated. Don Ottavio's "Il mio tesoro" (2.2; p. 224) takes on great amorous intensity in its minor section, an intensity that Donna Anna's climactic aria, "Non mi dir" (2.4; p. 230) also possesses in abundance. She responds to her lover's use of the Petrarchan word "crudele," rejecting its applicability to her heart, which is constant, tender, and full of reciprocating love. Thus Mozart has softened the acerbity of her character without removing either her somewhat aggressive piety or a hint of ironic ambiguity in treating this lofty dame. Her noble and brilliantly accompanied aria must be viewed as a masterpiece, however grave and elevated, of love and sensibility.

Against these richly human and not always attractive portrayals of female humanity the character of the Don develops its essential ambivalence. That ambivalence lies deep within the overture, which combines somber tragic strains with the sparkling music of seductive gallantry. Even the catalog aria ("Madamina!" 1.2; p. 176), which is sung by Leporello to the outraged Donna Elvira, portrays a libidinous machine whose function it is not to enjoy love but to produce a longer and ever longer list. But at the same time the reading of the list has its caressing side (consider the phrase beginning "nella bionda"), and its very size and comprehensiveness have an almost superhuman grandeur. The champagne aria ("Finch'han dal vino," 1.3; p. 194), for all its brilliant intensity, shows more than anything else that the Don is preoccupied with increasing the length of his list; but concurrently he is capable of the alluring "Deh, vieni" (2.1; p. 216), surely a pure essence of nighttime pleasurable longing, the very apotheosis of the serenade. The concluding scene presents a man of complete sensuality—he loves food and wine as well as women—and brings punishment to a murderer and a rapist. Off he goes to hell, his usual courage deserting him as he confesses to a "tremore insolito" (2.5; p. 238), a shudder that the audience must have shared as the solemn statue precipitates him into the infernal flames. These are real enough in the Don's last aria, in Leporello's heated and frightened imagination, and in most productions. But before the music is well over, the Christian hell has been cooled considerably; and Zerlina, Masetto, and Leporello finally consign him not to the hands of an angry God but to the company of Prosperpine and Pluto:

> Resti dunque quel birbon
> Con Prosperpina e Pluton!
> [2.5; p. 240]

Not much can be concluded from all this, but it is not out of character that the opera should remain somewhat ambiguous about the nature of the hero's final punishment.

The opera is full of contradictions, and the central one about the hero—is he more criminal than lover, or more lover than criminal?—has produced a formidable body of critical analysis. The problem cannot be easily resolved. If Lovelace, despite Richardson's unrelenting moralizing, was nevertheless attractive even to contemporary readers of *Clarissa*, what shall one say of the Don, to whom Mozart gives immortal music? That music makes several inescapable points: the hero possesses, despite his sins—and in deep ways because of them—dignity, courage, and vital force; he knows how to woo and win; and though his appetite is boundless and unappeasable, he is no mere automaton of sensuality, or he would not arouse fascination in his victims and in the creative spirits that have through the centuries contributed to his immortality. He causes love—and hate and rage and dismay, too—in others; he produces sensual passion in a humanity that is doomed to suffer for yielding to his charms, which nevertheless beget some of its only real joys. The "antichissima canzon" (p. 242) of jollity which the joyful peasants sing at the close must surely express more than relief at his disappearance and satisfaction at his postmortem torments. Mozart could not have escaped perceiving that from his doomed hero springs whatever is energetic and life-enhancing in the ensemble of men and women who live in his opera. The more one thinks about it, the deeper the paradox becomes, and in the end it seems unresolvable. It is perhaps as unresolvable as the very relations of love and sensuality: sensuality can be an enormous evil, and yet love cannot be realized fully without it.

Don Giovanni is a flawed work, but more fervent thought and an intenser artistic concentration would not have boiled out the foreign matter. The opera is flawed as Chaucer's *Troilus*, Milton's *Paradise Lost*, and Richardson's *Clarissa* are flawed. Each of these works produces considerable residual dissatisfaction because we cannot without protest allow heaven to have its way in defeating what we have loved or admired about the earthly and even the hellish: the physical love of Troilus and Criseyde, the magnificent rebelliousness of Satan, the energetic charm of Lovelace. The eighteenth century came to perceive that no life could be called good unless sex and sensibility united. Mozart's *oeuvres* demonstrate his dedication to that fusion. *Don Giovanni*, uniquely a work without very much sensibility in it, portrays eros divided from the heart. The Fall, as we know, can come from division, and it is inevitable therefore that the stone statue will win in the end. But so necessary is libidinous energy to ideal union that even in its separated state it possesses the attractions of beauty and dignity. Blake and many others were made Satanists by the poetic power of Milton's Son of the Morning. The same impulses could easily make Juanists of all who care very deeply about the energies that generate life.

"Così fan tutte"

Così fan tutte (1790) possesses a geometrical structure that seems at first inflexible and even mechanical. One lover appears to be a mirror image of the other, one couple balances the other; and the handsome, loving, and aristocratic four are opposed in values to Despina and Don Alfonso, both disenchanted and worldly wise—one in the manner of an experienced and observant maidservant, the other in the manner of the gray-haired *boulevardier.* Into these shapely, sparkling, and symmetrically aligned vessels Mozart pours the champagne of laughing music. Much in *Così* fulfills the expectations of the subtitle, which calls it an *opera buffa,* and music and words unite exquisitely to produce the lightsome frolic of comic intrigue. The overture's sparkling music in the major key almost reconciles us to the assertion that "*all* women do it," the title phrase whose musical equivalent is repeated in the concluding resolution. Don Alfonso, warning the two men about their "pazzo desire" (1.1; p. 250) to learn the secret of the human heart, reveals worldly wisdom of the highest comic order; and when the girls sing antiphonally of love (embroidering the word "amore," 1.2; p. 256) and declare their happiness, one is perhaps justified in not taking the protestation of feeling too seriously. The ball is tossed back and forth a bit too nonchalantly and merrily. The girls' united desire for death as their lovers depart is more theatrical than real; and the lovers, one senses, are guilty of stylized insincerity in the farewell, as "Mio cor," "Idolo mio," "Mio ben," "Mia vita" fall glibly from the handsome lips. The girls' weeping is undermined by Don Alfonso's cynical asides, "Io crepo se non rido" (1.5; pp. 260, 262). Such light musical satire insinuates the whole plot—the arrival of the men in impenetrable disguises as Turks, the farcical use of the huge magnet, the "fall" of the women, the double entendre of Despina (who sings that a girl of fifteen ought to know "dove il diavolo ha la coda," 2.1; p. 290), Mr. Worldly Wiseman's triumphant singing of the title phrase at the end, and the vigorous praise of *ragion* and *riso* as redemptive values in love and life by the concluding chorus. Besides all this, it is unclear—perhaps deliberately so—whether the original sets of lovers reunite at the end or whether they remain paired as they were while the men were in disguise. However this may be—in production it has been interpreted both ways—this is in one aspect a highly masculine opera, and its wit enforces the lesson that human weakness must be realistically accepted and that romantic excess is ridiculous and fruitless, though apparently not really all that dangerous after all.

But actually the satiric-comic view is far from just to the subtle characterization, the emotional tensions, and the genuine love that is demonstrably present. The second trio between the lovers and Don Alfonso ("E la fede delle femmine / Come l'araba fenice," 1.1; p. 252), in which the faith of woman is declared to be as real as the Arabian phoenix, begins musically like the serpent in Eden, coil upon coil—and at least suggests, if it does not demonstrate, that the ladies will undergo a genuine Fall rather than a minor human slip. In the trio of the two girls and Alfonso, the music responds to the words: hope for a gentle wind and calm waves is translated into lovely lilting music that is mostly benign but turns ominous as the harmony shifts on the last word, "desir" (1.6; p. 262). The first response to the return of the gallants, now disguised and therefore tempters, is not merely conventional outrage but a subtle interweaving of hope and fear. Fiordiligi reveals, in her rejection of the "Turkish" lover assigned to her, that she is a leader, and her aria "Come scoglio" (1.11; p. 274) is noble, majestic, difficult—but also perhaps excessively artificial and even inhumanly formidable.[68] Against such morality Guglielmo's "Non siate ritrosi" (p. 274) is a marvel of flirtatious insinuation. Ferrando's incomparably beautiful "Un' aura amorosa" (1.12; p. 278), full of ravishing melody, is also full of *hubris,* for it will be his beloved Dorabella who will be faithless first. If we ask what overcomes the girls' will, the music, not the libretto, may provide the answer. It is not the pathetic, as one would expect in an age of sensibility, but the physically passionate, as the breathing, sighing music suggests.

The brisk music that ends act 1 assures us that all will be well in the end even if sexual feeling for the wrong man is aroused. This is surely a comedy, we say, and it will end in the equilibrium of a marriage based on a clear, commonsensical vision of reality in love. And so it does. But the temptation by passion and the fall into sensuality and faithlessness are complexly rendered, as if to show that Mozart is much more interested here in the nuances of real feeling than in the permanent structures of rational insight. As we could have anticipated, Dorabella falls almost at once—and in response to a conventional enough conceit about the exchange of hearts sung by Guglielmo ("Il core vi dono," 2.5; p. 296). The richer nature of Fiordiligi undergoes torment: "Per pietà" (2.7; p. 300) is a dark, foreboding, and difficult aria, representing Mozart at his most profound and most subjective; and Ferrando responds to the discovery of his beloved's faithlessness in a cry of pain and love in passionate music ("Tradito, schernito," 2.9; p. 304). Fiordiligi's yielding is slow and difficult and, by a dramatic irony, made possible only by the grief of the betrayed Ferrando, which makes his delicate appeals to her full of suffering and dismay. It is a rich bit of musical characterization that makes his postlapsarian pain the means of finally bringing down his fair quarry. Fiordiligi, morally much more serious than her laughing, flirtatious younger sister, yields only when she encounters real suffering. Thus both girls make that typically

68. See Singer, pp. 97–98; Charles Rosen, *The Classical Style: Haydn, Mozart, Beethoven* (New York: Viking Press, 1971), p. 315, suggests that this aria expresses "mock grandeur." Rosen also finds that Fiordiligi becomes more natural as she yields, that the music becomes "correspondingly more human," and that the whole opera achieves "warmth" as well as irony (ibid.).

eighteenth-century journey from innocence to experience—each in her own way: one with easy, untortured grace, the other with an expense of spirit. But in the end both make the crossing without trauma, and the Fall is only superficially like that of our first mother. The secularism of the Enlightenment has leavened the loaf, and the conventions of comedy, one of the favorite artistic forms of the period, are here brilliantly exploited. The girls are now mature enough to transcend their humiliation as they join the men in the "bella calma" that prevails at the end. On the surface this is a male triumph, and the women submit meekly enough to it: the masculine wager, "così fan tutte," has been won. But here, as almost everywhere in Mozart, the art invites us beneath the formal and conventional surface. The qualities of combined physical attraction and sympathy for distress—sex and sensibility, in short—that emerged in the Fall are apparently not shed like a temporary outer garment. If the music can be trusted, all the lovers go to a future that promises to be prolific and joyful. Fussy piety and romantic excess do not survive in the Mozartian world. But it would be a mistake to think that the cynical realism of the laughing old man and the giggling maid fully explain the harmony achieved. It is much too late in cultural time for a reincarnation of Etherege and Congreve. We are here in the world of Goldsmith and Austen, where sensibility permeates but does not destroy sense.[69]

"The Magic Flute"

In *Così fan tutte* sensibility is fairly implicit; and it is easy to see why sentimental or moral critics might find either sensuality or cynicism to be offensively prominent. It is not surprising that the nineteenth century tended to neglect this opera, which had to wait until our own day for its greatest triumphs. *The Magic Flute* (1791) became popular at once, capturing German cities large and small before the turn of the century and all the major Western capitals, including New York, by the end of the first third of the nineteenth century.[70] The reasons for this nineteenth-century triumph should be obvious: the opera is ideal, moral, and, in the best eighteenth-century sense of the term, sentimental. It is an appropriate climax to my investigation because in it eros and sensibility are both present and unite in an equilibrium that had become increasingly a Western ideal. Love is here present in both real and ideal forms, but these are not locked in conflict. Conflict there is, but it lies

69. Since *Così* is peculiarly the discovery of our century, it is not surprising that twentieth-century performances and criticism of them do not necessarily reflect the historical interpretation given here. Kenneth Furie, reviewing Solti's London recording, calls the opera "a tangled fable of psychological and sexual ambiguity" (*High Fidelity* 24 [Oct. 1974]: 82). Peter Hall's Glyndebourne production of 1978 apparently makes Alfonso a "depressed misanthrope," Despina "street-smart, sluttish," the plot a cruel analysis of the lovers in which sex is a physical wound and the body an irresistible tyrant. See Peter Conrad's review in the *New Statesman*, 14 July 1978, pp. 59–60.

70. *The Great Operas of Mozart*, p. 328.

elsewhere than between the "Natur-Mensch" Papageno, the bird-catcher, and Tamino, the hero, who grows into the mature and manly "Freundschaft und Liebe" with Pamina which he says he seeks (2; p. 360). Our sympathy for both the *Vogelfänger* and the prince means there can be no real conflict at all between them, although they constitute an important intellectual antithesis. We love Papageno—and of course his Papagena—though the limitations of his wit can be exasperating as well as amusing; and of course we love Tamino—and his beloved and his bride—for the natural, uninhibited love that wells up in them, just as we respect them for their disciplined attainment of "Schönheit und Weisheit" (2; p. 382). Where, then, does the conflict lie? Essentially between Sarastro and the Queen of the Night, and it represents a cosmological and ontological division of reality into light and dark, good and evil, superstition and reason. *The Magic Flute* represents in its depths—depths which the many simple allegorical interpretations that have been offered are all inadequate to plumb—a Zoroastrian struggle between ultimate health and ultimate alienation. But its immediate subject is love—love between a real man and a real woman, who, however, bear symbolic meanings; familial love that involves fathers and mothers; and a future conjugal intimacy that will produce offspring. The emphasis of word and music is inescapable: lovers are at the center of the action, and they are more real than metaphorical. In its core the opera celebrates not so much abstract virtue, wisdom, and discipline as virtuous, wise, and disciplined love. If that is true, what does the basic philosophic antithesis between good and evil translate itself into? Into a conflict between primitive and mature love, between the dangerous persistence in the psyche of regressive forces and the progressive attainment of wisdom. It is therefore not fortuitous that the word *manly* is prominent in the opera, where it does not suggest primarily virility, though that Figaro-like and Giovanni-like quality is by no means excluded, but the ideal of an adult enlightenment. Another way of putting all this is to invoke a central theme of eighteenth-century art and say that *The Magic Flute* treats of the initiation of innocents into experience.

First to be considered are the forces that conspire against mature love. Some of these can be attractive indeed, particularly at the beginning of the hero's search. The three maidens who serve the Queen of the Night create at once a kind of sexual allure that reminds one of the energetic libido of Don Giovanni himself and indeed of all the sensual music that Mozart ever wrote.[71]

71. For a summary and analysis of various scholarly and critical views of whether the original dramatic scheme was changed in mid-course—whether, that is, the Queen of the Night and her court were good at first and then changed to evil—see Robert Craft, "Playing with 'The Magic Flute'" in *New York Review of Books*, 27 Nov. 1975, p. 18. I believe my analysis, which interprets the dark forces as regressive and the attainment of the light as a progress toward maturity, is not inconsistent with Jacques Chailley's important "essai d'explication du livret et de la musique": *"La Flûte enchantée": Opera maçonnique* (Paris: Robert Laffont, 1968).

They admire the hero and his appearance and greet him with attractive zest; they present him with Pamina's portraits (images and likenesses are sexually important in Mozart and all eighteenth-century art); they give to Papageno the glockenspiel that later saves him from suicide and preserves him for fruitful wedlock; above all, they give him the golden flute itself, created by Pamina's father, an Orphic instrument that both creates and controls desire and leads the loving pair through water and fire into a realm where sex and sensibility become fruitful and interacting contraries without which there can be no progression. They serve the dark queen and fear Sarastro as a wicked magician, and hence they must be regarded as potentially mischievous creatures despite their own endowments and their gifts. But their mischief is complex, and they cannot be thought, *tout simplement,* to represent desire. Is it not they who *destroy* a snake, which must possess some significance as a sexual symbol? Can they therefore be regarded as benefactors who tried to keep the hero from his own physical nature? This combination of attractiveness and limitation suggests that the maidens are neither good nor evil in any absolute sense but regressive, signifying primitive elements in our being that keep us from maturity. Monostatos the Moor— a descendant, surely, of Osmin in *The Abduction*—may represent another aspect of sensibility, one that would have preserved the snake and let it grow into an obsession.[72] He is a buffoon and is lustful to boot ("Weiss ist schön," he sings as he contemplates kissing Pamina: 2; p. 364), aggressive, even murderous in his intentions; but for all that— partly *because* of all that—he is human ("Bin ich nicht von Fleisch und Blut?" p. 364, he asks, reminding us of Shylock's questions). And in love he is not all that dangerous ("[Er] schnäbelt, tändelt, herzt und küsst," p. 364), and his music of lust and bluster tends at times to be shallow, spinning like a top, but at others full of verve and charm. We know that he will be defeated, and at the end he is in fact made to disappear quickly, with the Queen of the Night, as though through a trapdoor.

And what of her? She plots the murder of the fatherly paragon, she believes in revenge, and she uses those fatal enemies of *Aufklärung,* delusion and superstition ("Blendwerk und Aberglauben": 2; p. 358), against the brotherhood. Yet she is a mother, whom the daughter Pamina loves at the beginning and who reciprocates that filial affection. In her first aria she is appealingly "pathetic" and calls Tamino her "lieber Sohn" (1; p. 340), apparently desiring none but the best for her daughter. And she is given music of great coloratura

72. For a discussion of the snake as a sexual symbol, see Robert Spaethling, "Folklore and Enlightenment in the Libretto of Mozart's *Magic Flute,*" *Eighteenth-Century Studies* 9 (Fall 1975): 45–68, esp. p. 52. Spaethling goes on, however, to show that an emendation in Mozart's own hand changed "dem grimmigen Löwen" to "der listigen Schlange" (p. 63)—perhaps a last-minute change that should warn us not to interpret the snake in a way that would be inappropriate for a lion. Blake, in *Songs of Innocence and Experience* (see esp. "The Little Girl Lost" and "The Little Girl Found"), uses the lion as a symbol of sexual initiation.

energy and brilliance, which, however, upon examination seems itself to be a reversion from the new and beautiful simplicities that are overtaking Western music to the floridity and elaboration of outworn styles, the rococo and the baroque. Again we must ask, as we did about the three maidens who serve her, what kind of mischief this combination of actually fearsome and potentially lovable qualities can represent. Again the key lies in the term "regressive," here applied to a motherhood that means well, that in its nature can be regarded as good, but that by selfish domination is now prepared to impede the progress of the young and loving to maturity and independence. If this is true, Mozart is a modern "affective individualist"—affective because the primary emphasis is upon love, individual because he is purging a single man and a single woman of residual and potential evil, and modern because he views evil as immaturity, as the persistence of the primal, and as fully controllable by discipline and purpose.

The good Sarastro and his priests are given music of the highest simplicity and sublimity, music that carries over into the age of sensibility the quiet, hymnlike beauty and tenderness of Bach's chorales, without, however, a trace of the Christian "pathetic" that arises, for example, from contemplating the Crucifixion. The enemies of night are Apollonian apostles of the sun, which shines here in the brightness of the *siècle des lumières*—"One *clear, unchang'd*, and *Universal* Light," to quote Pope (*Essay on Criticism*, 1.71). "Sweet Science reigns," to quote Blake in one of his apocalyptic climaxes that bears more relation to Enlightened sensibility than to Romantic rapture (*Vala, or The Four Zoas*, last line). The priests of Mozart's temple of wisdom are at once men of enlightenment and sensibility, and it is of the last importance to stress that both reason and feeling beckon the lovers to adult manliness and adult femininity. Certainly one feature of the religion of Isis and Osiris is that, though it frustrates the lust of the Moor, it is by no means the enemy of sexuality and seems to favor the sharp differentiation of the sexes. No Cherubino of dubious or ambivalent sexuality appears in this decisively male-female world, for which nevertheless the sexual energy of the Italian operas is one kind of preparation.

But sexual attraction pure and simple has its own levels, and the inexpressibly sublime music that the bass Sarastro and his ministers produce cannot be attained by the likes of Papageno. Within his limitations he too wins our love and even a kind of respect. He has charm and verve, and after suffering that verges on the suicidal, he finally attains a fully integrated natural sexuality. He may be childlike, but he is not childish, and unlike that of the queen and the maidens, his is not a dangerous reversion. In fact it is not reversion at all, since he escapes from the realm of Night. If he cannot fully achieve the worship of the sun of reason and sensibility, he is led to the highest fulfillment his good but limited nature can reach. His music is simple,

melodic, charming, physical, and fresh; but it does not have the rich moral
sublimity of "In diesen heil'gen Hallen" (2; p. 366), where revenge is not
known, where enemies are forgiven, and where the hand of friendship beckons to joy. It is, however, given to him to sing the joys of physical union in
an excited, sexually suggestive patter duet ("Pa-pa-pa," 2; p. 380) that, unlike
Swift's "little language," is entirely free of morbidity. It would be possible, of
course, to take much too seriously the union of "Mann und Weib, und Weib
und Mann" (1; p. 348) and the production of innumerable offspring, but it is
perhaps not too solemn to say that Mozart has in this natural pair realized one
aspect of Goethe's "Ewig-Weibliche."

The central action of the opera is the attainment of a compassionate as well
as a passionate humanity by Tamino and Pamina. Both begin in innocence,
and their first state is attractive and big with promise. Tamino's love aria, the
magnificent but almost overstated larghetto, "Dies Bildnis ist bezaubernd
schön," exalts rapture: he envisions being not only "warm und rein" but in
"voll Entzückung," a rapture in which he presses her to his "heissen Busen"
(1; p. 340). If the prince begins in a purely physical, though extremely beautiful palpitation,[73] Pamina's innocence is tearful—she grieves over losing a
mother. But she too is attractive in her preprobatory condition. Besides being
beautiful, she is openly, unabashedly in love with a man ("Ich höre das Wort
Liebe gar zu gern": 1; p. 348), and Mozart—in no mean achievement if we
remember the immemorial impediments to giving women full expression of
their feelings—presents a modern heroine who is free of hypocritical concealments and even excessive modesty. Her emotions are outraged by the
delays she must encounter: at one point she is close to suicide and is saved only
by learning that Tamino "liebet dich allein" (2; p. 376). I have mentioned the
sharp distinction of the sexes in the opera, which also assigns slightly different
roles to each. The man, at once more religious and realistic, accepts sooner the
need for discipline and submission. While Pamina languishes in love, Tamino
accepts the test, and in music of unimaginable beauty the two separate ("lebe
wohl," 2; p. 372); she triumphs with the man as virtually an equal and reappears with him after the sublime crossing into the brilliant light at the
temple gate. That light streams from the sun of reason and humanity, and
Pamina and Tamino achieve an ordered and stable love. Along with
Beethoven—indeed the music of Sarastro and his priests strongly anticipates
some of the choruses of *Fidelio*—Mozart has achieved a secular version of
Milton's Edenic vision.

Deeply passionate physical love thus unites with compassion and reason to
create friendship between man and woman, the highest conceivable expres-

73. As an example of one popular view of Mozart, an Italian servant somewhere in Aldous
Huxley's writings—I wish I had the exact reference—prefers Verdi or Puccini, because Mozart
"non palpita."

sion of humanity. How often have we not in these pages encountered the separation of love and friendship, a division so frequent that one might pardonably conclude that it is indigenous to our culture, if not to human nature itself! But the vision of Mozart in this opera unites them. Again, how often in the literature of the Restoration and the eighteenth century have we not encountered conclusions in which the rewards of heterosexual friendship are postponed either to a Christian afterlife or, more often, to a vague and religiously neutral hereafter! But neither Christian nor pagan immortality is important in *The Magic Flute*, where mention of the afterlife is made only incidentally, when Sarastro says that if Tamino should die during his trials (and the High Priest knows very well he will not), he would then enter into the joy of the gods before the others (2; p. 358). Tamino of course survives to enjoy life with Pamina, just as Bethoven's Florestan emerges from the death and hell of prison to be reunited in society with Leonore. In the great operas of sensibility, the realization of ordered energy is simply not allowed to die; the achievement of stable love continues on earth as the pursuit of happiness. Gluck, Mozart, and Beethoven circumvent the religions of guilt and prevent them from permanently thwarting the union of sex and sensibility.

In *Black Lamb and Grey Falcon* Rebecca West makes the black lamb she saw sacrificed on a sacred rock in gratitude for the birth of a child a symbol of sacrifice in the name of religion; the lamb is made to signify the "repulsive pretense that pain is the proper price of any good thing."[74] As one who represented the diametrically opposite values, her own values, Miss West named Wolfgang Amadeus Mozart.

74. See Martin Green's review of *Rebecca West: A Celebration*, ed. Samuel Hynes, in *Saturday Review*, 15 Oct. 1977, p. 25.

Appendixes

Appendix A

Milton and the Visual Arts

For systematic accounts of Milton and the visual arts, see Roland M. Frye, *Milton's Imagery and the Visual Arts* (Princeton, N.J.: Princeton University Press, 1978), and the essays by J. B. Trapp, Roy Daniells, and John Dixon Hunt in *John Milton: Introductions*, ed. John Broadbent (Cambridge: Cambridge University Press, 1973), pp. 162–225. Frye (pp. 101–10) discriminates the several visual concepts of the tempting Satan available to Milton and illustrates each with important works of visual art. By Milton's time the two most frequent forms were the snake pure and simple or a hybrid, a serpent with a human head or torso (p. 102). Of the latter, the head of a woman on the body of a serpent was the most popular from the late twelfth century and on (p. 103). I agree that this type could not have seemed appropriate for the Satan, who was tempting Eve, any more than did the snake with the head of a putto or a child. Frye believes that Milton thought of the zoological form, an erect serpent. Indubitably. But did he think *only* in those terms? Frye tends to underplay the sexual element in the Fall, contrary, it seems to me, to the forceful implications of the imagery and of what has gone on before in the mind of Eve. For the type of temptation I believe she underwent, I have chosen Van der Goes's salamander (who lives in the flames of hell, and who symbolizes sexual passion) with a tempting male visage that has about it some suggestions of ambiguity (pl. 3). Frye recognizes the existence of this type of Satan (p. 102 and pl. 162), but finds that it was limited in popularity to the fifteenth century and that it is not relevant to Milton, who does not hint at the existence of these creatures in *Paradise Lost*. The truth is that no painted form is a satisfactory equivalent to Milton's famous beast; but a human male head, with suggestions of phallic animality in the body, can be thought of as representing his larger purposes. For the use of the salamander in a sexual connection see Swift's poem addressed to Baron Cutts (above, p. 149).

Appendix B

Chronology of Plays Referred To

Because the plays discussed in chapter 3 and subsequent chapters are not presented in strict chronological order, it may be helpful to provide a brief chronological scheme for the Restoration and early eighteenth-century drama relevant to this study. I am indebted to Robert D. Hume, *The Development of English Drama in the Late Seventeenth Century* (Oxford: Clarendon Press, 1976). The reader may wish to refer to this appendix and to the pages in Hume, in order to get his chronological bearings and to pursue further the historical context of each play selected for discussion. The dates of first performance of a play are given in parenthesis after its first mention in the text.

1. 1663–64: plays of love and honor, of which Dryden's *Rival Ladies* is one example. These romantic tragicomedies were congenial to expressions of tender love and were in fact the most popular plays of the earlier 1660s. Smut, profanity, sexual explicitness came later. It is important and relevant to a basic thesis of this study that the Restoration theater should begin not in sexual license but in delicacy and refinement (see Hume, pp. 241, 249).

2. 1664–75: heroic plays. Note that these did not suddenly flower with the production of *The Indian Queen* (1664) but appeared slowly and unsystematically (p. 250).

3. Early 1670s: "The dominant serious type in the early seventies is the horror play" (p. 290).

4. 1675–77: height of Carolean drama. Dryden, Shadwell, Etherege, Wycherley, Lee, and Otway "were all at or near" the peak of their powers (p. 269). These years also saw the finest achievements in London sex comedy (p. 305).

5. Late 1670s: heroic tragedy in blank verse with emphasis on pathos. Ritual heroic exaltation declines and tragic emotions rise (p. 317).

6. Early 1680s: production of truly pathetic plays by Otway and Banks, of which *The Orphan* (1680) is a landmark (pp. 350–51).

7. 1690s: an active period after the doldrums of the late 1680s. Comedy is divided between plays of a hard glitter and plays of tender humanity (p. 380). Serious plays, which include tragicomedies, tragedies with both heroic and pathetic elements, and operas undergo a resurgence (p. 397). The heroic, when it appears, is on a more human scale.

8. 1697–1710: a period which produced what Hume with reluctance calls Augustan drama (p. 432). This included many new tragedies, the revival of heroic modes and horror in plays mostly of dismal quality (p. 458) and, most significantly, of "humane comedy." This last type has been named by Shirley Strum Kenny, who regards it as distinct from both comedy of wit and comedy of manners and also from sentimental comedy. It includes works of Cibber, Farquhar, Steele, Vanbrugh, Congreve; its chief characteristic is its good nature and believable humanity. See "Humane Comedy," *Modern Philology* 75 (Aug. 1977): 29–43.

APPENDIX C

Watteau, "Le pèlerinage à l'Ile de Cythère"

In opposition to the traditional interpretation, Michael Levey has argued cogently and influentially for the view that the painting represents not a search for future bliss but a departure from Venus's island *after* a day of pleasure. See "The Real Theme of Watteau's *Embarkation for Cythera,*" *Burlington Magazine* 103 (May 1961): 180–85. This interpretation has the great merit of explaining fully the sadness that pervades the canvas and of accounting for many of the details. Not all, however; and I am not willing to abandon the framework provided by the traditional interpretation until the following details have been confronted and interpreted. (1) The love animation increases as the pilgrims move toward the boat: there seems to be more embracing, more joy. (2) The boat itself and the Cupids who adorn, guide, and in a sense propel it suggest motion toward something that lies ahead, not away from something achieved. The oarsman is muscular, his body tensed in anticipation, and he too suggests onward and upward motion. (3) If the boat is departing from what is indeed the island of Cythera, then the statue of Venus should be the point of highest energy. It is far from that: it is armless, the expression on the face is dead or perhaps matronly or even respectable. The garlanding may therefore represent a preliminary offering to a representation only as the couples proceed on their way to the real goddess and her kingdom. (4) The light is not indisputably a sunset light but is instead ambiguous; it could as easily be dawn light. Levey, in a later discussion of Watteau, in which he reaffirms the interpretation of the article, says, rightly, that "ambiguity is one characteristic of Watteau's art" (Wend Graf Kalnein and Michael Levey, *Art and Architecture of the Eighteenth Century in France* [Harmondsworth, Eng.: Penguin Books, 1972], p. 14). That quality is best served if we do not look on the scene as categorically either an embarkation or a departure. We may come closest to the profundity of the picture if we see it as a movement toward a naked consummation (the true isle of Cythera) that is as likely to disappoint as the day of clothed foreplay, which had its own blend of joy and sorrow. The details noted by Mirimonde (see above p. 288 and n.18) seem to support the traditional interpretation: the Cupids carry torches that symbolize passion; the stern of the boat is made of the shell of Venus; the nude statue in the stern is a "Victory," celebrating the triumph of Venus (pp. 17–18).

Index

Abelard, 161; *Historia calamitatum mearum*, 130. *See also* Pope, *Eloisa to Abelard*

Addison, Joseph, 14, 103 n.10, 160, 190; *Spectator*, 14, 187

Aden, John M., 149 n.

Admiration, 65 and n.21, 99

"Affective individualism," 1, 2, 216 and n.50, 279, 313, 329

Agapē, 2–3, 4 and n.10, 75, 131, 289, 291. *See also* Religion

Aitken, George A., 166 n.16, 167, 168 n.19

Alcoforado, Marianna, 113. *See also* Portuguese Nun

Aldridge, A. Owen, 103 n.11

Allan, David, 281

Allestree, Richard, 186

Amour de soi, 223, 224

Amor-désir, 75

Amour-propre, 223

Amour-tendresse, 22, 75

Anacreon, 103 and n.10, 105, 312

Anchor, Robert, 263 n.40

Anderson, Howard, 167 n.17

Androgyny, 32 and n.19, 42 n.29, 141, 318. *See also* Hermaphrodite

Angel, *angélisme*, 84, 119, 125, 152–53, 163–64, 188, 189, 192, 200, 208 and n., 266 and n.44, 296; defined, 152

Antal, Frederick, 284 n.13

Aphrodite, 106. *See also* Venus

Apollinarius, 34

apRoberts, Ruth, 272 n.

Ariès, Philippe, 47 n.41

Ariosto, Lodovico, 162 and n.6

Aristotle, 32, 90, 212

Arnold, Matthew, 23

Astarte, 106

Astell, Mary, 166

Atkins, Stuart Pratt, 260 n.

Atkinson, Geoffroy, 72 n., 73 n.5, 74 n.6

Auden, W. H., 317 n.

Audra, Emile, 122 n.49

Auerbach, Erich, 70–71, 190 and n.15

Augustine, Saint, 30 and nn.12, 13, 34, 107

Ault, Norman, 278 n.1

Austen, Jane, 11–12, 163, 218, 261 n.33, 303, 326; *Emma*, 269; *Mansfield Park*, 269; *Northanger Abbey*, 269, 271; *Persuasion*, 269 n.; *Pride and Prejudice*, 268–69; *Sense and Sensibility*, 8, 9, 11, 12, 247, 268–74

Babb, Lawrence, 101 n.3, 145 n.16

Bach, Johann Sebastian, 22, 58, 278, 286, 288–91, 297, 329

Bacon, Francis, 44, 259

Bailey, Benjamin, 21 n.43

Bailey, Margery, 275 n.59

Bailey, Nathan, 6 n.16

Baker, David Erskine, 94 n.

Bale, John, Bishop of Ossory, 101 n.2

Ball, F. Elrington, 153 n.

Banks, Thomas, 169

Barbeau, Anne T., 69 n.28

Barkan, Leonard, 318 n.63

Barker, Arthur, 21 n.44

Barker, Jane, 70

Barre, François Poulain de la, 166

Barreno, Maria Isabel, 113 n.27

Barrow, Isaac, 180, 184

Barry, Elizabeth, 90–91 and n.27

Barry, James, 15, 283, pls.1a, 1b

Bartel, Roland, 262 n.36

Barthelme, Donald, 1

Bateson, F. W., 138 n., 141 n.11

Battestin, Martin C., 181 n.37

Baxter, Richard, 74 and n.9

Bayley, John, 1, 3
Bearne, Colin, 43 n.32
Beating, in schools, 10
Beaty, Frederick L., 1
Beaumarchais, Pierre de, 318, 319 n.
Beaurline, L. A., 52 n.
Beckford, William, 180
Beethoven, Ludwig van, 48, 286, 317, 330, 331; *Fidelio*, 15, 39, 294–97
Behn, Aphra, 77–80, 105, 122; *The Dumb Virgin*, 78 and n.17; *The Fair Jilt*, 77–78 and n.16; *Love Letters to a Gentleman*, 113; *Oroonoko*, 77, 78–80
Belgion, Montgomery, 47 n.40
Bell, Clara, 290 n.23
Bell, John, 284 n.13
Bellarmine, Cardinal (Saint Robert), 31
Bellenot, Jean-Louis, 240 n.29
Berington, Joseph, 131 n.66
Bernard, Saint, 31 and n.17
Bernard, J. H., 153 n.
Bernbaum, Ernest, 162 n.5, 172 n.25, 175 n.28
Bernini, Giovanni Lorenzo, 101, 284, 285
Bible, 19–20, 187, 208, 225, 236; *Song of Solomon*, 18, 164 and n.10, 236
Blacklock, Thomas, 122
Blake, William, 11 and nn.25, 26, 70, 77, 88, 177, 185, 203, 222, 244, 246, 251, 262, 266, 273, 279 and n.4, 283, 303, 323, 328 n., 329
Blamires, Harry, 43 n.31
Blanchard, Rae, 166 nn.13, 15, 167 n.17
Blankenburg, Walter, 290 n.23
Bloch, John, 317 n.
Bloom, Eric, 286 n.
Blount, Martha (Pope's "Patty"), 8, 121 n.47, 138–42, 160, 278 n.2
Blount, Teresa, 138–40
Blow, John, 105
Blunt, Anthony, 108 n.19
Boas, Frederick S., 175 n.28
Boase, T. S. R., 282 n.10
Boccaccio, Giovanni, 8, 50, 53 n.5, 54
Boismortier, Joseph Bodin de, 288
Bolingbroke, Henry St. John, 1st Viscount, 150
Bossuet, Jacques Bénigne, 74 and n.8, 221
Boswell, James, 12 n., 88 n., 252 and n.20,

262, 263 n.38, 274–75
Botticelli, Sandro, 45
Boucé, P.-G.,183 n.40
Boucher, François, 198 n., 284 n.14, 285, 302, 318
Bouguereau, Adolphe William, 311 n.55
Bouilly, Jean Nicolas, 294 and n.30
Boulton, James T., 251 n.15, 263 n.39
Bowers, Fredson, 52 n.
Bowles, William Lisle, 127 n.60
Boydell, John, 280 n.
Boyette, Purvis E., 27 n.4
Bradshaigh, Lady, 189 n.10, 196 n.27, 202 n.33
Brady, Frank, 252 n.20, 253 n.24
Brady, Valentini P., 75 n.11
Brandes, Georg, 264 n.
Braudy, Leo, 208 n.
Breast-feeding, 10
Bretonne, Restif de la, 246
Bridges, Gwendolyn, 198 n.
Brissenden, R. F., 6 n.16, 8 n.21, 72 n., 161 n.3, 271 n.55
Broadbent, J. B., 1, 3 and n.4, 27 n.4
Broder, Nathan, 317 n.
Bronson, Bertrand H., 304 n., 306 n.
Brontë, Charlotte, *Jane Eyre*, 131
Brooke, Tucker, 3
Brookner, Anita, 314 and n.59
Brophy, Brigid, 270 n.52
Brower, Reuben, 58 n.12
Browne, Norman O., 149 n.
Brujn, Nicolas de, 45
Burden, Dennis H., 44 n.35
Burgelin, Pierre, 238 n.
Burke, Edmund, 65 n.22, 207, 263
Burlington, Richard Boyle, 3d Earl of, 278 n.2
Burnet, Gilbert, 146 n.18
Burney, Edward Francis, 283
Burney, Fanny, 18, 270–71
Burton, Robert, 30, 101 n.3, 255
Butt, John, 123 n.52, 278 n.1
Byron, George Gordon, 6th Baron, 127 and n.61, 180; *Childe Harold's Pilgrimage*, 92–93, 246; *Don Juan*, 22, 35; *Manfred*, 70

Calzabigi, Ranieri, 286 n., 293 n.
Canfield, J. Douglas, 117 n.41, 174 n.26

Canova, Antonio, 251, 297

Carnochan, W. B., 135 n.5

Carracci, Annibale, 103 n.11

Carroll, John, 119 n., 161 n.4, 189 n.10

Casanova, Giacomo G., 241, 284

Cash, Arthur H., 259 n.31

Catamite, 6, 73

Chailley, Jacques, 327 n.

Champion, Larry S., 57 n., 149 n.

Chandler, Alice, 270 n.52

Chapone, Sarah, 206 n.40

Charity, emblem of, 183, 311–12 and
  n.55

Charles II, 51, 134

Charleton, Walter, 102

Charmet, Raymond, 284 n.14

Chatterton, Thomas, 263 n.38

Chaucer, 50, 53 n.5, 107 n.18; *Parson's
  Tale,* 31; *Troilus,* 58, 130–31, 323

Chesterfield, Philip Dormer Stanhope,
  Earl of, 271 n.55

Chesterton, G. K., 261 n.33

Cheyne, Dr. George, 190, 194 n.22

Christopher, Georgia B., 25 n., 38 n.

Chrysippus, 29

Cibber, Colley, 118, 163

Cicero, 129 n.

Cirillo, A. R., 29 n.9, 32 n.19, 42 n.29

Clark, Kenneth, 285 n.15, 297 n.37

Cleland, John, 252 and n.20; *Fanny Hill,*
  100, 252

Cockshut, A. O. J., 1, 182 n.

Coeur sensible, 97, 178, 199, 239, 241, 243,
  268, 275, 277, 312, 316. *See also* Delicacy; Sensibility

"Coffee" (Swift's idiosyncratic use of the
  term), 153–55

Cogan, Thomas, 101 n.3

Colardeau, Charles Pierre, 227

Coleridge, Samuel T., 17, 166, 220, 261
  and n.34, 273

Collier, Jeremy, 74 and n.8, 103 n.11, 136

Collins, William, 125

Colony, Joyce, 25 n.

Compassion. *See* Pathetic

Concernment. *See* Pathetic

Congreve, William, 8, 100, 134, 250 n.14,
  268, 275, 307, 326; *The Mourning Bride,*
  12, 82, 88–90, 118, 274; *The Way of the
  World,* 8 and n.21, 135, 136–37, 143

Conrad, Peter, 326 n.69

"Conscious," 68 and n.27, 111, 136;
  defined, 172 and n.25

Constable, John, 303

Cooke, Arthur L., 83 n.

Cooper, Martin, 293 n.

Corcoran, Mary Irma, 48 n.43

Corman, Brian, 136 n.

Correggio, Antonio Allegri da, *Ganymede,*
  45, 103 n.11, 284, pl.2

Couperin, François, 300

Cowley, Abraham, 76, 77, 103 n.10, 154
  n.30

Cowper, William, 166, 247, 252 n.18,
  262, 268, 271

Craft, Robert, 327 n.

Crane, Ronald S., 73 n.4, 75, 76 n.13

Crashaw, Richard, 13, 102, 290

Creech, Thomas, 104

Creichton, Captain John, 157

Crocker, Lester G., 243 n.

Croft, Herbert, 262–63 and n.38

Cromwell, Henry, 138

Cupid, 4, 109, 259, 274, 280, 281 and n.6,
  284, 298, 303, 312, 315, 320 n.66. *See
  also* Venus

Curran, Stuart, 42 n.30

Curtis, Lewis P., 248 n.1

Cutts, John, Baron of Gowran (Swift's
  "Salamander"), 149, 333

Da Costa, Maria Velho, 113 n.27

Dadelsen, Georg von, 289 n.

Daghlian, Philip B., 167 n.17

Damon, S. Foster, 222 n.6

Daniells, Roy, 333

Dante, 20; *Inferno,* 18, 107; *Paradiso,* 31
  n.17

Darwin, Erasmus, 249 n.8

Davenant, Sir William, 60

David and Jonathan, 203, 305

Davis, Herbert, 88 n., 146 n.18, 157 n.

Dean, Winton, 304 n., 307 n.48, 308 n.,
  310 n.51

Dearing, Vinton A., 52 n.

Death, 262–64; associated with love, 17,
  18–19, 40, 46–47, 89–90, 129–30,
  175–76, 210, 293, 319. *See also* Suicide

Debussy, Claude, 309

Defoe, Daniel, 16, 58, 78, 104, 164–65,

166, 169, 189, 191; *Conjugal Lewdness*, 102, 159 n., 189 and n.13; *Moll Flanders*, 179

Delicacy, 102–3, 105, 193, 197, 198 and n., 201, 250, 266–67, 288, 300, 304, 305. *See also* Feminizing of the psyche; Sensibility

Deloffre, F., 113 n.29, 115 n.32

Dennis, John, 98–99, 101, 103 n.11, 112, 172, 193 n., 220

Descartes, René, 4 and n.9

De Selincourt, Ernest, 54 n.7

De Troy, Jean-François, 297

"Dialogue between Two Young Ladies, Lately Married," 132

Dickens, Charles, 164

Diderot, Denis, 16–17, 175, 180, 206 n.40, 213, 248 n.1, 266–67, 311, 314

Dido, 106–12, 118, 280–81

Digeon, Aurélien, 180 n.34

Dingley, Rebecca, 155

Divorce, 47–48; Milton on, 33

Dixon, Peter, 139 n.9

Dobrée, Bonamy, 65 n.20, 121 n.45

Domenichino, Il, Domenico Zampieri, 315

Donne, John, 3, 102, 262, 290

Doody, Margaret Anne, 186 n.3, 188 n.7

Downey, James, 222 n.6

Downs, Brian W., 215 n.

Draper, Eliza, 259 n.31

Dronke, Peter, 114 n.30

Dryden, John,13, 22, 50–71, 74, 75, 77, 82, 91, 98, 100, 103, 104 n.13, 108–11, 122, 128, 129, 132, 136, 186, 188, 189, 199, 218, 250 n.14, 274, 275, 279, 286, 287, 304 and n., 306, 309, 316, 321; *All for Love*, 60–62, 97, 258; *Amboyna*, 65 n.22; *Aureng-Zebe*, 13, 56, 67–69, 78, 79, 122 n.48; I *Conquest of Granada*, 54 n.7, 66; II *Conquest of Granada*, 56, 67; "A Defence of an Essay of Dramatic Poesy," 65 n.21; *Don Sebastian*, 13, 56–58, 78, 94, 122 n.48, 179; *An Essay of Dramatic Poesy*, 59; *Fables*, 9–10, 54; "The Grounds of Criticism in Tragedy," 59, 65; "Heads of an Answer to Rymer," 59; *The Hind and the Panther*, 55; *The Indian Emperour*,

63–64; *The Indian Queen*, 56, 60, 62–63; *Marriage A-la-Mode*, 52; *To Mrs. Anne Killigrew*, 51; *Oedipus*, 55–56; *Religio Laici*, 19–20, 55; *The Rival Ladies*, 60; *Secret Love*, 51; *The Tempest*, 55, 60; Translations from Lucretius, 53; Translations from Ovid, 54–55; *Tyrannick Love*, 13, 64–65, 122 n.48; "The Vindication of the Duke of Guise," 55 n.

Dubois-Ferrière, Muriel, 284 n.14

Dugard, Samuel, 95 n.39

Duncombe, John, 212 n.

Dunton, John, 134, 232

D'Urfé, Honoré, 75

D'Urfey, Tom, 133

Dürr, Alfred, 290 n.23

Dusinberre, Juliet, 31 n.16

Dussinger, John A., 186 n.1, 212 n.

Eaves, T. C. Duncan, 189 nn.9, 12, 194 nn.21, 23, 196 n.26, 204 n.35, 213 n.47

Edwards, Calvin R., 44 n.34

Effeminacy, 41 and n., 42 n.29, 46, 85, 104, 223, 284 and n.14. *See also* Feminizing of the psyche; *"Haec-vir"*; Homosexuality; Narcissism

Ehrenpreis, Irvin, 151 n.26, 155 n., 167 n.17

Einstein, Alfred, 286 n., 292 n.27

Eliot, T. S., 50, 57, 90, 109

Elizabeth I, 36

Elledge, Scott, 6 n.13, 65 n.22, 121 n.45

Elliott, John R., Jr., 32 n.19

Ellrodt, Robert, 32 n.19

Emasculation, 126–27

Empson, William, 9 n.24

Epictetus, 276

Epstein, William H., 252 n.21

Erämetsä, Erik, 7

Eros, 2, 3, 4 and n.10

Ethē, 5

Etherege, Sir George, 134, 137, 187, 252, 268, 275, 326; *The Man of Mode*, 135–36

Euripides, 54 n.8, 215

Evans, Thomas, 56 n.

Evelyn, Mrs. John, 66

Family, 1–2, 216–17

Farquhar, George, 47, 182 n.
Father, fatherhood, 87–88, 205–8, 231, 264–65, 313
Faulkner, William, 23
Fawkes, Francis, 103 n.10
Feminizing of the psyche, 86, 105, 141, 163, 197, 304
Ferré, Jean, 297 n.39, 320 n.65
Feuillerat, Albert, 42 n.29
Fiedler, Leslie, 1, 32 n.19, 48 n.43, 218 n.
Fielding, Henry, 58, 134, 160, 166, 169, 178–85, 191; *Amelia*, 11, 12, 15, 180–85, 214, 274; *Joseph Andrews*, 172, 178–79; *Shamela*, 191; *Tom Jones*, 11, 179, 181
Fish, Stanley, 25 n.
Fitzwilliam, T. W., 280 n.
Flaxman, John, 251
Fleetwood, William, 171, 187, 206–7
Fleming, Anne Taylor, 44 n.36
Ford, John, *'Tis Pity She's a Whore*, 57
Foster, James R., 113 n.27
Fowlie, Wallace, 1
Fox, George, 75
Foxon, David, 51 n.3, 100 n., 103 nn.10, 11
Fragonard, Jean Honoré, 302
France, 72 and n., 73 and n.5, 75, 166, 221, 229, 297
Franklin, Benjamin, 253
French romances, 75
Freud, Sigmund, 36 n.24, 42, 47, 156, 200, 216 n.51, 222, 261, 267, 295
Fréval, Jean Baptiste de, 194 n.21
Fried, Michael, 283 n.11, 314 n.57
Friedlaender, Walter, 297 n.36
Friedman, Arthur, 212 n., 262 n.36
Friendship, 160, 185, 305; in *Clarissa*, 200–203; in *La Nouvelle Héloïse*, 232–34; Milton's ideal of, 24, 28, 34–35, 47, 133, 142; in Pope, 138–42; in Swift, 151–57. *See also* David and Jonathan; Homoerotic love
Frost, William, 53 n.5
Frye, Roland M., 48 n.43, 333
Fujimura, Thomas H., 53 n.6
Fuller-Maitland, J. A., 290 n.23
Furie, Kenneth, 326 n.69
Fuseli, Henry, 43 n.33, 107, 281, 283

Gagen, Jean Elisabeth, 104 n.12
Gainsborough, Thomas, 303
Galen, 101 n.3
Garrick, David, 88 n., 248 n.1, 276
Gautier, Théophile, 301
Gay, John, 92, 304 n.
Gay, Peter, 21
Genius, natural *vs.* artificial, 114
Gentleman's Journal: or the Monthly Miscellany, 105
Gerber, Rudolf, 292 n.
Ghosh, J. C., 91 n.28, 94 n., 95 n.41
Gibbon, Edward, 20 and n.41
Gilbert, Sandra M., 36 n.24
Gilliam, J. F., 43 n.32
Gillray, James, 103, 107, 282 n.10
Gilmore, Thomas B., Jr., 149 n.
Gilson, Etienne, 121 n.46
Girodet-Trioson, 316
Girolamo da Carpi, 284
Gluck, Christoph Willibald, 21, 48, 278, 286 and n., 288, 291–93, 294, 331; *Alceste*, 15, 293; *Orfeo ed Euridice*, 15, 84, 291–93
Goes, Hugo van der, 44, 333, pl.3
Goethe, Johann Wolfgang von, 180, 260–68, 274, 314 n.59, 330; *Elective Affinities*, 260; *Faust*, 260; *Werther*, 19, 82, 247, 260–68, 269; *Wilhelm Meister*, 58, 168, 260, 264
Golden, Morris, 216 n.49
Goldoni, Carlo, 286 n.
Goldsmith, Oliver, 92, 250, 252 n.18, 262 and n.36, 265, 268, 326
Goldstein, Malcolm, 117 n.41
Goncourt, Edmond and Jules de, 301
Gorer, Geoffrey, 269 n.
Gorges, Sir Arthur, 44 n.34, 259 n.30
Gosse, Edmund, 114 and n.31
"Gothic" effects, 73, 77, 89, 109, 117, 119, 123, 127, 173, 174, 175, 176, 263, 287
Gray, James, 16 n.34
Gray, Thomas, 91, 131, 166, 172 n.25, 222, 247
Greatness of soul (mind), 54, 61, 65 n.21, 78, 171, 172 n.25, 188, 197, 198, 207, 214. *See also* Heroism; Sublime
Green, Martin, 331 n.
Greenacre, Phyllis, 146 n.18

Greene, Donald J., 73 n.4, 76 n.13, 149 n.
Gregory, Dr. John, 271 n.55
Gregory of Nyssa, 34
Greuze, Jean-Baptiste, 198 n., 282, 297,
    310–16, pls.24–32
Griffin, Dustin H., 125 n.
Griffiths, Ralph, 248
Gros, Baron Antoine, 316
Grube, G. M. A., 30 n.10
Guilleragues, Gabriel de Lavergne de,
    113 n.29, 114
Guthkelch, A. C., 74 n.9, 101 n.4, 146
    n.17
Guyon, Bernard, 238 n.

Haac, Oscar A., 246 n.37
Hackman, Rev. James, 262 n.37, 263 and
    n.38
"Haec-vir," 36, 38, 284
Hagstrum, Jean H., 6 n.14, 16 n.34, 42
    n.30, 141 n.12, 180 n.33, 222 n.6, 245
    n., 263 n.40, 284 n.14, 290 n.20
Halifax, William, 1st Marquis of, 205–6
Halkett, John, 25 n., 28 n., 33 n.21, 38 n.
Hall, Peter, 326 n.69
Haller, William and Malleville, 35 n.
Halsband, Robert, 125 n., 126 n.
Ham, Roswell G., 56 n., 82 n., 90 n.26
Hamilton, Lady Emma, 282 and n.10
Hammond, James, 251
Handel, George Frideric, 48, 188, 278,
    286, 288, 303–10, 312
Hardwicke, Philip, 1st Earl of, 275
Hardy, Thomas: Jude the Obscure, 27; Tess
    of the D'Urbervilles, 131, 164
Harris, Jocelyn, 15 n., 187 n.4
Harrison, T. W., 111 n.24
Hart, Sophie C., 121 n.45
Harth, Phillip, 208 n.
Hartley, David, 251–52 and n.18
Hartman, Geoffrey, 150 n.25
Haydn, Joseph, 48–49, 278, 288, 294
Hayley, William, 282
Hayman, Francis, 283
Haywood, Eliza, 102, 186
Hazlitt, William, 106
Hazo, Robert G., 160 n.
Henry VIII, 157
Hercules at the Crossroads, 84
Hermaphrodite, 29, 32 and n.19, 42 n.29,

81, 138–39, 141, 193 n., 284. See also
    Androgyny; Narcissism
Heroic drama, 62–70, 132, 287
Heroism, domestication of, 67–68, 132,
    162, 210, 214–15
Herz, Gerhard, 290 n.21
Hierarchy, between men and women,
    35–36, 37, 226
"High souls," 120. See also Greatness of
    soul
Highmore, Susanna, 189 n.10
Hill, Christopher, 101 n.2, 206 n.40
Hilles, Frederick W., 195 n.25
Hinnant, Charles H., 54 n.7
Hoare, Henry, 123
Hobbes, Thomas, 65 and n.21
Hogarth, William, 283, 303, 311; Industry
    and Idleness, 177; Marriage à la
    Mode, 177; A Rake's Progress, 177–78,
    pls.8, 9
Homer, 187
Homoerotic love, 202–3, 232–34 and n.,
    295, 305
Homosexuality, 45–46, 103 n.11, 146 and
    n.18, 222
Honor, 143–45. See also Virginity
Hooker, Edward Niles, 44, 99 n., 111
    n.23
Hopkins, Charles, 70
Horowitz, Louise K., 4 n.9, 116 n.39
Horta, Maria Teresa, 113 n.27
Houghton, Walter E., 208 n.
Houlahan, Michael O., 253 n.24
"Hovingham Master," 108 and n., pl.7
Howard, George E., 33 n.20
Howard, Robert, 62
Howes, Alan B., 248 n.2
Hughes, John, 122, 127, 129 n., 160, 304
    n.
Huguelet, Theodore L., 252 n.18
Hume, David, 122, 161, 185 n.41, 262; A
    Treatise of Human Nature, 13, 60 n.17,
    86 n., 185
Hume, Robert D., 48 n.42, 55 n., 56 n., 65
    n.21, 66 n.23, 69 n.28, 81 n., 86 n., 91
    n.30, 136 n., 334
Hunt, John Dixon, 333
Huxley, Aldous, 330 n.
Hyde, Anne, Duchess of York, 105
Hynes, Samuel, 331 n.

Ibsen, Henrik, 121, 175
Illo, John, 43 n.32
Imagination: and love, 17–18, 129, 282–83; and morbid love, 78 and n.17; and masturbation, 224–25, 236, 242; and sensibility, 270–71
Imlay, Gilbert, 14
Immortality, 131, 210–11, 239–41, 258, 266, 331. *See also* Religion
Incest, 20, 42–43, 55–56, 56–58 and n.12 74, 82–83, 92, 94, 98, 146, 179–80, 212 266–67, 283, 314 n.59. *See also* Narcissism; Oedipal triangle
Innocence: frontier with experience, 95, 194, 256–57, 299, 303, 312–13, 318, 325–26, 327

Jacobson, Howard, 54 n.8
James, Duke of York, 66 n.25
Jeffreys, George, 212 n.
Jensen, H. James, 59 n.15, 65 n.22, 98 n.
Jerome, Saint, 34
Johnson, Elizabeth (Tetty), 7–8
Johnson, Esther (Swift's Stella), 8, 151, 155–59, 160
Johnson, James Turner, 31 n.15, 33 n.20
Johnson, Samuel, 7–8, 12, 16, 22, 70, 77, 88 and n., 92, 99, 117 and n.41, 121 n.45, 169, 181, 198, 213, 218, 221–22, 247, 249, 251, 262, 268, 273, 283; *Dictionary,* 6, 8, 172 n.25, 270 and n.53; Life of Addison, 165; of Dryden, 60 and n.18, 69; of Milton, 283 n.12; of Otway, 93; of Pope, 122 n.50, 130; of Rowe, 118; "Preface to Shakespeare," 131
Jonathan. *See* David and Jonathan
Jones, Ben, 222 n.6
Jones, Ernest, 267 n.47
Jong, Erica, 169 n.
Josephus, 46 n.
Juvenal, 198

Kallman, Chester, 317 n.
Kalnein, Wend Graf, 335
Keats, John, 21, 51, 125, 240–41, 266
Keener, Frederick M., 130 n.64
Keller, Abraham C., 72 n., 74 n.6
Kenny, Shirley Strum, 170 n., 334
Kerman, Joseph, 292 n.26

Keynes, Geoffrey, 11 n.25, 262 n.35
Kimpel, Ben D., 189 nn.9, 12, 194 nn.21, 23, 196 n.26, 204 n.35, 213 n.47
King, Bruce, 62 n., 69 n.29, 111 n.24
Kinkead-Weekes, Mark, 200 n.30, 204 n.35, 209 n.43
Kinsley, James, 250 n.52
Kirsch, Arthur, 69 n.28
Klopstock, Friedrich Gottlieb, 265
Kneller, Sir Godfrey: Hampton Court beauties, 133–34; *Lady Middleton,* pl.5
Knott, John R., 48 n.43
Knox, John, 104
Knox, Vicesimus, 59 n.16
Korshin, Paul J., 252 n.19
Köster, Patricia, 102 n.7
Kott, Jan, 45
Krehbiel, H. E., 295 n.32
Krieger, Murray, 111 n.24, 130 n.64
Krutch, Joseph Wood, 16
Kunzle, David, 314 and n.59

La Bruyère, Jean de, 113
Laclos, Choderlos de, 113, 213, 246; *Les liaisons dangereuses,* 276–77
La Fontaine, Jean de, 300
Lamont, Claire, 250 n.52, 274 n.
Lancret, Nicolas, 198 n., 297, 302
Landon, H. C. Robbins, 294 n.29
Lang, Paul Henry, 294 n.30, 307 nn.48, 49
Langbaine, Gerard, 57
Lane, Helen R., 113 n.27
Larat, P. and J., 113 nn.27, 28
Laslett, Peter, 101 n.2
Lavin, Marilyn Aronberg, 279 n.4
Lawrence, D. H., 198 n.
Leach, Clifford, 94 n.
Le Comte, Edward, 1, 24 n., 27 n.6, 36 n.24, 46 n.
Lee, Nathaniel, 19, 55, 81, 82–88, 90, 98, 189, 213, 218, 308; *Caesar Borgia,* 84–86; *Lucius Junius Brutus,* 87–88; *The Princess of Cleve,* 86; *The Rival Queens,* 82; *Theodosius,* 86; *The Tragedy of Nero,* 82–84
Lee, Vernon, 57
Lely, Sir Peter: "The Windsor Beauties," 105–6, 133, 134; *Lady Jane Needham,* pl.4

Le Moyne, François, 284
Leonardo da Vinci, 279 n.4
Lesbianism, 193 n., 217
Lessing, Gotthold Ephraim, 175
L'Estrange, Sir Roger, 113, 114 n.31
LeSueur, Eustache, 103 n.11
Lettres d'une religieuse portugaise, 112–17.
    See also Portuguese Nun
Levey, Michael, 319 n., 335
Lewis, C. S., 1, 3 n.6, 9, 27 n.5
Lewis, Wilmarth Sheldon, 261 n.33
Lillo, George, 121 n.45, 129, 162, 179,
    180, 208, 218, 274; *The London Mer-
    chant,* 173, 175–77
Lister, Raymond, 280 n.
"Little language," Swift's, 155–56, 330
Locke, John, 10
Lodge, Thomas, 46 n.
Loftis, John, 52 n., 94 n., 162 n.5
Longyear, R. Morgan, 294 n.30
Love, Harold, 111 n.24
Lovejoy, Arthur, 151
Lucretius, *De rerum natura,* 53
Lukacs, Georg, 263 n.40
Lumley, Elizabeth, 259 n.31
Lust, 40–41, 124
Luther, Martin, 31
Lynch, Kathleen M., 135 n.5

MacCannell, Juliet Flower, 223 n.9
MacDonald, Robert H., 224 n.12
Mack, Maynard, 122 n.49, 123 n.53, 130
    n.64
Mackail, J. W. 110 n.
Mackenzie, Henry, 163, 251, 252, 266
MacMillan, Dougald, 52 n.
Macpherson, James, 267
Madness, 82, 83, 84, 85–86, 124 n.55, 215
Maisch, Herbert, 43 n.32
Man of Feeling, 3, 75–76, 120, 183, 210,
    230, 241, 252, 292, 296, 316; carica-
    tured, 282
Mandeville, Bernard, 180
Manley, Mary de la Rivière, 102
Marcuse, Herbert, 1, 30 n.11, 37, 88
Marivaux, Pierre de, 75, 221
Marlowe, Christopher, 107 n.18
Marriage, 132, 136, 146, 160, 162,
    182–85, 185 n.41, 215, 225, 274–75,

318; aims of, 33 and nn.20, 21, 47, 255;
    in Beethoven, 295–97; between first
    cousins, 95 n.39; Milton on, 26–34;
    Pope's Eloisa on, 128–29; in Rousseau,
    230–31; Swift on, 146–48
Martin, Ruth and Thomas, 317 n.
Marvell, Andrew, 19
Masturbation, 224 and n.12, 243 n., 270
    n.53
Mayo, Robert D., 212n.
Mayoux, Jean-Jacques, 253 n.24
Mazarin, Duchess of, 105
Mazzeo, J. A., 39 n.
McBurney, William H., 96 n., 175 n.30
"Melmoth, Courtney," 248. *See also* Pratt,
    Samuel Jackson
Metastasio, Pietro, 286 n.
Michel, Emile, 108 n.
Michelangelo Buonarroti, 45, 103 n.11,
    284, 311
Michelet, Jules, 22–23, 246 n.37
Milhous, Judith, 55 n.
Miller, Henry K., 212 n.
Milton, John, 10, 13, 18, 24–49, 50, 56,
    75, 77, 98, 100, 104, 133, 134, 142, 146,
    153, 160, 163, 168, 185, 187, 189, 190,
    199, 203, 208, 215, 255, 274, 279, 283,
    285–86, 297, 321, 330, 333; *Apology for
    Smectymnuus,* 29 n.8; *Areopagitica,* 30
    n.11, 39; *Christian Doctrine,* 34; *Comus,*
    25, 39; Divorce Tracts, 15, 24, 26,
    27–30; *History of Britain,* 36 n.24;
    Paradise Lost, 14, 15, 21, 25–29, 37–44,
    46, 105, 145, 149, 161, 169, 183, 187,
    199, 292, 310, 314 n.59, 323; *Samson
    Agonistes,* 25, 36–37
Miner, Earl, 53 n.6, 58 n.12, 60 n.17, 104
    n.13, 245 n.
Minturno, 65
Mirimonde, A.-P. de, 288 n., 335
Miyoshi, Masao, 58 n.13
Moers, Ellen, 189 n.9, 193–94
Montagu, Lady Mary Wortley, 124–27
Montaigne, 129 n.
Monteverdi, Claudio, 287, 292 n.26
Moore, George, 273–74
Moore, John Robert, 95 n.40
Moore, Robert Etheridge, 112 n.25
Moore, Thomas, 103 n.10

Morgan, Bayard Quincy, 260 n.
Morgan, Charlotte E., 112 n.26
Morris, David B., 124 n.55
Motion (meaning emotion), 98 n., 115
Motteux, P. A., 105
"Mouvemens." *See* Motion
Moynihan, Robert D., 206 n.39
Mozart, Wolfgang Amadeus, 5, 15, 21,
    48, 196, 278, 286, 316–31
Mueller, Martin, 107 n.18
Munhall, Edgar, 310 n.52, 314 n.59
Murdoch, John, 8, 271
Music, love in, 15, 278–79, 285–97. *See
    also* Handel; Mozart
Myers, Robert Manson, 306 n.

Narcissism, 24, 41–46, 77, 81–82, 128,
    145–46, 163, 211, 217, 223–24, 263,
    283, 285, 288, 318. *See also* Effeminacy;
    "*Haec-vir*"; Homosexuality; Incest
Needham, Gwendolyn Bridges, 198 n.
Nelson, Horatio, Viscount, 282 n.10
Neumann, Werner, 290 n.23
Newman Ernest, 292 n.25
Newton, Isaac, 251
Nichols, John, 166, 246 n.37
Nickalls, John L., 75 n.12
"Nicky Nacky," 95–96
Nicoll, Allardyce, 121 n.45, 175 n.29
Niebuhr, Reinhold, 77
Nomos, 2, 3
Noonan, John T., 31 n.15
Novak, Maximillian E., 52 n., 81 n., 189
    n.13
Noyes, George R., 51 n.2, 107 n.16, 110
Nussbaum, Felicity A., 142 n.
Nygren, Anders, 1, 4 and n.10

O' Connor, Mark, 111 n.24
OED. See Oxford English Dictionary
Oedipal triangle, 238, 243–44, 261,
    264–67. *See also* Incest
O'Hehir, Brendan, 130 n.64
Okes, Nicholas, 56 n.
Oldmixon, John, 103 n.10, 165
Onania, 224 n.12
Onanism, 242, 270 n.53. *See also* Mastur-
    bation
Opie, John, 281–82

Oppens, Kurt, 289 n.
Otway, Thomas, 19, 81, 82, 90–98, 100,
    121 n.45, 173, 189, 199, 213, 218, 220,
    250, 274, 314 n.59; *Don Carlos*, 92, 98;
    Familiar Letters, 91; *The Orphan*, 78, 92,
    93–95, 217; *Venice Preserved*, 95–98
Ovid, 19, 44 n.34, 52–53 and n.5, 54–55,
    91, 103 and n.11, 104, 111, 112, 122,
    154 and n.30, 169, 250, 304, 320 n.66
Oxford English Dictionary, 6, 8, 9

Pagliaro, Harold E., 130 n.64, 212 n., 271
    n.55, 294 n.29
Painting, love in, 15, 278–85. *See also*
    Greuze; Watteau
Paley, William, 267 n.46
Parker, William R., 24 n.
Parnell, Paul E., 162 n.5, 163 n.7
Pascal, Blaise, 221
Pascal, Roy, 260 n.
Pater, Jean-Baptiste, 297, 302
Pathé, 5, 58
Pathetic, the, 5–6, 73, 98, 173, 198; and
    Christ's passion, 58, 130–31, 165–66,
    286–87, 329; in Dryden, 58–59;
    "pathetic vehemence," 65–71
Pathic, 5–6, 73
Pathos. *See* Pathetic
Patrick, J. Max, 44 n.35
Patterson, Frank Allen, 24 n.
Paul the Apostle, 20, 32, 35, 36 n.24, 170,
    263–64
Paulson, Ronald, 178 n., 183 n.40, 279
    n.4
Pedicord, Harry William, 174 n.26
Pepys, Samuel, 51, 242 n.31
Perugino, Il, Pietro Vannucci, 315
Peruzzi, Baldassare, 284
Peterborough, Charles Mordaunt, 3d
    Earl of, 137
Pettit, Henry, 122 n.49, 213 n.45
Philia, 2, 3
Philips, Ambrose, 103 n.10
Philips, Katherine, 105
Phillips, James E., Jr., 36 n.23
Phillips, William, 269 n.
Philo Judaeus, 29 n.9
Pike, E. Royston, 6 n.12
Pilkington, Matthew, 303 and n.

Pity, 65 and n.21, 286. *See also* Pathetic

Plato, 3–4, 5, 28, 29, 30, 32, 62, 255

Platonic love, 76, 77

Pleasure-pain, 115. *See also* Sensibility, bitter and sweet

Pointon, Marcia R., 43 n.33, 283 n.12

Pope, Alexander, 6, 8, 16, 50, 122–25, 134, 137–45, 166, 180, 188, 212 n., 218, 223, 268, 275, 278, 303, 304 n., 308, 309, 329; *The Dunciad,* 123–24, 143; "Elegy to . . . an Unfortunate Lady," 122 and n.50; *Eloisa to Abelard,* 11, 12–13, 111 and n.24, 118, 121–32, 133, 145, 152, 227–28; *Epistle to a Lady,* 8, 137, 141–42; *An Essay on Man,* 28, 123, 145; *Imitations of Horace,* 123 and n.52; *Rape of the Lock,* 137, 142–45, 297

Pornography, 100 n.

Porterfield, Allen W., 264 n.

Portuguese Nun, 112–17, 122, 128

Posner, Donald, 259 n.29, 285 n.16, 297 n.38, 298 n.40

Potter, Robert, 251

Pottle, Frederick A., 252 n.20, 262 n.37, 268

Poussin, Nicolas, 107, 108 and n.19, 286–87, 299

Powell, Nicolas, 281 n.6

Pratt, Samuel Jackson, 248 n.3

Prestage, Edgar, 113 n.27

Prévost, Antoine François, 221

Price, Martin, 124 n.55, 144 n.

Prior, Matthew, 103 n.9, 165, 250 n.13

Prostitution, 241–42

Proudfoot, L., 111 n.24

Prud'hon, Pierre-Paul, 316

"Prue." *See* Scurlock, Mary

Purcell, Henry, 105, 112 and n.25, 287–88

Quennell, Peter, 252 n.19

Quinlan, Maurice, 252 n.18

Racine, Jean Baptiste, 56, 60 n.17, 91, 286

Radcliffe, Mrs. Anne, 271

Radzinowicz, Mary Ann Nevins, 39 n.

Rameau, Jean-Phillippe, 288 and n.

Ranum, Patricia M., 47 n.41

Raphael Sanzio, 45, 280, 302

Rawson, C. J., 181 n.36, 193 n.

Ray, Martha, 263 and n.38

Reed, Joseph W., 262 n.37

Reiman, Donald H., 124 n.56

Reinert, Otto, 62 n.

Religion, 130, 265; associated with love, 17, 19–23, 289, 290–91. *See also* Agapē; Pathetic

Rembrandt van Rijn, 103 n.11

Reni, Guido, 279 n.4, 315

Renoir, Pierre Auguste, 314 n.56

Reynolds, Joshua, 17, 107, 108 n.19, 279–81 and n.6, 303, pl.10

Richardson, Samuel, 7, 11, 16, 22, 50, 70, 100, 117, 119 n., 132, 161–62, 164, 166, 169, 181, 186–218, 219–20, 247, 248, 250, 287, 291, 295, 303, 311, 312, 314 n.59; *Sir Charles Grandison,* 12, 13, 14–15, 187, 188, 214–18, 268 and n.49, 274, 278, 294, 305–6; *Clarissa,* 3, 6, 7, 8, 12, 13, 118, 170, 172, 173, 186, 195–213, 227–29, 240, 247, 256, 260, 275, 277, 281–82, 283, 305, 307 n.49, 313, 316, 323; *Pamela,* 20, 166, 191–95, 312

Richardson, Tony, 179

Ridgway, R. S., 23 n.

Rilke, Rainer Maria, 113

Roberts, Warren, 75 n.10

Rochester, John Wilmot, Earl of, 48 n.44, 82, 86, 91, 101 n.2

Rodes, David Stuart, 52 n., 81 n.

Rodin, François Auguste René, 301

Rogers, Daniel, 35

Rogers, Pat, 139 n.9, 141 n.11

Rollins, Hyder Edward, 21 n.43

Romano, Giulio, 280, 281

"Romantic," "Romantick," 73 and n.4, 77, 121, 122, 123, 127, 139, 140, 145, 189, 234–41, 279, 280 n.

Romanticism, 51, 58, 77

Romney, George, 169, 251, 282, 283, 303, pl.12

Roscoe, William, 43 n.33

Rose, Mark, 1, 30 n.13, 31 n.15, 36 n.25, 41 n.

Rosen, Charles, 124 n.56, 325 n.

Rosenblum, Robert, 281 n.7, 314 n.59

Rothstein, Eric, 69 n.28, 73 n.3, 87 n., 93 n.36, 182 n., 212 n.

Rougemont, Denis de, 1, 47, 160

Rougeot, J., 113 n.29, 115 n.32

Rousseau, G. S., 183 n.40, 212 n.

Rousseau, Jean-Jacques, 11, 14, 16, 20, 77, 162, 180, 206 n.40, 213, 219–46, 247, 250, 260, 261, 262, 266, 272 n., 274, 277, 278, 291, 292, 295, 296, 303, 314 n.59; *The Confessions,* 222, 241–46, 248, 249, 264; *Emile,* 220, 221–27, 230, 236, 241; *Narcisse,* 223 and n.10; *La nouvelle Héloïse* 3, 12, 22, 173, 219, 221, 227–41, 245, 247, 256, 264, 272 n.

Rowe, Elizabeth Singer, 102, 164 and n.10

Rowe, Nicholas, 6, 70, 93, 100, 180, 199, 208, 218, 250, 274; *The Fair Penitent,* 12, 117–21, 129; *Jane Shore,* 173–75, 198

Rowe, Theophilus, 164 n.9

Rowlandson, Thomas, 103, 261 and n.33, 282 and n.10, 283, pls.12, 13

Rubens, Peter Paul, 77, 103 n.11, 107–8, 129, 280, 297, pl.6

Rubin, James Henry, 311 n.54

Runciman, Alexander, 281, pl.11

Runte, Roseann, 246 n.37

Ryskamp, Charles, 251 n.17

Sacks, Sheldon, 212 n.

Sade, Marquis de, 213, 241, 271

Sainte-Beuve, Charles A., 113

Saint-Evremond, Charles de, 65 n.21, 105

Saint-Paulien, 298 n.41, 302 n.

Saint-Pierre, Bernardin de, 246

Saintsbury, George, 65 n.22, 66 n.25

Salmon, Thomas, 194

Samuel, Irene, 29 n.8

Sandburg, Carl, 90

Sappho, 102, 103 and nn.10, 11

Satan, Sin, and Death. *See* Narcissism

Sayers, Dorothy L., 107

Scatology, 138, 148–49 and n.22

Scherer, Jacques, 223 n.10

Schering, Arnold, 289 n.

Schiff, Gert, 282 n.10

Schiller, Friedrich, 229

Scott, Sir Walter, 65 n.22

Scurlock, Mary (Steele's "Dear Prue"), 166–68

Segrais, Jean Regnauld de, 110

Selden, John, 19, 20

Seneca, 276

Sense, 7–9, 59, 137–38, 174 and n.27, 271–72; "Good Sense," 122

Sensibilité, 113, 115, 121, 235

Sensibility, 5, 7–9, 172 n.25, 173, 181 and n.36, 183, 195–99, 216, 219, 224–25, 248–49, 267, 270–74, 282, 293, 316; bitter and sweet, 239, 289, 319. See also *Coeur sensible;* Delicacy; Pleasure-pain

Sensible, 7–9, 172, 232. See also *Coeur sensible*

"Sensorium," 248, 249

Sensuality. *See* Sexuality

Sentiment, sentimental, 5, 6–7, 72 n., 73, 160–63, 168, 189, 190, 193, 247–48, 260, 268, 279, 287, 298–99

"Sentire," 5

Settignano, Valerio da, 280

Settle, Elkanah, 82

"Sex in minds [souls]," 134, 169 and n., 232

Sexuality, 1–2, 5, 132; in Austen, 269–70; Dryden, 51–58; Eden, 26–27; Goethe, 264–67; Greuze, 312, 313–15; Handel, 305, 306–9; Mozart, 318–19, 320, 323, 325–26, 327–28, 329; Pope, 124 and n.55, 125–27, 129, 138–41; Richardson, 190, 191–93, 199–204, 209, 215; Rousseau, 224–26, 237, 241–45; Sterne, 252–59; Swift, 147, 148, 149–51, 153–55, 159; Watteau, 284–85, 297–98, 299–302

Shadwell, Thomas, 90 n.26

Shaftesbury, Anthony Ashley Cooper, 3d Earl of, 166 n.13, 197

Shakespeare, William, 6, 45, 168, 187, 234, 247, 258, 266; *Antony and Cleopatra,* 60, 61, 62; *As You Like It,* 45; *Cymbeline,* 150–51; *Hamlet,* 92, 267 and n.47; *King Lear,* 18, 215; *Macbeth,* 169; *Much Ado about Nothing,* 51, 268; *Romeo and Juliet,* 49; Sonnets, 18, 19; *The Tempest,* 55; *Twelfth Night,* 317

Sheffield, John, Earl of Mulgrave, 67 n., 82

Shelley, Percy B., 17, 35, 37, 61, 77, 88, 99, 164, 179, 180 and n., 246, 251, 275, 308

Shenstone, William, 251

Sherbo, Arthur, 162 n.5

Sherburn, George, 121 n.47, 123 n.51, 141 n.11, 278 n.2

Sheridan, Richard Brinsley, 268

Sherman, Stuart Pratt, 57

Shesgreen, Sean, 178 n., 179 n.

Shilleto, A. R., 101 n.3

Shinagel, Michael, 252 nn.19, 21

Sibelius, Jean, 114

Sidney, Sir Philip, 36, 42 n.29, 104, 203

Signorelli (Luca da Cortona), 45

Sinfield, Mark, 257 n.27

Singer, Irving, 1, 2, 3, 107 n.18, 295 n.32, 296 n.34, 316 n., 318 nn.62, 63, 319 n., 320 n.66, 325 n.

Sirluck, Ernest, 26 n.

Smirke, Robert, "Death of Héloise," 130 n.64

Smith, D. Nichol, 74 n.9, 101 n.4, 146 n.17

Smith, John Harrington, 52 n., 135 n.4

Smith, Logan Pearsall, 73 n.4

Socrates, 28, 30, 62, 208 n.

Sodomy, 83, 146 n.18, 189 n.13, 193 n., 270 n.53. See also Homosexuality

Southam, B. C., 270 n.52

Southerne, Thomas, 173; Oroonoko, 80–82

Southey, Robert, 9 n.24

Spacks, Patricia Meyer, 124 n.55, 128 n., 250 n.12, 256, 271 n.54

Spaethling, Robert, 328 n.

Spearman, Diana, 186 n.1

Spears, Monroe K., 165 n.11

Spector, Robert D., 206 n.40

Spenser, Edmund, 4, 32 and n.19, 36, 38–39, 43, 44 n.34, 59, 75, 104, 178, 189, 199

Spiegelman, Willard, 109 n.21

Spitta, Philipp, 290 n.23

Spitzer, Leo, 113 n.29

Sponsalia per verbo de futuro, 182. See also Marriage

Stanley, Thomas, 103 n.10

Starobinski, Jean, 223 n.10, 239 n., 244 n.

Steele, Richard, 68 n., 88, 134, 160, 162, 165–72, 182, 185, 190, 199, 218, 274, 287, 291; The Christian Hero, 165–66; The Conscious Lovers, 165, 170–72, 177, 205, 298; The Ladies Library, 166; Letters to Prue, 166–68; Spectator, 170; Tatler, 14, 82, 145, 165

Steen, Jan, 285

Stein, Arnold, 25 n.

Steinbeck, John, 312

Steinhauer, Harry, 260 n.

Stella. See Johnson, Esther

Stendhal (Marie Henri Beyle), 113, 319 n.

Stephen, Leslie, 22

Sterba, Edith and Richard, 295 n.32

Sterne, Lawrence, 10, 11, 12, 22, 73, 102, 163, 170, 175, 242 n.31, 274, 275, 276; Journal to Eliza, 248, 249; Sentimental Journey, 7, 11, 242, 248, 316; Tristram Shandy, 5, 9 n.23, 12, 248–49, 253–59, 269

Sternfeld, Frederic, 294 n.29

Stevens, Wallace, 19

Stewart, J. Douglas, 106 n., 134 n.1

Stone, Lawrence, 1, 2, 10, 11, 19, 31 n.15, 35 n., 74 n.7, 99, 101 n.3, 103 n.11, 166, 168 n.20, 205, 206 n.39, 216, 224 n.12, 242 n.31, 252 n.18, 275 n.60

Stout, Gardner D., 248 n.3

Strachey, James, 156 n.33, 200 n.29

Strong, Roy, 108

Stroup, Thomas B., 83 n.

Sublime, the, 65 n.22, 98, 115, 167, 173, 206, 207, 211, 213, 235, 261, 263, 269, 306, 309. See also Burke, Edmund; "Gothic" effects

Suicide, 117, 118, 236, 262 and n.36, 263, 266. See also Death

Sullivan, Maureen, 162 n.5

Summers, Joseph H., 24 n., 25 n., 42 n.30, 43 n.31

Summers, Montague, 52 n., 58 n.13, 78 n.16

Swedenberg, H. T., Jr., 111 n.23, 141 n.12

Swift, Jonathan, 8, 16, 86, 133, 134, 145–59, 187–88, 268, 275; The Battle of

the Books, 145; "A Beautiful Young
Nymph Going to Bed," 148; *Cadenus
and Vanessa,* 3, 151–53, 154–55; "On
the Death of Mrs. Johnson," 157–58
and n.36; "The Description of a Salamander," 149; *Gulliver's Travels,* 146
n.18, 147; *Journal to Stella,* 155–57; *The
Legion Club,* 158; "Mechanical Operation of the Spirit," 74 and n.9, 101 and
n.4; "Memoirs of Capt. John
Creichton," 157 n.;"Phyllis, or the
Progress of Love," 146–47; "The Progress of Marriage," 147; Stella poetry,
152–53, 156, 158; "Thoughts on Various Subjects," 148 and n.21
Sympathy, 60 n.17. *See also* Pathetic

Taine, Hippolyte A., 95
Tanner, Tony, 270 n.52
Tate, Nahum, 112
Tave, Stuart M., 272 n.
Taylor, Aline M., 93 nn.32, 37
Taylor, G. Rattray, 30 n.14
Taylor, Jeremy, 170, 187, 206; *The Rule
and Exercises of Holy Living,* 159 n., 207
Teresa, Saint, 101
Tertullian, 34
Tetty. *See* Johnson, Elizabeth
Thayer, Alexander W., 295 n.32
Thomson, James, 160, 172 n.25, 185,
197, 282; *Autumn,* 13 and n.30; *Spring,*
13
Tibullus, 154 n.30
Tiepolo, G. B., 107
Tillich, Paul, 4
Tillotson, Geoffrey, 13 n.29, 122 n.48,
127 n.61, 145 n.15
Tillyard, E. M. W., 25 n.
Tinker, Chauncey B., 105 n., 279 n.3
Tompkins, J. M. S., 267 n.46
Tonson, Jacob, 103 n.11
Towers, A. R., 181 n.35
Tracy, Clarence, 62 n.
Trahard, Pierre, 220 n., 221 nn.4, 5
Trapp, J. B., 333
Trask, Willard R., 295 n.32
Traugott, John, 253 n.24
Très riches heures, 45
Trilling, Lionel, 272 n.

Trinquesse, Louis, 303–4, pl.21
Trowbridge, Hoyt, 130 n.64
Trunz, Erich, 260 n.
Turner, J. M. W., 107, 303

Underwood, Dale, 101 n.2
Ut pictura poesis, 278
Utter, Robert Palfrey, 198 n.

Valency, Maurice, 1, 32n.18
Vanessa. *See* Vanhomrigh, Esther
Van Ghent, Dorothy, 204 nn.35, 36
Vanhomrigh, Esther (Swift's Vanessa),
151–55
Van Loo, Carle, 103 n.11, 283
Varina. *See* Waring, Jane
Velázquez, Diego, 284–85
Venus, 3 and n.6, 53 and n.6, 79,
109,148, 259, 274, 281 n.6, 284, 285,
290, 298, 299, 300, 301, 303, 311, 320,
335. *See also* Cupid
Versini, Laurent, 219 n.1
Vertu, 221
Vice solitaire, le, 17, 224, 236 and n. *See also*
Masturbation; Onanism
Vieth, David M., 48 n.44, 87 n.
Virgil, 32, 107 and n.18, 109, 110, 111,
122, 154 n.30
Virginity, ideal of, 31, 142
Voisine, Jacques, 219 n.1, 246 n.37
Voltaire, 22, 262
Vouet, Simon, 107

Waith, Eugene M., 60 n.17, 66 n.24, 69
n.28, 93 nn.34, 35
Waller, A. R., 76 n.14
Waller, Edmund, 154 n.30
Walpole, Horace, 134, 166, 180, 246 n.37
Walsh, William, 76
Warburton, William, 145
Ward, Charles E., 59 n.14, 77 n.
Ward, H. C., 121 n.45
Waring, Jane (Swift's Varina), 148, 151
Warner, James H., 219 n.1
Warton, Joseph, 6, 65 n.22, 121 n.45, 127
and n.60, 215
Waterhouse, Ellis K., 279 n.4, 280 n., 281
n.6

Watson, George, 53 n.5, 59 n.16, 65 and
n.21, 107 n.16, 108, 110
Watson, Philip S., 4 n.10
Watt, Ian, 188 n.6, 191 n., 193 n., 198 n.
Watteau, Jean-Antoine, 198 n.,259 n.29,
284–85, 288 and n., 297–303, 310 and
n.53, 315, 318, 319–20, 335, pls.16–20
Wertz, Margaret C., 114 n.30
Wellesz, Egon, 294 n.29
Wellington, James E., 127 n.61, 129 n.
Werth, Helmut, 294 n.29
Wesley, John, 248
West, Rebecca, 331
Westcomb, Sophia, 119 n., 189 n.11
Whaples, Miriam K., 316 n.
Whately, William, 35
Whicher, George F., 102 n.8
Wilcoxon, Reba, 53 n.6, 100 n.
Wilenski, R. H., 279 n.3, 281 n.6
Wilkes, John, *Essay on Woman*, 252, 282
Williams, Aubrey, 74 n.8
Williams, Harold, 147 n., 148 n.20, 150
n.23, 154 n.29
Williams, Murial Brittain, 183 n.39
Williams, Raymond, 9 n.24
Wills, Garry, 8 n.18, 314 n.56
Wilson, Arthur M., 229 n.
Wilson, John Harold, 91 n.27

Wilt, Judith, 209 n.42
Wimsatt, William K., 252 n.20
Winchilsea, Countess of (Anne Finch),
197, 309
Wind, Edgar, 47 n.41, 281
Winn, James Anderson, 125 n., 127 n.59,
139 n.8
Winton, Calhoun, 166 n.16
Wittreich, Joseph A., 42 n.30
Wolfe, Don M., 26 n.
Wollstonecraft, Mary, 14
Woman, position of, 30–31, 35–37, 104,
164–65, 208, 211
Wood, Paul Spencer, 51 n.2
Woodbridge, Kenneth, 123 n.54
Woolf, Virginia, 36 n.24
Wordsworth, William, 54 n.7, 99, 109 and
n.21, 245 and n.
Work, James A., 5 n., 249 n.7, 250 nn.10,
11, 257 n.27
Wright, H. Bunker, 165 n.11
Wright, Joseph, 281
Wright, Walter Francis, 195 n.24
Wycherley, William, 150, 187, 252

Young, Edward, 213

Zeno, Apostolo, 286 n.